Lecture Notes in Computer Science 13391

More information about this series at https://link.springer.com/bookseries/558

Marijn Janssen · Csaba Csáki · Ida Lindgren ·
Euripidis Loukis · Ulf Melin ·
Gabriela Viale Pereira ·
Manuel Pedro Rodríguez Bolívar ·
Efthimios Tambouris (Eds.)

Electronic Government

21st IFIP WG 8.5 International Conference, EGOV 2022
Linköping, Sweden, September 6–8, 2022
Proceedings

Springer

Editors
Marijn Janssen
Delft University of Technology
Delft, The Netherlands

Csaba Csáki
Corvinus University of Budapest
Budapest, Hungary

Ida Lindgren
Linköping University
Linköping, Sweden

Euripidis Loukis
University of the Aegean
Samos, Greece

Ulf Melin
Linköping University
Linköping, Sweden

Gabriela Viale Pereira
Danube University Krems
Krems an der Donau, Austria

Manuel Pedro Rodríguez Bolívar
University of Granada
Granada, Spain

Efthimios Tambouris
University of Macedonia
Thessaloniki, Greece

ISSN 0302-9743 ISSN 1611-3349 (electronic)
Lecture Notes in Computer Science
ISBN 978-3-031-15085-2 ISBN 978-3-031-15086-9 (eBook)
https://doi.org/10.1007/978-3-031-15086-9

This Springer imprint is published by the registered company Springer Nature Switzerland AG
The registered company address is: Gewerbestrasse 11, 6330 Cham, Switzerland

Preface

The EGOV-CeDEM-ePart 2022 conference, or for short EGOV2022, is now in the fifth year of its existence after the successful merger of three formerly independent conferences, i.e., the IFIP WG 8.5 International Conference on Electronic Government (EGOV), the Conference for E-Democracy and Open Government Conference (CeDEM), and the IFIP WG 8.5 International Conference on Electronic Participation (ePart). This larger, united conference is dedicated to a broad area of digital or electronic government, open government, smart governance, artificial intelligence, e-democracy, policy informatics, and electronic participation. Scholars from around the world have found this conference to be a premier academic forum with a long tradition along its various branches, which has given the EGOV-CeDEM-ePart conference its reputation of the leading conference worldwide in the research domains of digital/electronic, open, and smart government as well as electronic participation.

The call for papers attracted completed research papers, and work-in-progress papers on ongoing research (including doctoral papers), project and case descriptions, as well as workshop and panel proposals. This volume contains only full papers. All submissions were assessed through a double-blind peer-review process, with at least three reviewers per submission, and the acceptance rate was 46%. The acceptance rate was higher than in the previous years as there were many high-quality papers. The review time took 39 days this year, thanks to the contributions of the many Program Committee (PC) members.

The review process was focused on ensuring a double-blind reviewing and avoiding any conflicts of interest. Authors submitted their papers to a particular track. The track chairs handled the papers within their own track by assigning reviewers and proposing acceptance decisions. The lead track chair became part of the editor of the proceedings, in addition to the general chairs. Track chairs were not allowed to submit to their own track, nor were persons from the same university or close collaborators of a track chair to avoid any conflict of interest. Track chairs could either submit to another track or to the 'track chairs' track. The latter was handled by the general chairs. The general chairs checked if there was any conflict of interest among the papers submitted to each track, if so, then papers were moved to another track. The track chairs checked that all papers were submitted anonymously. If not, the authors were asked to resubmit within days. Track chairs assigned the reviewers and selected the Program Committee members in such a way that there were no conflicts of interest. After at least three reviews were received, the track chairs made a proposal for a decision per paper. The decisions were discussed in a meeting with the general and track chairs to ensure that the decisions were made in a consistent manner per track.

The conference tracks of the 2022 edition present the evolution of the topics and the progress in this field. The papers were distributed over the following tracks:

- General E-Government and E-Governance
- General E-Democracy and E-Participation
- ICT and Sustainability Development Goals

- AI, Data Analytics, and Automated Decision Making
- Digital and Social Media
- Digital Society
- Emerging Issues and Innovations
- Legal Informatics
- Open Data
- Smart and Digital Cities (Government, Districts, Communities and Regions)

Among the full research paper submissions, 36 papers (empirical and conceptual) were accepted for this year's Springer LNCS EGOV proceedings (vol. 13391) from the General E-Government and E-Governance; AI, Data Analytics, and Automated Decision Making; Emerging Issues and Innovations; Open Data; and Smart and Digital Cities tracks. The LNCS ePart proceedings (vol. 13392) contain the completed research papers from the General E-Democracy and E-Participation, ICT and Sustainability, Digital and Social Media, Legal Informatics, and Digital Society tracks.

The papers included in this volume have been clustered under the following headings:

- Public Services
- Social Media
- Open Government and Open Data
- AI, Bots and Data Analytics
- Smart Cities
- E-Government Evaluation

As in previous years and per the recommendation of the Paper Awards Committee, under the leadership of Noella Edelmann from Danube University Krems, Austria, and Evangelos Kalampokis from the University of Macedonia, Greece, the IFIP EGOV-CeDEM-ePart 2022 Conference Organizing Committee granted outstanding paper awards in three distinct categories:

- The most interdisciplinary and innovative research contribution
- The most compelling critical research reflection
- The most promising practical concept

The winners in each category were announced during the obligatory awards ceremony at the conference.

Many people behind the scenes make large events like this conference happen. We would like to thank the members of the Program Committee, the reviewers, and the track chairs for their great efforts in reviewing the submitted papers. We would also like to express our deep gratitude to Ulf Melin and Ida Lindgren and their local organization team for hosting the conference.

The EGOV-CeDEM-ePart 2022 conference was hosted by the Division of Information Systems and Digitalization, at the Department of Management and Engineering, Linköpings Universitet (LiU). LiU conducts world-leading, boundary-crossing research in fields including materials science, IT, and hearing. In the same spirit, LiU offers many innovative educational programs, many of them with a clear vocational focus, leading to qualification as, for example, doctors, teachers, economists and engineers. LiU has 35,900 students and 4,300 employees on four campuses. The conference was held at the largest campus - Campus Valla – which is situated just outside the city center of Linköping. We were very happy to be hosted here, enjoying the newly opened building, and had many in-depth discussions advancing the EGOV-CeDEM-ePart field.

We hope that the papers help to advance your research and hope that you will enjoy reading them.

September 2022

Marijn Janssen
Csaba Csáki
Ida Lindgren
Euripidis Loukis
Ulf Melin
Gabriela Viale Pereira
Manuel Pedro Rodríguez Bolívar
Efthimios Tambouris

Organization

Conference Chairs

Marijn Janssen	Delft University of Technology, The Netherlands
Noella Edelmann	Danube University Krems, Austria
Ida Lindgren	Linköping University, Sweden
Jolien Ubacht	Delft University of Technology, The Netherlands
Thomas Lampoltshammer (Lead)	Danube University Krems, Austria
Euripidis Loukis	University of Aegean, Greece
Ulf Melin	Linköping University, Sweden
Peter Parycek	Fraunhofer Fokus, Germany, and Danube University Krems, Austria
Gabriela Viale Pereira	Danube University Krems, Austria
Manuel Pedro Rodríguez Bolívar	University of Granada, Spain
Gerhard Schwabe	University of Zurich, Switzerland
Efthimios Tambouris	University of Macedonia, Greece
Csaba Csáki	Corvinus University of Budapest, Hungary

Program Committee Chairs

Joep Cromvoets	KU Leuven, Belgium
Csaba Csaki	Corvinus University, Hungary
Lieselot Danneels	Ghent University, Belgium
Noella Edelmann	Danube University Krems, Austria
Katarina L. Gidlund	Mid Sweden University, Sweden
J. Ramon Gil-Garcia	University at Albany, SUNY, USA
Sara Hofmann	University of Agder, Norway
Marijn Janssen	Delft University of Technology, The Netherlands
Evangelos Kalampokis	University of Macedonia, Greece
Robert Krimmer	University of Tartu, Estonia
Thomas Lampoltshammer	Danube University Krems, Austria
Habin Lee	Brunel University London, UK
Katarina Lindblad-Gidlund	Mid Sweden University, Sweden
Ida Lindgren	Linköping University, Sweden
Euripidis Loukis	University of the Aegean, Greece
Rony Medaglia	Copenhagen Business School, Denmark
Francesco Mureddu	The Lisbon Council, Belgium
Anna-Sophie Novak	Danube University Krems, Austria

Panos Panagiotopoulos	Queen Mary University of London, UK
Peter Parycek	Danube University Krems, Austria
Manuel Pedro Rodríguez Bolívar	University of Granada, Spain
Marius Rohde Johannessen	University of South-Eastern Norway, Norway
Iryna Susha	Utrecht University, The Netherlands
Efthimios Tambouris	University of Macedonia, Greece
Jolien Ubacht	Delft University of Technology, The Netherlands
Gabriela Viale Pereira	Danube University Krems, Austria
Shefali Virkar	Danube University Krems, Austria
Anja Wüst	Berner Fachhochschule, Switzerland
Anneke Zuiderwijk	Delft University of Technology, The Netherlands

Chair of Outstanding Papers Awards

Noella Edelmann	Danube University Krems, Austria
Evangelos Kalampokis	University of Macedonia, Greece

Ph.D. Colloquium Chairs

Ida Lindgren	Linköping University, Sweden
J. Ramon Gil-Garcia	University at Albany, SUNY, USA
Gabriela Viale Pereira	Danube University Krems, Austria

Web Master

Gilang Ramadhan	Delft University of Technology, The Netherlands

Program Committee

Karin Ahlin	Mid Sweden University, Sweden
Salah Uddin Ahmed	University of South-Eastern Norway, Norway
Suha Alawadhi	Kuwait University, Kuwait
Valerie Albrecht	Danube University Krems, Austria
Cristina Alcaide Muñoz	University of Alcalá, Spain
Laura Alcaide-Muñoz	University of Granada, Spain
Konstantina Alexouda	International Hellenic University, Greece
Leonidas Anthopoulos	University of Thessaly, Greece
Ari-Veikko Anttiroiko	Tampere University, Finland
Wagner Araujo	United Nations University, Portugal
Karin Axelsson	Linköping University, Sweden
Luiza Azambuja	Tallinn University of Technology, Estonia
Dian Balta	Fortiss, Germany
Kristina Belancic	Danube University Krems, Austria

Peter Bellström	Karlstad University, Sweden
Lasse Berntzen	University of South-Eastern Norway, Norway
Christina Bidmon	Utrecht University, The Netherlands
Radomir Bolgov	Saint Petersburg State University, Russia
Alessio Maria Braccini	University of Tuscia, Italy
Paul Brous	Delft University of Technology, The Netherlands
Matthias Buchinger	Technische Universität München, Germany
Kelvin Joseph Bwalya	University of Johannesburg, South Africa
Jesus Cano	National University of Distance Education (UNED), Spain
Iván Cantador	Universidad Autónoma de Madrid, Spain
João Carvalho	University of Minho, Portugal
Luiz Paulo Carvalho	Federal University of Rio de Janeiro, Brazil
Youngseok Choi	University of Southampton, UK
Wichian Chutimaskul	King Mongkut's University of Technology Thonburi, Thailand
Vincenzo Ciancia	Istituto di Scienza e Tecnologie dell'Informazione "A. Faedo", Consiglio Nazionale delle Ricerche, Italy
Antoine Clarinval	Université de Namur, France
Taiane Coelho	Federal University of Parana, Brazil
Andreiwid Sheffer Corrêa	Federal Institute of Sao Paulo, Brazil
María E. Cortés Cediel	Universidad Complutense de Madrid, Spain
J. Ignacio Criado	Universidad Autónoma de Madrid, Spain
Joep Crompvoets	KU Leuven, Belgium
Peter Cruickshank	Edinburgh Napier University, UK
Jonathan Crusoe	Gothenburg University and University of Borås, Sweden
Csaba Csaki	Corvinus University, Hungary
Frank Danielsen	University of Agder, Norway
Lieselot Danneels	Ghent University, Belgium
Gabriele De Luca	Danube University Krems, Austria
Athanasios Deligiannis	International Hellenic University, Greece
Monica Denboer	Università di Bologna, Italy
Edna Dias Canedo	Universidade de Brasília, Brazil
Devin Diran	TNO, The Netherlands
Bettina Distel	Universität Münster, Germany
Ioanna Donti	International Hellenic University, Greece
David Duenas-Cid	Gdansk University of Technology, Poland
Noella Edelmann	Danube University Krems, Austria
Gregor Eibl	Danube University Krems, Austria
Tove Engvall	University of Agder, Norway

Montathar Faraon	Kristianstad University, Sweden
Shahid Farooq	Government of the Punjab, Pakistan
Asbjørn Følstad	SINTEF, Norway
Marcelo Fornazin	FGV EBAPE, Brazil
Mary Francoli	Carleton University, Canada
Jonas Gamalielsson	University of Skovde, Sweden
Luz Maria Garcia	Universidad de la Sierra Sur, Mexico
Francisco García Morán	European Commission, Luxambourg
Mila Gasco-Hernandez	University at Albany, SUNY, USA
Alexandros Gerontas	University of Macedonia, Greece
J. Ramon Gil-Garcia	University at Albany, SUNY, USA
Dimitris Gouscos	University of Athens, Greece
Malin Granath	Linköping University, Sweden
Stefanos Gritzalis	University of Piraeus, Greece
Divya-Kirti Gupta	Indus Business Academy, India
Mariana Gustafsson	Linköping University, Sweden
Sebastian Halsbenning	Universität Münster, Germany
Marcus Heidlund	Mid Sweden University, Sweden
Moreen Heine	Universität zu Lübeck, Germany
Marissa Hoekstra	TNO, The Netherlands
Wout Hofman	TNO, The Netherlands
Sara Hofmann	University of Agder, Norway
Tomasz Janowski	Gdańsk University of Technology, Poland
Marijn Janssen	Delft University of Technology, The Netherlands
Marius Rohde Johannessen	University of South-Eastern Norway, Norway
Björn Johansson	Linköping University, Sweden
Luiz Antonio Joia	Getulio Vargas Foundation, Brazil
Hong Joo Lee	Catholic University of Korea, South Korea
Gustaf Juell-Skielse	Stockholm University, Sweden
Yury Kabanov	National Research University Higher School of Economics, Russia
Natalia Kadenko	Delft University of Technology, The Netherlands
Muneo Kaigo	University of Tsukuba, Japan
Evangelos Kalampokis	University of Macedonia, Greece
Nikos Karacapilidis	University of Patras, Greece
Evika Karamagioli	University of Athens, Greece
Areti Karamanou	University of Macedonia, Greece
Naci Karkin	Pamukkale University, Turkey
Jongwoo Kim	Hanyang University, South Korea
Fabian Kirstein	Fraunhofer FOKUS, Germany
Jens Klessmann	Fraunhofer FOKUS, Germany
Bram Klievink	Leiden University, The Netherlands

Ralf Klischewski	German University in Cairo, Egypt
Michael Koddebusch	European Research Center for Information Systems, Germany
Robert Krimmer	University of Tartu, Estonia
Peter Kuhn	Fortiss, Germany
Zoi Lachana	University of the Aegean, Greece
Mariana Lameiras	United Nations University, Portugal
Thomas Lampoltshammer	Danube University Krems, Austria
Habin Lee	Brunel University London, UK
Azi Lev-On	Ariel University, Israel
Matthias Lichtenthaler	Bundesrechenzentrum, Austria
Johan Linåker	RISE Research Institutes of Sweden, Sweden
Katarina Lindblad-Gidlund	Mid Sweden University, Sweden
Ida Lindgren	Linköping University, Sweden
Nuno Lopes	DTx - Digital Transformation CoLAB, Portugal
Euripidis Loukis	University of the Aegean, Greece
Rui Lourenço	University of Coimbra, Portugal
Michalis Loutsaris	University of the Aegean, Greece
Tangi Luca	Joint Research Centre - European Commission, Spain
Luis F. Luna-Reyes	University at Albany, SUNY, USA
Bjorn Lundell	University of Skövde, Sweden
Ahmad Luthfi	Delft University of Technology, The Netherlands
Johan Magnusson	University of Gothenburg, Sweden
Heidi Maurer	Danube University Krems, Austria
Keegan McBride	Hertie School Centre for Digital Governance, Germany
John McNutt	University of Delaware, USA
Rony Medaglia	Copenhagen Business School, Denmark
Ulf Melin	Linköping University, Sweden
Sehl Mellouli	Laval University, Canada
Ana Melro	University of Aveiro, Portugal
Tobias Mettler	University of Lausanne, Switzerland
Morten Meyerhoff Nielsen	United Nations University, Portugal
Yuri Misnikov	University of Leeds, UK
Francesco Mureddu	The Lisbon Council, Belgium
Marco Niemann	European Research Center for Information Systems, Germany
Anastasija Nikiforova	University of Tartu, Estonia
Anna-Sophie Novak	Danube University Krems, Austria
Galia Novakova-Nedeltcheva	Politecnico di Milano, Italy
Hannu Nurmi	University of Turku, Finland

Ann O'Brien	NUI Galway, Ireland
Svein Ølnes	Vestlandsforsking, Norway
Monica Palmirani	University of Bologna, Italy
Panos Panagiotopoulos	Queen Mary University of London, UK
Peter Parycek	Danube University Krems, Austria
Samuli Pekkola	Tampere University, Finland
Rob Peters	HU University of Applied Sciences Utrecht, The Netherlands
Luiz Pereira Pinheiro Junior	Universidade Positivo, Brazil
Vigan Raca	Ss. Cyril and Methodius University of Skopje, North Macedonia
Michael Räckers	European Research Center for Information Systems, Germany
Luis Felipe Ramos	University of Minho, Portugal
Barbara Re	University of Camerino, Italy
Nicolau Reinhard	University of São Paulo, Brazil
Britta Ricker	Utrecht University, The Netherlands
Nina Rizun	Gdansk University of Technology, Poland
Manuel Pedro Rodríguez Bolívar	University of Granada, Spain
Alexander Ronzhyn	University of Koblenz-Landau, Germany
Boriana Rukanova	Delft University of Technology, The Netherlands
Per Runeson	Lund University, Sweden
Øystein Sæbø	University of Agder, Norway
Amir Sahi	Bern University of Applied Sciences, Switzerland
Rodrigo Sandoval-Almazan	Universidad Autonoma del Estado de Mexico, Mexico
Verena Schmid	Danube University Krems, Austria
Hendrik Scholta	University of Muenster and ERCIS, Germany
Johanna Sefyrin	Linköping University, Sweden
Uwe Serdült	Ritsumeikan University, Japan
Kerley Silva	University of Porto, Portugal
Anthony Simonofski	Université de Namur, Belgium
Søren Skaarup	IT University of Copenhagen, Denmark
Leif Sundberg	Mid Sweden University, Sweden
Iryna Susha	Utrecht University, The Netherlands
Proscovia Svärd	Mid Sweden University, Sweden
Efthimios Tambouris	University of Macedonia, Greece
Lörinc Thurnay	Danube University Krems, Austria
Jean-Philippe Trabichet	HEG Genève, Switzerland
Andrea Trentini	University of Milan, Italy
Jolien Ubacht	Delft University of Technology, The Netherlands
Sélinde van Engelenburg	Delft University of Technology, The Netherlands

Colin van Noordt	Tallinn University of Technology, Estonia
Marco Velicogna	IRSIG-CNR, Italy
Gabriela Viale Pereira	Danube University Krems, Austria
Shefali Virkar	Danube University Krems, Austria
Gianluigi Viscusi	Imperial College London, UK
Flurina Wäspi	Berner Fachhochschule, Switzerland
Frederika Welle Donker	Delft University of Technology, The Netherlands
Guilherme Wiedenhöft	Federal University of Rio Grande, Brazil
Elin Wihlborg	Linköping University, Sweden
Peter Winstanley	Semantechs Consulting, UK
Stijn Wouters	Katholieke Universiteit Leuven, Belgium
Anja Wüst	Berner Fachhochschule, Switzerland
Maija Ylinen	Tampere University of Technology, Finland
Chien-Chih Yu	National Chengchi University, Taiwan
Thomas Zefferer	A-SIT Plus GmbH, Austria
Dimitris Zeginis	University of Macedonia, Greece
Qinfeng Zhu	University of Groningen, The Netherlands
Sheila Zimic	Mid Sweden University, Sweden
Anneke Zuiderwijk	Delft University of Technology, The Netherlands

Additional Reviewers

Lucana Estevez	San Pablo CEU University Foundation, Spain
Stanislav Mahula	KU Leuven, Belgium
Simon Hunt	University of Manchester, UK

Contents

Public Services

Evaluating the Impact of Trust in Government on Satisfaction with Public Services

Wivian A. dos R. Correa(✉), Gabriela Y. Iwama, Marilia M. F. Gomes, Glauco V. Pedrosa, Wander C. P. Silva, and Rejane M. da C. Figueiredo

University of Brasilia (UnB), Brasilia, DF, Brazil
wivian.reis@aluno.unb.br, {glauco.pedrosa,rejanecosta}@unb.br

Abstract. User satisfaction with public services has been monitored by several countries. Although many studies relate satisfaction with perceived quality, indirect aspects may also influence satisfaction. In this paper, we investigate the impact of trust in government on user satisfaction with Brazilian public services, along with two other dimensions: usability and perceived quality. A quantitative survey was carried out with 171 users of 7 public services. Data were analyzed using Structural Equation Modeling to understand the role of trust as a mediator of satisfaction with public services. It was observed that trust has a low direct correlation with service satisfaction. On the other hand, perceived quality has a high correlation with trust. This demonstrates that other dimensions apart from perceived quality must be considered in the evaluation of public services.

Keywords: Public services · Evaluation of services · User satisfaction · Perceived quality · Trust in government

1 Introduction

The relationship between government and citizens has been transformed by the use of Information and Communication Technologies (ICTs). The adoption of ICTs enables the government to strengthen relations with citizens through the digital transformation of public services, which optimizes services and reduces bureaucracy. Despite that, the evaluation of digital services and user satisfaction is not so noticeable. Satisfaction is related to the customer's assessment of the service provided by the company, based on their expectations and perceptions of quality [1]. Measuring user satisfaction is a complex task due to the inherent characteristics of the service [2]. Assuming this, we can measure some aspects that define satisfaction when taken together, such as ease of finding the service desired, delivery time, and the cost of the service.

The relationship between customer satisfaction and service quality has received much attention [3–5]. Although the relationship between quality and satisfaction is complex, quality in general acts as a significant predictor of satisfaction, and this relationship is essential to generating behavioral intentions [6, 7]. User expectations regarding service quality have a direct and positive effect on their satisfaction [8].

Published by Springer Nature Switzerland AG 2022
M. Janssen et al. (Eds.): EGOV 2022, LNCS 13391, pp. 3–14, 2022.
https://doi.org/10.1007/978-3-031-15086-9_1

In recent years, trust has also become an important factor in the adoption of electronic government [9], and it even influences whether people will use e-government [11]. Though there is no widely accepted definition of trust [12–14], it can be divided into topics such as the user's trust in digital systems, the user's trust in the security of the information provided through the digital mode, and the user's trust in the government. Thus, trust is not limited to interpersonal relationships, since it also involves relationships between the person and the organization, as well as between organizations or institutions [10].

Yet the impacts of trust in the satisfaction with the efficiency and effectiveness of public services are not so perceptible or directly measurable. To solve this issue, the Structural Equation Modeling (SEM) proves valuable to measure unobservable variables related statistically to people's perceptions or attitudes. This shows that academic research and technological innovation management may be powerful resources in public and private organizations [15].

Furthermore, the ease of access and navigation, that is, the usability of the system, is a key factor for the population to use electronic government. According to [16], "the variables use and user satisfaction are mutually dependent. While, logically, usage precedes user satisfaction, changes in the level of satisfaction also influence usage". Given this, this work considers usability as a potential measure to affect user satisfaction.

As satisfaction is a measure influenced by cognitive and affective aspects, this study tests the direct and indirect impacts of trust in the government in the assessment of citizen satisfaction. It also tests the predictive power of perceived quality on the user's satisfaction with the public services, using the SEM method. The central question of this paper is: what is the effect of service quality and usability on satisfaction? And what is the mediating role of trust, considering the latent nature of the variables of interest?

2 Definitions and Related Works

The hypotheses and measures chosen are based on the study [16], which developed a model for evaluating public services in Brazil. This work reviewed evaluation models such as SERVQUAL, DeLone and McLean Model and Technology Acceptance Model (TAM), which were applied in works in the context of public services. This study [16] explains that [17] used the SERVQUAL model to conduct a survey of users of digital government websites in Singapore, [18] applied the DeLone and McLean model to evaluate general digital government services in China and [19], evaluate digital public systems in India with the TAM model. Thus, the items were kept due to their theoretical relevance.

2.1 Service Quality and Satisfaction

Traditionally, user satisfaction is defined as the fulfilment of their wants and needs [20]. More recently, the formation process of satisfaction began to be considered as part of satisfaction [21]. Thus, in addition to the user's general satisfaction, factors involved in the process are also measured, such as quality of service and quality of system [22].

Therefore, knowing the quality perceived by users about a given service is essential for the redesign and improvement of that service.

Several definitions for service quality are found in the literature. Two main approaches can be presented: one based on the user, and the other, based on the production [23, 24]. In the user-oriented approach, quality can be defined as suitability for use and is commonly measured by the assessment of satisfaction with user preferences. In the production-based approach, quality can be defined as the fulfilment of requirements, that is, as the service's conformity with best practices.

The literature also differentiates quality in terms of user satisfaction and perception of quality. The perception of quality is considered a more cognitive assessment, while user satisfaction is considered a more effective assessment of the service [25].

2.2 Trust in Government

Trust tends to be conceptualized in the literature on trust in government as a correlate or cause of a wide variety of social behaviors that have significant direct or indirect consequences for political outcomes, such as effective and stable governance [26]. The question of interest to politicians is how trust is formed and sustained and, therefore, how (in fact, if) the decline in trust in government can be reversed by political actions and decisions.

Although the issue of political trust and its consequences is inherently interdisciplinary, different disciplines and fields of study have their own concerns. For example, political scientists are concerned with the nature, the reasons and the political significance of public confidence in institutions, such as governments, politicians, judiciary, the media, professions and armed forces [26]. They are also concerned about the political consequences of trust or the lack of it. Trust, or its absence, is translated into political results through institutional, structural and behavioral mechanisms, including civic participation, contributing to campaigns and voting.

Political economists tend to view trust based on assumptions of rational behavior and formal reasoning [26]. Trust can reduce the costs of economic transactions, including those between the public and the government. Also, trust can allow the maintenance of balance and stability in repeated interactions, provided that it has the appropriate institutional design. In law, trust tends to be the basis for the acceptance and social legitimacy of the rule of law and legally constituted government institutions. An important role of legal institutions is to promote and sustain that trust.

3 Methodology

To estimate the direct and mediating effects of trust in government on user satisfaction, a Confirmatory Factor Analysis (CFA) was conducted, and SEM was used. The instruments and the procedures for data collection are described below.

3.1 Subjects

A total of 171 volunteers participated in the present study. Of them, 131 (77%) evaluated a partially digitized service, while the others evaluated a completely digitized service. As for gender, age and education, 55, 7% were women, 56, 5% were between 20 and 24 years old, and the majority had incomplete higher education (74, 8%). The sample of this study was part of a larger study aimed at proposing a citizen-oriented evaluation of all Brazilian public services, including services offered in-person only [16].

3.2 Measures

Public Service Quality. To measure the quality of public services, the authors used a self-report questionnaire developed to measure specific aspects of quality, such as reliability, information quality and time adequacy [27], based on previous studies [28–31]. Before the study, semantic evaluations were made in a pilot study to ensure all the questions were understandable. The final version of the questionnaire was composed of 16 items measuring Service Quality and Usability based on an agreement scale from 1 (Strongly Disagree) to 5 (Strongly Agree).

Trust in Government. A questionnaire measuring trust in government used in previous studies was translated to Brazilian Portuguese [9, 32, 33]. It consists of three items related to the perceived government's integrity.

Satisfaction. Three questions were taken from [34] to measure user satisfaction. The items refer to a cognitive and affective global evaluation of the service provided, such as "the service provided exceeded my expectations".

3.3 Procedure

Volunteers were invited through social media to participate in an online study about the evaluation of public services. Those who accepted to participate chose to evaluate one of the following services: a) issuance of criminal records; b) passport issuance for Brazilian citizens; c) emission of employment record cards; d) enrollment in the National Secondary Education Examination; e) obligatory military conscription; f) income tax filing; and g) emission of the International Certificate of Vaccination and Prophylaxis. After choosing the service, participants answered the items on the questionnaire in random order. Informed consent was waived according to Resolution 510/2016 of the National Health Council, which dismisses the ethical review of studies of public opinion.

3.4 Data Analysis

CFA for the hypothesized factorial model was conducted to evaluate the measures. More parsimonious, alternative models for the measurement model were tested to evaluate the pieces of evidence of validity based on the internal structure of the final model used in the hypothesis testing. The hypothesis of the influence between latent variables was tested using SEM, according to Fig. 1. In all the models, the Weighted Least Squares with Mean and Variances Adjusted estimation method was used since it does not have assumptions about the distribution of the variables observed and performs better for ordinal data [35, 36]. All analyses were conducted in R v. 3.6.1 [37], using the lavaan package [38, 39].

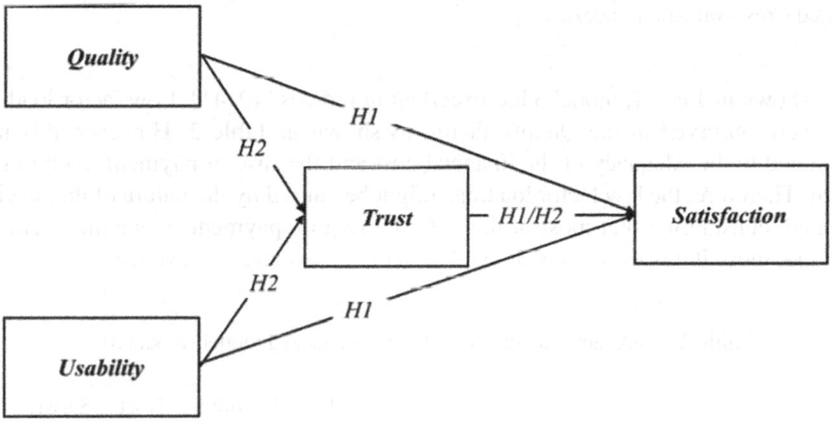

Fig. 1. Structural model used to test the hypotheses of direct (H1) and indirect effects (H2).

4 Results

4.1 Measurement Model Evaluation

To evaluate the measurement model used in the hypothesis testing, alternative CFA models were compared. Table 1 shows the fit indices for five alternative models. In the null model, none of the variables observed is caused by any latent variable. In the unifactorial model, all variables observed were caused by the same latent variable. Model 1 tests a measurement model with two correlated factors: one with Service Quality and Usability items and the other with Satisfaction and Trust items. Model 2 tests a measurement model with three factors: one for Service Quality and Usability items, one for Satisfaction, and another one for Trust. Model 3, the hypothesized model, tests a measurement model with four factors: Service Quality, Usability, Satisfaction and Trust.

Table 1. Fit indices of CFA models.

Model	χ^2	df	CFI	TLI	RMSEA	SRMR	ECVI
Null	1579	300	0	0	0.158	0.298	27.146
Unifactorial	492.3	275	0.83	0.815	0.068	0.088	2.947
Model 1	339.7	208	0.879	0.866	0.061	0.078	1.970
Model 2	262.9	206	0.948	0.941	0.040	0.064	1.523
Model 3	233.9	203	0.972	0.968	0.030	0.057	1.373

Note: χ^2 = Chi-squared with Satorra-Bentler correction; df = degrees of freedom; CFI = Comparative Fit Index; TLI = Tucker-Lewis Index; NFI = Normed Fit Index; RMSEA = Root Mean Square Error of Approximation; SRMR = Standardized Root Mean Square Residual; ECVI = Expected Cross-Validation Index.

As shown in Table 1, model 3 has excellent fit indices [40, 41]. Low factor loadings (<.4) were observed in the Quality factor, as shown in Table 2. However, this item was related to the adequacy of the financial cost and the ease of payment to obtain the service. Therefore, the low factor loadings might be caused by the nature of the services evaluated, considering that most of them do not require payment. Since the overall fit was good, those items were maintained due to their theoretical relevance.

Table 2. CFA factor loadings for the hypothesized model (model 3).

	Quality	Usability	Trust	Satisfaction
The service was completed within the stated period	0.545	—	—	—
The financial cost for obtaining the service was adequate	0.233	—	—	—
The time to obtain the service was adequate	0.747	—	—	—
The effort to obtain the service was adequate	0.713	—	—	—
The contact information provided was up to date	0.635	—	—	—
The information regarding the service was relevant to me	0.604	—	—	—
The service did what it promised	0.577	—	—	—
The information provided is secure	0.524	—	—	—

(continued)

Table 2. (*continued*)

	Quality	Usability	Trust	Satisfaction
The payment system was easy to use	0.312	—	—	—
Information about the service was easily found	—	0.693	—	—
The support provided by the system helped in using the service	—	0.428	—	—
The service could be performed with just a few clicks	—	0.464	—	—
The website layout was pleasant	—	0.616	—	—
The information and contents were easy to understand	—	0.691	—	—
The information generated by the service could be used and easily understood	—	0.709	—	—
The pages loaded properly	—	0.551	—	—
The government is reliable	—	—	0.794	—
The government is honest	—	—	0.810	—
The government is interested in my welfare	—	—	0.780	—
I am satisfied with the service received	—	—	—	0.676
My expectations were exceeded with the service received	—	—	—	0.656
I consider the service provided has the ideal quality	—	—	—	0.757

As shown in Table 3, correlations between factor scores were all positive and statistically significant, showing a strong relationship between the latent variables. Reliability indices, shown in the diagonal of Table 3, were all above the cut-off to be considered adequate (>.7).

Table 3. Pearson correlation between factor scores.

Factor	Quality	Usability	Trust	Satisfaction
Quality	.77			
Usability	.85**	.77		
Trust	.55**	.48**	.84	
Satisfaction	.96**	.88**	.62**	.74

Diagonals represent omega reliability indices [42].
Note: * means $p < .05$; ** means $p < .01$.

4.2 Hypothesis Testing

Table 4 shows the SEM results, with the regression coefficients of the direct effect of quality and usability on satisfaction, as well as their indirect effect mediated by trust. As shown in Fig. 2, the perception of service quality has a direct positive effect on user satisfaction and trust in government. Contrary to our hypothesis, the direct effect of trust in the government, as well as its effect as a mediator, was not statistically significant. As can be seen in Table 4, a great part of the variance in user satisfaction was explained by the perception of service quality, while trust remains largely unexplained.

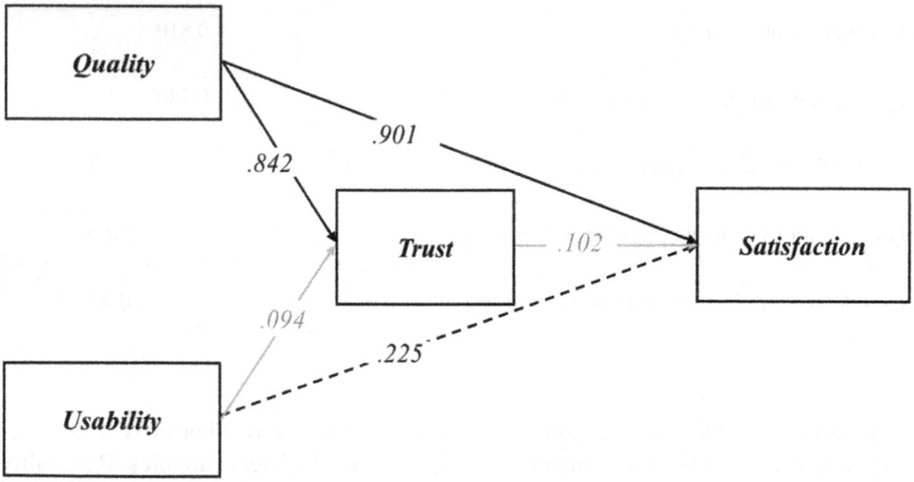

Fig. 2. Graphical representation of the structural model tested. Continuous, dashed and gray lines represent regression coefficients with, respectively, $p < 0.05$, $p < 0.08$ and $p \geq 0.08$.

Table 4. Statistical results for satisfaction and trust in government

Effect	B	p	LL	UL	SE
Quality→Satisfaction	0.901	0.000	0.415	1.387	0.248
Usability→Satisfaction	0.225	0.058	– 0.008	0.457	0.119
Trust→Satisfaction	0.102	0.114	– 0.024	0.229	0.065
Quality→Trust	0.842	0.016	0.157	1.527	0.350
Usability→Trust	0.094	0.631	– 0.290	0.479	0.196
Indirect effect of quality	0.086	0.122	– 0.023	0.195	0.056
Indirect effect of usability	0.010	0.659	– 0.033	0.052	0.022
Satisfaction–R^2	0.828				
Trust–R^2	0.248				

Note: Regression coefficients (B), lower (LL) and upper limit (UL) of the 95 CI of the regression coefficient, statistical significance (p), standard error (SE) for the direct and indirect effects, and coefficient of determination (R^2) for Satisfaction and Trust in Government.

5 Discussion and Final Considerations

This study aimed at testing the impact of the perception of public service quality on user satisfaction, considering trust in the government. In comparison to usability, the perception of quality was the greatest predictor of satisfaction, as reported by previous studies [43]. Though trust in government was significantly predicted by the quality and usability of public services in this study, it did not obtain predictive power on user satisfaction. These results point out that the general quality of the service, such as having adequate time and efforts for execution, is more essential for user satisfaction than trust in government or usability. This finding can serve as input for the strategic allocation of resources to promote the quality of public services.

The impact of quality on trust in government is also important for the strategic planning of the Federal Public Administration as a whole. An improvement in public services can promote an increase in confidence in the government, which is relevant for the probability of using electronic public services [9]. In the long run, enhancing confidence in government can be essential for the success of digital transformation.

Previous studies suggest that the relationship between satisfaction and trust depends on the type of service provided to the citizen [44]. Therefore, future studies should investigate the role of trust in government according to the different areas of public services, such as education, health, civil etc. We suggest to examine the hypotheses tested in this study for the types of public services in Brazil, since trust was found to be important for the adoption of electronic services in developing countries [45].

The role of the usability of electronic or digitized services can also be further investigated. Individual factors can affect the adoption of electronic services, such as age group or computer literacy [46, 47]. Usability can also be more important for specific services, which require more than one interaction, for example [48].

The use of SEM enabled a better understanding of the perception of public service quality by the user and can assist in the construction of indicators that will focus on the permanent improvement and evaluation of these services. Additionally, they will contribute to the digital transformation, which seeks to develop methodologies, models and tools that promote the automation of public services aimed at citizens and organizations.

References

1. Zeithaml, V., Bitner, M., Gremler, D.: Marketing de Serviços - A Empresa Com Foco No Cliente, 6th edn. Amgh, Porto Alegre (2014)
2. Lovelock, C., Wirtz, J., Henzo, M.: Marketing de Serviços: Pessoas, Tecnologia E Estratégia, 7th edn. Pearson Prentice Hall, São Paulo (2011)
3. Parasuraman, A., Zeithaml, V.A., Berry, L.L.: Servqual: a multiple-item scale for measuring customer perception of service quality. J. Retail. **64**(1), 12–40 (1988)
4. Bolton, R.N., Drew, J.H.: Linking customer satisfaction to service operations and outcomes. In: Rust, R.T., Oliver, R.L. (eds.) Service quality: new directions in theory and practice, pp. 173–200. Sage Publications, Newbury Park (1994)
5. Dabholkar, P., Shepherd, C., Thorpe, D.: A comprehensive framework for service quality: an investigation of critical conceptual and measurement issues through a longitudinal study. J. Retail. **76**(2), 139–173 (2000)
6. Cronin, J.J., Taylor, S.A.: Measuring service quality: a re-examination and extension. J. Mark. **56**(3), 55–68 (1992)
7. Ryu, K., Han, H.: Influence of physical environment on disconfirmation, customer satisfaction, and customer loyalty for first-time and repeat customers in upscale restaurants. In: International CHRIE Conference-Refereed Track, pp. 1–8. ScholarWorks@UMass Amherst, Amherst (2010)
8. Fornell, C., et al.: The American customer satisfaction index: nature, purpose and findings. J. Mark. **60**, 34–50 (1996)
9. Belanger, F., Carter, L.: Trust and risk in e-government adoption. J. Strateg. Inf. Syst. **17**(2), 165–176 (2008)
10. Lewicki, R., Bunker, B.: Developing and maintaining trust in work relationships. In: Kramer, R.M., Tyler, T.R. (eds.) Trust in Organizations: Frontiers of Theory and Research, pp. 114–139. Sage Publications, Thousand Oaks (1996)
11. Abu-Shanab, E.: Antecedents of trust in e-government services: an empirical test in Jordan. Transform. Gov. People Process Policy **8**(4), 480–499 (2014)
12. Belanger, B., Hiller, J.S., Smith, W.J.: Trustworthiness in electronic commerce: the role of privacy, security, and site attributes. J. Strat. Inf. Syst. **11**, 245–270 (2002)
13. Lee, M.K.O., Turban, E.: A trust model for consumer internet shopping. Int. J. Electron. Commer. **6**(1), 75–91 (2001)
14. Lewis, J.D., Weigert, A.: Trust as a social reality. Soc. Forces **63**(4), 967–985 (1985)
15. Azevedo, A., Mazzoni, M., Silveira, M.: Academic research in technology innovation management and related thematic area in Brazil. Int. J. Innovation **8**(1), 271–284 (2013)
16. Silva, W.C.P.D., et al.: Avaliação da Qualidade Em Serviços Públicos: Relatório Técnico (2019)
17. Srivastava, S., Teo, T., Nishant, R.: What is electronic service quality? In: ECIS 2011 Proceedings, p. 85. AIS Electronic Library (2011)
18. Wang, Y.-S., Liao, Y.-W.: Assessing eGovernment systems success: a validation of the DeLone and McLean model of information systems success. Gov. Inf. Q. **25**(4), 717–733 (2008)

19. Bhattacharya, D., Gulla, U., Gupta, M.P.: E-service quality model for Indian government portals: citizens' perspective. J. Enterp. Inf. Manag. **25**(3), 246–271 (2012)
20. Ives, B., Olson, M.H., Baroudi, J.J.: The measurement of user information satisfaction. Commun. ACM **26**(10), 785–793 (1983)
21. Brown, S.A., Venkatesh, V., Goyal, S.: Expectation confirmation in information systems research. MIS Q. **38**(3), 729–756 (2014)
22. Antonopoulou, M., Kotsilieris, T.: A literature review of user satisfaction models towards information system success. Int. J. E-Serv. Mobile Appl. **11**(2), 71–87 (2019)
23. Juran, J.M.: Quality Control Handbook, 3rd edn. McGraw-Hill, New York (1974)
24. Crosby, P.B.: Quality is Free: The Art of Making Quality Certain, 1st edn. McGraw-Hill, New York (1979)
25. Oliver, R.L.: Satisfaction: A Behavioral Perspective on the Consumer, 1st edn. McGraw-Hill, New York (1997)
26. Keele, L.: Social capital and the dynamics of trust in government. Am. J. Polit. Sci. **51**(2), 241–254 (2007)
27. Soares, V.A., et al.: Evaluating government services based on user perspective. In: Proceedings of the 20th Annual International Conference on Digital Government Research, pp. 425–432. Association for Computing Machinery, New York (2019)
28. Fassnacht, M., Koese, I.: Quality of electronic services: conceptualizing and testing a hierarchical model. J. Serv. Res. **9**(1), 19–37 (2006)
29. Sá, F., Rocha, Á., Gonçalves, J., Cota, M.P.: Model for the quality of local government online services. Telematics Inform. **34**(5), 413–421 (2017)
30. Deng, H., Karunasena, K., Xu, W.: Evaluating the performance of e-government in developing countries: a public value perspective. Internet Res. **28**(1), 169–190 (2018)
31. Parasuraman, A., Zeithaml, V.A., Malhotra, A.: ES-QUAL: a multiple-item scale for assessing electronic service quality. J. Serv. Res. **7**(3), 213–233 (2005)
32. Carter, L., Bélanger, F.: The utilization of e-government services: citizen trust, innovation and acceptance factors. Inf. Syst. J. **15**(1), 5–25 (2005)
33. McKnight, D.H., Choudhury, V., Kacmar, C.: Developing and validating trust measures for e-commerce: an integrative typology. Inf. Syst. Res. **13**(3), 334–359 (2002)
34. Urdan, A.T., Rodrigues, A.R.: O modelo do índice de satisfação do cliente norte-americano: um exame inicial no Brasil com equações estruturais. Rev. de Administração Contemporânea **3**(3), 109–130 (1999)
35. Brown, T.: Confirmatory Factor Analysis for Applied Research, 1st edn. Guildford, New York (2006)
36. Flora, D.B., Curran, P.J.: An empirical evaluation of alternative methods of estimation for confirmatory factor analysis with ordinal data. Psychol. Methods **9**(4), 466–491 (2004)
37. R Core Team. https://www.R-project.org/. Accessed 27 Apr 2020
38. Rosseel, Y.: Lavaan: an R package for structural equation modeling. J. Stat. Softw. **48**, 1–36 (2012)
39. Hirschfeld, G., Von Brachel, R.: Multiple-group confirmatory factor analysis in R – A tutorial in measurement invariance with continuous and ordinal indicators. Pract. Assess. Res. Eval. **19**(7), 1–12 (2014)
40. Hu, L.T., Bentler, P.M.: Fit indices in covariance structure modeling: sensitivity to underparameterized model misspecification. Psychol. Methods **3**(4), 424–453 (1998)
41. Schumacker, R.E., Lomax, R.G.: A Beginner's Guide to Structural Equation Modeling, 3rd edn. Routledge Academic, New York (2010)
42. McDonald, R.P.: Test Theory: A Unified Treatment, 1st edn. Lawrence Erlbaum, Mahwah (1999)

43. Santa, R., MacDonald, J.B., Ferrer, M.: The role of trust in e-government effectiveness, operational effectiveness and user satisfaction: lessons from Saudi Arabia in e-G2B. Gov. Inf. Q. **36**(1), 39–50 (2019)
44. Morgeson, F.V., Petrescu, C.: Do they all perform alike? an examination of perceived performance, citizen satisfaction and trust with US federal agencies. Int. Rev. Adm. Sci. **77**(3), 451–479 (2011)
45. Mustafa, A., Ibrahim, O., Mohammed, F.: E-government adoption: a systematic review in the context of developing nations. Int. J. Innovation **8**(1), 59–76 (2020)
46. Phang, C.W., Sutanto, J., Kankanhalli, A., Li, Y., Tan, B.C., Teo, H.H.: Senior citizens' acceptance of information systems: a study in the context of e-government services. IEEE Trans. Eng. Manag. **53**(4), 555–569 (2006)
47. Chatzoglou, P., Chatzoudes, D., Symeonidis, S.: Factors affecting the intention to use e-government services. In: 2015 Federated Conference on Computer Science and Information Systems (FedCSIS), pp. 1489–1498. IEEE (2015)
48. Moraes, G.H.S.M., Meirelles, F.S.: User's perspective of eletronic government adoption in Brazil. J. Technol. Manag. Innov. **12**(2), 1–9 (2017)

Adoption of Public e-services versus Civic Tech Services: On the Issue of Trust and Citizen Participation in Ukraine and Belarus

Olga Matveieva[1], Vasil Navumau[2], and Mariana Gustafsson[3](✉)

[1] Dnipro University of Technology, Av. Dmytra Yavornytskoho, 19, Dnipro, Ukraine
[2] Center for Advanced Internet Studies and Institute of Social Movements, Ruhr-University Bochum, Universitätsstraße 150, Bochum, Germany
[3] IEI, Linköping University, 581 83 Linköping, Sweden
mariana.s.gustafsson@liu.se

Abstract. Belarus and Ukraine embarked on digitalisation relying on an international experience. Ukraine experienced difficulties in building infrastructure and connecting their regions and faced challenges in providing training and raising citizen awareness on advantages of the digital services. Yet, the digitalization reform proceeded from the principles of citizen-centeredness and e-participation. Belarus, on the contrary, was quick in building the basic infrastructure and training their public officials. However, the e-government was oriented rather on technical aspects and inter-sectoral communication, than on the needs of the citizens. Despite the differences in both cases, the level of trust, the basic prerequisite for the quality e-services, has been low (Ukraine) or non-existent (Belarus). This paper uses multi-method approach to examine citizen trust and their adoption of e-services in developing political or administrative regime contexts that are characterized by low trust, variable digital literacy, and variable access to information. A key finding is that in both countries it was the historical legacy of access to free services, that was one of the barriers to building a sustainable and reliable system of e-services. However, while Ukraine started to improve their infrastructure and building trust towards digital services during the COVID-19 pandemic, in Belarus the authorities' ineffective management of the pandemic has led to sharp decrease in trust towards authorities. As a result, rudiments of an alternative system of public-services' delivery, based on the people-to-people model, have been launched by the civil society.

Keywords: Citizen trust · E-government · Ukraine · Belarus

1 Introduction

As both Ukraine and Belarus embarked on digital transformation of government and public service delivery, their journeys entailed various challenges of adoption and use by society actors that may bring fundamental implications for the state building and their civil society. Notably, the period between August 2020 and February 2022 was marked by

Published by Springer Nature Switzerland AG 2022
M. Janssen et al. (Eds.): EGOV 2022, LNCS 13391, pp. 15–30, 2022.
https://doi.org/10.1007/978-3-031-15086-9_2

a rapid digitalisation in public services in Ukraine. During the same time, pluralistic civic tech initiatives were launched in Belarus. Ukraine and Belarus pursue different trajectories in the e-government development. Although governmental digitalisation policies and IT-solutions are available on the market, the public e-services are either unknown for most users, not user-friendly or non-functional [1]. Characteristic for both countries is that certain e-services are more used than others, commonly urban regions are front runners, while rural regions lag and are struggling with broadband infrastructure and computer literacy of the inhabitants. As an example, most popular services in Ukraine in 2020 were passport registration; application for subsidies and social benefits; services related to personal transport; pension provision services. Among the 47% of people who have not used e-services in 2020, almost a quarter did not know how to do it, and 21% had no access to the Internet [2].

Authorities and local policies did little to enhance the public interest representation mechanisms online and to establish the channels of digital communication between the citizens and the government agencies. That said, digitalisation of public services in Belarus and Ukraine, are carried in parallel to substantial public administration reforms, especially in the latter case. Digitalisation of public services, both as a concept and as an intervention, needs to be linked with the objectives and priorities of the on-going administrative and welfare reforms. A disconnected, fragmented digitalisation efforts will pose further challenges and complicate public administration reform. That said, among the public officials there is a widely accepted stereotype, that such a reform is very costly, while its benefits cannot be easily calculated [3].

An underlying challenge drawing on political instability and the soviet legacy was citizens' general mistrust in public administration and their political leaders [4]. The practice shows that most initiatives were carried with a shortage of expertise on e-services demand on the local level and an absence of citizen perspective as primary beneficiaries of public welfare. A wide coverage of internet infrastructure, including countryside and remote rural areas is still a challenge that constrains equitable access to governmental information and e-services [5].

The systemic changes affecting legitimacy and trust, via stakeholders' participation, the costs and the risks that digital transformation brings into public administration and public services need to be investigated for the different political and administrative contexts to define how the level of public trust shapes participation. The quality of government, including public digital services in Ukraine and Belarus so far shows that the political interest, the administration, and citizen digital literacy, score lower in comparison to other countries [6]. Such results imply that the challenges, the capabilities, and the solutions at national level so far are fragmented and not sufficient. Therefore, more granular knowledge on adoption of e-government through citizen-centric e-services in transitioning societies is crucial for both e-government research and practitioners in public services.

To summarize our argument, in the context of on-going digitalisation, governmental provision of e-services and their adoption by the citizens in political and administrative regimes generates different practices of citizen engagement and participation that are worth to follow closer. In the context of developing or changing political and administrative regimes, with low or no trust between citizens and the government, where governmental e-services are fragmented or non-existent, while citizen digital literacy and access to information is widely variable, there may emerge new practices of citizen-to-citizen services as an alternative to governmental services, but also as a mode of resistance and coping with suppression. The aim of this paper is to examine citizen adoption of e-services, in developing political or administrative regime contexts characterized by low trust, variable digital literacy and variable access to information.

2 Literature Review

E-government has been defined as governmental authorities' use of digital technologies to provide information, communicate and deliver public services to citizens, businesses, and other governmental authorities [7]. Studies addressing e-government adoption and use by the citizens are in abundance [8–12]. Among predicting factors that influence citizen attitudes towards e-government were found: service utility, service usability, habits of internet use, but also trust in government and citizen satisfaction with government performance [13]. In addition, UK citizen studies have found information quality and service quality, but also citizen prior experience with e-services, their expectations and service outcome satisfaction, as well as social influence were important predictors of adoption and use of e-government [14].

Despite a wide field and growing e-government research, citizen-to-citizen (C2C) services have not been sufficiently covered in current research [15]. Technology mediated citizen interaction has earlier been approached as alternative coordination mechanisms in the context of missing or incomplete governmental services [16]. A few years later, looking into the plethora of citizen co-production models of cooperation with government, Linders [17] proposed a unified typology of along three categories: 'citizen sourcing', 'government as a platform' and 'do-it-yourself government'. Citizen co-production of e-services and other types of collective action were believed to affect public administrative paradigms and the re-distribution of roles and responsibilities between governments and their citizens. New public management norms in public administration, treating the citizen as customer or client to be served, with public services as modes of mass production has been challenged by practices of citizen sourced services and the new framing of technology-enabled, active citizenry that engaged in service co-production [17].

Saylam and Yıldız [15], took citizen co-production a step further and analyzed C2C services, their integration in the e-government domain and their implications upon the quality of e-Government. They argued that C2C interactions when systematical and integrated in the e-Government they form an important 'value chain' that can affect the e-services in critical ways. They argued that the main beneficial effects of C2C interaction are support of governmental decisions, increase of volume of e-services and enhancing of quality of services. Among the disadvantages they identified distribution of misinterpreted or manipulative information [15].

eParticipation research still needs to thoroughly explain citizen participation versus non-participation, their long-term commitment and deeper engagement with e-Government. Yetano and Royo [18] have emphasized the challenge of long-term citizen commitment in participation in government interventions. The problem involves both in engaging the citizen to participate and if successful, to sustain their engagement in long-term collaboration. Their study, focusing on citizen participation in a two-year project of monitoring citizen behavior for reducing CO2 emissions in two Spanish cities found that access and use of digital technologies was not sufficient to attract and sustain citizens' longer term commitment [18]. Rather person-to-person interaction, a combination of onsite and digital activities, using different communication channels and timely follow ups were more effective.

Social capital [19], in terms of social ties, commitment to- and trust in local community and government have been found to be significant in deeper and frequent citizen engagement [20]. In other words, social capital elements for engagement with government in co-production of e-services seem to pre-condition the elements of technology adoption and use of digital services. Literature on social capital and trust in post-soviet societies in Europe has discussed the soviet legacy for the political culture in the development of post-soviet regimes, the nature of old and new political elites and the issue of citizen trust for democratization processes [21].

3 Ukraine and Belarus: Two Different Backgrounds for E-government, Citizen Trust and Participation

3.1 Ukraine

Ukraine, has been enjoying a dynamic rise in digital services, provided by the state, a trend, characteristic for the last 5 years. Ukraine became independent after the collapse of the USSR in 1991. After the ineffective spell of Kravchuk (who was at the helm between 1991 and 1994) and the corruption-plagued two terms of Kuchma (1994–2004), in 2004 Ukraine experienced the first revolution (dubbed Orange Revolution), which altered political landscape of the country. It was not merely political, but a cultural movement [22]. For the first time, Ukrainians openly expressed their desire to move closer to Europe, to embrace European political and civic values, instead of participating in quasi-integration projects initiated by Russia based on the conservative views of its political elite. In 2014 Ukraine once again expressed its European vector of development by overthrowing the Russia-supported president Yanukovich in the EuroMaidan revolution. This has led to a military conflict with Russia, followed by annexation of Crimea and the war in the Eastern Donbas region that extended to the entire country in 2022. Another important factor for understanding the peculiarities of Ukraine's trajectory of development in both economic and political spheres is the existence of strong business-political networks, that are still having control over certain economic branches, and that creates opportunities for corruption. Freedom House considers Ukraine to be a hybrid regime (with the score 3.36) [23].

Still, after 2014, the country implemented a set of reforms, which led to a gradual shift in the political environment: decentralization and digitalization proved the most crucial ones of them. 41-year-old actor Volodymir Zelensky, who came to the presidential power in 2019 following the businessman Poroshenko, and being supported by a parliamentarian majority, continued the reforms [24]. However, his best efforts to fight the oligarchy by closing several media channels and launching charges against them, were met with strong resistance from the judiciary as entrenched interests fought to preserve the status quo [25]. That said, Zelensky continued the decentralization program for more transparent and accountable governance, an intervention known as 'EGOV4UKRAINE', launched by his predecessor. Importantly, within the program the government launched the data exchange system "Trembita" (the Ukrainian analogue of the Estonian "X-Road"). Despite multiple systems being adopted, in general, e-government in Ukraine is developing fragmentarily, unevenly and at a rather slow pace: only some components of e-government have been implemented or partially implemented. Still, despite its shortages of digital infrastructure (0.5492, which is lower score compared to the Eastern European neighbors), Ukraine made a substantial progress in E-Gov Index in the last years, thanks to its highly developed human capital (0.8591): the country jumped from 82nd in 2018 spot to 69th in 2020 [26].

The Covid-19 pandemic gave Ukraine an additional impetus in its development of various digital solutions. At the initial stages of the pandemic, Ukraine was progressing in digitalisation reform which required a political will and financial backing for making relevant political decisions and providing practical solutions on implementation of a nation-wide digitalisation initiative in 2010 [27]. The project was focused on providing comprehensive services for the general public and for vulnerable groups of citizens; raising the level of digital literacy; developing solutions for improving regulatory framework and citizen's skills; bridging the digital gap between generations and social groups. The focus was also put on intergeneration cooperation to solve the problem of digital gap. Ukrainian government introduced the "Diia" mobile application in early February, serving as the main channel of digital communication between the government and the citizens. Within a week, it had been installed by more than one million Ukrainians [28].

3.2 Belarus

Belarus' geographical location, strong cultural and economic ties with Russia proved to be crucial for the geopolitical orientation of the country and its leaning to the Eastern vector in their regime development. In 1994, after a brief democratic opening, the country chose its first president Alexander Lukashenka, who gradually accumulated the power in his own hands, fighting his opponents via direct repressions and cooptation (and sometimes assassinations) thus establishing an autocratic regime. He created a heavily centralized decision-making system, which marked all the processes in the country for years to come. In 2009–2015 Belarus adopted an 2010–2015 Informatization Strategy, the logical continuation of "Electronic Belarus" (2002), one of the aims of which was creation of the normative base and infrastructure for e-services. In 2011 the government approved the program of accelerated development of ICT-mediated services, which included subprogram called "E-government". Despite the first and subsequent strategies of informatization proclaiming principles of efficacy and citizen-centeredness as the core of the development of Belarus, in fact, the actual policies turned out far from the initial idea.

As experts have pointed out, the focus of the e-documents has been rather on technocratic expansion of the state, rather than on establishment of the e-participation structures and the channels of communication between government and citizens [29]. The attention is devoted to the creation of the single system of digital document exchange and the unification of the governmental websites. The situation has not changed significantly over the 2010s, with the subsequent document (2016–2022 Informatization Strategy) launching rather information services, than transactional. As of 2021, Unified Electronic Services Portal (portal.gov.by) is providing more than 149 services for individuals and 197 – for companies, with most of them being purely informational. 45 administrative procedures are available, and merely 19 of them – purely digital, having a "low social significance".

The Covid-19 pandemic and the political crisis after the 2020 presidential elections has influenced the situation in Belarus in a fundamental way, leading to major worsening of the situation in all spheres. In the latest *Nations in Transit* comparative report, published by Freedom House, Belarus has been labeled a consolidated authoritarian regime, having the lowest possible National Democratic Governance Rating (1.00 with the highest being 7.0) and receiving the Democracy Score of 1.29 [30]. Amid severe repressions implemented to civil society, political opposition, independent media, and the representatives of certain professions (such as teachers and medical professionals), the capacity of the government to provide high-quality services ultimately decreased. Lukashenka was channeling all efforts and resources available on countering revolution and fell behind other Eastern European countries in struggling against the pandemic.

Finally, the trends of e-government development in Ukraine and Belarus in the period between August 2020 and February 2022 differ significantly due to the varying political, economic and social context, with the differences becoming even more pronounced after the pandemic and the political crisis in Belarus which started from August 2020, after mass falsification of presidential election results. For example, according to the statistics by International Telecommunication Union (ITU) from 2017, Belarus held 32nd place out of 167 countries in ICT Development Index, while Ukraine was on the 79th place [31]. As of 2020, Belarus also performed significantly better than Ukraine in E-government Readiness Index, resting on a 40th place, while Ukraine taking 69th spot (still a significant breakthrough as compared to previous year - the country improved its position by 13 positions) [32].

To summarize, despite solid performance in the international indexes and both countries naming digital economy and e-government as priorities, they still fall behind with regards to material (infrastructure) and non-material (digital literacy) components, crucial for the dynamic development of e-services. More than that, the policies with regards to e-government development neither entailed the mechanisms of e-participation nor established reliable communication channels between the citizens and the government agencies. The lack of trust in public administration and political leaders, the legacy of the common Soviet past, has been among the most important challenges for the political administration to overcome.

4 Material and Methods

The analysis in this paper is based on empirical material from two country cases studies. Ukraine case included 34 interviews and document analyses. 27 structured, questionnaire-based interviews targeted citizens in Dnipro who had experience with e-services. The snowball sample included alumni of Dnipropetrovsk institute of public administration, and the residents of Dnipro city, knowledgeable of the administrative reform. The respondents belonged to different age groups (3, 7% of youth under 21 y.o., 3, 7% of youth of 22–25 y.o., 55, 6% of citizens of 26–39 y.o., 14, 8% of citizens of 40–50 y.o., 18, 5% of citizens of 51–65 y.o., and 3, 7% of citizens of 66 y.o. and older) and gender groups (63% of women and 37% of men). The respondents professional background came from business, civil service, education, healthcare, construction work, trade and services, and agriculture.

The questionnaire consisted of four groups of questions: (1) "Vision of change"; where does the digitalization reform lead: which achievements of the digitalisation reform are successful; how the work of local authorities in this regard could be estimated? (2) "Analysis of existing problems": availability of the Internet, mobile phone, computer, and other devices; preferences among digital and paper formats of services; easement of e-services; trust for authorities and e-services; e-participation; common e-services and individual problematic experience; needs and demands. (3) "Values engrained into the e-services" (citizen-centeredness, trust, participation for all, support, and inclusion). (4) "The "digital citizen" in the digital society": how the role and responsibilities of the citizens could be described or imagined; which kind of knowledge, information, or improvements from authorities is needed? Importantly, the small population of the respondents and its coverage of digitally active users makes it non-representative and presents an important limitation of our material.

7 semi-structured interviews with Dnipro city council representatives were included. The informants were responsible for the strategy work on digital transformation of the city. The interview and document analysis served as a basis for research input to "Dnipro Smart City Concept". In addition, we relied on document analysis (such as "Digital Agenda of Ukraine – 2020", "Concept and the Action Plan for the Development of the Digital Economy and Society of Ukraine for 2018–2020") and other secondary data (relevant literature on the topic along with the international ratings, such as Freedom House, Heritage Foundation, and UN E-Gov Survey).

The Belarus case involved mapping of more than 70 civic tech initiatives in the social domain and at the grassroots level during the first wave of mass mobilization in Belarus, highlighting the innovations. Some of these initiatives targeted the literal absence of civil rights, while others aimed to support and re-educate former public officials, who lost their jobs for political reasons. At the same time, decision-making bodies emerged and crystallized at the local level, as people organized themselves in urban districts to solve daily problems, while also expressing their civic stance during the protest and publishing the coverage on social media, particularly on Telegram channels. Additionally, we conducted 3 semi-structured interviews with the representatives of civil society, preoccupied with the topic of digitalization in Belarus, to test the findings of our mapping exercise (e-government expert, civic tech activist, civic tech developer). The document analysis included national documents, related to e-service infrastructure and their regulations, such as National Program of Advanced Development of Services in ICT, subprogram "Electronic Belarus", as well as reported data ITU, Freedom House, Heritage Foundation, UN E-Gov Survey.

The limitations of the Belarus material is that it covers a certain amount of civic tech initiatives, providing rather a snapshot of a highly dynamical and fluid environment.

Also, the study did neither include any initiatives, launched by the state, nor analysis of the current state-of-the-art of the system of e-services in Belarus and its perception by the citizens. This is due to the fact, that it is neither possible to receive any reliable information from the official sources (as a rule it is propaganda-shaped) nor conduct interviews with the public officials (who are reluctant to speak to representatives of civil society or Western academia).

5 Results and Analysis

5.1 (Pre-war) Ukraine: Challenges of Citizen Trust that Underly Multiple Digitalisation and Decentralization in Public Administration

Our analysis in the Ukrainian case study has involved assessing Dnipro local authorities' capacity for a deeper organizational and digital transformation, its efficacy and readiness for providing highly demanded citizen-centered e-services of high quality. We have also analyzed the citizens' readiness for contributing to societal and economical change through e-participation and the role of trust in local authorities.

We found that the opinions of representatives of local authorities and of the interviewed citizens were somewhat divided. The representatives of the local authorities admitted that their organizations did not enjoy a high level of trust among the citizens. However, referring to the pre-war time (2020–2022), they experienced a significant progress in the digitalization of services, the optimization of the entire service delivery system, the removal of many systemic barriers to make government to citizen interactions, convenient, open, and user-friendly. The civil servants recognized the pace of the national reforms in the sphere of digitalization and decentralization of power as one of the main factors in the success of the transformations at the city level. The digitalisation reforms provided expanded access of the cities to new high-quality digital solutions proposed by the state, on the one hand. On the other hand, under the decentralization reform, they provided an opportunity for self-government bodies to actively participate in the acceleration of these processes at the expense of their own capabilities and budgets, which previously proved impossible under the centralized governance.

Thus, in addition to a centralized, national web portal of electronic services (the Portal Diia (2022), the residents of Dnipro have received an extensive system of local services. However, the interviewed residents of the city were not equally optimistic in their reflection of their attitude towards the available e-services. 40% of respondents expressed distrust in e-services, 20% of them reported that they did not use them at all, and 60% say replied that they use them sometimes. Nevertheless, the general picture was that the respondents were mostly satisfied with the direction of the digitalization of public services in their city.

The majority (60%) of the respondents preferred choosing e-services over traditional ones that involved visiting the service centers, time-consuming queuing, and the paperwork. They noted that the convenience of the reform could not be overestimated and hoped in the reforms' positive results. In terms of consumption, those who used the e-services recognized them as convenient and therefore used them more often. However, the increasing consumption of e-services did not concur with an increase of citizen participation in the public community development initiatives.

While the respondents recognized the digitalization reform among the more successful reforms of independent Ukraine (1991–2021), nevertheless, the challenge with citizen trust and active participation in social transformations through the use of the e-democracy and e-participation involve an array of problematic issues [33]. Considering the global ranking of Ukraine in the e-democracy index (39/100), we should emphasize the low level of e-service consumption and community engagement by using e-petitions, participatory budgeting, online voting for local development initiatives and projects, using platforms and instruments of local development and decision-making). We observe insufficient progress in the component of e-participation which depends on trust, digital literacy, and activism. Our interview results confirm that the low level of citizens' community engagement may partly be explained by the historically low level of trust for the authorities. The reason was in resistance to major reforms in Ukraine in 2020, which canceled the democratic achievements of 2019 (40/100 in the rating) as President Zelensky initiated the termination of employment of key politicians who led the reforms. That decreased citizens' trust in authorities which seemed to prioritize their own political interests over national ones. At the end of 2021, only 27% of Ukrainians trusted their president, and 50% did not [34].

While the governmental solutions and policy measures on activating and engaging the population was fragmentary and non-systemic during 2020 until 2022, the escalation of violence due to the Russian invasion, in February 2022, may prove a radical change in citizen trust and engagement with the government. As the government headed by President Zelensky had shown strong ability to resist massive Kremlin's attacks, evidence of citizens united supportively to use all the available e-tools available to stop Russian aggression while demonstrating never-before-seen trust in authorities.

5.2 (Post - 2020 Elections) Belarus: No Political Trust, but Citizen-to-Citizen Trust Through Civic-Tech Initiatives as Service Alternatives to Suppressive Government

Our findings in the Belarus case revealed a set of problems hindering the improvement of the e-services in Belarus. Our interviewees mentioned the following problems: the lack of transparency and accountability. There is a formal procedure of civil society mediation on the projects, but the authorities set the agenda and the discussion is commonly a purely formal process, the orientation on the formal aspects in the implementation of digitalisation to progress in ratings. There is lack of cooperation and trust between the stakeholders, due to the fallout between the authorities and the civil society. There is neither cooperation nor discussion on priorities and problems of digitalisation between the parties that are driven by different visions of priorities and tasks for the actors in the process of digital transformation. There is a lack of understanding about the methods and the tools for promoting their interests through digital platforms among the NGOs, and a lack of positive examples of cooperation between the different players. In addition, the multiple governmental websites, that are still not using HTTPS protocols, provide a low level of information security.

That said, the interviewees acknowledged that one of the key challenges faced by the Belarusian society was the dramatically reduced level of trust, which occurred initially due to the poor treatment of the pandemic, and after the brutal repressions of the civil society in 2020 presidential elections. Particularly, according to the research by Douglas, Elsner [35] at ZOiS, the trust in all of the Belarusian political institutions has been weak, with the same scores being characteristic for the judiciary, executive, legislative powers as well as the security apparatus. Along with the negative attitude to the violence, this lack of trust, has become one of the main reasons for the protests [35].

Notably, because of this lack of political trust, the citizens started self-organizing in different initiatives. The most striking feature of the civic initiatives, which emerged during the 2020–21 Belarusian protests was their evolution into important problem-solving instruments amid fundamental social and political uncertainty. Activists were decisive in situations when the authorities tried to block every possible channel of communication, to both direct assistance to those in need and maintain societal aspirations for political and social transformations, by employing creative ideas and developing digital solutions to act as mediators between the Belarusian diaspora and the protesters. The challenges they faced were multiple, from finding financial sources to support those who lost their jobs because of their political views, to developing applications enabling communication between arrested protestors, their relatives, and human rights defenders.

Consequently, the civil society organizations have introduced multiple initiatives and contributed to building networks of solidarity and uncovered truthful information about key events in Belarus. We have traced and analyzed around 70 civic initiatives that fall under the name "civic tech" initiatives by actively using the technological innovations in their activities. The initiatives covered various areas, including financial assistance of arrested protesters, crowdsourcing, medical help, assistance to strike committees, assistance to students, assistance to those arrested, self-help instruments, public initiatives incubators, police crime watchers, support to former 'siloviki' (riot police), support with reeducation, black-listing of companies, tools for recounting of votes, sociological research, civic control of justice system, psychological support, alternative schools, support for independent media and sportsmen union. For the most part, the initiatives were focused on providing direct assistance to citizens who suffered from the brutal repressions, launched by the authorities to suppress the mass protests. The initiatives aimed at supporting different groups of victims: young people who lost their jobs; families who lost their breadwinners as a result of arrest; retirees who, due to the risk of coronavirus infection and the turbulent situation on the streets, could not buy basic necessities; students and schoolchildren who could not go to school on September 1, or whose parents were persecuted because of voicing the political opinion.

Consequently, a rise in Belarusian civic activism has managed to launch multiple civic initiatives, based on crowdfunding and crowdsourcing, thus solving acute public needs (normally addressed by public welfare services) and have served, in a manner, as a substitute to the system of services, that should be provided by the state.

5.3 Political Trust and Citizen Non-engagement Understood Through the Soviet Legacy of Public Services

Delving into the historical roots for citizens' low trust in the authorities, we could turn back to the era of the USSR, in which Ukraine spent 72 years (1919–1991). The experience of building socialism in a totalitarian state had a significant impact on the values and attitudes of the citizens. Some of our respondents called this impact as "established mentality". The totalitarian regime, organized according to the principles of "the dominant head" and "population weaned to participate", has significantly affected civic trust and civic engagement with the authorities [36]. Citizens got used to the fact that they were guaranteed a minimum package of social benefits and services, the access to which never required active participation in design or development. In addition, personal "obedience" and tactics of "non-intervention" in the processes of societal and state's development during this long historical period brought more benefits than the active position of a citizen, especially if appeared to be in opposition to the ruling communist party [37]. "Respectable" or "good citizen" in the USSR meant "convenient" and "not interfering." This contributed to the development of habits of "non-intervention" in problems "not concerning the obedient citizen", the rejection of entrepreneurial initiative, which was associated with fraud, in favor of a guaranteed social contract of employment in the "state sector" [38]. The uniform distribution of benefits in a socialist state in equally small volumes has resulted in the low quality of services, which could hardly be called citizen-centric or user-friendly [39]. The low quality of the guaranteed state services was offset by a constant state propaganda about "the greatness of the most powerful nation in the world", so it was never challenged by the people due to the lack of comparison with other existent approaches and service quality [40].

The transition to the capitalist model of services was extremely challenging for three generations of Ukrainian citizens, which were "accustomed" to the "free" services that were included in the "package" by default. Attempts by subsequent governments of Ukraine to build a public understanding of dependencies inevitably resulted in condemnations and a statement of their «weak leadership», inability to "give their people the necessary package of benefits in the required volume" [41, 42]. Very few presidents and presidential candidates of Ukraine dared to raise this topic, as this inevitably ended in a large-scale loss of electoral sympathies (as in the examples of Yushchenko and Poroshenko). Conversely, politicians who promised an alternative to the Soviet "package" were successful (as in the examples of Kuchma, Yanukovych) [43]. Yet a classical example was the presidency of Yanukovych, whose reign is still considered by many Ukrainians as "times of prosperity of Ukraine" [44]. The reason for the "growth of prosperity" was his obedience or cooperative attitude to the Putin regime and anti-Ukrainian policies (disregard to Ukraine's course to European integration) grounded in the constant economic incentives for the adoption of laws that strengthened Russian representation and its influence on the territory of Ukraine to the detriment of its national interests.

When the economically inefficient and anti-Ukrainian policies of Yanukovych were replaced by the pro-Ukrainian policies of Poroshenko, which relied on the consolidation of Ukrainian citizens to restore it, everyone could feel how difficult it was to find themselves in open market conditions. The rejection of state paternalism in order to boost the development of a competitive economic environment has thus become a serious stress test for Ukrainians. Many could not withstand this pressure and could not adapt to conditions where there would no longer be "free" services for everyone. Due to this reason, after the pragmatic Poroshenko, the Ukrainians chose the populist and "politically neutral" Zelensky, who promised again to make "everything accessible" [45]. His promise was based on a previously agreed course on Ukraine's integration into the European digital space for creation of a single digital market [46].

By the end of Zelensky's presidency term (prior to the war), it became clear that they could not provide for "a free paradise" for Ukrainians, leaving many disappointed again, with unfulfilled promises. Distrust of the institution of power was again growing, because many Ukrainians were accustomed to measuring the success of management by access to free public services [47].

According to the results of our interviews, only 20% of the respondents recognized the reform of the digitalization of public services as very successful. Half of all respondents found it difficult to assess this issue. At the same time, 67% of respondents said that if they had a choice, they would always prefer electronic services to traditional ones (in paying utility bills, making a doctor appointment, filling in tax declaration). But the answers about trust and distrust in the authorities were distributed approximately equally (37% said they feel the influence of the e-services industry on the development processes in their city, 30% said they do not trust the institution of power as such, and the development of e-services does not change this). A positive observation was that 69% of those interviewed "see changes in the responsiveness of local authorities towards citizens, as well as an increase in their accountability to the people". 22% of respondents, however, did not agree with that.

In general, trust in the digital environment, without reference to the actions of the authorities, was expressed by only 52% of respondents. 37% noted that they did not trust the government because of the insufficient level of security and data protection. Also, 51.9% of the respondents stated that they participated in the process of improving the system of electronic services in their city (for example, took part in community discussions, commented on social media); 33.3% expressed such a readiness, but specified that they did not know how to do that; only 15% said that they did not care about it at all, and that the local authorities were themselves responsible for the services.

As for the trust in government's services, respondents expressed the greatest confidence in national electronic services (the portal and the mobile application for DIIA-services) (62%), 32% of respondents admitted that they still preferred contacting local authorities and administrative services centers. Referring to the problems that they faced with e-services, 59.3% named technical problems or failed attempts to navigate the service without someone's help, 48% noted the inconvenience of using the sites, the applications or the portals of the e-services. 29.6% admitted that they did not considered the accessed e-services as a citizen-centric.

As the main criteria for trust in digital services, the majority of respondents named the availability and free of charge service, saving personal time when receiving it, the speed of obtaining results, citizen-centricity and convenience of the service, as well as the safety and security of personal data. As a result, 77.8% of respondents admitted that the development of digital services will help to create a common space managed by citizens. Here the trust in the authorities is gradually increasing, but there is still work to be done on the quality of services and their information security.

Finally, as the Russian – Ukrainian war is unfolding at the moment of writing, it is important to note that citizen trust in government seems to undergo significant changes. President Zelensky and his team have raised mass popularity after proving a strong military resistance and care for the unity of the country. As Ukrainians were used to experience lack of practical proofs of governmental bodies' ability to get the desired result (long awaited and planned economic uprise, promised digital transformation and infrastructural smartisation in a couple of years), demonstration of practical capabilities in defense operations during the war is currently generating an increase in trust in- and engagement of the citizens with the authorities to defend their local communities.

6 Concluding Remarks

The analysis of both cases highlights the role of citizen trust for their engagement with authorities and citizens' participation in the development of public e-services. Citizen-centric public services pre-suppose an underlying trustful collaboration legacy among the citizens, public servants, and welfare service providers. In post-soviet countries, such as Belarus and Ukraine, the key role in this process was traditionally assigned to government officials, who were directly responsible for decision-making, rather than the involvement of capacities of civil society organizations, business, and citizens.

Ukraine and Belarus – although in different ways, are still developing a culture of civic participation in public service production, which is due to the long-term historical period of authoritarian governance. In the Ukrainian case we can observe a gradual civic alignment with the authorities (especially highlighted by the civic engagement during the war), while in the Belarusian case we register the rise of civic tech initiatives, driven by the emerging trust among the citizens. As during the Soviet period the citizens had access to free and state-guaranteed package of basic, albeit low quality services, the practice of constructively engaging with authorities for public service development is still not in place. Considering that this citizen-government non-engagement model, common for post-Soviet countries, is an important integral component of the socio-political legacy in Belarus and Ukraine, building trust between government and civil society is still a challenging task.

However, the experience of social movements, collective actions and revolutions aimed at overthrowing the oppressive government (Ukraine in 2014 or Belarus in 2020), brought people closer to understanding their specific role in developing a system of public services that can be trusted and improved. The hope is that fair, democratic elections, and an open information policy will foster formation of collective habit of participation. The experience of a joint overcoming of barriers towards building a democracy (mass peaceful protest in Belarus, and the Russian war in Ukraine, uniting people around democratic values), strengthens ties within the system of productive interactions between government and citizens.

As we have showed, in Belarus the 2020–2021 protests led to an explosive emergence of civic initiatives in response to the brutal actions of the authorities and rigged elections. Civic activists employed creative and innovative methods to resist the authorities, promote their agenda, and advocate for human rights. Doctors, lawyers, IT professionals, and ex-policemen combined, launching multiple initiatives to solve different problems related to the protests and help those in need. They provided reliable information about the COVID-19 pandemic and offered financial and organizational support for arrested protesters. In the absence of reliable national media-sources, Telegram channels played a vital role in the dissemination of messages, connecting activists with each other, and facilitating the arrangement of collective actions. Almost every initiative mentioned above had its own Telegram channel, with some developing more specific applications to solve urgent and emerging problems.

Proceeding from mutual trust it becomes possible to rebuild welfare services in organizational and technological terms, which can eventually lead to a citizen-centric e-government. As our findings show, trust-based civic initiatives arise both in Ukraine and Belarus: while in the former case they complement the government's efforts in the struggle against the aggressors, in the latter case they are providing a system of services, alternative to those of an authoritarian government. Despite different dynamics in both situations, civic activists proceed from the principles of user-friendliness, accountability and transparency. The development and interpenetration of e-services shape the dynamics of governance smartisation in its aspiration to incorporate new processes into managerial structures. There is a trust-based co-creation of these new processes in the triad of people, government and technologies. Its goal is to jointly design a productive, sustainable and comfortable environment for the citizens based on their needs.

Thus, the establishment of basic civil trust, which has been a complicated issue for the post-Soviet societies, allows launching a transformative transition of society to the level of active participation. It is no longer just the identification of issues of concern, but the formation and joint development of community technologies with raised added value.

Acknowledgement. *A part of this research was possible due to the public financial support by Swedish Institute, in the project 'Link for Change: Engaging stakeholders for user-centric digital public services'.*

References

1. OECD et al.: SME Policy Index: Eastern Partner Countries 2020. OECD Publishing, Paris, Brussels (2020)
2. Ministry of Digital Transformation of Ukraine. Every second Ukrainian used at least one eservice during 2020 (2021). https://voladm.gov.ua/new/kozhen-drugiy-ukrayinec-skoristavsya-schonaymenshe-odniyeyu-e-poslugoyu-protyagom-2020-roku-doslidzhennya/
3. Kosenkov, A.: IT-country: the reverse side of the digitalization of Belarus. [«IT-strana»: obratnaya storona tsifrovizatsii Belarusi]. EuraZia expert (2019)
4. Reznik, V.: Factors of trust in power as an object of theoretical typology. Soc. Dimensions Soc. 227–240 (2012)
5. Solonar, M., Limarenko, Y., Rozenkov, D., Snizhko, V.: Digitalization in every house: when stable internet will finally appear in Ukrainian villages [Didzhytalizatsiya v kozhnu khatu: koly v ukrayinskykh selakh nareshti z'yavytsya stabilnyy internet]. Results of the week [Pidsumky tyzhnya] (2021)
6. Akhvlediani, T.: Digital Literacy in times of the Covid-19 in the Eastern Partnership Countries. In: EaP CSF COVID-19 Policy Paper for Eastern Partnership Civil Society Forum, in #PrepareEaP4Health. Eastern Partnership Civil Society Forum (2021)
7. Islam, P.: Citizen-centric e-government: the next frontier. Harvard Kennedy Sch. Rev **7**, 103–109 (2007)

8. Yera, A., Arbelaitz, O., Jauregui, O., Muguerza, J.: Characterization of e-government adoption in Europe. Plos One **15**(4), e0231585, 1–22 (2020)
9. Wouters, S., Janssen, M., Crompvoets, J.: Governance challenges of inter-organizational digital public services provisioning: a case study on digital invoicing services in Belgium. In: Electronic Government Proceedings of the 19th IFIP WG 8.5 International Conference, EGOV 2020. Linköping. Springer International Publishing, Sweden (2020). https://doi.org/10.1007/978-3-030-57599-1_17
10. Tsutskiridze, M., Bereza, A.: The impact of e-government on the level of corruption. Baltic J. Econ. Stud. **6**(2), 93–99 (2020)
11. Sonnenberg, C.: E-government and social media: the impact on accessibility. J. Disabi. Policy Stud. **31**(3), 1–11 (2020)
12. Pariso, P., Marino, A.: From digital divide to e-government: re-engineering process and bureaucracy in public service delivery. Electron. Gov. Int. J. **16**(2), 314–325 (2020)
13. de Souza, A.A.C., d'Angelo, M.J., Filho, R.N.L.: Effects of predictors of citizens' attitudes and intention to use open government data and government 2.0. Gov. Inf. Q. **39**(2), 101663 (2022)
14. Alruwaie, M., El-Haddadeh, R., Weerakkody, V.: Citizens' continuous use of eGovernment services: the role of self-efficacy, outcome expectations and satisfaction. Gov. Inf. Q. **37**(3), 101485, 1–11 (2020)
15. Saylam, A., Yıldız, M.: Conceptualizing citizen-to-citizen (C2C) interactions within the Egovernment domain. Gov. Inf. Q. **39**(1), 101655 (2022)
16. Flanagin, A.J., Stohl, C., Bimber, B.: Modeling the structure of collective action. Commun. Monogr. **73**(1), 29–54 (2006)
17. Linders, D.: From e-government to we-government: defining a typology for citizen coproduction in the age of social media. Gov. Inf. Q. **29**(4), 446–454 (2012)
18. Yetano, A., Royo, S.: Keeping citizens engaged: a comparison between online and offline participants. Adm. Soc. **49**(3), 394–422 (2017)
19. Putnam, R.D.: Bowling Alone: The Collapse and Revival of American Community. Simon and Schuster, New York (2000)
20. Choi, J.-C., Song, C.: Factors explaining why some citizens engage in E-participation, while others do not. Gov. Inf. Q. **37**(4), 101524, 1–12 (2020)
21. Åberg, M., Sandberg, M.: Social Capital and Democratisation: Roots of Trust in Post-Communist Poland and Ukraine. Routledge (2017)
22. Dickinson, P.: How Ukraine's orange revolution shaped twenty-first century geopolitics. Atlantic Council, in Atlantic Council. A. Council, Editor (2020). https://www.atlanticcouncil.org/blogs/ukrainealert/how-ukraines-orange-revolution-shaped-twenty-first-century-geopolitics/. Accessed 08 Nov 2022
23. Freedom House: Ukraine countries in transit 2021 (2022). https://freedomhouse.org/country/ukraine/nations-transit/2021
24. Alekankina, K.:With the autograph of Volodymyr Zelensky: which reforms has the president supported [Z avtohrafom Volodymyra Zelens_koho: yaki reformy pidtrymav prezy-dent]. VoxUkraine (2020)
25. Khomenko, S: Historical chance or great corruption: what is the law against oligarchs in fact about [Istorychnyy shans chy velyka koruptsiya: pro shcho naspravdi zakon proty oli-harkhiv] (2021). https://www.bbc.com/ukrainian/features-58675569
26. United Nations, E-government development index. Ukraine 2020 (2021)
27. Ministry of Economic Development and Trade of Ukraine, Digital Agenda for Ukraine (2010)
28. Marysyuk, K.B., Tomchuk, I.O., Denysovskyi, M.D., Geletska, I.O., Khutornyi, B.V.: 'Diia. Digital state' and E-government practices as anti-corruption Tools in Ukraine. WSEAS Trans. Environ. Dev. **17**, 885-897 (2021)

29. Sokolova, M.: E-Government in Belarus: how to overcome the informatization inertia. [Jelektronnoe pravitel'stvo v Belarusi: preodolet' inerciju informatizacii] (2010)
30. Freedom House Belarus. Freedom in the world 2021 (2021). https://freedomhouse.org/country/belarus/freedom-world/2021
31. #ITUdata. ICT Development Index (2017). https://www.itu.int/net4/ITU-D/idi/2017/index.html
32. United Nations. UN E-Government Knowledgebase. E-Government Development Index (EGDI) (2020). https://publicadministration.un.org/egovkb/en-us/data-center
33. Dom. From decentralization and digitalization to the land market - how reforms are being implemented in Ukraine [Vid detsentralizatsiyi ta tsyfrovizatsiyi do rynku zemli — yak vprovadzhuyut′ reformy v Ukrayini] (2021). https://kanaldom.tv/uk/vid-deczentralizacziyi-ta-czifrovizacziyi-do-rinku-zemli-yak-vprovadzhuyut-reformi-v-ukrayini-video/
34. Kyiv International Institute of Sociology. Dynamics of trust in social institutions during 2020–2021: results of the telephone survey (2021). https://www.kiis.com.ua/?lang=ukr&cat=reports&id=1093&page=1
35. Douglas, N., Elsner, R., Krawatzek, F., Langbein, J., Sasse, G.: Belarus at a crossroads. Attitudes on social and political change. ZOiS Report, **3** (2021)
36. Gudkov, L.: Returning totalitarianism [Vozvratnyy totalitarizm]. New literature observation (2022)
37. Gaiduk, K., Rakova, E., Silitsky, V. (eds.): Social contracts in modern Belarus [Sotsial'nyye kontrakty v sovremennoy Belarusi]. Belarus Institute for Strategic Studies. Minsk (2009)
38. Ziegler, C.E.: Worker participation and worker discontent in the Soviet Union. Polit. Sci. Q. **98**(2), 235–253 (1983)
39. Anthony, C.: Poverty in the former Soviet Union steadily declines. The Borgen Project (2020). https://borgenproject.org/poverty-in-the-former-soviet-union-declines/
40. Meduza. In the USSR, everything was the best! In fact, no. The main myths about the "golden age" - the late Soviet Union [V SSSR vse bylo samoye luchsheye! Na samom dele net Glavnyye mify o «zolotom veke» — pozdnem Sovetskom Soyuze] (2016). https://meduza.io/feature/2016/12/09/v-sssr-vse-bylo-samoe-luchshee-na-samom-dele-net
41. Strakhova, V.: Ukraine: in a quest of the leader [Ukraina: v Poiskakh Lidera]. VoxUkraine (2015)
42. Shurkhalo, D.: The strength of the Bolsheviks was the weakness of the Ukrainian government - historian Mykhailo Kovalchuk [Syla bil′shovykiv polyahala v slabkosti ukrayins′koho uryadu – istoryk Mykhaylo Koval′chuk]. RadioLiberty (2017)
43. Chervonenko, V.: Five presidents of Ukraine: what are they remembered for [Pyat' prezidentov Ukrainy: chem oni zapomnilis'] (2019). https://www.bbc.com/ukrainian/features-russian-48348011
44. Grigoriev, V.:Ukrainians consider Yanukovych the best former president, and Tymoshenko is more likely to be seen as the new president - the results of a sociological survey [Luchshim byvshim prezidentom ukraintsy schitayut Yanukovicha, a v kachestve novogo vidyat skoreye Timoshenko – rezul'taty sotsoprosa]. KievVlast (2018)
45. Gavrilyuk, V., Khudyakova, A.: The year after the election: an analysis of the implementation of Zelensky's program [Rik pislya vyboriv: analiz vykonannya prohramy Zelens′koho]. Word and deed (2020)
46. Duchovna, O.: Ukraine "in digits": directions of reform. Judical newspaper, pp. 45–46 (2019)
47. Mordvinov, O., Zhelyabin, V.: Some approaches to assessing the effectiveness of public administration [Deyaki pidkhody do otsinyuvannya efektyvnosti derzhavnoho upravlinnya]. State Reg. Ser. Pub Adm. **3**, 49–54 (2009)

Applying Central Data Catalogues to Implement and Maintain Digital Public Services. A Case Study on Catalogues of Public Administration in Poland

Szymon Mamrot(✉), Filip Nowak, Katarzyna Rzyszczak, Łukasz Kaczmarek, and Jacek Krzywy

Łukasiewicz Research Network–Poznań Institute of Technology, ul. Estkowskiego 6, 61-755 Poznań, Poland

{szymon.mamrot,filip.nowak,katarzyna.rzyszczak,lukasz.kaczmarek, jacek.krzywy}@pit.lukasiewicz.gov.pl

Abstract. With a great number of e-government portals, public administrations across the world face a challenge to properly manage the information related to digital public services. Ensuring data reliability, completeness and validity are crucial to ensure e-services uptake by users.

The paper aims at presenting the case study of the Polish initiative to develop Catalogues of Public Administration (KAP), which will serve as a reference source for the delivery of digital public services. Centralisation and harmonisation of service-related information are expected to improve the delivery of e-services and decrease resources dedicated to maintenance. The case-study method was used to present how to implement and maintain digital public services by the application of a central data catalogue.

The efficiency of two business processes related to e-service description update and public entity data update executed within the KAP system have been evaluated by using process simulations. In contrast to a standard approach to organize and make public datasets available in public catalogues, in the presented use case the primary purpose is to provide and effectively manage digital public services. Apart from increasing the reliability of information and resources savings, it will allow for conscious decision-making for the elimination of administrative barriers which burden citizens and entrepreneurs.

Keywords: Public e-services management central data catalogue · e-government

Track: General E-Government and E-Governance Track

1 Introduction

The Covid-19 pandemic has shown that electronic handling of public services is the only effective way for citizens and businesses. Public administrations around the world

M. Janssen et al. (Eds.): EGOV 2022, LNCS 13391, pp. 31–46, 2022.
https://doi.org/10.1007/978-3-031-15086-9_3

have faced the challenge of the rapid deployment of digital services that have so far been handled in the traditional, paper-based manner [1]. In addition, the pandemic itself made it necessary to launch new e-services or update existing ones. Research [2] shows that during the pandemic, the importance of the quality of the information provided by the public administration has increased significantly.

The functioning of public services is regulated by the law, which is subject to frequent changes. In the first three quarters of 2021, 1205 legal acts of the highest rank (laws, regulations, and international agreements [3]) were passed in Poland. Changes in the law pose a serious challenge in terms of ensuring that e-services are up-to-date.

In order to launch and maintain digital public services, the government needs easy access to reliable data. Reliable data is source data, i.e. data from the place of its creation. The data must be complete and up-to-date, in particular compliant with current legal regulations. The data should be controllable, which means that it should be possible to check it at any time during its life cycle. On the one hand, the data should be open or accessible to authorised users, but at the same time, it should be secured against unauthorised modification (intentional or accidental). The article addresses the problem of multiple data sources, which are not consistent and reliable.

In this paper, we describe how the implementation and maintenance of digital public services can be improved by using a central data catalogue. Data catalogues are detailed inventories of all data assets that enable data consumers to find and understand a relevant dataset for the purpose of extracting business value [4]. Data catalogues help to collect, organize, access, and enrich metadata to support data discovery and governance [5].

A central data catalogue not only provides data for e-services but also allows for the collection of information that facilitates the management of digital services on a national level. Importantly, the use of a data catalogue improves data quality while reducing data maintenance costs. Although literature offers a number of researches related to public data management, their availability thanks to the open data concept as well as communication between data catalogues in e-government, their consistency, quality and their interoperability in the specific context of public service related information, is not sufficiently investigated. European countries have tackled this problem by developing national data models based on the Core Public Service Vocabulary Application Profile (CPSV-AP) provided by ISA [6]. This data specification ensures the format is machine-readable, allowing the information to be easily searched and shared. It enables harmonization of the way public services are described and guarantees interoperability across domains and public authorities of all government levels across Europe. The solution adopted by Poland differs from most of the solutions adopted by the European states by allowing only one central source of information. In this way, apart from solving interoperability issues, the quality and reliability of presented information can be easily ensured.

The case study method [7] was used to present the benefits of the central data catalogue application. The two processes that are crucial for providing reliable data related to public service delivery (public entity data update and service description update), have been analysed and evaluated by business process simulations.

The paper is organized as follows. In Sect. 2 the most important governance challenges of delivering digital public services are presented. Section 3 shows how the data catalogue can be applied to implement and maintain digital public services. Section 4 presents the results of the analysis of two processes executed within the system "Katalogi Administracji Publicznej" (KAP), which is an example of a central data catalogue, implemented in Poland. Section 5 concludes the paper and shows the areas for future research.

2 Governance Challenges of Delivering Digital Public Services

The digitalization of public administration in Poland started around the year 2000. The act of 6 September 2001 on access to public information, introduced the obligation to publish, in a form of teleinformatic publication, the Public Information Bulletin. Since then, the e-government idea has been realized in a dispersed and often inconsistent way. Digital services have been created bottom-up at the local or regional level or by central authorities. It is estimated that there are over 4,300 e-government websites in Poland (estimation made within the KAP project). The costs of building and maintaining such a large number of dispersed services (often duplicating each other) are extremely high and the use-value of such architecture is low [8]. The situation results in a number of problems which all together hinder the development of effective e-government and the proper management of public services. The problem is common not only in Poland but also other EU countries. Different public service models, data dispersed across various registers, unstructured information, and formats, which enable further processing [9], impact the quality and the efficiency of the public service provision, increase administrative burdens, and make public service provision more costly [10]. According to The ISA^2 Programme[1], this situation constitutes a major obstacle for the Single Market. Collecting information from a number of e-Government portals – local, regional and national ones, especially if searching for information abroad, is a perplexing task.

- The silo approach

Most of the electronic systems in Poland, as well as many EU states, that are at the disposal of the central institutions, were designed according to the "silo principle". In literature, the silo structure has a bad reputation [11, 12] and is claimed to hinder effective governance. Silos are also blamed for the integration problems within public administration. However, as Ian Scott and Ting Gong noticed, the gist of the problem is not the silos structure itself but the lack of effective coordination mechanisms between them [13]. The existence of stand-alone systems, which do not communicate, has many negative results affecting efficient e-service delivery and e-service management. As the

[1] The ISA^2 Programme supports the development of digital solutions that enable public administrations, businesses and citizens in Europe to benefit from interoperable cross-border and cross-sector public services. ISA^2 was running from 1 January 2016 until 31 December 2020.

OECD stated in their Digital Government Studies, "The lack of an overarching data governance model can lead to the proliferation or duplication of data standards and technical solutions for data sharing, thus hindering data interoperability across different organisations and sectors, and affecting the possibility of integrating data, processes and organisations" [14].

- The lack of coherent data models

As the information on public services is developed separately by each public body within diverse e-government portals, different data models are applied. As a result, users receive different scopes of information and levels of detail. In the context of information heterogeneity, semantic interoperability in e-Government remains a crucial issue [15]. Semantics is one of four interoperability layers described by the European Interoperability Framework [16]. It can be achieved by applying the generic data models in various systems [17] and is perceived as a way to integrate heterogeneous, distributed information and the applications of different public agencies. This challenge was addressed by the ISA^2 Programme, to support EU Member States by the provision of a common data model – (CPSV-AP), which has been described in the Introduction.

- Low quality of data

As the results from the KAP initiative show, the data published on the e-government portals differs not only as far as the scope and level of details are concerned but also accuracy and timeliness. Ensuring high quality of information scattered through numerous portals is a challenging task as it requires the engagement of a large number of entities. As this is an additional workload for public institutions, many of them fail to keep the information updated and continuously improve their quality. In turn, different versions of the same service description can be found, and therefore the user needs to investigate on his own which one is the most reliable. Reflections on the user-friendliness of the text or considerations related to the language used (e.g. applying plain language rules) are often beyond the interest of the public bodies.

According to the guidelines on how to build catalogues of public services [18] to optimize the quality and efficiency of services, published by the ISA^2 Programme, public service providers need to be able to describe their services only once in a machine-readable format to allow for the widespread dissemination of the information across all channels. Redundancies in the form of obsolete services, obsolete descriptions, and duplications, should be avoided. The need for the harmonisation and quality levels of existing service descriptions gains importance when thinking about accessing the information on public services in a cross-border context. The Single Digital Gateway [19] is an example of an initiative that is expected to provide citizens and businesses information which is accurate, and of high quality. Having one version of the information is the only way to make it possible. Currently, with information scattered in various portals across public agencies, the effort should be made to centralise and harmonise service-related information.

Furthermore, Myrseth, Stang and Dalberg [20] claim that high-quality metadata is also crucial for the successful governance of e-services as it supports the monitoring and improvement of the content in an e-government metadata repository.

- Data stewardship and sustainability

Whilst in the case of public services, which are within the responsibility of central bodies, the information owner is known, the services offered by local and regional bodies have many stewards/managers. As there is no one data owner, the responsibility to manage information is dispersed. As a consequence, a number of bodies need to handle updates and ensure the sustainability of service-related data. Apart from the workload in hundreds or even thousands of institutions, this poses the risk of their own interpretation of the law. This in turn negatively affects the information quality and credibility.

The chaos in information delivered resulting from the factors mentioned above negatively affects the image of public bodies and weakens their accountability. Proper information management contributes to the overall e-government success. Management of information, understood as knowledge management, enables to manage e-government content eloquently in order to make it more usable and accessible and to keep it updated [21]. With more and more data available, the need to have control over information is becoming a priority.

Apart from the unnecessary burden of the public bodies related to workload, duplicated responsibility to manage the data, and impact on their image, the end-users also suffer consequences. Citizens and businesses searching for information are lost in a number of information sources, which are not coherent, reliable, and up-to-date. Looking for complete data on several platforms, and comparing and checking its correctness, makes the process the utmost ineffective and unfriendly. In addition, it happens that the authorities present different interpretations of the provisions, including the requirements, attached documents, or the form of their submission, often to the disadvantage of the applicant.

The existence of a number of e-government portals can be of value for the user when they are able to cooperate for the delivery of high quality, consistent and reliable information. Proper information management can then become part of the user-centric strategy of the public administration.

3 Data Catalogues in Public Administration

The simplified e-service lifecycle consists of three stages: implementing the e-service, maintaining and development of the e-service and withdrawing the e-service [22]. At each stage, access to the appropriate data set is required.

Enabling electronic execution of public service requires access to data about how it is handled, such as who is authorized to submit an application, what public entity is competent to handle it, what is the deadline, cost, etc. Any change to this data may result in the need to update or withdraw the e-service.

It is, therefore, crucial to provide 'data curation', which can be defined as the process of organizing and managing a dataset to meet specific requirements [23]. Acquiring appropriate datasets is only the first step in this process. The key is to ensure that data is effectively managed and organized so that well-defined datasets are understandable and easily accessible.

Data curation can be easily achieved by implementing data catalogues. Dave Wells [23] defines a data catalogue as a collection of data along with tools to search and manage the data. Data catalogues first focus on an inventory of available data and then link these datasets with a great deal of information about them. With data catalogues, datasets can be quickly searched, accurately evaluated, and the data needed can be consciously selected for further analysis. One of the main differences between databases and data catalogues is that databases usually contain raw data while data catalogues include a fully curated collection of datasets that have already been standardized, cleaned and prepared for further use [24].

Ehtisham Zaidi, and Guido De Simoni [25] indicate that a data catalogue creates and maintains an inventory of data assets through the discovery, description and organisation of distributed data sets.

The use of a data catalogue improves data management, since it:

- allows to unambiguously identify the owner of the data (data steward),
- introduces a process to facilitate the data lifecycle management,
- enables implementation of a data model for objects (core elements) and relations between objects,
- makes it possible to share data in an automated way (API).

An example of a central data catalogue, implemented in Poland, is "Katalogi Administracji Publicznej". KAP is a central, reference data catalogue, providing standardized, consistent, reliable and complete information for providing digital public services in Poland. KAP will make data available for service portals and other domain systems of administration thanks to API.

There are five core elements of the KAP ontology, which are presented on the Figure below. A life event is a factual or legal occurrence that generates a specific need of a citizen or business, which can be addressed by handling a public service. A public service is an obligation or entitlement of citizens, business entities or organizations, defined by law in a direct or indirect manner, which public administration is obliged to fulfil. A public digital or electronic service (e-service) refers to public service provided using digital technologies wherein the interaction with a public sector organisation is conducted by an IT system [26, 27]. A public entity is an entity that is competent to define a description of a public service or implement an e-service. A document is an input or output to a public service and may be in electronic or paper form (Fig. 1).

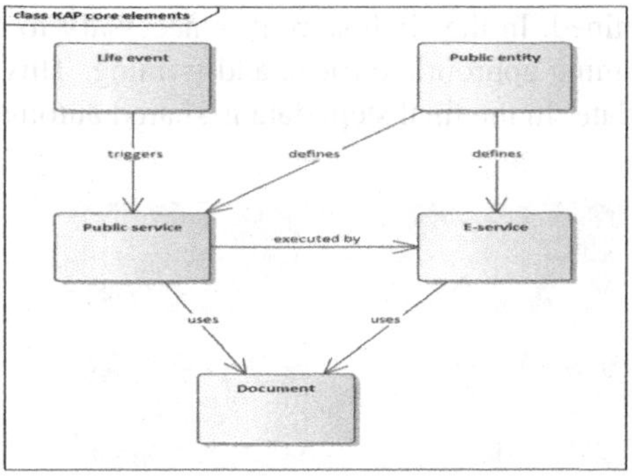

Fig. 1. KAP core elements

KAP is a system that provides various catalogues, but from the point of view of managing digital public services, four of them are relevant:

- the Catalogue of Public Entities, in which the primary object is the public entity.
- the Catalogue of Public Services, in which the primary objects are public service and a life event.
- the Catalogue of Electronic Public Services, in which the primary object is an e-service.
- the Catalogue of Documents' Templates, in which the primary object is a document.

The experience with the KAP implementation shows that the process of implementing a data catalogue for the purpose of digital service management should include the following steps (Fig. 2).

In the first step, it is necessary to define a logical data model for the objects that will be collected in the data catalogue. The model defines an entity as a representation of an object (public services, entities, e-services), attributes that indicate the main characteristics of the entity, and relationships between the entities. In the case of a catalogue system, dependencies may apply to entities in other catalogues. In the second stage, business processes are designed to manage the data, especially its maintenance. Before designing the business processes, it is necessary to decide on the data maintenance model.

In the case of a data catalogue for managing digital public services, three models can be considered - central, distributed and hybrid. In the central model it is a dedicated team that is responsible for keeping the data up-to-date and ensuring quality. The distributed model assumes that it is the competent offices that maintain the data. In the hybrid model the responsibility for maintenance is shared between the team and the respective public entities. The catalogue is implemented based on the designed processes and logical data model. It is important that the implemented system allows for the management of data through a GUI and its automatic retrieval through an API.

A key step is to identify data sources that can be used to feed the catalogue. In this regard, it is important to verify the quality of the data that will be used for the catalogue. The fifth stage involves verification and adjustment of the collected data to the model implemented in the catalogue. At this stage, data is supplemented and relationships between objects are defined. In the sixth step, it is necessary to define procedures for data maintenance, assigning appropriate roles, and training. This ensures that the data is complete and up-to-date. In the final step, data is shared automatically via API.

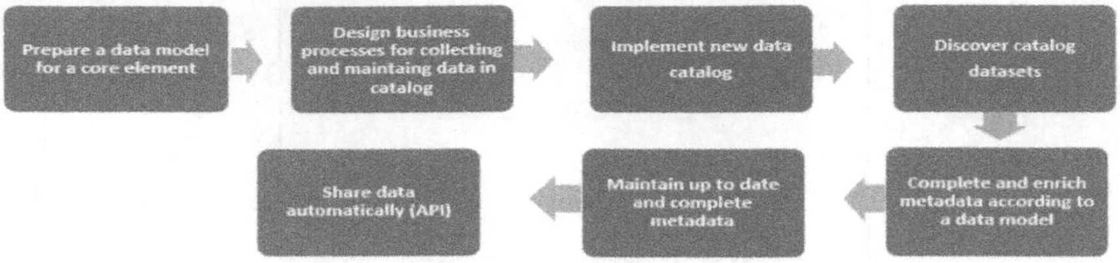

Fig. 2. The process of implementing a data catalogue

4 A Case Study on Catalogues of Public Administration in Poland

This part of the article presents results of the analysis of two processes executed within the system KAP – the process of updating the step-by-step description of a public service (4.1.) and the data (contact and related data) of the public authority (4.2) – which aim at ensuring reliable and up-to-date information on the e-government portals. This part of the research was conducted in accordance with the following phases (Fig. 3).

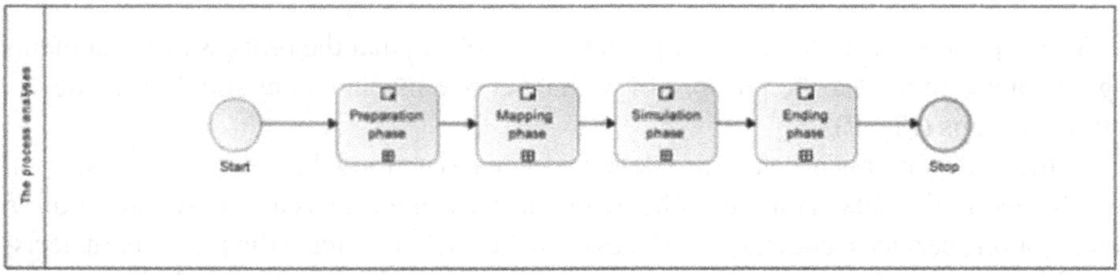

Fig. 3. The phases of the business processes efficiency analysis

The preparatory phase included collecting basic information and preparing assumptions on the basis of conducted research. A scenario was built according to the currently running process which was to be tested. The AS-IS scenario includes, among others, information about the number of people working within the examined process, hours of resource availability (working time), determination of process transactions, their quantity, and the time when processes will be generated.

The process mapping phase is divided into two parts: AS-IS mapping and TO-BE mapping. The purpose of the AS-IS mapping is, on the one hand, to reflect the course of processes in accordance with the practice of their application and, on the other hand, to prepare conclusions showing the identified discrepancies in relation to the references contained in the arrangements with the process owner. The purpose of TO-BE mapping is to illustrate the planned changes and then check their correctness and logic using process analysis.

The simulation phase is divided into two parts: preparation and simulation of the AS-IS model and preparation and simulation of thee TO-BE model. The purpose of simulating the AS-IS model is to verify whether the AS-IS prepared map reflects the actual state of the current process. After preparing the current state map of the process (AS-IS), it is parameterized and calibrated on the basis of historical data. The conditions for the simulations are the same for the AS-IS and TO-BE processes, which allows to compare the results. The assumptions for the simulations scenarios were made based on the experience from the Biznes.gov.pl portal, but are relevant for all governmental portals in Poland. Within the ending phase, the results of process simulation are analyzed in order to evaluate whether the achieved effectiveness is sufficient. The effectiveness is measured, based on the level of Key Performance Indicators (KPI). These KPIs are the times of the processes, cost of processes and the use of resources [28].

4.1 The Process of Updating the Description of Public Services

The public service description contains basic information such as the competent office, required fees, deadline for handling the matter, etc. As a rule, the public service description contains a redirect to the e-service.

As part of the research, the process of updating the description of the public service by the competent entity was analyzed. A model of the AS-IS process was prepared, which is currently in place, as well as a model of the TO-BE process, which will eventually be introduced with the launch of KAP (Fig. 4).

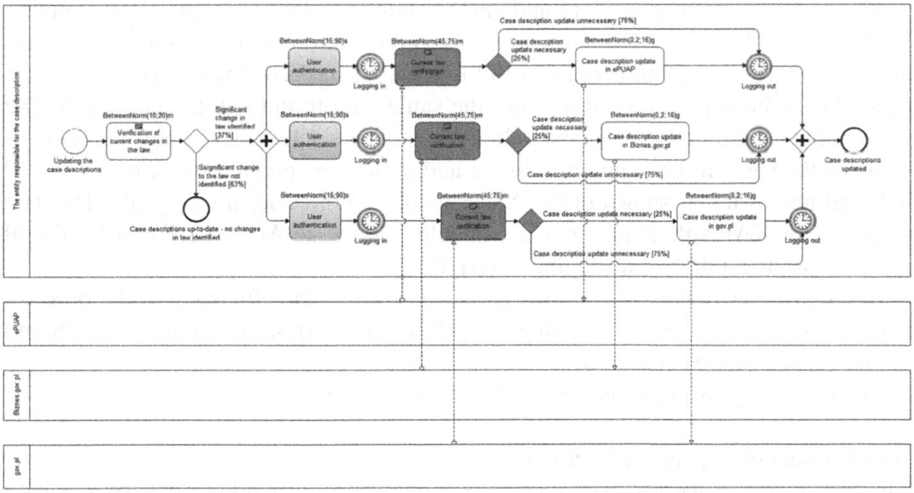

Fig. 4. Update of the public service description – AS-IS

Currently, a public entity is required to update the public service description in three different systems – Business.gov.pl (Point of Single Contact), Gov.pl and ePUAP (Electronic Platform for Public services). Updating the public service description is caused primarily by changes in the law. The figure shows the process, which begins with monitoring changes in legal regulations and then assessing the impact of those changes on the public service description. If significant changes are detected, the entity updates the public service description. Currently, changes are made in three different portals, which requires the use of separate content management systems (Fig. 5).

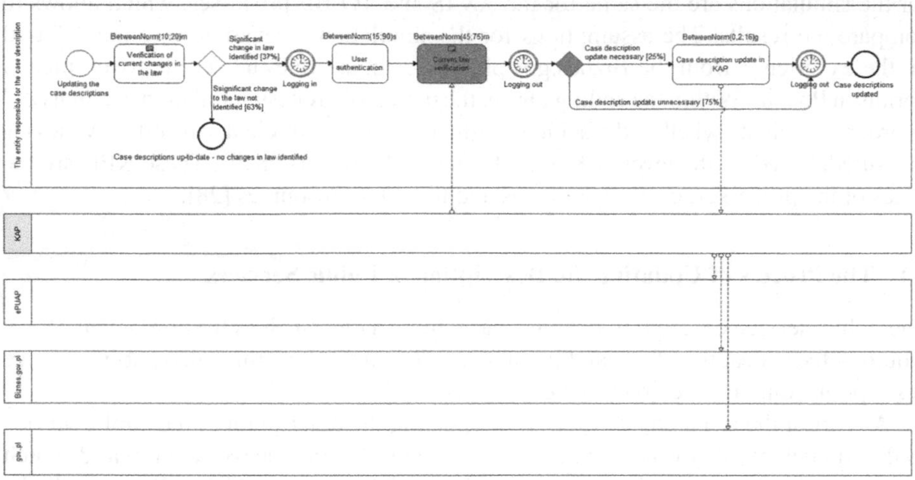

Fig. 5. Update of the public service description – TO-BE

The figure shows the process of updating the public service description after launching the KAP. In this model, a single source of complete reference data on public services handled by the public administration, resulting from its tasks defined by law, was introduced. This eliminates the need to enter the same data in three different portals. The entity responsible for describing the public service after detecting changes while monitoring of the law will be required to log in and update the public service only in KAP GUI, and not, as it was shown in the AS-IS model, in three separate portals. The data entered in the KAP will then be made available through an API. The use of KAP will reduce the cost and time of managing descriptions.

In order to verify how the introduced changes affect the efficiency of the process, simulations of the process of updating the public service description in the AS-IS and TO-BE versions were conducted.

The following assumptions were made for the simulations:

- one transaction is generated per day,
- average hourly wage (gross): is PLN 38.5 - 6475.37/21 working days/8 h (which was determined based on statistical information on employment and remuneration in the national economy in 2020 in the public administration sector available from the Central Statistical Office),
- the detection of a significant change in the law is at the level of 37% (determined on the basis of experience resulting from the law monitoring conducted for the needs of maintaining the service in the Biznes.gov.pl project),

- the time needed to verify the need for an update ranges from 10 to 30 min on average (defined on the basis of experience resulting from monitoring laws affecting the public service on the Biznes.gov.pl portal),
- the average time needed to update a public service description after detecting significant changes in the law ranges from 20 min to 16 h (determined on the basis of a survey conducted among experts involved in introducing update changes in public services on the Biznes.gov.pl portal),
- the number of working days per month is 21 (Figs. 6 and 7).

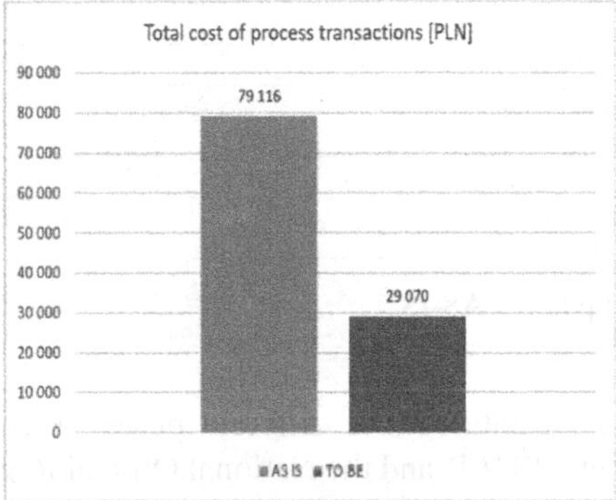

Fig. 6. Total cost of process transactions

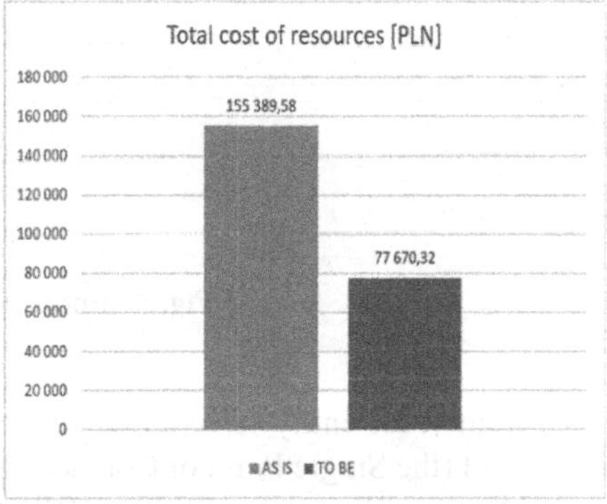

Fig. 7. Total cost of resources

Thanks to the use of KAP, the overall use of resources necessary for updating public service descriptions will decrease by 26%, and the average work time will be reduced by 21%. In addition, the introduction of KAP will significantly reduce the costs related to updating. The cost of process transactions will be reduced by 63%, while the total cost of resources will be reduced by 50%. By centralizing information about public services, introducing updates will be easier, faster and cheaper.

4.2 The Process of Public Entity Data Update

In order to provide an e-service, it is necessary to identify the entity responsible for the execution of the e-service. The KAP will collect and make available reliable, complete, up-to-date, high-quality, standardized data of public entities for the purpose of providing public services, thanks to API.

The process of updating public entity data was analyzed in order to verify whether the introduction of KAP will improve the efficiency of the process. For this purpose, a model of the AS-IS process was prepared, which is currently functioning, as well as a model of the TO-BE process, which will ultimately be introduced with the launch of KAP (Fig. 8).

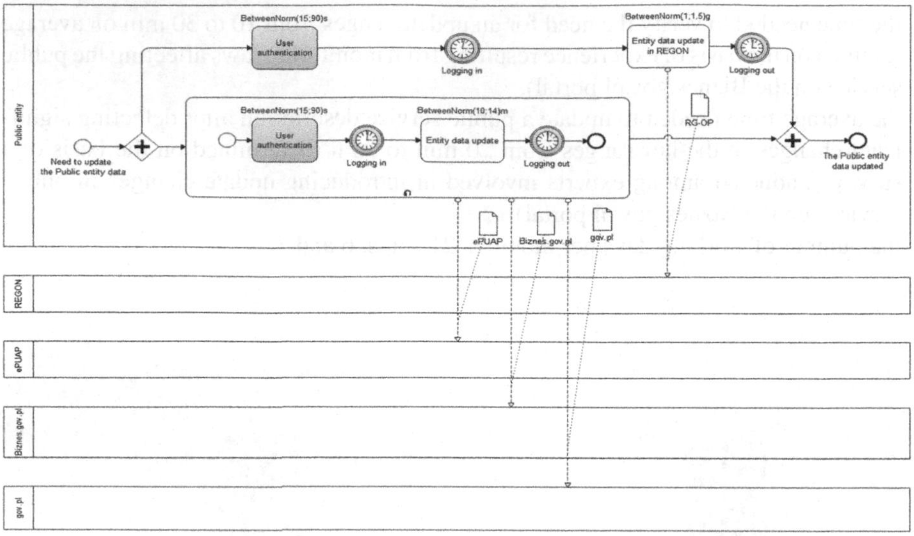

Fig. 8. Entity data update – AS-IS

Currently, an entity is required to update its data in four different places: Business.gov.pl (the Single Point of Contact), gov.pl, ePUAP, and the National Official Register of National Economic Entities (REGON). The basis for updating the entity's data is a change of the entity's data as a result of e.g. change of location, change of structure, change of name. The need for updating may also be caused by a change of legal regulations affecting the entity's data. The figure shows the process that begins with the need to modify the entity's data, and then the steps made by the entity to update its data in four different places (Fig. 9).

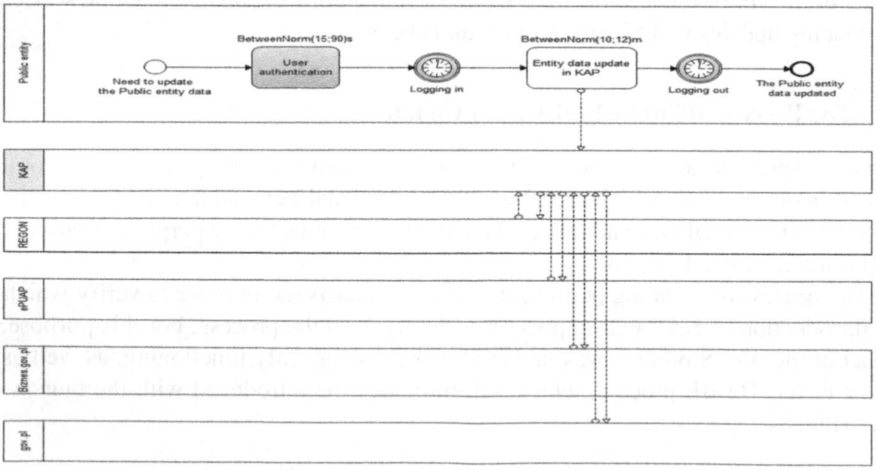

Fig. 9. Entity data update – TO-BE

The figure shows the process of updating the entity data after launching KAP. In this model, a single source of complete reference data on public entities was introduced. Thus, the need to enter the same data on 3 different portals and in the REGON register was eliminated. The entity responsible for its data will be obliged to log in and update data only in KAP GUI, and not as it was shown in the AS-IS model in three separate portals and in the REGON register. Data entered in KAP GUI will be made available via API. In order to verify how the introduced changes affect the efficiency of the process, simulations of the process of updating the data of the entity in the AS-IS and TO-BE versions were carried out.

The following assumptions were made for the simulation:

- in the process of updating public entity data (AS-IS and TO-BE), the number of 78,000 public entities was assumed (KAP project assumption),
- the number of data updates per office per year is 0.3 (determined on the basis of experience from working on the Biznes.gov.pl portal),
- the number of updates per month (all offices) is 1,950 (78,000 * 0.3 / 12 months),
- the average time of updating the data of the entity is from 10 min to 1.5 h - depending on whether the change takes place on the portal or in the REGON register (the data results from the experience of working at the Biznes.gov.pl portal) (Figs. 10 and 11).

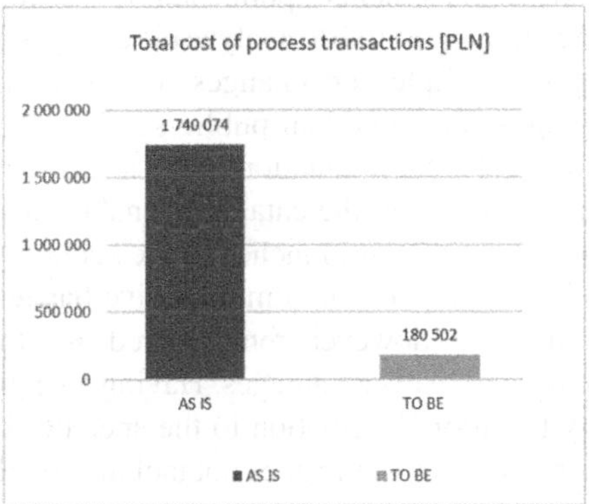

Fig. 10. Total cost of process transactions

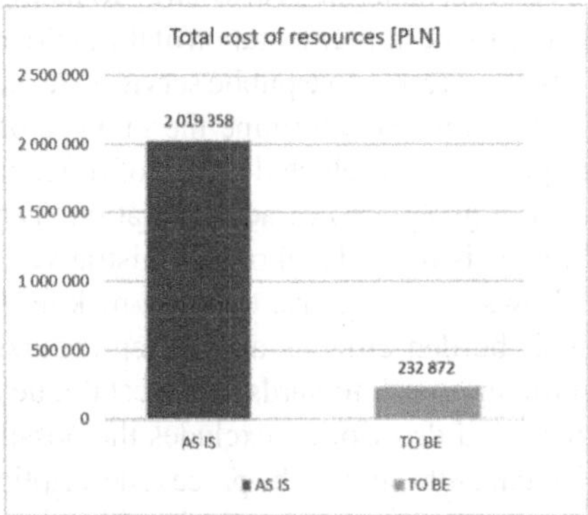

Fig. 11. Total cost of resources

Currently, the entity data management and maintenance is scattered across many different systems. The process related to the management and maintenance of entities' data is carried out on various portals as well as in the REGON register, which is time-consuming and expensive. Thanks to the introduction of KAP, the updating of data of entities will be performed in one place, and thus the overall use of resources will decrease by 11%, and the average working time will be reduced by 86%. Moreover, the introduction of KAP will significantly reduce the costs related to updating. The cost of process transactions will be reduced by 89%, while the total cost of resource use will be reduced by 88%. Thanks to the centralization of information about entities, updating them will be easier, faster and cheaper.

5 Conclusions

In the case of public administration, data catalogues are primarily used to organize and make open datasets available [29, 30]. In this article a concept of using a data catalogue for the purpose of providing and managing digital public services is presented. The use of a central data catalogue allows to reduce the problems pointed out in the second section of the article to a large extent. Proposing a central data catalogue as an element of state information architecture is an answer to the problem of silos in public administration. In this way, the central data catalogue provides a reference data source for all platforms offering e-services, both at the central and local levels. As indicated in the third section, one of the steps in the implementation of the data catalogue should be the development and agreement of a single data model for the basic data objects. In addition, the collected data from various dispersed sources should be aligned with the applicable data model in the catalogue. Through data verification and completion activities, the catalogue will be a reliable data source. The quality of the data, however, depends on whether the data that will initially feed the catalogue are continuously maintained. Therefore, it is important to develop data maintenance processes with clear roles for each entity in these processes.

Importantly, the launch of the data catalogue should not impose new obligations on the public administration. The fourth section proves that appropriately designed data maintenance processes make it possible to keep the data up-to-date while reducing the costs and time of the process. In addition to providing data for digital public services, the central catalogue is also a tool to facilitate the management of public administration. Thanks to the implementation of the data catalogue, it is possible to analyze the changes in the flow of respective public services, resulting for example from changes in regulations. It is possible to determine the number of changes for individual public services in a perspective of a selected period of time, which enables the evaluation of the stability of law in a given area of administration. The data included in the catalogue enables also an analysis of the level of administrative burden in particular branches of the economy. It allows for conscious decision-making for the elimination of administrative barriers which burden citizens and entrepreneurs. It must be, however, remembered that the central approach towards a data catalogue also has some disadvantages. Having a single referenced description excludes the possibility to tailor information to the specifics of the local authorities. The process description is more generic and does not include details that could be provided at the local level.

Further research activities could focus on the application of machine learning for a real-time data discovery and automatic cataloguing of data assets. This will contribute to the concept of augmented data catalogues [25].

References

1. Mazzucato, M., Kattel, R.: COVID-19 and public-sector capacity. Oxford Rev. Econ. Policy **36**(Supplement_1), S256–S269 (2020). https://doi.org/10.1093/oxrep/graa031
2. Alamsyah, N., Zhu, Y.: We shall endure: exploring the impact of government information quality and partisanship on citizens' well-being during the COVID-19 pandemic. Gov. Inf. Q. **39**(1), 101646 (2022). https://doi.org/10.1016/j.giq.2021.101646. ISSN 0740-624X
3. Barometr Prawa. https://barometrprawa.pl/. Accessed 21 Feb 2022

4. https://www.ibm.com/topics/data-catalog. Accessed 19 May 2022
5. https://www.oracle.com/big-data/data-catalog/what-is-a-data-catalog/. Accessed 19 May 2022
6. ISA^2. https://ec.europa.eu/isa2/actions/accessing-member-state-information-resources-european-level. Accessed 10 Feb 2022
7. Yin, R.K.: Case Study Research: Design and Methods, vol. 5. Sage publications, New York (2009)
8. Kierunki Działań Strategicznych Ministra Cyfryzacji w obszarze informatyzacji usług publicznych. https://www.gov.pl/web/cyfryzacja/kierunki-dzialan-strategicznych-ministra-cyfryzacji-w-obszarze-informatyzacji-uslug-publicznych. Accessed 02 Feb 2022
9. Domeyer, A., Hieronimus, S., Klier, J., Weber, T.: Government data management for the digital age. McKinsey & Company (2021). https://www.mckinsey.com/industries/public-and-social-sector/our-insights/government-data-management-for-the-digital-age
10. Joinup. https://joinup.ec.europa.eu/collection/semantic-interoperability-community-semic/solution/core-public-service-vocabulary/about. Accessed 03 Feb 2022
11. Daglio, M., Gerson, D., Kitchen, H.: Building organisational capacity for public sector innovation. In: Background Paper prepared for the OECD Conference Innovating the Public Sector: from Ideas to Impact, Paris (2014). https://www.oecd.org/innovating-the-public-sector/Background-report.pdf
12. Crawford Urban, M., Abondoning Silos, Mowat Research # 178 (2018). https://munkschool.utoronto.ca/mowatcentre/wp-content/uploads/publications/178_abandoning_silos.pdf
13. Scott, I., Gong, T.: Coordinating government silos: challenges and opportunities. Glob. Public Policy Governance **1**(1), 20–38 (2021). https://doi.org/10.1007/s43508-021-00004-z
14. OECD, The path to becoming a data-driven public sector. OECD Digit. Gov. Stud. 23–57 (2019). https://doi.org/10.1787/059814a7-en
15. Ching-Chieh, K., Tsui, E.: Semantic interoperability for enhancing sharing and learning through e-government knowledge-intensive portal services. Int. J. Knowl. Syst. Sci. **1**(2), 39–48 (2010). https://doi.org/10.4018/jkss.2010040104
16. European Commission, European Interoperability Framework (EIF) for European public services. Annex 2. Towards interoperability for European public services (2010)
17. Ryhänena, K., Päivärintab, T., Tyrväinenc P., Generic data models for Semantic eGovernment interoperability: Literature Review. IOS Press (2014). https://www.diva-portal.org/smash/get/diva2:993528/FULLTEXT01.pdf
18. ISA^2, Guidelines on how to build catalogues of public services at one-stop-shop portals and improve user experience. https://ec.europa.eu/isa2/sites/default/files/docs/publications/1._catalogue_of_services_guidelines.pdf. Accessed 08 Feb 2022
19. Regulation (EU) 2018/1724 of The European Parliament and of the Council of 2 October 2018 establishing a single digital gateway to provide access to information, to procedures and to assistance and problem-solving services and amending Regulation (EU) No 1024/2012
20. Stang, J., Dalberg, V., Myrseth, P.: A data quality framework applied to e-government metadata: a prerequsite to establish governance of interoperable e-services. In: International Conference on E-Business and E-Government (ICEE), pp. 1–4 (2011). https://doi.org/10.1109/ICEBEG.2011.5881298
21. Gupta, R., Singh, J.: Knowledge management and innovation in (e) government. Int. J. Inf, Comput. Technol. **4**(16), 1637 (2014). ISSN 0974-2239. https://www.ripublication.com/irph/ijict_spl/ijictv4n16spl_04.pdf. Accessed 10 Feb 2022
22. Heeks, R.: Implementing and Managing eGovernment: An International Text. Sage Publications, New York (2006). https://doi.org/10.4135/9781446220191
23. Wells, D.: Introduction to Data Catalogs. Eckerson Group (2019). https://www.alation.com/wp-content/uploads/Data-Catalogs-Intro-Dave-Wells-Alation.pdf

24. https://www.explorium.ai/blog/why-you-need-data-catalogs-not-databases/. Accessed 19 May 2022
25. Zaidi, E., de Simoni, G.: Augmented data catalogs: now an enterprise must-have for data and analytics leaders. Gartner Research (2019)
26. Jansen, A., Ølnes, S.: The nature of public e-services and their quality dimensions. Gov. Inf. Q **33**(4), 647–657 (2016). https://doi.org/10.1016/j.giq.2016.08.005
27. Lindgren, I., Østergaard Madsen, C., Hofmann, S., Melin, U.: Close encounters of the digital kind: a research agenda for the digitalization of public services. Gov. Inf. Q. **36**(3), 427–436 (2019). https://doi.org/10.1016/j.giq.2019.03.002
28. Ragin-Skorecka, K., Nowak, F.: Process analysis as a tool to improve the organization's operations. Studia i Prace WNEiZ US **48**, 77–88 (2017). https://doi.org/10.18276/sip.2017.48/2-07
29. Kučera, J., Chlapek, D., Nečaský, M.: Open government data catalogs: current approaches and quality perspective. In: Kő, A., Leitner, C., Leitold, H., Prosser, A. (eds.) EGOVIS/EDEM 2013. LNCS, vol. 8061, pp. 152–166. Springer, Heidelberg (2013). https://doi.org/10.1007/978-3-642-40160-2_13
30. Maali, F., Cyganiak, R., Peristeras, V.: Enabling interoperability of government data catalogues. In: Wimmer, M.A., Chappelet, J.L., Janssen, M., Scholl, H.J. (eds.) EGOV 2010. LNCS, vol. 6228, pp. 339–350. Springer, Heidelberg (2010). https://doi.org/10.1007/978-3-642-14799-9_29

No-Stop Government: Expected Benefits and Concerns of German Young Adults

Irisa Murataj(✉) and Maximilian Schulte

University of Muenster, Leonardo-Campus 3, 48149 Muenster, Germany
imurataj@uni-muenster.de

Abstract. This paper further investigates the concept of no-stop government and its implementation as an innovative approach in the process of public services delivery. The no-stop government aims to proactively provide public services to its citizens. No-stop government is expected to reduce the citizens' effort in triggering such processes as they will not have to contact or fill in any forms as previously required by public organizations. Accordingly, researchers are discussing barriers and enablers of this concept, mainly focusing on the government's perspective. At the time of writing, no research addresses citizens' views on their understanding of the concept of no-stop government. The contribution of this paper is to provide an analysis of German young adults' expected benefits and concerns regarding no-stop government services. The results found are then discussed and compared with previous findings. Our research results indicate that most of the benefits and concerns of citizens have already been studied in other contexts and are consistent with previous research findings. For example, citizens expect to save a lot of time if such services are offered, but they are also concerned about potential issues with privacy protection and legislative requirements. In addition, some perspectives contradicted other scholars' results. By way of illustration, our study found that automated procedures are likely to lead to less discrimination than manual ones, while other research on automated child support payments showed the opposite. Finally, we provide some guidance for the future work of other research teams and practitioners.

Keywords: No-stop government · Proactive service delivery · Digital public services · Proactive government

1 Introduction

Citizens communicate constantly with the government in their everyday lives by sending requests for public services. In the current decade, some public services are handled digitally to ease the interaction between citizens and public organizations. Those services are tagged as digital public services within the concept *of digital government*, which was examined by various researchers [16, 21, 24]. Advancements accustomed to digital public services lead to more efficient processes from the government's perspective [1, 21]. Despite high private usage of the internet, a study from the Institut

Published by Springer Nature Switzerland AG 2022
M. Janssen et al. (Eds.): EGOV 2022, LNCS 13391, pp. 47–59, 2022.
https://doi.org/10.1007/978-3-031-15086-9_4

der Deutschen Wirtschaft shows that digitalization matters, and Germany lags behind comparable countries significantly [12]. In 2021, 52% of Germans used e-government services, with 47% of them seeing the lack of consistency in services as the main barrier to an increase in usage of online government services [10]. Despite the switch to digital government, citizens are still responsible for initiating the process of receiving a specific governmental service. They must fill in the necessary data required on forms that are provided by public organizations. Citizens complain about the comprehensiveness of the forms' technical content as well as that they find it tiresome to enter the same information several times [22]. At this point, government organizations are taking under discussion the concept of providing public services proactively, resulting in a concept called "no-stop government". In this scenario, all the services will be delivered to eligible citizens in the background without their demand for a certain service [22]. As other researchers are discussing enablers and barriers of no-stop government implementation from a different perspective, the citizens' opinions on this topic have not been taken yet into consideration from existing literature [22]. Therefore, the purpose of this paper is to engage in a discussion of citizens' stance by exploring the following research question: What are the expected benefits and concerns of German young adults regarding no-stop government services? We refer to concerns as what their major issues will be in terms of their interests following a no-stop government. We conducted face-to-face semi-structured interviews with eight German young adults in the age range of 18 to 27 years old to collect in-depth information from their responses.

In a brief overview, our paper has the following structure: Sect. 2 provides a summary of the work of other scholars. Furthermore, definitions of main concepts allied with the no-stop government concept are explained. Then, in Sect. 3, we elaborate on the research design. It describes our approach and methods for conducting, transcribing, and analyzing the interviews as part of the qualitative research. Results are delivered in Sect. 4. Within this section, we present our findings in two distinct categories: expected benefits and expected concerns. In the next step, in Sect. 5, we discuss citizens' expected benefits and concerns regarding estimated barriers and benefits from the government perspective presented by other scholars on the no-stop government implementation. Lastly, Sect. 6 incorporates our conclusions compared to the existing work, highlighting what should be open for discussion in the future. The limitations of our study are also listed in this part of the paper.

2 Research Background

2.1 No-Stop Government

The research field of digital governance first emerged in the 1990s, and it is also referred to as electronic government, electronic governance, or by similar terms [7, 9, 11]. The concept also has various meanings, leading to a wide range of definitions and criticism of the "definitional vagueness of the e-government construct" [21, p.2, 26]. In this paper, we will stick to the term "digital government" and follow the World Bank's definition from 2015 of e-government as "the use of information technologies by government agencies capable of transforming relationships with citizens, businesses, and other government entities" [23, p.1]. Within the concept of digital government lies the concept of digital public services, which describes a service provided by a government agency to a citizen electronically. A simplified perspective on digital public services of the framework by Lindgren and Jansson was used by Scholta et al. to create an understanding of the next step for these types of services [16, 22]. According to Scholta et al. the next step is to proactively provide such services to address negatively assessed circumstances in current services provided by the state (e.g., filling out forms and the passive role of the government) [21]. This proactive provision of services, especially fully automated services, introduces the concept of no-stop government [13]. Linders et al. point out that in traditional models of previous research, a one-stop online portal that is personalized and unified is already considered the holy grail of digital governance, showing that the concept of no-stop shop government services is even more ambitious [15]. In their paper of 2019, Scholta et al. also see the no-stop government as the last step in the stage model of further developing governmental services [22].

2.2 Related Work

The difficulties in introducing functioning digital government services in general and no-stop government services, as well as the corresponding barriers and enablers, have already been the subject of research in the past. This section also presents research findings on barriers related to digital governance broadly, as no-stop shop services are a subset of the former. Distel et al. for example reviewed 36 relevant articles on the rejection of digital government services in general and classified barriers into six different categories, revealing the complexity of the topic [6]. In a paper from 2006, Pieterson et al. showed general user barriers to the implementation of digital government to be accessibility, trust in government, control of data, and privacy concerns [19]. Chan et al. examined the design characteristics of digital public services and defined three categories of service perceptions to help improve citizens' acceptance and experience of these services. Within the three categories, we find a total of 10 design characteristics, including, for example, privacy protection, transparency, convenience, and accessibility of services [4]. In a paper from 2016, Ayachi et al. also highlight the accessibility of services as a barrier to citizen adoption. They propose that governments should provide services in a "personalized citizen-centric approach" to increase the number of citizens using them [2, p. 1]. Even though this barrier only applies to digital public services that are not part of no-stop services, accessibility seems to be an important factor in digital governance. The privacy concerns of citizens might have also been pointed out by Meijer in a paper from 2015. According to the researcher, the image that citizens have of the government is important because citizens will not digitally interact with a government that is not trustworthy. He also highlights the shortage of time in citizens' daily lives that prevent the adoption of new technologies but also interaction with the government in general [18].

Scholta et al. found that the usual barriers that prevent the application of a no-stop government are "current legal regulations, distributed power, unintegrated back-end processes, incompatible legacy systems, privacy, limited resources, and rejection by citizens." [22, p.23], while enablers are "support of top management, process management, trust, employees with key competencies, citizen focus, and smart devices" [22, p.23]. This shows that for proper implementation of no-stop services, governments need to overcome obstacles related not only to technical issues but also to legislation and especially to citizens' opinions on this type of service provision. Scholta et al. also point to the need for more research on how governments can overcome those barriers [22]. Despite research on barriers to implementing these types of concepts, the question of citizens' views on such approaches remains unanswered. Our paper addresses this research gap by providing an analysis of the expected benefits and concerns of German young adults. We believe that the opinion and legitimate criticism of the citizens is an important factor for the development of a no-stop government and can contribute decisively to the introduction of realistic and feasible concepts of this kind.

3 Research Design

The research question was designed to investigate the standpoint of German young adults on the implementation of no-stop government services in their everyday lives. Accordingly, we conducted individual semi-structured in-depth interviews [5] with citizens as an exploratory approach to learn more about their perspectives regarding no-stop government. We used this type of interview as citizens were not familiar with the concept and we had to guide them through its definition [5]. We made use of predefined open-end questions [5, 8] and additional questions that emerged during the conversation, to elicit as much information as possible from our interviewees.

All interviews were conducted in December 2021, and both authors were involved in carrying out interviews separately. Our sample of German young adults consists of eight citizens aged 18 to 27 years old. We selected this age range to create a sample group of citizens who are old enough to have experience with requesting public services but at the same time young enough to still be considered digital natives. It was important to survey only digital natives, as they use more technology in their everyday lives than people of older generations and tend to be more tech-savvy. Since some of our questions are related to issues that require a certain level of technical understanding and also the ability to imagine concepts that might sound futuristic to people who did not grow up in a digitalized world, we think the age range of our sample group fits our research goal. To get fewer biased opinions and a more diverse set of answers, we decided to equally include men and women in our study, resulting in four women and four men. To avoid the given structures of government services being included in the evaluation of the proposed ideas, we decided to exclude former employees of government agencies from the sample group. Initially, we planned to carry out six interviews, but during the conduct of the first interviews, we realized that it might be beneficial to do more. We decided to include two more interviewees in our study to broaden the range of perspectives and then soon realized that answers in certain areas were becoming redundant. Therefore, we decided that the sample size of eight interviewees is the right amount for our research goal. More details about our interviewees' backgrounds are presented in Table 1, page 5.

Each interview was organized into two main parts. The first part of the interview included generally warming up questions and getting into the context. We mainly asked about their experience with public services, what would they like to change about the actual process of perceiving those services, and how would they feel in case they did not have to fill in any forms. In the second part of the interview, we provided a short explanation of the main concept, no-stop government services, followed by direct questions on their perception of the benefits and concerns of no-stop government services. In the subsequent step, we discussed further one potential benefit (time-saving) and one concern (data privacy issue) put forward by our side. Furthermore, we also discussed what would a perfectly designed proactively delivered service look like in their opinion. Mainly, interviews lasted approximately 30 to 40 min each. They were recorded via an mp3 recorder provided by the university and voice memo software on our smartphones. Due to actual pandemic restrictions, we had to arrange them as video conferences using Zoom software in prescheduled appointments. Our final data were the interview transcriptions on which we applied intelligent transcription [3, 14]. We transcribed every word of our interviewees except for their pauses and filler words, alongside straightening out the grammar to have a more comprehensive text [25].

The analyzing process consisted of four steps in which we were involved separately and together. At first, in the initial round, only one of us read the data and assigned general codes: *expected concerns, expected benefits, and digitalization of services* to various excerpts using the structural coding method. In the second step, the other researcher of our team had to detect specific concerns and benefits and label them accordingly [17]. Next, we worked together on some other rounds of coding by re-evaluating the previously codes segments and dividing them into two main categories: *expected benefits; expected concerns.* At this step, we also resolved some conflicts related to labeling and selecting coding segments. Our main purpose in the third step was thematic analysis coding to search for recurring themes and patterns along with the data set [20]. Lastly, we turned codes and categories into a set of findings and quoted citizens' standpoints as supportive arguments.

Table 1. Description of interviewees' background.

ID	Interviewees	Age	Professional background	Location
I1	Interviewee 1	20	*Student:* Biology (B.Sc.)	Flensburg
I2	Interviewee 2	25	*Student:* Electrical Engineering (M.Sc.)	Karlsruhe
I3	Interviewee 3	24	*Student:* Strategic Communication (M.Sc.) *Working student:* Communication Coordinator	Muenster
I4	Interviewee 4	25	*Student:* Computer Science (M.Sc.) *Working Student:* Software Developer	Aachen
I5	Interviewee 5	26	*Student:* Information Systems (M.Sc.)	Muenster
I6	Interviewee 6	27	*Student:* Theater Directing (B.A.)	Berlin
I7	Interviewee 7	24	*Student:* Social Work (B.A.)	Aachen
I8	Interviewee 8	27	*Student:* Social Work (B.A.)	Cologne

4 Results

The results listed in this section are extracted from the coding analysis of the transcripts of the 8 interviews conducted with German young adults. Our findings are structured in two main categories, a) *expected benefits* and *b) expected concerns* as an output of coding which is subsequently elaborated in more detail. The number and order of benefits and concerns are not related to the frequency of the observed patterns. Furthermore, we present our results below in Table 2 and include a short description respectively.

Table 2. List of results divided into benefits and concerns.

a) Expected benefits	Description
1. Time-saving	Contacts between citizens and the government decrease
2. Fewer errors (citizen)	Standardized processes result in fewer errors
3. Fewer errors (government)	Automated application process results in fewer errors
4. Less effort	Less effort for citizens with paperwork
5. No deadlines	Deadlines cannot be missed by citizens anymore
6. Government grants	Total amount of state aid might increase
7. Government reputation	Increase of positive image of the government
8. Government budget	Net-positive effect on the government budget
9. Data safety	Integrity of data is secured through automation
10 Less discrimination	Unbiased decision-making when set up properly
b) Expected concerns	Description
1. Data privacy	Centralized data on citizens pose certain risks
2. Data safety	Government may not be able to secure important data
3. Decision making	Expectation of errors in automated decision-making
4. Human interaction	Problem of the lack of human interaction
5. Less control	Expectation of less control over system decisions
6. Potential outliers	Importance of detection and handling of outlier cases
7. High costs	Expectation of high costs for well-functioning systems
8. Legislation issues	Current legislation is not suitable for no-stop services
9. Potential unemployment	Expectation of job losses for state employees

4.1 Expected Benefits

Time-Saving: Our interviewees elaborated on how an implemented no-stop government could save time in their daily lives. Interactions between citizens and state institutions are based on requirements that the state places on the citizen. Since the majority of these requirements, such as the re-registration of the address, could be automated, all interviewees are convinced that they would have less contact with public organizations and save time accordingly (based on Interviewee with ID **I7** as identified in Table 1. We will use the same method to refer to the interviewees for the remaining of our results): *"That you don't need to spend time to go to the agencies."* (I7) This saved time could be used for, what interviewees consider more important things: *"[...] it would just save my time, which I can then put to more productive means like studying or working [...]."* (I4).

Fewer Errors (Citizen): Not only could the time spent by citizens be prevented but the interviewees were also convinced that many mistakes made by citizens in processing applications could be prevented. It was assumed that eliminating steps such as submitting, sending, or filling out various forms with personal data would result in fewer errors in the corresponding processes, where the same information often has to be entered manually multiple times: *"I think it would be helpful to reduce errors from the individual people because it would be optimized and much, much easier."* (I3).

Fewer Errors (Government): The interviewees also believe that mistakes made by government employees happen regularly. *"[...] it's always the whole government that is doing stuff wrong, at least for the people I work with when I am doing social work. I think if these processes would be easier that would go away."* (I7) According to the interviewees, these errors could be prevented by providing no-stop government services. *"[...] generally, there is less risk for errors with lots of digitized government because everything will always happen in the exact same way."* (I4).

Less Effort: Citizens also struggle to grasp the language used when filling out forms or reading through documents. Accordingly, not having to deal with data entry for specific public services, would make their life easier as it requires less effort from their side: *"[...] it takes away the paperwork and all of the tedious things that you have to do right now."* (I3).

No Deadlines: Another highlighted positive aspect was the avoidance of missing deadlines. Interviewees consider life more dynamic now than it was when most public organizations were established. Everyday activities taking place in citizens' lives require optimized time management, therefore it is not considered easy to spare time for an appointment at short notice. Especially considering the relatively short opening hours of most public organizations, the deadlines seem unnecessary and disproportionate: *"It is sometimes really difficult to find a schedule if you are a student or working actively. It would be difficult to find a timeframe where I can go there [...]."* (I5) Therefore, a no-stop government could also reduce penalties and associated costs of not being on time with citizens' requirements for a specific service.

Government Grants: The implementation of no-stop government services and therefore proactivity of certain services could also lead to more benefits for citizens in total, according to the interviewees. Since many services are not used by all possible candidates, the population would obtain more services: *"[...] more benefits in general. I think there are way more benefits we are entitled to out there than we realize."* (I8).

Government Reputation: Receiving governmental support without being forced to trigger the process as a citizen, could also lead to an increase of positive perception towards the government: *"So I think it's the cost of public services also kind of related to governments and maybe political attitudes or how content we are with the government."* (I6).

Government Budget: Although this would result in higher government spending on certain services, interviewees believe that the overall government deficit would not increase due to the funds saved by automated processes: *"And I think this would save a lot of money, even though more people are going to get entitled for some things. But all this money is going back into the economy by spending and taxes. So, I think this would be a net-positive outcome."* (I8) In addition, the interviewees believe that the introduction of such procedures would save public organizations' staff time, which in turn would further reduce spending.

Data Safety: According to our interviewees, another benefit of a no-stop authority service is that the data required for such automated processes is more secure when processed automatically than when processed by public organizations' workers: *"[...] nobody could steal your data. The chance of data getting in the wrong hands is lower."* (I2).

Less Discrimination: Another potential benefit that was mentioned, is less discrimination in governmental decision-making. If the systems are set up properly, interviewees expect the governmental support mechanisms to be more objective: *"[...] the institutions try to abolish discrimination more and more. And I think that also with the change of generations of people working in public service institutions, this might become easier."* (I6).

4.2 Expected Concerns

The coding of the conducted interviews also reveals potential downsides that German young adults see as a result of the implementation of a no-stop government.

Data Privacy: Our interviewees are concerned with data privacy when it comes to automated processes by the government. Since such technologies would require some sort of integration of data about every citizen, the population could become too transparent (*"citizens made of glass"* (I2)), which furthermore could lead to dystopian scenarios. Interviewees consider an authority that holds every data point on every citizen in a centralized manner as too powerful. Combining for example data about personal finances, health records, metadata, and such, without the citizen's knowledge would not be desirable. In fully automated systems, it would be needed to know what data points the public organizations hold on individuals, how they use them and to have to possibility to restrict access to the data: *"[...] if things work automatically and you don't quite know which information is held about you and what database and how the information is transferred or which information is transferred to which institution."* (I6).

Data Safety: The interviewees not only mentioned data privacy as a concern, but they also draw attention to issues regarding data safety. Public organizations storing crucial data about every citizen in a centralized manner have potential safety considerations. Information could get lost or erased, get into the hands of people that should not have access to it, get manipulated with false information, or just supplemented with incorrect data by accident. Given the current state of technology in public organizations, the interviewees are concerned about the ability to handle the volume and nature of such data: *"[…] can we trust the I.T. infrastructure of the public institutions at the moment to handle this amount of data, which would need to be relatively easily accessible?"* (I4).

Decision-Making: Another concern is the possible implementation of errors in the decision-making processes. If the ruling of entitlement for certain services is automated but the technological realization is flawed, there is no way to check the decision-making process for the affected residents: *"[…] if you are not involved in the process of proving to be entitled, maybe you're not getting services because someone decided wrong."* (I8).

Human Interaction: This disadvantage gets reinforced by less human interaction between public organizations and citizens since no questions can be asked, or concerns are communicated. When considering a fully realized no-stop government, the concerns go even further: *"I think it wouldn't be a wise decision to make it all automatic so that people are not getting disconnected from government services."* (I8).

Less Control: Despite potential errors that could lead to false decisions, interviewees are generally concerned about not being in control of the process with more automatization and less human interaction. Being confronted with final decisions made by computer systems leads to the need for an independent contact point to review decisions: *"And so I think if the whole responsibility is at the government side to provide these services and also to automatically work with the information they get, then there maybe should be like checks and balances […] like a second service that can be notified if something isn't working, because the responsibility for gathering the information and rendering the service is kind of in the same hand."* (I6).

Potential Outliers: Furthermore, if decisions are automated, systems might not be able to track individual problems or handle exclusive cases: *"[…] when you look at society as a whole that when you optimize things like this, you have to generalize, and you have to make a lot of generalized assumptions about people's situations."* Assigning individual cases to categories might be impossible since citizen's issues might vary a lot: *"[…] generalizing individual cases like this could be very problematic because you need to have some kind of flexibility with regards to what kind of person you have in front of you."* (I3).

High Costs: Another concern is the costs that would be necessary to set up a well-functioning system. The investment that would be needed to realize the concepts are considered immense by our interviewees even if it would pay for itself over time: *"[…] the main barrier would be probably the upfront investment. Like it would be relatively costly to develop these services in the beginning and they will pay off slowly over time […]."* (I4).

Legislation Issues: Interviewees are worried about the legal issues related to the process of getting the public services just in the background. They would prefer to get notified and to have legal documentation associated with the service received: *"[...] makes me a little bit curious how the legal part of proving my rights (or whatever) would be [...] satisfied at some point."* (I5).

Potential Unemployment: Due to the automatization of government services, interviewees think a lot of public organizations' workers can lose their jobs. Mostly, the workers answered the hotline and provided real-time help to get citizens through a problem they might have encountered: *"A lot of unnecessary work would probably fall away because they have a generalized system of how stuff works."* (I3) It can be considered as a problem for society in general. *"That might be a concern of society, that people who are at the moment working in jobs where they are interacting with people, where they are trying to help people with their concerns that they might lose their job."* (I1).

5 Discussion

The findings presented in the results section show different expected benefits and concerns regarding the realization of the no-stop government public services. In this section, we discuss and critically reflect on the statements of our interviewees and show common, as well as contradictory expected benefits and concerns. Most benefits and concerns mentioned by our interviewees coincide with the findings of previous research, but we also found contradictory results.

One benefit that was mentioned by all our interviewees was the time-saving aspect of no-stop government service, but also less effort regarding paperwork and that there are no deadlines to be missed. These findings coincide with the results of other researchers. According to Scholta et al. citizens find filling out forms tedious and expect government agencies to provide information or services without the citizen asking for it [22]. The principal guidelines developed by Linders et al. show that information and services should be brought to citizens so that they no longer have to worry about the timing and sequencing of services, which confirms our research findings. They also suggest that officials should be equipped with mobile devices to improve the efficiency of paper-based processes, which our respondents also viewed as unnecessary and old-fashioned [15]. Our interviewees also expect government employees to make fewer mistakes in a no-stop service environment, which coincides with Linders et al.'s principal guidelines. As routine tasks are done automatically and sophisticated information systems are implemented, civil servants have more time for the rest of their responsibilities [15].

The most mentioned concern of our interviewees was data privacy issues, which are compatible with the findings of other researchers. Scholta et al. found that for Austrian citizens, data privacy concerns are among the most important since to provide no-stop services the government would have to have access to large amounts of data on its citizens: "In Austria, the topic of the 'transparent citizen' is still an issue" [22, p.19]. If citizens do not want to share data with the government, which according to our findings many have concerns about, no-stop government services are impossible to realize, which is explicitly stated by Meijer [18]. Additional to Scholta et al.'s findings, our results on citizens' concerns about privacy protection also coincide with Pieterson et al. and Chan et al. [4, 19]. Scholta et al. also show concern about data safety, which furthermore coincides with our results. The authors recommend using encryption methods and avoiding data leaks to gain the trust of citizens since can share their data only if they think that the government is protecting and keeping them private. This issue of trust and control of data was also pointed out by Pieterson et al. [19]. Furthermore, similar to our findings, one expert interviewee in Scholta et al.'s paper clarified that the government needs to make great efforts to "stop accidentally finding personal information when you are not legitimately entitled to do that" [22, p.21]. This concern was also explicitly mentioned in our interviews. The concern of less human interaction in a no-stop government environment has also been the subject of study by other researchers. In Linders et al.'s proposed principal guidelines citizens should be able to call the government at a single point of service. Thus, the guidelines proposed by Linders et al. involve enhanced human interaction, as desired by our respondents [13]. One of the usual barriers that prevent the application of a no-stop government pointed out by Scholta et al. are existing laws. Citizens express the same concern regarding legislation as they would prefer to have legal evidence connected to the received services. This concern about the requirement of comprehensive adaptions of the underlying legal foundations is congruent with the results of Scholta et al., who stated that in many cases current laws do not allow delivering a service to a recipient without his or her explicit consent [21, 22]. Furthermore, the potential concern about the high costs of implementation of no-stop government services due to outdated systems also coincides with the findings of Scholta et al. who state "incompatible legacy systems" as a typical barrier [22, p.23].

Another one of our findings from the conducted interviews is potentially less discrimination through automatization in no-stop government services. Our respondents believe that increasing automation could eliminate discriminatory factors in decision-making. This result is at odds with the research findings of Karl Kristian Larsson, who showed that a fully automatic child support procedure discriminates against low-income households. Although the process offered ideal conditions for automation, low-income citizens had to submit a disproportionate number of manual applications [13]. The above-mentioned concern about data safety was both stated as a potential benefit and concern in our results. According to these findings, citizen data could be safer in the hands of public organizations if no-stop government services would be implemented, and these institutions are modernized. This is in direct contradiction to the findings of Scholta et al. and Pieterson et al. [19, 22].

6 Conclusions

In this paper, we further investigate the concept of no-stop government as an innovative approach to public service delivery requiring no initial trigger from citizens. By examining literature presented in different journals, we were able to summarize key enablers and barriers related to no-stop government implementation which have been studied so far by other scholars. On the other hand, previous work has not brought into light citizens' stance regarding this issue. By conducting interviews with German young adults, we discovered that there are several expected benefits and concerns from their side that mainly coincide with the government's perspective but also contradict some of their standpoints.

As an open issue for the future, we would like to conduct more interviews with different age groups to include as many citizens' perspectives on no-stop government implementation as possible. Additional and deeper data collection processes could take place and focus groups could be a solution to reach a higher number of young adults. Additionally, we would like to mention the limitations of our research. To start with, our interviewees had some difficulties with fully expressing themselves as they were native German speakers and it was required for them to use English when providing their answers. Furthermore, only one age group was interviewed, which limits the potential variety of opinions and does not fully represent the German population. Moreover, the size of our sample group could be increased to achieve a wider perspective on the given topics, although we think our sample group was big enough to draw legitimate conclusions from the given answers. Hopefully, these initial findings trigger the need to take into consideration citizens' experiences and expected perspectives in using public services through digital communication channels.

The purpose of this paper was to contribute to the research on no-stop government with citizens' stance on the benefits and concerns about its implementation. As a result, other scholars can take into consideration citizens' main expected benefits and concerns when discussing further key barriers and enablers of no-stop government services. At the same time, the government can make use of this research on digital public service delivery by correcting interaction processes with citizens and emphasizing clearly the benefits of no-stop government services.

References

1. Axelsson, K., Melin, U., Lindgren, I.: Public e-services for agency efficiency and citizen benefit—Findings from a stakeholder centered analysis. Gov. Inf. Q. **30**, 10–22 (2013)
2. Ayachi, R., Boukhris, I., Mellouli, S., Ben Amor, N., Elouedi, Z.: Proactive and reactive e-government services recommendation. Univ. Access Inf. Soc. **15**(4), 681–697 (2015). https://doi.org/10.1007/s10209-015-0442-z
3. Califf, C.B., Sarker, S., Sarker, S.: The bright and dark sides of technostress: a mixed-methods study involving healthcare IT. MIS Q. **44**, 809–856 (2020)
4. Chan, F.K.Y., Thong, J.Y.L., Brown, S.A., Venkatesh, V.: service design and citizen satisfaction with e-government services: a multidimensional perspective. Public Admin. Rev. **81**, 874–894 (2021)
5. Dicicco-Bloom, B., Crabtree, B.F.: The qualitative research interview. Med. Educ. **40**, 314–321 (2006)
6. Distel, B., Ogonek, N.: To adopt or not to adopt: a literature review on barriers to citizens' adoption of E-government services (2016)
7. Ebbers, W.E., Pieterson, W.J., Noordman, H.N.: Electronic government: rethinking channel management strategies. Gov. Inf. Q. **25**, 181–201 (2008)
8. Given, L.M.: The Sage Encyclopedia of Qualitative Research Methods. Sage Publications, Los Angeles Calif (2008)
9. Grönlund, Å., Horan, T.A.: Introducing e-gov: history, definitions, and issues. CAIS **15**, 39 (2005)
10. Jahn, S.,et al.: egovernment monitor 2021 (2021)

11. Klievink, B., Janssen, M.: Realizing joined-up government—Dynamic capabilities and stage models for transformation. Gov. Inf. Q. **26**, 275–284 (2009)
12. Klös, Hans-Peter, 2021, Digitalisierung des Staates in Deutschland. Need for Speed, IW-Kurzbericht, Nr. 64, Köln
13. Larsson, K.K.: Digitization or equality: when government automation covers some, but not all citizens. Gov. Inf. Q. **38**, 101547 (2021)
14. Limpaecher, A., Ho, L.: The essential guide to coding qualitative data. https://delvetool.com/guide. Access 01 Mar 2022
15. Linders, D., Liao, C.Z.-P., Wang, C.-M.: Proactive e-governance: flipping the service delivery model from pull to push in Taiwan. Gov. Inf. Q. **35**, S68–S76 (2018)
16. Lindgren, I., Jansson, G.: Electronic services in the public sector: a conceptual framework. Gov. Inf. Q. **30**, 163–172 (2013)
17. McLellan, E., MacQueen, K.M., Neidig, J.L.: Beyond the qualitative interview: data preparation and transcription. Field Methods **15**, 63–84 (2003)
18. Meijer, A.: E-governance innovation: barriers and strategies. Gov. Inf. Q. **32**, 198–206 (2015)
19. Pieterson, W., Ebbers, W., van Dijk, J.: Personalization in the public sector. Gov. Inf. Q. **24**, 148–164 (2007)
20. Saldaña, J.: The Coding Manual for Qualitative Researchers. SAGE, Los Angeles, London (2016)
21. Scholta, H., Lindgren, I.: The long and winding road of digital public services—one next step: proactivity. In: Fortieth International Conference on Information Systems (2019)
22. Scholta, H., Mertens, W., Kowalkiewicz, M., Becker, J.: From one-stop shop to no-stop shop: an e-government stage model. Gov. Inf. Q. **36**, 11–26 (2019)
23. Sudan, R., Bhatia, D., Melhem, S., Lewin, A. and Petrov, O.: e-government (2015). https://www.worldbank.org/en/topic/digitaldevelopment/brief/e-government
24. Twizeyimana, J.D., Andersson, A.: The public value of e-government–a literature review. Gov. Inf. Q. **36**, 167–178 (2019)
25. Braun, V., Clarke, V.: Successful qualitative research: a practical guide for beginners (2015)
26. Yildiz, M.: E-government research: reviewing the literature, limitations, and ways forward. Gov. Inf. Q. **24**, 646–665 (2007)

Omni-Channel Overtures Defining the Concept and Its Applicability in Public Sector Channel Management

Willem Pieterson[1(✉)], Christian Østergaard Madsen[2], and Wolfgang Ebbers[3]

[1] Pieterson Strategic, London, UK
willem@pieterson.com
[2] Research Centre for Government IT, Department of Computer Science, IT University of Copenhagen, Copenhagen, Denmark
chrm@itu.dk
[3] Erasmus School of Social and Behavioural Sciences, Department of Public Administration and Sociology, Erasmus University Rotterdam, Rotterdam, The Netherlands
ebbers@essb.eur.nl

Abstract. The channel landscape and citizens' channel behaviors are continuously evolving. This challenges how governments manage service delivery and their available service channels. To address these challenges, a new type of strategy has surfaced in the literature on private sector channel management; omni-channel management. But could the omni-channel concept be applied in the public sector context as well? More importantly: could it address the current challenges in the channel landscape? Currently no comprehensive studies exist that examine omni-channel management in a public sector setting. Therefore, we present relevant developments in the channel landscape and discuss how an omni-channel approach could be applied in the public sector.

Keywords: Service delivery · Channel management · Omni-channel · Channel strategy · e-Government

1 Introduction

Public sector service delivery is continuously evolving. Technological developments continuously create new public service delivery channels [1]. Subsequently, these changes are reflected in a) how citizens and other public sector clients adopt and use different channels [2] and b) how governments incorporate these changes in their channel and service delivery strategies [3].

While several models and frameworks outlining such channel strategies for public sector organizations have been published in the last decades e.g. [4–6], fewer publications have emerged recently. Moreover, in a review of the literature, Madsen and Hofmann [3] conclude that the majority of the literature in eGovernment and public administration in general has focused on either a) barriers towards channel strategies (e.g., legal, structural,

Published by Springer Nature Switzerland AG 2022
M. Janssen et al. (Eds.): EGOV 2022, LNCS 13391, pp. 60–72, 2022.
https://doi.org/10.1007/978-3-031-15086-9_5

and/or organizational, or b) the adoption of and migration towards digital channels (e.g., websites and self-service applications). Main question this paper asks is whether existing channel approaches that focus on so-called 'multi-channel management' are sufficient today. This is especially relevant as an increasing number of studies, most notably in the context of private sector sales and service delivery, focus on a new type of channel strategy: omni-channeling [7–9]. Furthermore, the channel landscape is evolving rapidly, the number of available channels is still increasing [1] and citizens' channel behaviors are evolving [2]. The goal of this paper is to address this main question. Specifically, we address the following research questions:

- RQ1. What have been the key changes in the channel landscape and channel behaviors in the past decades?
- RQ2. What types of channel strategies have been developed that address these developments and to what extent do these strategies suffice in the current landscape?
- RQ3. To what extent is an omni-channel approach applicable for public sector service delivery and what are the key elements of such an approach?

We answer these questions using existing publications on channel behavior and channel management. We collected these publications using a process inspired by a hermeneutic literature review [10]. In Sect. 2, we briefly discuss this method. Subsequently, in Sect. 3, we discuss the key changes in the channel landscape, thus seeking to answer the first research question. Section 4 provides an overview of various channel strategies and discusses several associated key challenges, thereby answering the second research question. Section 5 discusses definitions of omni-channel management from the literature, provides a public sector appropriate definition of the concept and discusses key elements of the omni-channel concept. Building on this analysis, we present an agenda to create a framework for omni-channeling in the public sector as well as the main conclusions and points of discussion in Sect. 6.

2 Method

Our search for papers on omni-channel management in digital government research is inspired by the hermeneutic literature review process [10]. This regards a literature review as an iterative process, whereby researchers gradually develop an understanding of a body of literature. Moreover, it recognizes that researchers may have existing knowledge of the area in question. The authors have studied channel choice (CC) and multichannel management (MCM) for more than fifteen years and published extensively on this topic. Our previous work includes three literature reviews on CC and MCM [3, 11, 12]. We began by revisiting the pool of papers for the previously published literature reviews. We supplemented this pool with a new search for papers in January 2022. The search was conducted using Publish or Perish with Google Scholar as an underlying search engine [13]. The benefit of this approach is the wide range of results it yields. We used the following keywords: omni-channel (and 'omnichannel'), digital government and e-government. Of the initial forty papers identified with omni-channel in the title, only three concerned omni-channel management in digital government [14–16]. We did, however, identify multiple papers, which presented the omni-channel concept in a private sector setting. Finally, we downloaded the latest version (17.5) of the Digital Government Reference Library (DGRL) [17] and conducted a keyword search using "omni-channel" as well. This search did not yield any additional results.

We began our reading and synthesis of the literature by focusing on papers in a digital government setting. Guided by our research questions, we sought to capture and describe (1) the historical development in the channel landscape and citizens' channel behavior, and (2) the historical development in public organizations' channel strategies and the associated key challenges. Next, we focused on capturing how the omni-channel concept is presented in the extant literature. Here, we included papers from both a public sector and private sector setting. More specifically, we searched for (1) definitions of the omni-channel concept, and (2) key features according to the literature. Having presented our research approach, we now turn to our findings.

3 Background: A Changing Channel Landscape

Next, we focus on key developments in the channel landscape. This concerns technological developments and the rise of new channels and subsequently changes in citizens' channel behaviors. Thus, this section seeks to answer the first research question.

3.1 Changes in the Channel Landscape

The channel landscape has continuously evolved in the past decades, with new channels added to the ways citizens and public organizations interact [1]. Historically, the public encounter, i.e. the "interaction of citizens and [government] official as they communicate to conduct business" [18, p. 4] occurred via traditional channels: In person meetings (office or counter), telephone conversations and physical letters [1, 18].

In the 1990's, the world wide web offered a means to present information visually on websites. As the websites matured, they also allowed citizens to both retrieve and submit information ideally without any help from public officials [19]. Hereby, the technical foundation for digital self-service was in place. Finally, two more digital channels, electronic mail, and chat, became popular.

In the 2000s, social media such as social networking sites, blogs and wikis appeared. While these were mostly used by private companies and citizens, public organizations began to use social media to present information to citizens and to engage with them online for consultation or co-creation purposes [20].

The 2000s also saw the increased adoption of smartphones, which added additional channels and features to the government-to-citizen interaction. This interaction had historically taken place in government offices, and then moved into citizens homes with the electronic channels. Now, smartphones afforded citizens even more freedom with regards to when and where they could interact with public organizations. Further, smartphones added additional channels such as SMS text messages (which often serve as reminders of upcoming meeting or a source of receipts), and mobile apps for specific services, including the handling of digital ID.

Finally, recent years have seen a rise in a new type of channels, fueled by the development in artificial intelligence and robotization. These channels offer direct interaction and support to citizens without the inclusion of a traditional caseworker or other type of public sector employee. Pieterson et al. [1] classify this generation of service channels in three groups. *Software agents* include chat bots (text), conversation bots (spoken language), and intelligent agents, which can both response to inquiries and solve various tasks. The remaining two groups are *virtual robots*, which have a visual appearance for instance on a website, and physical *social robots*, which can either have a humanoid or non-humanoid form. These robotic channels are potentially able to substitute for some of the costlier interaction citizens have with frontline staff and caseworkers. The emergence of these new channels and the public demand to interact through different means have increased the interaction complexity and made governmental multi-channel management even more important [5].

3.2 Changes in Channel Behaviors

The remarkable increase in the number and types of communication channels available have given citizens a greater choice of channels. For public organizations, however, the increase in channels also creates new tasks and additional costs, as they must develop these channels, and present and harmonize their content across multiple channels. Further, there may be costs related to training staff and adjusting business processes.

Recent empirical studies have studied how the shifting channel landscape has influenced citizens CC and offer several important findings. First, a study from the Netherlands showed that Dutch people's needs and expectations regarding public organizations' service provision has shifted towards digital channels [2]. Similarly, official EU statistics show a clear increase in citizens' use of digital channels in recent years [21]. Second, recent studies also show that citizens and businesses rarely substitute new channels for the old ones. Rather the traditional channels, especially the telephone, is still the preferred channel for complex problems. For instance, citizens may call to ensure that they have understood information on a website correctly, or that a public organization have received information submitted via a self-service application [2, 22]. Third, since the introduction of electronic channels, studies show an increase in both the amount and types of channels citizens and businesses use to interact with public organization [5, 21], as well as the total volume of traffic across channels [12]. Fourth, citizens needs are shifting. For example, citizens need clarity about how to communicate with whom and why, e.g. because messages increasingly run the risk of being 'lost', especially when governments communicate through digital channels [23].

While previous CC studies mostly focused on CC as a discrete event, i.e., citizens' choice of a single channel for a specific task, newer CC studies find that citizens may use a variety of channels either sequentially or simultaneously, and across both private companies and public organizations throughout a public encounter [2, 24]. The increase in the complexity of citizens' channel use and expectation may be partly caused by their experiences with services offered by private companies [25], but also by the fact that citizens are increasingly expected to solve tasks through self-service applications that were previously conducted for them by public organizations [19]. Further, governments often seek to create seamless user journeys across public organizations with point of departure in specific life events [26].

To summarize, we see an increasing fragmentation of populations in their channel behaviors and this creates customer journeys that occur across channels and organizations in flexible and different configurations for different types of customers [27].

4 Channel Strategies

Governments deploy various channel strategies to deal with the different behaviors and demands of citizens [4–6, 28]. With the changing channel landscape and demands and channel behaviors of the population these strategies have evolved over time from relatively rudimentary approaches to sophisticated strategies dealing with channels, their relations and beyond. Following new technological breakthroughs, different generations of channel strategies appear. Below, we summarize these generations and discus shortcomings of existing approaches vis-à-vis the changes discussed above.

Generations of (Multi) Channel Strategies

Pieterson and Van Dijk [29] provide an overview of different perspectives on channels and how they could be positioned. They argue that the basic forms of channel management entail very little management; channels can either exist in parallel to each other, where most services are offered via different channels in parallel, or channels can replace each other where the functionality of one channel entirely replaces another.

When the channel landscape started changing in the late 1990s (see [12]), both practitioners and scholars started to rethink their approaches towards channel management. For government organizations, digitalization brought opportunities, but also new challenges related to managing public service encounters across multiple channels and organizations [28]. Furthermore, the growth of digital technologies resulted in a drastic increase in the number of channels [1] and in longer and more varied customer journeys [24]. This gave rise to a shift in thinking from 'multiple channels' (where several channels are managed independently) to 'multi-channel' approaches, where the 'supplemental characteristics' of channels are being stressed [12, p. 58]. In this, channels can refer to each other or be used for different purposes, depending on their characteristics. These multi-channel strategies themselves have evolved over time in three generations:

1. Basic/supplemental multi-channel strategies

   The underlying idea for these strategies is that different channels have different properties that render them suitable for different tasks. This builds upon communication theories such as Media Richness Theory [30] that suggest that channels, and media, vary in their properties thus rendering them suited for different types of problems. In the private sector such channel strategies were suggested by various authors [31, 32] and several government agencies followed or suggested supplemental strategies in the early 2000s, such as in the UK, and Australia.
2. Integrated multi-channel strategies

   While the idea of channels supplementary value seems logical, there are challenges. These include the need to switch channels and flaws in channel choice decision making [12], citizens habits that could hamper the best channel choice [22] and legal requirements to offer channels to all citizens thus sacrificing task-channel fit for accessibility [12]. To deal with these obstacles, more integrated channel strategies were developed. In its basic form this points to the referral between channels and the possibilities to guide citizens from one channel to another, thus facilitating their customer journeys. The integrated multi-channel management model developed by Ebbers, Pieterson and Noordman [4] is an example of such an integrated approach.

3. Blended/advanced multi-channel strategies

   Integrated multi-channel strategies also have drawbacks. One challenge is that it focuses on channel integration, but not on the underlying elements that are required to make channel integration succeed, such as (organizational) coordination, as well as content and systems integration. Third generation multi-channel strategies focus on integration with other elements of the service delivery space. For example, Gagnon et al [6] focus on the importance of meeting client needs expectations using the available channels while added more contextual variables, such as personnel, technology, cooperation, and regulations. The Wirtz and Langer [5] framework analyses strengths and capabilities of a large set of channels and adds elements of the organization (e.g., levels of centralization). This could facilitate, for example, concurrent channel usage. Kernaghan [28], finally, presents the integrated channel delivery continuum along which organizational integration can occur, from informal relationships (cooperation), to coordination, collaboration, convergence and finally consolidation, the complete "uniting and harmonizing" of the organization [28, p. 125].

   Thus, multi-channel strategies have clearly evolved over time and have increased in scope and depth to keep up with changes in the channel landscape. However, the question remains whether current strategies are sufficient to deal with the latest changes. The answer, in our view, is no. In the next section, we address the key challenges to the successful deployment of multi-channel strategies.

4.1 Key Challenges

The following are these key challenges:

- Channel multiplexity

  All models tend to treat contacts as independent incidents (e.g., I have a question and choose channel X). As mentioned above, empirical studies [24] show that many contacts are highly interdependent and of a *multiplex* nature. This interdependence requires such things as a *memory* in transfer between channels, so that citizens don't have to repeat their questions. Further, a *link* is required between contacts across channels when subsequent contacts are part of one customer journey (e.g., when I call to enquire about a form I just submitted online, the agent must see that I submitted this and where I am in my journey). Thus, the growth in channels has resulted in longer and more varied customer journeys [24], necessitating the need to approach channel management from a customer journey perspective, rather than a 'contact incident' perspective.
- Static channel features

  All models discussed in this publication take a relatively static approach towards channel characteristics and task channel fit [4–6]. They assume that channel properties

are 'fixed' and that therefore certain channels are better suited for certain tasks than others. This ignores that channel characteristics are evolving, for example when users gain more experience with the use of a channel and that the combination of channels could augment their use (e.g., through blending and applications such as co-browsing). Thus, rather than being discrete and static entities, the current reality of channels is one of 'fluidity' and current channel management models do not account for this.
- Increasingly fragmented population
  As discussed in the previous section, the number of channels increases and citizens have started diverging in their (digital) skillsets, behaviors, and channel expectations [1, 2]. As a result, different customer segments might have different preferences for different channels in different parts of the customer journey. Thus, a static 'one size fits all' model of task-channel fit might not satisfy the need of today's dynamic and varied population needs. Channel management models typically rely on the idea of task-channel fit (e.g. [4–6]) and do not account for variety among different segments of the population.

The notion that existing channel approaches are insufficient is not completely new, but still recent and not targeted as the challenges presented in this contribution. In the private sector literature, academics in the mid 2010 started to argue that channel management should focus on the "synergetic management of the different channels and touch points" [7, p. 176] and improve service delivery following the realization that more integrated (and fluid) approaches are needed. More recently, Madsen and Hofmann [3] in a review of the public sector literature argued that newer channel strategies are needed to deal with the high number of channels. In our view newer strategies need to address all key challenges.

5 An Omni-Channel Approach

In this section we discuss the core of such a new type of channel strategies: omni-channel management. While this concept is gaining ground in the private sector, it has not been extensively used in public sector contexts. In this section we discuss definitions of the concept before presenting a definition tailored to public sector service delivery. Subsequently we discuss key elements of such an omni-channel strategy, and we discuss the applicability of key elements to the public sector and an agenda to create a model for the public sector.

5.1 Defining the Omni-Channel Concept

So, what is omni-channel management? The word 'omni' itself is a Latin word meaning "all" and "universal". Various definitions in the (mostly marketing and/or sales) literature of the concept exist. The following are examples:

- "an integrated sales experience that melds the advantages of physical stores with the information-rich experience of online shopping" [33, p. 65]
- "a unified approach that manages channels as intermingled touch points to allow consumers to have a seamless experience within an ecosystem." [8]

- "the synergetic management of the numerous available channels and customer touch points in such a way that the customer experience across channels and the performance over channels is optimized" [7].

While these definitions differ in certain areas, they are similar in most. They emphasize the need to unify or integrate channels fully and to manage these as 'synergetic' as possible [34]. This suggests that, rather than seeing channels as separate entities, they need to be regarded from a symbiotic or holistic point of view. This entity of channels is used to manage client interactions and the touchpoints between client and organization take place using a non-predefined collection of communication cues [35].

While the definitions above focus on 'customers, often 'sales' or 'retail', they are clearly aimed at private sector (sales) settings. The public sector context, obviously, is different (see [12] for a discussion). For example, citizens (as opposed to private sector clients) often have no choice between providers and governments have an obligation to serve all clients. This has some implications for the potential of omni-channel strategies. Private sector organizations can typically target select segments of the population [36] and thus choose to deploy a limited set of channels to target their audiences. This makes the design and management inherently simpler than for governments that need to serve *all* citizens via an appropriate set of channels. Furthermore, typically citizens have more roles in their relationship with governments than just being 'consumers' of public services. They also have duties and obligations, vote and they could participate in policy processes and typically the same set of channels is used for a multitude of purposes [37]. This further complicates channel management in the public sector and necessitates inclusion as an element of a definition of omni-channel service delivery in the public sector. Given this and based on the definitions above, we propose the following definition of omni-channel management in the public sector:

> *"Omni-channel management is the holistic management of all available service channels in which all channels are fully integrated and allow the seamless delivery of all services to all segments of the population".*

5.2 Key Features of the Omni-Channel Concept

But how exactly is this different from existing multi-channel strategies? To answer this question, we need to study the features of omni-channel strategies. The public sector literature in this area is scarce. As mentioned above, our review has only yielded three studies [14–16]. None of these provide a definition of the concept tailored to the public sector. Two of the publications build upon the private sector literature in explaining the concept [15, 16], the third is a work in progress paper [14] that does not provide a definition. However, this publication does mention features of omni-channel management in the public sector, based on a non-academic report [35]. The publication argues that the success of omni-channel management depends on integration on four levels: a) organizational, b) services and processes, c) IT systems and d) data. The private sector literature provides more insights. Shi et al. [38] provide an overview of five dimensions that define the omni-channel experience of retail customers:

1. Connectivity. The extent to which the cross-channel service content and information are linked and interconnected
2. Integration. The extent to which customer perceives all information systems and management operations are unified and integrated well across channels.
3. Consistency. The extent to which customers experience both content and process consistency of interactions across channels.
4. Flexibility. The extent to which customers are provided with flexible options and experience the continuity when migrating tasks from one channel to another channel.
5. Personalization. The extent to which a customer perceives that the omni-channel retailer provides its customers with individualized attention.

In addition, Burford and Resmini [39] found that information coherence and cross-channel experience are the two most essential aspects in omni-channel design. Saghiri et al. [40] focus on integration and see the concept as a truly integrated approach across the whole retail operation that delivers a seamless response to the consumer experience through all available channels, thus emphasizing both integration and the seamless nature of the customer journey. This 'seamless' aspect of omni-channeling appears often in the literature. The underlying reason appears to be twofold. First, omni-channel customers tend to move freely between the different channels, all within a single transaction process [41]. These customers expect a seamless purchasing experience across channels and touch points [7]. Second, different customer segments use different configurations of channels. 'Mono channel' users, for example, use one channel throughout their journey, while other users engage in 'showrooming' or 'webrooming' and finally some users frequently switch between channels in every stage of the process [9].

From this brief overview, several key features of an omni-channel approach emerge that are relevant for the public sector:

- All channels are strongly linked (connected) so that all content is in-sync and interconnected. This facilitates a consistent experience throughout the customer journey
- Channels and the underlying organization, systems, processes, and data-sources are highly integrated to facilitate the interconnectedness of channels.
- There is a high level of flexibility; citizens have options to choose relevant entry points and they are transferred or migrated seamlessly across channels and/or phases of their journey. This flexibility should also facilitate high levels of personalization and requires integration on the behavioral level; we need to fully understand the diversity in behaviors of the different segments of the population.

These features depart from the existing multi-channel strategies. None of the multi-channel approaches discussed above emphasize the full integration and connection between channels, the integration of aspects such as data, and the levels of flexibility needed to create seamless customer journeys.

6 Conclusions and Discussion

This study was guided by three research questions. Regarding RQ 1, we saw that the channel landscape and channel behaviors are constantly evolving. We have more channels than ever to manage, and channel behaviors are increasingly complex. Citizens use different channels for different service delivery processes and may also display *multiplex* behaviors of using various channels simultaneously or consecutively in one service interaction. Regarding RQ 2, we presented and discussed different types of channel strategies and three generations of multi-channel strategies. We noted how current strategies are ill suited to deal with today's channel landscape and multiplex channel behaviors.

Lastly, regarding RQ 3, we discussed approaches to omni-channeling from the private sector and presented a suitable definition for the public sector. We presented key elements from the literature that comprise an omni-channel approach and differentiate it from existing multi-channel strategies. These are a) the links between channels and synchronization of content, b) high levels of integration of the underlying organization, systems, processes and data, and c) high levels of flexibility to create seamless customer journeys either through citizen choice or through channel migration.

However, several key challenges must be addressed to develop a working concept:

- Public sector agencies must serve their entire population. With the increase in the complexity of citizens' channel behaviors, developing an omni-channel approach that works for everyone becomes a massive challenge, especially if the customer journeys must be seamless. Work is needed to develop omni-channel models that combine the behaviors of different segments in the population with the available channels or communication cues and different parts of the customer journey.
- While most publications agree that high levels of integration across various areas (e.g., organization, process, data, and behavior) are needed, few address *how* this integration can be achieved. With factors such as siloing and resistance to change, the organizational challenges alone will be big. Thus, realistic omni-channel strategies should not just describe what the strategy entails, but also how to achieve it.
- The complex nature of channel behaviors combined with channel multiplexity and fragmentation in the population make it a necessity to develop some level of organizational memory. Only if the organization measures and remembers how their clients are interacting with them can it migrate clients successfully and create more pro-active and personalized customer journeys. Thus, a mechanism to create memory must be built into any omni-channel framework.
- The continuously evolving channel landscape teaches us that there is little use for static approaches towards channel features and channel strategies. If we want to develop robust and somewhat future proof omni-channel strategies, we must develop and build in the appropriate mechanisms to a) continuously improve customer journeys and b) update channel strategies.

Our main recommendation is to build upon this review and take the key conclusions and observed challenges into the development of new omni-channel strategies. These new omni-channel strategies are by no means a silver bullet that will solve all existing challenges in service provision, but represent a step forward towards more inclusive, efficient, and effective public service delivery.

References

1. Pieterson, W., Ebbers, W., Madsen, C.Ø.: New channels, new possibilities: a typology and classification of social robots and their role in multi-channel public service delivery. In: Janssen, M., et al. (eds.) EGOV 2017. LNCS, vol. 10428, pp. 47–59. Springer, Cham (2017). https://doi.org/10.1007/978-3-319-64677-0_5
2. Pieterson, W.J., Ebbers, W.E.: Channel choice evolution: An empirical analysis of shifting channel behavior across demographics and tasks. Gov. Inf. Q. **37**(3), 101478 (2020). https://doi.org/10.1016/j.giq.2020.101478
3. Madsen, C.Ø., Hofmann, S.: Multichannel management in the public sector: a literature review. Electron. J. e-Government (EJEG), **17**(1), 20–35 (2019). https://issuu.com/academic-conferences.org/docs/ejeg-volume17-issue1-article538/1
4. Ebbers, W.E., Pieterson, W.J., Noordman, H.N.: Electronic government: rethinking channel management strategies. Gov. Inf. Q. **25**(2), 181–201 (2008). https://doi.org/10.1016/j.giq.2006.11.003
5. Wirtz, B.W., Langer, P.F.: Public multichannel management – an integrated framework of off- and online multichannel government services. Public Organ. Rev. **17**, 563–580 (2016). https://doi.org/10.1007/s11115-016-0356-0
6. Gagnon, Y.C., Posada, E., Bourgault, M., Naud, A.: Multichannel delivery of public services: a new and complex management challenge. Int. J. Public Adm. **33**(5), 213–222 (2010). https://doi.org/10.1080/01900690903405535
7. Verhoef, P.C., Kannan, P.K., Inman, J.J.: From multi-channel retailing to omni-channel retailing: introduction to the special issue on multi-channel retailing. J. Retail. **91**(2), 174–181 (2015). https://doi.org/10.1016/J.JRETAI.2015.02.005
8. Shen, X.L., Li, Y.J., Sun, Y., Wang, N.: Channel integration quality, perceived fluency and omnichannel service usage: The moderating roles of internal and external usage experience. Decis. Support Syst. **109**, 61–73 (2018). https://doi.org/10.1016/J.DSS.2018.01.006
9. Cortiñas, M., Chocarro, R., Elorz, M.: Omni-channel users and omni-channel customers: a segmentation analysis using distribution services. Span. J. Mark. - ESIC **23**(3), 415–436 (2019). https://doi.org/10.1108/SJME-06-2019-0031/FULL/PDF
10. Boell, S.K., Cecez-Kecmanovic, D.: A hermeneutic approach for conducting literature reviews and literature searches. Commun. Assoc. Inf. Syst. **34**(1), 12 (2014). https://doi.org/10.17705/1CAIS.03412
11. Madsen, C.Ø., Kræmmergaard, P.: Channel choice: a literature review. In: Tambouris, E., et al. (eds.) EGOV 2015. LNCS, vol. 9248, pp. 3–18. Springer, Cham (2015). https://doi.org/10.1007/978-3-319-22479-4_1
12. Pieterson, W.: Channel choice: citizens' channel behavior and public service channel strategy. Enschede: University of Twente (2009). https://doi.org/10.3233/978-1-58603-973-8-50
13. Harzing, A.W.K., van der Wal, R.: Google scholar as a new source for citation analysis. Ethics Sci. Environ. Polit. **8**(1), 61–73 (2008). https://doi.org/10.3354/ESEP00076
14. Kosenkov, A., Pappel, I., Giannoumis, G.A.: Omnichannel public engagement: from theory to practice. In: Proceedings of Ongoing Research, Practitioners, Posters, Workshops, and Projects of the International Conference EGOV-CeDEM-ePart 2019, pp. 237–240 (2019). https://biblio.ugent.be/publication/8626904/file/8626906#page=251. Accessed 16 Mar 2022
15. Rey-Moreno, M., Medina-Molina, C.: Omnichannel strategy and the distribution of public services in Spain. J. Innov. Knowl. **1**(1), 36–43 (2016). https://doi.org/10.1016/J.JIK.2016.01.009

16. Schenk, B., Dolata, M., Schwabe, C., Schwabe, G.: What citizens experience and how omni-channel could help–insights from a building permit case. Inf. Technol. People (2021). https://doi.org/10.1108/ITP-06-2020-0374/FULL/XML
17. Scholl, H.J.: Digital Government Reference Library (DGRL) Version 17.5, 17 Mar 2021. https://faculty.washington.edu/jscholl/dgrl/. Accessed 17 Mar 2022
18. Goodsell, C.T., The Public Encounter. Where State and Citizen Meet. Indiana University Press, Bloomington (1981)
19. Madsen, C.Ø., Lindgren, I., Melin, U.: The accidental caseworker – how digital self-service influences citizens' administrative burden. Gov. Inf. Q. **39**(1), 101653 (2022). https://doi.org/10.1016/J.GIQ.2021.101653
20. Hofmann, S., Beverungen, D., Räckers, M., Becker, J.: What makes local governments' online communications successful? Insights from a multi-method analysis of Facebook. Gov. Inf. Q. **30**(4), 387–396 (2013). https://doi.org/10.1016/j.giq.2013.05.013
21. Eurostat: ICT usage in households and by individuals 2022. https://ec.europa.eu/eurostat/web/digital-economy-and-society/data/database. Accessed 17 Mar 2022
22. Madsen, C.Ø., Kræmmergaard, P.: How to migrate citizens online and reduce traffic on traditional channels through multichannel management: a case study of cross-organizational collaboration surrounding a mandatory self-service application. In: Innovative Perspectives on Public Administration in the Digital Age, IGI Global, pp. 121–142 (2018)
23. Ebbers, W.E., van de Wijngaert, L.A.L.: Paper beats ping: on the effect of an increasing separation of notification and content due to digitization of government communication. Gov. Inf. Q. **37**(1), 101396 (2020). https://doi.org/10.1016/j.giq.2019.101396. [1–8]
24. Madsen, C.Ø., Hofmann, S., Pieterson, W.: Channel choice complications. In: Lindgren, I., et al. (eds.) EGOV 2019. LNCS, vol. 11685, pp. 139–151. Springer, Cham (2019). https://doi.org/10.1007/978-3-030-27325-5_11
25. Margetts, H.: Public management change and e-Government: the emergence of digital Era governance. In: Chadwick, A., Howard, P.N. (eds.) Routledge Handbook of Internet Politics, pp. 114–128. Routledge, London; New York (2009)
26. Scholl, H.J., Klischewski, R.: E-government integration and interoperability: framing the Research Agenda. Int. J. Public Adm. **30**(8), 889–920 (2007)
27. Madsen, C.Ø., Christensen, L.R.: Integrated and seamless? single parents' experiences of cross-organizational interaction. Sel. Pap. IRIS **9**(9) (2019)
28. Kernaghan, K.: Changing channels: managing channel integration and migration in public organizations. Can. Public Adm. **56**(1), 121–141 (2013). https://doi.org/10.1111/CAPA.12006
29. Pieterson, W., van Dijk, J.: Governmental service channel positioning: history and strategies for the future. In: Grönlund, Å., Scholl, H.J., Andersen, K.V., Wimmer, M.A. (eds.) Electronic Government. Communication Proceedings of the Fifth International EGOV Conference 2006, pp. 53–60 (2006)
30. Daft, R.L., Lengel, R.H.: Organizational information requirements, media richness and structural design. **32**(5), 554–571 (1986). https://doi.org/10.1287/MNSC.32.5.554
31. Payne, A., Frow, P.: The role of multichannel integration in customer relationship management. Ind. Mark. Manage. **33**(6), 527–538 (2004). https://doi.org/10.1016/J.INDMARMAN.2004.02.002
32. Neslin, S.A., Shankar, V.: Key issues in multichannel customer management: current knowledge and future directions. J. Interact. Mark. **23**(1), 70–81 (2009). https://doi.org/10.1016/J.INTMAR.2008.10.005
33. Rigby, D.K.: The future of shopping. Harvard Bus. Rev. 2022. https://hbr.org/2011/12/the-future-of-shopping. Accessed 05 Mar 2022

34. Lee, Z.W.Y., Chan, T.K.H., Chong, A.Y.L., Thadani, D.R.: Customer engagement through omnichannel retailing: the effects of channel integration quality. Ind. Mark. Manage. **77**, 90–101 (2019). https://doi.org/10.1016/J.INDMARMAN.2018.12.004
35. Pieterson, W.: Multi-channel management in PES: from blending to omni-channelling. Luxembourg (2017). https://doi.org/10.2767/73549
36. Mintrom, M.: Market organizations and deliberative democracy: choice and voice in public service delivery. **35**(1), 52–81 (2016). https://doi.org/10.1177/0095399702250346
37. Pieterson, W.: Citizens and service channels: channel choice and channel management implications. Int. J. Electron. Gov. Res. **6**(2), 37–53 (2010). https://doi.org/10.4018/jegr.2010040103
38. Shi, S., Wang, Y., Chen, X., Zhang, Q.: Conceptualization of omnichannel customer experience and its impact on shopping intention: a mixed-method approach. Int. J. Inf. Manage. **50**, 325–336 (2020). https://doi.org/10.1016/J.IJINFOMGT.2019.09.001
39. Burford, S., Resmini, A.: Cross-channel information architecture for a world exposition. Int. J. Inf. Manage. **37**(6), 547–552 (2017). https://doi.org/10.1016/J.IJINFOMGT.2017.05.010
40. Saghiri, S., Wilding, R., Mena, C., Bourlakis, M.: Toward a three-dimensional framework for omni-channel. J. Bus. Res. **77**, 53–67 (2017). https://doi.org/10.1016/J.JBUSRES.2017.03.025
41. Kim, J.C., Chun, S.H.: Cannibalization and competition effects on a manufacturer's retail channel strategies: Implications on an omni-channel business model. Decis. Support Syst. **109**, 5–14 (2018). https://doi.org/10.1016/J.DSS.2018.01.007

Use of Commercial SaaS Solutions in Swedish Public Sector Organisations under Unknown Contract Terms

Björn Lundell[1](✉), Jonas Gamalielsson[1], Andrew Katz[1,2], and Mathias Lindroth[3]

[1] University of Skövde, Skövde, Sweden
{bjorn.lundell,jonas.gamalielsson}@his.se,
andrew.katz@moorcrofts.com
[2] Moorcrofts LLP, Marlow, UK
[3] ACF Legal International AB, Malmö, Sweden
mathias.lindroth@acflegal.org

Abstract. Lawful and appropriate use of cloud-based globally provided Software-as-a-Service (SaaS) solutions by a public sector organisation (PSO) for data processing and maintenance of digital assets presupposes an investigation of all relevant contract terms. Having obtained, analysed, and filed all relevant contract terms when using a SaaS solution is a prerequisite for good administration. Identifying and obtaining all relevant contract terms for a SaaS solution involves significant obstacles which in practice may be impossible to overcome for each PSO. This paper addresses how PSOs investigate contract terms prior to adoption, and why PSOs use a globally provided SaaS solution without having identified and obtained all relevant contract terms. Through a review of responses to questions and public documents from Swedish PSOs we analysed how each PSO had investigated contract terms and licences for the Microsoft 365 (M365) solution prior to adoption and use of the solution in each PSO. We find that no PSO had investigated all relevant contract terms prior to use of M365, which implies that each PSO uses M365 under unknown contract terms. Further, we find that all PSOs use M365 for data processing of its digital assets under unknown contract terms and that each PSO has significant dependence and trust in its supplier.

1 Introduction

Market concentration involving a few dominant global providers of cloud-based Software-as-a-Service (SaaS) solutions has caused concern amongst nations and public sector organisations for disproportionate supplier dependence [30]. When a public sector organisation (PSO) acquires and uses a SaaS solution from a global provider, such as Microsoft 365 and Google Workspace, this implies that data processing and maintenance of the organisation's digital assets may be exposed to many sets of regulations applicable in different countries and different lock-in effects, which imposes a number of legal, technical and societal challenges [8, 9, 11, 22, 26, 27, 35, 37, 40, 51, 53, 57, 66, 69]. Previous research shows that many Swedish PSOs have acquired a specific globally provided SaaS solution (Microsoft 365) without having addressed critical issues,

M. Janssen et al. (Eds.): EGOV 2022, LNCS 13391, pp. 73–92, 2022.
https://doi.org/10.1007/978-3-031-15086-9_6

including the need to identify, analyse, and maintain all contract documents containing all applicable contract terms and the need to obtain all necessary licences, before use of the acquired SaaS solution [34, 35]. Should a PSO have been unable to identify all contract terms governing the use of a specific SaaS solution it follows that it is impossible to assess if use of the specific solution is lawful and appropriate[1] for the PSO. Such a situation has potentially severe consequences[2]. The overarching goal of this paper is to report on *how* a PSO investigates contract terms for a globally provided SaaS solution prior to adoption, and *why* a PSO uses such a solution without having identified, obtained and analysed all relevant contract terms.

Several studies show a range of technical, economic, and legal issues which cause challenges related to use of cloud based SaaS solutions [10, 28, 35]. Major issues include the use of complex and time limited contract terms for such solutions [1, 37, 70]. In the EU, there are several initiatives that seek to address data sovereignty and concern over lawfulness and appropriateness of using cloud based SaaS solutions from global providers by seeking alternatives. For example, in France, two suppliers have announced plans to establish a new EU-based company (Bleu) for offering a version of Microsoft 365 to the French market. Similarly, a number of Swedish based PSOs have explored the potential for lawful and appropriate provision of Microsoft 365 to the PSOs in the Swedish market and concluded that the provider has, so far, been unwilling to engage in such arrangements [16]. Further, there are also a number of related initiatives at EU (e.g. GAIA-X [24]) and national levels (e.g. the collaborative initiative by eSam [17]).

In Europe, lawfulness and appropriateness concerning data processing and maintenance of a PSO's digital assets has been an ongoing issue for decades. For example, on 11 May 1973 the Swedish Data Act came into force which implied that data processing outside Sweden was unlawful where protection according to European conventions could not be guaranteed [7]. On 24 May 2014 the EU adopted the General Data Protection Regulation (GDPR) which has applied since 25 May 2018 [14]. With the establishment of the EU and its Charter of Fundamental rights, the GDPR, and the decision in the so called Schrems II case (Case C-311/18) by the Court of Justice of the European Union on 16 July 2020 [5] there is an increasing concern amongst many individuals and organisations related to privacy. The importance of data sovereignty, interoperability and avoiding different types of lock-in effects have also been recognised, and several

[1] Throughout this paper, the phrase 'lawful and appropriate' refers to all the requirements imposed on each PSO within the EU in accordance with all applicable law and regulation, and also the principles of good administration whether codified or not. The concept of 'good administration' originates in the Charter of Fundamental Rights of the European Union [13] and has been further developed in the Committee of Ministers Recommendation to member states on good administration [6]. Good administration encompasses the fundamental principle of the rule of law and a general duty of care. In Sweden, the principle of the rule law is codified in the Constitution [58] and the principles of good administration in the 2017 Administrative Procedure Act [19].

[2] For example, adoption and use of a SaaS solution under unknown contract terms may involve data processing and maintenance of digital assets under conditions which violate (one or several) laws and regulations, including the Swedish Public Access to Information and Secrecy Act [54], the 2017 Administrative Procedure Act [19], regulations provided by the Swedish National Archives [59, 60], GDPR [14], and the Constitution [58].

stakeholders have articulated concern over lawfulness and appropriateness related to use of cloud based SaaS solutions [16, 17, 22, 35, 29, 66, 69, 61]. Further, there are also a number of other technical and legal challenges which become especially challenging when using SaaS solutions in a public sector context, such as requirements for longevity of digital assets over very long life-cycles [35].

This study addresses the following research questions:

RQ 1: How do public sector organisations that use commercial globally provided SaaS solutions investigate contract terms prior to adoption?
RQ 2: Why do public sector organisations use commercial globally provided SaaS solutions for data processing and maintenance of its digital assets without having identified and obtained all relevant contract terms?

The paper addresses lock-in effects amongst PSOs related to use of globally provided SaaS solutions under unknown and unclear contract terms. First, the study contributes insights and explanations related to how PSOs adopting the Microsoft 365 (M365) solution seek to investigate contract documents containing all relevant contract terms prior to adoption and use of M365. In particular, the study highlights work practices used amongst PSOs related to preconditions for an investigation of all relevant contract terms, which include strategies used for identifying and obtaining all relevant contract documents containing all contract terms prior to adoption. Second, the study presents explanations of why PSOs use the M365 solution for data processing and maintenance of digital assets without having identified and obtained all relevant contract terms that would allow each PSO to investigate under which terms the PSO uses M365.

2 On Standard Essential Patents and Contract Terms for SaaS Solutions

An investigation of all relevant contract terms and conditions for use of cloud based SaaS solutions from global providers illuminates significant challenges [1, 8, 10, 35, 37].

The European Commission has expressed concern for absence of interoperability and lock-in effects when organisations use cloud solutions: "In general, each vendor has an incentive to achieve dominance through lock-in which inhibits interest in standardised, industry-wide approaches. Thus despite numerous attempts to develop standards for clouds, mostly led by suppliers, there is a strong risk that clouds **will lack interoperability and data portability** (withdrawal of data). The latter is crucial feature for competition as a distributed data environment cannot be easily moved to another platform." [8].

Research shows that interoperability and avoidance of format lock-in presupposes use of formats which technically and lawfully can be (and has been) implemented in software under different conditions to allow for data processing and maintenance of digital assets [11, 33]. Investigations of several formats that providers of widely used cloud based SaaS solutions have (or claim to have) implemented show that it may be impossible to clarify conditions and acquire all patent licences for standard essential patents (and all necessary rights) to allow for implementation in software [33]. Such circumstances prevent a PSO to establish an effective exit plan that can be executed at short notice. Further, contract terms for the M365 solution require the customer to acquire several third party patent licences for specific formats to allow for lawful use of M365 and to allow for lawful long term maintenance of digital assets exported from M365 [35].

Many PSOs which use globally provided SaaS solutions for data processing and maintenance of their digital assets are unable to export their assets into formats which can be interpreted by other software applications independently of the specific SaaS solution initially used [35]. Hence, for reasons of data sovereignty and ability for each PSO to maintain full control of its digital assets it follows that ICT standards and their implementation in open source software "are of strategic importance to any organization wishing to address challenges related to lock-in, interoperability, and long-term maintenance" [36].

Across the EU, each PSO is expected to observe the principles of *good administration.* The notion of good administration originates in Article 41 of the Charter of Fundamental Rights of the European Union [13] and has been further developed, inter alia, in the Committee of Ministers Recommendation to member states on good administration [6]. Good administration encompasses several concepts, including principles of objectivity, proportionality, efficiency and an obligation of availability. Also, and even more importantly, it includes the fundamental principle of the rule of law and a general duty of care. The principles of good administration are codified by various means in many member states. In Sweden, for instance, the principle of the rule of law is codified in Chapter 1, Sect. 1, paragraph 3 of the Constitution [58], and several provisions explicitly labelled "good administration" are contained in Sects. 5 through 8 of the 2017 Administrative Procedure Act [19]. Notably there is also a provision in the following section, Sect. 9, of the same act which stipulates that administrative matters shall be processed in writing [19]. The question of whether it would be in keeping with good administration not to read the contract terms for mission-critical tools is bordering on the rhetorical. A PSO that does not acquire all the contractual documents, studies them thoroughly and preserves them, disregards the concept of good administration in its core. Further, if a PSO does not have access to the contract terms it is impossible to undertake any meaningful analysis of the lawfulness and appropriateness of a particular solution.

During 2020 and 2021 a large PSO, the municipal board of the City of Stockholm, undertook an investigation of the potential adoption of the M365 solution [67, 68] and presents three main reasons for refraining from use of M365 in a report presented on 9 December 2021 [69]. One main reason concerns unknown and dynamic contract terms, which implies that the PSO would use M365 under unclear conditions since the supplier may unilaterally change the conditions any time. As stated in the report (our translation): "It is not possible to check under what conditions the service delivered. The city has no influence over the conditions and the agreement can be changed at any time." [69].

It should be noted that all dynamic contract terms are not illegal, or even inappropriate. Many types of agreements need to contain provisions that allow for adjustment in relation to external factors. Even clauses that allow one party to unilaterally change the terms to their advantage need not be problematic. For example, price adjustment clauses often give one party the right to increase prices within certain limits. On the other hand, it is very hard to imagine a situation where it is justified to allow one party a broad and far reaching arbitrary right to unilaterally alter central contractual conditions.

Two PSOs (the Swedish Tax Agency and the Swedish Enforcement Authority) decided on 3 May 2021 that Microsoft Teams cannot be lawfully used. The decision presents a detailed analysis which draws from eSam's group of legal experts who concluded on 23 October 2018 [15] that "if information is made technically available to an IT service provider that is bound by the rules of another country due to ownership conditions, according to which the service provider may be obliged to provide information, the information should be considered divulged" [66]. In addition, the decision stresses that "authorities must accept the terms and conditions of Microsoft Online Services" and highlights concerns related to "risk of unauthorised disclosure through the provision of data to the US authorities by Microsoft". Specifically, the decision clarifies that this "may occur due to US extraterritorial surveillance legislation – FISA 702 in particular. A request for data by US authorities can entail unauthorised disclosure and data transfer to a third country, in breach of the General Data Protection Regulation" [66].

Over the years, Microsoft has authorised many organisations based in several jurisdictions to access customer data (including personal data) as subprocessors [42, 43, 44, 45, 46, 47, 48, 49]. Further, a recent analysis shows that "Microsoft does not offer a sovereign country cloud to countries, with the exception of the cloud for the federal USA government and the cloud for China." [52].

Research shows that some Swedish PSOs have recognised that they are bound by contract terms for the M365 solution which imply that a PSO's data processing and maintenance of digital assets may involve organisations and staff based in several third countries, including China, India, Serbia, USA, and United Arab Emirates [34, 35]. Further, Microsoft's list of subprocessors that was provided on 23 November 2021 includes organisations based in these (and several other third) countries [48].

3 Research Approach

During research design and conduct of the study we considered validity threats and aspects of trustworthiness, which also considered experiences from prior research on research methods [25, 31]. The research design for the study was informed by experiences from previous research on qualitative techniques conducted in the software systems domain, which includes the first author's experiences from research on Glaser's strand of Grounded Theory [32]. Based on previous experiences, it is essential for researchers in the area to be 'knowledgable' in conditions for use of the technologies under investigation [32], which for the present study necessitates understanding of both technical and legal issues related to investigations of contract terms for, and conditions for use of, globally provided SaaS solutions in PSOs.

The study considered investigations of contract terms for the M365 solution amongst Swedish PSOs under the government, regional PSOs, and local authorities (municipalities) with a view to explaining why each PSO uses M365 without them having identified and obtained all relevant contract terms.

We undertook a systematic review of *how* Swedish PSOs that use the M365 solution investigated contract terms prior to adoption and analysed reasons for *why* the same PSOs use M365 without having identified and obtained all relevant contract terms as follows. First, through an extensive review of publicly available information we identified indications of use of the M365 solution by 140 PSOs[3]. The review considered various types of sources, including information published via websites provided by each Swedish PSO, news articles published by various media (including newspapers and trade press), press releases and promotion material from different suppliers, and public presentations at various practitioner events. Each one of the 140 PSOs for which we identified indication of use of the M365 solution falls into one of the following three categories of PSOs: PSOs under the government (Swe. 'Statliga förvaltningsmyndigheter')[4], regional PSOs[5], and local authorities (municipalities[6]). Second, we requested public documents (supplemented with specific questions in case requested documentation was missing) from each PSO (via email) related to its use of the M365 solution. Data collection focused on obtaining information and documentation of analyses related to contract terms and licences, and other conditions for use of M365 that each PSO had conducted prior to adoption and use of M365. Third, we reviewed the availability of all relevant contract terms, all necessary licences, and other conditions for use of M365 based on documentation we requested from each PSO. Further, we reviewed information obtained in response to specific questions (that were asked to probe reasons for why specific documentation of contract documents and analyses were missing). We analysed the contract terms and licences provided as part of that documentation with a view to considering whether each PSO had obtained (and filed) all relevant contract terms, and all licences necessary for using M365 (as detailed in our broader review of the applicable M365 contract terms).

The study was initiated on 20 June 2021 and data collection has been ongoing for more than eight months. A large number of requests for information and data sources have been sent (via email and via letters) to representatives for each PSO. Data collection became a tedious and complex process, which to large extent can be explained by the complexity of the subject matter. Several respondents perceived requests difficult to understand which lead to further dialogues, in many cases involving synchronous communication (via phone dialogues, video meetings, and physical meetings) involving different representatives for each PSO. Representatives for many PSOs were curious and eager to learn more about what was being requested which lead to constructive dialogues where several representatives expressed that they have learnt a lot that will be useful for further projects.

However, data collection also experienced that representatives for several PSOs (explicitly or implicitly) expressed frustration and unwillingness to provide requested documentation. In several cases, respondents refused to respond to questions and refused

[3] None of the 140 PSOs constitute a publicly owned company.

[4] There were 251 governmental agencies (Swe. 'Statliga förvaltningsmyndigheter') in Sweden on 24 May 2022 according to Statistics Sweden [63].

[5] There were 21 regions in Sweden on 31 December 2020 [64].

[6] There were 290 municipalities in Sweden on 30 December 2020 [65]. Most municipalities own several publicly owned companies and may be organised into several different agencies.

to provide public documents[7]. Several PSOs even refused to acknowledge whether requested public documents existed in their organisation (or were missing)[8]. During data collection, it became apparent that (in order to be able to respond to questions) several PSOs requested information from other sources, including their licensing partner. PSOs commonly obtain their licences for M365 through a licensing partner: one of a number of authorised Microsoft resellers. The information so obtained often contributed to misconceptions and misunderstandings, partly caused by the fact that several statements provided by licensing partners were incorrect or misleading. During several phone dialogues with respondents for various PSOs we also perceived a sense of frustration over their supplier's inability to provide them with the information they needed to clarify all applicable contract terms.

4 Observations on Investigations of Contract Terms Prior to Adoption

Based on the information that has been provided during the study, we find that each PSO that uses the M365 solution does so without prior analysis of all relevant contract terms and without having procured all necessary licences that would allow for data processing and maintenance of digital assets over long life cycles. Hence, each PSO that uses the M365 solution do so under unknown and unclear conditions which imposes significant risks for different types of lock-in effects that may prevent sustainable and lawful maintenance of digital assets. Further, we find that no PSO has identified all relevant contract terms for the M365 solution before use. In addition, we find that no PSO maintains documentation of all relevant contract terms they are bound by for their use of the M365 solution. Hence, we find that since no PSO had obtained and filed documentation of all relevant contract terms it follows that each PSO fails to fulfil expectations of good administration.

The study has made a number of observations concerning *how* PSOs investigate contract terms prior to adoption of the M365 solution which reveal a number of issues that contribute to explain an inappropriate practice related to investigations of contract terms prior to adoption and continued use of the solution.

First, we find that no PSO had investigated the need for acquiring all relevant contract terms and licences prior to adoption and use of the M365 solution. Moreover, no PSO

[7] In Sweden, the "constitutional right of access to public documents is delineated by the Swedish Public Access to Information and Secrecy Act (OSL) (2009:400)" [22]. We find that the vast majority of PSOs made a serious effort to provide the requested public documents they had access to within a six month time period, whereas some PSOs did not respond at all. In fact, despite a strong emphasis on transparency for public sector organisations (and in particular related to research studies) in Sweden some PSOs devoted significant efforts in arguing for why they were not obliged to provide the requested public documents as required under Swedish law [54].

[8] In acknowledging the depth of the data collection, we find that several PSOs lacked requested information (including documents containing decisions, licenses, and contract terms). Instead, PSOs referred to their supplier since requested information were not maintained by each specific PSO.

had investigated the need for acquiring all relevant contract terms and licences related to several formats that would allow for data processing and maintenance of digital assets during and after use of the M365 solution. For example, the contract terms for M365 express, concerning the HEVC format standard, [55]: "*Customer must obtain its own patent license(s) from any third party H.265/HEVC patent pools or rights holders before using Azure Media Services to encode or decode H.265/HEVC media.*" Hence, since H.265/HEVC and many other standards, such as the H.264/AVC format standard [33], are normatively referenced (via other standards) in the ISO/IEC 29500 standard it follows that digital assets that are exported from M365 (and stored locally as '.docx' files) may impinge on patents that have been declared as standard essential for the ISO/IEC 29500 standard (and including all its normative references) in the ISO and ITU-T patent databases. This includes patents which may be standard essential patents (SEPs) for these formats even if those have not been declared in any of these patent databases. In addition we find that no PSO had investigated the need for acquiring all relevant contract terms and licences related to several other format standards, including the PDF/A-3 (ISO/IEC 19005–3) format standard (and including all its normative references), used by M365 prior to adoption and use of the M365 solution. For these reasons, use of M365 for export of digital assets in all these formats without prior having acquired all contract terms for all relevant licences for all formats used would prevent maintenance of digital assets. Further, findings from the study show that no PSO had realised the implications of being unable to use M365 for export of digital assets to the PDF/A-1 format which is the appropriate version of the PDF/A format (that is also required in Sweden for long-term archiving). Hence, it follows that all PSOs that use M365 cannot fulfil Swedish archiving requirements for long-term maintenance of digital assets.

Second, concerning contract terms and conditions for future use of the M365 solution, we find that no PSO had investigated relevant contract terms and conditions that will be (and currently are) applicable for use of M365 during a time frame of less than three years[9]. Further, no PSO had access to any contract terms and licences for M365 on perpetual terms (amongst the PSOs that had access to a subset of relevant contract terms we find that all those PSOs had access to time-limited contracts for a time period of three years). Specifically, we find that no PSO had investigated the cost of acquiring all necessary licences (including costs for all necessary patent licences) and considered other technical and legal issues, such as under which jurisdictions future provision of M365 may allow for lawful use by a PSO in Sweden.

Third, we find that no PSO had investigated how each PSO's contract terms for the M365 solution allow for involvement of external staff and subprocessors (based in different jurisdictions) for data processing and maintenance of digital assets. Further, the vast majority of PSOs seem unaware of that conditions for use of the M365 solution change over time and that each PSO's contract terms for M365 allow for data processing through use of subsidiaries and subcontractors in numerous jurisdictions, including but not limited to China, Serbia, USA, and United Arab Emirates [45, 46, 47, 48, 49]. We find that only one PSO identified that its relevant contract terms for use of the M365

[9] The data collection during conduct of the study obtained responses from PSOs (in response to requests for public documents and supplementary questions) during the time frame after 20 June 2021 and until 14 March 2022 (when the manuscript was prepared).

solution (on 22 September 2021) allowed for data processing through use of specific subcontractors in these (and many other) jurisdictions [45, 46]. However, we observed that the same PSO's contract terms for use of M365 more recently (on 4 March 2022) referred to a different set of subcontractors [48, 49]. We find that no PSO had investigated under which conditions data processing through use of M365 would be exposed to regulations and laws in these (and several other) jurisdictions under previous, current, and any future contract terms that each PSO is bound by. Further, no PSO had investigated relevant legislation concerning security and privacy issues related to use of M365 for data processing in China and Serbia, including NIL [38, 62] and Säkerhetsskyddslagen [56].

Fourth, we find that the vast majority of PSOs have failed to investigate contract terms and legislation in all countries where data processing may take place. This implies that each PSO's data processing and maintenance of digital assets take place under unknown conditions. We observe that many PSOs seem to assume that digital assets will be stored in Europe, even though several recognise that each PSO's contract terms allow for data processing outside the EU. For example, we identified several PSOs that recognised that their data processing will take place outside EU and some PSOs (e.g. [23, 20]) explicitly mention that digital assets may be stored outside EU. We identified several PSOs that expressed uncertainty and concern over lawfulness of data processing outside the EU. For example, a legal analysis presented by a data privacy officer at a PSO identifies Sect. 702 of FISA [18] and EO 12333 [12] as main inhibitors which prevent lawful data processing that involves US-based providers under the GDPR and therefore recommends that no new contracts should be signed with US-based providers before lawful transfer of data to the US is possible.

Fifth, we find that PSOs have limited understanding of relevant contract terms that apply to each PSO and that there is far reaching dependence and significant trust in recommendations provided by each PSO's supplier. For example, several PSOs do not maintain any contract documents and instead refer to the supplier's current website when trying to identify which contract terms they are bound by. This is despite having signed a contract ('Program Signature Form') which states that they have received several contract documents and information provided via websites and referenced documents: "*By signing below, Customer and the Microsoft Affiliate agree that both parties (1) have received, read and understand the above contract documents, including any websites or documents incorporated by reference and any amendments and (2) agree to be bound by the terms of all such documents.*" Further, we find that several PSOs have negotiated with the Swedish company Microsoft AB which for several years has been wholly owned by the Bermuda-based company MBH Limited [41]. Hence, PSOs have been engaged in such negotiations despite the fact that Bermuda has been listed on the "EU list of non-cooperative jurisdictions for tax purposes" [3, 4].

Sixth, we observed a widespread practice amongst PSOs to adopt the M365 solution by explicitly referring to the solution when renewing old contracts and when using framework contracts. We find that no PSO had investigated alternative solutions by public procurement prior to renewal of contract terms for the M365 solution. In one case, we identified that adoption of the M365 solution through explicit reference to the solution for a new PSO which was established during conduct of the study actually preceded the formal establishment of the PSO that handles very sensitive personal data. We approached the new PSO just after it became operational and found the relevant contract terms for the newly established PSO's M365 solution had not been obtained and investigated prior to adoption and use of M365.

5 Observations on why SaaS Solutions are Used Without Having Obtained All Contract Terms

Based on the information that has been provided during the study, we find a range of different explanations as to why each PSO that uses the M365 solution agreed to sign (or renew) contracts without having investigated all relevant contract terms and without having procured all necessary licences that would allow for data processing and maintenance of digital assets over long life cycles. Overall, amongst the vast majority of PSOs we find stark dependence and trust in recommendations from the supplier and significant unawareness related to risks associated with different types of lock-in effects.

The study has made a number of observations concerning *why* PSOs use the M365 solution for data processing and maintenance of its digital assets without having identified and obtained all relevant contract terms prior to adoption and use of M365.

First, we note widespread misconceptions among PSOs concerning the importance of obtaining (and filing) all relevant contract terms and acquiring all relevant licences (including all necessary patent licences) prior to adoption and use of the M365 solution by each PSO in order to investigate opportunities for lawful data processing and maintenance of digital assets during and after use of M365. No PSO had investigated the need for obtaining (and filing) all relevant contract terms and licences related to several formats prior to use of M365. During conduct of the study, we found that many PSOs acknowledged (and elaborated through many discussions by phone[10] with representatives for many PSOs) that they were unaware of the implications of the contract terms for M365 each PSO had accepted. However, many PSOs also conveyed misleading information concerning patents (related to several formats used by M365) that had been provided to them by their suppliers. Several PSOs also passed on misleading and incorrect information, which we find may have contributed to severe misunderstandings of how standard essential patents (SEPs) may impinge on various formats used for representing digital assets. During dialogues with representatives for several PSOs we found significant unawareness of the implications of formats used and contract terms for M365, and in particular related to how various stakeholders have declared SEPs related to several format standards (including ITU-T H.264/AVC, ITU-T H.265/HEVC, ISO/IEC 29500, ISO 32000–1, and ISO 19005–3) in several patent databases maintained by various standard setting organisations (including ITU-T and ISO). Some PSOs expressed

[10] From in-depth discussions with more than twenty representatives for different PSOs we find that each PSO's initial adoption of the M365 solution was preceded by stark trust in the supplier and note that these representatives (with few exceptions) acknowledged that they had no issue with continued use of the solution despite the fact that they lack access to all contract terms. However, some representatives expressed concern over the fact that they lack access to (and are unable gain access to) all relevant contract terms and perceived they (and their PSO) had been misled by the supplier.

stark frustration over the misleading information provided by their suppliers when they realised that they had been misled, whereas some PSOs insisted in their beliefs. For example, several PSOs (who upon request provided digital assets in the "docx-format") insisted on the incorrect belief that the ITU-T H.264/AVC and ITU-T H.265/HEVC formats are not normatively referenced (via other standards) by ISO/IEC 29500 and some PSOs had even been misled to believe that the ITU-T H.264/AVC format is provided under royalty-free conditions. Overall, we find that these misconceptions may have contributed to the incorrect belief that there is no need for acquiring licences for all these formats used, despite the fact that all PSOs need to maintain digital assets over very long time periods (i.e. both during and after use of M365). We note that some PSOs expressed that they will never stop using M365, a view which we find to be peculiar in light of legislation concerning public procurement and requirements for long-term maintenance of digital assets each PSO needs to account for.

Second, we find that, with few exceptions, PSOs seem unconcerned over the fact that they lack access to and have omitted to investigate relevant contract terms and conditions (including cost for all necessary licences) that will be (and currently are) applicable for use of M365 during a time frame of less than three years. A majority of PSOs express that they do not plan to abandon M365. Overall, we note that most PSOs seem to be confident with the supplier and licensing partner for the M365 solution they use. Some even express how grateful and satisfied they are as part of marketing material for the solution. However, there are also several PSOs which express concern over the contract terms and licences they are bound by. For example, representatives for several PSOs expressed stark concern for being locked-in and they lack (and cannot comprehend how to establish) an effective exit plan from M365. One representative for a large PSO that already uses the M365 solution expressed during a meeting that for a PSO that has not yet adopted M365 it would be "completely insane" (Swe. 'helt vansinnigt') to adopt and use the solution under current conditions as it is "unlawful" (Swe. 'inte lagligt').[11]

Third, we find that no PSO had investigated and documented any decisions concerning whether or not applicable contract terms for each SaaS solution used for the PSO's data processing and maintenance of its digital assets allow or forbid exposure to laws and regulations in jurisdictions such as Bermuda, China, India, North Korea, Russia, Serbia, USA, and United Arab Emirates. Further, we also find that no PSO seemed concerned over the fact that applicable contract terms for the M365 solution may unilaterally be changed by the supplier and that current contract terms for M365 allow for data processing in countries which (for privacy, security, and tax reasons) are seen highly inappropriate by the EU and the Swedish Security Service. Overall, we find that many PSOs seem totally unaware of the conditions under which they use M365.

Fourth, we find that many PSOs are unaware of how a PSO's own use of the M365 solution for data processing may cause issues in light of the Schrems-II case [5]. We note that many PSOs are unaware of the contract terms and conditions under which they use M365, some justify their use with the explanation that they need the M365 solution. Many PSOs consider their use of the M365 solution unproblematic and they

[11] The meeting was held in Swedish. During the meeting, the representative elaborated on several unresolved legal issues of which the essence was that for a PSO it would now be completely reprehensible to adopt the M365 solution for use in a PSO.

have no intention of abandoning use of M365 as a consequence of the Schrems-II case. However, several PSOs also express concern over continued data processing through use of US-based providers. For example, the outcome of a legal analysis conducted by a data protection officer recommended that the PSO should not sign any new contracts for continued use of M365. Overall, we note that many PSOs seem to hope for changed legislations and several seem to rely on the recommendations from their supplier.

Fifth, we find that several PSOs have accepted and signed contracts for the M365 solution without having obtained all relevant contract terms in all applicable contract documents. Further, no PSO had investigated and documented any decisions which prohibit procurement of SaaS solutions provided by suppliers that have business operations in countries that have been included in the EU list of non-cooperative jurisdictions for tax purposes in tax havens.

Sixth, we find a widespread practice amongst PSOs is to express explicit preference for the M365 solution when accepting new contract terms and renewing contracts for M365. We find that no PSO had investigated changes between old and new contract terms and conditions for use of the M365 solution when renewing contracts for M365. Overall, we identified no reasonable explanation as to why many PSOs seem to use the M365 solution under conditions that were unknown to each PSO and without having acquired all necessary licences that would allow for data processing and maintenance of the PSO's digital assets over long life cycles independently of the M365 solution.

6 Analysis

Findings show that many PSOs have significant trust and stark dependence on their suppliers of the M365 solution, especially with respect to interpretations and filing of contract terms and conditions for use of the solution. For example, no PSO had investigated conditions for use of different formats prior to adoption and use of the M365 solution. Further, many PSOs seem to rely exclusively on recommendations from their suppliers and lack independent documentation from investigations of contract terms and conditions for a PSO's opportunities for lawful use of M365 for its data processing and maintenance of digital assets. Some PSOs even acknowledged that they only trust recommendations from their supplier, with reference to the huge resources large companies have. Overall, we identified no indication of that any representative for any PSO had read all contract terms for the M365 solution before signing the contract. Hence, we find that each PSO uses the solution under contract terms that are unknown to them. This suggests significant deficiencies in terms of adherence to administrative regulations and public procurement laws [21].

The study confirms and extends previous research which has identified work practices amongst PSOs that omit to investigate contract terms and licences for several formats used, which cause format lock-in and other types of problematic lock-in effects. This imposes significant risks since format lock-in prevents long-term maintenance of digital assets [33]. Further, such lock-in also causes interoperability problems, which in turn may significantly inhibit competition in public procurement projects. To allow for competition in the context of public procurement, it is critical to only express mandatory requirements for specific standards and formats provided under conditions which allow for implementation by software projects under different licences, including all open source software licences. Previous studies have recognised concern for absence of interoperability and different types of lock-in effects, specifically format lock-in, as particularly challenging in the context of cloud based SaaS solutions [8, 29, 33, 35]. For these reasons, it may be unsurprising that the Swedish National Procurement Services stipulates that when organisations use their framework agreements "they are allowed only to reference open standards when expressing a mandatory requirement which refer to a standard in public procurement projects" [36].

For every PSO, the importance of ensuring data processing and maintenance of its digital assets beyond the time frame for its current contract with any provider of a SaaS solution must be recognised. This presupposes that a PSO has obtained all necessary licences on perpetual terms for all formats used for representing the PSO's digital assets. It is critical that each format used for representing a PSO's digital assets can be interpreted by software applications that are available for many decades. For this reason, a PSO that uses a format for which there is no software application that can process its digital assets independently of the SaaS solutions currently used is exposed to significant risks.

Legal and privacy issues have been ongoing concerns related to potential use of outsourcing and cloud-based SaaS solutions for data processing and maintenance of digital assets amongst stakeholders in large organisations for several years (e.g. [1, 29, 56]). For example, a study which investigated adoption of M365 in two large organisations "raised the question of data integrity, such as patent and loss of data" and highlighted concern over privacy issues as follows: 'The following citation describes the issue of data integrity at UniSwed [anonymised name for a Swedish University]: "Privacy and data integrity are important issues – can we rely on the service providers to safeguard our data? Can we read different logs from here; can others read the information, US government (referring to the reports of NSA surveillance of data centres)?" (IT Manager, UniSwed, September, 2013)' [39].

Further, we find that contract terms for the M365 solution express rather broad rights which may cause issues if a PSO wishes to process digital assets for which they lack copyright or sub-licensing rights. For example, in case copyrighted material sent to a PSO should be processed by the M365 solution since the provider of M365 requires a royalty-free licence for the digital assets being processed. Specifically, the contract terms state: "*To the extent necessary to provide the Services to you and others, to protect you and the Services, and to improve Microsoft products and services, you grant to Microsoft a worldwide and royalty-free intellectual property license to use Your Content, for example, to make copies of, retain, transmit, reformat, display, and distribute via communication tools Your Content on the Services. If you publish Your Content in areas of the Service where it is available broadly online without restrictions, Your Content may appear in demonstrations or materials that promote the Service. Some of the Services are supported by advertising.*" [50] We find that such contract terms may inhibit use of M365 by a PSO which seeks to process digital assets for which they lack all copyright or sub-licensing rights.

Findings from the study show that several decision makers representing different PSOs are uneasy with their observation that the provider of the M365 solution can unilaterally change the contract terms and conditions for use of M365, potentially implying data processing of a PSO's data in unknown and problematic jurisdictions. Further, the study shows that only one PSO recognised that a PSO's data processing may involve staff and organisations in several countries (through use of subcontractors and subprocessors), such as China and Serbia. Many PSOs have identified that a PSO's data will be transferred to a country outside the EU. In addition, we note that only one Swedish PSO that investigated possibilities for lawful use of the M365 solution had approached IMY (the Swedish Data Protection Authority) for advice [67, 68, 69, 27]. Specifically, during 2020 and 2021 the municipal board of the City of Stockholm undertook an investigation of the potential adoption of M365 and presented three main reasons for refraining from using M365 in a report presented on 9 December 2021 [69]. One main reason concerns legal and privacy issues: "Due to current legislation in the field of intelligence, US cloud service providers cannot provide sufficient guarantees for the protection of personal data and are therefore deemed not to be able to be used at present." ([69] (our translation)) Further, the City of Stockholm also finds that contract terms for M365 can "be changed at any time" and that it is impossible for the PSO to determine if a tool can or cannot be lawfully used [69]. The observation that the provider of M365 unilaterally can change the contract terms confirms previous research, which has reported that cloud service providers "typically reserve the right to change contract terms and policies unilaterally" [37].

Related to contract terms issued by the provider of the M365 solution, we find that besides the City of Stockholm there are also other PSOs that have reached similar conclusions when observing that acceptance of such contract terms "would necessitate the continuous review" of contract terms as the provider continuously changes the solution [66]. For these reasons, we note that several PSOs seek alternative solutions and have identified that there are lawful alternative solutions which may be appropriate for PSOs. For example, as identified by a group of Swedish PSOs: "it is clear that suitable legal alternatives to US-based cloud services are available" [17].

Finally, the plans to establish a new EU-based company (Bleu) that seeks to offer a lawful provision of Microsoft 365 to the French market [2] has so far not received any public attention in Sweden. Hence, we find that it is an open question as to if (and if so when) a new Swedish-based company (which is 100% independent of the US-based current provider of M365) will be established and if such a company will be able to provide a special version of M365 which would fulfil Swedish PSOs' requirements for lawful and appropriate data processing and maintenance of digital assets. Besides having obtained all licences and all necessary rights as a licensor, one example of a necessary customisation of the special version of M365 will be to provide support for export of digital assets to the PDF/A-1 format.

7 Discussion and Conclusions

Lawful and appropriate use of a cloud-based Software-as-a-Service solution by a public sector organisation presupposes full control over the organisation's data processing and maintenance of its digital assets during and beyond the life cycle for the specific cloud-based solution currently used. Full control of an organisation's data processing includes an ability to export the organisation's own digital assets in formats which can be lawfully and appropriately processed independently of the solution initially used to create and process the exported assets.

The study shows that all public sector organisations have omitted to obtain and investigate the relevant contract terms for the specific Software-as-a-Service solution (Microsoft 365) they use. Further, prior to adoption and use of the Microsoft 365 solution no public sector organisation had investigated if contract terms and conditions for their use of Microsoft 365 would allow for lawful and appropriate data processing and maintenance of digital assets over long life cycles.

Findings show that public sector organisations place significant dependence and trust in their suppliers, which may have contributed to the observation that no organisation had identified and obtained all relevant contract terms and licences prior to their adoption and use of the Microsoft 365 solution. Hence, all relevant contract terms are unknown to all investigated organisations that use the solution. In particular, the study identified significant unawareness and misconceptions amongst representatives for public sector organisations concerning the role of standard essential patents which may impinge on formats implemented and used by organisations that use the Microsoft 365 solution for data processing and maintenance of digital assets. Further, the study also identified misconceptions amongst some suppliers and licensing partners which some public sector organisations had consulted during conduct of the study.

The study reveals a, potentially very, concerning situation for public sector organisations since the investigation identified no organisation which has been able to establish that its use of the adopted SaaS solution is lawful and appropriate. Based on the information that has been provided by respondents during conduct of the study, findings from the study show a distinct risk that many public sector organisations are dependant upon solutions which do not allow them to adhere to all legal requirements and the principles of good administration. They are thereby experiencing a dilemma, where they have to choose between systematically violating the law or neglecting tasks they have been entrusted with. Our findings suggest that there may be different reasons for a public sector organisation not analysing the contract terms before deploying a particular solution. In some instances, a public sector organisation has blindly trusted the advice of its partner or the supplier, and actively chosen not to perform any analysis of their own. In other cases, the public sector organisation has tried but not succeeded in acquiring all applicable contract terms, or have not had access to the competence necessary to analyse these. With regard to the Microsoft 365 solution, the study shows that it is extremely difficult, if at all possible, for a user to identify and obtain all applicable contract terms, and contract terms are difficult to analyse even for specialists. Obviously, such difficulties does not excuse the omission by a public sector organisation to act under the laws but it may explain how and why this occurs on such a large scale.

We find that a conceivable, and potentially very effective, policy implication from the study would be to propose and introduce, in law or policy, an obligation for any provider offering a Software-as-a-Service solution to a public sector organisation, to always provide all contract terms at one and the same time in a cohesive format. A corresponding obligation for a public sector organisation in connection with adoption of such a solution to ascertain that all contact terms have been obtained and filed, would clarify the responsibilities of all parties involved.

We acknowledge that requests for public information sent to the official register at each public sector organisation have been handled differently by different organisations. Moreover, we note that there has been interactions and communications between different public sector organisations and their suppliers, which have caused that responses and reactions from some organisations have been influenced by views expressed by other organisations (such as other public sector organisations and suppliers). For example, instead of providing requested documents containing contract terms, some public sector organisations have been influenced by other organisations that have referred to their supplier or declined to provide requested documents. In some such cases we conjecture that the behaviour of a public sector organisation (and its supplier) during data collection may have been an attempt to hide an absence of good administration.

Finally, findings from the study show an overwhelming and rather worrying unawareness of how contract terms for the Microsoft 365 solution allow for involvement of staff representing various subcontractors and subprocessors based in different countries when a public sector organisation uses the solution for its own data processing of digital assets.

Acknowledgement. This research has been financially supported by the Swedish Knowledge Foundation (KK-stiftelsen) and participating partner organisations in the SUDO project. The authors are grateful for the stimulating collaboration and support from colleagues and partner organisations.

References

1. Bradshaw, S., Millard, C., Walden, I.: Contracts for clouds: comparison and analysis of the terms and conditions of cloud computing services. Int. J. Law Inf. Technol. **19**(3), 187–223 (2011)
2. Capgemini: Capgemini and Orange announce plan to create "Bleu", a company to provide a "Cloud de Confiance" in France. Capgemini, Orange, Joint Press Release, 27 May 2021
3. CEU: The EU list of non-cooperative jurisdictions for tax purposes, 15429/27, Council of the European Union, 5 December (2017)
4. CEU: The revised EU list of non-cooperative jurisdictions for tax purposes – Council conclusions, 12 March 2019, 7441/19, Council of the European Union, 12 March (2019)
5. CJEU: The Court of Justice invalidates Decision 2016/1250 on the adequacy of the protection provided by the EU-US Data Protection Shield. Judgment in Case C-311/18, Press Release No 91/20, Court of Justice of the European Union, Luxembourg, 16 July (2020)
6. CM: Recommendation CM/Rec(2007)7 of the Committee of Ministers to member states on good administration, The Council of Europe, 20 June 2007
7. Datalag: Datalag (1973:289), SFS 1973:289, 11 May 1973. http://rkrattsbaser.gov.se/sfst?bet=1973:289
8. EC: Communication from the Commission to the European Parliament, the Council, the European Economic and Social Committee and the Committee of the Regions: Unleashing the Potential of Cloud Computing in Europe, SWD(2012) 271 final, European Commission, Brussels (2012)
9. EC: Shaping Europe's Digital Future, Communication from the Commission to the European Parliament, the Council, the European Economic and Social Committee and the Committee of the Regions. European Commission, Communication, COM (2020) 67 final, 19 February 2020

10. EDPS: Outcome of own-initiative investigation into EU institutions' use of Microsoft products and services. European Data Protection Supervisor, European Union, 2 July 2020
11. Egyedi, T.: Standard-compliant, but incompatible?! Comput. Stan. Interfaces **29**(6), 605–613 (2007)
12. EO: Executive Order 12333 - As amended by Executive Orders 13284 (2003), 13355 (2004), and 13470 (2008). The White House, 4 December 1981
13. EU: Charter of the Fundamental Rights of the European Union, C 326/392, Official Journal of the European Union, 26 October (2012)
14. EU: Regulation (EU) 2016/679 of the European Parliament and of the Council of 27 April 2016 on the protection of natural persons with regard to the processing of personal data and on the free movement of such data, and repealing Directive 95/46/EC (General Data Protection Regulation), Official Journal of the European Union, 4 May (2016)
15. eSam: Rättsligt uttalande om röjande och molntjänster, VER 2018:57, eSamverkansprogrammet, 23 October 2018
16. eSam: Uppföljning av möten mellan eSam och Microsoft (letter to Microsoft Sverige AB, sent by the chair of eSam), Dnr. 8–731121, eSamverkansprogrammet, 27 October 2021
17. eSam: Digital collaboration platform for the public sector, eSamverkansprogrammet, 18 November 2021
18. FISA: Section 702 FISA, The Senate of the United States, Congressional Bills 110th Congress, U.S. Government Publishing Office, 20 June 2008
19. FL: Förvaltningslag (2017:900), SFS nr: 2017:900, 28 September 2017. https://rkrattsbaser.gov.se/sfst?bet=2017:900
20. Forte: Personuppgiftspolicy för Forte.se, Forskningsrådet för hälsa, arbetsliv och välfärd, Stockholm. https://forte.se/om-webbplatsen/personuppgiftspolicy-for-forte-se/. Accessed 8 Mar 2022
21. Furberg, P., Westberg, M.: Måste myndigheter följa lagarna? Om utkontraktering och legalitet i digital miljö. Juridisk tidskrift, 2, 406–417 (2020/21)
22. Försäkringskassan: Cloud Services in Sustaining Societal Functions–Risks, Appropriateness and the Way Forward. Swedish Social Insurance Agency, Dnr. 013428–2019, Version 1.0, 18 November 2019
23. Försvarsmakten: Behandling av personuppgifter i Mitt Försvarsmakten. Försvarsmakten, Stockholm. https://www.forsvarsmakten.se/sv/information-och-fakta/for-dig-som-privatperson/personuppgifter/behandling-av-personuppgifter-i-mitt-forsvarsmakten/. Accessed 8 Mar 2022
24. GAIA: Project GAIA-X: A Federated Data Infrastructure as the Cradle of a Vibrant European Ecosystem. Federal Ministry for Economic Affairs and Energy (BMWi), Berlin, October 2019
25. Guba, E.G.: Criteria for assessing the trustworthiness of naturalistic inquiries. Educ. Commun. Technol. **29**(2), 75–91 (1981)
26. IMY: Integritetsskyddsrapport 2020: redovisning av utvecklingen på it-området när det gäller integritet och ny teknik. Integritetsskyddsmyndigheten, IMY rapport no. 1, Stockholm, 28 January 2021
27. IMY: Förhandssamråd om Azure AD och Teams. Dnr. DI-2021–1513, Integritetsskyddsmyndigheten, Stockholm, 2 June 2021
28. Kahn Pedersen: Public cloud services for private businesses in Sweden. Kahn Pedersen, Advokatfirman Kahn Pedersens skriftserie 2020, 3 (2020)
29. Kammarkollegiet: Förstudierapport: Webbaserat kontorsstöd. Dnr 23.2–6283–18, National Procurement Services, 22 February 2019
30. Lianos, I., McLean, A.: Competition Law, Big Tech and Financialisation: The Dark Side of the Moon. Centre for Law, Economics and Society, Research Paper Series: 5/2021, Faculty of Laws, UCL, London (2021). ISBN 978–1–910801–39–0

31. Lings, B., Lundell, B.: On transferring a method into a usage situation. In: Kaplan, B. et al. (eds.) Information Systems Research: IFIP Working Group 8.2 – IS Research Methods Conference – "Relevant Theory and Informed Practice: looking forward from a 20 year perspective on IS research", Kluwer, Boston, pp. 535–553 (2004)
32. Lings, B., Lundell, B.: On the adaptation of grounded theory procedures: insights from the evolution of the 2G method. Inf. Technol. People **18**(3), 196–211 (2005)
33. Lundell, B., Gamalielsson, J., Katz, A.: Implementing IT standards in software: challenges and recommendations for organisations planning software development covering IT standards. Eur. J. Law Technol. 10(2) (2019)
34. Lundell, B., Gamalielsson, J., Katz, A.: Addressing lock-in effects in the public sector: how can organisations deploy a SaaS solution while maintaining control of their digital assets? In: Virkar, S. et al. (eds.) CEUR Workshop proceedings: EGOV-CeDEM-ePart 2020, vol. 2797, pp. 289–296 (2020). ISSN 1613–0073
35. Lundell, B., Gamalielsson, J., Katz, A., Lindroth, M.: Perceived and actual lock-in effects amongst Swedish public sector organisations when using a Saas solution. In: Scholl, H.J., Gil-Garcia, J.R., Janssen, M., Kalampokis, E., Lindgren, I., Rodríguez Bolívar, M.P. (eds.) EGOV 2021. LNCS, vol. 12850, pp. 59–72. Springer, Cham (2021). https://doi.org/10.1007/978-3-030-84789-0_5
36. Lundell, B., et al.: Effective strategies for using open source software and open standards in organizational contexts – experiences from the primary and secondary software sectors. IEEE Softw. **39**(1), 84–92 (2022)
37. Lynn, T.: Dear cloud, I think we have trust issues: cloud computing contracts and trust. In: Lynn, T., Mooney, J.G., van der Werff, L., Fox, G. (eds.) Data Privacy and Trust in Cloud Computing. PSDBET, pp. 21–42. Springer, Cham (2021). https://doi.org/10.1007/978-3-030-54660-1_2
38. Mannheimer Swartling: Applicability of Chinese National Intelligence Law to Chinese and non-Chinese Entities, Mannheimer Swartling AB, Stockholm, January 2019
39. Melin, U., Sarkar, P., Young, L.: Fashions in the cloud – a case of institutional legitimacy. In: Proceedings of the Twentieth Americas Conference on Information Systems (AMCIS 2014), Savannah, pp. 7–10, August 2014. https://aisel.aisnet.org/amcis2014/
40. Michels, J.D., Millard, C., Turton, F.: Contracts for Clouds, Revisited: An Analysis of the Standard Contracts for 40 Cloud Computing Services. Queen Mary University of London, School of Law, Legal Studies Research Paper No. 334/2020 (2020)
41. Microsoft: Årsredovisning Microsoft Aktiebolag: Räkenskapsår 2016–07–01 – 2017–06–30. Microsoft Aktiebolag, Org.nr 556233–4804, 23 February 2018
42. Microsoft: Microsoft Core Online Services Subprocessor List. Microsoft, 22 February 2019
43. Microsoft: Microsoft Online Services Subprocessors List. Microsoft, 5 September 2019
44. Microsoft: How does Microsoft handle your data in the cloud? Subprocessors and Data Privacy. Microsoft, 2 March 2020
45. Microsoft: Microsoft Online Services Subprocessors List. Microsoft, 31 July 2020
46. Microsoft: Microsoft Commercial Support Subcontractors. Microsoft, 13 August 2021
47. Microsoft: Microsoft Online Services Subprocessors List. Microsoft, 24 September 2021
48. Microsoft: Microsoft Online Services Subprocessors List. Microsoft, 23 November 2021
49. Microsoft: Microsoft Commercial Support Subcontractors. Microsoft, 28 January 2022
50. Microsoft: Microsoft Services Agreement. Published 1 April 2021, Effective 15 June 2021 (2022). https://www.microsoft.com/en-us/servicesagreement. Accessed 7 Mar 2022
51. Mitchell, A.D., Samlidis, T.: Cloud services and government digital sovereignty in Australia and beyond. Int. J. Law Inf. Technol. **29**(4), 364–394 (2022)
52. Nas, S., Terra, F.: DPIA report Diagnostic Data processing in Microsoft Teams, OneDrive, SharePoint and Azure AD, Privacy Company, Version 1.1, 16 February 2022

53. Opara-Martins, J.: A decision framework to mitigate vendor lock-in risks in cloud (SaaS category) migration, Ph.D. thesis, Bournemouth University (2017)
54. OSL: Offentlighets- och sekretesslag (2009:400), SFS nr: 2009:400, 20 May 2009
55. OST: Volume Licensing: Online Services Terms, June, Microsoft (2020)
56. Regeringskansliet: Granskning av Transportstyrelsens upphandling av it-drift, Ds 2018:6, February 2018. ISBN 978–91–38–24768–6, ISSN 0284–6012
57. Regeringskansliet: Säker och kostnadseffektiv it-drift: rättsliga förutsättningar för utkontraktering. Delbetänkande av It-driftsutredningen, Statens Offentliga Utredningar, SOU 2021:1, Stockholm (2021). ISBN 978–91–525–0001–9, ISSN 0375–250X
58. Kungörelse, R.F.: (1974:152) om beslutad ny regeringsform, SFS nr: 1974:152, 28 February 1974. https://rkrattsbaser.gov.se/sfst?bet=1974:152
59. Riksarkivet: Riksarkivets föreskrifter och allmänna råd om elektroniska handlingar (upptagningar för automatiserad behandling), Riksarkivets författningssamling, RA-FS 2009:1, Riksarkivet (2009). ISSN 0283–2941
60. Riksarkivet: Riksarkivets föreskrifter och allmänna råd om tekniska krav för elektroniska handlingar (upptagningar för automatiserad behandling), Riksarkivets författningssamling, RA-FS 2009:2, Riksarkivet (2009). ISSN 0283–2941
61. Roshanbin, S., Melin, D.: Digital samarbetsplattform för offentlig sektor. eSam, 24 November 2021
62. Säpo: Säkerhetspolisens årsbok 2019. Säkerhetspolisen, Stockholm 2019. ISBN: 978–91–86661–17–5
63. SCB: Välkommen till det allmänna myndighetsregistret, Statistiska Centralbyrån (Statistics Sweden), Örebro (2022). https://myndighetsregistret.scb.se/. Accessed 24 May 2022
64. SKR: Länskod, regioner och folkmängd, Sveriges Regioner och Kommuner, Stockholm (2022). https://catalog.skl.se/catalog/1/datasets/77. Accessed 24 May 2022
65. SKR: Kontaktuppgifter till kommunerna, Sveriges Regioner och Kommuner, Stockholm (2022). https://catalog.skl.se/catalog/1/datasets/38. Accessed 24 May 2022
66. SKV/KFM: Decision: Memorandum regarding the replacement of Skype in the Swedish Tax Agency's and Swedish Enforcement Authority's operations. The Swedish Tax Agency, Reference no.: 8–958696, The Swedish Enforcement Authority, Reference no.: KFM 10419–2021, 3 May 2021
67. Stockholm: Konsekvensbedömning avseende dataskydd för tjänsten Azure AD och Teams med begränsad funktionalitet. Stadsledningskontoret, Stockholm Stad, 18 February 2021
68. Stockholm: Kompletteringar till förhandssamråd med IMYs dnr DI-2021–1513. Dnr KS 2021/232, Stadsledningskontoret, Stockholm Stad, 13 March 2021
69. Stockholm: Underlag för inriktningsbeslut avseende Microsoft 365 och andra molntjänster. Dnr KS 2021/581, Stadsledningskontoret, Stockholm Stad, 9 December 2021
70. Wagle, S.S.: Cloud Computing Contracts. In: Leh-mann, A., Whitehouse, D., Fischer-Hübner, S., Fritsch, L., Raab, C. (eds.) Privacy and Identity Man-agement. Facing up to Next Steps. Privacy and Identity 2016. IFIP Advances in Information and Commu-nication Technology(), vol. 498, pp. 182–198. Springer, Cham (2016). https://doi.org/10.1007/978-3-319-55783-0_13

Design Principles for EU Cross-Border Services

Sophie Maierhofer and Simon Schimpe(✉)

Department of Information Systems, Westfälische Wilhelms-Universität Münster, Schlossplatz 2, 48149 Münster, Germany
{smaierh1,s_schi53}@uni-muenster.de

Abstract. Successful cross-border labor services are an important requirement for providing free movement of workers in the European Union. This paper focuses on identifying possible improvements in European cross-border labor using digital technologies based on the current challenges of the German-Dutch cross-border collaboration. To achieve this research goal, initially, factors impacting the success of cross-border services are described based on literature from the field of public sector digitalization and the experiences of The Once-Only Principle Project, which represents a current digitalization effort of the European Union (EU). To assess the current state of cross-border labor, four interviews with German and Dutch cross-border experts are conducted. The results of these interviews are then mapped to the factors found in the literature. Finally, five design principles for successful EU cross-border services are derived, namely a Top-Down Approach, Standardization, Adaptability, Accessibility, and Communication, and their projected effects on cross-border services are described.

Keywords: European Digital Decade · Cross-border services · Design principles · Drivers · Barriers · Once-Only Principle

1 Introduction

Ever since the introduction of the EU single market in 1993, the European Union has been striving to improve the conditions for citizens and provide the four freedoms guaranteed by the single market: Free movement of goods, capital, services, and people [5].

Despite the policies, individual citizens and institutions still need to overcome a number of obstacles to make the single market work [4]. Therefore, solutions are urgently needed. An important enabler is the introduction of cross-border services. Labor cross-border services, for example, allow a seamless working experience independent of country borders. There are ongoing efforts, such as the Once-Only Principal Project (TOOP), to reduce administrative barriers. The European Commission's European Digital Decade campaign also intends

Published by Springer Nature Switzerland AG 2022
M. Janssen et al. (Eds.): EGOV 2022, LNCS 13391, pp. 93–105, 2022.
https://doi.org/10.1007/978-3-031-15086-9_7

to strengthen an EU-coherent labor market and encourages every country to establish citizen-friendly administrative procedures [13]. The four aims set out for the digital decade are: (1) a digitally skilled population and highly skilled digital professionals; (2) secure and sustainable digital infrastructure; (3) digital transformation of businesses; and (4) digitalization of public services [6].

The focus of this paper is cross-border services at the German-Dutch border which was particularly motivated by the accessibility to data and information as a good-practice model of European cross-border practices due to long-standing cross-border relations in this region. An additional factor was that despite this traditional cooperation and relationship there are still existing challenges that hinder easy movement of people between the Netherlands and Germany.

Ever since the establishment of the Dutch-German border cooperation, the EUREGIO, in 1958, it has acted as an inspiration and role model for many other cross-border cooperation projects throughout Europe. With an extensive catchment area, high frequency of cross-border movement, and high financial impact, the Dutch-German border region is still to date of immense importance in regards to continuous improvement and development of cross-border activities [22].

This paper aims to analyze the development of European cross-border services by digitalization. Its research goal is to identify possible improvements in European cross-border labor using digital technologies based on the current challenges in the German-Dutch cross-border collaboration. Therefore, factors that impact the success of cross-border services will be described based on available literature, followed by the main research, interviews that have been conducted with German and Dutch cross-border labor experts. The results of the interviews are presented and mapped according to the theoretical factors for successful cross-border services. Finally, design principles for successful EU cross-border services are presented based on both theoretical and empirical findings.

2 Factors Impacting the Success of Cross-Border Services

Several researchers have provided categories of drivers and barriers for digital technologies in general and for projects of the EU in particular. In order to explore the current state of cross-border labor, their results will be reviewed.

One of the currently most relevant efforts in European cross-border digitalization is the Once-Only Principle (OOP). Its goal is to reduce “administrative burdens for citizens and businesses when fulfilling government-imposed administrative requirements and consuming public services” [16]. This is done by reusing data that has already been provided by citizens and businesses to the government and making it available through digital public sector databases. In 2017, the European Commission initiated TOOP to start the implementation of OOP [16].

As part of TOOP, research has been conducted on drivers and barriers for successful implementation. Research has recently been summarized [16]. The terms drivers and barriers are used as the positive or negative expression of the influencing factors of OOP [16]. This means that every factor can either be a driver or a barrier, depending on the context of the project [16]. The authors also consider the time dimension, as the influence of factors can vary between different stages of implementation [16]. To extend the amount of reviewed literature, the authors also used the adjacent fields of "e-government, interoperability, public sector innovation, as well as acceptance of technology" [16] in addition to OOP research. As [16] summarizes, the authors of all reviewed papers are in agreement that the factors influencing digitalization projects are manifold and have to be viewed in combination. Additionally, all authors recognize the need for factors to extend further than the technological dimension.

Although the research papers use different names for these factors, they represent "fairly consistent models" [16] that extend the technological domain and also consider the external context. The most recent summary [16] deals specifically with factors for EU cross-border service. This classification of factors will be explained in the following.

2.1 Technological Factors

The level of technological progress is an essential driver for the successful implementation of a cross-border service [16]. This is expected as the implementation of cross-border services has high technological demands that are easier met with a solid foundation of an organization's own technical systems. Still, [16] shows that a high technological readiness may be a barrier, too. Three main categories of technological factors are found to be particularly important in the context of OOP and other cross-border services [16].

Interoperability. "The ability of two or more software components to cooperate despite differences in language, interface, and execution platform" [21] is called interoperability, which can be viewed as the most challenging aspect of modern cross-organizational information systems [17]. On the one hand, interoperability can be viewed from a technical perspective [19]. Technical interoperability is a prerequisite for any implementation of cross-border services, resulting in a high relevance and focus for this issue [16]. On the other hand, there is semantic interoperability, which entails the content of the shared information and data. The goal is for all organizations to share a common understanding of the processes, which include the sharing of data, the correct translation of documents and texts but also the semantics of the documents [9]. As [16] shows, this part of the cross-border collaboration is not sufficiently covered all the time, resulting in a missing common understanding that puts a project's overall success at risk.

Data Management and Data Quality. There are many issues that can emerge from bad data quality and turn this factor into a barrier. Two of the possible effects of bad data quality are the issues of identity matching [20] and record matching [7]. These two issues result from e-government systems and databases that have not been designed with cross-border applications in mind and therefore lack sufficient identifiers [16]. This leads to problems with the unique identification of citizens or businesses in different systems. In general, information systems and databases in use play a significant role in the success of cross-border services [16].

Security and Trust. Cross-border services rely on mutual data and document exchange, so transparency between all beneficiaries is crucial. For transparency to be implemented by all participating countries, shared trust is essential [10]. The answers provided by the countries to the questionnaire [16] revealed that countries with a high level of technological progress can be held back from participating in cross-border services by countries with a lower level.

Another impact on trust in digital services is bad data and system quality [18]. A lower level of technological progress can imply lower security standards and an increased risk for technologically progressed countries when sharing data cross-border [16]. Implementation of appropriate digital authentication methods and digital signatures are two security factors mentioned [16].

As [10] shows, dependence is a precondition for building trust. It is, therefore, essential to create incentives for the implementation of cross-border services for further developed countries, as they are disadvantaged in comparison to countries already benefiting from the implementation of the service itself. The implementation of cross-border services might even lead to high costs and additional work to adapt their own systems and standards to cross-border applications [16]. Therefore, the positive effects of cross-border services need to be examined and publicly communicated to create an incentive which is independent of the countries' technological progress levels.

2.2 Organizational Factors

Organizational factors are internal to an organization. In case of EU cross-border services, they thus relate to each member state. Based on [16], there are two main areas of concern in organizational factors.

Financial Costs. The lack of financial resources is one of the organizational factors that is most often named in the survey on the OOP [16]. From the start of the project to the end, its importance was even amplified. In 2020, it was the factor with the highest negative impact on OOP implementation [16].

Organizational Structure. The factor with the second most negative impact on OOP implementation in 2020 was a lack of human resources, which is also based on costs, but it can lead to additional problems in the organization. Structural and procedural changes and the organization's overall culture are viewed as important factors [3,16]. Cross-border knowledge transfer networks, for instance, can be a driver for the implementation of cross-border services [8]. On the flip side, one of the most common barriers to a successful implementation are governmental silos [12]. Another finding of the OOP survey is that the installation of an internal IT department which is responsible for the implementation of the cross-border service also positively impacted the implementation time [16]. This finding amplifies the importance of an organization's structure for the overall implementation success.

2.3 Institutional Factors

Institutional factors are concerned with the rules and laws surrounding an organization which impact the implementation of the cross-border service. The two main areas of institutional factors are legal constraints and political decisions. Both of these areas affect organizations heavily [1] by laying the foundation for all organizational actions, decisions and innovations.

2.4 Actors

Apart from the organization itself, there are many actors that impact the implementation of a cross-border service, especially but not exclusively, if the organization is based in the public sector. The first factor is politics which has already been described as an institutional factor. In addition to the overall political vision and individual decisions, the successful implementation of a cross-border project also depends on the willingness of individual government officials and politicians during the project [16]. This willingness is oftentimes driven by the demands of the public and businesses in particular [15]. Therefore, for any cross-border project to be successfully implemented, clear communication of the expected benefits and possible disadvantages is required [16].

2.5 Other Factors

There are more factors that do not fit into the prior categories but are still highly relevant for the success of implementation. First of all, the adoption of new technologies plays a big role in the service's success. In the context of the EU, the adoption might differ between member states and is also highly individual. There are several individual traits that can influence the adoption of a new technology, including age, level of education, experience with a specific or related technology, the degree of voluntary use, and gender [16]. Secondly, the expected outcomes of the implementation of a cross-border service play an important role. Based on the findings of [16], this can be viewed as the even more critical factor. For this reason, it is essential to communicate properly about the expected benefits the service can deliver to set clear expectations and motivate organizations to participate.

3 Research Methodology

This paper employs a qualitative research approach built on semi-structured interviews as the primary research method. A literature review was undertaken to provide a research context to the four interviews conducted in December 2021.

Initially, a thorough concept-centric literature research of relevant, existing papers and studies was conducted. Throughout, the "iterative review approach" was performed where the researchers first start with a broad literature search to gain general knowledge about the new concepts and themes using search terms such as "EU Single Market", "Drivers/Barriers of digitalization", or "European cross-border services" before then refining and extending the initial search with more explicit search commands such as "Digital Decade", "E-government", "The Once-Only Principle", or "EUREGIO" to attain specific insights into the topic by examining additional related work until no new concepts of the domain can be found [2]. The goal was to understand the current state and planned projects regarding European cross-border services, as well as to define common drivers and barriers specifically in the German-Dutch border region.

In the second step of the research phase, based on the literature findings, four semi-structured interviews lasting 30 to 45 min, with two administrative employees, one executive, and one project manager involved in cross-border activities, were carried out. The two administrative employees work for a European institution which offers individual, free-of-charge information and supports citizens and businesses regarding any issue related to working, living, or studying in the German-Dutch-Belgian border region. The third interview partner is an employee at a middle-sized German company located close to the Dutch border. The company not only operates cross-border but also founded a subsidiary company in the Netherlands. The fourth interview was conducted with a team member of an EU project regarding public sector digitalization. Interview partners were specifically chosen based on the variety of tasks they performed in facilitating cross-border relations, and their different approaches, experiences, and understanding of requirements for successful cross-border services. The aim was to thus achieve a more diverse and therefore representative overview of the current situation in the German-Dutch border region.

For this purpose, a rough interview guideline consisting of the following six broad topics and themes was compiled: Employees, taxes, retirement, unemployment, corporate law, and digitalization. These categories were then further adapted to the specific profession and the task of the interviewees. The answers to the open-ended interview questions were then further processed by performing a qualitative analysis through a thematic as well as a content analysis. Thematic analysis is a method for describing data, but it also involves interpretation to identify, analyze, and report repeated patterns [11]. Content analysis is a research technique for making replicable and valid inferences from data to their context and seeks to analyze within a specific context in terms of the meanings someone attributes to them [14].

4 Current Challenges with Cross-Border Services in the German-Dutch Border Region

Based on the findings in the literature, four interviews were conducted to gain further insights and expertise from people involved in cross-border activities in the German-Dutch border region. The subsequently presented findings align with the literature research and fall into the same five categories described before.

Technological Factors. Interoperability is a factor mentioned. As a variety of software services and online communication tools are in use, system compatibility is not always given. Interviewee 1, who is an administrative employee, for instance, recognized the different organizational use of video communication tools which presents a barrier to efficient data exchange, especially for technically challenged clients. Interviewee 1 also mentioned the lack of multiple language offerings for digital services, highlighting semantic interoperability as a barrier. A required German border entry document during COVID-19 provided by border authorities was available in many languages except Dutch, despite the high number of Dutch commuters.

Interviewee 4, a team member of an EU project regarding public sector digitalization, stressed the coordination need for record and identity matching (credentials, voter registration), as this can cause problems for cross-border services or election registrations.

Concerning data security, one of the interviewed administrative employees suggested additional hardware for official use, as work computers containing private data are a technological and data protection challenge.

The differences in technological progress are a barrier in practice, as all interviewees stressed major cultural differences concerning the implementation of digital solutions. In the Netherlands, well-functioning systems, such as DigiD, provide online client identification for interaction with governmental, educational, healthcare institutions, or pension funds. In Germany, this is not the case. Therefore, incentives to develop reward systems for good practice models are needed. Interviewee 1 mentioned the difficulty for authorities to access required private data for administrative purposes, such as information from a client's social security account or data stored by the tax office in the Netherlands. In Germany, data from the online tax office ELSTER cannot be shared due to German privacy concerns, whereas in the Netherlands, sharing personal information is common. Different current states of digitalization, standards, and structures discussed by all interview partners, lead to barriers for cross-border solutions.

Organizational Factors. For local authorities, costs for developing, implementing, and maintaining digital services present a barrier. Financial resources for required technical equipment or for hiring internal or external experts to deal with challenges arising from cross-border digitalization are often times unavailable. In addition, according to administrative employee, with digital services in place, higher expectations of users for continuous improvement and extension of these services arise.

Expansion of the recruiting market for companies can be a driver, but is oftentimes rather a barrier due to legal and administrative concerns. All interviewees emphasized cross-border employment advantages benefitting companies. Information is key due to the specifics of individual cases. Interviewee 2, the second interviewed administrative employee, suggested a designated expert at company level for the early stages of recruitment to prevent additional administrative work later.

Institutional Factors. Varying national legal residency requirements lead to administrative and legal barriers concerning social security, healthcare, taxes, and retirement issues, as worker and residency registration do not align according to second administrative employee. For these reasons, company expansions are often executed by founding daughter companies as mentioned by Interviewee 3, an employee at a middle-sized German company located close to the Dutch border. One reason is a deficiency in recognition of educational qualifications, legal documents, and institutional credentials. In addition, regarding to the interviewed administrative employees, authorities in charge often lack knowledge and are located far from the border.

Improvements - as stated by the EU project team member - can be achieved via personal and organizational data sharing to improve efficiency. However, there is a general reluctance to share both personal and organizational data with third parties.

Actors. Communication between authorities and organizations is viewed as a barrier. Specific requirements are ignored or not adapted to meet cross-border needs. Online questionnaires meet only national needs and lack essential information for the other country, especially with social security issues. These disparities were noticed by one of the administrative employees and can lead to miscommunication and problematic exchanges between the authorities involved.

The other interviewed administrative employee additionally stated that not knowing whom to contact leads to longer and faulty processes. For example, a unit dealing with taxes is mistakenly contacted concerning healthcare. Data protection issues subsequently prevent the forwarding of requests to the responsible department.

Communication, open-mindedness, and flexibility are key drivers, especially in crises. A perfect example is the forced rapid digitalization due to COVID-19 in the past two years, which all interview partners stressed.

Other Factors. One of the administrative employees mentioned that despite existing digital services, personal consultations are crucial, especially for those technologically challenged by age and digital fatigue. However, both interviewed administrative employees stressed that services cannot always be generalized because individual, tailor-made consultation is required. Additionally they mentioned that younger people see opportunities with available solutions, which only require official confirmation. Language was a concern for all interview partners, with one administrative employee and the EU project team member viewing bilingualism as an immense driver for the border region.

5 Deriving Design Principles for Cross-Border Services

In this section, based on the described theoretical and empirical findings, five design principles for successful cross-border services are presented. Table 1 additionally shows their assumed impact on the five categories of factors for successful cross-border services.

Top-Down Approach. To allow for a better-structured development of digital services that can successfully be applied cross-border, general guidelines and rules need to be established by the EU to be implemented top-down through a hierarchical structure. First of all, information needs to be gathered from different countries, institutions, and implementation fields to allow for an analysis of the data as a basis for developing an applicable structure. Thereby, necessary recommendations and documentation can be provided, and specifications as well as required data input types can be determined. Thus, the requirements of all relevant countries are included in the development phase.

Standardization. Standardization and unification of the systems used are key to improving cross-border services. For example, by establishing sufficient identifiers for individuals and organizations in different systems, the often-discussed barrier of identity matching and record matching can be avoided. Through standardized processes and services, it can also be ensured that there are standardized educational qualifications as well as acceptance of certificates cross-border. This can reduce a lot of effort and time-consuming procedures for cross-border students, workers, and companies and thereby simplify all cross-border services simultaneously.

Adaptability. Regardless of the required standardization of services, it is equally important to still allow for individual adaptations to meet the specific requirements and needs of member states. As mentioned in literature and during the interviews, there are various technical systems in place, which require a newly developed service to be adaptable, ensuring a successful implementation process. In addition, to deal with highly individual cases, it is crucial to allow for some degree of freedom on how certain users, for example authorities or countries, can adapt services in terms of their specific needs, such as national laws or different cultural backgrounds.

Accessibility. Furthermore, the technological standards and structures in place require services to be accessible by a wide variety of existing systems. Regardless of the technological difficulty or financial and human resources, the service needs to be easily implemented, connected, and maintained. In addition, it needs to be user-friendly and create visible advantages regardless of the background, language, or culture of the users. Since some end-users still try to avoid digital reliant services, the ease of use and understanding of the benefits need to be made obvious. For these reasons, accessibility is linked to the concept of usability which describes some of the aforementioned criteria.

Communication. The final principle is communication, which plays a significant role in all aspects of cross-border activities and public services. It is crucial that overlying guidelines and rules are not only determined but also efficiently and effectively communicated. In addition, countries with higher existing standards need to be encouraged, possibly through incentives, to cooperate with others in order to ultimately achieve a higher level of digitalization overall and successfully implement cross-border services. It is important to create a positive image by ensuring and encouraging honest promotion of the services to support the acceptance of the offerings which can help with e.g., data privacy concerns or the general willingness to share data.

Exemplary Application. To illustrate these design principles for successful digital cross-border services, one specific case will be discussed, which was mentioned by Interviewee 2, one of the administrative employees, that is that the lack of governmental coordination can lead to breaches of social security laws. In the Netherlands, questions concerning a previous registration in the German system are not asked. This has legal and financial consequences when accepting employment in the German public sector, as then the German social security laws apply also for a Dutch citizen. As Interviewee 2 stressed, this is not a matter of unwillingness by the Dutch officials, but simply a lack of knowledge that this information is relevant for cross-border employment. Therefore, based on the suggested five design principles, the following recommendations can be made: As a first step, a top-down approach by the EU needs to be initiated, whereby the requirements of the member states regarding social security are gathered and summarized to develop a generalized questionnaire and guidelines. Then, standardized identifiers for citizens can be established, so that once a citizen applies for social security in one country, their history is made available to authorities in the others. Data privacy issues need to be considered throughout this process. It is crucial to adapt the catalog of questions for every country. Then, this service needs to be made easily accessible for technological systems used in the Netherlands and possibly differing technological standards in Germany. Finally, communication channels between the authorities should be pre-determined to deal with additional questions that might arise within the process. Responsibilities in this process need to be clearly defined and communicated. A public information campaign should be initiated in order to make the improvements widely known to the public, including citizens and businesses.

Table 1. Design principles for EU cross-border services mapped to factors impacting the success of cross-border services

	Technological factors	Organizational factors	Institutional factors	Actors	Other factors
Top-down approach	– Ensure same data security standards – Guidelines for implementation	– Reduce financial costs – Less organizational changes	– Determine legal regulations	– Less dependence on individuals' willingness	– Increase adoption rates through education programs
Standardization	– Interoperability – Standardize data schemata	– Less dependence on internal IT department	– Provide clarity of rules and laws	– Consistent communication of expected outcomes	– Standardized acceptance of certificates and qualifications
Adaptability	– Incorporate different tools and technologies	– Integrate into existing organizational structures	– Allow flexibility in interpretation of norms and regulations	– Increase public acceptance	– Adapt to individual traits (e.g., gender, age, education)
Accessibility	– Data exchange with pre-existing systems	– Cost-efficient usage of the service	– Efficient implementation of regulations	– Reduce administrative burdens	– Easier access regardless of individual background
Communication	– Incentivization	– Establish communication structures and knowledge transfer networks	– Contact points to support businesses and citizens	– Public promotion of services	– Personal and individual consultation

6 Conclusion

This paper's research goal was to identify possible improvements in European cross-border labor using digital technologies based on the current challenges in the German-Dutch cross-border collaboration. For this purpose, first a literature-based framework of factors influencing the success of cross-border services has been presented. This framework was heavily based on the work of [16], which presents the results of the implementation of the Once-Only Principle in several European pilot projects. This framework of influencing factors was then used to categorize the results from interviews that have been conducted with cross-border labor experts in the German-Dutch border region. Then, it was possible to derive a list of design principles for successful cross-border services based on the literature and interviews. These design principles have been presented in extensive detail and are this paper's main contribution.

Even though these results are based on extensive literature research and interviews with experts from different fields, this paper has several limitations. First and perhaps most importantly, the number of interviews was limited to four and the results, therefore, cannot be generalized to a larger context. Additionally, TOOP has been used as the main source which was reasonable as it is a well-researched and publicized EU project that was implemented a short time before the publication of this paper. Still, taking a higher number of cross-border projects into consideration would lead to more stable results.

Future research that aims to verify or challenge this paper's results should therefore focus on more extensive empirical research that allows for more stable results. Ultimately, it is important to understand the reasons why cross-border services succeed or fail, in order to be able to implement successful ones in the future and thereby support European Commission's digitalization efforts.

References

1. Bekkers, V., Tummers, L., Voorberg, W.: From public innovation to social innovation in the public sector: a literature review of relevant drivers and barriers. Erasmus University Rotterdam, Rotterdam (2013)
2. Vom Brocke, J., Simons, A., Riemer, K., Niehaves, B., Plattfaut, R., Cleven, A.: Standing on the shoulders of giants: challenges and recommendations of literature search in information systems research. Commun. Assoc. Inf. Syst. **37**(1), 9 (2015)
3. Cave, J., Botterman, M., Cavallini, S., Volpe, M.: EU-wide digital once-only principle for citizens and businesses. Policy options and their impacts. European Commission, DG CONNECT (2017)
4. Duch-Brown, N., Martens, B.: Barriers to cross-border ecommerce in the Eu digital single market. Technical report, Institute for Prospective Technological Studies Digital Economy Working Paper (2015)
5. European Commission, Directorate-General for Internal Market, I.E., SMEs: Single market: 25 years of the Eu single market. Publications Office (2018)
6. European Commission, Directorate-General for Communications Networks, Content and Technology: communication from the commission to the European parliament, the council, the European economic and social committee and the commit-

tee of the regions; 2030 digital compass: the European way for the digital decade. European Commission (2021)
7. Fan, W., Jia, X., Li, J., Ma, S.: Reasoning about record matching rules. Proc. VLDB Endow. **2**(1), 407–418 (2009)
8. Ferguson, S., Burford, S., Kennedy, M.: Divergent approaches to knowledge and innovation in the public sector. Int. J. Public Adm. **36**(3), 168–178 (2013)
9. Heiler, S.: Semantic interoperability. ACM Comput. Surv. (CSUR) **27**(2), 271–273 (1995)
10. Kelton, K., Fleischmann, K.R., Wallace, W.A.: Trust in digital information. J. Am. Soc. Inform. Sci. Technol. **59**(3), 363–374 (2008)
11. Kiger, M., Varpio, L.: Thematic analysis of qualitative data: AMEE guide no.131. Med. Teach. **42**(8), 846–854 (2020)
12. Kommission, E., und Medien, G.I.: Study on eGovernment and the Reduction of Administrative Burden: final report. Publications Office (2014)
13. Krimmer, R., Kalvet, T., Toots, M., Cepilovs, A., Tambouris, E.: Exploring and demonstrating the once-only principle: a European perspective. In: Proceedings of the 18th Annual International Conference on Digital Government Research, pp. 546–551 (2017)
14. Krippendorff, K.: Content Analysis, vol. 1. Oxford University Press, New York, NY (1989)
15. Kuklinski, J.H., Quirk, P.J., Jerit, J., Rich, R.F.: The political environment and citizen competence. Am. J. Polit. Sci. **45**(2), 410–424 (2001)
16. Leosk, N., Põder, I., Schmidt, C., Kalvet, T., Krimmer, R.: Drivers for and barriers to the cross-border implementation of the once-only principle. In: Krimmer, R., Prentza, A., Mamrot, S. (eds.) The Once-Only Principle. LNCS, vol. 12621, pp. 38–60. Springer, Cham (2021). https://doi.org/10.1007/978-3-030-79851-2_3
17. Mocan, A., Facca, F.M., Loutas, N., Peristeras, V., Goudos, S.K.: Solving semantic interoperability conflicts in cross-border e-government services. Int. J. Semant. Web Inf. Syst. (IJSWIS) **5**(1), 1–47 (2009)
18. Purwanto, A., Zuiderwijk, A., Janssen, M.: Citizens' trust in open government data: a quantitative study about the effects of data quality, system quality and service quality. In: The 21st Annual International Conference on Digital Government Research, pp. 310–318 (2020)
19. Vernadat, F.B.: Technical, semantic and organizational issues of enterprise interoperability and networking. Annu. Rev. Control. **34**(1), 139–144 (2010)
20. Wang, G.A., Atabakhsh, H., Chen, H.: A hierarchical naïve bayes model for approximate identity matching. Decis. Support Syst. **51**(3), 413–423 (2011)
21. Wegner, P.: Interoperability. ACM Comput. Surv. (CSUR) **28**(1), 285–287 (1996)
22. Wolf, U., Hollederer, A., Brand, H.: Cross-border cooperation in Europe: what are euregios? Gesundheitswesen **68**(11), 667–73 (2006)

Challenges and Potentials of the Use of Convertibles in Emergency Management

Flemming Götz(✉) and Maria A. Wimmer(✉)

University of Koblenz, Universitätsstrasse 1, 56070 Koblenz, Germany
{fgoetz,wimmer}@uni-koblenz.de

Abstract. Digitalization in public services constantly progresses. Aspects investigated in research on digital public services range from strategic subjects to organizational, semantic and technical concepts and solutions, and also include user interaction and the hardware used thereby. This work investigates the use of 'convertible devices" in emergency management from a user perspective. We study challenges and potentials of using convertible devices to support the workers of Crisis Response Organizations (CROs). A qualitative study investigates the emphasized influences of such convertibles on the work within a CRO. The results from the first cohort indicate a positive influence from the perspective of the CRO workers related to the convertible device usage. The participants argue that the device could serve as a laptop, as well as a tablet computer and possibly reduce the number of devices in use. However, the complex interplay of hardware, software, human behavior, emergency management scenarios and environment variables such as mobile network coverage reveal also various challenges for the convertible device usage. According to the participants, the full potential of the hardware could not be exploited. As possible reasons, inter alia, a lack of software support and optimization for pen and touchscreen input, as well as a heterogeneous system environment from a user's perspective have been identified.

Keywords: Convertible devices · Digitalization in emergency management · Potentials and challenges · Qualitative research

1 Introduction

In emergency management, different governmental and non-governmental organizations (NGO) as well as networks of volunteers collaborate on complex tasks of civil protection [1]. Over time, more and more of these tasks are supported by Information and Communication Technologies (ICT) [2, 3]. As civil protection is a central responsibility of public authorities, the ongoing digitalization process for civil protection is a substantial part of e-government strategies [4].

In Germany, the main workforce of Crisis Response Organizations (CRO) like the German Red Cross (DRK), the German Federal Agency for Technical Relief (THW) or the German fire brigades and welfare organizations are operating based on voluntary

Published by Springer Nature Switzerland AG 2022
M. Janssen et al. (Eds.): EGOV 2022, LNCS 13391, pp. 106–122, 2022.
https://doi.org/10.1007/978-3-031-15086-9_8

engagement [5]. Hence, emergency response and civil protection heavily rely on people, who have another profession, while also investing a certain amount of their time without any wage or just for a small recompense [6, 7]. Voluntary workers in emergency management and disaster response are usually participating in their CRO for a longer time. In case of emergency or disaster events, voluntary workers are released from their main employing organizations to support their CRO in a certain role to undertake organized measurements against the disaster. Beyond rescue tasks in emergency events, CROs are also involved in all other phases of disaster management, including prevention, protection, mitigation, response and recovery [8].

Voluntary work for CROs is characterized by the management of unplanned disasters [9]. In combination with the duties in private work and family life, voluntary work demands high flexibility and an effective personal time management. As digitalization promises to make many tasks more time and location independent, it is also a chance for making any kind of voluntary engagement more attractive and effective.

Recently, hybrid tablet/laptop devices (further shortly referred to as "convertibles") have been promoted as all-in-one solution combining the advantages of laptops and tablet computers [10]. Convertibles are tablet computers, which offer the possibility to attach a portable keyboard, so that these can be "converted" into a laptop.

In order to explore the potentials of using convertibles in CRO works, the BKS-Portal.rlp[1] team and its involved institutional actors started a longitudinal study in 2020 to investigate the potentials and challenges regarding the usage of convertibles in the context of emergency management. The main research question for the study on the convertible use in CROs is: how can the software/application portfolio that CRO workers already use in their emergency management tasks be used by them more easily, more flexibly (through mobile device) and more intensively through the support of a convertible? In this paper, we present first insights from the initial two surveys with the first cohort. The empirical research is qualitative.

The paper is structured as follows: the next section outlines the foundations of the research, including a review of the status and progress of digitalization and emergency management. Further aspects outlined are the emergency management in Rhineland-Palatine, the context of our study, as well as the significance of mobile-enabled digital work for emergency management and possible advantages of convertible devices derived from similar research projects. Section 3 describes the setup of the empirical study and the developed questionnaire. In Sect. 4, the research results of the first two interrogations of the eight convertible users are summed up and interpreted. This is followed by a summary of identified challenges, potentials and a brief discussion of first findings (cf. Sect. 4.5). We conclude in Sect. 5 with a summary of the research conducted, with a reflection on the limitations of the work, and an outlook on further research.

[1] BKS-Portal.rlp (https://bks-portal.rlp.de) – Project to develop and support emergency management and underlying administrative processes between public and non-profit organizations in Rhineland-Palatine (Germany) with digital services.

2 Foundations: Digitalization, Emergency Management and Mobility

The ongoing digitalization in emergency management is heavily dependent on the digitalization of the public sector. Although CROs are usually independent organizations with their own structure, their existence and acting are based on laws and regulations. In Rhineland-Palatine (Germany) for example, around 51.000 people are engaging voluntarily as firefighters in about 2.250 regional units.[2] Regulations define, how governmental authorities interact with CROs and vice versa. The regulations aim at guaranteeing a basic degree of protection against various natural and human-made hazards and disasters. To achieve such public safety and civil protection, the CRO and formal CRO units need to be properly equipped with the needed technical and coordination facilities, and they need to be supported in the coordination and cooperation in missions. Examples are the provision of governmental funds for expensive equipment or the obligations of reporting on actions and delivering of information from the CROs to government agencies. In cases of larger disaster events, units of voluntarily working CROs may be directly subordinated to governmental emergency management units.

During disasters, the effective collaboration of various government-led and voluntary specialized organizations is crucial. It is a topic under investigation in various research projects [11]. The interorganizational interaction among these actors creates a significant bureaucratic overhead, which is induced by the many processes between government and CRO units and by the legal requirements to precisely document every action and decision. Administrative burdens result e.g. from redundantly maintaining data in multiple data bases. Thus, inconsistencies occur, data records may be not up to date and data needs to be merged from various data sources with costly efforts, for example to create a statistical overview of available equipment and staff to serve as decision basis for government officials. In emergency management, the overhead of redundantly maintained data must be regarded as especially expensive and as a severe burden straining the valuable time of volunteers and government CRO workers. At worst, it may also result in poor data quality leading to wrong or delayed decisions from the authorities, which could be fatal.

Many inter-organizational processes in this domain are not digitalized yet due to various reasons such as: the number of disaster management organizations, which can possibly interact with each other; a very heterogeneous IT-system landscape; and a lack of regulations and willingness of public authorities toward standardization of data formats, interfaces, and processes in the field.

To overcome the inhibitors of smooth digital interaction, different approaches are being promoted and developed. In terms of ad-hoc collaboration along disasters, highly flexible architectures are being designed to support the matching of offers and demands of any kind of digital resources from various organizations as a decentral solution [2, 12]. Other more centralized approaches try to establish a common use of the same software product for specific use cases [13, 14]. In any case, the availability of digital services and their integration is a fundamental requirement for digitalization in emergency management. As the focus of this paper lies on the potentials and challenges to

[2] https://mdi.rlp.de/de/unsere-themen/bevoelkerungsschutz-und-rettungsdienst/feuerwehr/personal (retrieved at 16.03.2022).

access software and digital solutions from anywhere and at any time, with the use of convertibles, architectures and implementations are not discussed further.

Mobility is a very important factor in the context of emergency management, since disasters or accidents may occur everywhere. CRO workers therefore need to be able to collaborate, coordinate and be able to access data and communication facilities from anywhere, as communication and reporting is crucial for coordinating joint forces. Most CROs have special technical units or roles, which are supposed to establish communication, ensure documentation and reporting etc. Already while driving to the hazardous event, the participants of the mission can be recorded digitally, and first information can be obtained. In a study, Karl et al. summarize that various research projects have documented the benefits and possibilities to make use of mobile devices for example to warn inhabitants, to gather important geoinformation about the affected area or for the application of crowdsourcing and social media [15].

Enabling digital work from anywhere is a significant need in emergency management. With mobile devices, CRO workers, particularly voluntary actors, can contribute on the fly and between mission actions, for example, by sharing information, answering questions, editing and preparing documents, or communicating wherever they have a sufficient network connection.

With digitalization, many tasks can be accomplished in a more flexible way, not always needing to meet physically or to go to a specific location of CRO institutions. Thus, voluntary work could be better integrated into private and "normal" work life [16, 17]. This also could help to reduce stress and increase personal safety [18]. Various tasks from different areas of activity such as administration, organization and knowledge management, virtual training/e-learning options or communication and public relations can be accomplished or supported via software applications and web services.

Haski-Leventhal and McLeigh argue that CRO work for emergency management usually can be accomplished at four locations: at home, at work, in a building of the CRO or at the site of the hazardous event. In addition, people who work voluntarily are also often engaging for multiple organizations and may contribute work at different locations [19]. Especially in larger CROs with several organizational levels such as the fire brigades, higher functionaries must be able to move to different departments residing at different locations. Hence, mobile digital work enables volunteers and formal CRO workers in emergency management to be more flexible and available when needed, and it helps to better connect and support each other within the network of rescue teams.

In order to facilitate mobile work of CRO staff, convertibles offer new potentials. Such convertibles represent recent technological advancements and offer "all-in-one" devices with various input options (touchscreen, pen, keyboard etc.) as well as sufficient computing and battery power for the most daily use cases [10]. This new generation of devices combines different features of laptops and mobile devices such as tablets to transition to the ultimate mobile workstations. Hence, this new generation of devices looks promising to meet the demand of a maximum of mobility and flexibility for CRO workers as argued before. Therefore, we conducted a pilot study in Rhineland-Palatine (Germany)[3] as is outlined in the next section.

[3] In collaboration with the Ministry of the Interior and Sports (MdI) Rhineland-Palatinate.

3 Setup of the Study

The study is conducted using literature analysis and deductive empirical research following the research framework of Österle et al. [20]. The research framework is designed for empirical research. It represents an iterative cycle, starting with defining the research problem and establishing the scientific foundations for the investigation. Subsequently, research and practice interact to advance the solutions and to test them in practice. Lastly, the results are evaluated, and next innovations are triggered. The goal of the pilot study is to explore challenges and potentials of using convertibles by CRO workers in emergency management from a user's perspective. Our hypotheses are that with the use of convertibles in their CRO work i) participants face several challenges; and ii) participants recognize potentials. To verify the hypotheses and to gather deeper insights into the challenges and potentials of using convertibles in emergency management, a longitudinal approach was selected for the general research design. Several cohorts are foreseen and the overall pilot study aims to investigate possible changes regarding to the situation of the CRO workers at three different points in time: a) before the convertibles were given to the participants, b) after approximately 6 months of using them, and c) after another year of use of the convertible. In this paper, we provide first insights from surveying the first cohort at points a) and b).

The first cohort comprises eight CRO workers that have been equipped with convertibles. All eight participants work in one or more CROs, voluntarily or as part of their professional job in a CRO. The participants were selected by the directors of the BKS-Portal.rlp[4] project because of their engagement for the development of the central digital disaster management platform for Rhineland-Palatine, for example by giving feedback on developments or by contributing new requirements.

Even though the small number of participants, these actors offered a complex scenario with different roles, different software in use by each municipal CRO of the participants and with varying personal skills regarding ICT usage. The setup of this group mirrors the complex and very heterogeneous characteristics in the domain of civil protection.

To gather the relevant information for the study at the first and second instance, two questionnaires with open and closed questions were developed, which the CRO workers filled (either with pen or on the computer) and sent back to the study team. To reduce problems of understanding on both sides (for the research team as well as for the participants) the two questionnaires were reviewed and pretested by at least two members of the collaborating institution. Additionally, the research team could be contacted to clear questions regarding to the understanding of the questionnaires, mainly by telephone and virtual conference sessions due to the geographical distribution of the participants and the ongoing Covid-19 pandemic.

The two questionnaires were divided into several sections each. The first questionnaire first asked demographic data and basic information about the participants' roles in the possibly multiple CROs they work for. Since the group was the same in the second questionnaire, this part was not asked again. The second section queried information about the currently used software and personal computing devices to get an

[4] https://bks-portal.rlp.de.

overview about the participants' digital work environment before and after they started to use their convertible device. In the third question block, the participants were asked to describe the usage scenarios for hard- and software in the context of their work, and which devices they primarily use for a specific work scenario. A total of twelve predefined usage scenarios were defined (e.g. coordinate or distribute tasks, document ideas, search or retrieve information, etc.). Additionally, further questions on possible barriers, inhibitors, connectivity, offline support and media type support were asked to encourage the participants to think of further aspects related to the usage of mobile computing devices within their daily work. In question block four, the participants were asked regarding positive and/or negative impacts when using innovative technologies and devices in the context of their CRO works in emergency management. The second questionnaire also asked about the perceived performance and usability features of the convertible in use, i.e. the experiences from the first six months. Finally, the participants were asked in both questionnaires about general feedback regarding the device and the study. The next section presents the main findings of the first and second instance of surveying the first cohort.

4 Interpretation of Results and Discussion

In this section, the first results of the study (surveying the first cohort in two questionnaires) are presented following the basic structure of the questionnaire, which was used to gather the feedback of the convertible users.

4.1 Demographic Information and Organizational Affiliation

Seven of the eight participants indicated their age between 36 and 50 years. Only one participant indicated to be between 21 and 35 years old. Figure 1 depicts the participants and their organizations by regional level and type. Five of the eight participants work voluntarily for a CRO as well as in their main job position (e.g., in a public administration responsible for crisis management and response). Three of the study participants work only voluntarily in a CRO. Among the eight participants, seven work for firefighting departments. This is caused by their selection through the BKS-Portal.rlp project, which is mainly used by fire fighters and administration officials responsible for fire departments and civil protection.

Four participants additionally work voluntarily for aid organizations and one for the Federal Agency for Technical Relief. One participant only works for a single organization, while the others work for more than one CRO (voluntarily and main job). Of these others, half of the participants work voluntarily in one CRO, while the rest is engaged even in three or four positions.

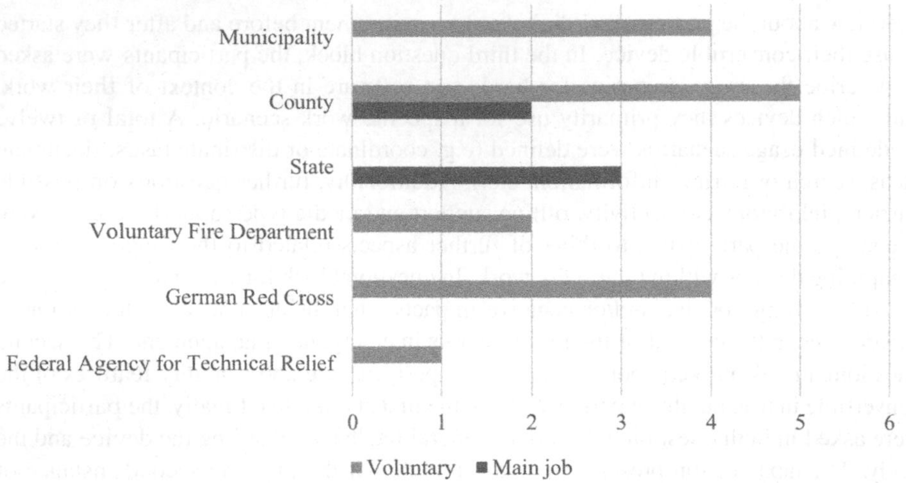

Fig. 1. Study participants by organizational regional level and type (n = 8, multiple affiliations possible)

Overall, the participant group represents highly experienced and voluntary workers with a primary job background related to fire departments and public administration.

4.2 Used Devices and Software Applications for Emergency Management

Of the eight participants, three participants were equipped with a laptop, and other two participants received a tablet and/or smartphone by one of their CROs before they received the convertible device for the purpose of this study (see Fig. 2). Figure 2 also indicates whether the device was provided by the voluntary CRO or by the responsible public administration unit they work in.

Participants who were not equipped with a mobile device from their CRO stated to use primarily their private mobile devices for their work in context of emergency management/response.

The query regarding the software products used on the devices resulted in a variety of 34 different software products and web services. Among these software products are classical standard software like MS Office Suite, Document Cloud Services or Adobe PDF Reader, and various specialized products for emergency management like MP-Feuer, ARIGON, Firebird, Command X, Group Alarm or BKS-Portal.rlp. Although the investigation for software products and web services was not systematic and cannot be expected to be complete in any way, the number of products, which is used by the (voluntary) CRO workers without IT-background emphasizes the high significance of software support within the context of emergency management.

Figure 3 depicts the results from the second interrogation regarding the ten most used software products by device. Participants were asked to rate each of the five devices (Desktop-PC, Laptop, Smartphone, Tablet and Convertible) from 1 (low usage) to 5 (high usage) and the ratings finally were added up. Like for the software products in use, the presented data are highly biased by the selection of the participants in the first

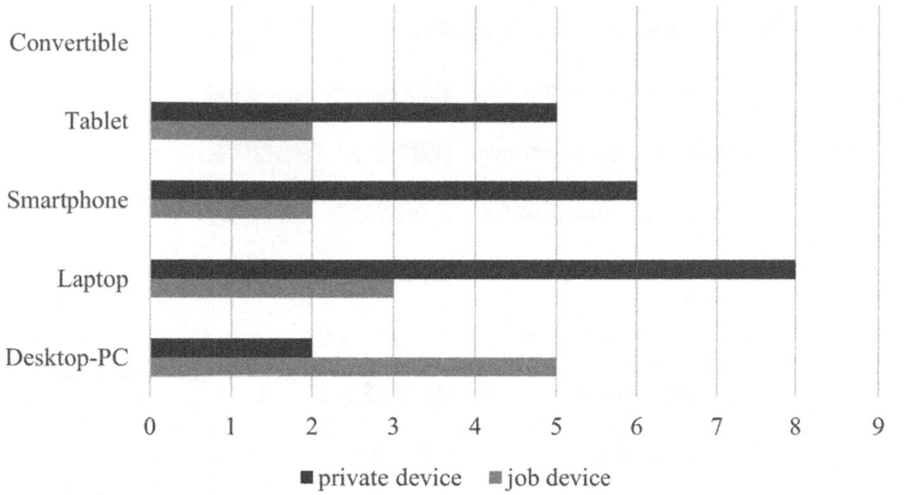

Fig. 2. Available devices of the participants before they have been equipped with convertibles (n = 8)

cohort. Hence, the indications provide an impression about the selected participants' digital work that is subject in this study, but the data are by no means representative for the typical CRO worker in Rhineland-Palatinate. The identified software tools can be (with blurring boundaries regarding to overlapping functionality) generally categorized in standard software (e.g. office suite, document management or communication tools) and domain specific software for disaster management support (e.g. web portal for disaster management, alarm pager, security or training management). Additionally, the rating for the mobile devices remarks the significant role of devices like mobile phones, tablets and convertibles within the regarded user group. The top ten rated software products are used with any kind of mobile devices. Interestingly – and confirming the need of flexible and mobile access to it, the BKS-Portal.rlp (web portal, web conferencing and Nextcloud talk) is accessed through the convertible by seven out of eight persons. Only two of the software products are not used on a smartphone (LEVESO training management and ARIGON). Further research is needed to understand whether these limitations result from a lack of support or optimization for small screen sizes or mobile operating systems.

4.3 Mobile Usage Scenarios in Emergency Management

To get an impression of common usage scenarios in the context of emergency management and which devices are typically used for a specific application scenario, the participants were asked in the first interrogation to provide further information about the use cases of software tools. The resulting answers were then evaluated by the research team to identify usage scenarios, which were used as possible options in the second questionnaire. Overall, 12 typical usage scenarios were identified. Although this list cannot be expected to be complete, no additional answers have been provided in the second questionnaire indicating that the identified scenarios may cover a large part of the usage

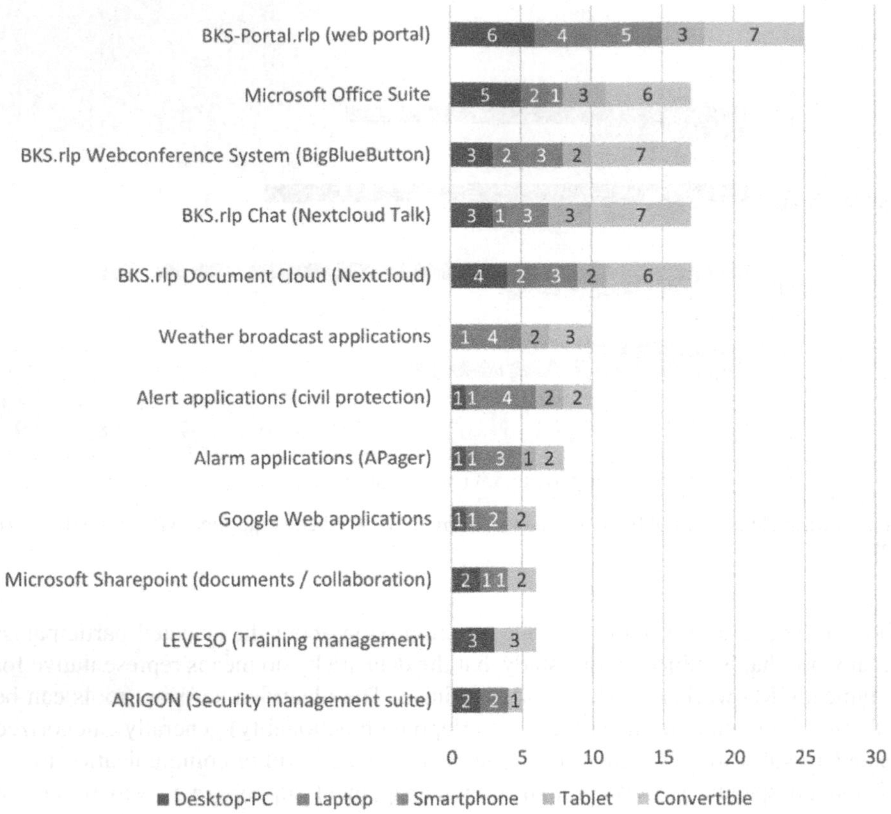

Fig. 3. Web and software applications by device usage (n = 8)

scenarios in perspective of the participants. Figure 4 depicts an overview of identified usage scenarios and the devices used at the second survey instance. For each scenario, multiple devices could be added once, so that the highest number for one device is at max. Eight. Regarding the results, in every scenario a participant stated to use more than one device for a specific scenario. The most devices per scenario included "polls and surveys", "organization of events", "synchronous communication", "information sharing" and "information search". Administrative tasks are mainly accomplished by only one or two devices. The lower number of participants using a tablet computer for any of the usage scenarios is limited by the fact that only two participants have been equipped with such a device by one of their organizations as well as the statement of multiple participants that the convertible was able to "replace" a tablet computer or a laptop for most of the tasks. Seven of the eight participants indicated to use their convertible for most of the given scenarios, which indicates that the device was a suitable option to support most of the usage scenarios of the CRO workers participating in the study.

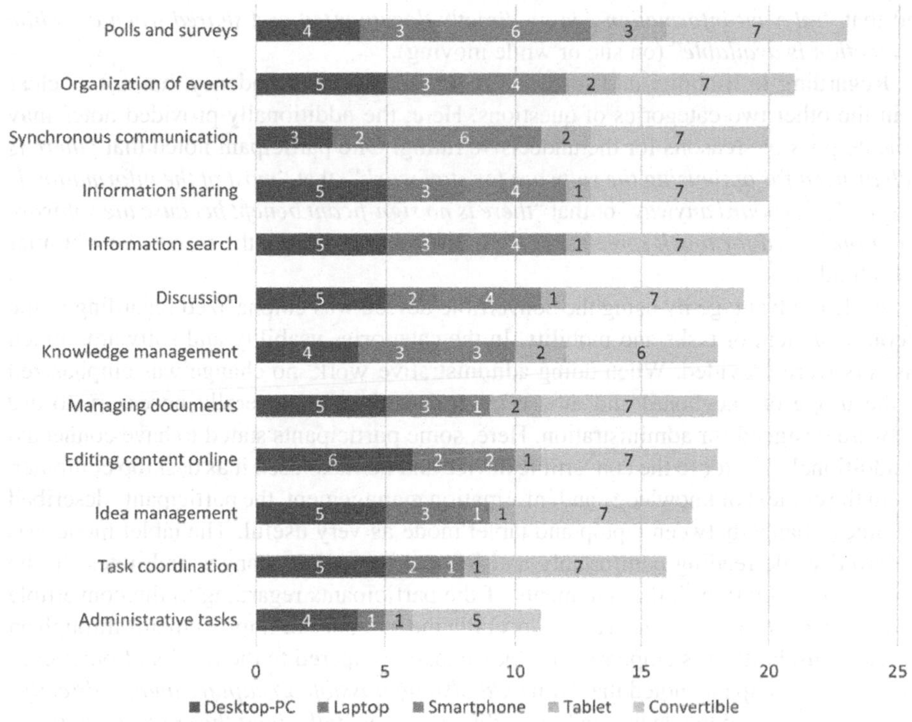

Fig. 4. Common usage scenarios and devices (n = 8)

After the first six months of convertible usage, the participants were asked to evaluate if the given scenarios were experienced as improved in a certain context of emergency management work. The predefined scenarios were *staff work*, *administrative work*, *organization/coordination*, *knowledge and information management*, *operations support*, *training* and *public relations work*. For each usage scenario, the participants were asked to rate their experience either positive (+), neutral (o) or negative (-) in four categories: 1. An improvement of the task itself was experienced, 2. an increased usability was perceived, 3. Improved software was available for the specific task for the convertible device or 4. Improvement resulted from increased mobility. Due to the different CRO work positions of the participants, the number of responses varied for the different contexts and scenarios. Whereas for "staff work" 40 points were given by the participants, only 6 points were distributed for usage scenario "public relations work". For the scenario "staff work", most of the participants emphasized that many tasks related to the given scenarios seem to be easier with a convertible. A participant stated that thanks to the convertible device "*all data can be kept on one device*". Another participant added that some tasks would not even be possible on the laptop.

The possibility to use the convertible device everywhere is clearly regarded as advantage. For example, one participant wrote that an "*easy shift of the workplace is possible quickly and easily*", and that it would be possible to be "*quickly ready for operations*" and that "*relevant information can be directly documented and shared when a mobile connection is available*" (on site or while moving).

Regarding to usability and software, there is a positive tendency, but not as clear as in the other two categories of questions. Here, the additionally provided notes may indicate possible reasons for the undecisive rating. One participant noted that "*there is a clear need for optimizing the software for staff work*", that "*most of the information is entered by keyboard anyway*" or that "*there is no significant benefit because the software is not optimized for touch screen usage*". In the other contexts, the results were similar to each other.

A clear advantage by using the convertible device was emphasized regarding to the accomplishment of tasks and mobility. In the categories usability and software, mixed answers were provided. When doing administrative work, no change was emphasized as the usage of "keyboard and mouse" was described as generally necessary to use software designed for administration. Here, some participants stated to have connected an additional monitor to the convertible device and de facto used it as desktop computer.

In the context of knowledge and information management, the participants described the quick change between laptop and tablet mode as very useful. The tablet mode was preferred while reading comfortably and for making quick changes and notes. In the context of "operations", the statements of the participants regarding to the convertible devices were clearly positive. Here, especially the category of improvements through an increased usability was emphasized as advantage compared to the results of other contexts. The participants noted that "*it would also be possible to capture images directly*" using the camera of the device and to be able to easily "*talk about the current situation*" via video conferencing tools. Also, the "*creation and sharing of quick drawings to share possible operation tactics*" by using the touch screen with fingers or the digital pen was regarded useful.

Next questions investigated challenges, barriers, inhibitors, as well as environmental factors influencing the usage of the convertible devices. In comparison to the results from the answers of the first questionnaire (before the participants have been equipped with convertibles), the results of the second questionnaire indicate some positive tendency: In the first interrogation, the five participants, who also worked for government institutions in parallel to their voluntary work, indicated to expect difficulties to use the convertibles for the main job because of the strict security policies regarding to the use of "external" devices in their job. Contrary to these expectations, the results of the second questionnaire indicate that a solution was found in all cases and the devices could be used within the administration networks without constraints. Regarding availability of mobile network connections along emergency missions, the eight participants indicated to expect difficulties in the first questionnaire. According to a participant, "*the availability of mobile network connections will be critical to use any web service in the field. Based on previous experiences, this will not be possible everywhere and it depends on the coverage of the specific network provider*". Recalling the above described distinguished software portfolio of the participants, a number of web services and application software is used via the convertibles for exchange of information and for communication in field missions. In the second questionnaire, the participants' assessment regarding the quality of mobile network connections varied from "very good" to "insufficient". Different factors may influence this, for example: work area of the participant, mobile network provider or current local demand. Although the limited number of participants do not provide a representative sample, still the mobile network availability represents a key requirement for many use cases of mobile devices within the context of disaster management. As there was and is no guarantee for a sufficient mobile network connection especially when mobile network infrastructure may have been damaged or destroyed by a large disaster, the participants indicated relevant data that should be available on the convertible in offline mode, for example: "*any data relevant for incident and hazard management*", "*contact information*", "*all info included in the disaster management plans*", "*maps and geographical information*", "*basic information about equipment, organizations and staff*". Furthermore, functionality provided by software to support incident and disaster management should also be available in offline mode, such as tools to "*report or document the situation and its development*". This would make it possible to gather and document information immediately and to upload and merge it with other reports as soon as a network connection is available.

4.4 Perspectives on Convertible Device Usage in Emergency Management

In the fourth part of the questionnaire, the participants were asks to describe positive and negative aspects regarding to the usage of the convertible devices for their work from several perspectives such as "flexibility", "communication", "decision making", "efficiency", "device portfolio" and "user acceptance". All perspectives were introduced by an explanation and by examples to create a common basis of understanding. In the first questionnaire, the participants were asked to describe their expectations, while in the second questionnaire they indicated to which extent the expectations could be confirmed. In the analysis of the data, we could compare the results of both.

On *flexibility*, the eight participants reported mainly positive expectations such as the "*possibility to work more independent*", to be able to "*gather data directly in the field*" or to "*do voluntary work in between*". Two participants mentioned negative aspects like an "*expectation of availability all around the clock*" and "*increasing lack of separation between private and work life*". Interestingly after the first usage period, only positive statements were provided on flexibility, indicating that the convertible devices had no additional negative impact in comparison to previously available mobile devices such as smartphone, tablet computer or laptop. Regarding to "*communication*", the participants expected to be better available, to be able to react faster on incoming messages or to communicate via more secure applications. Negative expectations were overlapping with the answers to flexibility and included concerns about a high demand for availability and an overflow of messages. In the second questionnaire, seven of the participants gave positives responses about the influence of the device usage on their communication behavior. The combination of "*a lightweight device with a relatively large screen, integrated microphone and video camera as suitable for video conferences*" was perceived as benefit by four of the eight participants. Two responses confirmed the negative expectations for quick responses and a possible negative influence on the own work life balance. One participant notated additionally that the possibly negative effects were not caused by the availability of the device itself, but from a lack of self-control about its usage. The expected benefits related to "decision making" included "*availability of information on one device*", "*more up to date information*" and "*quick access to relevant information*". Here, all expected positive aspects have been regarded as confirmed by the participants. Additionally, respondents mentioned that the larger screen size of the convertible device made it easier to retrieve information and to display them in a better way in comparison of using a smartphone screen. As only negative expectation, an overwhelming information flood was mentioned by one participant in the first interrogation, which was confirmed in the second questionnaire by the statement "*that it is necessary to be able to handle the large amount of information available*".

Positive expectations related to efficiency included: "*it will not be necessary to use multiple devices and interrupt the workflow to accomplish a task*", "*prevent synchronization conflicts leading to inconsistencies*" and to be "*more efficient when it is possible to use all applications and data on one device*". In the second questionnaire, the positive expectations were confirmed without exceptions. A negative assumption was spotted in the first questionnaire by a respondent as follows: "*tasks need be accomplished quicker everywhere at any time*". This negative expectation was, however, not confirmed by any of the participants in the second questionnaire. Instead, one participant complained about the number of applications and software systems to be used, describing the current system landscape for emergency management as "very heterogeneous". Although this annotation is not directly related to the convertible device, it is important regarding to the possibility to work efficiently.

Regarding to the influence of the available convertible on the "device portfolio" of the users, all eight participants expected that the new convertible will be able to replace either a laptop, a tablet computer or both devices and serve as "two in one device". This expectation was confirmed by the answers to the second questionnaire. Negative expectations which were not confirmed in the answers of the second questionnaire included that "*data needs to be organized better for synchronization*" and that "*more hardware and additional components will be difficult to handle*". A respondent argued that possible data inconsistency problems could be successfully prevented by using a document cloud synchronization application. Thus, a possible negative effect caused by multiple hardware devices was solved by a software solution.

Most answers related to the *user acceptance* of the device as additional category in the second questionnaire were related to the input options and usability of the convertible. Six of eight participants stated to use the touchscreen of the device regularly or to make "more and more use of it within daily work". Only one participant mentioned to use the pen as input option and another one mentioned to use the device as a pure laptop replacement without making use of any other input options than the keyboard. The new input options of the convertible provided new possibilities for interacting with the software on the device. This occurred to offer potentials and challenges at the same time. The participants indicated that software products were not optimized for the new input options. Especially the feedback that the touchscreen usage increased over time may lead to the assumption that the users had to decide when to use the right input option and had to adjust their behavior accordingly.

4.5 Synthesis of Identified Challenges and Potentials

The results presented in the previous subsections indicate a number of challenges and potentials spotted by the participants. Table 1 summarizes these identified potentials and challenges, grouped into four categories: 1. Hardware (exclusively related to the physical convertible device), 2. Software, 3. Technical environment and 4. Emergency management scenarios and human behavior. Potentials and challenges of the categories 2–4 are mainly software and context related, and thus, not specific to the usage of a convertible device. Indeed, the aspects raised possible impacts of the usage of any other personal mobile computing device as well.

Table 1. Overview of identified challenges and potentials related to the usage of convertible devices in the context of emergency management

Category	Potentials	Challenges
1. Hardware	P1.1 More input options (touchscreen, digital pen) P1.2 Reduced number of devices in use (tablet and laptop) P1.3 Lightweight device P1.4 Integrated camera and microphone	C1.1 Management of devices and hardware accessories
2. Software	P2.1 Offline support and synchronization P2.2 Consistent workflows on one device P2.3 Data, information and applications available on one device	C2.1 Missing software optimizations for input options C2.2 Heterogeneous software system landscape C2.3 Data management needs to be improved
3. Technical environment		C3.1 Quality and availability of mobile network connections
4. Emergency management scenarios and human behavior	P4.1 More flexible work possible P4.2 Gathering data, photos and videos directly on site P4.3 Enabling quick video conferencing P4.4 Enabling better decision-making based on more / on up-to-date information	C4.1 Selection of the most suitable input option C4.2 Expectation of availability, fast responses and work performance C4.3 Possible information and communication overflow

With four potentials and only one aspect categorized as challenge, the hardware (1) of the convertible device primarily offers benefits. The provision of multiple input options (P1.1) was categorized as potential but could be regarded as a challenge in a perspective of human-computer interaction at the same time, because the participants stated to sometimes have felt indecisive on which input option to use. This example shows that a potential may be a challenge at the same time, and vice versa. Further, a potential could weaken or even equalize a challenge completely; e.g., some participants indicated that the convertible potentially replaces a laptop and/or a tablet (P1.2). The management of devices and accessories was described as challenge (C1.1) but could be less of an issue with a reduced number of devices.

Concerning the hardware, the initially assumed benefits through increased mobility have been confirmed by the statements of the participants. The "multimedia" device with two cameras, microphone and several interfaces (P1.4) seems to close the gap between devices primarily designed for mobility like tablet computers and laptops. Thus, quick video conferencing as well as gathering data, photos and videos on site are also perceived potentials with the convertible device.

Several participants of the study argued that various software (2) products they use in CRO works do not fully support all hardware and input options yet (C2.1). Additionally, a heterogeneous system environment (C2.2) and concepts for data management (C2.3) have been emphasized as challenges. Beyond the challenges, new possibilities with features like offline support and synchronization (P2.1), as well as consistent workflows (P2.2) and the opportunity to have all data on one device (P2.3) have been spotted as potentials.

With regard to the technical environment (3), the quality and availability of mobile network connections (C3.1) was regarded as a challenge in some regions. However, a key requirement is to support mobility and flexibility in various mobile scenarios in the context of emergency management.

Regarding emergency management scenarios and human behavior (4) overall, crucial potentials are more flexible work possible (P4.1), including gathering data, photos and videos directly on site (P4.2), and quickly enabling video conferencing (P4.3). To confirm the observations of for example Pipek et al. [1], a high demand for collaboration software supporting for example coordination, communication, as well as document exchange and editing was spotted. Another benefit is the availability of up-to-date information for better informed decision-making (P4.4). Drawbacks of increased flexibility and ubiquitous computing are fears of high expectations regarding to personal availability, fast responses and work performance (C4.2). Both have been reported in multiple responses and may be regarded primarily as social and organizational challenge in the category. Along this, also a possible information overflow (C4.3) was spotted by the participants.

Some more general insight from the study is that CROs are challenged to adopt technical and organizational solutions to mitigate the challenges, and to protect their workers from unnecessary workload and stress alike.

5 Conclusion and Future Research

In this paper, we investigated the use of convertible devices in emergency management. The findings of the first two questionnaires of the cohort of eight CRO workers indicated several changes driven by the adoption of convertible devices as technological innovation. In scope of the qualitative empirical research was the exploration of challenges and potentials of convertible usage in emergency management. The analysis of the results of the two queries resulted in a set of eleven potentials and eight challenges of convertible device usage in emergency response.

While the list of challenges and potentials can by no means be considered to be complete or verified, these represent first insights on how CRO workers can be supported with the usage of convertible devices. The answers provided by the participants partially included hints about possible solutions for CRO workers to exploit some of the potentials and to overcome various challenges. Overall, the results provide a starting point to understand the added value of convertible devices in the field. However, as argued in the previous section, a number of the challenges identified are not necessarily related to the convertible usage, but represent issues external to the device usage. To resolve such challenges, these need to be addressed at macro-level strategic-political decision-making. Therefore, the findings will also be communicated to the upper echelons of formal ministerial officials. The research will be continued with a third interrogation of the first cohort. A second cohort is now receiving convertibles, so the second iteration of questionnaires will be initiated.

Some limitations of this work are that challenges and potentials could only be analyzed with a limited set of eight participants within this research. The third questionnaire shall dig into more details considering the use of a convertible device in the different work contexts in emergency management such as administrative work, incident management, staff training or public relations work and scenarios of mobile computing device usage.

The qualitative approach applied in this study was appropriate to observe the changes from a user's perspective by making use of two questionnaires, which were answered before receiving and after using the convertibles for a while. The third round of query is a next step in our research. To gather additional information and to verify the answers of the participants of the first peer group, another set of convertible devices has been purchased for the BKS-Portal.rlp project and the first questionnaire data are being collected from the second peer group. Ultimately, beyond the analytical research, further research is planned to derive concrete recommendations for CROs and voluntary workers to support them in mobile emergency management scenarios.

Acknowledgement. The authors are very grateful to the eight participants of the first peer group for their time and inputs to the study. We are also grateful to Jörg Kohlbeck who supported us in the conduction of the second survey and in the analysis of the findings. Finally, we are very thankful to the Ministry of the Interior and for Sports Rhineland-Palatinate for financing the convertible devices.

References

1. Pipek, V., Liu, S.B., Kerne, A.: Crisis informatics and collaboration: a brief introduction. Comput. Support. Coop. Work (CSCW) **23**(4–6), 339–345 (2014). https://doi.org/10.1007/s10606-014-9211-4
2. Elahraf, A., et al.: A framework for dynamic composition and management of emergency response processes. IEEE Trans. Serv. Comput. **10**, 14 (2019)

3. Feuerwehr, B., Köln, B.: Deutsche Hochschule der Polizei: SoKNOS – ein Forschungsprojekt im Bereich öffentlichen Sicherheit, Berlin, Köln, Münster-Hiltrup (2010)
4. Fleron, B., Pries-Heje, J., Baskerville, R.: Digital organizational resilience: a history of Denmark as a most digitalized country. In: Proceedings of the Annual Hawaii International Conference on System Sciences, pp. 2400–2409. IEEE Computer Society (2021)
5. Kigge, A.: The voluntary welfare associations in Germany: an overview, ZeS-Arbeitspapier, No. 03/2009, Universität Bremen, Zentrum für Sozialpolitik (ZeS), Bremen, Germany (2009)
6. Freeman, R.B.: Working for nothing: the supply of volunteer labor. J. Labor Econ. **15**, 140–166 (1997)
7. Dangermond, K., Elbers, M.J., Tonnaer, C.: Legal status of (on-call) volunteer firefighters in Europe. Instituut Fysieke Veiligheid, Arnhem, Netherlands (2019)
8. Reese, S., Stienstra, L.R.: National preparedness: a summary and select issues. A Congressional Research Service (CRS) Report (2021)
9. Schryen, G., Wex, F.: Risk reduction in natural disaster management through information systems: a literature review and an IS design science research agenda. Int. J. Inf. Syst. Cris. Response Manag. **6**, 38–64 (2014)
10. O'Donnell, P., McKelvey, N., Curran, K., Subaginy, N.: The rise of the tablet. IGI Global (2015)
11. Ley, B., Ludwig, T., Pipek, V., Randall, D., Reuter, C., Wiedenhoefer, T.: Information and expertise sharing in inter-organizational crisis management. Comput. Support. Coop. Work (CSCW) **23**(4–6), 347–387 (2014). https://doi.org/10.1007/s10606-014-9205-2
12. Braune, S., et al.: A service-oriented architecture for emergency management systems. In: Reussner, R., Pretschner, A., Jähnichen, S. (eds.) GI-Edition, Software Engineering 2011–Workshopband. Lecutre Notes in Informatics, pp. 225–232. Gesellschaft für Informatik e.V., Karlsruhe (2011)
13. Qi, G., Wu, Y., Chen, A.: Analysis and design of modern emergency management platform. In: Proceedings - 2010 IEEE International Conference on Emergency Management and Management Sciences, ICEMMS 2010, pp. 468–471. IEEE (2010)
14. Bartoli, G., Fantacci, R., Gei, F., Marabissi, D., Micciullo, L.: A novel emergency management platform for smart public safety. Int. J. Commun. Syst. **28**, 928–943 (2015)
15. Karl, I., Rother, K., Nestler, S.: Crisis-related apps. Int. J. Inf. Syst. Cris. Response Manag. **7**, 19–35 (2015)
16. Cote, M., Hasskamp, B., Chevuru, P., Verma, M.: Empty boot, quiet sirens: the state of non-career firefighting in Minnesota, Minneapolis (2014)
17. Linsdell, G.: Catastrophic work/life balance: emergency responder role conflict and abandonment–implications for managers. In: Australian & New Zealand Disaster and Emergency Management Conference, pp. 225–240, Brisbane, Australia (2012)
18. Smith, T.D., Hughes, K., DeJoy, D.M., Dyal, M.A.: Assessment of relationships between work stress, work-family conflict, burnout and firefighter safety behavior outcomes. Saf. Sci. **103**, 287–292 (2018)
19. Haski-Leventhal, D., McLeigh, J.D.: Firefighters volunteering beyond their duty: an essential asset in rural communities. J. Rural Commun. Dev. Firefighters **4**, 80–92 (2009)
20. Österle, H., Brenner, W., Hilbers, K.: Unternehmensführung und Informationssystem. Vieweg+Teubner Verlag, Stuttgart (1992)

Social Media

Real-Time Stance Detection and Issue Analysis of the 2021 German Federal Election Campaign on Twitter

Arthur Müller(✉), Jasmin Riedl, and Wiebke Drews

University of the Bundeswehr Munich, 85577 Neubiberg, Germany
arthur.mueller@unibw.de

Abstract. Real-time large-scale data streams provided by Twitter create new possibilities for political scientists to nowcast political events. We developed a pipeline to process, analyze and aggregate data for presentation on a web application. During the 2021 German federal election campaign, expressed stances on competing political parties and their front-runners were analyzed in real time. State-of-the-art linguistic neural networks were reused and adapted by post-training and fine-tuning for detecting stances toward political actors. Furthermore, a dictionary-based approach was adopted to analyze the salient topics during the campaign across 32 (policy) issues. Within stance detection, a decrease in performance over time became visible, which can largely be attributed to a shift in issue focus on Twitter during the election campaign. This is emphasized with concrete empirical examples. During the final phase of the campaign, qualitative monitoring was maintained to ensure the validity and reliability of our findings. Based on this, potential error sources are presented, and possible solutions for future research are offered.

Keywords: Stance detection · Issue analysis · Twitter · Nowcasting · 2021 German election campaign

1 Introduction

National election campaigns are the epitome of democratic competition. To boost electoral fortunes, political actors must be able to listen and react to the concerns of their (potential) constituencies in a timely manner [26]. Because digital platforms have become decisive arenas for political actors to compete over policies and votes [41], social media platforms open new and exciting avenues for public opinion research.

Public opinion is commonly analyzed by means of population surveys that are static in time or by traditional media with journalistic gatekeepers. New textual data abounding on social media allow meticulous and unmediated analyses of salient (policy) issues and public perceptions of parties and their front-runners [11]. More strikingly, social media data enable unprecedented, real-time analyses of public opinion to nowcast political events [7]. Although social media analytics

Published by Springer Nature Switzerland AG 2022
M. Janssen et al. (Eds.): EGOV 2022, LNCS 13391, pp. 125–146, 2022.
https://doi.org/10.1007/978-3-031-15086-9_9

cannot fully replace surveys, not least due to a lack of representativeness of the population as a whole, they may complement understandings of elections in a time marked by an increased volatility with rising numbers of undecided and swing voters [31].

This paper provides novel insights into how political debates on social media can be analyzed under real-time conditions based on a case study of the 2021 German federal election campaign on Twitter.[1] The analysis focuses on stances toward parties and their leading candidates as well as the salience of (policy) issues expressed in tweets commenting on the German election. The paper presents the findings of the analysis and addresses opportunities and limitations of real-time analyses of Twitter data. In the process of conducting the stance detection[2] and issue analysis, specific challenges arose with respect to political speech: over time, a decrease in the performance of the models in terms of the accuracy of predicting stances was observed that is ascribed to a shift of salient issues addressed in tweets. More specifically, exogenous shocks such as the German flood disaster in July 2021 and the evacuation mission in Afghanistan in August 2021 gave rise to novel topical priorities and related vocabulary, i.e., hashtags and terms, that were previously unknown to the models. Target-dependent stances in the context of such new issues were thus more difficult to detect. By focusing on the opportunities and challenges of our real-time analysis, this paper paves the way for future endeavors in the field of electoral nowcast.

In the following sections, we first provide an overview of the 2021 German federal election and detail the proposed research approach for real-time analysis of Twitter data. We then describe the procedure of data collection, the training and results of supervised stance detection models and the findings obtained from the issue analysis. Finally, we elaborate on monitoring, problem solving and error analysis and conclude with a summary of insights.

2 Case Study: The 2021 German Federal Election Campaign

Germany has a federal and parliamentary form of government that had at its core seven political parties in the 2021 federal election. On a simplified left-right-scale,[3] these parties included: DIE LINKE, SPD, Bündnis 90/Die Grünen, FDP, CDU, CSU and AfD. Two parties—CDU and CSU—build a conservative alliance called *Union*. None of the parties holds an absolute majority of seats,

---

[1] The results presented here are part of the larger interdisciplinary research project SPARTA (Society, Politics and Risk with Twitter Analysis). The WebApp is accessible via: https://dtecbw.de/sparta?lang=en.

[2] Stance detection means inferring user's attitude towards a predefined entity or topic. See Sect. 5 for details.

[3] In contrast to two-party systems, Germany has a more advanced multidimensional political space [12], although spatial models may work with a simplified left-right-scale.

meaning that governments are usually based on coalitions.[4] As a result, election campaigns are less confrontational than in two-party systems such as the USA or the UK, at least between potential coalition partners. Simultaneously, Germany is characterized by strong cooperative elements between the state and federal levels (cooperative federalism) and fierce competition between majority and opposition parties in parliament. Therefore, a mixture of both consensual and competitive elements characterizes the German political system and becomes noticeable during election campaigns [27,29,38].

Recently, election campaigns have increasingly focused on social media as decisive arenas in which to win or lose votes. The 2017 German federal election is argued to have been the turning point in this regard since party strategists and observers began to regard social media not just as experimental and peripheral venues but as central battlegrounds for winning election campaigns [41]. In the context of a global pandemic and a younger electorate [5], data-driven and digital campaigning [36] further increased during the 2021 election campaign, both in terms of quantity and quality.

The growing importance of digital tools in German election campaigns is further reflected in a steady increase of scholarly literature on the topic. Already in 2009, Tumasjan et al. [43] analyzed a German federal election by means of a LIWC-based dictionary approach [33]. They found that Twitter chatter corresponded to offline political programs and candidate profiles and that the number of mentions of political parties in tweets closely predicted the 2009 election outcome. In contrast, Jungherr et al. [24] refuted a relationship between Twitter mentions and electoral chances of parties for the 2013 federal election. Moreover, the authors found that the distribution of topics mentioned on Twitter differs from those stressed in traditional media and population surveys, even though such topics are related to real-life events. Hence, one can conclude that Twitter is not representative of a population as a whole, particularly in terms of a user demographic that is predominantly male, college educated and under 50 years old [13]. Similarly, Stier et al. [41] found that during the 2017 federal election, candidates and their direct audiences prioritized different topics in social media messages than the mass audience did, and the authors ascribed this to the affordances of platforms. Additionally, Ceron et al. [6] revealed that parties' issue emphasis on Twitter fluctuates frequently and depends on exogenous shocks in real life, among other factors. Meier et al. [32] further showed that topic trends on Twitter are time sensitive and depend on the electoral cycle [4]. It is therefore evident that Twitter communication during German election campaigns is extremely dynamic and volatile.

While there is increasing scholarly interest in the topic of digital campaigning, all studies cited thus far analyzed German election campaigns retrospectively (i.e., after election day). In contrast to previous research, our analysis is a nowcasting [7] of stances on parties and candidates as well as salient issues during

[4] The 2021 election resulted in a coalition government made up of SPD, Bündnis 90/Die Grünen and FDP.

the 2021 German federal election campaign. In other words, all relevant tweets were harvested, preprocessed and analyzed in real time.

Some previous research has focused on real-time analyses of Twitter during elections in other contexts. Soler et al. [40] focused on three Spanish elections during 2011 and 2012 and provided a web application (WebApp) that was able to display numbers of mentions of political parties and candidates in tweets. Wang et al. [45] suggested a real-time pipeline to classify tweets using sentiment analysis for the 2012 U.S. presidential election to be presented on a WebApp. The authors employed a Naïve Bayes classifier. Kagan et al. [25] considered the 2013 Pakistani and 2014 Indian elections and applied sentiment analysis based on the adjective-verb-adverb approach (AVA). Gupta et al. [20] analyzed the 2017 Indian elections in the federal state of Punjab in real-time. The authors trained and compared different architectures of sentiment analysis classifiers (for example a multi-layer perceptron) on data collected from GitHub and achieved high evaluation performance. Although stance prediction is a sentiment related task [42], it is questionable how far sentiment models trained on data from a foreign domain can be transposed to the prediction of stances in political language [22,35]. Hitesh et al. [23] focused on the 2019 Indian elections and performed sentiment analysis using a Random Forest classifier and their own annotated dataset.

However, none of these publications employed the current state-of-the-art pretrained neural transformer-based language models for predicting stance (or even sentiment) in real time, which impose additional requirements on the scalability of the processing pipeline architecture. Additionally, there is a lack of accounts of the technical realization of such pipelines. Moreover, in contrast to previous research, we added issue analysis to our pipeline, which enabled us to make assumptions about the change of issues over time in conjunction with expressed stances. From the perspective of stance detection, many unsupervised or semi-supervised approaches based on network structures of user or tweet connections (e.g., follower or retweet graphs) have achieved impressive classification performance [9,14,34,37]. However, these methods are not applicable in the real-time streaming setting for tweets. Of alternative methods that could be employed, little research has concentrated on stance detection for the German language [18,21,44]. In particular, none of the existing studies investigated tweets as the information source or considered target entities of German political parties or candidates during election campaigns. Language employed on Twitter is quite different from grammatically clean and structured German language used in newspapers [21] or surveys [18,44]. Thus, there is a lack of annotated German tweet datasets and available pretrained neural classification models for this case study. Our approach aims to fill these gaps.

3 Real-Time Analysis Approach

To monitor the 2021 German federal election, we implemented a pipeline-based architecture that fetches tweets using Twitter API. Tweets were processed via

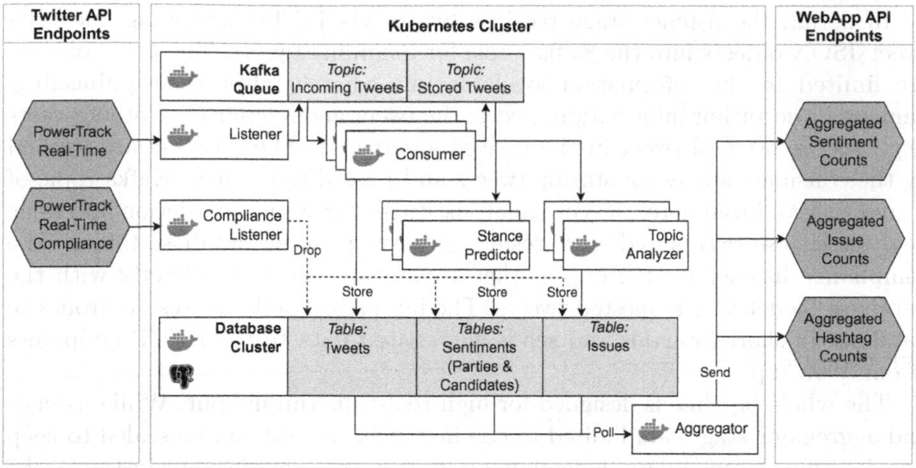

Fig. 1. Architecture of the pipeline used for real-time processing of tweets

different pipeline stages, and results of the nowcasting were finally published on a WebApp from August 1, 2021 until election day (September 26, 2021). The overall results were summarized and archived as soon as the new German government was formed in December 2021.[5]

Figure 1 gives an overview of the implemented real-time architecture. On the left- and right-hand sides the inputs and outputs of the pipeline are depicted, while the middle box contains the pipeline itself. The main lane begins by reading the tweet stream from the PowerTrack API[6] endpoint, which is controlled by specific filter rules (see Sect. 4), and finishes by sending data to the endpoints of our WebApp for further visualization. The second pipeline lane handles incoming messages about deleted tweets from the Compliance Firehose API[7] which need to be deleted in our data storage to comply with data protection regulations. We employ a Kubernetes[8] cluster with one master and two GPU-enabled worker nodes to orchestrate different Docker[9] containers as parts of the pipeline: (1) Apache Kafka[10] for building a tweet-processing queue in-memory; (2) the PostgreSQL[11] relational database for persisting tweets with enriched information; and finally, (3) custom pipeline stages with the logic for storage, analysis and aggregation of tweet data.

[5] The archived summary can be found at: https://dtecbw.de/sparta/germanelection.
[6] https://developer.twitter.com/en/docs/twitter-api/enterprise/powertrack-api.
[7] https://developer.twitter.com/en/docs/twitter-api/enterprise/compliance-firehose-api.
[8] https://kubernetes.io/.
[9] https://www.docker.com/.
[10] https://kafka.apache.org/.
[11] https://www.postgresql.org/.

In detail, the listener stage receives tweets via HTTP streaming and puts tweet JSON objects into the Kafka topic for incoming tweets. The tweet objects are limited to the information available immediately after their publishing, namely: basic author information, text of the tweet and references to other tweets (e.g., to the original tweet in the case of a retweet). These tweets are fetched by the consumer stages for storing tweets and passed to the next Kafka topic of stored tweets. From here, the core analysis stages for stance prediction and issue analysis choose tweets and store results to corresponding database tables. The compliance listener reads from another stream and interacts directly with the database by deleting requested tweets. The final stage polls the results from the database in short intervals and sends aggregated data to the HTTP endpoints of our WebApp.

The whole pipeline is designed for high real-time throughput. While listener and aggregator stages are limited to one instance, the rest can be scaled to keep up with the streamed data depending on its own complexities. For instance, the execution time of the stance predictor per tweet is very long compared to the consumer. The predictor preprocesses the tweet text and then passes it to the stance detection model using a GPU (see Sect. 5). Additional scaling can be done by processing batches of tweets on a single GPU. On the hardware level, these stages are supported by NVIDIA's multi-instance GPUs, which can be split into smaller virtual GPUs, enabling them to run more stages in parallel and cope with the high data pressure.

4 Data Collection and Units of Analysis

The filter rules for the real-time stream consisted of 428 hashtags (e.g., *#kanzlerduell* or *#btw21*), 701 keywords (e.g., *Bundeskanzlerkandidat*), 110 user mentions (e.g., *@ArminLaschet*) and 111 Twitter accounts as direct tweet sources (e.g., *from: Die_Gruenen*). The filter rules were directly related to the federal election and its central actors and included hashtags and keywords about the German federal election in general (e.g., its name), the election outcome (e.g., potential future coalitions), specific actions related to the election (e.g., going to the ballot box), and the campaign and surrounding events (e.g., TV debates). Moreover, hashtags, keywords and—if available—user mentions and Twitter accounts of central actors such as parties, parliamentary groups, state-level party associations and leading candidates were used to find the relevant tweets. In order to establish the filter rules, an extensive monitoring of German political talk on Twitter preceded the real-time analysis. User mentions and Twitter accounts of the above-mentioned actors were evaluated for their authenticity. Moreover, the list of filter rules was extended with novel, relevant hashtags arising during the election campaign. For this purpose, a list with new hashtags not previously included in the filter rules was issued and qualitatively examined on a weekly basis. Only German-language tweets were considered. The tweets were processed and stored in a relational database according to German IT security standards and data protection regulations.

Table 1. Numbers of collected tweets (including retweets) published by party accounts and their leading candidates as well as mentions of them in tweets from July 1 until September 26, 2021. Since multiple mentions per tweet are possible, the overall sum in the right column is higher than the total number of all harvested tweets.

Political parties		
	Tweets published by	Mentions of
AfD	2,735	1.801 mio
Bündnis 90/Die Grünen	3,830	2.595 mio
CDU	3,839	4.039 mio
CSU	1,004	1.533 mio
DIE LINKE	6,109	1.002 mio
FDP	3,949	1.096 mio
SPD	5,312	2.958 mio
Sum	26,778	15.024 mio
Leading candidates		
	Tweets published by	Mentions of
Annalena Baerbock	107	1.297 mio
Dietmar Bartsch	333	0.041 mio
Tino Chrupalla	62	0.054 mio
Armin Laschet	137	3.187 mio
Christian Lindner	192	0.308 mio
Olaf Scholz	256	0.966 mio
Alice Weidel	80	0.159 mio
Janine Wissler	257	0.059 mio
Sum	1,424	6.072 mio

Tweets were collected from July 1, 2021 until election day on September 26, 2021. Overall, 18,094,931 tweets and retweets were harvested (i.e., 8,093,480 tweets excluding retweets). For the stance detection and the training of the neural language models, the first period until July 26 was considered the initiation period, and the subsequent nine weeks until election day served to illustrate nine evaluation periods (see Sect. 5 for details). The initiation period was much longer than the single evaluation periods. Data collected from this time interval was used to train the first initial stance detection model. Its ability to generalize was then tested on future data from the evaluation periods week by week, and subsequently adjusted using new incoming data aimed to adapt to the issue shift of political discussion on Twitter.

From August 11, the findings of the real-time analysis were published on a WebApp. For this purpose, all tweets were categorized according to three units of analysis or authorship: the German election Twittersphere (i.e., all German language tweets commenting on the election campaign); tweets from the seven main political parties, including federal and state-level party accounts (approximately 17 per party); and tweets from the accounts of the seven parties' leading candidates. AfD and DIE LINKE had two front-runners each who were analyzed jointly. The three groups—Twittersphere, parties and leading candidates—formed the basis of the real-time analysis. The middle column of Table 1 shows the numbers of tweets published by political parties and their leading candidates.

For each tweet from the German election Twittersphere, the stance detection revealed whether it expressed a stance in favor of or against one or more parties or leading candidates (or neither of the two). The right column of Table 1 summarizes the numbers of mentions of these targets in tweets. Additionally, the (policy) issues (e.g., economy, security) discussed in tweets by the German election Twittersphere, the parties, and the candidates were identified. To that end, a dictionary approach with a list of 32 issues and 1,402 related terms was employed. Finally, the hashtags most frequently used by each group as well as their activity levels (i.e., the number of tweets published on a daily level) were tracked.

5 Stance Detection to Predict the Tone in German Election Tweets

Stance detection, elsewhere called viewpoint or support detection [1], is commonly defined as inferring a user's attitude *(favor, against, neither)* toward a predefined entity or topic by using the user's utterances regarding this target. The objective of stance detection is related to that of sentiment analysis, yet while sentiments are uttered using specific sentimental signal words, stances may be expressed in a more nuanced way [42].

Although impressive results have been achieved via stance detection using techniques of unsupervised [9,34] or semi-supervised [14] machine learning, these are not applicable in real-time streaming since they rely on network graphs of user accounts or retweets. Instead, our analysis focused on the content of tweets and trained neural network models in a supervised manner to predict stances toward multiple mentioned targets. Here, neural models based on BERT architecture have exhibited the best performance [10]. Thus, we used a fine-tuned RoBERTa model [30] similar to UNITOR [17]. However, UNITOR only predicts stances toward one predefined target, which is different from our multiple-target approach. The approach by Li and Caragea [28], which uses target pairs to predict two expressed stances, is also not applicable here since the number of entities per tweet could vary. Hence, the final neural network ensemble for the stance detection, which is described in detail in the following sections, was formed by three pretrained and fine-tuned transformer-based models of the same type, based on the pretrained multilingual RoBERTa model [2].

5.1 Training Dataset and Annotation

To train and test datasets, we used three stance classes (*favor, against, neither*) for seven party entities (*CDU, CSU, SPD, Bündnis 90/Die Grünen, AfD, DIE

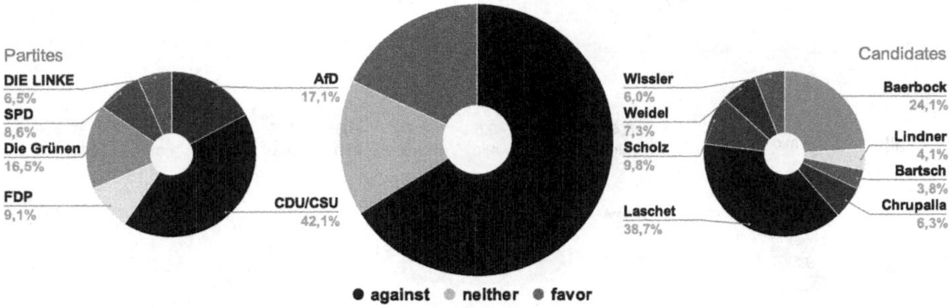

Fig. 2. Distribution of stance classes and target entities in the training dataset. Die Grünen refers to Bündnis 90/Die Grünen.

LINKE, FDP) and eight leading candidate entities (*Laschet, Baerbock, Scholz, Lindner, Chrupalla, Weidel, Wissler, Bartsch*). However, a single tweet could be mapped to multiple entity-stance pairs (e.g., *against-Laschet* and *favor-SPD*). The position of referred entities in the text of the tweet was not explicitly annotated because this was subsequently undertaken by the Named Entity Recognition procedure (see Sect. 5.2). A tweet could also be assigned to a party entity even if there was no literal mention of its name in the text due to specific hashtags (e.g., *#rotrotgrün → DIE LINKE, SPD, Bündnis 90/Die Grünen*), keywords (e.g., *Sozialdemokraten → SPD*), individual names (e.g., *Jens Spahn → CDU*) or user mentions associated with a party, for example.

The datasets were annotated by three coders. Inter-rater reliability was measured based on a random sample of 450 tweets. The coders annotated 75% of tweets identically across all 45 classes, which indicates a high level of agreement. From this set, the coders discussed all tweets annotated differently by at least one of the coders until unanimity was reached. Thereafter, each of the coders individually annotated their share of the training and testing datasets.

The final annotated training dataset had highly unbalanced distributions regarding stances and target entities, as shown in Fig. 2. The same applies to tweets labeled for testing purposes during the evaluation periods. Empirical observations during the election campaign reflected this imbalance: tweets disproportionately included stances against rather than in favor of parties or candidates. Moreover, central figures such as Annalena Baerbock, then leading candidate of Bündnis 90/Die Grünen and current foreign minister, and Armin Laschet, leading candidate of CDU/CSU, received comparatively more attention than other political actors. The same also applies to the populist extreme-right AfD. It is worth highlighting that tweets mentioning more than one target entity or even expressing different stances are counted multiple times in the presented statistics. For instance, approximately 13% of tweets in the training dataset expressed stances on different entities using distinct polarities (i.e., one actor was mentioned positively and another negatively in a single tweet).

To augment the training dataset and improve the prediction models, we tried two techniques: pseudo-labeling and chain-translation. Pseudo-labeling labels

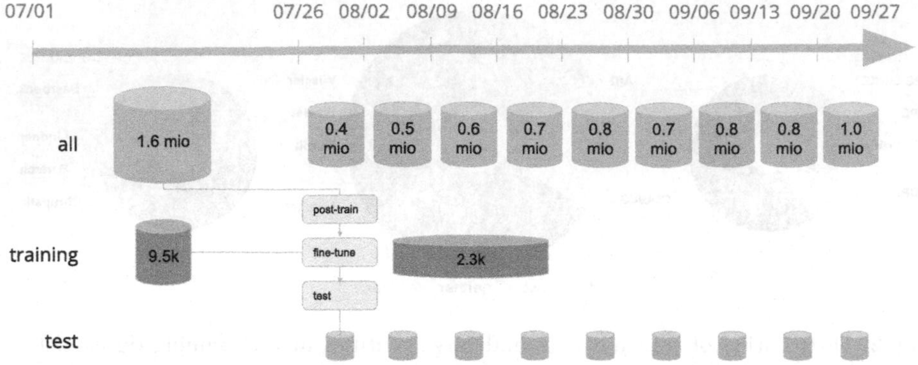

Fig. 3. Iterative training and evaluation procedure for stance detection models. Containers at the top represent all collected unique tweets without retweets in the corresponding period, which were used for the unsupervised post-training of models. Containers in the middle represent labeled training datasets for the supervised fine-tuning of models and were uniformly sampled from collected unique tweets of a corresponding period. Containers at the bottom are uniformly sampled unique tweets that were annotated in every evaluation period and used for model testing.

new data with the same model to gather more automatically annotated data. For this purpose, models trained on non-augmented datasets were used first.

Unfortunately, no improvement could be achieved using these models. Additionally, we used existing pretrained models previously developed for sentiment analyses with a confidence threshold of 0.98 to acquire reliably classified sentimental tweets only. Using this method, we found very few tweets and the overwhelming majority of them had a negative sentiment attached to them. Due to an already existing imbalance in the training datasets toward negative stances, there was no added value in augmenting those datasets with more negative items. For the approach of chain-translation, we employed the neural translation library *Argos Translate*[12]. In two to three steps, tweets were translated into another language (e.g., Spanish, Arabic or Russian), and then back to German. This technique worsened the performance of models because translation distorted the meaning of political language rather than augmenting it by new variants of text.

As indicated in Fig. 3, models for supervised stance detection were trained using two parts of the dataset (containers in the middle). The first trainings were executed every week after the initiation period ended on July 26, 2021 and were based on 9,500 tweets that were published between July 1 and 25, 2021. Following the end of the fourth evaluation period on August 22, 2021, subsequent rounds of training were conducted on an extended dataset, which included 2,300 additional tweets published between August 2 and 18, 2021. All models were tested on the evaluation set of approximately 150 to 200 tweets from the subsequent evaluation period (containers at the bottom). However,

[12] https://pypi.org/project/argostranslate/.

before post-training, fine-tuning and prediction, the tweets underwent various preprocessing steps briefly described below.

5.2 General Preprocessing, Chunking, Named Entity Recognition and Target Assignment

Several steps of preprocessing were needed before the text of a tweet could be used to train the neural network and ultimately predict the stances within these tweets:

- Remove retweet prefixes, URLs and email addresses, dates and numbers.
- Remove any type of quotation marks and special characters (e.g., slash, asterisk).
- Replace ampersand *&* with the German word *und*.
- Transform capitalized words to lowercase by considering their part of speech (PoS), since German nouns start with a capital letter (e.g., *NICHTS* to *nichts* or *BUNDESTAG* to *Bundestag*).
- Transform abbreviations to their full length (e.g., *d.h.* to *das heißt*).
- Transform emojis into two forms only: positive and negative. Here the *emosent*[13] library is used to obtain sentiment value for each emoji. Positive emojis are translated to *thumbs up* and negative to *thumbs down* and neutral emojis are omitted.
- Remove duplicate words or multiple emojis in a row.
- Remove user mentions at the beginning of tweets if there is more than one. This applies to tweets that are replies to multiple Twitter accounts. In this case, the target of utterance is not clearly determinable unless it occurs elsewhere in the tweet text. Hence, such user mentions are counted as neutral target entity mentions.
- Remove all other user mentions after Named Entity Recognition finishes.
- Split hashtags utilizing camel case patterns and names of parties and leading candidates.

In addition to these more general tasks, the tweets were also split into chunks before they were passed to the model for training and prediction. This is because the models are trained to recognize the stance toward a target entity by considering a certain part of the tweet text that includes this entity. However, the model is unable to distinguish between different stances toward multiple target entities in the same part of the text. Hence, the tweet texts were separated into chunks that consisted of concatenated clauses (parts of sentences) that contained a target entity.

For this purpose, a tweet's text was divided into clauses using a pretrained neural parser called *benepar*[14]. Mentions of parties and candidates were then identified in each clause and assigned to corresponding target entities. Finally, adjacent clauses with references to the same target were concatenated into

[13] https://github.com/FLAIST/emosent-py.

[14] https://github.com/nikitakit/self-attentive-parser.

chunks. Clauses without any assignment were used as contextual information preceding or following those with associated targets. Some of the chunks therefore contain overlapping clauses.

Consider the following example of a tweet with five clauses and four target entity references:

> [1] **@c_lindner** is insane. [2] At a time when people are often reluctant to vote for **Scholz** or **Laschet**, [3] and are still crossed with government parties after the flood, [4] **FDP** candidate for chancellor could come in between 20–30%. [5] Where is the courage that is invoked at every party conference.[15]

Here, the tweet was split into three chunks; the third clause is associated with the first and second chunks. As is shown, the candidates *Scholz* and *Laschet* cannot be further separated and are both included in the second chunk.[16]

1. [1] **@c_lindner** is insane.
2. [2] At a time when people are often reluctant to vote for **Scholz** or **Laschet**,
   [3] *and are still crossed with government parties after the flood,*
3. [3] *and are still crossed with government parties after the flood,*
   [4] **FDP** candidate for chancellor could come in between 20–30%.
   [5] Where is the courage that is invoked at every party conference.

To determine the stance targets (party, candidate), lists of specific hashtags, keywords, handles of Twitter users, and full names of political actors associated with the targets were manually compiled. These lists contained 2,000 hashtags, 500 keywords, 104 Twitter handles of party accounts, the names and Twitter handles of 1,500 MPs and those of 350 key actors associated with parties (i.e., prominent and well-known political personalities). The lists were maintained and, when necessary, updated during the election campaign. The recognition of the above mentioned entities (e.g., hashtags) and assignment to target entities performed with a macro F1-score of 0.91 over 15 targets.

5.3 Post-training and Fine-Tuning of Stance Detection Models

To further enrich the knowledge of the models for stance detection, information about sentiments was integrated [17] by reusing models pretrained for sentiment detection: the German-Sentiment-BERT [19] and the multilingual Twitter-XLM-RoBERTa-Sentiment [2].

Drawing on Xu et al. [47], the pretrained sentiment models were further post-trained using the Masked Language Model objective on the data collected from

[15] Original German tweet text: @c_lindner hat was an der Waffel. In einer Zeit wo Leute oft nur widerwillig Scholz oder Laschet wählen, und nach der Flut noch sauer auf Regierungsparteien, könnte FDP Kanzlerkandidat oder Kandidatin zw. 20–30% kommen. Wo ist der Mut der bei jedem Parteitag beschworen wird.

[16] Although there are many similar examples, according to our training dataset, the polarity assigned to these targets only differs in 1.7% of the cases.

the same period of time as the first training dataset (July 1 to 25, 2021). For this purpose, the base layers (including embeddings, encoder and pooler) of both pretrained sentiment models were reused, but the final three-class classification layers were replaced by the Masked Language Model prediction layers with randomly initialized model weights. For the implementation, we used the HuggingFace library [46]. The post-training was conducted on preprocessed (chunking not included) full tweets' texts for three epochs (rounds) with a batch size of 64 tweets and maximal sequence length of 100 using Adam optimizer with a learning rate of 10^{-5}. For both pretrained models, we followed the training procedure of RoBERTa [30], in which 15% of input tokens (word parts) were randomly selected in each tweet and each epoch for the masking procedure.

Following the original BERT paper [10], the post-trained models were then fine-tuned and cross-validated over 10 randomly sampled folds, which were balanced in terms of the three stance classes. The validation folds consisted of 10% of the sampled folds. As architecture for the fine-tuned models we reused the architectures of the German-Sentiment-BERT and Twitter-XLM-RoBERTa-Sentiment without any change. Their base layers were reused from the corresponding post-trained models, but the final layers were replaced by new three-class classification layers with randomly initialized model weights. The fine-tuning was conducted on tweet chunks for eight epochs with a batch size of 16 tweet chunks using the same maximal sequence length and optimizer settings as above. After seven to nine epochs, trained models began to overfit; thus, a mean number of epochs was selected for all models trained on different random folds to compare them fairly in cross-validation.

After the initial training, we repeated the procedure on a weekly basis during nine subsequent evaluation periods, as presented in Fig. 3. Thereby, the post-trained model from the previous evaluation period was reused and further post-trained on recently collected data from the current week. It was then fine-tuned with the training dataset and eventually tested with data from the following week. In the fourth evaluation period (the week after August 16, 2021), the training dataset was extended by additional items to improve the model's performance. This extended dataset was used in all subsequent periods.

5.4 Results: Ups and Downs in Stance Detection Performance

The models were evaluated using the mean macro F1-score over 10 runs on sampled folds. Figure 4 compares this score across different models based only on the superior Twitter-XLM-RoBERTa-Sentiment model. We omitted the complete results of the German-Sentiment-BERT for better readability of the figure since it performed worse in general. For instance, the best BERT-based model scored 0.05 points of macro F1 below the best RoBERTa-based model for the initiation period. The initiation period (init) on the left-hand side of the figure represents the average performance over 10 validation folds. The testing datasets from the evaluation periods are represented on the x-axis and indicated with the date of the first tweet they contain (i.e., 07/26, 08/02). The performances of the models tested on all datasets are illustrated by the lines in Fig. 4.

Fig. 4. Mean macro F1-score of trained stance model for the initiation (referenced as *init*) and nine evaluation periods week-by-week: (1) bottom line: untuned Twitter-XLM-RoBERTa-Sentiment model; (2) middle line: RoBERTa sentiment model fine-tuned on the stance detection task using the initial training set; (3) top line: RoBERTa sentiment model post-trained on large tweet corpora from the initiation period and subsequently fine-tuned; and (4) dots: RoBERTa models iteratively post-trained on data from the preceding week, fine-tuned and predicted only on data from the following week.

The untuned off-the-shelf sentiment model (bottom line) performed worst but still better than random allocation by chance. The model that was fine-tuned on the stance dataset from the initiation period (middle line) improved throughout the process except on the datasets from 08/02 and 08/16. On average and for all testing datasets (initiation period excluded), the model increased in performance by 9%. The model that performed best (top line) was post-trained by applying the masked language objective to data from the initiation period. The mean F1-score improved by 7.5% with an F1-score of approximately 61.5% on average. Adaption of the model by post-training to a specific language, which is used in politically motivated tweets, also seems to have helped in the evaluation periods 08/02 and 08/16. The performances of these models were tested on all datasets.

In contrast, subsequent models that were iteratively post-trained on data from the preceding week were tested on the testing set from the following week only. An exception was made for the model from the last evaluation period, which was tested on data from the same week. These models are depicted as differently shaped points in Fig. 4. Models tested on data prior to 08/23 still used the initial training set only, while the subsequent models used an extended training set. Their performance is compared to the initially post-trained model (top line). Although all subsequently post-trained models improved slightly on their validation sets, there is no consistency in terms of prediction performance for future data. There is an increase in performance for 08/02, 08/09 and 08/23; a decrease for 08/16, 08/30, 09/06 and 09/20; and no change for 09/13.

When taking the mean value over all evaluation periods, we found no significant difference from the initially post-trained model. However, when considering the performance of these models on data from the preceding week (i.e., the data they were post-trained on), we measured a slight improvement of approximately

1.3% on average. A similar effect is evidenced for the period 09/20 in Fig. 4, where two F1-scores are presented and the model post-trained on more recent data performs better. This effect can be beneficial for retweets, where the original text comes from the past and is only retweeted in the future so that the model has knowledge about the same text due to its post-training. Furthermore, there is an interesting finding for the period 08/23, during which additional data were added to the training set. At least for this future prediction, an increase of performance by 4% is visible, but it drops below the top line in the next period.

One can therefore conclude that fine-tuning alone does not feed sufficient knowledge to the model to improve it for all time periods. Initial post-training of the model is highly beneficial and allows the model to adapt to political language in tweets. Furthermore, iterative post-training led to ambivalent results, considering its ability to generalize to further data while still slightly improving on past data. Finally, one can speculate that iteratively adding new training data from recent periods of time can improve models in the short term. We hypothesize that the decrease in performance is caused by newly arising issues addressed in novel tweets, which may be countered by integrating more recently labeled data.

For production usage in the pipeline, the three models that performed best on the validation dataset and on all testing sets from the preceding evaluation period were selected for each period. These models were combined by means of the majority voting principle to form an ensemble. This strategy produced the best results (i.e., 2% better than a single model selected by the best validation accuracy only).

6 Salient Topics: Issue Analysis and Issue Shifts

A dictionary approach was applied to analyze the salient issues discussed by the election Twittersphere, parties and candidates in real time. A dictionary contains a list of words that correspond to different categories. For the issue analysis, a custom dictionary was created that includes 1,402 terms and expressions, which were assigned to 32 policy issues and non-policy valence issues. The terms and topics were gathered as part of an in-depth press review and monitoring of the public debate on Twitter from July 1 until September 26, 2021. New expressions and topics were added when necessary (e.g., to match current events like the flood disaster in Germany or to extend the vocabulary to include international crises, such as the evacuation mission in Afghanistan).

Based on a fully automated pipeline, each tweet was analyzed as to whether it contained any terms included in our dictionary, and if so, which ones. A single tweet could match more than one issue; for example, a tweet commenting on Covid-19 testing regulations in schools was assigned to both education and health.

A fully automated topic modeling for short texts using SeaNMF [39] was also undertaken. However, the results were less clear and required significant human interpretation. Moreover, most of the topics generated by the topic modeling

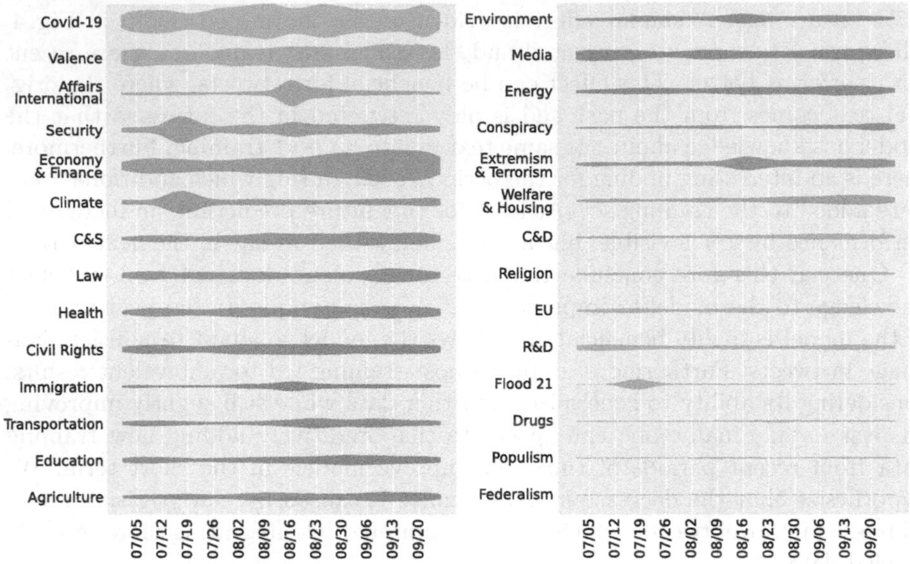

Fig. 5. Distribution of issues discussed by the Twittersphere during the 2021 German federal election

focused on events and personalities, which reflects the specific events-centered and strongly personalized character of Twitter communication. Hence, the topics and terms discovered by the model were mostly already included in the issue dictionary. Therefore, solely the dictionary approach was continued to map (policy) issues.

Over time, there was a shift in the issues the German election Twittersphere, parties, and leading candidates addressed. This empirical observation offers an intuitive explanation for the decrease in F1-scores (see Fig. 4) of the post-trained and fine-tuned models (top line in Fig. 4), particularly for two periods of the evaluation phase. The first, sharper decrease on August 2, 2021 (testing data from August 2 to 8, 2021) can be explained by the following shift in issue focus:

From July 14, 2021, the election campaign shifted its attention to the flood disaster in the German region of Ahrtal and discussions on Twitter accompanied this catastrophe (especially the issues *Flood 21*, *Security*[17] and *Climate*). However, this debate was relatively short lived and decreased substantially at the end of July 2021, which Fig. 5 reflects. The initial training dataset contained numerous tweets commenting on the flood and related themes while the latter also dominated the election campaign and parties' communication strategies at the time. Consequently, when the issue focus on Twitter changed, this also effected the F1-score of our model trained on that dataset.

The same observation holds true for the second decrease in the post-trained and fine-tuned model's F1-score. On August 16, the German defense forces (Bun-

[17] Disaster Control (Katastrophenschutz) is substantial during catastrophic events.

deswehr) began evacuating Germans and local employees working for the German forces in Afghanistan. The evacuation mission massively increased Twitter communication regarding international affairs; extremism & terrorism, and to some extent, issues of security and immigration, as illustrated in Fig. 5. Clearly, talk on Twitter was shaped by the events in Afghanistan as well.

7 Classification Errors and Qualitative Monitoring

During the real-time analyses, several challenges were encountered that could have had a potential impact on the real-time presentation of findings on the WebApp. For example, stance detection output could be erroneous if tweets about parties or candidates were classified incorrectly. Accordingly, (policy) issues can only be detected if appropriate strings are stored in the issue dictionary. To analyze all tweets about the 2021 German federal election campaign, filter rules had to be set correctly.

Potentially erroneous real-time analyses are problematic because scientific results have to be valid and reliable; the expectations of those visiting the WebApp, namely to receive reliable information about the tone, topics and hashtags during the election campaign on Twitter, need to be fulfilled. Moreover, nowcasting and publishing such results in real time is unprecedented in the German context. Consequently, the contribution of this research also lies in exploring previously unknown territory, including limitations and errors.

Besides the shift in issue focus, the trained models suffered from a few well known problems from a linguistic perspective, such as misunderstanding of irony and sarcasm [16]. For instance, emojis used in a sarcastic manner may be misleading. Furthermore, tweets including rhetorical questions could be classified incorrectly because stances are not expressed explicitly. For example,

> "We have to build more social housing. I am doing this in NRW[18]." says #Laschet in the #Triell[19]. **Is that so?**[20]

The first part of the tweet (""We have to build more social housing. I am doing this in NRW." says #Laschet in the #Triell.") has to be classified as *neither* because it is neither in favor of nor against an entity (topic or politician). The second part of the tweet ("Is this so?") is a critical rhetorical question and turns the classification into *against*. However, the neural network incorrectly predicted the latter as *neither*.

In general, we found that language used in political discussions is more nuanced than emotional terms used in sentiment analysis. The latter usually

[18] NRW is the German federal state of North Rhine-Westphalia, where Armin Laschet was governor at the time.

[19] Triell was the TV debate between the leading candidates of CDU/CSU, SPD and Bündnis 90/Die Grünen.

[20] Original German tweet text: "Wir müssen mehr Sozialwohnungen bauen. Ich mache das in NRW." sagt #Laschet im #Triell. Ist das so?

have a strong negative or positive polarity that can be misleading for rather subtle political stances. This was one of the main challenges for our models. The same holds true for double negation. More generally, comparisons between any kind of objects (persons, issues, etc.) and contrasting descriptions seem to be difficult for the neural network to detect. Typical examples include the following:

> **No means is too dirty** for the bloc party and the bought media to **discredit** the AfD.[21]

> The outrage spectacle with a **dangerous** mixture of facts and untruths reveals **fears** of losing power, as the Greens have a plan to combine climate protection and prosperity. #Kretschmann #btw21 #dBDK21[22]

The former should be predicted as *favor* for the AfD, but was classified as *against* for the AfD. The same is true for the second example regarding Bündnis 90/Die Grünen: the tweet was classified as *against* although it should have been *favor*.

Since our results are visible in real time on a publicly accessible WebApp, presenting valid data is key, especially due to the political actuality of the work. To improve data validity and increase certainty, the plausibility of the findings was continuously monitored and checked qualitatively.

The qualitative review included the following routines:

- Manual checking of the results on the WebApp starting every morning at 6:00 AM, then hourly until 6:00 PM.
- The stance graph was checked for plausibility and positive or negative outliers.
- Cross-checking of each leading candidate's number of tweets in our database and on the candidates' Twitter account.
- Verification and, if necessary, correction of the automated stance prediction of the 100 most retweeted tweets for each entity (parties and candidates), every morning at 7:00 AM and for the last 24 h.

In cases that outliers in terms of positive or negative stances on parties or candidates were displayed on the WebApp, such findings were validated in both a qualitative and quantitative manner. For example, the contextual situation (e.g., larger press interviews, party congresses or a party's or candidate's position on an event) was first qualitatively investigated to check whether this could explain peaks in our stance detection. Second, the automated stance classification of tweets in our database was reviewed. For the respective time period and stance target, an output of the stance results (descending by the number

[21] Original German tweet text: Der Blockpartei und den gekauften Medien ist kein Mittel zu dreckig um die AfD in Misskredit zu bringen.

[22] Original German tweet text: Das Empörungsspektakel mit einem gefährlichen Gemisch aus Fakten und Unwahrheiten zeigt die Angst vor Machtverlust, da die Grünen einen Plan haben, wie sich Klimaschutz und Wohlstand verbinden lassen. #Kretschmann #btw21 #dBDK21.

of retweets) was extracted; reviewed for mistakes; and if necessary, manually corrected. Corrected results were then swiftly made visible on the WebApp.

The importance of the qualitative review is highlighted by two examples. First, it was observed that the number of tweets in favor of the AfD usually increased between 4:00 AM and 6:00 AM. After checking the database, it became apparent that AfD supporters engaged in so-called retweeting campaigns around 4:00 AM. Second, stances on the CSU suddenly improved on August 15, 2021 due to misleading filter rules (or Name Entity Recognition list). The filters that enabled the collection of tweets included all federal ministers. Gerd Müller (CSU) was the former Federal Minister for Economic Cooperation and Development. However, Gerd Müller is also the name of a famous German soccer player who died on August 15. This sudden bereavement was unforeseen and the ambiguity of the name had not been considered for the filter criteria. To avoid further outliers, we excluded the name from the analysis after mid-August. Besides these daily routines, events such as TV debates, election rallies and the election day itself were regularly monitored.

8 Conclusion

Based on the case study of the 2021 German federal election campaign, this paper examines how political debates on Twitter can be analyzed under real-time conditions. The analysis employed a stance detection based on different fine-tuned neural models. Salient (policy) issues discussed on Twitter during the election campaign were also monitored and their evolution linked to the performance of the stance detection models.

We faced challenges when employing our stance detection such as a decrease in performance due to shifts in issue focus and challenges attributed to political language (e.g., misleading signal words due to sarcasm and irony and a more subtle tone compared to sentimental wordings).

Future endeavors in the field of electoral nowcast should invest in methods to ease the effects of issue shifts for stance detection by retraining models on additional data, as suggested by Bechini et al. [3]. Such data should consist of consecutive training sets that correspond to newly emerging events. This allows for consideration and inclusion of changes in salient topics discussed on Twitter. Alternatively, topic modeling can be integrated into an unsupervised iterative pretraining of models. Moreover, one could pretrain a RoBERTa model on the Next Sentence Prediction (NSP) task using keywords extracted by a topic model as input. This approach may enrich the representation of tweets. Additionally, more attention could be given to the stance target. For instance, a BERT-based architecture suggested by Gao et al. for target-dependent sentiment analysis [15] focuses more strongly on the target entity for prediction instead of considering the whole tweet text uniformly. Finally, integration of more syntax information may improve the identification of related signal words to avoid unrelated and favor-related words as well as their connection to target entities. Dai et al. [8] already suggested this for aspect-based sentiment analysis. Each of these approaches represents valuable and promising tools for future research in the field, which we hope this paper helps to pave the way for.

Acknowledgements. This research is funded by dtec.bw—Digitalization and Technology Research Center of the Bundeswehr [project SPARTA]. We would like to thank all team members of SPARTA, in particular, the core team that worked so hard to make our real-time monitoring during the 2021 German election campaign possible: Andreas Neumeier, Benedikt Radtke, Martin Riedl and Johannes Steup.

References

1. Aldayel, A.: Stance detection on social media: state of the art and trends (2021). https://doi.org/10.1016/j.ipm.2021.102597
2. Barbieri, F., Anke, L.E., Camacho-Collados, J.: XLM-T: a multilingual language model toolkit for Twitter (2021). https://arxiv.org/abs/2104.12250v1
3. Bechini, A., Bondielli, A., Ducange, P., Marcelloni, F., Renda, A.: Addressing event-driven concept drift in twitter stream: a stance detection application. IEEE Access **9**, 77758–77770 (2021)
4. Beck, P.A.: The electoral cycle and patterns of American politics. Br. J. Polit. Sci. **9**(02), 129 (1979). https://doi.org/10.1017/S0007123400001691
5. Bundeswahlleiter: Heft 4 Wahlbeteiligung und Stimmabgabe nach Geschlecht und Altersgruppen. Wahl zum 20. Deutschen Bundestag am 26, 4 Sept 2021 (2022)
6. Ceron, A., Curini, L., Drews, W.: Short-term issue emphasis on twitter during the 2017 German election: a comparison of the economic left-right and socio-cultural dimensions. German Polit. 1–20 (2020). https://doi.org/10.1080/09644008.2020.1836161
7. Ceron, A., Curini, L., Iacus, S.M.: Politics and Big Data. Nowcasting and Forecasting Elections with Social Media. Routledge (2017)
8. Dai, J., Yan, H., Sun, T., Liu, P., Qiu, X.: Does syntax matter? A strong baseline for aspect-based sentiment analysis with RoBERTa (2021)
9. Darwish, K., Stefanov, P., Aupetit, M., Nakov, P.: Unsupervised user stance detection on Twitter. In: Proceedings of the International AAAI Conference on Web and Social Media, vol. 14, pp. 141–152 (2020)
10. Devlin, J., Chang, M.W., Lee, K., Toutanova, K.: BERT: pre-training of deep bidirectional transformers for language understanding (2019)
11. Dong, X., Lian, Y.: A review of social media-based public opinion analyses: challenges and recommendations. Technol. Soc. **67**, 101724 (2021)
12. Downs, A.: An Economic Theory of Democracy. Harper and Row, New York (1957)
13. Duggan, M., Ellison, N., Lampe, C., Lenhart, A., Madden, M.: Demographics of key social networking platforms. Pew Research Center (2015). http://www.pewinternet.org/2015/01/09/demographics-of-key-social-networking-platforms-2/
14. Fraisier, O., Cabanac, G., Pitarch, Y., Besançon, R., Boughanem, M.: Stance classification through proximity-based community detection **18** (2018). https://doi.org/10.1145/3209542.3209549
15. Gao, Z., Feng, A., Song, X., Wu, X.: Target-dependent sentiment classification with BERT. IEEE Access **7**, 154290–154299 (2019)
16. Ghosh, S., Singhania, P., Singh, S., Rudra, K., Ghosh, S.: Stance detection in web and social media: a comparative study (2020). https://github.com/prajwal1210/Stance-Detection-in-Web-and-Social-Media

17. Giorgioni, S., Politi, M., Salman, S., Croce, D., Basili, R.: UNITOR @ sardistance 2020: combining transformer-based architectures and transfer learning for robust stance detection (2020)
18. Göhring, A., Klenner, M., Conrad, S.: DeInStance: creating and evaluating a German corpus for fine-grained inferred stance detection (2021). https://huggingface.co/dbmdz/bert-base-german-cased
19. Guhr, O., Schumann, A.K., Bahrmann, F., Böhme, H.J.: Training a broad-coverage German sentiment classification model for dialog systems, pp. 11–16 (2020)
20. Gupta, Y., Kumar, P.: Real-time sentiment analysis of tweets: a case study of punjab elections. In: Proceedings of 2019 3rd IEEE International Conference on Electrical, Computer and Communication Technologies, ICECCT 2019 (2019). https://doi.org/10.1109/ICECCT.2019.8869203
21. Hamdi, A., et al.: A multilingual dataset for named entity recognition, entity linking and stance detection in historical newspapers (2021). https://doi.org/10.1145/3404835.3463255
22. Hardalov, M., Arora, A., Nakov, P., Augenstein, I.: Cross-domain label-adaptive stance detection (2021)
23. Hitesh, M.S., Vaibhav, V., Kalki, Y.J., Kamtam, S.H., Kumari, S.: Real-time sentiment analysis of 2019 election tweets using word2vec and random forest model. In: 2019 2nd International Conference on Intelligent Communication and Computational Techniques, ICCT 2019, pp. 146–151 (2019). https://doi.org/10.1109/ICCT46177.2019.8969049
24. Jungherr, A., Schoen, H., Jürgens, P.: The mediation of politics through Twitter: an analysis of messages posted during the campaign for the German federal election 2013. J. Comput. Mediated Commun. **21**(1), 50–68 (2016). https://doi.org/10.1111/JCC4.12143
25. Kagan, V., Stevens, A., Subrahmanian, V.S.: Using Twitter sentiment to forecast the 2013 Pakistani election and the 2014 Indian election. IEEE Intell. Syst. **30**(1), 2–5 (2015). https://doi.org/10.1109/MIS.2015.16
26. Klüver, H., Spoon, J.J.: Who responds? voters, parties and issue attention. Br. J. Polit. Sci. **46**(3), 633–654 (2016)
27. Lehmbruch, G.: Parteienwettbewerb im Bundesstaat: Regelsysteme und Spannungslagen im Politischen System der Bundesrepublik Deutschland. VS Verlag für Sozialwissenschaften, Wiesbaden (2000)
28. Li, Y., Caragea, C.: A multi-task learning framework for multi-target stance detection, pp. 2320–2326 (2021)
29. Lijphart, A.: Patterns of Democracy. Government Forms and Performance in Thirty-Six Countries, Yale University Press, New Haven (2012)
30. Liu, Y., et al.: RoBERTa: a robustly optimized BERT pretraining approach (2019)
31. Mainwaring, S., Gervasoni, C., España-Najera, A.: Extra- and within-system electoral volatility. Party Polit. **23**(6), 623–635 (2017)
32. Meier, F., Bazo, A., Elsweiler, D., Bazo, A.: Using social media data to analyse issue engagement during the 2017 German federal election (2021)
33. Pennebaker, J.W., Booth, R.J., Francis, M.E.: Linguistic inquiry and word count: Liwc [computer software], p. 135. liwc. net, Austin, TX (2007)
34. Rashed, A., Kutlu, M., Darwish, K., Elsayed, T., Bayrak, C.: Embeddings-based clustering for target specific stances: the case of a polarized Turkey (2020)
35. Reuver, M., Verberne, S., Morante, R., Fokkens, A.: Is stance detection topic-independent and cross-topic generalizable? - A reproduction study (2021). https://webis.de/events/sameside-19/

36. Roemmele, A., Gibson, R.: Scientific and subversive: the two faces of the fourth era of political campaigning. New Media Soc. **22**(4), 595–610 (2020)
37. Samih, Y., Darwish, K.: A few topical tweets are enough for effective user stance detection, pp. 2637–2646 (2021)
38. Scharpf, F.W., Reissert, B., Schnabel, F.: Politikverflechtung: Theorie und Empirie des kooperativen Föderalismus in der Bundesrepublik. Monographien Ergebnisse der Sozialwissenschaften 1. Scriptor-Verl., Kronberg (1976)
39. Shi, T., Tech, V., Kang, K., Choo, J., Reddy, C.K.: Short-text topic modeling via non-negative matrix factorization enriched with local word-context correlations, p. 10 (2018). https://doi.org/10.1145/3178876.3186009
40. Soler, J.M., Cuartero, F., Roblizo, M.: Twitter as a tool for predicting elections results (2012). https://doi.org/10.1109/ASONAM.2012.206
41. Stier, S., Bleier, A., Lietz, H., Strohmaier, M.: Election campaigning on social media: politicians, audiences, and the mediation of political communication on Facebook and Twitter. Polit. Commun. **35**(1), 50–74 (2018)
42. Sun, Q., Wang, Z., Li, S., Zhu, Q., Zhou, G.: Stance detection via sentiment information and neural network model. Front. Comput. Sci. **13**(1), 127–138 (2019). https://doi.org/10.1007/s11704-018-7150-9
43. Tumasjan, A., Sprenger, T.O., Sandner, P.G., Welpe, I.M.: Predicting elections with twitter: what 140 characters reveal about political sentiment. In: Proceedings of the International AAAI Conference on Web and Social Media, vol. 4, no. 1, pp. 178–185 (2010)
44. Vamvas, J., Sennrich, R.: X-Stance: a multilingual multi-target dataset for stance detection (2020). https://doi.org/10.5281/zenodo.3831317
45. Wang, H., Can, D., Kazemzadeh, A., Bar, F., Narayanan, S.: A system for real-time Twitter sentiment analysis of 2012 U.S. presidential election cycle, pp. 8–14 (2012). http://t.co/qEns1Pmi
46. Wolf, T., et al.: Transformers: state-of-the-art natural language processing (2019). https://github.com/huggingface/
47. Xu, H., Liu, B., Shu, L., Yu, P.S.: BERT post-training for review reading comprehension and aspect-based sentiment analysis (2019)

Assessing the Suitability of Social Media Data for Identifying Crisis Events in Smart Cities: An Exploratory Study on Flood Situations

Magaywer Moreira de Paiva(✉), José Viterbo(✉), and Flávia Bernardini(✉)

Institute of Computing, Fluminense Federal University, Niterói-Rj, Brazil
magaywermp@id.uff.br, {viterbo,fcbernardini}@ic.uff.br

Abstract. Social media have been used to extract different types of information. The objective of this exploratory research was to investigate the characteristics necessary to identify crisis events with social media, analyzing the aptitude of messages produced in three crisis events that hit cities in the southeastern region of Brazil. In total, 3,042 Twitter posts were analyzed based on three essential dimensions for event identification: semantic, temporal and geographic information. The results show that users actually write messages about urban floods in Brazilian cities. However, it is possible to observe differences in volume, agility and location properties posted in areas with different numbers of populations. In addition, most posts lack information. Naturally, this limits the automatic use of these messages. Before applying some automatic detection technique, managers can investigate the data that circulates in a certain region and employ strategies to improve the use of this data.

Keywords: Open government data · Crowdsourcing · Participatory sensing · Decision making · Emergency situation

1 Introduction

Social media has been widely used to see what users are talking about. These data can be applied both in processes of prediction of elections [6] and to extract demands from the population [13]. Social media can also be used to detect the occurrence of events in the real world [5] and obtain the location of these events [2]. Knowing the location of an event can be especially important for events that create risk situations or temporary inconvenience to people. In this work, we call these events a crisis event. Some examples are flood, hurricane, fire, earthquake, typhoon, traffic accident and civil disturbance [11].

In Smart Cities, social media data generated during crisis events has been exploited to support local government decision making [20]. In this scenario, users are potential data transmission agents at the event location [16]. Through

M. Janssen et al. (Eds.): EGOV 2022, LNCS 13391, pp. 147–162, 2022.
https://doi.org/10.1007/978-3-031-15086-9_10

the collaborative process, Crowdsourcing, this data can be used to identify current problems [14], assess damages [12] or extract the "Wisdom of the Crowd" [21]. During the most severe events, access to information can mean the difference between life and death for people in risky places [4]. In this way, social media have the potential to turn it possible to create an immense network of users warning about crisis events.

The need to quickly and automatically identify recurring crisis events in a city can motivate the development of computer systems that use social media data. Currently, the investment in Machine Learning algorithms for event detection is notorious according to Kruspe et al. [11]. The identification of events is necessarily linked to the time interval [3] and a location [2] in which the event occurred. However, these systems can be complex and involve challenges related to semantic, temporal and geographic information [1,19]. Essentially, these systems rely on user participation with a non-negligible amount of publications about the event, provided during the event and with location data. Therefore, before starting to develop a system, it is interesting to verify if the available data are adequate: if the data set has the necessary dimensions to identify a crisis event. We consider three questions to evaluate a dataset: (1) Does the information allow us to reliably detect a crisis event? (2) is the information transmitted in a timely manner? and (3) does the information make it possible to know where the crisis event is in progress?

This work aims to carry out an exploratory analysis on data produced in social media to verify if there is support for the implementation of automatic event identification systems in the area of interest. For this, we manually analyzed Twitter data shared during 3 urban flooding events that hit the southeastern region of Brazil during spring 2020. We describe the volume, temporal distribution and properties of the location found in Twitter posts within the area of interest and point out possible strategies to take advantage of this data in the context of Smart Cities. In the next section, we present the features of Twitter that allow event identification. Section 3 presents other works that also studied crisis events. In Sect. 4, we show the steps applied to analyze the events. Section 5 describes the results obtained in each event, while Sect. 6 details the discussion related to these results. We end with a conclusion and suggestions for future work in Sect. 7.

2 Using Social Media Interaction in Real Events

Event detection essentially depends on semantic, temporal and geographic information [1,19]. On Twitter, users can register a 280-character text message in their posts. A Twitter post includes a timestamp and may contain other metadata (e.g. geolocation, self-declared user profiles, and message language). The text message and timestamp can be exploited to extract semantic and temporal information about events. The text message can describe a specific event and the timestamp indicates when the post was made. However, the text message can express an event that has already happened, is happening, or could happen. Therefore, the text message may be time-shifted (i.e. not published at the time the event was in progress). In this context, posts about an ongoing event can be filtered considering temporal attributes of the text message [8]. The temporal idea of the message can indicate whether a post is suitable for detecting a crisis event as it happens.

Location is another piece of information that can be used to define whether a post is related to an event. There are two properties of the location that can be considered to define where the event is happening: the source (i.e. where it was extracted from) and the level of granularity (i.e. what area it comprises). On Twitter, a post can express some location in the text message (i.e. location mentioned in user-written text), geolocation field (i.e. location attached in real-time by user) and user profile text (i.e. location filled in when setting up user account) [22]. These localization sources can be exploited in isolation (e.g. only the geolocation [7], only the text message [3]) or combined with each other (e.g. the geolocation and the text message [2,4]). Regarding the level of granularity, the location can be differentiated into exact coordinates (i.e. longitudes and latitudes) and place names (e.g. the name of a neighborhood, a city or a country) [10]. Place names can be broken down into levels that represent how close the location is to becoming an exact coordinate (i.e. the lowest level of granularity). In this context, granularity levels can be defined based on local political-administrative divisions [4] or geographic scales of the map [15]. However, the lack of data to identify the exact location poses a challenge for event identification [1]. There are cases where only the location up to a certain level of granularity is considered (e.g. city [7] and point [3]) and others are discarded.

3 Crisis Event Interaction Analysis

In the literature, several approaches for detecting crisis events in social media data are presented. We can group these approaches into: filtering by characteristics (e.g. keywords or location); crowdsourcing; or, machine learning-based [11]. In addition to event detection, it is possible to extract insights into user interactions on social media during crisis events. Arapostathis [4] analyzes 10 categories of messages related to the flood in Messinia, southern Greece. Among the classification categories were considered: identification of rainfall and consequences of the flood. One of the main findings of this research is to observe that messages about the consequences of the flood can be detected three hours after the first notification of occurrence of the identification of rain and the first reports of human death start from the fourth hour of the event.

Hong et al. [9] study the communication of citizens and local governments during 18 snowstorms in the State of Maryland, USA. Both posts are labeled with topics taken from the posts themselves. This study shows that users use social media to report problems and concerns during snowstorms. This can be used by local governments to adjust the priority of information to be published and pay attention to traffic accidents in certain regions. This study showed that local governments can also take actions to improve disaster relief performance: make their profiles better known on social media; and strategically choosing the information they share to meet citizens' need for specific information.

Villodre and Creator [18] propose a taxonomy of user roles to define which and how users virtually participate during emergency situations. This study examines the relationships between roles, crisis phases and types of actors for a flood event in Sant Llorenç, Mallorca, Spain. The results show the variations of certain roles played in different phases of crisis events and what types of users are predominant. For example, in the crisis response phase, ordinary users play a "retweeter" role, sharing situational information and calls to action. In the post-crisis phase, celebrities play the same role, sharing irrelevant information. This and other contributions can help crisis coordination to direct user behavior during crises.

Previous analyzes focused mainly on perceptions that explain the relationship between content and qualitative aspects. In contrast to these works, we focus on a process to extract quantitative information that seeks to indicate the feasibility of implementing automatic crisis event detection systems. Wang [19] defines time, content, space and network as the important dimensions for disaster identification. These dimensions correspond respectively to the information that can be extracted from Twitter: in the timestamp; in the text message; in the geolocation field and in the text of the user's profile; and, in retweet references. Afyouni et al. [1] corroborates the first three dimensions as the main resources to extract events from social media. Therefore, our work seeks to assess whether the data available during a crisis event allow us to define these three dimensions: dimension of time (D-T), dimension of content (D-C) and dimension of space (D-S). Thus, we are interested in analyzing the characteristics and volume of information shared on Twitter and verifying whether the data is suitable for automatically identifying crisis events.

4 Material and Methods

In this work, we have gathered information related to a crisis event and data from Twitter. A key issue when analyzing social media data is to sample the massive amount of data available. Our aim is to investigate the suitability of social media to identify crisis events. Therefore, we need to assess three dimensions (e. D-A, D-C and D-S) of the data available during actual crisis events. In other words, posts made during the event must have the following characteristics: describe the event (D-C), indicate the idea of an event in progress (D-T), include some location that is within an area of interest (D-S). To do this, we perform four research steps: (a) data collection (i.e. retrieving a set of Twitter posts and information about the crisis event); (b) selection of candidate publications (i.e. using the event time range to create a set of posts); (c) message filtering (i.e. separating posts based on D-C and D-T); and, (d) location recognition (i.e. separating posts based on D-S). In this work, we apply the search steps manually. Figure 1 presents a flowchart of the research steps with the activities numbered 1 to 7.

Data Collect. We mainly use news published on the web to validate the days when events occurred and extract information about them (Act. 1). Validation of the occurrence of events can also be done through government agencies (e.g.

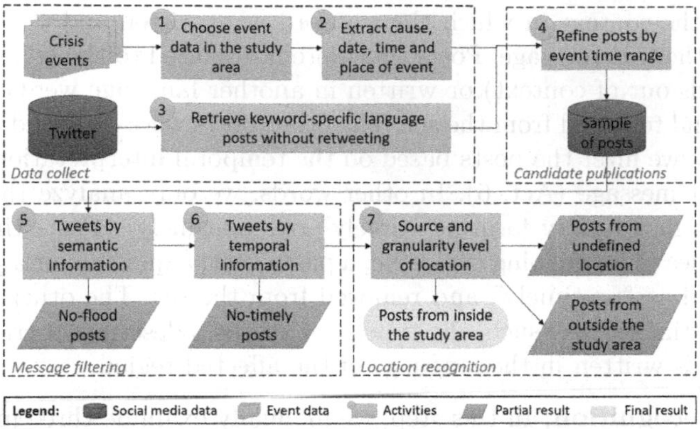

Fig. 1. Flowchart with the research steps

security agencies, monitoring agencies and civil defense) or other communication vehicles (e.g. television and magazine). For each event, we look for the cause, the start date and time, the end date and time, and the place reached (Act. 2). The collection of Twitter posts and news was done in parallel and used keywords about the crisis event that were written in the language of the region where the event took place (Act. 3). The keywords were defined in an exploratory way, observing news about the event and other studies about the event. In addition, we apply two filters available on Twitter. We removed posts that were not identified with the language of the region affected by the event to avoid text messages written in another language or referring to crisis events in other countries. We remove posts generated by retweets to avoid a large mass of data being repeated or shared by users who were not at the event site.

Candidate Publications. We identified the region affected by the event and its estimated duration in the information collected in the previous step. So, we chose some event to cross-reference the event's temporal information with the Twitter posts. At this point, we use the event start and end date and time to select a set of publications made during the event (Act. 4). With this clipping, we separated the publications that may contain information related to problems faced by users during the event. To increase the temporal scope of the publication clipping, we increased the range of hours studied based on the duration of the event. We consider hours before at the beginning of the event and hours after at the end of the event. By studying the event hours earlier at the beginning, it is possible to investigate whether there were already signs of problems and compare it with information about the event obtained in the previous step. Already with the study of the event hours after the end it is possible to observe if the event really stops causing problems.

Message Filtering. First we filter the posts by the semantic information contained in the text message (Act. 5). In other words, we only analyze D-C and classify posts in a binary form as "event" or "no-event". This was determined by checking the context in which the keyword was written and the meaning it expresses in the text message. Posts that were not related to the crisis event (i.e. with keywords out of context) or written in another language were classified as "no-event" and removed from the set. The other posts were classified as "event". Subsequently, we filter the posts based on the temporal interpretation extracted from the text message (Act. 6). In other words, we only analyze the D-T and classify posts in a binary form as "timely" or "no-timely". Posts that did not express the idea of an ongoing event (i.e. a past event, a question or a possibility) were classified as "no-timely" and removed from the set. The other posts were classified as "timely". As such, the timely set of posts describes a crisis event in progress and is written in the language of the affected region.

Location Recognition. In this step, we manually examine three metadata to extract some location information. We use the following order of precedence to determine the location of each post: (1) the text message; (2) the geolocation field; and, (3) the text of the user's profile. The granularity was divided into 6 levels based on political-administrative divisions. From lowest to highest level, we use: (1) point; (2) street; (3) neighborhood; (4) city; (5) state; and, (6) country. To determine the location of the post, we consider the source of the location with less granularity, respecting the order of precedence and discarding contradictory information between the sources (Act. 7). Therefore, we analyze the D-S and classify the posts as "inside", "outside" or "undefined" Thus, in the inside posts, the location pointed inside the study area. In outside posts, the location pointed outside the study area. In undefined posts, the location did not point to a determinable location (i.e. inside or outside). Note that the set of inside posts represents the posts with the potential to identify points affected by the crisis event within a study area. Therefore, we analyzed the volume, temporal distribution and location detail of this set of posts.

5 Results

This exploratory study was applied to Twitter data on urban flooding events in Brazilian cities. Twitter was explored in this research, as it has adherence within the study area, its use is characterized by the immediate sharing of messages and it has an API (Application Programming Interface) that allows the collection of messages and metadata in a structured way. Even so, other social media with similar characteristics (i.e. local membership, immediate sharing and ease of data collection) could also be explored.

To validate the occurrence of events, we use news published on the web by the Brazilian press. Data collection was carried out over 76 d: September 16, 2020 to November 30, 2020. We selected three events based on population: two events that affected the two most populated cities in Brazil and one event that affected another city with less than 10 The objective was to study data sharing in cities with significantly different populations.

Data Collect. We retrieved the flood news from are important news company in Brazil, the G1 news portal[1] with only one keyword written in Portuguese ("alagamento", which means flood in English). We found 192 news items that were published on 56 different days in 2020: 8 d in September, 21 d in October and 27 d in November. Social media data was collected based on different words found in the news. In September, posts were collected with 5 keywords in Portuguese[2]. Subsequently, we added to the search set 11 words with verb tense variations in Portuguese[3]. Thus, in October and November, the posts were collected with 16 keywords. During the 76 d, 55,073 posts were collected, with an average of 724 posts per day: 2,985 in September, 23,237 in October and 28,851 in November.

The selected flood events had a relevant amount of news related to their occurrence. The events affected cities in the same region of Brazil (i.e. southeast) but occurred in different states. *Ev1:* the first event affected the city of Rio de Janeiro (over 6 million inhabitants[4]) and other cities in the same metropolitan region. *Ev2:* the second event affected the city of São Paulo (over 12 million inhabitants[5]) and other cities in the same metropolitan region. *Ev3:* the third event affected some cities in the state of Espírito Santo (capital Vitória, Vila Velha, Serra and Cariacica). These cities have an estimated population of less than 530,000 inhabitants[6].

The selected events were caused by rain in the same season of the year (i.e. spring) but in different months. According to the news found *Ev1* had a rain time of approximately 26 h (Sept., 22nd at 6 pm to 23rd at 8 pm) and *Ev2* had a rain time of approximately 4 h (Oct., 20th at 2 pm to 6 pm). In *Ev3* rain had a time interval of approximately 14 h (Nov., 24th at 10 am to 25th at 0 am). In this case, we used precipitation data from the National Institute of Meteorology (INMET)[7], because the news found did not inform the estimated time of rain. These events are interesting because they make it possible to study in isolation the social media data generated during the same season of the year and in nearby areas.

Candidate Publications. In this step, we use the date and duration of the rain to select the sample of candidate posts (i.e. potentially related to the urban flood event). Before that, we added 6 h at the beginning and at the end of the rain to increase the temporal coverage. In this way, *Ev1* have a new time range totaling 38 h (i.e. Sept., 22nd at 12:00 pm to 24th at 2:00 am) and we selected 980 posts with 5 flood-related keywords in that time range. *Ev2* have a new time range totaling 16 h (i.e. Oct., 20th at 08:00 am to 21st at 00:00 am) and we selected 1269 posts with 16 flood-related keywords in that time range. *Ev3* have

[1] https://g1.globo.com. Last accessed: Jan. 30th 2022.
[2] "alagamento", "enchente", "inundação", "inundações" and "inundado".
[3] "alaga", "alagada", "alagado", "alagando", "alagar", "alagou", "inunda", "inundada", "inundando", "inundar" and "inundou".
[4] https://sidra.ibge.gov.br/tabela/6579#resultado. Last accessed: Jan. 30th 2022.
[5] https://sidra.ibge.gov.br/tabela/6579#resultado. Last accessed: Jan. 30th 2022.
[6] https://sidra.ibge.gov.br/tabela/6579#resultado. Last accessed: Jan. 30th 2022.
[7] https://portal.inmet.gov.br/paginas/catalogoaut#. Last accessed: Jan. 30th 2022.

a new time range totaling 26 h (i.e. Nov., 24th at 04:00 am to 25th at 06:00 am) and we selected 852 posts with 16 flood-related keywords in that time range.

Message Filtering. We analyzed the message from the post sets selected in the previous step to remove the no-event posts (i.e. unrelated to the urban flood event). So, we selected: 794 event posts out of 980 (or 81.02%) in *Ev1*, 1010 event posts out of 1269 (or 79.35%) in *Ev2* and 410 event posts out of 852 (or 48.12%) in *Ev3*. Next, we analyze the event post sets to remove the no-timely posts (i.e. posts whose message was not interpreted as a message describing an ongoing urban flood). So, we selected: 447 timely posts out of 794 (or 56.30%) in *Ev1*, 652 timely posts out of 1007 (or 64.75%) in *Ev2* and 204 timely posts out of 410 (or 49.76%) in *Ev3*.

Posts within the Study Area. We group the posts timely according to available location in relation to a study area. The study area was defined based on the area affected by the crisis event. Events may manifest in different cities at the same time due to variability associated with rain and users may not be specific when reporting an event location. Considering the development of an automatic event detection system, posts can be captured by bodies that monitor the entire state (e.g. meteorology agency) and guidelines can be passed to the responsible agencies in each city (e.g. civil defense). Therefore, we defined a study area with more geographic coverage than the affected area. Therefore, posts were considered within the study area when the location of the post had the same state described in the flood news. In *Ev1*, the study area was the state of Rio de Janeiro (RJ), from 447 timely posts, we get: 294 inside posts, 61 outside posts and 92 undefined posts. In *Ev2*, the study area was the state of São Paulo (SP), from 652 timely posts, we get: 346 inside posts, 109 outside posts and 197 undefined posts. In *Ev3*, the study area was the state of Espírito Santo (ES), from 204 timely posts, we get: 73 inside posts, 72 outside posts and 59 undefined posts. Figure 2 presents the results of the Twitter data decomposition steps from the selected to the dataset within the study area for each event.

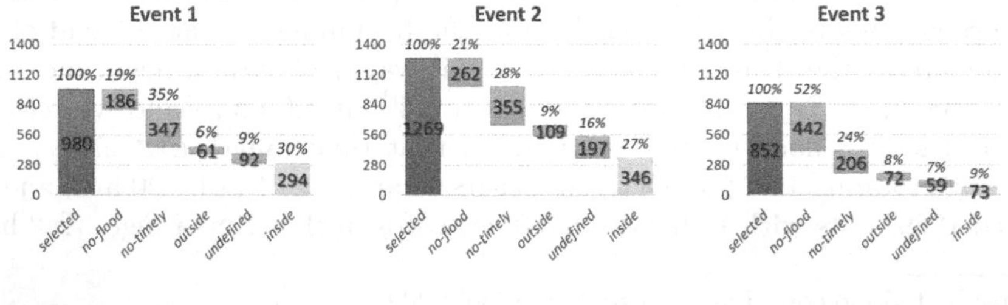

Fig. 2. Twitter data decomposition steps: starting at selection up to data inside the study area

Temporal Distribution of Information. In all cases, we did not find any inside posts or news published during the first 6 h before the rain event. Therefore, we do not include this time interval in our representations. Figure 3 presents the temporal distribution of inside posts and news published during and after the rain for the three events. *Ev1* was represented with 32 h (i.e. 26 h of rain). *Ev2* was represented with 10 h (i.e. 4 h of rain). *Ev3* was represented with 20 h (i.e. 14 h of rain). The graph shows the cumulative number of publications for each hour of the event and the markings of the moment when some news about the event was published.

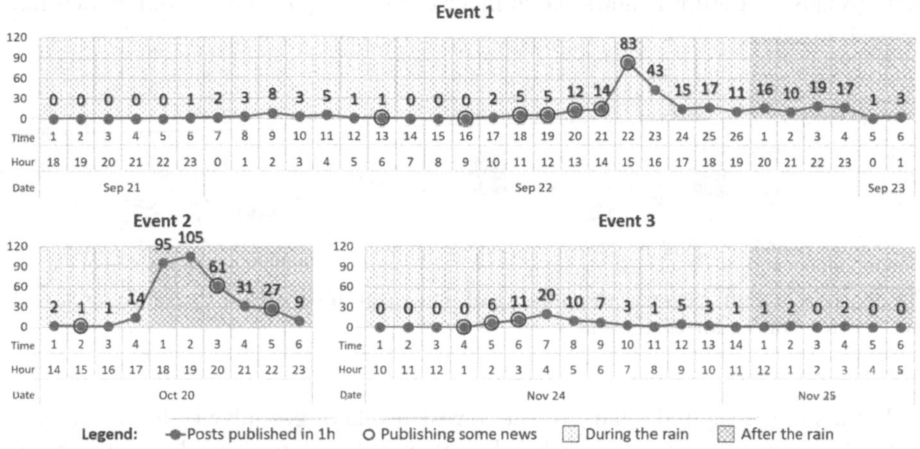

Fig. 3. Temporal distribution with posts accumulated per hour, marking the moment when some news was published start and end of the rain in each event

In *Ev1* (RJ), the first posts were published after 5 h of rain. The time between the first post and the publication of news was more than 7 h. During this period 23 posts were made. In this case, most posts were published during the rain event: 229 posts (77.98%) against 65 posts (22.11%). Furthermore, the peak of posts published per hour happened after 21 h of rain or 4 h before the end of the rain, 83 posts per hour.

In *Ev2* (SP), the news describes a fast and intense rain. In the first hour of rain, 2 posts inside were found. In the second hour of rain, the first news about the floods was published. In this event, most of the posts were published after the rain ended: 328 posts (94.80%) against 18 posts (5.20%). In addition, the three highest rates of posts occurred between the end of the rain and 3 h after the end of the rain, respectively: 95, 105 and 61 posts per hour.

In *Ev3* (ES), the first posts were published after 4 h of rain. However, about 1 h before, there was already some news published about flooding. Most of the posts were published during the rain event: 68 posts (93.15%) versus 5 posts (6.85%). In this case, the peak of posts happened after 6 h of rain or 7 h before the end of the rain: 20 posts per hour. Also, no posts were collected after 4 h of the end of the rain.

Location Breakdown. Subsequently, we investigated the source used to extract the location of posts inside (i.e. text message, geolocation field and profile text).

In *Ev1*, of 294 posts within RJ, the location was extracted from the text message in 169 posts (57.48%), from the geolocation field in 14 posts (4.76%) and profile text in 111 posts (37.76%). In *Ev2*, of 346 posts within SP, the location was extracted from the text message in 201 posts (58.09%), from the geolocation field in 13 posts (3.76%) and profile text in 132 posts (38.15%). In *Ev3*, from 73 posts within ES, the location was extracted from the text message in 46 posts (63.01%), from the geolocation field in 3 posts (4.11%) and profile text in 24 posts (32.88%). Figure 4 shows the number of posts separated by source location for each event.

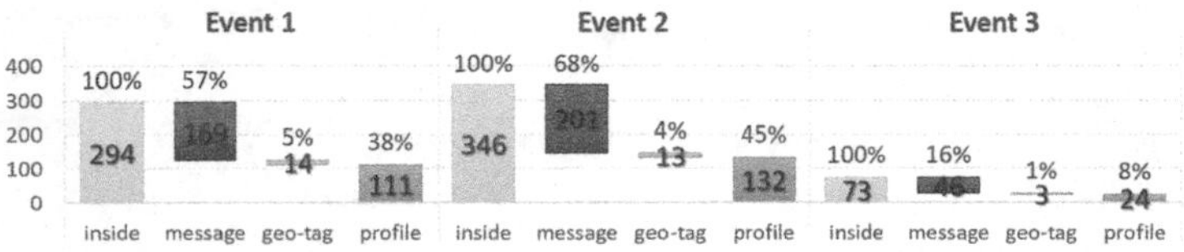

Fig. 4. Relationship between the number of posts obtained within the study area and the location source for each event

We also investigated what are the lowest levels of granularity found in each source (i.e. point, street, neighborhood, city or state). A post inside must contain at least one state-level location. Figure 5 shows the number of posts separated by source and granularity levels obtained in each event.

In *Ev1* (RJ), the text message (169 posts) was used to inform the state in 12 posts (7.10%), city in 49 posts (28.99%), neighborhood in 64 posts (37.87%), street in 28 posts (16.57%) and dot in 16 posts (9.47%). The geolocation field (14 posts) was used to inform the city in 13 posts (92.86%) and neighborhood in 1 post (7.14%); The text in the profile (111 posts) was used to inform the state in 14 posts (81.98%), city in 77 posts (81.98%) and neighborhood in 20 posts (18.02%).

In *Ev2* (SP), the text message (201 posts) was used to inform the state in 17 posts (8.46%), city in 61 posts (30.35%), neighborhood in 43 posts (21.39%), street in 46 posts (22.89%) and dot in 34 posts (16.92%). The geolocation field (13 posts) was used to inform the city in 12 posts (92.31%) and neighborhood in 1 post (7.69%); The text in the profile (132 posts) was used to inform the state in 5 posts (93.18%), city in 118 posts (93.18%) and neighborhood in 9 posts (6.82%).

In *Ev3* (ES), the text message (46 posts) was used to inform the city in 27 posts (58.70%), neighborhood in 13 posts (28.26%), street in 5 posts (10.87%) and dot in 1 post (2.17%). The geolocation field (3 posts) was used to inform only city; and, the text in the profile (24 posts) was used to inform the state in 7 posts (91.67%), city in 15 posts (91.67%) and neighborhood in 2 posts (8.33%).

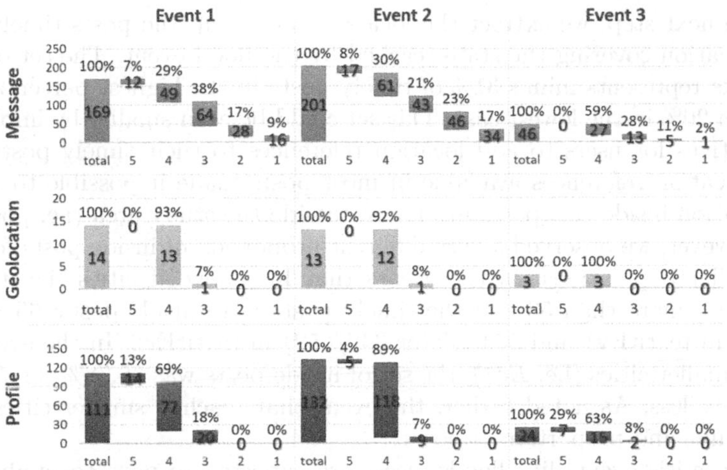

Fig. 5. Relationship between source and localized granularity level for all events: 5) state-level; 4) city-level; 3) neighborhood-level; 2) street-level; and, 1) point-level

6 Discussions

After applying the steps described in this work, we hope that it is be possible to build insights on: (a) the volume of posts within the study area (i.e. "does the information allow us to reliably detect a crisis event?"); (b) the temporal distribution of these posts (i.e. "is the information transmitted in a timely manner?"); and, (c) the detailing of the location of these posts (i.e. "does the information make it possible to know where the crisis event is in progress?"). Understanding these aspects allows assessing the suitability of the available data for automatic identification of the crisis event in a given area and planning strategies to improve user participation.

Posts within the Study Area. Twitter users write about urban flooding at the time the event occurs. In the events studied, we can observe a rate of event posts greater than 15 posts per hour (i.e. 20.89 in *Ev1*, 62.94 in *Ev2* and 15.77 in *Ev3*). Even in the worst event, that volume of 15 posts per hour can be compared to the volume of readings a water level sensor would take during the same time interval. Therefore, there is a relevant participation of users to talk about urban floods. Afterwards, we delete the no-timely posts. In the first two events, timely posts represent more than 56% of event posts (i.e. 56.30% (or 447/794) in *Ev1* and 64.75% (or 652/1007) in *Ev2*). In the third event, the result was 49.76% (or 204/410) in *Ev3*. As in the previous filtering, the third event had fewer posts and a lower percentage of timely posts. However, almost half of the posts collected with different terms related to the flood refer to the event and expressed the idea of a flood in progress. During unknown events, this information can be used by governments to detect events that are happening. Note that on average 1 timely post was collected in less than 8 min. This frequency of timely posts can provide important information for the context of Smart Cities.

In the next step, we extract the location and group the posts timely based on the location covering the state reached by the flood event. The set of undefined posts represents minus 31% of timely posts in the highest percentage and more than 20% in the lowest case. This set could be even smaller by implementing incentives for users to add location references to their timely posts. Even so, the location references available in most posts made it possible to identify some location inside (i.e. posts inside) or outside the study area (i.e. posts outside). However, we observed a very different proportion of inside posts for cities with smaller populations. In the events that hit crowded cities (i.e. the first two events), more than 53% of the timely posts were inside posts: 65.77% (or 294/447) in textitEv1 and 53.07% (or 346/652) in textitEv2. In the event that reached smaller cities (i.e. *Ev3*), the set of inside posts was 35.78% (or 73/204), almost 18% less. As noted earlier, the event that reached smaller cities had a lower volume and proportion of posts.

During crisis events like floods, users are expected to post posts about the event that is happening with some location information. Furthermore, we can expect greater participation with timely posts than no-timely posts and a greater participation with inside posts than no-inside posts. We can consider that in the course of separating the classes, the proportion of posts should be higher for the class of interest. Thus, in crowded cities, an algorithm may simply consider most timely posts and inside posts as criteria for deciding whether there are flood events. The same can't be applied to smaller cities that don't have the most timely posts, let alone posts inside. Therefore, the identification of events in crowded cities can be more reliable than small cities.

Temporal Distribution. Naturally, we didn't find any inside posts before the rain event. This may indicate that our filtering steps have achieved good accuracy. Inside posts presented variations of posts per hour. In the event with long rainy weather (i.e. first event and third event), there was a spike in posts during the rain. In the event with the fastest rain (i.e. second event), there was a spike in posts after the rain. Floods caused by rain usually dissipate some time after the rain has ended. However, in cases of rain concentrated in a few hours, the problems may persist for some time. In this context, the flood reaches its maximum level and is exhausted with the passage of time without rain. This pattern can be observed in the messages published during the event. Messages peak and the volume of posts decreases after some time, especially when there is no more rain. The occurrence of the flood event and the problems caused by it reflected in the variation in the volume of posts published per hour. Therefore, the message pattern can be related to the type of event and can be used in conjunction with burst or spike-based techniques for event detection.

The time analysis allows you to show if there are publications about the event that were published before confirmation by online news. In the event that reached populous cities (i.e. first event and second event) we can observe this behavior. In the event that reached smaller cities (i.e. third event), the posts about flooding were published after the first news about the problem. Posts collected before any news could have been posted by users who were in the place where the flood was starting. These posts can provide important information for accident prevention and alert people who are nearby. Otherwise, posts published after some news may have been generated with information replicated from the news. In more populous cities, Twitter users demonstrated greater agility than in small towns. Therefore, it may be more favorable to detect flood events in a timely manner in crowded cities.

Location Breakdown. In all events the location with the smallest levels of granularity was extracted from the text message (i.e. average of 58.35%). The second most used font was the text in the profile (i.e. average of 37.45%) and lastly the geolocation field (i.e. average of 4.21%). In the event that hit populous cities, text message was used more than 61% of the time to inform one of the 3 lowest levels (i.e. point, street and neighborhood). In the event that reached smaller cities, the text message was used less than 42% of the time for the same purpose (i.e. almost 20% less). On the other hand, posts whose location was extracted from the profile text or from the geolocation field presented mainly the city level (i.e. average of 78.65% for the profile text and average of 93, 33% for the geolocation field) and only a small part presented the neighborhood level (i.e. average of 11.61% for the profile text and average of 6.67% for the field of geolocation).

Text message had the widest range of granularities and was the only source that reported point and street levels. As such, more than half of the inside posts were written by users interested in describing the event and adding a location along with the text message. In this way, we can suggest the possibility of investing in the development of Machine Learning and Artificial Intelligence tools to extract the location inserted in the text message.

Locations with state and city levels represent the granularities with the largest geographic area and allow identifying which regions have flooding problems. However, due to the large geographic area they represent, these levels do not contribute to directing emergency actions and identifying flood points in a city. At the same time, neighborhood and street-level locations represent geographic areas that can be significantly large in populated cities. However, these levels can be combined with other information such as relief information or flood history to derive areas or points that are likely to be flooded. This type of procedure requires the storage and processing of more data from the informed neighborhood or street. Therefore, these granularities can contribute to the direction of emergency actions and identification of flood points, but they represent location classes that can be used with limitations or delays.

The point level can assist in directing emergency actions without extra processing or combining with other information. However, the isolated use of posts with point references represents a use of less than 10% of the posts about flooding in progress in the study area: 5.44% in *Ev1*, 9.83% in *Ev2* and 1.37% in *Ev3*. If it is possible to use the street and neighborhood levels, the utilization improves, but it is still less than 44% in all cases: 43.88% (or 129/294) in *Ev1*, 38.44% (or 133/346) in *Ev2* and 28.77% (or 21/73) in *Ev3*. Therefore, user participation will hardly be used if the location references are incomplete. In view of this, developing new ways to facilitate the entry of complete location information can take advantage of users' participation interest.

Data Validation and Enhancement. The occurrence of each event was validated by the news and the results showed that much of the data would be lost because it does not present a complete location. In this sense, the locations were extracted, but not validated. Within the context of Smart Cities, managers can apply Crowdsourcing and gamification techniques to validate the affected regions. Another important piece of information is the time when the event occurred. In this work we consider the interpretation of text messages to infer the temporality of the event. However, managers may be interested in validating the timing of events. Some possible strategies might be to interact with people and ask for missing information, contact people nearby in nearby locations, or send people to the location to confirm that the event is happening. In general, managers can encourage the publication of messages with the necessary characteristics. One approach that may be promising is to produce interfaces using specific techniques for the design of Crowdsourcing applications [17].

7 Conclusions and Future Work

This work presents a study that provides an a priori perception of the needs for the implementation of automatic event detection systems and an evaluation that quantifies the contribution of users in a given region to local and recurrent crisis events. Before applying any automatic detection technique, public managers and crisis managers in governmental organizations and the public sector can pay more attention to the characteristics of the messages that circulate in a given region about the recurring problems in a region. We consider the volume of posts during the crisis event, the temporal distribution of posts and news about the event, and a breakdown of available location.

After discarding messages that did not happen within a time interval, that do not specifically deal with an ongoing event and that do not refer to a study area, we found that in the scenario of crowded cities it is possible to identify posts related to the event. crisis and published before any news about the event. This behavior can be observed even for faster events. On the other hand, in scenarios of cities with significantly smaller population, we found that the volume of messages about the crisis event in progress within the study area is lower and the messages are published after some news. In both scenarios we performed a detailed location study. We have verified that the smallest levels of granularity are inserted in the text message and the point, street and neighborhood levels are extracted in a small part of the posts.

Therefore, the development of automatic event detection systems can be supported by user participation in crowded cities. As we manually extract in our work, it is also possible to use natural language processing on Twitter data to automatically extract timely semantic, temporal and geographic information within a study area. However, only a small part of the posts identify the full location. This type of assessment can provide support for decision-making by local governments regarding investment in technological solutions for Smart Cities. Note that when defining a set of keywords, we left out other posts and we don't know if these posts could present adequate information to identify an event. In the future, the development of a Twitter alert post sharing interface with the proper information should be considered. This can leverage user participation by enriching shared location and encourage new user participation. Consequently, this approach can bring better results for recurrent flood event detection and identification solutions implemented in this area.

Acknowledgement. This study was financed in part by the Coordenação de Aperfeiçoamento de Pessoal de Nível Superior - Brasil (CAPES) - Finance Code 001

References

1. Afyouni, I., Al Aghbari, Z., Razack, R.A.: Multi-feature, multi-modal, and multi-source social event detection: a comprehensive survey. Inf. Fusion **79**, 279–308 (2022)
2. Alkouz, B., Al Aghbari, Z.: SNSjam: road traffic analysis and prediction by fusing data from multiple social networks. Inf. Process. Manag. **57**(1), 102139 (2020)
3. Alsmadi, I., O'Brien, M.: Event detection in twitter: a content and time-based analysis. arXiv preprint arXiv:2111.05274 (2021)
4. Arapostathis, S.G.: A methodology for automatic acquisition of flood-event management information from social media: the flood in Messinia, South Greece, 2016. Inf. Syst. Front. **23**(5), 1127–1144 (2021). https://doi.org/10.1007/s10796-021-10105-z
5. Erfanian, P.Y., Cami, B.R., Hassanpour, H.: An evolutionary event detection model using the matrix decomposition oriented dirichlet process. Expert Syst. Appl. **189**, 116086 (2022)
6. Filho, W.P., Rosseti, I., Viterbo, J.: On tweets, retweets, hashtags and user profiles in the 2016 american presidential election scene. In: Proceedings of the 18th Annual International Conference on Digital Government Research, pp. 120–128. dg.o 2017. Association for Computing Machinery, New York, NY, USA (2017). https://doi.org/10.1145/3085228.3085230
7. Gao, Y., Wang, S., Padmanabhan, A., Yin, J., Cao, G.: Mapping spatiotemporal patterns of events using social media: a case study of influenza trends. Int. J. Geogr. Inf. Sci. **32**(3), 425–449 (2018)
8. Gutierrez, C., Figuerias, P., Oliveira, P., Costa, R., Jardim-Goncalves, R.: Twitter mining for traffic events detection. In: 2015 Science and Information Conference (SAI), pp. 371–378. IEEE (2015)
9. Hong, L., Fu, C., Wu, J., Frias-Martinez, V.: Information needs and communication gaps between citizens and local governments online during natural disasters. Inf. Syst. Front. **20**(5), 1027–1039 (2018). https://doi.org/10.1007/s10796-018-9832-0
10. Huang, Q., Wong, D.W.: Activity patterns, socioeconomic status and urban spatial structure: what can social media data tell us? Int. J. Geogr. Inf. Sci. **30**(9), 1873–1898 (2016)
11. Kruspe, A., Kersten, J., Klan, F.: Detection of actionable tweets in crisis events. Nat. Hazard. **21**(6), 1825–1845 (2021)

12. Li, L., Bensi, M., Cui, Q., Baecher, G.B., Huang, Y.: Social media crowdsourcing for rapid damage assessment following a sudden-onset natural hazard event. Int. J. Inf. Manag. **60**, 102378 (2021)
13. Lima, P.C.R., Barcellos, R., Bernardini, F., Viterbo, J.: Using geocoding and topic extraction to make sense of comments on social network pages of local government agencies. In: Parycek, P., et al. (eds.) EGOV 2018. LNCS, vol. 11020, pp. 263–274. Springer, Cham (2018). https://doi.org/10.1007/978-3-319-98690-6_22
14. Monteiro, M., Vasconcelos, L., Viterbo, J., Salgado, L., Bernardini, F.: Assessing the quality of local e-government service through citizen-sourcing applications. In: 2021 IEEE 24th International Conference on Computer Supported Cooperative Work in Design (CSCWD), pp. 1178–1183 (2021). https://doi.org/10.1109/CSCWD49262.2021.9437746
15. Rehman, F.U., Afyouni, I., Lbath, A., Khan, S., Basalamah, S.: Building socially-enabled event-enriched maps. GeoInformatica **24**(2), 371–409 (2020). https://doi.org/10.1007/s10707-020-00394-y
16. Sadiq, R., Akhtar, Z., Imran, M., Ofli, F.: Integrating remote sensing and social sensing for flood mapping. Remote Sens. Appl. Soc. Env. **25**, 100697 (2022)
17. Vasconcelos, L., Trevisan, D., Viterbo, J.: Engagement by design: a card-based approach to design crowdsourcing initiatives. In: 2022 IEEE 25th International Conference on Computer Supported Cooperative Work in Design (CSCWD), pp. 353–358 (2022). https://doi.org/10.1109/CSCWD54268.2022.9776308
18. Villodre, J., Criado, J.I.: User roles for emergency management in social media: understanding actors' behavior during the 2018 majorca island flash floods. Gov. Inf. Q. **37**(4), 101521 (2020)
19. Wang, Z., Ye, X.: Social media analytics for natural disaster management. Int. J. Geogr. Inf. Sci. **32**(1), 49–72 (2018)
20. Yigitcanlar, T., et al.: Detecting natural hazard-related disaster impacts with social media analytics: the case of Australian states and territories. Sustainability **14**(2), 810 (2022)
21. Zhang, Y., Zong, R., Wang, D.: A hybrid transfer learning approach to migratable disaster assessment in social media sensing. In: 2020 IEEE/ACM International Conference on Advances in Social Networks Analysis and Mining (ASONAM), pp. 131–138. IEEE (2020)
22. Zheng, X., Han, J., Sun, A.: A survey of location prediction on twitter. IEEE Trans. Knowl. Data Eng. **30**(9), 1652–1671 (2018)

Health Fake News in the Covid-19 Pandemic in Brazil

Ana Paula Tavares[1](✉), Luiz Antonio Joia[1], and Marcelo Fornazin[2]

[1] Getulio Vargas Foundation, R. Jorn. Orlando Dantas, 30, Botafogo, Rio de Janeiro, RJ, Brazil
anapaula.dstavares@gmail.com, luiz.joia@fgv.br

[2] Fundação Oswaldo Cruz (FIOCRUZ) and Fluminense Federal University, Av. Gal. Milton Tavares de Souza, São Domingos, RJ, Brazil

Abstract. Digital technologies are revamping the world, creating opportunities to increase social well-being while generating challenges associated with sustainable development. The growing popularity of social media, along with the dissemination of information, has led to the emergence of fake news. The misinformation linked to the Covid-19 pandemic has been prolific and a major barrier to dealing with this crisis. In this sense, this study aims to address the underlying challenges and opportunities associated with digital technologies initiatives implemented in Brazil to deal with the spread of health fake news during the Covid-19 pandemic. By analyzing a single longitudinal case study, we investigate how digital technologies were used by government, media groups and civil society to articulate common interests and enforce fundamental rights such as privacy and freedom of expression in a digitally connected society.

Keywords: Fake news · Infodemic · Digital transformation · Sustainable development · Health

1 Introduction

Digital technologies are reshaping the world, providing opportunities to foster prosperity, human well-being, and sustainability. Conversely, increasing challenges, risks, and ethical issues have been impacting individuals, organizations, and society at large, setting forth questions about the complex and multi-faceted relationship between ICTs and sustainability [1]. In this context, could democracies be jeopardized by the power of social media and false news? The Nobel Peace Prize 2021 was awarded to two journalists who have championed freedom of expression [2], revealing that social media is being used to spread fake news, harass opponents, create chaos, and manipulate public discourse. Likewise, evidence suggests that people tend to unknowingly believe in seemingly personal, independent, algorithmic recommendations more than in someone else's recommendations [3].

ICTs have a key role to play in expanding participation, transparency, and accountability to sustain collective action in the world's transition to a digitally united society

Published by Springer Nature Switzerland AG 2022
M. Janssen et al. (Eds.): EGOV 2022, LNCS 13391, pp. 163–177, 2022.
https://doi.org/10.1007/978-3-031-15086-9_11

[4]. Notwithstanding, building a strong ethical agenda to promote a better and equitable world requires a critical understanding of ICT within the development context [5] to mitigate the digital divide and generate social value, in particular for marginalized communities [4, 6–9]. Precisely, ethical dilemmas, such as trust in unknown virtual sources of information, and the use of social media as a source of reliable dialogue, raised important concerns that should be addressed considering local contexts and local actors involved [3]. Low and middle-income countries (LMIC) have different types of vulnerable groups, with specific needs. Understanding each group's particular needs and designing programs to promote their social and economic inclusion must contribute to developing their capacities and ensure that they are neither discriminated against nor manipulated by outsiders [3, 10].

According to the United Nations' Sustainable Development Goals (SDG), information for decision-making and participation should be one of the world's top priorities by 2030 [11]. The UN Agenda emphasizes that, in a sustainable development context, everyone is a user and provider of information in a broad sense. That includes data, information, experience, and knowledge [11]. Therefore, the need for information and freedom of speech arises at all levels, from decision-makers at the national and international levels to grassroots groups and ordinary people. In LMIC, for example, citizens do not have the capacity to assess which digital information is meaningful and reliable, or even to identify fake news [12]. In Brazil, for instance, 9 out of 10 citizens have been exposed to health fake news during the Covid-19 pandemic, which places the country among the world's most concerned people (82%) with the spread of false information and fake news [13]. Thus, evidence indicates that citizens' digital literacy, and particularly their skills needed to identify fake news or trolls, are not sufficient for them to participate in democratic processes and reliable online dialogues [14].

That way, the abovementioned issues have led to a question still unanswered: how were digital technologies used by government, media groups and civil society to deal with the spread of health fake news and articulate common interests during the Covid-19 pandemic in a LMIC like Brazil?

2 Theoretical Background

2.1 Contextualizing Digital Technologies and Ethical Dilemmas

Digital technologies are transforming economic, political, technological, social, and environmental systems [3] creating opportunities for enhancing people's well-being while raising sustainability challenges [15]. So far, most research has focused on the development and implementation of digital technologies [16] but little attention has been paid to reflecting on and anticipating the unintended effects of same, which can severely impact not only socio-technological systems but also society in general. Coping with unintended effects and more precisely ethical dilemmas are major elements for sustainability learning [17]. The digital transition, which has been accelerated by the outbreak of the Covid-19 pandemic, raised concerns about loss of privacy, cyberterrorism, digital oligarchy, and exclusion, to name just a few [12, 14,18–21]. Some experts assert that sustainability effects should be approached considering a normative component "assigned according to the values, norms, objectives of the stakeholders involved"

[3, p. 4]. Thereby, what might be positive to one group or culture, might have wicked effects on another.

In such a context, providing personal data to digital platforms such as health apps or global tech companies, like Google or Facebook, allows the access of people to products and services while enabling data usage for promoting business and political purposes. As asserted by Zuboff [22], these business models are a new form of "surveillance capitalism", by which personal data is exploited and controlled using algorithms that analyze information to make important decisions. Such activities replace human cognitive operations with those accomplished by computers, raising another ethical dilemma associated with the asymmetry of power, trust, and free choice. In fact, taking ownership of private information collected due to free access of users requires regulation and laws to avoid backlash against how companies use this information gathered [22]. Tackling misinformation and web misuse is a wicked and complex problem that affects the lives of millions and, therefore, cannot be addressed with simplistic narratives [23]. So far, several countries such as China and Russia have stepped out of the global network for the sake of "cyber sovereignty" [3]. Also, European countries and Brazil, for instance, have established a general data protection regulation to harmonize data privacy laws[1]. The dynamics of power over the Internet put big digital industries in a position of much control in different countries, whereas nations, especially poor ones, have limited control over the Internet. Consequently, it is paramount to identify vulnerabilities and unintended effects of misinformation in the Global South to provide a local viewpoint which entails a trustworthy and well-grounded ethical agenda to promote sustainable development in the region.

2.2 Infodemic: The Age of Fake News and Misinformation

The World Health Organization (WHO) classified the misinformation associated with the Covid-19 pandemic as a "mass infodemic[2]" and one of the main problems to mitigate this outbreak [24]. Disinformation is not a new trend. In fact, it predates the Covid-19 pandemic [25], being propagated by the same tools traditionally used to disseminate public health information. However, today, the digitally connected world has amplified this phenomenon, which has impacted society in general. Disinformation is therefore defined as false or inaccurate information, or especially information whose purpose is to deliberately mislead [24]. The term fake news, which has become a major phenomenon in the context of Internet-based media [26], refers to the mass production and propagation of false information to intentionally distort facts in order to attract, deceive, misinform and mislead audiences, manipulate public opinion, and discredit or exalt an institution or a person to obtain economic and political advantages [27].

[1] What Governments do. Retrieved from https://privacyinternational.org/learn/what-governments-do.

[2] An infodemic is too much information including false or misleading information in digital and physical environments during a disease outbreak. It causes confusion and risk-taking behaviours that can harm health. It also leads to mistrust in health authorities and undermines the public health response. Retrieved from https://www.who.int/health-topics/infodemic#tab=tab_1.

Fake news has increased with the rise of social media algorithms, putting a lens on political polarization, post-truth politics, and confirmation bias [28]. To cope with such ethical dilemmas and contribute to sustainable development, fact-checking institutes, such as the International Fact-Checking Network (IFCN), Poynter and other checking platforms, have been developed worldwide by journalists and experts. Despite that global effort, the spread of fake news has led to an unsettling loss of confidence in institutions, such as the press, science, and intellectual groups. In fact, during the outbreak of the Covid-19 pandemic, information and guidelines that contradicted scientific knowledge disseminated fear and impacted the mitigation of the pandemic especially in developing regions [25]. Furthermore, most citizens are unable to assess which digital information is meaningful and reliable. This sheds light on the lack of digital awareness to identify fake news and to engage in reliable online democratic dialogues [3].

2.3 A Multilevel Framework for Digital Technologies and Disinformation Analysis

Bringing together the theories on contextualist ICT innovation [7, 29, 30] social shaping of technology [31, 32], and structuration view of technology [33–35], we present below an empirical framework combining the central concepts of this study: social groups, technologies, and discourses. The social constructivist [36] approach allows the understanding of the acceleration of digital transformation in the pandemic, addressing conceptual relationships such as technology/society, agency/structure, and technical reasoning/institutional dynamics [7]. That way, technology could be considered as part of a broader social context, raising questions concerning the way specific categories of technologies and social actors' clusters are formed and shaped, leading to specific socioeconomic outcomes.

According to Pozzebon and Diniz [37], contextualism allows the perusal of actions and perceptions of human actors in the light of historically situated context within which such actions happen, as well as perceptions are shaped [30]. Pettigrew [29] emphasizes three elements - context, process, and content - and claims that these three elements are equally important and should be considered altogether. The present study adapted these three elements to investigate the digital transformation changes at the community level considering: the social groups where the ICT artifact is being used; the discourses to understand how social groups influence the negotiation process taking place around the implementation and use of an ICT artifact; and the technologies being implemented, used by particular actors at a certain level of analysis.

Another theoretical influence on the present study is the structuration view of technology based on Giddens' structuration theory, which has been developed by some researchers such as Barrett and Walsham [33], Orlikowski [34], and Walsham [35]. The concept of technology-in-practice, derived from the structuration theory, explains how social groups, negotiating meanings and applications of a given ICT, adapt them locally and what are the consequences of it. According to the theory, different cultures will be involved differently with local adaptations or appropriations. Furthermore, the concept of improvisation - which arises intuitively from emergencies or crises to solve a problem [38] and in response to unexpected opportunities or actions [39] - makes room for research in this area in the Brazilian context. In fact, improvisation is frequent in developing regions due to their less stable political and economic environments [39]. That way, Table 1 presents the main dimensions of the Multilevel and Pluralistic Conceptual Framework developed by Pozzebon and Diniz [37], considering the three abovementioned theoretical perspectives: contextualism, social shaping of technology, and structuration view of technology, as explained below.

Table 1. Framework components.

Components	Dimensions	Concepts
Actors	Context	Social groups
Digital technologies	Content	Technology-in-practice
Discourses	Process	Mechanisms of negotiation

'Actors' refer to the social setting in which the ICT artifact is being implemented and used. It helps define the boundaries of the investigation and includes the identification of different relevant social groups. Social groups, in turn, refer to a group of people who share a common geographical space, a common social class, a common professional occupation, to name a few. It also includes the identification of interpretive frames for each social group, allowing the recognition of shared and conflicting perceptions, expectations, and interests that characterize the community context [37, 40, 41]. 'Digital Technologies' refer to the socio-technical characteristics of the ICT artifact being implemented, as used by specific actors at a given level of analysis (individual, social groups, society). The technologies-in-practice resulting from the process of negotiation is both intended and unintended, and their choice emerges from the literature on digital transformation in addition to the analysis of the mini-cases [33–35]. 'Discourses' refer to the understanding of how social groups influence the negotiation process taking place around the implementation and use of a given ICT artifact. The implementation of ICT in a community or region can be seen as an opportunity to change information flow, resource allocation and responsibility attributions [35, 37].

3 Research Method

This study is based on qualitative methodology, being designed as a single longitudinal case study [42] grounded on an interpretive approach [36, 43–46]. The case study method is a great opportunity to gain an in-depth view of a contemporary event within its real context [47]. This approach is especially useful to define the boundaries between the phenomenon and the context, along with the interpretations and knowledge of the constructed reality gathered through the investigation [48]. The adopted criterion for selecting the case study was based on three main components: relevance, reliability, and impact on society - relevance to research and practice; reliability in the sense that the research method produces consistent results; and impact on society via (i) the understanding of societal issues that influence socio-economic development, and (ii) the reframing of debates and assumptions about the topic investigated. These criteria provide a unique research opportunity to understand an important phenomenon through a real-life case. Moreover, based on Klein and Myers' [43] set of principles for conducting and evaluating interpretative studies, this research presents below a set of criteria proposed by Pozzebon [36] that will guide the qualitative research project and the procedures to support the quality of the work [45]. Such criteria consider the adopted ontological and epistemological assumptions, namely: authenticity, plausibility, criticality, and reflexivity. The research method was developed considering the following steps. First, the case study was analyzed through data collection. The data collection procedure comprised a logbook of events recorded during the outbreak of the Covid-19 pandemic from March 2020 to October 2021. The procedure conducted sought consistent and trustworthy data and information collected through several methods like observation [49] and document analysis [48].

Besides, the data collection included the analysis of the studies on the use of ICTs in Brazil during the pandemic, released by the Center for Studies on Information and Communication Technologies (Cetic.br) in collaboration with the Observatory for the Information Society in Latin America and the Caribbean (OSILAC)[3]. The systematic search for fake news and disinformation in public databases was directed by the International Fact-Checking Network (IFCN), Index on Censorship, International Press Institute (IPI) and First Draft News of the Poynter Institute, along with media websites, governmental organizations, intergovernmental organizations, health professionals, NGOs, think tanks, and academic publications. The following keywords were used: "disinformation", "disinformation", "Covid-19", "coronavirus", "epidemic" and "pandemic". This information is essential to monitor and assess the socioeconomic impact of ICTs to support the development of public policies that can guarantee society's access to the digital arena, as well as allow the comparison of the Brazilian reality with that of other countries [24]. Table 2 presents the synthesis of the data collection (Table 3).

After data collection, the theoretical framework was applied to the case "to understand the meaning or knowledge constructed by people [...] and the way people make sense of their world and their experiences in this world." [48, p. 137). Theoretical perspectives were then articulated through a primary codification of actors and technologies, aiming to seek and identify concepts and find relationships between them. This was followed by the analysis of discourses in a dialogue between the theory and the field. Finally, specific outcomes were presented based on the analysis of the selected single case. The criteria to define the outcomes considered the results of the case at the societal level and how technologies, actors and discourses have impacted such results.

---

[3] This research follows the methodology developed by the 'Partnership on Measuring ICT for Development', an international initiative that aims to improve the quality and availability of data and indicators on the evolution of the Information Society worldwide [24].

Table 2. Summary of data collection.

Data source	Description	Period	Role
Public documents	Articles in the media, annual reports, books, podcasts, websites	October 2020 to October 2021	Important for establishing the chronology of main events and for understanding different viewpoints
Observation	Field notes from participation in public conferences/events	October 2020 to October 2021	Important for understanding the dynamics of interactions among the social groups and the discourses that emerged
Cetic.br Survey[4]	Studies and research reports on the use of ICTs in Brazil during the Pandemic	January 2021 to October 2021	Important for monitoring and evaluating the socioeconomic impact of ICTs for development

4 Health Fake News During the Covid-19 Pandemic in Brazil

Nine in every 10 Brazilians have been exposed to fake news about the pandemic, which is typically shared via WhatsApp groups [50]. Besides, seven in 10 said they believed in the information they received. The risks of fake news have gained new urgency because of the seriousness of the health issue. Thus, to combat fake news, the Ministry of Health created a channel called "Health without Fake News" to analyze viral news and determine whether it was true or false. To manage the Covid-19 situation more carefully, the former ministry created a specific channel for information related to the pandemic. Also, Brazil's Congress has pushed for legislation to stop this flood of disinformation. The bill, however, has raised fears about freedom of speech and government surveillance. Despite the discussion around information transparency, fake news has been rampant and the spread of same has contributed to discrediting science and global public health institutions, thereby weakening people's adherence to the necessary preventive care [25].

Brazil has seriously looked towards the increasing influence of fake news after the 2014 Presidential elections and mostly during the impeachment of the President, in 2016. According to BBC Brazil [51], in 2016, three out of the five most-shared articles on Facebook in Brazil were fake. Such awash in misinformation led independent journalists to set up the first fact-checking website in Brazil, called 'To the Facts' [51]. Despite the growing number of fake news that has affected science, education, human rights, business and the environment, misinformation about the Covid-19 pandemic in Brazil has contaminated people's understanding of the different aspects of the coronavirus disease and its effects, by focusing on beliefs instead of facts. Thus, people started to decide based on prejudice, ideological polarization and political identity, showing

[4] This research follows the methodology developed by the 'Partnership on Measuring ICT for Development', an international initiative that aims to improve the quality and availability of data and indicators on the evolution of the Information Society worldwide [24].

disbelief and cynicism to deal with the great complexity and change imposed by the Covid-19 pandemic [52].

5 Results

The Ministry of Health has taken steps to check viral news, while the Brazilian Congress has pushed for legislation to stem the flood of disinformation. Platforms that do not meet this new reality are supposed to be subject to fines of up to 10% of the group's sales in Brazil in the previous year. In 2020, the most watched YouTube channels about Covid-19 were the biggest fake news outlets [25]. Brazilians are the most concerned people in the world with the dissemination of false information and fake news (82%), with 63% of Internet users using social media as source of information compared to 47%, eight years ago [53]. In essence, 54% of Internet users asserted that the risk of making personal data available in the pandemic outweighs its benefits. Furthermore, the main concerns about the use of their personal data are financial loss due to bank fraud and identity theft [21]. Conversely, despite the general concern, a study revealed that roughly seven out of ten Brazilians believed in at least one type of fake news about the pandemic: "from doubtful remedies to coffee to prevent de virus; to relatives of Covid-19 victims being forced to accept the coronavirus as the cause of death listed on death certificates" [52, p. 8].

To disseminate the denial narrative led by President Bolsonaro, organizations used pages and profiles on social networks and digital platforms such as YouTube and Twitter. The PIC also identified that "not only did public communication agencies failed in their mission to combat rumors and disinformation, but they actively participated in the process of creation and distribution of fake news" [24, p. 3]. On Facebook, for example, disinformation campaigns were initiated with posts created by fake accounts and then digital influencers were hired to disseminate this information, many of them paid by agencies hired by the Special Secretariat for Communication of the Presidency (Secom), in expenses that added up to almost one million dollars. Brazil lacks laws and regulations that classify those actions as crimes and, therefore, punish people who disclose false information. This context highlights the importance of improvements in Brazilian legislation to punish fake news in Criminal Law. In addition, social media and digital platforms must provide open data[5] and information on user identification and social media profiles to hold offenders accountable. The PIC's report also states that "it is essential to tighten the rules for publishing and monetizing content, preventing attacks on public health or any other purpose against the public interest" [54, p. 4]. The first response from the big tech companies came in July 2021, when YouTube removed videos

[5] Data are open if any individual is free to use, reuse or redistribute them, subject, at most, to measures that preserve their origin and openness. There are two dimensions to data openness: (i) the data must be legally open - that is, it must be placed in the public domain or under liberal terms of use and with minimal restrictions; (ii) the data must be technically open - meaning that it must be published in non-proprietary, machine-readable electronic formats so that anyone can access and use it through common and available free software tools. The data must also be publicly available and accessible on a public server, without password or firewall restrictions. To make open data easier to find, most organizations have created and managed open data catalogs. World Bank [56].

from Bolsonaro's official channel in which he recommended using hydroxychloroquine and ivermectin against Covid-19, despite scientific evidence that these drugs are not effective in treating the disease. Moreover, in October 2021, Facebook and YouTube removed another video by President Bolsonaro in which the leader made a false claim that Covid-19 vaccines were linked with developing AIDS [53]. Multiple solutions have been developed by digital platforms such as changing their architecture/code, reducing the reach of fake news, changing algorithms, and tagging fallacious content. However, despite several initiatives implemented by social media and government platforms, the emergence of new technological channels such as Telegram - present in more than 53% of Brazilian smartphones in 2021 (against 35% in 2020) and used to spread fake news, selling weapons and drugs - highlights the urgent need to control the dissemination of harmful information and access to open data [53].

After analyzing the case study and surveying the scientific literature, three main discourses related to digital technologies initiatives for the management and mitigation of the Covid-19 pandemic were perceived, namely: (1) Sustainable Development; (2) Data Privacy & Citizenship; (3) Transparency, Accountability & Participation. Sustainable Development encompasses prosperity, social inclusion, environmentally oriented policies, inclusive good governance, and peace. Fake news, however, exacerbates inequalities and challenges to improve living conditions through improvements in digital literacy and health care. Data Privacy & Citizenship aims to make the digital environment a safe and reliable place, conducive to services and consumption and in which citizens' rights are respected. The pandemic made visible the growing volume of commercial and financial online transactions and the provision of public services virtually, reducing the boundaries between the online and offline worlds. In line with this, there have been important legislative improvements, however, the rise of fake health news during the pandemic contributed to discrediting science and public health institutions. Finally, Transparency, Accountability & Participation involve expanding channels for citizen collaboration in public policymaking to achieve online transparency, accountability, inclusion, and participation.

Table 3. Summary of the case study.

Components	Actors	Description
Social groups	Government	Initiatives from Brazilian Legislative and Judiciary such as the 'Fake News Bill' were developed to mitigate this issue, while the Executive has been accused of promoting the spread of health fake news and reducing in quantity and quality the data available about the pandemic
	Private companies	Social media platforms have been developing multiple solutions such as changing their architectures/codes to use, reducing the reach of fake news, changing algorithms, and tagging fallacious content. Yet, no one has been claimed responsible for the misinformation spread across digital platforms

(continued)

Table 3. (*continued*)

Components	Actors	Description
	Media groups	Media Groups had to reinvent themselves bringing good journalism using both new formats and channels or by strengthening accessible fact-checking initiatives. Also, reduced data available about the pandemic urged the creation of a partnership between the media groups to collect Covid-19 statistics directly from the States' health departments
	Academia	Academia has acted with qualified research and the development of new methodologies/indicators to respond to the challenges imposed by the infodemic
	Civil society	Organized civil society has acted on the basis of advocacy, raising awareness about the harmful effects of misinformation for democracies, as well as developing media and information literacy tools
Technologies	Artificial intelligence (AI)	AI is a double edged-sword: (1) applied to detect and limit the spread of disinformation or to provide context and extra information on individual items and posts; (2) applied to create AI bots and fake profiles to spread misinformation
	Social media	Social media is also a double edged-sword: (1) monitoring and fact-checking are vital tools for measuring and understanding the infodemic as they uncover the continuously changing topics of viral misinformation; (2) it is one of the main enablers of fake news
	Big data analytics	Access to open data to analyze the information disseminated in digital platforms along with the identification of fake accounts and digital influencers involved in the infodemic dynamics
	Mobile	Monitoring of the number of smartphones and digital platforms used to disseminate misinformation (e.g., WhatsApp, Telegram, etc.)
	Cloud computing	Data storage and protection has been constantly expanding. Cloud computing plays an important role in detecting fake news on social media, while allowing the spread of misinformation
Discourses	Sustainable development	Pursuit of prosperity, social inclusion, environmentally oriented policies, inclusive good governance, and peace
	Data privacy & citizenship	Make the digital environment a safe and reliable place, conducive to services and consumption and in which citizens' rights are respected
	Transparency & participation	Expand channels for citizen collaboration in public policymaking to achieve online transparency, accountability, inclusion, and participation

6 Discussion

The case of fake health sheds light on the intended and unintended effects of digital technologies during the pandemic, both as enablers of fake news and as relevant tools to mitigate same. Unforeseen outcomes show how digital platforms, transparency and participation are critical in the aggregation and convergence of common interests from government, private companies, media groups and citizens. The present study revealed those outcomes, examining relevant social groups to define the boundaries of the investigation while providing evidence of intended and unintended consequences of digital technologies for society at large. Thus, government, civil society, private companies, academia and media play an important role in mitigating the pandemic, by exposing their shared and conflicting perceptions, expectations and interests in relation to the digital technologies used to combat the coronavirus. Eliminating misinformation is not a panacea. Multisectoral participation and collaboration are key for gaining a holistic understanding of this issue as well as the needs of citizens. In relation to technologies and their socio-technical characteristics, mobile devices, big data analytics, artificial intelligence, cloud computing and social media were used by the selected actors, showing the impact of digital technologies initiatives in increasing the dissemination of fake news and, therefore, shedding light on issues related to media culture and ethical dilemmas associated with promoting better conditions for the population during the Covid-19 outbreak.

In essence, responding to the main challenges accrued from the infodemic to promote sustainable development is a complex task, as it requires a set of interventions that, according to Unesco [55], should consider three main dimensions, namely, supply, demand, and transmission. Supply encompasses official transparency by governments and open data, in line with Right to Information law and policy. Demand relates to promote partnership with agencies such as WHO, while building resilience among audiences by intensifying its online media and information literacy initiatives [55]. Transmission refers to the promotion of Internet Universality as a means to align digital development to sustainable development. This involves advancing norms and indicators based on the ROAM[6] (Rights, Openness, Accessibility, Multi-stakeholder participation) principles agreed by member states. Thereby, it is possible to provide a viewpoint wherein the rights to freedom of expression and access to information are strong remedies to the dangers of disinformation. Mostly, to enable accountability, transparency and participation with reliable information, it is notorious the need of: (i) monitoring and investigative responses; (ii) law, governance and policy responses, as well as "counter-disinformation" campaigns; (iii) curation and technological responses relevant to institutions mediating content; (iv) normative, ethical, educational, empowered, and credible responses targeted to citizens [24].

7 Conclusions

The contribution of this study is twofold. First, it contributes to academic research by investigating and categorizing the impact of digital technologies on the spread of disinformation, analyzing the proliferation of health fake health in the context of a global pandemic. In addition, the work intends to add to the IS body of knowledge by shedding light on the application of a theoretical framework to investigate the role of social groups, technologies and discourses in the Brazilian context, in the midst of a health crisis. Second, from a managerial point of view, this study presents a set of

[6] ROAM principles of human Rights, Openness, Accessibility, Multi-stakeholder participation. Retrieved from: https://en.unesco.org/internet-universality-indicators.

reflections that can help policymakers identify the unforeseen consequences of fake news in a pandemic, which is a learning opportunity for them to be better prepared to deal with possible future outbreaks.

Future research can re-examine the assumptions underlying this work, which can be addressed through in-depth analysis of the impact of the digital divide on the spread of fake news in an LMIC such as Brazil. Furthermore, the role of digital inclusion and literacy in the empowerment and participation of diverse vulnerable and underserved groups can also be verified to strengthen democracy in developing countries in the context of a pandemic.

The current Brazilian context, with political and economic turmoil associated with a still huge digital divide and strong social inequalities, highlighted the debate around the role of digital technologies to mitigate the Covid-19 pandemic. The absence of adequate regulations, political instability and digital illiteracy are impacting the digital trajectory of the country towards a more transparent, inclusive, and empowered society.

References

1. Corbett, J., Mellouli, S.: Winning the SDG battle in cities: how an integrated information ecosystem can contribute to the achievement of the 2030 sustainable development goals. Inf. Syst. J. **27**(4), 427–461 (2017)
2. Nobel Prize: The Nobel Peace Prize 2021: Announcement. https://www.nobelprize.org/prizes/peace/2021/press-release/ (2021)
3. Viale Pereira, G., et al.: South american expert roundtable: increasing adaptive governance capacity for coping with unintended side effects of digital transformation. Sustainability **12**(2), 718 (2020)
4. Heeks, R., Ospina, A.V.: Conceptualizing the link between information systems and resilience: a developing country field study. Inf. Syst. J. **29**(1), 70–96 (2019)
5. Walsham, G.: Are we making a better world with ICTs? Reflections on a future agenda for the IS field. J. Inf. Technol. **27**(2), 87–93 (2012)
6. Kleine, D.: ICT4WHAT? - using the choice framework to operationalise the capability approach to development. In: 2009 International Conference on Information and Communication Technologies and Development (ICTD). IEEE (2009)
7. Avgerou, C.: Discourses on ICT and development. Inf. Technol. Int. Dev. **6**(3), 1–18 (2010)
8. Teles, A., Joia, L.A.: Assessment of digital inclusion via the actor-network theory: the case of the Brazilian municipality of Piraí. Telematics Inform. **28**, 191–203 (2010)
9. Walsham, G.: ICT4D research: reflections on history and future agenda. Inf. Technol. Dev. **23**(1), 18–41 (2017)
10. AbuJarour, S.A., et al.: Empowering refugees with technology: best practices and research agenda. In: Proceedings of the European Conference on Information Systems (2017)
11. United Nations.: The 17 Goals. Department of Economic and Social Affairs Sustainable Development. https://sdgs.un.org/goals (2021)
12. Makhortykh, M., Urman, A., Roberto, U.: How search engines disseminate information about COVID-19 and why they should do better. The Harvard Kennedy School (HKS) Misinformation Review, 1 (2020)

13. Reuters Institute.: Digital News Report 2021, Reuters Institute for the Study of Journalism, 10th edn. (2021)
14. Pan, S.L., Zhang, S.: From fighting COVID-19 pandemic to tackling sustainable development goals: an opportunity for responsible information systems research. Int. J. Inf. Manag. **55**, 102196 (2020)
15. Linkov, I., Trump, B., Poinsatte-Jones, K., Florin, M.V.: Governance strategies for a sustainable digital world. Sustainability **10**(2), 440 (2018)
16. Vial, G.: Understanding digital transformation: a review and a research agenda. J. Strateg. Inf. Syst. **28**(2), 118–144 (2019)
17. Scholz, R.W.: Environmental Literacy in Science and Society: From Knowledge to Decisions. Cambridge University Press, Cambridge, UK (2011)
18. Kim, S., Kim, S.: The crisis of public health and infodemic: analyzing belief structure of fake news about COVID-19 pandemic. Sustainability **12**(23), 9904 (2020)
19. Pramiyanti, A., Mayangsari, I.D., Nuraeni, R., Firdaus, Y.D.: Public perception on transparency and trust in government information released during the COVID-19 pandemic. Asian J. Public Opin. Res. **8**(3), 351–376 (2020)
20. Shirish, A., Srivastava, S.C., Chandra, S.: Impact of mobile connectivity and freedom on fake news propensity during the COVID-19 pandemic: a cross-country empirical examination. Eur. J. Inf. Syst. **30**(3), 1–20 (2021)
21. Fernández-Torres, M.J., Almansa-Martínez, A., Chamizo-Sánchez, R.: Infodemic and fake news in spain during the COVID-19 pandemic. Int. J. Environ. Res. Public Health **18**(4), 1781 (2021)
22. Zuboff, S.: Surveillance capitalism and the challenge of collective action. In: New Labor Forum, vol. 28, no. 1, pp. 10–29. SAGE Publications, Los Angeles (2019)
23. Web Foundation.: 30 years on, what's next #ForTheWeb?, World Wide Web Foundation. https://webfoundation.org/2019/03/web-birthday-30/ (2019)
24. Cetic.br.: Infodemic: disinformation and media literacy in the context of COVID-19, Internet Sectorial Overview, 3 September 2021 (2021)
25. Galhardi, C.P., Freire, N.P., Minayo, M.C.D.S., Fagundes, M.C.M.: Fact or fake? An analysis of disinformation regarding the Covid-19 pandemic in Brazil. Cien. Saude Colet. **25**, 4201–4210 (2020)
26. Molina, M.D., Sundar, S.S., Le, T., Lee, D.: "Fake news" is not simply false information: a concept explication and taxonomy of online content. Am. Behav. Sci. **65**(2), 180–212 (2021)
27. Cambridge Dictionary.: Meaning of fake news [Internet]. Cambridge Dictionary. https://dictionary.cam-bridge.org/pt/dicionario/ingles/fake-news (2021)
28. Borney, N.: 5 reasons why 'fake news' likely will get even worse. 9 May 2018. USA Today. https://www.usatoday.com/story/opinion/2018/05/09/fake-news-donald-trump-journalism-video-audio-facebook-twitter-column/590006002/ (2018)
29. Pettigrew, A.M.: Longitudinal field research on change: theory and practice. Organ. Sci. **1**(3), 267–292 (1990)
30. Walsham, G., Sahay, S.: GIS for district-level administration in India: problems and opportunities. MIS Q. **23**(1), 39–56 (1999)
31. MacKenzie, D., Wajckman, J.: The Social Shaping of Technology. Open University Press, Philadelphia
32. Bijker, W.E., Law, J.: Shaping Technology/Building Society: Studies in Sociotechnical Change. MICT Press, Cambridge (1999)
33. Barrett, M., Walsham, G.: Electronic trading and work transformation in the London insurance market. Inf. Syst. Res. **10**(1), 1–21 (1999)

34. Orlikowski, W.J.: Using technology and constituting structures: a practice lens for studying technology in organizations. Organ. Sci. **11**(4), 404–428 (2000)
35. Walsham, G.: Cross-cultural software production and use: a structurational analysis. MIS Q. **26**(4), 359–380 (2002)
36. Pozzebon, M.: Conducting and evaluating critical interpretive research: examining criteria as a key component in building a research tradition. In: Kaplan, B., Truex, D.P., Wastell, D., Wood-Harper, A.T., DeGross, J.I. (eds.) Information Systems Research. IFIP International Federation for Information Processing, vol. 143, pp. 275–292. Springer, Boston, MA (2004). https://doi.org/10.1007/1-4020-8095-6_16
37. Pozzebon, M., Diniz, E.H.: Theorizing ICT and society in the Brazilian context: a multilevel, pluralistic and remixable framework. BAR - Brazilian Adm. Rev. **9**(3), 287–307 (2012)
38. Weick, K.: The collapse of sensemaking in organizations: the mann gulch disaster. Adm. Sci. Q. **38**(4), 268–282 (1993)
39. Silva, L.: Outsourcing as an Improvisation: a case study in Latin America. Inf. Soc. **18**(2), 129–138 (2002)
40. Sahay, S., Robey, D.: Organizational context, social interpretation, and the implementation and consequences of geographic information systems. Account. Manag. Inform. Technol. **6**(4), 255–282 (1996)
41. Bartis, E., Mitev, N.: A multiple narrative approach to information systems failure: a successful system that failed. Eur. J. Inf. Syst. **17**(2), 112–124 (2008). https://doi.org/10.1057/ejis.2008.3
42. Stake, R.E.: Case studies. In: Denzin, N.K., Lincoln, Y.S. (eds.) Strategies of Qualitative Inquiry Sage Publications, California, pp. 445–454 (1998)
43. Klein, H.K., Myers, M.D.: A set of principles for conducting and evaluating interpretive field studies in information systems. MIS Q. **23**, 67–93 (1999)
44. Mitev, N.N.: Postmodernism and criticality in information systems research: what critical management studies can contribute. Soc. Sci. Comput. Rev. **24**(3), 310–325 (2006)
45. Pozzebon, M., Petrini, M.: Critérios para condução e avaliação de pesquisas qualitativas de natureza crítico-interpretativa. In: Takahashi, Adriana Roseli Wünsch. Pesquisa Qualitativa em Administração: fundamentos, métodos e usos no Brasil. São Paulo, Atlas, pp. 51–72 (2013)
46. Walsham, G.: Interpretive case studies in IS research: nature and method. Eur. J. Inf. Syst. **4**(2), 74–81 (1995)
47. Yin, R.K.: Case Study Research, Design and Methods, 4th edn. Sage Publications, London (2008)
48. Yazan, B.: Three approaches to case study methods in education: Yin merriam, and stake. Qual. Rep. **20**(2), 134–152 (2015)
49. Myers, M.D.: Qualitative Research in Business & Management. Sage, London (2013)
50. Financial Times.: Spread of fake news adds to Brazil's pandemic crisis. https://www.ft.com/content/ea62950e-89c0-4b8b-b458-05c90a55b81f (2020)
51. Reuters, Editorial: Fake news hurts trust in media, mainstream outlets fare better: poll. Reuters, 31 October 2017. https://www.reuters.com/article/us-media-fakenews-idUSKBN1D002S (2017)
52. Columbia Global Centers: Brazil and Its Challenges: Searching for Truth, Battling Misinformation. Annual Report 2020–2021 (2021)
53. Reuters, Editorial: Facebook, YouTube take down Bolsonaro video over false vaccine claim. https://www.reuters.com/world/americas/facebook-takes-down-bolsonaro-video-over-false-vaccine-claim-2021-10-25/ (2021)
54. El País.: Bolsonaro é "líder e porta-voz" das 'fake news' no país, diz relatório final da CPI da Pandemia, Relatório Final da CPI da Pandemia. https://brasil.elpais.com/brasil/2021-10-20/bolsonaro-e-lider-e-porta-voz-das-fake-news-no-pais-diz-relatorio-final-da-cpi-da-pandemia.html (2021)

55. Unesco.: Disinfodemic: Dissecting responses to COVID-19 disinformation, Policy Brief 2. https://en.unesco.org/sites/default/files/disinfodemic_dissecting_responses_covid19_disinformation.pdf (2020)
56. World Bank.: Open Data Essentials. http://opendatatoolkit.worldbank.org/en/essentials.html (2022)

Open Government and Open Data

How May an OGD Solution Help You? – An Information Behaviour Perspective

Jonathan Crusoe[1,2(✉)]

[1] Faculty of Librarianship, Information, Education and IT, Swedish School of Library and Information Science, University of Borås, 503 32 Borås, Sweden
jonathan.crusoe@hb.se

[2] Swedish Center for Digital Innovation, Department of Applied IT, University of Gothenburg, 405 30 Gothenburg, Sweden
jonathan.crusoe@ait.gu.se

Abstract. Information seekers express information behaviour (IB) when they seek or utilise information, which can help them work effectively, solve problems, or pursue hobbies. They can distil information from data. A growing source of data is open government data (OGD). While OGD is too raw for direct use, OGD solutions can help seekers to interpret and act on OGD. Previous OGD research lacks knowledge about the match between seekers' IB and OGD solutions' design. Therefore, this paper explores offered help of OGD solutions to seekers' IB, assuming a general set of IB since it tends to propend between technologies. This paper used qualitative content analysis to analyse OGD solutions, aiming for saturation. First, a code frame was built from previous IB research. Second, 74 OGD solutions were selected through purposive sampling. Third, 37 OGD solutions were subsume coded, because of saturation, whereas the remaining 37 OGD solutions were checked for negative cases. The findings show that an OGD solution can help a seeker by (1) providing a base or frame for interpretation, (2) taking a proactive or active role in the distillation of information from OGD, and (3) contextualising its help to a seeker's life. The findings unravelled the assumed general set of IB to reveal a new possible data behaviour (DB); where a seeker focuses on transforming and distributing information, distilled from OGD, to possibly satisfy the needs of other seekers.

Keywords: Open government data · Solution · Information behaviour · Data behaviour

1 Introduction

People, as information seekers, express information behaviour (IB) when they seek or utilise information [2]. These behaviours help seekers to satisfy information needs, which can originate from attempts to satisfy primary needs (e.g.,

M. Janssen et al. (Eds.): EGOV 2022, LNCS 13391, pp. 181–195, 2022.
https://doi.org/10.1007/978-3-031-15086-9_12

find food or shelter) [24,31]. The behaviours are unselfconscious, as seekers, for example, solve problems rather than seek or utilise information [2]. When seekers satisfy their needs, they can work effectively, solve problems, or pursue hobbies [24]. IB can also involve data since information can be distilled or drawn from them [5]. A growing new source of data is open government data (OGD), which is shared by public organisations for anyone to reuse freely [16,20]. OGD could enable seekers to determine the attractiveness of potential investments, scrutinise conclusions drawn from public data, and gain new insights into the public sector [16].

One OGD challenge is that seekers can be unable to directly use OGD for any meaningful purpose in their life, as the data are too raw [29]. On such cases, solutions (e.g., interactive maps and newspaper reports [7]) play a vital role to help seekers interpret and act on OGD and related information [15]. However, while the value of OGD comes from its use [20], seekers can seem irrational and chaotic in their IB, as they jump between needs [10]. They tend to minimise their seeking efforts, as they prioritise ease of access and use over quality [2], aiming for quick wins [24]. It is, as such, important to design solutions considering IB [24,26]. While previous OGD research has understood solutions as outputs, business models, and domain contributors [e.g., 7,17,21], it lacks knowledge about the match between seekers' IB and solutions' design. It can, therefore, be difficult to design helpful solutions based on OGD.

This paper explores OGD solutions' offered help to seekers' IB. **Help** means to make it possible or easier for someone by doing part of the work or by providing, for example, advice or support [28]. This paper analyses OGD solutions from an IB perspective to identify offered help, which is possible since seekers' IB tends to propend between technologies [2]. This paper is a step towards understanding how OGD solutions can be designed to be helpful for seekers. It limits its scope towards European OGD websites because of context familiarly and accessibility. This research was guided by the following research question:

- How have European OGD websites offered help to seekers in their information behaviour?

This paper starts by presenting previous research about IB and OGD solutions, which has guided this study. It then presents the used research approach and findings. It ends with a discussion about OGD solutions' offered help, the IB assumption, and implications, and conclusion.

2 Previous Research

2.1 Information Behaviour

The concept of IB originates from the discipline of information science [32]. IB has developed from several streams, such as library visitation, research diffusion, and social information usage [2]. IB encompasses the many ways in which seekers can interact with information [2]. One conclusion from previous IB research is that patterns in the seekers' IB emerge again and again even if new technologies are introduced. New technologies often offer better speed and use, while replicating social structures and interactions [2]. Based on this conclusion, this paper assumes a general behavioural set for seekers' IB that consists of *needing, seeking, using, or distributing* information [26,32]. This set was used to analyse the empirical material. The set includes four modes of IB: being aware (a seeker soaks up information in its environment), monitoring (a seeker maintains a back-of-the-mind alertness for interesting information), browsing (a seeker actively exposes itself to information driven by curiosity rather than a search for answers), and searching (a seeker actively seeks information that can satisfy its information need) [1].

A seeker can experience an information **need** when it encounters (1) information, (2) a curiosity, or (3) a knowledge gap [10,24,31]. An aware seeker who encounters information starts by using it. The encounter can happen when it conducts daily tasks or seeks other information [10]. It could give rise to new needs [30], such as a curiosity or knowledge gap. On the other hand, a curious seeker has to decide if it is going to stay aware (wait for an information encounter) or browse for information [1]. The latter means the seeker starts to seek information in the hopes of a meaningful information encounter [1]. Lastly, a seeker who experiences a previously encountered knowledge gap could reuse a solution that helped it last time. It can then, hopefully, move quickly from seeking information to using information. However, for new gaps, the seeker might need to gather information to concretise its need through reflections or social interactions [30]. If a seeker cannot express its need, its interactions with solutions can be awkward where it can demand information it does not need [19,24]. Moreover, a seeker **seeks** information by either browsing to encounter it or searching to find it [1]. This behaviour involves a search for solutions and information within solutions [24,30] (this paper focuses only on the latter). The seeker could follow references, explore content, surveil solutions, or talk with peers and experts [19,30,31]. In the seeking, a seeker can sample a number of solutions and then select from the options [1]. A seeker who cannot find sought-after information can give up. On the other hand, if the seeker finds the sought-after information, it can continue to use it. Furthermore, a seeker **uses** information when it, for example, interprets information for some purpose and evaluates information quality [24]. Information use is further explained in Sect. 2.2. Finally, a seeker **distributes** information when it shares the information beyond the used solution. For example, it can take the opportunity to share information with other seekers [31] or seek to reference the solution in other solutions (e.g., cite a study) [19,30]. The act of sharing information could give rise to an information encounter for other people.

2.2 Solutions

In information use, a seeker and a solution interact with a certain division of labour. A solution could help a seeker by doing part of some work or by providing data or information. Together, they can collect, store, process, and distribute data and information [5]. A solution that visualises data can, for example, help a seeker by acquiring, parsing, filtering, mining, representing, and refining the data. It can also allow the seeker to interact with the process by changing, for example, the data source or filter parameters. This change then propagates through the solution's work to change the presented information [12]. As such, the seeker can *customise* the offered help, which is both the solution's work and provided information.

Previous OGD research has approached OGD solutions from two broad approaches. First, this research has classified OGD solutions in practice. [7] explains a solution could help a seeker transform data to facts, data, information, interface, and service. [11] focus on the data to service transformation with related data, themes, and topics (e.g., list of first names, politics, and economics). [17] have grouped solutions into single-purpose apps (process data to a visualisation), interactive apps (enable seekers to share reviews or other information), information aggregators (combine multiple datasets that are then processed for presentation), comparison models (help seekers compare entities), open data repositories (help seekers search for data), and service platforms (allow seekers to search, import, clean, process, and visualise information). [21] classify solutions by domain (e.g., mobility and health) and features (e.g., GPS, payment, and problem resolution). Second, previous OGD research as designed and evaluated OGD solutions. [13] develop a solution using open crime data to offer safe urban navigation. [25] implements a storytelling solution where a seeker can reuse or upload data to then develop custom visualisations using a simple programming language. [8] develop a solution that presents the journeys of agricultural products from farms to stores. [18] implement a solution where a seeker can tag and link issues in governmental budget data, but also visualise and vote on these links. [4] demonstrate a solution where a seeker can explore and see big open linked data to answer questions about, for example, politicians, companies, and government funding.

3 Research Approach

This qualitative study explored the offered help from OGD solutions through artefact studies [14]. A qualitative approach was required to gain a deeper understanding of a specific phenomenon [23], enabling the construction of a rich interpretive description. An artefact study generates detailed empirical material concerning the functions and properties of artefacts, giving limited information about seekers' views and use of said artefacts [14]. The approach of studying artefacts instead of seekers was possible, as the underlying propensities of seekers' IB emerge again with each wave of technology [2]. However, this assumption is also a limitation of this study that is later discussed (see Sect. 5.2). The study applied qualitative content analysis (QCA) on the empirical material [27], following these steps: (1) build a code frame, (2) select and segment OGD solutions, (3) subsume code the segments. The study iterated between Steps 2 and 3, aiming for saturation (further data collection no longer sparks new insights or reveals new properties) [6].

First, a code frame was built to give a structure for the empirical material [27]. It followed a mixed QCA approach where previous research is used to define generic concepts whereas specific concepts (help) are derived from the empirical material and sorted following the generic concepts [27]. Previous IB research guided the attention of this study, while empirical material refined and developed the code frame. Table 1 presents the initial code frame. The main concept is the focus of this study, while the generic concepts are explained in Sect. 2. The analytical questions were used in Step 3.

Table 1. A code frame for OGD solutions' offered help with references.

Main Concept		
OGD solutions' help offered to seekers' IB		
Generic Concepts	**Analytical Questions**	**References**
Need	(1) How does the solution help a seeker encounter information or a curiosity? (2) How does the solution help a seeker concretise, formulate, or express its need?	[1, 10, 19, 24, 30, 31]
Seek	(1) How does the solution help a seeker browse to encounter or search to find data or information?	[1, 19, 24, 30, 31]
Use	(1) How does the solution help a seeker by providing data or information? (2) How can the seeker customise this help?	[5, 7, 12, 17, 24]
Distribute	(1) How does the solution help a seeker share or spread its data or information?	[19, 30, 31]

Second, select and segment OGD solutions. This step started with desktop research to identify sources of OGD solutions. Multiple sources contribute towards data triangulation, improving the study's validity [22]. A source was relevant if it presented OGD solutions as use cases (indicating practitioners perceive them as helpful), being European (researcher familiarly with context), and written in English or Swedish (researcher proficiency). In total, six relevant websites were identified: (1) the European Data Portal, (2) the Swedish Open Data Portal, (3) Swedish Traffic Lab, (4) JobTech Development initiative by the Swedish Public Employment Service, (5) the Irish Open Data Portal, and (6) EuroStat visualisation Tools[1]. This study's focus on saturation [6] meant that purposive sampling [9] was used to select OGD solutions. An OGD solution was considered relevant if it was a website, its language in English or Swedish, being European (familiarity with context), accessible to the public (free to use), not gamified (as gamified solutions were perceived to focus more on having fun than

[1] The 2nd and 4th websites have since the data collection been updated and removed the use cases. The empirical material was still included in this study.

satisfying information needs), and usable (not broken or retired). The sampling aimed for variety, as such OGD solutions with new or unique functions and properties were prioritised, while familiar OGD solutions were only included if more evidence was needed. In total, 74 solutions were hand-picked for this study. The hand-picked solutions were prepared for analysis through segmentation, where the empirical material is divided into segments that can be coded and related to the code frame [27]. Screenshots were taken to capture important functions and properties for each hand-picked solution (using qSnap). When needed, files were downloaded (e.g., PDF guides or datasets stored in CSV). The final result was 798 segments divided over 74 solutions.

Third, the segments were analysed with subsumption coding. Subsumption coding is used if the researcher has an idea about the main concept [27]. The coding started by examining the segments, one solution at a time, to answer the analytical questions in Table 1. The examination of a solution's functions and properties could generate multiple answers to one analytical question. If an answer matched a specific concept from the code frame, the answer was merged with the existing specific concept. Else, a specific concept was created and given a tentative name. On the other hand, if the collected segments for a solution could not give a proficient answer, the solution was revisited for further data collection. Saturation was reached once 37 solutions had been analysed (451 segments). Sixteen of the 37 analysed solutions verified previously identified concepts without adding new concepts. Saturation needed to be ensured, as such the segments for the remaining 37 solutions were examined for negative cases. No negative cases were identified, improving the validity of the study [22]. This step ended with a refinement of the specific concepts by giving them final names and merging similar specific concepts.

4 Findings

This section presents this paper's findings following the code frame (see Table 1): needing, seeking, using, and distributing OGD and related information, hence on content. Footnotes are used to present good examples of OGD solutions offering a certain help. Table 2 presents an overview of the final code frame based on Table 1. The generic concepts and concepts are defined from previous research (see Sect. 2), while the various ways of help (specific concepts) are derived from the empirical material.

4.1 Need

When a seeker needs certain content either because of curiosity or gap, an OGD solution can help the seeker encounter content or formulate its information need.

Table 2. Overview of the final code frame. # = occurrences of certain help.

Generic Concept	**Need**				**Seek**			
Concept	*Encounter*	#	*Formulate*	#	*Browse*	#	*Search*	#
Help (Specific Concept)	Insights	8	Themes	29	Filter	12	Scan	15
	Suggest	8	Questions	4	Flip	8	Comb	7
	Setup	11	Nudge	8	Traverse	13		

Generic Concept	**Use**						**Distribute**	
Concept	*Represent*	#	*Support*	#	*Adapt*	#	*Share or Spread*	#
Help (Specific Concept)	Comparative	21	Elucidate	23	Acquisition	11	Refer	24
	Movement	15	Understand	24	Customisation	15	Embed	8
	Relative	11	Facilitate	13	Personalise	11	Extract	25

An OGD solution can create an **encounter** in three ways. First, it can provide *insights*, which are highlights in or conclusions from the content[2]. The insights can range from content panels to articles. Second, the OGD solution can *suggest* content to the seeker, such as top rankings, alternatives, and new content[3]. Third, the OGD solution can *setup* its content in an initial structure to create an encounter upon a seeker's arrival to the page[4]. On the other hand, a seeker might need help **formulating** its information need, including the potential for an OGD solution to satisfy it. A common approach amongst OGD solutions is to use *themes* where an OGD solution position itself within a topic or issue, such as European legal documents[5] or archaeology (See footnote 3). This approach leaves broad leeway for a seeker to identify an overlap between its need and the solution's content. Another approach is that an OGD solution presents *questions* it aims to answer using OGD[6]. This approach restricts the possible overlap between the need and content, but presents a clear purpose for the OGD solution. Alternatively, a seeker might need help in its interaction with an OGD solution. An OGD solution can *nudge* the seeker towards certain actions, such as "Click on a country" or a search field containing example keywords (e.g., "Germany" or "Clean energy")[7].

4.2 Seek

When a seeker seeks certain content because of curiosity or gap, an OGD solution can help it browse or search its content. A seeker can **browse** content when the OGD solution gives access to most or all its content (at once) where the seeker

[2] Commuting in Ireland 2016 - https://public.tableau.com/app/profile/arup.ireland/viz/CommutingInIreland2006-2016/CommutinginIreland.

[3] Ariadne - https://portal.ariadne-infrastructure.eu/.

[4] Eurostat - Regions and Cities Illustrated https://ec.europa.eu/eurostat/cache/RCI/.

[5] Lexparency - https://lexparency.org/.

[6] Shedding light on energy in the EU - https://ec.europa.eu/eurostat/cache/infographs/energy/.

[7] Keep.eu - https://keep.eu/.

needs to filter, flip through, or traverse this content. The seeker can *filter* the content to reduce it, which enables it to encounter relevant content or identify patterns. The content can be divided into a list of categories[8] or presented as a dashboard. In the latter, a seeker can wrangle the content by applying keywords and changing parameters (See footnote 2). The seeker can *flip* through the OGD solution's content by scrolling through lists or moving between tabs[9]. The hierarchy of content is flat with no opportunity to filter the content. On the other hand, the seeker can *traverse* the content by moving between categories or subsets of the content. The content is divided over a multi-level hierarchy. In an aggregation, this help can enable the seeker to drill into the statistics looking at how parts become a whole[10].

A seeker can **search** for content when an OGD solution offers the functionality to scan or comb its content. A search brings out some selected content from a larger body of obfuscate content. A seeker can *scan* the content by using simple keyword searches where the solution presents a list of results[11]. A seeker can *comb* the content when it uses keywords combined with various parameters and sliders, which allows the seeker greater granularity or delicacy when selecting content[12].

4.3 Use

When a seeker uses certain content, an OGD solution can help by representing the content, supporting the seeker's interpretation of the content, and adapting its help to the seeker's needs.

A seeker might need help when distilling or drawing information from OGD. An OGD solution can provide and combine various **representations** of OGD for this purpose. An OGD solution can provide a *comparative* representation where similarities or differences are made clearly visible, such as bar charts or map charts[13]. An OGD solution can also provide a *movement* representation, highlighting the transfers of data between nodes or changes in data over time. It can be presented in Sankey diagrams or line charts (See footnote 6). Another approach is to provide a *relative* representation where the relations, occurrences, density, relativity, or concentrations of the content are important. It can be interactive maps, word clouds, or heat maps (See footnote 3).

A seeker might need **support** to interpret the content. An OGD solution can help to *elucidate* content by providing various approaches to see it. Eluci-

---

8 Irish Heritage Map - https://www.heritagemaps.ie/WebApps/HeritageMaps/index.html.

9 YouthMetre - https://youthmetre.eu/youthmetre/.

10 Where Your Money Goes - https://whereyourmoneygoes.gov.ie/en/.

11 Platsminnen (eng. "Place Memories") was publicly available on data collection, but later became commercialised - https://www.platsminnen.se/.

12 OpenOpps - https://openopps.com/.

13 Which country suits EU best? - https://public.tableau.com/shared/2DQ98NPYG?:toolbar=n&:display_count=n&:origin=viz_share_link.

dation can involve giving a statistical overview that is potentially represented (See footnote 7). It can also be that the same OGD is presented using different representations side by side, enabling the drawing of different information (See footnote 4); or showing and hiding layers on a map[14]. On the other hand, an OGD solution can attempt to help a seeker to *understand* its content. This help can be allowing to change the content's language[15]; bestowing certain colour meanings to values (e.g., map charts using one colour for low values and another colour for high values)[16]; or explaining terminology or patterns (See footnote 6). Alternatively, a seeker might want help an OGD solution cannot directly offer, but could enable. Thus, the OGD solution can *facilitate* social communication where it asks other seekers to contribute to improving its help. A seeker could be asked to review a product[17] or be able to create groups and discuss the content (See footnote 5). This help can also involve the organisation of communities, supporting the usage of content (See footnote 20); or the presentation of contact information to help seekers to, for example, find where to buy a product (See footnote 17) or contact a politician[18].

A seeker might need to **adapt** an OGD solution's offered help, which could happen in three ways. First, an OGD solution can allow a seeker to adapt its *acquisition* of content, by allowing the seeker to upload content (See footnote 8) or request content[19]. Second, a seeker might want to add *customisation* to the offered help. On such occasions, the OGD solution can provide tools to, for example, draw or measure (See footnote 8). It can include the ability to save the present view for later (See footnote 14). Another approach is to customise the OGD solution's work, such as asking it to notify the seeker when its content changes (See footnote 12). Third, a seeker might want to *personalise* the offered help. The solution can allow the seeker to switch content representation, change comparisons, or create representations of content (See footnote 20). The seeker can provide personal content, which the OGD solution uses when processing OGD into information (See footnote 13).

4.4 Distribute

When a seeker wants to distribute some content, an OGD solution can enable it to **share or spread** it. A seeker might want to *refer* to the content by sharing a link or on social media (See footnote 12). A seeker might want to *embed* the content in other solutions, such as through an iframe or API[20]. Lastly, a seeker

14 Ireland's Marine Atlas - https://atlas.marine.ie/.

15 What Europe does for me - https://www.what-europe-does-for-me.eu/.

16 Atlas of the Sky - https://ec.europa.eu/transport/modes/air/aos/aos_public.html.

17 GoodGuide helps seekers to find health products. Sadly, it was discontinued after data collection.

18 MEPRanking, MEPVote, and MEPTwitter were publicly available on data collection, but have since then commercialised - http://www.mepsoftware.eu/mepranking.php.

19 GetThere.ie - https://getthere.ie/.

20 OpenSpending - https://openspending.org/.

might want to *extract* the content by, for example, downloading a visualisation or the underlying OGD or printing a map (See footnote 8). The extracted content can be spread to other seekers and solutions without being dependent on the OGD solution. On the other hand, the two previous ways of help are dependent on the existence of the solution.

5 Discussion

This paper explored how OGD solutions can help seekers' IB (see Sect. 4), which is a step towards designing helpful OGD solutions. Previous OGD research argues that the value of OGD comes from its usage [20] where the processing of OGD *"[...] is simply the hoop [seekers] have to jump through to gain answers to their questions"*. [16, p. 265]. This paper extends this focus by including the needing, seeking, and distributing OGD and related information (hence on content). This section discusses patterns in how OGD solutions can help seekers, the assumed general set of IB, and implications for OGD practice and OGD research.

5.1 How May an OGD Solution Help You?

Seekers can be unable to meaningfully use OGD, as it is too raw [29]. This paper's findings contain patterns, showing that OGD solutions have multiple ways to overcome this challenge, as such help a seeker's IB. Generally, the hand-picked OGD solutions help seekers following three patterns, each containing an important range of help. This subsection discusses the three patterns in relation to previous OGD research, helping to interpret the findings from an IB perspective. An OGD solution can, at various locations in a seeker's IB, provide help that is specifically different, but generally similar, as such patterns emerged in the findings.

First, the findings' *represent* and *theme* mean an OGD solution can help a seeker interpret OGD by providing a base or frame for interpretation. This pattern is in line with previous OGD research, such as single-purpose apps, comparison models, and open data repositories [17] or data to facts [7]. It is open-ended and multivocal, as a seeker could reach various conclusions from the same OGD. It requires the seeker to possess certain previous knowledge else the OGD can be unintelligible. In addition, the findings' *elucidate* and *understand* mean an OGD solution can attempt to make OGD more comprehensible to a seeker. This addition could reduce the demand on a seeker's previous knowledge. Previous OGD research presents OGD solutions designed for the first pattern, such as [8] present an OGD solution that can help a seeker follow the journey of agricultural products and [4] give an OGD solution that can help a seeker explore OGD for answers. In the findings, the occurrences of certain help for the first pattern together with previous OGD research indicate the first pattern to be common, which could be because it is easy to design and allows for more diverse usage.

Second, the findings' *insight* (as highlights), *suggest*, *setup*, *questions*, and *nudge* mean an OGD solution can take a proactive role in the distillation of information from OGD. This pattern is noticeable in previous OGD research, such as being similar to [7]'s data to information and [17]s' information aggregators. The OGD solution can shepherd the seeker towards actions and content it believes could satisfy the seeker's needs. It can help the seeker formulate its need or encounter interesting content, but increases the requirements for the OGD solution to be designed with consideration to the seeker's IB. Furthermore, the findings' *insight* (as conclusions), *understand* (as explanations), and *personalisation* mean an OGD solution can have an active role in the distillation of information from data. This help reduces the workload for a seeker, but can restrain the ability to see alternative conclusions. It further adds to the requirement of fitting a solution's design with a seeker's IB. In previous OGD research, [13] present a good example of an OGD solution that offers safe urban navigation. This solution allows a seeker to enter a start location and a destination where the app then calculates a safe route for the seeker to follow. In the findings, the occurrences of certain help for the second pattern together with previous OGD research show the second pattern to be rarer in relation to the first pattern. This rarity could come from that it is more complex to design or requires data analytical expertise, but also knowledge about the seeker's need and its IB.

Third, the findings' *browse*, *search*, *adapt*, and *facilitate* mean an OGD solution can contextualise its help or content, making it meaningful to the life of a seeker. This pattern is in line with previous OGD research, such as [17]s' interactive apps, information aggregators, and service platforms and [7]'s data to interface. In its simplest form, it allows a seeker to influence the help of an OGD solution to, for example, find relevant content. Continued influencing can allow the seeker to understand the "thinking" of an OGD solution, as such formulate how it could best express its need to find relevant content [19,24]. In a more advanced form, this pattern enables a seeker to adapt the help of an OGD solution similar to *customise* in Sect. 2.2 and Sect. 4.3. This adaptation helps an OGD solution to contextualise its help to the life of the seeker. On the other hand, in a more complex form, an OGD solution helps a seeker build new meanings on the solution's help and content within a context. This help can possibly allow a seeker to make an OGD solution valuable in its life and context. However, it requires that the solution is designed to be contextualised for the seeker's life. Previous OGD research also contains OGD solutions designed following the third pattern. For example, [18] present an OGD solution where seekers can create new meanings about budget data, while [25] gives an OGD solution where a seeker can create custom visualisations and share them with others. In the findings, the occurrences of certain help for the third pattern together with previous OGD research indicate the third pattern to be more popular than the second, but less than the first. This ranking is unexpected, as it could be concluded that contextualisation is more difficult than proactively or actively help a seeker distil information from OGD. However, an OGD solution can provide both the second and third pattern (e.g., [13]s' OGD solution provides a personalised route based on seeker's input). In addition, an OGD solution that focuses on the third pattern can facilitate social communication, as such enables its seekers to generate content (driving the contextualisation). Furthermore, the first pattern acts as a base for the other two patterns out of necessity to interpret OGD or related information.

5.2 Assuming the Seeker' IB

This paper has assumed a general set of IB, as seekers' IB tends to be propend between technologies [2]. This assumption was useful to analyse the hand-picked OGD solutions. It provided structure and direction for the analysis and made intricate details in the OGD solutions' offered help comprehensible. However, the assumption lead to a realisation about the findings' help of *refer* and *extract.* IB states that a seeker unselfconsciously seeks information to satisfy needs [2, 24], while previous OGD research presents a spectrum between (1) satisfying needs and (2) creating information for others based on OGD [e.g., 3,7,17]. A good example is the difference between a single-purpose app and an open data repository [17] or data to data [7]. The two sides overlap as a seeker in both cases can get help with needing and seeking content whereas using and distributing it differ. On the first side of the spectrum, a seeker uses and distributes content following previous IB research, including the distillation of OGD into information (see Sect. 2). Previous OGD research has designed OGD solutions for this side [e.g., 8,13,25]. On the second side of the spectrum, a seeker extracts or embeds content into an OGD solution (see Sect. 4.4), which can partly be understood through previous OGD research [e.g., 3,7,11]. This type of seeker needs and seeks OGD for the purpose to transform it into information, which could be used by others to satisfy needs. However, previous OGD research has not provided a name for this set of behaviours, as such it is labelled data behaviours (DB) to differentiate them from IB, highlighting a new research avenue.

5.3 Implications

This paper has some implications for OGD practitioners and OGD researchers. OGD developers can use the findings (see Sect. 4) as a basis for designing OGD solutions, ensuring they have covered vital options. It can help them to think about how their design help seekers' IB. They are recommended to consider how they are making OGD and related information meaningful for seekers and how they are making their OGD solutions adapt to or facilitate seekers' IB. On the other hand, OGD researchers can use this paper's findings to further study OGD solutions' offered help, but also as a basis for evaluating their helpfulness.

6 Conclusion

Previous OGD research lacks knowledge about the match between seekers' IB and solutions' design. As such, this paper has explored the help offered by OGD solutions (focusing on European OGD websites), revealing how they have tackled the rawness challenge of OGD [29]. It is a step towards designing OGD solutions that are helpful for seekers' IB, but also extends the previous argument that the value of OGD comes from its usage [16,20]. The paper's findings show that an OGD solution can help a seeker following three patterns. First, an OGD solution can provide a base or frame for interpretation, which can be enhanced to ease the comprehension of the OGD, lowering the demand on a seeker's previous knowledge. Second, an OGD solution can take a proactive or active role in the distillation of information from OGD, reducing a seeker's workload. Third, an OGD solution can contextualise its help to a seeker's life, making OGD meaningful for the seeker. Furthermore, the usage of an IB perspective for the study of OGD solutions revealed an unnamed set of seeker behaviours, concerning the creation of information from OGD for others. This set was labelled data behaviours (DB) to highlight a new research avenue and differentiate DB from IB.

This paper has some limitations. The analysis was driven by the researcher's interpretations rather than that of practitioners, as such open to bias. The analysis reached saturation once 37 of 74 OGD solutions had been analysed where no negative cases were identified in the remaining OGD solutions. The sample consisted of hand-picked OGD solutions where all were European websites. It is possible that other mediums can provide other help and other contexts constrain offered help in new ways. This paper's findings can be used to understand and describe OGD solutions, but not explain or predict their possible helpfulness. While previous IB research has helped to ground the findings, the findings needs further validation in other contexts.

References

1. Bates, M.J.: Toward an integrated model of information seeking and searching. New Rev. Inf. Behav. Res. **3**(1), 1–15 (2002)
2. Bates, M.J.: Information behavior. Encycl. Libr. Inf. Sci. **3**, 2381–2391 (2010)
3. Begany, G.M., Gil-Garcia, J.R.: Understanding the actual use of open data: levels of engagement and how they are related. Telematics Inform. **63**, 101673 (2021)
4. Böhm, C., et al.: Govwild: integrating open government data for transparency. In: Proceedings of the 21st International Conference on World Wide Web, pp. 321–324. ACM New York, NY, USA (2012)
5. Checkland, P., Holwell, S.: Information, Systems and Information Systems. Wiley, Hoboken (1997)
6. Creswell, J.W., Creswell, J.D.: Research Design: Qualitative, Quantitative, and Mixed Methods Approaches. Sage publications, California (2017)
7. Davies, T.: Open data, democracy and public sector reform - a look at open government data use from data.gov.uk (2010). http://www.opendataimpacts.net/report/wp-content/uploads/2010/08/How-is-open-government-data-being-used-in-practice.pdf
8. Deng, D., Mai, G.-S., Shiau, S.: Construction and reuse of linked agriculture data: an experience of taiwan government open data. In: Ichise, R., Lecue, F., Kawamura, T., Zhao, D., Muggleton, S., Kozaki, K. (eds.) JIST 2018. LNCS, vol. 11341, pp. 367–382. Springer, Cham (2018). https://doi.org/10.1007/978-3-030-04284-4_25

9. Denscombe, M.: The Good Research Guide: For Small-scale Social Research. McGraw Hill, New York (2010)
10. Erdelez, S.: Information encountering: it's more than just bumping into information. Bull. Am. Soc. Inf. Sci. Technol. **25**(3), 26–29 (1999)
11. Foulonneau, M., Martin, S., Turki, S.: How open data are turned into services? In: Snene, M., Leonard, M. (eds.) IESS 2014. LNBIP, vol. 169, pp. 31–39. Springer, Cham (2014). https://doi.org/10.1007/978-3-319-04810-9_3
12. Fry, B.J.: Computational information design. Ph.D. thesis. Massachusetts Institute of Technology (2004)
13. Galbrun, E., Pelechrinis, K., Terzi, E.: Urban navigation beyond shortest route: the case of safe paths. Inf. Syst. **57**, 160–171 (2016)
14. Goldkuhl, G.: The generation of qualitative data in information systems research: the diversity of empirical research methods. Commun. Assoc. Inf. Syst. **44**, 572–599 (2019)
15. Hunnius, S., Krieger, B.: The social shaping of open data through administrative processes. In: Riehle, D., et al. (eds.) Proceedings of The International Symposium on Open Collaboration, pp. 1–5. Association for Computing Machinery (2014)
16. Janssen, M., Charalabidis, Y., Zuiderwijk, A.: Benefits, adoption barriers and myths of open data and open government. Inf. Syst. Manag. **29**(4), 258–268 (2012)
17. Janssen, M., Zuiderwijk, A.: Infomediary business models for connecting open data providers and users. Soc. Sci. Comput. Rev. **32**(5), 694–711 (2014)
18. Kim, N.W., et al.: Budgetmap: engaging taxpayers in the issue-driven classification of a government budget. In: Proceedings of the 19th ACM Conference on Computer-Supported Cooperative Work & Social Computing, pp. 1028–1039 (2016)
19. Kuhlthau, C.C.: Inside the search process: information seeking from the user's perspective. J. Am. Soc. Inf. Sci. **42**(5), 361–371 (1991)
20. Lee, D.: Building an open data ecosystem: an irish experience. In: Estevez, E., Janssen, M., Soares Barbosa, L. (eds.) Proceedings of the 8th International Conference on Theory and Practice of Electronic Governance, pp. 351–360. Association for Computing Machinery (2014)
21. Mainka, A., Hartmann, S., Meschede, C., Stock, W.G.: Mobile application services based upon open urban government data. In: iConference 2015 Proceedings, pp. 1–15. iSchools (2015)
22. Mays, N., Pope, C.: Assessing quality in qualitative research. BMJ **320**(7226), 50–52 (2000)
23. Myers, M.D.: Qualitative Research in Business and Management. Sage Publications Limited, California (2013)
24. Nicholas, D., Herman, E.: Assessing Information Needs in the Age of the Digital Consumer. Routledge (2010)
25. Petricek, T.: Tools for open, transparent and engaging storytelling. In: Sartor, J., D'Hondt, T., De Meuter, W. (eds.) Companion to the first International Conference on the Art, Science and Engineering of Programming, pp. 1–2 (2017)
26. Pettigrew, K.E., Fidel, R., Bruce, H.: Conceptual frameworks in information behavior. Annual review of information science and technology (ARIST), **35**(43–78) (2001)
27. Schreier, M.: Qualitative Content Analysis in Practice. Sage publications (2012)
28. The Cambridge Dictionary: Help. Cambridge University Press (2019). https://dictionary.cambridge.org/dictionary/english/help. Accessed 01 Oct 2019

29. Weerakkody, V., Irani, Z., Kapoor, K., Sivarajah, U., Dwivedi, Y.K.: Open data and its usability: an empirical view from the citizen's perspective. Inf. Syst. Front. **19**(2), 285–300 (2017). https://doi.org/10.1007/s10796-016-9679-1
30. Westbrook, L.: User needs: a synthesis and analysis of current theories for the practitioner. RQ **32**(4), 541–549 (1993)
31. Wilson, T.D.: On user studies and information needs. J. Documentation **37**(1), 3–15 (1981)
32. Wilson, T.D.: Models in information behaviour research. J. Documentation **55**(3), 249–270 (1999)

Open Technologies for Public Tendering. Blockchain Technology Impact on Transparency and Efficiency of Public Procurement Processes

Manuel Pedro Rodríguez Bolívar(✉) and Manuel Prados Prados

University of Granada, 18071 Granada, Spain
{manuelp,maprados}@ugr.es

Abstract. Although public procurement accounts for a substantial share of the GDP and is recognised as a relevant aspect in public administrations, it is not always conducted efficiently and transparently. In this regard, the evaluation of these aspects in public procurement processes is essential and it is mainly focused on the analysis of both competition and financial and administrative efficiency (cost and time savings) of these processes. The implementation of emerging technologies promises to ensure transparency and access to public tenders, increasing competition, simplifying processes for contract award and management, driving time and cost savings. Considering the lack of a strong empirical grounding of the impact of emerging technologies on these aspects, this research addresses this research gap by aiming to analyse the transparency, in terms of competition, and the efficiency, in terms of cost and time savings, of public procurement processes performed under Blockchain technology (BCT) based platforms. Findings reveal a great impact of BCT based platforms especially on cost and time savings, deriving avenues for future research.

Keywords: Blockchain · Public procurement · Transparency · Efficiency · Emerging technologies

1 Introduction

Governments are increasingly recognising the great power of public procurement to solve many of the key policy challenges that the countries are facing, including the fight against corruption and collusion, market access for SMEs, citizens' trust in public authorities, innovation and environmentally and socially sustainable growth [1]. In fact, public procurement accounts for a substantial share of the GDP - 14% in Europe [2], 12% in OECD countries (see https://www.oecd.org/gov/public-procurement/), plays a key role in the OECD [3] to be used for achieving smart, sustainable and inclusive growth while ensuring the most efficient use of public funds [4].

Nonetheless, although considered a critical aspect to all government functions, it requires being analysed [5] to be conducted efficiently and transparently [6]. This way, the evaluation of these systems is essential, particular in terms of measuring the impact

Published by Springer Nature Switzerland AG 2022
M. Janssen et al. (Eds.): EGOV 2022, LNCS 13391, pp. 196–211, 2022.
https://doi.org/10.1007/978-3-031-15086-9_13

of public procurement on policy objectives [3] focused, especially, on both transparency and financial efficiency and effectiveness of public spending [7].

Up to now, traditional public procurement processes have been demonstrated to be inefficient and corruption, outright bribery and collusive practices have found here a good ground for growing [8]. Under this framework, the adoption of new technologies in procurement has increased transparency (improving the trust of bidders) and competition (improving the financial efficiency) [9] and revolutionised the way vital upstream supply networks are managed [10] and innovation [3]. It has demonstrated to create public value through the dissemination of information and knowledge [11], enabling purchase and supply chain practices [12].

In the last years, the implementation of emerging technologies is aimed at ensuring transparency and access to public tenders, increasing competition, simplifying processes for contract award and management and reducing costs [3]. Although Blockchain technology (BCT) has been widely tested in various domains, BCT implementation in public procurement area is of particularly relevance. Specifically, distributed ledger (DLT) solutions can truly complement e-gov reforms enhancing trust-building practices [13, 14], speeding up various public information management procedures, and providing a platform for delivering public services over encrypted communication channels [15]. It has made to increase the interest in using BCT to solve problems of scale and trust inherent in responsible business conducts [16].

Indeed, BCT promises to have a high impact on transparency, integrity, autonomy, and overall speed-up procurement cycles [17] and put emphasis on the need of assessing the potential scenarios of a wider uptake of public DLT-based network [18]. This assessment is especially important on transparency, effectiveness, and savings of the public procurement system for benchmarking purposes with the aim at supporting strategic policy making on public procurement in public procurement processes [3].

Nonetheless, academic research in the implementation of emerging technologies in this field often lacks a strong theoretical and empirical grounding [19]. Thus, to acquire a high level of knowledge about DLT implementation, the European Parliament [18] points out that the use of cases is essential and, at this respect, it welcomes research aimed at improving assessment of the potential opportunities and challenges of emerging technologies in support of better decision-making processes in public procurement. Lindman et al. [20] also indicates that experimentation with BCT is important, but those lessons and takeaways should be shared.

In brief, this study addresses this research gap by aiming to analyse the transparency, in terms of competition, and the efficiency, in terms of financial and administrative efficiency, of public procurement processes performed under BCT based platforms. The main research question is: do BCT based platforms for public procurement improve transparency (competition) and efficiency (cost and time savings) compared to web-based procurement processes?. In addressing the research aims, as a first approach to this topic, this study draws on the comparison of an example of public purchasing of reusable face masks that protect against Covid-19 performed under a BCT based platform in the Region of Aragon (Spain) -leading example in Europe [17] up to May 2021- vs those under web-based platforms in all Spanish public entities up to 31st May 2021.

2 BCT and Its Potential Impact on Public Procurement

Traditional public procurement processes have been perceived as a clerical and order placing function which has limited the improvement of transparency and fraud combat [21]. This way, in the last decades, public administrations have been aware of the need of implementing information technology in public procurement processes to increase transparency, efficiency of interaction and removal of corruption in public competitive procedures [22]. In this regard, it seems clear that public sector procurement has progressed over the years because of the electronic technology boom, which impels digital procurement practices on public sector entities [23].

However, the steps taken into digital public procurement can be separated into two main stages. At the beginning, public entities used non-disruptive technologies -called "basic digital technologies" by Kosmol et al. [19]- and only tried to upload on electronic means all the phases of the procurement process and all the information needed for the tender. As noted, this stage does not provide changes in the procurement procedures but only in the way of access to the process, usually through the Internet – e-procurement web systems- [24, 25].

Nonetheless, in the last years, the development of emerging technologies (ETs) such as big data, internet of things (IoT), machine learning, artificial intelligence (AI), remote sensing, cloud computing, social media communication and blockchain, is providing the governments with the capacities for disrupting the way that public procurement processes are being performed [26]. In this research, we focus our attention on the BCT implementation in the public procurement process due to its main features revolving around decentralised registers, immutability, trust, coordination, or security [27], which impact notably, among others, on two main aspects of public procurement processes: transparency (immutability of the BCT system) and efficiency (speed, performance, error free, cost savings) – [28, 29]. In fact, both the principle of transparency and the efficiency are fundamental and underlying principles of EU public procurement rules [1, 30].

Regarding transparency, BCT implementation in public procurement processes should result in improving transparency by creating a window on governmental functioning in these processes. This emerging technology can help to fight against both corruption by creating reputation lists accessible to all participants [31] and collusive practices by increasing trust in the public procurement system [32]. In this regard, competition is a key aspect of transparency in public procurement processes making them more efficient.

Indeed, competitive processes help public procurement process to both be more transparent [33] and provides less perception for corruption in public tenders [34], building trust in institutions among citizens [33]. In addition, the greater competition among suppliers, the lower awarding prices because of the lowest cost bidders' selection [35]. As the OCDE [3] indicates, competitive procedures should be the standard method for conducting procurement as a means of driving efficiencies, fighting corruption, obtaining fair and reasonable pricing, and ensuring competitive outcomes. Therefore, the following research question is derived:

RQ1. Do BCT based platforms increase transparency in public procurement processes through increasing bid competition compared to those web-based platforms?

Concerning efficiency, according to the OECD [5], the primary objective of public procurement is to deliver goods and services necessary to accomplish government missions in a timely, economical, and efficient manner. Prior research has indicated that using an electronic and automated system from purchase posting up to the issuance of contract is perceived to be efficient [36]. In fact, the e-procurement system's ability to reduce procurement costs is likely one of the most important factors for e-procurement systems adoption [37–40] mainly for fiscally stressed and managerial innovative state governments [41].

Nonetheless, empirical experiences indicate that one main challenge of e-procurement platforms is the adoption of fully privately run and competing platforms [42]. This way, compared to web-based, the European Parliament [18] has recognised that DLT systems, especially blockchain technologies, reduce intermediation costs in a trusted environment between the transacting parties and allows peer-to-peer exchange of value that can empower citizens. Therefore, the following research question is derived:

RQ2. Do BCT based platforms reduce cost of supplies in public procurement processes compared to those web-based platforms?

Finally, BCT based platforms for public procurement is not only expected to reduce costs, but also to produce efficient administrative procedures. In this regard, recent research has indicated that BCT can introduce time savings because it reduces the time spent for both processing documentation [31] and handling reporting and meetings making all processes automated [43].

Therefore, the following research question is derived:

RQ3. Do BCT based platforms produce time savings in public procurement processes compared to those web-based platforms?

3 Empirical Research

3.1 Sample Selection and Data Collection

According to Mackey and Cuomo [44], prior research has focused mainly on electronic data transfer and/or e-procurement systems, whereas fewer articles have discussed emerging technologies solutions. Therefore, this paper focuses its attention on a BCT based platform for public procurement processes adopted by the Regional Government of Aragon in Spain. This BCT based platform was created for processing simplified open procurement procedures (see procurement process for selecting a firm to create this BCT platform in the Spanish National Procurement Platform [59]), is considered a leading example of BCT experience in Europe for public procurement process [17] -the first one in Spain- and integrates the interaction between the red Ethereum (public BCT) and Hyperledger (private BCT). The first one was used for both validating of the smart contracts and making all the processes public, whereas the second one was used for firms to make all interactions in the process (upload their offers, sign their offers, etc.).

The process to participate in a procurement process based on this BCT platform is simple: a) the tendering process is disclosed, which is accessible to all potential tenders;

b) The tender registers its offer into the system with electronic fingerprint, creating a Hash code; c) The tender submits all the data an documentation included into its offer; d) After the offering deadline, the manager of the contract can admit or exclude offers explaining all the motives involved in this decision; e) A smart contract is applied for scoring all offers taking into account the criteria defined at the beginning of the procurement process; f) The tendering process is awarded to one of the tenders.

To compare transparency (competition) and efficiency (cost and time savings) of procurement processes undertaken in this BCT based platform vs traditional e-procurement mechanisms (usually through Internet), we performed a search of simplified open procurement processes undertaken in the BCT based platform of the Regional Government of Aragon and we only found one process performed and finished (up to 31st May 2021). This process, with reference expedient number HAP SCC 17/2020 was addressed to acquire 35,000 reusable face masks that protect against Covid-19.

Later, we performed a search on the Spanish National Procurement Platform about simplified procurement processes in e-procurement web systems with the aim of acquiring the same type of reusable face mask to protect against Covid-19. In Spain all public administrations are enforced to publish all their public procurement processes into this Spanish National Procurement Portal (art. 334 of the Royal Legislative Decree 3/2011, of November 14, approving the revised text of the Public Sector Contract Law). The search was performed following different phases. Initially, we made a search on the Internet with the aim at identifying all common public procurement vocabulary codes (CPVs) in which reusable face masks could be tendered. This resulted in the following CPV list: 18100000-Work clothes, special work clothes and accessories; 18143000-Protective clothing; 33000000-Medical, pharmaceutical, and personal hygiene items and equipment; 33140000-Expendable medical supplies; 33770000-Paper articles for sanitary use; and 33771000-Paper products for sanitary use.

After that, we introduced in the search query form of the Spanish National Procurement Platform the following text in each aspect: a) Type of contract: supplies; b) CPV code: those indicated above; c) Procedure: Simplified open; and d) Publication date between: 01/January/2020 and 31/May/2021.

This search query resulted in 2,546 procurement processes listed in 123 screen pages. Then authors read all simplified open procurement processes to capture those whose aim was the acquisition of reusable face masks and, finally, 11 were found. Considering that fully open procurement procedures are like those of simplified open procedures regarding the competition, we made again the same search query but widening to fully open procurement procedures. This new search query resulted in 5,603 procurement processes listed in 281 screen pages, resulting finally in adding 14 procurement processes incorporated to our sample selection.

In brief, this research compares the transparency (competition) and efficiency (cost and time savings) of one simplified open procurement procedure performed under the BCT based procurement platform (the only one performed under this environment) vs a total of 25 open procurement procedures performed under t e-procurement web systems, all of them (performed under BCT based platform or under e-procurement web systems) addressed to acquire reusable face masks that protect against Covid-19.

In all procurement processes selected in the sample selection (BCT or e-procurement), we collected the following data of this reference expedient: reference number, contracting authority, object of the contract, CPV code, dates of publication of: a) the announcement; b) deadline for submitting offers; c) the opening of economic offers; d) the evaluation of offers; e) award and formalization. We also collected information about the estimated value of the contract, the budget base of the tender, the volume of masks to be supplied, the number of washings of the reusable face masks promised by the seller, the technical characteristics of the masks, the estimated unit price per mask, the place of execution of the contract, the bidding companies (distinguishing between these the successful bidder, those excluded and those not awarded), and finally the unitary amount offered by each bid company.

3.2 Research Methodology

Prior research has put emphasis on different stages in e-procurement processes -see for example, Knudsen [45], Afolabi et al. [46], Afolabi et al. [47] or Aguiar and Grillo [48]. From a holistic point of view, the United Nations [58] distinguished two main phases in the e-procurement process, namely the pre-award phase (e-Notification, e-Submission, e-Evaluation and e-Awarding) and the post-award phase (e-Ordering, e-Invoicing and e-Payment). Similarly, as outlined by Costa et al. [42] or Tavares [49], e-procurement process is typically subdivided into two broader steps: e-Tendering (e-Noticing, e-Submission, and e-Decision + e-Auctions) and e- Execution (covering the remaining steps). In our research, we have focused on the e-tendering phase, this is the process form the e-noticing to e-awarding phase.

Concerning the measurement of transparency, as RQ1 is focused on analysing competition in public procurement processes, we have used, as main indicators, the following: a) total number of bid companies in each procurement process; b) number of bid SMEs involved in the procurement process; and c) total number of bid companies whose headquarter is in a different location to the Region of Aragon.

The first measure seeks to know if BCT based platforms are more easily accessed for bid companies, introducing higher competition in the procurement process. The second one seeks to know if BCT based platforms could help to promoting equal-balanced power environments where SMEs can be easily involved with other bigger firms in competitive environments for awarding public procurement processes. The third indicator seeks to know if BCT based platforms for public procurement processes can help to attracting bid companies in a more globally environment, increasing competition into the public procurement process. Finally, descriptive statistics have been used for all the indicators measured.

As for the financial efficiency (RQ2), we have used the cost (€)/efficiency indicator, defined as the unitary price per washing of the reusable face masks analysed. This is, the mathematical equation is, as follows:

$$cost\ (€)/efficiency = \frac{\textit{Unitary price of reusable face mask}}{\textit{Number of washing}} \tag{1}$$

This indicator has been applied not only to the final successful tender, but also to the initial estimated value of the product object of the public procurement process (reusable face masks), prior to the execution of the procurement process (the expected cost of the reusable face mask in each one of procurement process undertaken -the BCT based platform and e-procurement web system-).

In addition to the data obtained from the bid companies involved in both the BCT based procurement process and the e-procurement web systems, we have made a search at the date of the research regarding the price of the same or similar type of reusable face masks to protect against Covid-19 (same technical features) on all Spanish companies selling this type of face masks on the web published by the Association of Consumer Office in Spain (companies whose reusable face masks accomplished the international UNE 0065:2020 standard) -see Table 1-, with the aim at making differences regarding the market value of this type of masks and the cost saving obtained on each one of the different procurement processes analysed. We have restricted our search to Spanish firms on the web due to two main reasons: a) the need to have the market context into account; and b) Because all bid submissions were performed by Spanish registered bid companies according to the Spanish regulatory framework of public procurement.

Table 1. Spanish firms on the web selling the same type of face masks selected in this research and the market value of face masks to protect against Covid-19 at the date of the research.

Company name	Webpage[b]	Number of washings[c]	Unitary price
Tecteltic On-Line, S.L.	https://www.mimetikal.com	30	7.43 €
Quíquere Ecobags, S.L.	https://rewinder.eco	40	8.18 €
Different Brand	https://differentbrand.com	80	12.36 €
Belpla, S.A.	https://mascarillas.belpla.com	25	0.82 €
Fh2h, Lda	https://maskk.com	20	6.60 €
Actual Colors Bcn, S.L.[a]	http://www.windxtreme.eu	50	9.19 €
Actual Colors Bcn, S.L.[a]	http://www.windxtreme.eu	50	9.50 €
Parafarmic Parafarmacia Online, S.L.	www.parafarmic.com	50	8.60 €
Alser, Regalos Publicitarios, S.L.	www.alserregalos.com	25	1.89 €
Jgn Informatica S.L.	https://tecnopata.es	50	7.43 €
Dosfarmashop Online Sl	https://www.dosfarma.com	50	7.85 €

(continued)

Table 1. *(continued)*

Company name	Webpage[b]	Number of washings[c]	Unitary price
Mascarillas Zero S.L.	www.mascarillaszero.es	20	9.01 €
Virto Industrial	www.virtoindustrial.es	50	1.45 €
Textiles Montecid S.L.	https://www.hippyssidy.com	10	2.95 €

[a]This company offers two different, but similarly, reusable face masks to protect against Covid-19 at different prices
[b]Some webpages could not be working nowadays because firms finished working on this item.
[c]This is the number of washings promised by the seller.

Finally, concerning the time saving produced in the public procurement process (RQ3), this research is based on the time of the stamping documents uploaded on the BCT based platform/e-procurement web systems on each one of the different stages or phases of the e-tendering process. As the fully open and simplified open procurement processes can be different in time periods, we have compared here the simplified open procurement process under the BCT based platform vs the simplified open procurement procedures under the e-procurement web systems (11 public procurement processes as noted previously in the sample selection section). The following time measures were defined in our research: a) Total time from noticing to awarding; b) Noticing time; c) Submission time of offers; c) Open period time of offers; d) Evaluation time of offers; e) Awarding time.

3.3 Analysis of Results

According to the report of the Spanish National Commission of the Competition Market (NCCM) [50] entitled "E/CNMC/004/18 Radiografía de los Procedimientos de Contratación Pública en España" (Radiography of Public Procurement Processes in Spain), the mean number of bid companies in the public procurement processes is about seven per procurement process. Data of this research regarding the competition in the sample procurement processes in Table 2 (RQ1) shows that the number of bid companies in all procurement processes (including those performed under BCT based platforms and e-procurement web systems) is higher than the mean mentioned previously in the NCCM report.

Concretely, the mean number of bid companies in public procurement process of reusable face masks to protect Covid-19 performed under e-procurement web systems (14 approximately) is higher than that performed under the BCT based platform (8), and both are over the mean displayed by the NCCM [50]. Data also suggest that the competition per sample procurement process is high considering that it reaches eight in the BCT based platform, and that only three public e-procurement processes in web systems show a small number of bid companies (lower or equal to 6).

Table 2. Competition analyses in the sample public procurement processes.

	BCT based platform[a]	E-procurement web systems				
	Number	Mean	Median	Max	Min	Standard deviation
Number of bid companies per public procurement process	8	14.3462	13	40	4	8.3662
Number of bid companies with headquarters different from the location of the public procurement process	5	13.6000	11	35	4	7.5664
Number of bid companies with headquarters different from the province of the public procurement process	3	10.6400	10	24	2	5.2032
Number of bid companies with headquarters in the location of the public procurement process	3	1.3200	1	5	0	1.5470
Number of bid companies with headquarters in the province of the public procurement process	5	4.2800	3	22	0	5.5115

[a]As there is only one simplified open public procurement process under BCT based platform, we show the frequency obtained in this process.

As for the financial efficiency (RQ2), we can observe in Table 3 that the procurement process under BCT based platform is more efficiency than that performed under e-procurement web systems. This higher cost/efficiency in BCT based platforms can be seen comparing not only the final successful tender, but also comparing the cost savings obtained in the procurement process concerning the expected cost before performing the procurement process.

This way, while in BCT based procurement processes the average cost/efficiency of the bids submitted (0.0541 €) is less than 79.68% compared to the average initially expected cost/efficiency for the process (0.2663 €), in procurement processes under e-procurement web systems only a reduction of 42.50% has been achieved. It means that the range of improvement inside the procurement process is higher in BCT based procurement processes. This is also reflected in the capability of BCT based procurement processes to save higher costs in acquiring supplies concerning the market value of the items.

In addition, we can observe that procurement processes under BCT based platforms obtain cost savings regarding e-procurement web systems. Indeed, whereas reusable face masks were acquired at 0.0541 € per washing in the public tender under the BCT based platform, it was acquired at 0.1449 € per washing under e-procurement web systems. Also, data indicate that the median and the standard deviation are lower under the BCT based platforms than that under e-procurement web systems (0.0490 € vs 0.06904 € and 0.0275 € vs 0.2147, respectively). Therefore, it seems that public tenders using BCT based platforms are more cost efficient and more homogenous in terms of bid submissions than those using e-procurement web systems.

Table 3. Cost/efficiency analyses in the sample public procurement processes.

	Market research of face masks									
	Mean		Median		Max		Min		Standard Deviation	
Market value of the reusable face masks	0.1908 €		0.1779 €		0.4504 €		0.0290 €		0.1144 €	
	BCT Based Platform					E-procurement web systems				
	Mean	Median	Max	Min	St. Dev.	Mean	Median	Max	Min	St. Dev.
Expected cost before performing the procurement process	0.2663 €	0.1935 €	0.5300€	0.0635 €	0.2165 €	0.2520 €	0.1375 €	0.7667 €	0.0143 €	0.2381 €
The final successful tender in the procurement processes	0.0541 €	0.0490 €	0.1044 €	0.0088 €	0.0275 €	0.1449 €	0.0694 €	1.9000 €	0.0143 €	0.2147 €

* Data for the BCTbased platform is the data obtained on the unique case collected.

Finally, Table 4 collects information about the analysis of the time savings in the public procurement process comparing the different analysed platforms (BCT vs e-procurement web systems -RQ3-). We can see the higher time spent in public procurement processes under e-procurement web systems compared to that of BCT based platform, regardless the high standard deviation of the data analysed (22.90). Indeed, the minimum number of days spent in the e-procurement processes account for 34 days, whereas the public procurement process under the BCT based platform spent 33 days.

In addition, the highest differences in time spent are produced on the awarding process, where procurement processes under e-procurement web systems are clearly more inefficient than that under BCT platform (see mean and median scores in Table 4). However, the time used for both the noticing and the submission time of offers are nearly the same.

Table 4. Time saving analyses in the sample public procurement processes (data in days).

	BCT based platform[a]	E-procurement web systems				
	Number of days	Mean	Median	Max	Min	Standard deviation
a) Total time from noticing to awarding	33.00	64.55	57.00	105.00	34.00	22.90
b) Noticing time	15.00	15.18	15.00	21.00	8.00	3.57
c) Submission time of offers	15.00	15.18	15.00	21.00	8.00	3.57
d) Evaluation time of offers	5.00	5.82	3.00	28.00	0.00	8.55
e) Awarding time	12.00	35.09	30.00	68.00	8.00	21.61

[a]As there is only one simplified open public procurement process under BCT based platform, we show the frequency obtained in this process.

4 Discussion and Conclusions

While there are many studies on e-procurement, there is still a long way to transition into a more intelligent execution of e-procurement-related activities [51]. Considering the need of empirical experiences to test the benefits of the implementation of emerging technologies into the public sector sphere, this research analyses the transparency, in terms of competition, and the efficiency, in terms of financial and administrative efficiency, of public procurement processes performed under BCT based platforms.

The main limitation of this research is the low number of simplified open public procurement processes under BCT based platforms. Although authors performed a deep search of all of them into the public administrations in Spain, up to now, only one public procurement process has been performed under this platform. Future research should widen the number of public procurement processes under BCT based platforms analysed and obtain more valid and consistent findings collecting data from other different products and different market environments to that under the COVID-19 pandemic. However, findings of this research seem to be clearly indicative of the impact of BCT based platform on competition and efficiency of public procurement processes.

Findings of this research suggest that competition is higher in public procurement processes under e-procurement web systems. This result could be produced by the difficulty of companies to adopt BCT in their organization and to attend to public procurement process under BCT based platforms due to the complexity of this emerging technology. Indeed, this research confirms prior research which indicate that excessively complicated digital systems could create implementation risks and challenges for new entrants or SMEs [3]. In this regard, the existence of personnel training projects in firms concerning emerging technologies like BCT and the standardization of BCT based procurement platforms could attract more enterprises to build up the capabilities of using these platforms [52].

In addition, another important finding of this research is that public procurement processes under BCT based platforms are more financial efficient than those under e-procurement web systems. This is especially relevant if we consider the lower number of bid companies in the BCT based platform experience of this research (lower competition), which could make us think that the higher competition in BCT based procurement processes, the higher difference in cost/efficiency concerning e-procurement web systems. In this regard, future research should deeply investigate this topic using other public procurement processes with higher competition in BCT based platforms.

Data also reveal that the range of improvement of cost savings inside the different types of public procurement processes (BCT vs e-procurement web systems) is much different. In fact, this finding makes us think in the need of distinguishing two different competition environments produced into the public procurement processes, which could be named as external and internal competition. The first one is produced by the number of bid companies that get into play in a public tender process. The second one is produced by the process itself, in other words, how the different aspects of the process foster competition in cost savings for awarding the public procurement process. Regardless other different factors, our research has identified the technology as one of the main factors that cause this internal competition for higher efficient public procurement processes.

In brief, the efficiency of the technology used in the procurement process can also produce higher competition in the public procurement processes. In this regard, future research should investigate both other factors that influence on the external and internal competition in public tenders and the capability of different technologies used for public procurement process to influence on the financial efficiency of the process.

Also, data indicate that public tenders using BCT based platforms are more homogenous in terms of bid submissions than those using e-procurement web systems (lower standard deviation of bid submissions). It could mean that both the immutability characteristic and the higher transparency involved in emerging technologies like BCT could make to foster competition in the procurement process, making bid companies to offer lower prices in the public tender due to their perception of the new high competition environment. This could make us to see BCT as a disruptive technology for reducing inefficiencies, if implemented appropriately.

Finally, concerning the time saving analyses produced in the public procurement process, our research demonstrates that public procurement process under BCT based platforms are time savings concerning those under e-procurement web systems, mainly concentrated in the lower awarding time spent into the process. The main reason could be that the other stages in the public procurement processes have limited time periods to be performed according to the Spanish regulatory framework, which makes difficult to save time in these stages (for example, there is a period of 15 days or over for bid submissions in simplified or fully open procurement processes). If the time restrictions weren't, it would be possible to obtain higher time savings using BCT based platforms in public procurement process. This way, future research should investigate in other contexts and/or countries the time saving analyses in the public procurement processes with the aim at obtaining new insights regarding the potential of BCT for time efficiency in these processes.

In any case, regardless findings of our research, BCT is in an earlier stage of development in its adoption in the public sector, which can involve some challenges derived from its implementation, including lack of training in emerging technologies of public officials [53], regulatory issues [54, 55], data protection [56], security issues [27, 57] or entrant barriers to the public tenders (especially for SMEs) due to the complexity of the technology [3]. Therefore, we agree with Parenti et al. [27] indicating that public managers and policymakers should make a thorough cost-benefit analysis to ensure the technology presents enough benefits to motivate a change for its use. In brief, the implementation of BCT in public procurement services, to be successful, needs to be valuable or vital, not only viable [20].

Future research should thus analyse new practical experiences and undertake cost-benefit analysis of BCT implementation. In addition, future research could analyse drivers/inhibitors of BCT implementation for public tendering processes. This way, public managers and policymakers could have great knowledge about the environment in which BCT platforms could be a good tool for transparency and efficient public procurement processes.

Nonetheless, this research is a first approach to this field of knowledge and findings suggest that, as far as the BCT technology advances in its implementation to public procurement process, it is expected higher benefits are going to come to the public entities and the society in general, including the reduction of corruption and collusive practices or the cost and time savings in the public tenders.

Acknowledgements. This research was funded by financial support from the Centre of Andalusian Studies (PR137/19), Ministry of Science, Innovation and Universities (RTI2018-095344-A100) and Regional Government of Andalusia, Spain (Research projects number P20_00314 and B-SEJ-556-UGR20).

References

1. European Union (EU): Public Procurement. European Semester Thematic Factsheet (2017). https://ec.europa.eu/info/sites/default/files/file_import/european-semester_thematic-factsheet_public-procurement_en_0.pdf. Accessed 06 Mar 2022
2. European Union (EU): Information from European Union Institutions, Bodies, Offices and Agencies European Commission. Notice on tools to fight collusion in public procurement and on guidance on how to apply the related exclusion ground. European Commission Communication (2021/C 91/01) (2021)
3. OECD: OECD Recommendation of the Council on Public Procurement (2015). https://www.oecd.org/gov/public-procurement/recommendation/. Accessed 04 Mar 2022
4. European Union (EU): Directive 2014/24/EU of the European Parliament and of the Council of 26 February 2014 on public procurement and repealing Directive 2004/18/EC
5. OECD: System Change in Slovenia. Making Public Procurement More Effective. OECD (2020). https://www.oecd-ilibrary.org/governance/system-change-in-slovenia_b050ef2f-en. Accessed 06 Mar 2022

6. Lindskog, H., Brege, S., Brehmer, P.O.: Corruption in public procurement and private sector purchasing. J. Organ. Transform. Soc. Change **7**(2), 167–188 (2010)
7. Da Silveira, V.A., da Costa, S.R.R., Resende, D.: A proposal to use blockchain technology in innovation ecosystems for sustainable purchases through the perception of public managers. In: 68th International Scientific Conference on Economic and Social Development, Aveiro, pp. 42–51 (2021)
8. Kashta, R.: Corruption and innovation in the Albanian public procurement system. Academicus Int. Sci. J. **10**, 212–225 (2014)
9. Pavel, J., Sičáková-Beblavá, E.: Do e-auctions really improve the efficiency of public procurement? The case of the Slovak municipalities. Prague Econ. Pap. **22**(1), 111–124 (2013)
10. Lorentz, H., Aminoff, A., Kaipia, R., Srai, J.S.: Structuring the phenomenon of procurement digitalisation: contexts, interventions and mechanisms. Int. J. Oper. Prod. Manag. **41**(2), 157–192 (2021)
11. Migiro, S.O., Ambe, I.M.: Evaluation of the implementation of public sector supply chain management and challenges: a case study of the central district municipality, North west province, South Africa. Afr. J. Bus. Manag. **2**(12), 230–242 (2008)
12. Malacina, I., Karttunen, E., Jääskeläinen, A., Lintukangas, K., Heikkilä, J., Kähkönen, A.K.: Capturing the value creation in public procurement: a practice-based view. J. Purch. Supply Manag. **28**(2), 100745 (2022)
13. Oruezabala, G., Rico, J.C.: The impact of sustainable public procurement on supplier management—the case of French public hospitals. Ind. Mark. Manag. **41**(4), 573–580 (2012)
14. Sparrevik, M., Wangen, H.F., Fet, A.M., De Boer, L.: Green public procurement–a case study of an innovative building project in Norway. J. Clean. Prod. **188**, 879–887 (2018)
15. Kassen, M.: Blockchain and e-government innovation: automation of public information processes. Inf. Syst. **103**, 101862 (2022)
16. OECD: OECD Blockchain Policy Forum. OECD (2018). http://www.oecd.org/finance/oecd-blockchain-policy-forum-2018.htm. Accessed 04 Mar 2022
17. Sánchez, S.N.: The implementation of decentralised ledger technologies for public procurement. Eur. Procure. Public Private Partnership Law Rev. **14**(3), 180–196 (2019)
18. European Parliament: Distributed ledger technologies and blockchains: building trust with disintermediation European Parliament resolution of 3 October 2018 on distributed ledger technologies and blockchains: building trust with disintermediation (2017/2772(RSP)) (2020/C 11/02) (2018)
19. Kosmol, T., Reimann, F., Kaufmann, L.: You'll never walk alone: why we need a supply chain practice view on digital procurement. J. Purch. Supply Manag. **25**(4), 100553 (2019)
20. Lindman, J., Berryhill, J., Welby, B., Barbieri, M.P.: The uncertain promise of blockchain for government. OECD Blockchain Policy Series, OECD Working Papers on Public Governance No. 43 (2020). https://www.oecd-ilibrary.org/docserver/d031cd67-en.pdf?expires=1646337898&id=id&accname=guest&checksum=B37D4E124555DAA39554E417ABE844C1. Accessed 03 Mar 2022
21. Erridge, A., Murray, J.G.: Lean supply: a strategy for Best Value in local government procurement? Public Policy Adm. **13**(2), 70–85 (1998)
22. Koscheyev, V., Hakimov, A.: Russian practice of using digital technologies in public procurement management in the construction industry. In: IOP Conference Series: Materials Science and Engineering, vol. 497, no. 1, p. 012009. IOP Publishing (2019)
23. Matthews, D.: Strategic procurement in the public sector: a mask for financial and administrative policy. J. Public Procure. **5**(3), 388–399 (2005)
24. Ronchi, S., Brun, A., Golini, R., Fan, X.: What is the value of an IT e-procurement system? J. Purch. Supply Manag. **16**(2), 131–140 (2010)
25. Schoenherr, T., Tummala, V.R.: Electronic procurement: a structured literature review and directions for future research. Int. J. Procure. Manag. **1**(1–2), 8–37 (2007)

26. Srai, J.S., Lorentz, H.: Developing design principles for the digitalisation of purchasing and supply management. J. Purch. Supply Manag. **25**(1), 78–98 (2019)
27. Parenti, C., Noori, N., Janssen, M.: A Smart Governance diffusion model for blockchain as an anti-corruption tool in Smart Cities. J. Smart Cities Soc. **1**(1), 71–92 (2022)
28. Kumar, S.: Blockchain: the solution to public sector corruption, 2 November 2017. Published in Articles: EE Publishers, Articles: PositionIT. https://www.ee.co.za/article/blockchain-solution-public-sector-corruption.html. Accessed 06 Mar 2022
29. Matyskevic, J., Kremer-Matyskevic, I.: Main features and considerations of blockchain technology implementation in E-procurement. Public Secur. Public Order **24**, 467–485 (2020)
30. Halonen, K.M.: Disclosure rules in EU public procurement: balancing between competition and transparency. J. Public Procure. **16**(4), 528–533 (2016)
31. Elalaoui Elabdallaoui, H., Elfazziki, A., Sadgal, M.: A blockchain-based platform for the e-procurement management in the public sector. In: Attiogbé, C., Ben Yahia, S. (eds.) MEDI 2021. LNCS, vol. 12732, pp. 213–223. Springer, Cham (2021). https://doi.org/10.1007/978-3-030-78428-7_17
32. Akaba, T.I., Norta, A., Udokwu, C., Draheim, D.: A framework for the adoption of blockchain-based e-procurement systems in the public sector. In: Hattingh, M., Matthee, M., Smuts, H., Pappas, I., Dwivedi, Y.K., Mäntymäki, M. (eds.) I3E 2020. LNCS, vol. 12066, pp. 3–14. Springer, Cham (2020). https://doi.org/10.1007/978-3-030-44999-5_1
33. Smith, J.J.S.: Competition and transparency: what works for public procurement reform. Public Contract Law J. **38**(1), 85–129 (2008)
34. Ochrana, F., Pavel, J.: Analysis of the impact of transparency, corruption, openness in competition and tender procedures on public procurement in the Czech Republic. Cent. Eur. J. Public Policy **7**(2), 114–134 (2013)
35. Baldi, S., Bottasso, A., Conti, M., Piccardo, C.: To bid or not to bid: that is the question: public procurement, project complexity and corruption. Eur. J. Polit. Econ. **43**, 89–106 (2016)
36. Thio-ac, A., Serut, A.K., Torrejos, R.L., Rivo, K.D., Velasco, J.: Blockchain-based system evaluation: the effectiveness of blockchain on E-procurements. Int. J. Adv. Trends Comput. Sci. Eng. **8**(5), 2673–2676 (2019)
37. Becker, J.: Systems and e-procurement-improving access and transparency of public procurement. Briefing requested by the IMCO Committee, European Parliament, Brussels, Belgium (2018)
38. Croom, S.: The impact of web-based procurement on the management of operating resources supply. J. Supply Chain Manag. **36**(1), 4–13 (2000)
39. Smith, A.D., Flanegin, F.R.: E-procurement and automatic identification: enhancing supply chain management in the healthcare industry. Int. J. Electron. Healthc. **1**(2), 176–198 (2004)
40. Bartsch, P., Lux, T., Wagner, A., Gabriel, R.: E-procurement in hospitals – an integrated supply chain management of pharmaceutical and medical products by the usage of mobile devices. In: Godara, B., Nikita, K.S. (eds.) MobiHealth 2012. LNICSSITE, vol. 61, pp. 406–412. Springer, Heidelberg (2013). https://doi.org/10.1007/978-3-642-37893-5_45
41. Reddick, C.G.: The growth of e-procurement in American state governments: a model and empirical evidence. J. Public Procure. **4**(2), 151–176 (2004)
42. Costa, A.A., Arantes, A., Tavares, L.V.: Evidence of the impacts of public e-procurement: the Portuguese experience. J. Purch. Supply Manag. **19**(4), 238–246 (2013)
43. Ogunlela, O.G., Ojugbele, O.H., Tengeh, R.K.: Blockchain technology as a panacea for procurement corruption in digital era. Int. J. Res. Bus. Soc. Sci. **10**(4), 311–320 (2021)
44. Mackey, T.K., Cuomo, R.E.: An interdisciplinary review of digital technologies to facilitate anti-corruption, transparency and accountability in medicines procurement. Glob. Health Action **13**(sup1), 1695241 (2020)
45. Knudsen, D.: Aligning corporate strategy, procurement strategy and e-procurement tools. Int. J. Phys. Distrib. Logist. Manag. **33**(8), 720–734 (2003)

46. Afolabi, A.O., Owolabi, J.D., Ojelabi, R.A., Oyeyipo, O., Aina, D.A.: Development of a web-based tendering protocol for procurement of construction works in a tertiary institution. J. Theor. Appl. Inf. Technol. **95**(8), 1595–1606 (2017)
47. Afolabi, A.O., Oyeyipo, O., Ojelabi, R.A., Tunji-Olayeni, P.F.: E-maturity of construction stakeholders for a web-based e-procurement platform in the construction industry. Int. J. Civ. Eng. Technol. (IJCIET) **8**(12), 465–482 (2017)
48. Aguiar Costa, A., Grilo, A.: BIM-based e-procurement: an innovative approach to construction e-procurement. Sci. World J. **4**, 1–15 (2015)
49. Tavares, L.V.: Public eTendering in the European Union: trust in evolution. Vortal, Lisbon (2010)
50. Spanish National Commission of the Competition Market (NCCM): "Radiografía de los procedimientos de contratación pública en España" (Radiography of Public Procurement Processes in Spain) (2019). https://www.cnmc.es/sites/default/files/2314114_6.pdf. Accessed 9 Sept 2021
51. Chan, A.P., Owusu, E.K.: Evolution of electronic procurement: contemporary review of adoption and implementation strategies. Buildings **12**(2), 198 (2022)
52. Huntgeburth, J., Parasie, N., Steininger, D., Veit, D.: Increasing the adoption of e-procurement services at the municipal level. e-Serv. J. J. Electron. Serv. Public Private Sect. **8**(3), 3–23 (2012)
53. Ubaldi, B., et al.: State of the art in the use of emerging technologies in the public sector. OECD Working Papers on Public Governance No. 34 (2019). https://ialab.com.ar/wp-content/uploads/2019/09/OECD-2019-State-of-the-Art-on-Emerging-Technologies-Working-Paper.pdf. Accessed 15 Mar 2022
54. Scholl, H.J., Rodríguez Bolívar, M.P.: Regulation as both enabler of technology use and global competitive tool: the Gibraltar case. Gov. Inf. Q. **36**(3), 601–613 (2019)
55. Scholl, H.J., Pomeshchikov, R., Rodríguez Bolívar, M.P.: Early regulations of distributed ledger technology/blockchain providers: a comparative case study. In: Proceedings of the 53rd Hawaii International Conference on System Sciences, pp. 1760–1769 (2020)
56. Berryhill, J., Bourgery, T., Hanson, A.: Blockchains unchained: blockchain technology and its use in the public sector. OECD Working Papers on Public Governance No. 28 (2018). https://www.pfmkin.org/sites/default/files/2020-02/185.%20Blockchains%20Unchained.pdf. Accessed 15 Mar 2022
57. Lin, I.C., Liao, T.C.: A survey of blockchain security issues and challenges. Int. J. Netw. Secur. **19**(5), 653–659 (2017)
58. United Nations: UN Procurement Practitioner's Handbook. Interagency Procurement Working Group (IAPWG) (2006)
59. https://contrataciondelestado.es/wps/portal/!ut/p/b0/04_Sj9CPykssy0xPLMnMz0vMAfIjU1JTC3Iy87KtUlJLEnNyUuNzMpMzSxKTgQr0w_Wj9KMyU1zLcvQjS1QNUnzStc2DA0wC8oLzQyKMq1QNzMsdbW31C3JzHQGlp2M1/

Assessing the Quality of Covid-19 Open Data Portals

Igor Garcia Ballhausen Sampaio(✉), Eduardo de O. Andrade, Flávia Bernardini, and José Viterbo

Universidade Federal Fluminense, Niterói, RJ, Brazil
igorgarcia@id.uff.br, {eandrade,fcbernardini,viterbo}@ic.uff.br

Abstract. Open data portals can be used for several purposes, including transparency leverage, access to information, and decision-making support. Recently, the pandemic broke out in the new coronavirus, causing the whole world to suffer its effects. As a result, several countries, institutions, and research teams have worked to understand the behavior of this new virus. Since then, several open data portals have emerged that have set out to disseminate regional, national, and even international information about Covid-19 information. Therefore, it is known that open data resources, together with data-based methodologies, provide many opportunities to improve the response of different administrations, especially to the virus. We identified the variables and methodologies necessary to analyze the fundamental aspects of the quality of Covid-19's open data portals and described the current aspects such as qualities, limitations, and difficulties found in these open data portals.

Keywords: Open data portals · Covid-19 · Open data covid portals · Open data quality

1 Introduction

Open data initiatives offer different solutions for opening government data to the public. Open data platform solutions provide simple tools to enrich government portals [6]. Therefore, open datasets and search, tagging, and downloading services represent an outstanding feature that allows the public to easily identify and quickly obtain the key datasets needed for not only Covid-19 searches but also how to source information in general.

The atypical pneumonia coronavirus disease (Covid-19) pandemic caused by a novel SARS-CoV-2 has significantly impacted global society. This impact includes both an economic and public health standpoint [7]. From an informative, analytical, and statistical point of view, data about the pandemic must become available. Therefore, several governments, institutions, and research teams have worked to provide data for analysis [2].

M. Janssen et al. (Eds.): EGOV 2022, LNCS 13391, pp. 212–227, 2022.
https://doi.org/10.1007/978-3-031-15086-9_14

Moreover, the consistent record of information related to Covid-19 is vital for understanding transmissibility, risk of geographic spread, transmission routes, and risk factors for infection [15]. With Covid-19 taking place in a much more digitized and connected world, the volume of data produced is unprecedentedly huge [18]. Furthermore, advanced computational models, such as those based on machine learning, have demonstrated outstanding potential to trace the origin or predict the future spread of infectious diseases. Therefore, it is imperative to take advantage of big data and smart analytics and put them to good use for public health [16].

Open data portals are known to be online platforms that provide access to open datasets and typically host the data of the host organization. Therefore, several initiatives for the evaluation of open data portals and methodologies for evaluations were proposed [19,31,38]. However, with the advance of the new coronavirus pandemic, several data portals emerged that began to offer data only about the global pandemic. However, no evaluation has been performed on these various covid data portals. Therefore, this work aims to carry out a methodological evaluation of Covid-19 open data portals, according to some criteria of good practices already established in traditional open data portals, based on a methodology already proposed in [21].

In this work, we conduct an assess the quality of this high volume of open data regarding Covid-19 in terms of its dissemination portals, using methodologies already established for evaluating government open data portals. It is challenging to identify suitable sources in many situations, especially for the general public. An example of this is the dissemination through repositories such as GitHub, which contains many significant datasets of global and regional scope. However, it can be challenging to discover them without proper guidance. For a particular person who is not a data scientist, or some computer professional, viewing and consuming information in this way is not the best way.

Furthermore, several other factors, such as languages, usability, and visualization, can be crucial in determining the quality of these portals. Another problem that can occur is the reliability of the data source provider, for instance. Therefore, this article aims to provide a qualitative analysis of the open data portals available to analyze the propagation and control of Covid-19. We try to use metrics already known to endure the usefulness of this article over time. For this, we searched several methodologies mentioned in the Sect. 2 in order to understand which would be the methodology that would best suit our problem, which is to evaluate Covid-19 open data portals.

The paper is organized as follows: we identify the main works related to Covid-19's open data portals and methodologies and methods for general evaluation of open data portals in Sect. 2. The methodology chosen for assessing the various Covid-19 portals and the most relevant open data institutions on a global scale addressing the pandemic is presented in Sect. 3. The assessment itself and the results obtained from the chosen methodology are presented in Sect. 4, including the results and suggestions for some possible improvements in these portals. Finally, in Sect. 5, we finish our work, pointing out the main conclusions that we can obtain from the research and possible future works.

2 Literature Review

Open data has received considerable attention in recent years. Open data policies are essential, as their objective is to guarantee the long-term transparency of government information and thus contribute to citizens' rights to public access to government information, which is considered a fundamental principle of democracy [39]. Governments and international organizations expressed perspectives that opening up access to their data would facilitate the creation of relevant benefits for society, organizations, and individuals [3]. Several works from literature explore and/or propose technologies to help citizens and government officers to improve their understanding on the features and issues of public spaces [4].

In order to make the administration of governments transparent and to make public information that is generated by the people, it is necessary that the portals are not merely repositories with data, without organization or a minimum of standardization. The need for intuitive portals that bring the population closer to data that help them gain a deeper insight into their surroundings, as well as generating solutions that help in everyday life has increased [29]. Hence, thousands of open datasets published by governments, organizations and companies, were made available through portals on internet [28].

With the knowledge of the growth and importance of open data portals, it is necessary to consider that providing low-quality data increases the cost of accessing and interpreting the data. These additional costs attributable to poor quality data depend on several factors. Such costs have been reported in the literature mainly for companies, stating that high-quality data are fundamental factors for the success of a company [35]. However, in Open Government Data (OGB), shreds of evidence show that disclosing data without proper quality control may jeopardize dataset reuse and negatively affect civic participation [35].

2.1 Covid-19 Open Data Portals

Just as open government data portals are vital in today's world [37], with the Covid-19 pandemic, the whole world has turned its eyes to the news and data about the new coronavirus [9]. However, research, news, information, and forecasts only became possible due to the scientific dissemination that we had during this period [12].

Therefore, another work better reviews the relevant open data sources to understand the worldwide dissemination of Covid-19 [1]. More than that, this work enumerates the variables necessary to obtain consistent epidemiological and forecasting models, but also in a set of auxiliary variables related to the study of their potential seasonal behavior, the effect of age structure, and the prevalence of secondary health conditions on mortality, and the effectiveness of government actions.

In one more work, the authors developed a comprehensive search for Covid-19 open-source datasets, organized based on the type of data and the application of the dataset [33]. Medical images, textual data, and speech data formed the main data types. The applications of the open-source dataset included Covid-19 diagnosis, infection estimate, mobility and demographic correlations, NPI analysis, and sentiment analysis.

Besides that, data sharing allows for creative innovation from archival datasets, generating new knowledge, promoting discoveries, formulating new hypotheses, creating new meanings connecting existing datasets, and verifying existing results [15]. Therefore, initiatives like [11,13,14] were only made possible by this open data policy.

During the development of this work, we had not identified any other research directed to the study of Covid-19 open data portals. However, when we revisited the bibliographic references, we noticed a recent work talking about the quality of Covid-19 open data portals [36].

The author focuses on developing a specific framework to evaluate Covid-19 portals, unlike this present work. We use pre-existing methodologies to evaluate open data portals, comparing Covid-19 portals and establishing the differences between conventional portals and Covid-19 ones. In addition, we found lessons from the Covid-19 data portals, setting up a discussion of what we can take and add to the world of open data portals in general.

2.2 Open Data Portals Evaluation

There are many government open data portal initiatives. Some of them dedicated to proposing frameworks and evaluation methodologies [10,20,24], others of comparative studies between open data portals [23,26,38] and even evaluation of a single open data portals country or region [8,17,30,31].

More generally, in [25] 42 national open data portals from different countries were analyzed, applying a common framework that allows their comparative analysis. The analysis shows that there are portals that can be considered leaders and an example of the less successful open data portals that were also identified. However, this study demonstrates that even more successful open data portals have room for improvement.

In [27], Brazilian OGD portals are evaluated according to different aspects related to the datasets available in each of the portals. The assessment considers the content and size of the datasets, frequency of updating, data formats, and data quality. In addition, we also consider evaluating other essential aspects of data integration and management perspectives, such as schema characteristics (for instance, size and types of attributes), schema quality problems, and heterogeneity between datasets.

Just as there are works that are dedicated to a single country, like the one mentioned above, we also have research that tries to cover a whole continent, as is the case of [5], which seeks to evaluate data portals in African countries with initiatives of open data. The countries selected in the work cited above have been determined based on their efforts to move towards requiring proactive disclosure of government data as part of their right to information laws.

Covid-19 open data portals differ from government data portals primarily in the layout structure of the pages where these portals are hosted. This difference is because Covid-19 portals contain only a specific theme, unlike government open data portals. We will hardly find separations by tags, keys, or search by theme, among others. Another critical difference is that covid data are usually time series, while government data may or may not be time series.

2.3 Frameworks and Methodologies

In recent years, the dissemination of Open Government Data (OGD) has kept a swift pace. However, evidence from professionals shows that disclosing data without adequate quality control can impair the reuse of the dataset and negatively affect civic participation [35]. Therefore, the need to build methodologies for evaluating these portals is evident [39].

At [32], the author conducted an in-depth assessment of selected cases to justify applying a proposed framework to understand the state of the government's open data initiatives. Subsequently, the work offers several observations in terms of policies and practices and the implication of developing an open portal of government data extracted from the application of the proposed structure.

Already in [38], a User Interaction Structure was developed, based on existing principles and evaluation methods, with concrete criteria in five dimensions: Access, Trust, Understand, Engage-integrate, and Participate. The framework was then used to evaluate the current OGD sites created and maintained by 34 US municipal government agencies.

As for open data mining in the scope of e-government, the framework proposed by [22] for open data mining is built to handle large amounts of data. This characteristic is fundamental, as open government data is growing enormously. Open data can be analyzed efficiently, and more helpful information can be extracted using this structure. The author also states that defining and implementing a framework for open data mining is only one step in the analysis of open data.

However, the work presented by [21] presents the benchmarking structure for assessing the quality of open data portals at the national level, as well as an in-depth analysis of the issues, challenges, and opportunities associated with these portals. To this end, the authors used a systematic review of the literature and content analysis methods and multidimensional with quantitative techniques.

3 Methodology

First, a bibliographic review of the most diverse methodologies proposed to evaluate open government data portals was carried out, seeking one that has more information and could fit well with the reality of the Covid-19 portals.

We followed some criteria to choose a methodology with some standards. These include: search strings: *open data portals evaluation*, *open data portals*, *open data covid portals*, *open data covid*, *open data portals framework*, *evaluation methodology open data portals* and recent methodologies (from 2017 onwards). The Covid-19 portals were chosen based on: portals of great international expression and the three largest Brazilian portals. This choice is because, in Brazil, many cases and deaths from coronavirus disease (COVID-19) have been reported. Becoming the second most affected country in the world, as of June 9, 2020 [34]. After that, the methodology was applied, and the analyzes were carried out.

As we understand that [21] was the work with more information, we found in literature, as described in Sect. 2 and this is the best fit for the scope of Covid-19's Open Data Portal. We chose it as a benchmarking framework for evaluating the open data portals of the new coronavirus. This choice is because it was the only work that detailed the framework created entirely and the methodology used to build it. Facilitating, therefore, the reproduction of this methodology for the case of the present work. Open data portals from Covid-19 can be understood as conventional open data portals, as they share some of the same characteristics. These characteristics are a data management system used to feed the portal, information about the authority that hosts the portal, and the governance model or institutional structure, among others.

The topics that were evaluated are presented below and are based on the benchmarking structure proposed by [21]. The framework used is divided into two parts. The first focuses on the general characteristics of the technical dimension, the availability and access dimension, and the communication and participation dimension. The second assesses the general characteristics of the datasets and their quality of metadata.

In total, 28 complete criteria (metrics) were used. Each criterion was assessed on a five-point Likert scale (1 = Strongly disagree, 2 = Disagree, 3 = Neutral, 4 = Agree, 5 = Strongly Agree) to measure agreement or disagreement with the proposed statements items below show. Consequently, each question can vary between one and five points, generating a total score between 28 (minimum) and 140 (maximum). In this work, 7 open data portals at the international and national level (Brazil) were evaluated, as can be seen in Table 1.

Authority and responsibility: Portals should provide information about the authority which hosts the portal and the governance model or institutional framework supporting data provision models;

Data management system: Portals should provide information about the data management system which is used to power the portal;

Language: Portals should offer more language versions to gain more users (attention) and improve the overall quality of this portal;

Free of charge: Portals should provide that all datasets and services are available free of charge and without any restrictions under open licenses;

Number of datasets: Portals should provide the number of datasets they include;

Number of applications (re-uses): Portals should provide the number of applications developed based on the open data re-used;
Search engine (filter): Portals should adopt and make visible an overall organization structure and provide strong dataset search capabilities and selection tools using different criteria for browsing through categories and browsing through filters;
API: Portals should provide API for stakeholders to develop applications using open data;
User account: Portals should support user account creation in order to personalize views and information shown;
Thematic categories and Tags (keywords): Portals should provide thematic categories of the datasets provided by the portal. The portal should distinguish categories (themes) from tags (keywords). Same tags should be used to classify data of the same type and category;
Forum (feedback): Portals should provide an opportunity to submit feedback on the data from the users to providers and a forum to discuss and exchange ideas among the users;
Request form: Portals should provide a form to request or suggest a new type or format type of open data;
Help (usability): Portals should include high-quality documentation and help functionality to learn how to use the portal and improve the usability;
Frequently Asked Questions (FAQ): Portals should provide a FAQ section to help resolve any potential issues;
Social media: Portals should be connected to a social media platform to create a social distribution channel for open data. OGD users and providers can inform each other about what they did with and learned from a dataset;
Title and description: Datasets should be provided together with their description and also how and for what purpose they were collected;
Publisher: Datasets should be provided together with their publisher to verify the authenticity of their source;
Release date and up to date: Datasets should be explicitly associated with a specific time or period tag. All information in the dataset should be up to date;
License: Datasets should provide license information related to using the published datasets. Datasets that don't explicitly have an open license are not open data;
Geographic coverage: Datasets should be determined if the coverage of data is on the national, regional, or local level;
Dataset URL: Datasets URL should be available for each dataset;
Dataset (file) size: Datasets (file) size should be available;
Number of views (visits): Total number of online views should be available for a dataset;
Number of downloads: Total number of downloads should be available for a dataset;
Machine-readable formats: Datasets should be provided in formats that are as convenient, easy to analyze, and modifiable as downloadable files in well-known formats;

Visualizations: Datasets visualization capabilities should be provided, e.g., as visualizations in charts or visualizations in maps;

User rating and discussion message: Datasets should provide capabilities allowing to collect user ratings and comments on a dataset or to discuss conclusions based on data use;

Table 1. The Covid-19 open data portals

Covid-19 open data portals	URL	Level
Johns Hopkins (JH)	https://coronavirus.jhu.edu/map.html	International
World Health Organization (WHO)	https://covid19.who.int/	International
Microsoft Bing (MB)	https://www.bing.com/covid	International
Oxford (Ox)	https://ourworldindata.org/coronavirus	International
Brazilian Government (BG)	https://covid.saude.gov.br/	National
Fiocruz (FC)	https://bigdata-covid19.icict.fiocruz.br/	National
Brasil IO (B-IO)	https://brasil.io/covid19/	National

4 Results and Discussion

In this work, only open data portals for Covid-19 are evaluated. Open government data portals, in general, are not the focus of this research. The comparison is based on the methodology described in the previous section, which assesses the state of open data in selected countries worldwide. Table 2 shows the results for each item in the benchmarking framework.

Based on the framework used in this work, the scores were distributed among the portals. The metrics used and described are discussed in the following paragraphs.

4.1 General Discussions and Observations

All evaluated portals provide the respective authorities responsible for hosting. In all portals, the portal's name already induces the authority responsible for it, except for Brasil IO, where a collaborative structure of 40 volunteers is established who, daily, compile and consolidate data on the portal. Each of the evaluated portals clearly explains the information sources of their portals and the data feed. Johns Hopkins uses several sources of information[1]such as the European Center for Disease Prevention and Control (ECDC), WorldoMeters, and COVID Tracking Project. The World Health Organization uses its regional offices as a source of information[2]. Microsoft Bing uses the sources[3] from the World Health Organization (WHO), Centers for Disease Control and Prevention

[1] https://github.com/CSSEGISandData/Covid-19.
[2] https://worldhealthorg.shinyapps.io/covid/.
[3] https://www.bing.com/covid/dev.

Table 2. Covid-19 portals evaluation results

Features	JH	WHO	MB	Ox	BG	FC	B-IO
Authority and responsibility	5	5	5	5	5	5	5
Data management system	3	5	5	5	5	5	5
Language	1	1	3	1	1	1	1
Free of charge	5	5	5	5	5	5	5
Number of datasets	5	5	5	5	5	1	5
Number of applications (re-users)	1	1	2	1	1	1	1
Search engine (filter)	5	5	5	5	5	4	5
API	3	3	4	3	2	1	5
User account	1	1	1	1	1	1	5
Thematic categories	5	5	5	5	5	5	5
Tags (keywords)	5	5	5	5	1	4	5
Forum (feedback)	5	2	1	5	1	1	5
Request form	5	5	5	5	1	3	5
Help (usability)	4	5	2	5	1	2	5
Frequently Asked Questions (FAQ)	5	5	5	5	1	1	5
Social media	2	5	5	5	1	1	1
Title and description	5	5	5	5	3	1	5
Publisher	5	5	5	5	3	5	5
Release date and up to date	5	5	5	5	5	5	5
License	5	5	5	5	1	1	5
Geographic coverage	5	5	5	5	5	5	5
Dataset URL	5	5	5	5	1	1	5
Dataset file (size)	5	1	5	5	1	1	5
Number of views (visits)	1	1	1	1	1	1	1
Number of downloads	1	1	1	1	1	1	1
Machine-readable formats	5	5	5	5	5	1	5
Visualizations	5	5	5	5	5	5	5
User rating and discussion message	5	2	1	5	1	1	5
Total	**112**	**108**	**111**	**118**	**73**	**69**	**120**

(CDC), national and state public health departments, BNO News, 24/7 Wall St., and Wikipedia. Oxford uses[4] data from Johns Hopkins, European Center for Disease Prevention and Control (ECDC), among others. The Brazilian Government draws on the Brazilian Ministry of Health as its source of information. Fiocruz uses the Brazilian Ministry of Health and the Johns Hopkins University itself, among others, as a source. Finally, Brasil IO supplies its portal through the daily bulletins released by the 27 Brazilian state health secretariats.

Only Microsoft Bing supports languages other than English in the international data portals. However, only when using its Widget for web pages[5]. As for the national portals (Brazil), none support any language other than Portuguese. All portals are free of any fees. That is, all access to information is entirely free. All portals, except Fiocruz, explain the amount of data made available. None of the portals explicitly use applications derived from their datasets. All portals provide search engines. However, Fiocruz lacks a little because it does not have a search bar.

Of all the portals, only Brasil IO provides a REST API for all data regarding Covid-19. Microsoft Bing only provides a Widget for HTML pages. Johns Hopkins and Oxford make their data available via Github. However, they do not have a built-in API. It is possible to make a GET request to our repositories, but this cannot be considered an API because the Brazilian Government and WHO only provide the download directly on the website via the user interface. However, the Brazilian Government makes available some OpenSUS datasets (Platform of open data of the Brazilian Unified Health System) related to Covid-19. Fiocruz does not provide data for download.

Only Brasil IO provides the creation of an account for the consumption of its REST API. All portals subdivide their data into categories, such as number of deaths, number of cases, and mortality rate. As for the tags, the Brazilian Government does not have them, and Fiocruz is a little confused as the tags are inserted within the categories. Johns Hopkins, Oxford, Microsoft Bing, and Brasil, IO use Github as a data repository. The tool already provides a forum for possible questions and debates regarding improvements. The Brazilian Government, WHO, and Fiocruz do not have a forum environment. Of all the evaluated portals, only the Brazilian Government portal does not have any communication channel for suggestions and improvements. Fiocruz has, however, only one e-mail available on the website.

As for usability, WHO, Oxfor, and Brasil IO provide usability support clearly and explicitly in their portals. Johns Hopkins also does, though it was harder to find on his website. Microsoft Bing and Fiocruz do not have usability help. The Brazilian government has nothing about it. Except for the Brazilian Government and Fiocruz, all portals have a part dedicated to the FAQ. WHO, Microsoft Bing, and Oxford have features to share their data on social networks. The other portals do not have this functionality. Johns Hopkins earned a higher score than the others (which do not have sharing functionality) as they have screens for

[4] https://github.com/owid/Covid-19-data/tree/master/public/data.

[5] https://github.com/microsoft/Covid-19-Widget.

news and updates about the pandemic. Except for the Brazilian government and Fiocruz (which does not provide any datasets for download), all other portals describe their datasets. As all evaluated portals make their sources available, it is possible to compare them with their respective origins.

All portals are updated at least daily. All portals have license information related to published datasets, except for the Brazilian government and Fiocruz. Internationally, all portals cover the entire world. At the national level (Brazil), all portals cover the Brazilian region. All portals had at least one URL to search for information more automatedly, except for the Brazilian government and Fiocruz. Only Johns Hopkins, Microsoft Bing, Oxford, and Brasil IO reported the size of their datasets. Unfortunately, none of the evaluated portals provide the number of visits to the portal nor the number of downloads of their datasets. All portals provide their information in the *CSV* format, except Fiocruz, which does not provide the data. Brasil IO, as it has an API, also makes data available in *JSON* format. Oxford provides, in addition to *CSV*, data in *XLSX* and *JSON* format. All portals have a data visualization area, such as maps, graphs (of different types), and tables, to perform the data's visual representation. Johns Hopkins, Oxford, and Brazil IO were the only portals that had an environment for discussions about insights over the datasets and a forum for debate.

From the presented evaluation, it can be noticed that the majority of Covid-19 open data portals in the world reached significant levels in the sense of opening a series of exciting and valuable datasets.

A significant difference that can be noticed between the Covid-19 open data portals concerning the government open data portals is the presence of KPIs (Key Performance Indicator). In the Covid-19 portals, it is common to see mortality rate, incidence rate, the total number of cases, the total number of deaths, and the incidence in 100,000 inhabitants. This point can be a good indication of several KPIs in government open data portals. We could exemplify the case of public safety datasets, the homicide rate per 100,000 inhabitants, the case of health datasets, and the number of ICU beds made available, among others.

Furthermore, the data update rate is another critical point that we can observe in the Covid-19 portals compared to government data portals. Data updates are daily. In traditional government portals, we sometimes see obsolete data without the regularity of publication. It is essential to note that providing updated data is expected in open data movement and is usually recommended in FOI access laws and acts. Change log is only available by CKAN [10]. However, by and large, Covid-19 portals follow the same "pattern" as government data portals.

updated data is a common practice in open data movement, and usually recommended in FOI access laws and acts, change log is only available by CKAN [10]. However, by and large, Covid-19 portals follow the same "pattern" as government data portals.

4.2 Lessons from Covid Open Data Portals

According to [13], providing information promptly for epidemiological outbreaks in order to initiate the necessary risk assessment and containment activities is of utmost importance. Therefore, we can see the importance of Covid-19 open data portals for studies around the disease, indeed serving as a basis for other cases.

In the absence of a methodology created specifically for evaluating open data portals for Covid-19, is it possible to evaluate open data portals for Covid-19 using pre-existing methodologies for evaluating open data portals in general? The conclusion of this work says yes. But why? Because the Covid-19 open data portals evaluated have the same characteristics found in open data portals in general, such as authority and responsibility, constant updating, API for data, and machine-readable formats.

The problems of open data government sites are mainly in the way data is presented by various government data repositories. There are no metadata standards, specifications, or protocols to achieve better discoverability and interoperability [23]. Therefore, the evaluation of open data portals is always based on other portals, causing methodologies and frameworks to emerge.

A crucial point observed during this work is based on the fact that Covid-19 portals build and present KPI. We can see very relevant indicators for the scenario in question, such as the mortality rate, infection rate, and vaccination rate. This scenario brings a new way of presenting this open data to improve the user experience (especially the layman) when accessing this information, which is public.

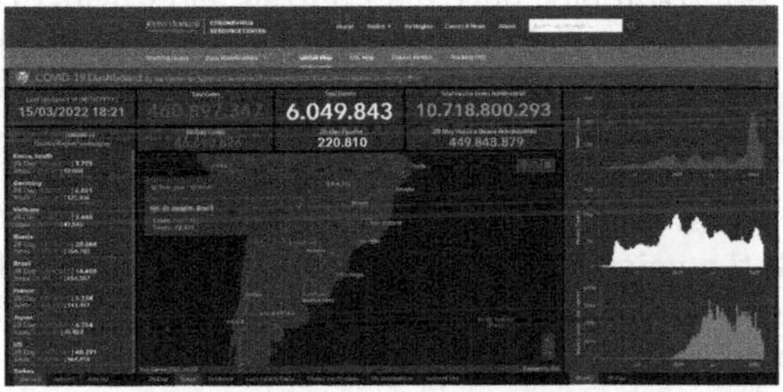

(a) John Hopkins COVID-19 Portal

(b) UK Open Data Government

Fig. 1. Comparison between the homepage of the John Hopkins Covid-19 open data portal and the UK government open data portal

Above, in Fig. 1, we can see a big difference between the homepage of the best-rated open data portal evaluated by [21] and the third-best place in the evaluation of this work.

5 Conclusion

This article presents an assessment of the quality of Covid-19 open data portals at the national and international level and an in-depth analysis of the issues, challenges, and opportunities associated with these portals. For this evaluation, a known and validated benchmarking framework for open data portals, in general, was used. Covid-19's open data portals are the interfaces between data from the most significant global pandemic and the general population. The excellent construction of these portals contributes to a better understanding of reality, and the different values added to this information.

We can see that evaluation metrics for government open data portals in general work well when we migrate from context, in this case, to Covid-19 data. Such portals must have a friendly interface with intuitive navigation. These portals must-have tools or search engines to quickly meet what the user wants and what the portal provides. Not least, these portals must reference the data sources so that we can have support in justifying the data presented and made available. This assessment can be used to direct missing aspects and possible improvements to those responsible for them. Finally, several observations and distinctions between traditional open data portals and Covid-19 portals are also made, trying to make a parallel to contribute to both modalities. However, the form of data availability, the use of APIs, and the visualization of Covid-19 open data portals and their functions differ, reflecting the lack of a model and establishing the need to create a technical standard to be followed. In particular, only Brasil.io provided an actual API.

Of course, all the points evaluated in this work are essential, but the main task is to provide a technical standard to be followed, like a framework. All construction must be thought of not only in terms of data quality but also in terms of users, who will have the right to use them as a tool, information, and metadata. Therefore, the results of this evaluation can be used to structure a pattern to be followed for not only Covid-19 open data portals but also open data portals in general.

Acknowledgements. This study was financed in part by the Coordenação de Aperfeiçoamento de Pessoal de Nível Superior - Brasil (CAPES) - Finance Code 001.

References

1. Alamo, T., Reina, D.G., Mammarella, M., Abella, A.: Covid-19: open-data resources for monitoring, modeling, and forecasting the epidemic. Electronics **9**(5), 827 (2020)
2. Alamo, T., Reina, D.G., Mammarella, M., Abella, A.: Open data resources for fighting covid-19. arXiv preprint. arXiv:2004.06111 (2020)

3. Barcellos, R., Bernardini, F., Viterbo, J.: Towards defining data interpretability in open data portals: challenges and research opportunities. Inf. Syst. **106**, 101961 (2022)
4. Barcellos, R., Viterbo, J., Miranda, L., Bernardini, F., Maciel, C., Trevisan, D.: Transparency in practice: using visualization to enhance the interpretability of open data. In: Proceedings of the 18th Annual International Conference on Digital Government Research, pp. 139–148 (2017)
5. Bello, O., Akinwande, V., Jolayemi, O., Ibrahim, A.: Open data portals in Africa: an analysis of open government data initiatives. Afr. J. Libr. Arch. Inf. Sci. **26**(2), 97 (2016)
6. Bogdanović-Dinić, S., Veljković, N., Stoimenov, L.: How open are public government data? An assessment of seven open data portals. In: Rodríguez-Bolívar, M.P. (ed.) Measuring E-government Efficiency. PAIT, vol. 5, pp. 25–44. Springer, New York (2014). https://doi.org/10.1007/978-1-4614-9982-4_3
7. Brimacombe, K.R., et al.: An opendata portal to share covid-19 drug repurposing data in real time. BioRxiv (2020)
8. Chatfield, A.T., Reddick, C.G.: A longitudinal cross-sector analysis of open data portal service capability: the case of Australian local governments. Gov. Inf. Q. **34**(2), 231–243 (2017)
9. Ciotti, M., et al.: Covid-19 outbreak: an overview. Chemotherapy **64**(5–6), 215–223 (2019)
10. Correa, A.S., Zander, P.O., Da Silva, F.S.C.: Investigating open data portals automatically: a methodology and some illustrations. In: Proceedings of the 19th Annual International Conference on Digital Government Research: Governance in the Data Age, pp. 1–10 (2018)
11. Crokidakis, N.: Data analysis and modeling of the evolution of covid-19 in Brazil. arXiv preprint. arXiv:2003.12150, vol. 26 (2020)
12. Desvars-Larrive, A., et al.: A structured open dataset of government interventions in response to covid-19. Sci. Data **7**(1), 1–9 (2020)
13. Dey, S.K., Rahman, M.M., Siddiqi, U.R., Howlader, A.: Analyzing the epidemiological outbreak of covid-19: a visual exploratory data analysis approach. J. Med. Virology **92**(6), 632–638 (2020)
14. Hamzah, F.B., et al.: Coronatracker: worldwide covid-19 outbreak data analysis and prediction. Bull. World Health Organ. **1**(32), 1–32 (2020)
15. Hu, T., et al.: Building an open resources repository for covid-19 research. Data Inf. Manag. **4**(3), 130–147 (2020)
16. Ienca, M., Vayena, E.: On the responsible use of digital data to tackle the covid-19 pandemic. Nat. Med. **26**(4), 463–464 (2020)
17. de Juana-Espinosa, S., Luján-Mora, S.: Open government data portals in the European union: considerations, development, and expectations. Technol. Forecast. Soc. Chang. **149**, 119769 (2019)
18. Kuhl, E.: Data-driven modeling of covid-19-lessons learned. Extreme Mech. Lett. **40**, 100921 (2020)
19. Machado, V., Mantini, G., Viterbo, J., Bernardini, F., Barcellos, R.: An instrument for evaluating open data portals: a case study in Brazilian cities. In: Proceedings of the 19th Annual International Conference on Digital Government Research: Governance in the Data Age, pp. 1–10 (2018)
20. Máchová, R., Hub, M., Lnenicka, M.: Usability evaluation of open data portals: Evaluating data discoverability, accessibility, and reusability from a stakeholders' perspective. Aslib J. Inf. Manag. (2018)

21. Máchová, R., Lněnička, M.: Evaluating the quality of open data portals on the national level. J. Theor. Appl. Electron. Commer. Res. **12**(1), 21–41 (2017)
22. Milić, P., Veljković, N., Stoimenov, L.: Framework for open data mining in e-government. In: Proceedings of the Fifth Balkan Conference in Informatics, pp. 255–258 (2012)
23. Nayek, J.K.: Evaluation of open data government sites: a comparative study. Libr. Philos. Pract. (2018)
24. Neves, F.T., de Castro Neto, M., Aparicio, M.: The impacts of open data initiatives on smart cities: a framework for evaluation and monitoring. Cities **106**, 102860 (2020)
25. Nikiforova, A.: Comparative analysis of national open data portals or whether your portal is ready to bring benefits from open data. In: IADIS International Conference on ICT, Society and Human Beings, pp. 21–23 (2020)
26. Nikiforova, A., McBride, K.: Open government data portal usability: a user-centred usability analysis of 41 open government data portals. Telematics Inform. **58**, 101539 (2021)
27. Oliveira, M.I.S., de Oliveira, H.R., Oliveira, L.A., Lóscio, B.F.: Open government data portals analysis: the brazilian case. In: Proceedings of the 17th International Digital Government Research Conference on Digital Government Research, pp. 415–424 (2016)
28. Pinto, H.D.S., Bernardini, F., Viterbo, J.: How cities categorize datasets in their open data portals: an exploratory analysis. In: Proceedings of the 19th Annual International Conference on Digital Government Research: Governance in the Data Age, pp. 1–9 (2018)
29. Reis, J.R., Viterbo, J., Bernardini, F.: A rationale for data governance as an approach to tackle recurrent drawbacks in open data portals. In: Proceedings of the 19th Annual International Conference on Digital Government Research: Governance in the Data Age, pp. 1–9 (2018)
30. Saxena, S.: Open government data (OGD) in six middle east countries: an evaluation of the national open data portals. Digit. Policy Regul. Gov. **20**(4), 310–322 (2018)
31. Saxena, S.: An evaluation of the national open government data (OGD) portal of the united Arab emirates. In: George, B., Paul, J. (eds.) Digit. Transform. Bus. Soc., pp. 191–209. Springer, Cham (2020). https://doi.org/10.1007/978-3-030-08277-2_12
32. Sayogo, D.S., Pardo, T.A., Cook, M.: A framework for benchmarking open government data efforts. In: 2014 47th Hawaii International Conference on System Sciences, pp. 1896–1905. IEEE (2014)
33. Shuja, J., Alanazi, E., Alasmary, W., Alashaikh, A.: COVID-19 open source data sets: a comprehensive survey. Appl. Intell. **51**(3), 1296–1325 (2020). https://doi.org/10.1007/s10489-020-01862-6
34. e Silva, L.V., et al.: Covid-19 mortality underreporting in Brazil: analysis of data from government internet portals. J. Med. Internet Res. **22**(8), e21413 (2020)
35. Vetrò, A., Canova, L., Torchiano, M., Minotas, C.O., Iemma, R., Morando, F.: Open data quality measurement framework: definition and application to open government data. Gov. Inf. Q. **33**(2), 325–337 (2016)
36. Wu, D., Xu, H., Yongyi, W., Zhu, H.: Quality of government health data in covid-19: definition and testing of an open government health data quality evaluation framework. Libr. Hi Tech. (2021)
37. Yang, T.M., Lo, J., Shiang, J.: To open or not to open? determinants of open government data. J. Inf. Sci. **41**(5), 596–612 (2015)

38. Zhu, X., Freeman, M.A.: An evaluation of us municipal open data portals: a user interaction framework. J. Assoc. Inf. Sci. Technol. **70**(1), 27–37 (2019)
39. Zuiderwijk, A., Janssen, M.: Open data policies, their implementation and impact: a framework for comparison. Gov. Inf. Q. **31**(1), 17–29 (2014)

Fostering Interaction Between Open Government Data Stakeholders: An Exchange Platform for Citizens, Developers and Publishers

Abiola Paterne Chokki(✉), Anthony Simonofski, Antoine Clarinval, Benoît Frénay, and Benoît Vanderose

University of Namur, Namur, Belgium
{abiola-paterne.chokki,anthony.simonofski,antoine.clarinval, benoit.frenay,benoit.vanderose}@unamur.be

Abstract. Open Government Data (OGD) consists of data released by publishers to drive the creation of innovative services by developers, and ultimately deliver value to citizens. However, the lack of communication between the different OGD stakeholders impedes the realization of this objective. The goal of this paper is to fill the technical aspects of this issue by identifying requirements needed in the design of a usable tool that can facilitate communication between OGD stakeholders. The stakeholders' requirements were identified from a literature review and validated through interviews with 9 stakeholders. Then, the identified features were integrated into the ODEON (Open Data Exchange solutiON) tool and its effectiveness in facilitating interaction between stakeholders was demonstrated through an evaluation with 22 stakeholders. This paper contributes to theory by proposing a list of 16 requirements to be implemented into a tool to facilitate communication between OGD stakeholders. Second, it contributes to practice by proposing a use case diagram listing the features needed to satisfy the requirements and a usable tool implementing them.

Keywords: Open government data · Requirements · Communication · OGD stakeholders

1 Introduction

In recent years, a number of Open Government Data (OGD) movements have emerged around the world, with data reuse being one of their main goals [1]. The stakeholders involved in the OGD process are subdivided in this study into three groups: citizens, developers and publishers [2–4]. Publishers release data to drive the creation of innovative services by developers, and ultimately deliver value to the citizens. OGD reuse can lead to several benefits, such as citizen participation in policy-making, collective problem solving, citizen empowerment, democratic accountability and development of innovative products and services [5]. However, it is a fact that even though a large amount of data is available, only a few people use it [3]. This lack of use is caused by the fact

Published by Springer Nature Switzerland AG 2022
M. Janssen et al. (Eds.): EGOV 2022, LNCS 13391, pp. 228–243, 2022.
https://doi.org/10.1007/978-3-031-15086-9_15

that there are many impediments to OGD use. Some of these are the result of a lack of communication between the different OGD stakeholders and therefore do not encourage them to take the first step to use or publish OGD [6, 7]. The term "communication" in this study refers to an interaction between OGD stakeholders for the purpose of creating a novel OGD-based service destined to citizens. Among these impediments, there is, for example, the unawareness of the usefulness of OGD (citizens), the unawareness of which services would be most useful to develop (developers) and the unawareness of which datasets to publish in priority (publishers) [5, 7–13]. In this study, we focus on the technical aspects of these impediments [10, 14, 15], which includes all other impediments to the use or publication of OGD that are not related to the social, emotional or motivational factors. For example, the *citizens' unawareness of the usefulness of OGD* impediment may result from social, emotional or motivational factors (e.g., citizens may not be interested in getting involved with OGD) or technical factors (e.g., few platforms demonstrate to citizens the usufulness of OGD).

Several methods and platforms have been proposed in the literature to overcome the technical aspects of the communication gap. For instance, hackathons have been put in place by public organizations (publishers) to promote the use of their published OGD to developers. However, this method does not generally involve the citizens [7]. In addition, OGD portals, where most OGD are published, do not provide a common space where, for example, all OGD stakeholders could collaborate to report certain issues on datasets and co-create new services [5, 10, 12]. In summary, even though many methods or platforms have been proposed to facilitate the communication between OGD stakeholders, none of them provides the complete functionality necessary to achieve this goal. Moreover, to the best of our knowledge, no study has been conducted in the literature to propose a list of requirements guiding the design of a usable tool that can facilitate the communication between OGD stakeholders.

This paper aims to address the mentioned gaps by first proposing a list of requirements needed in the design of a usable tool that can facilitate communication between OGD stakeholders, and then implementing them in a tool and evaluating it. Therefore, our research question is: *"How to design a tool that can facilitate communication between OGD stakeholders?"* To address this research question, we first conduct a literature review to collect the impediments of using and publishing OGD. Then, the impediments are used to derive requirements. The requirements are then presented to 9 stakeholders (1 publisher, 4 developers and 4 citizens) for validation and for gathering additional requirements, if any. Once the requirements are validated, a use case diagram listing the features needed to satisfy the requirements is proposed and the features are then integrated into a tool called ODEON (Open Data Exchange solutiON). Finally, we evaluate the ease of use and usefulness of the prototype by means of user testing with 22 stakeholders (9 citizens, 8 developers and 5 publishers). In doing so, we validate, using the implemented prototype as a proxy, the usefulness of the proposed requirements in addressing the technical aspects of the lack of communication between OGD stakeholders.

The remainder of this paper is structured as follows: we present the background related to OGD stakeholders, impediments to OGD use and publication and methods and platforms of communication between OGD stakeholders (Sect. 2). We then explain the design science research approach we followed (Sect. 3) and present the developed tool and its evaluation (Sect. 4). Finally, we discuss the findings and limitations of this study as well as avenues for future work (Sect. 5) and conclude with a summary of the contributions (Sect. 6).

2 Background

In this section, we first clarify the stakeholder types that we consider in this study. Then, we present previous work related to the impediments resulting from the lack of communication between OGD stakeholders. Finally, we present methods and platforms proposed in the literature to facilitate the communication between OGD stakeholders.

2.1 OGD Stakeholders

Many stakeholders are involved in the OGD process. In this study, we focus more on stakeholders who use OGD for private needs and whose interaction with public administrations is difficult, as well as on stakeholders who publish aggregated data on portals. Thus, stakeholders such as public servants who use OGD in their daily work and organizations that provide the data for publication are not considered here. Based on previous studies [2–4], we identify three roles that these stakeholders can hold: publishers, developers and citizens. Figure 1 summarizes the OGD process, and the three roles are defined below:

Publishers: These stakeholders are responsible for publishing the data online. This includes public organizations and governments.

Developers: These stakeholders create innovative services and applications with the data published by publishers.

Citizens: They represent most of the population who may eventually consume data via an application developed by developers.

It is important to note that a direct link between publishers and citizens is possible but difficult to establish due to the lack of technical skills of citizens to process the data themselves.

Fig. 1. OGD process. Publishers publish data that will be integrated into applications or services developed by developers. These will then be used by citizens.

2.2 Impediments to OGD Use and Publication

Several studies [5–13, 16–18] have focused on the impediments to OGD use and publication. Below, we present the impediments resulting from the technical aspects of the lack of communication between OGD stakeholders that demotivate them to use and to publish OGD.

From the citizens' perspective, we identified two main impediments. First, ***(IC1)*** many citizens are not aware of the existence and usefulness of OGD and the services that use them [5, 7]. Second, ***(IC2)*** the services developed with OGD are not used by citizens due to either unawareness of the services or mismatch between the services and their needs. Indeed, most of the time, they are not involved in the service design [7, 9].

From the developers' perspective, we identified six main impediments. First, ***(ID1)*** developers are not able to come up with a service idea that may be interesting for citizens due to a lack of knowledge of citizens' needs [9]. Second, ***(ID2)*** developers are not able to find examples of use case or success stories of OGD use to build on to propose services that may be interesting to citizens [9]. Third, ***(ID3)*** once developers have an idea of the service to implement, one of the issues is the data quality and the difficulty to communicate with the publisher to solve this issue [5, 9–13]. Fourth, ***(ID4)*** developers are sometimes unable to find the datasets needed to create the service due to the non-publication of these datasets by OGD providers and also the lack of discussion between the two parties to request the necessary datasets [5, 9, 10, 19]. Fifth, ***(ID5)*** developers often do not receive feedback from publishers after requesting datasets or asking some questions [5, 12]. Sixth, ***(ID6)*** developers often have no information about the datasets used in a specific project in order to replicate or improve it [16–18].

From the publishers' perspective, we identified three main impediments. First, ***(IP1)*** publishers are not motivated to publish data because most published datasets are not used, making the added value and economic impact of their publication efforts uncertain [13]. Second, ***(IP2)*** publishers are unaware of the datasets that they need to prioritize during the publication process [6, 7]. Third, ***(IP3)*** publishers do not know which projects are using their published datasets, as many users do not report their reuses [13].

The impediments, repeatedly reported in the literature, highlight the need for increased communication and collaboration among OGD stakeholders.

2.3 Methods and Platforms of Communication Between OGD Stakeholders

Many methods and platforms have been proposed in the literature to facilitate the communication between OGD stakeholders [20]. Reviewing each of them would be beyond the scope of this paper. Here, we focused on these popular (i.e. most cited or used in an OGD context) methods and platforms: hackathons, interviews, workshops, OGD portals and citizen participation platforms. Many extant platforms such as ADEQUATE [21], Github, Gitlab, Stack Overflow, gFoge, Jira, Redmine, Wiki, etc. can enable communication between users. However, in this study, we only reviewed platforms that are related to our research question i.e., that have already been used in previous studies to facilitate communication between users in the context of the OGD process and that clearly distinguish the role of each user in this process. Table 1 presents the methods and platforms reviewed, their strengths, and weaknesses.

All the gaps mentioned in the existing methods show that there is currently no method or tool that supports collaboration between OGD stakeholders adequately. This justifies the need to identify the necessary requirements such a tool should satisfy and to implement one fulfilling them. Therefore, we implemented ODEON, which differs from the methods and platforms reviewed in that it addresses each of their shortcomings. It is important to note that ODEON does not aim to replace existing OGD portals but rather proposes complementary communication features. Similarly, ODEON complements citizen participation platforms by allowing to link each service idea to some datasets available on OGD portals that can help to implement the idea.

Table 1. Strengths and weaknesses of methods and platforms of communication between OGD stakeholders.

Methods/Platforms	Strengths	Weaknesses
Hackathons [7, 20]	(1) enable developers to design, implement and present services for a specific issue, beyond the "product idea" level (2) physically reunite developers and publishers for several hours to several days, creating many opportunities for discussion (3) usually very focused on technological output, developers tend to oversee other aspects than code due to competition under tight schedule	(1) no consideration of citizens' needs (2) access limited to a certain type and number of participants (3) communication between these stakeholders is ephemeral (e.g., after the event, there is no possibility to report issues with the datasets or to request datasets) (4) no archiving option that allows, for example, other citizens or developers to know which reuses were implemented during the event (5) impossible to get feedback from participants who were not at the event on the solutions implemented
Interviews and workshops [6, 7, 19, 22, 23]	allows different OGD stakeholders to physically discuss to collect their needs or feedback	(1) access limited to a certain type and number of participants (2) communication between these stakeholders is ephemeral
OGD portals [5, 12]	(1) help local governments to publish and manage open data on the web (2) allow developers to submit their reuses or to see existing reuses	(1) can only handle reuses and datasets from the specific portal (2) citizens' needs are not considered (3) no common space to facilitate discussion among stakeholders (4) no archiving of the data issues and their status (5) developers are not able to collect feedback about the reuses they have submitted (6) publishers are not able to know which datasets to prioritize for publication
Citizen participation platforms (e.g., Citizenlab[1], Leuven make it happen[2]) [24]	(1) allow local governments to interact with the public (2) allow stakeholders to propose project ideas (3) allow stakeholders to vote on projects they are interested in (4) allow stakeholders to track the status of their projects (e.g., rejected or not)	(1) not focused on promoting the use of open data (2) unable to integrate publishers and developers into the project process (3) unable to track project progress after approval (4) unable to record existing reuses of open datasets (5) unable to link open datasets to projects (6) unable to request data to publishers (7) unable to report issues on open datasets (8) unable for publishers to know which datasets have priority for publication

[1] https://www.citizenlab.co/.
[2] https://leuvenmaakhetmee.be/.

3 Research Methodology

The Design Science Research (DSR) method [25, 26] was used to address the research question of this paper. It aims to develop solutions (design cycle) that meet defined objectives, contribute to the scientific knowledge base (rigor cycle) and provide utility in the environment (relevance cycle).

In the **rigor cycle**, we conducted a literature review to access existing knowledge on the impediments resulting from the technical aspects of the lack of communication between OGD stakeholders. These impediments were extracted from 12 articles returned by a search performed on the databases "Scopus" and "Science Direct" with the keywords ("open government data" or "open data") and ("features" or "impediments" or "barriers") and ("(re)use" or "publication" or "communication"). The results of the literature review are presented in Sect. 2.2. Once this step was completed, we used the identified impediments to formulate general requirements that should be implemented in a usable tool to solve these impediments. Next, interviews were conducted by the first author with 9 stakeholders (1 publisher, 4 developers and 4 citizens) to validate the suggested requirements and gather additional ones, if any. The interviews were handled in four steps. First, we briefly introduced participants to the utility of OGD with a concrete case of the use of OGD by the city of Namur, which developed an Intelligent Transportation System[3] based on the OGD it published. Second, we explained the context of our project by presenting the benefits and problems related to the lack of communication between OGD stakeholders. Third, we asked participants to suggest some requirements that can address these mentioned problems. Fourth, we showed participants the requirements we extracted from our literature review and asked them, on a scale of 1 (Totally irrelevant) to 5 (Totally relevant), how relevant they were and to justify their choice. Appendix A[4] summarizes the questions asked during the interviews. We took note of the participants' feedback and recorded the discussion with their agreement for transcription and later review. The interviews were later coded by the first author using short sentences to retain context and conceptual relations, and then reviewed by two other co-authors. Finally, we used the results of these interviews to provide a list of requirements that need to be incorporated into a usable tool to facilitate communication among OGD stakeholders.

In the **design cycle**, we used the validated requirements to propose a list of features that were then implemented in a tool called ODEON (Open Data Exchange solutiON). Once the features were implemented, we presented the tool to two stakeholders (a developer and a citizen) to get their feedback and integrate it before the evaluation phase.

In the **relevance cycle**, we evaluated the prototype through a user test with 22 stakeholders (5 publishers, 8 developers and 9 citizens) to assess its ease of use and usefulness in addressing the identified impediments, and to gather additional features for future versions. The publishers were recruited through contact forms available on their OGD portals. As for the developers and citizens, they were recruited through the following communication channels: first author's university mailbox and social media. The interviews were handled in four steps. The first two steps are identical to those of the rigor

[3] https://sti.namur.be/.

[4] https://doi.org/10.5281/zenodo.6332097.

cycle interviews. In the third stage we briefly presented the prototype's features to the participants in 10 min, and then gave them 20 min to perform scenarios related to their profile with ODEON. Citizens were invited to (1) explore existing projects, (2) suggest a new project with the content of their choosing, and (3) provide feedback on two projects of their choosing. Developers were asked to (1) explore existing projects, (2) suggest a new project with the content of their choosing, (3) request a dataset of their choosing they would be needed to develop the project they suggested in the second scenario, (4) report an issue with an existing dataset of their choosing, and (5) provide feedback on two other projects and two other datasets of their choosing. Finally, publishers were asked to (1) explore existing projects and (2) provide feedback on two projects and two dataset issues of their choosing. We encouraged them to perform think-aloud as they explored to gather qualitative data on their overall feeling and expectations. They were also given the opportunity to ask the interviewer questions if necessary. However, in accordance with user testing guidelines [27], the sequence of actions to perform the scenarios was not given to participants. Next, we collected participants' feedback through a questionnaire consisting of three types of questions: questions with a 7-point Likert scale (from "Strongly Disagree" to "Strongly Agree") based on the Technology Acceptance Model (TAM) [28] to assess the ease of use of prototype functionalities, the ease of use and usefulness of the prototype in solving the identified impediments, open-ended questions to gather general opinions and suggestions for additional features for future versions and to explain quantitative ratings, and questions on the respondent's profile. The questionnaire was pretested with two people to ensure that all kinds of errors that are associated with survey research are reduced [29]. Appendix B (see footnote 4) presents the questions contained in the questionnaire according to the stakeholder roles. After collecting participants' feedback, the median, mean and standard deviation were calculated for the Likert questions to evaluate the following aspects: (A1) ease of use of each prototype feature, (A2) overall ease of use of the prototype, (A3) usefulness of each prototype feature and (A4) overall usefulness of the prototype for facilitating communication between OGD stakeholders. The A1 (respectively A3) questions were used as a reference to understand the answers to the A2 (respectively A4) questions. These statistical measures were chosen because they are the most appropriate for analyzing Likert data and for having a central tendency measure [30]. Verbal thoughts and responses collected from the free text questions were coded using short sentences to retain context and conceptual relations.

4 Results

In this section, we first present the requirements that need to be incorporated into a usable tool to facilitate communication among OGD stakeholders. Next, we describe how the ODEON prototype was implemented to meet these requirements. Finally, we present the results of the evaluation of ODEON.

4.1 Requirements Identification for Communication Between OGD Stakeholders

Based on the identified impediments, we derived several requirements that were confronted with the participants during the rigor cycle interviews. Table 2 presents the requirements along with insights from the literature and interviewees.

Table 2. List of requirements to design a tool that can facilitate the communication between the OGD stakeholders along with insights from the literature and interviewees. "All" means that all participants were agreed that the requirement is relevant.

Requirements (C = citizens, D = developers, P = publishers)	Insights from	
	literature	# Participants
RC1. Inform citizens of existing projects based on OGD	IC1	All
RC2. Allow citizens to be involved in the service development process	IC2	All
RC3. Allow citizens to propose project ideas	IC2, ID1	All
RC4. Allow citizens to register existing projects	/	1
RC5. Allow citizens to define which requested projects should be prioritized	/	4
RD1. Allow developers to register existing projects	ID2	All
RD2. Inform developers about existing projects based on OGD	ID2	All
RD3. Allow developers to report issues related to the use of published datasets	ID3	All
RD4. Allow developers to request datasets that do not exist on the portals	ID4	All
RD5. Allow developers to provide feedback on projects and datasets	ID5	All
RD6. Inform developers about the datasets used in projects	ID6	All
RD7. Allow developers to propose project ideas	/	1
RD8. Allow developers to define which requested projects and data should be prioritized	/	4
RP1. Inform publishers about existing projects based on OGD	IP1	All
RP2. Inform publishers of priority data to be published	IP2	All
RP3. Inform publishers of projects using their datasets	IP3	All

4.2 ODEON System Description

We designed features that could meet the collected requirements and then implemented them in the prototype ODEON (source code available[5]). The following paragraphs explain how the implemented features meet the different requirements.

[5] https://github.com/chokkipaterne/odeon.

Provide a Form to Register a Project (RC4 and RD1). It allows developers and citizens to register an existing project in two steps. First, they fill in the following information: country, city, domain, title, access link, description, image and contact information. Then, they can add the datasets used in the project in three ways: by searching and selecting datasets directly from the OGD portals, by uploading files, or by using external links. To avoid duplicate entries, an auto-completion feature for the title field was added, as suggested by an interviewee. Regarding the addition of datasets related to a project from the OGD portals, ODEON provides a search option that allows users to search and select the desired dataset directly from any CKAN or OpenDataSoft portal using the APIs provided by these two systems.

Provide a Form to Suggest a Project (RC3 and RD7). The form to be filled in is similar to the project registration form, except that the access link is not requested, and developers and citizens can also skip the step of adding or requesting datasets for the project.

Display the List of Projects (RC1, RD2 and RP1). It displays all registered (existing and requested) projects.

Search Projects (RC1, RD2 and RP1). It allows stakeholders to search for specific projects among the registered projects based on the following criteria: keywords, domain, project type (requested or existing), country and city.

Display Details of a Specific Project (RD6). It allows stakeholders to see all information about a specific project: general information (title, description, country, comments, etc.) and data used or requested in the project.

Display Details of a Specific Dataset (RP3). It allows stakeholders to see all information about a specific dataset: general information (title, description, country, comments, etc.) and projects that use the dataset.

Provide a Form to Request Data (RD4). It allows developers and citizens to request data by filling in the following information: country, city, title, description and contact information.

Provide a Form to Comment a Specific Project (RC2 and RD5). It provides two options. The first option allows any user to provide general feedback on the project or respond to an existing comment. The second option allows developers to inform citizens of the progress of the project development.

Provide a Form to Comment a Specific Data (RD3). It provides two options. The first option allows any user to provide general feedback on the data or respond to an existing comment. The second option allows stakeholders to report data issues. The form has the following fields: comment type (general comment or report data issue), name, comment and attachment.

Display and Search Requested Data (RP2). It lists all the requested data. There is also a search option that allows filtering the display using the following options: country, state and keywords.

Display and Search Data Issues (RD3). It lists all data issues reported by stakeholders. There is also a search option that allows filtering the display using the following options: country, state and keywords.

Add a Voting Option for Requested Projects and Data (RC5 and RD8). It consists of adding a "Like" button for each requested project or data so that any user can click on the button to indicate that the requested project or data is relevant (Fig. 2).

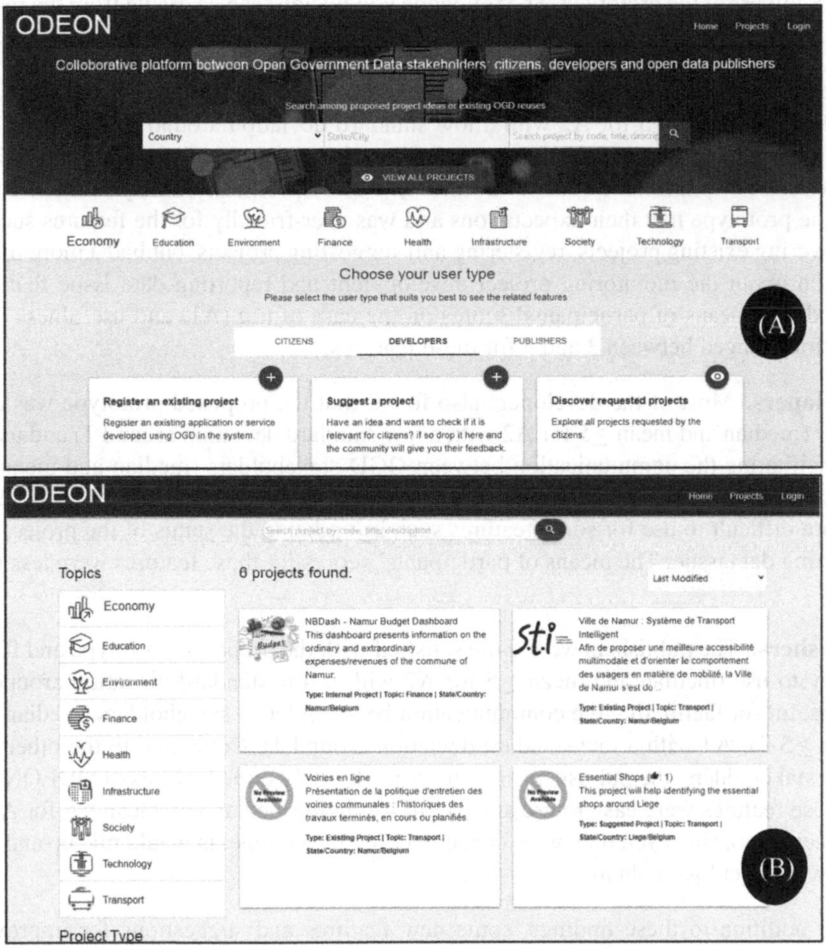

Fig. 2. Two pages of ODEON. (A) represents a portion of the homepage and (B) represents a portion of the project list page with available search options.

ODEON is a web application built using the Django framework. Figure 2 shows two pages of the prototype. (A) represents a portion of the homepage where the stakeholders can make a quick search of project or can access other features of the prototype based on their profile (citizen, developer or publisher) and (B) represents a portion of the project list page with available search options (keywords, topic, project type and location).

4.3 Evaluation

In total, 22 participants (9 citizens, 8 developers and 5 publishers) participated in the evaluation of ODEON and completed the questionnaire. Table 3 presents the median, mean and standard deviation (SD) for the Likert questions regarding the ease of use and the usefulness of the prototype. The following conclusions can be drawn from the results of Table 3, for the different stakeholders:

Citizens. Most of the citizens agreed that the proposed prototype was easy to use (median and mean $\geq$5 for A2 with a low standard deviation around 1) and useful for facilitating the communication between OGD stakeholders (median and mean $\geq$5 for A4 with a low standard deviation around 1). More specifically, many citizens found that the prototype met their expectations and was user-friendly for the features such as discovering existing projects, registering and suggesting projects, but had a more mixed opinion about the monitoring project development and reporting data issue features. Indeed, the means of participants' scores on the ease of use (A1) and usefulness (A3) questions ranged between 3 and 5 for these features.

Developers. Most of the developers also found that the proposed prototype was easy to use (median and mean $\geq$5 for A2 with a low standard deviation around 1) and useful for facilitating the communication between OGD stakeholders (median and mean $\geq$5 for A4 with a low standard deviation around 1). However, like the citizens, they found it more difficult to use for some features such as updating the status of the project and reporting data issue. The means of participants' scores for these features were less than 5.

Publishers. The publishers were quite satisfied with the proposed prototype and found it easy to use (median and mean $\geq$5 for A2 with a low standard deviation around 1) and useful for facilitating the communication between OGD stakeholders (median and mean $\geq$5 for A4 with a low standard deviation around 1). Compared to the other two OGD stakeholders, the publishers are concerned by only three features of ODEON and all these features were easy to use and useful for them (median and mean $\geq$5 for A1 & A3 questions). However, they were concerned that the comments would pile up and that they would get lost in them.

In addition to these findings, some new features and suggestions for improving the UI design were gathered from the verbal thoughts and answers to the open-ended questions provided by the participants. The new features are as follows. First, citizens and developers suggested having a feature that helps them to subscribe to a dataset or project to get weekly updates on the data or projects they have subscribed to. Second, publishers suggested having a monthly summary of requested datasets or data issues directly in their inbox. Third, for the discovery functionality of existing and requested projects, participants suggested moving the project type and location filters close to the search field to make them more visible. Fourth, participants suggested adding a status

Table 3. Median, mean and standard deviation (SD) of ease of use and usefulness questions.

	Citizens (N = 9)		Developers (N = 8)		Publishers (N = 5)	
	Median	Mean (SD)	Median	Mean (SD)	Median	Mean (SD)
A2. Ease of use of the prototype	5	5.19 (1.13)	5.5	5.25 (1.18)	6	5.7 (0.82)
A4. Usefulness of the prototype	5	5.36 (1.27)	5	5.67 (1.14)	6	6 (1.41)

attribute for projects to help to identify the current status of each project: requirements analysis, under development, development complete and abandoned project.

5 Discussion

This research contributes to theory in the following aspects. First, it extends previous studies related to impediments [5, 7–13], building on the previously identified impediments to propose a list of 16 requirements that should be implemented in a usable tool to facilitate the communication between OGD stakeholders. These identified requirements can also be used as reference by open data publishers or developers of citizen participation platforms to help them to know what features need to be added to their existing platforms to fully facilitate communication between OGD stakeholders. They can also be used by researchers to evaluate applications whose objective is to facilitate communication between OGD stakeholders. Second, unlike previous studies [5, 7–13] that focused only on a specific user profile or only on impediments, this research validates the identified impediments as well as the requirements through interviews with three different stakeholder roles. Third, the results obtained from the evaluation show that ODEON and the implemented features were easy to use and useful to address the technical aspects of the lack of communication between OGD stakeholders.

This research also contributes to practice in the following aspects. First, unlike previous studies [5, 7–13] that identified impediments without providing a list of features of a usable tool to address them, we derived a list of features from the requirements for each OGD stakeholder, and we present it as the use case diagram shown in Fig. 3. In this diagram, features are subdivided into data features and project features. The data features address the following impediments: data quality and lack of awareness of which data should be released first. The project features resolve other identified impediments, such as unawareness of the existing projects based on OGD, difficulty finding a project idea, lack of citizen involvement in project development, etc. Second, we provide access to the source code of ODEON (see footnote 5). This can be used as a starting point by developers to create their own online tool for facilitating the collaboration between OGD stakeholders or to improve the prototype. The use case diagram can be used as starting point as well.

However, this research has some limitations that will need to be addressed in future work. The first limitation concerns the representativeness of the participants in the evaluation. The number of participants may be small, but referring to previous studies [31,

32] 5 participants is a good baseline for usability tests and we also observed that our findings were reaching saturation at that point. However, to increase representativeness, we suggest using other communication channels or collecting data on-site in administrations, universities, workshops, hackathons or public places to recruit participants for the evaluation of the future prototype version. In this study, this was not feasible due to the COVID-19 situation. The third limitation is that we did not consider the discovery step of ODEON. Indeed, a multi-stakeholder collaboration platforms relies heavily on a community that needs to be attracted on the platform. One approach to address this issue will be to communicate about this prototype using social networks and by presenting it at open data workshops and hackathons. The fourth limitation is the non-generalization of the proposed requirements to other areas. Other researchers can start by investigating whether the existent platforms (e.g., Github, Wiki) can be adapted to the context of open data or whether the proposed requirements can be used or extend to other areas such as open data ecosystems, open government ecosystems, and open source software ecosystems. Future work will also include an implementation of the suggested new features and a field evaluation of ODEON, for example, by offering hackathon organizers to use it as meeting point between the stakeholders involved in the event.

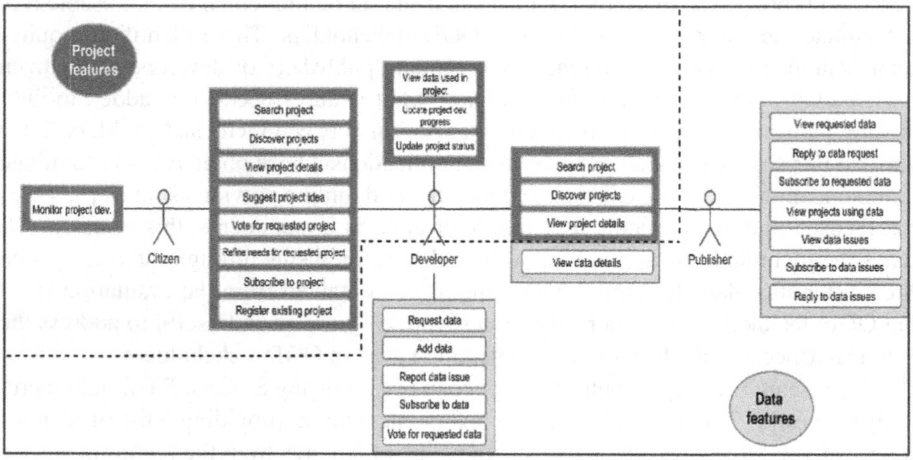

Fig. 3. Use case diagram of ODEON. The features are subdivided into two groups: the features related to the project (project features) and the features related to the data (data features).

6 Conclusion

The aim of this paper was to address the technical aspects of the lack of communication between OGD stakeholders (citizens, developers and publishers). To achieve that goal, we first identified the impediments resulting from the technical aspects of the lack of communication between OGD stakeholders that demotivate them to use and to publish OGD through a literature review. Then, through interviews with 9 stakeholders, we deducted and validated, the requirements that should be satisfied by a usable tool that addresses these impediments. Next, we implemented the ODEON prototype based on the collected requirements and used it as proxy to measure the extent to which the requirements were easy to use and useful to facilitate the communication between OGD stakeholders through an evaluation conducted with 22 stakeholders from the three different profiles.

The results of the literature review and successive evaluations have led to the proposal and validation of a list of 16 requirements along with a use case diagram of features that should be implemented in a usable tool to facilitate the communication between OGD stakeholders. These features are classified into two categories: data features and project features. Among the data features, the main ones are reporting data issues, requesting data and replying to data requests and issues. From the project features, the main ones are suggesting a project, discovering requested and existing projects, updating project development progress, and monitoring project development. Second, the evaluation results show that publishers are more satisfied with the proposed prototype compared to the citizens and the developers. Both latter stakeholders, however, were fully in agreement with the implemented features, but they just complained about the ease of use of some features and then gave us improvement suggestions that we plan to integrate in future versions.

References

1. Attard, J., Orlandi, F., Scerri, S., Auer, S.: A systematic review of open government data initiatives. Gov. Inf. Q. **32**, 399–418 (2015)
2. Gonzalez-Zapata, F., Heeks, R.: The multiple meanings of open government data: understanding different stakeholders and their perspectives. Gov. Inf. Q. **32**, 441–452 (2015)
3. Safarov, I., Meijer, A., Grimmelikhuijsen, S.: Utilization of open government data: a systematic literature review of types, conditions, effects and users. Inf. Polity **22**, 1–24 (2017)
4. Graves, A., Hendler, J.: A study on the use of visualizations for open government data. Inf. Polity. **19**, 73–91 (2014)
5. Janssen, M., Charalabidis, Y., Zuiderwijk, A.: Benefits, adoption barriers and myths of open data and open government. Inf. Syst. Manag. **29**, 258–268 (2012)
6. Gebka, E., Crusoe, J., Ahlin, K.: Open data reuse and information needs satisfaction: a method to bridge the gap. In: CEUR Workshop Proceedings, vol. 2797, pp. 41–49 (2020)
7. Gebka, E., Clarinval, A., Crusoe, J., Simonofski, A.: Generating value with open government data: beyond the programmer. In: 13th International Conference on Research Challenges in Information Sciences, pp. 1–2 (2019)
8. Crusoe, J., Melin, U.: Investigating open government data barriers: a literature review and conceptualization. In: Electronic Government, pp. 169–183. Springer, Cham (2018). https://doi.org/10.1007/978-3-319-98690-6_15
9. Crusoe, J., Simonofski, A., Clarinval, A., Gebka, E.: The impact of impediments on open government data use: insights from users. In: 13th International Conference on Research Challenges in Information Sciences, pp. 1–12 (2019)
10. Zuiderwijk, A., Janssen, M., Choenni, S., Meijer, R., Alibaks, R.S.: Socio-technical Impediments of open data. Electron. J. Electron. Gov. **10**, 156–172 (2012)
11. Martin, S., Foulonneau, M., Turki, S., Ihadjadene, M., Paris, U., Tudor, P.: Risk analysis to overcome barriers to open data. Electron. J. e-Gov. **11**, 348–359 (2013)

12. Beno, M., Figl, K., Umbrich, J., Polleres, A.: Open data hopes and fears: determining the barriers of open data. In: Proceedings of 7th International Conference for E-Democracy and Open Government, CeDEM 2017, pp. 69–81 (2017)
13. Polleres, A., Umbrich, J., Figl, K., Beno, M.: Perception of key barriers in using and publishing open data. JeDEM – eJ. eDemocr. Open Gov. **9**, 134–165 (2017)
14. Purwanto, A., Zuiderwijk, A., Janssen, M.: Citizen engagement with open government data: lessons learned from Indonesia's presidential election. Transform. Gov. People Process Policy. **14**, 1–30 (2020)
15. Lapointe, L., Rivard, S.: Research on user resistance to information technology. In: The Routledge Companion to Management Information Systems, pp. 183–201. Routledge (2017)
16. Matheus, R., Janssen, M., Maheshwari, D.: Data science empowering the public: data-driven dashboards for transparent and accountable decision-making in smart cities. Gov. Inf. Q. **37**, 101284 (2020)
17. Sarikaya, A., Correll, M., Bartram, L., Tory, M., Fisher, D.: What do we talk about when we talk about dashboards? IEEE Trans. Vis. Comput. Graph. **25**, 682–692 (2019)
18. Kitchin, R., Mcardle, G.: Urban data and city dashboards: six key issues. In: Data and the City (2016)
19. Chokki, A.P., Simonofski, A., Frénay, B., Vanderose, B.: Open government data for non-expert citizens: understanding content and visualizations' expectations. In: Cherfi, S., Perini, A., Nurcan, S. (eds.) Research Challenges in Information Science. LNBIP, vol. 415, pp. 602–608. Springer, Cham (2021). https://doi.org/10.1007/978-3-030-75018-3_42
20. Simonofski, A., Amaral de Sousa, V., Clarinval, A., Vanderose, B.: Participation in hackathons: a multi-methods view on motivators, demotivators and citizen participation. In: Dalpiaz, F., Zdravkovic, J., Loucopoulos, P. (eds.) Research Challenges in Information Science. LNBIP, vol. 385, pp. 229–246. Springer, Cham (2020). https://doi.org/10.1007/978-3-030-50316-1_14
21. Neumaier, S., Thurnay, L., Lampoltshammer, T.J., Knap, T.: Search, filter, fork, and link open data: the ADEQUATe platform: data- and community-driven quality improvements. In: Web Conference 2018 - Companion World Wide Web Conference, WWW 2018, pp. 1523–1526 (2018)
22. Crusoe, J., Gebka, E., Ahlin, K.: Open government data from the perspective of information needs - a tentative conceptual model. In: Viale Pereira, G., et al. (eds.) Electronic Government. LNCS, vol. 12219, pp. 250–261. Springer, Cham (2020). https://doi.org/10.1007/978-3-030-57599-1_19
23. Barbosa Tavares, R., Hepworth, M., De Souza Costa, S.M.: Investigating citizens' information needs through participative research: a pilot study in Candangolândia, Brazil. Am. J. Heal. Promot. **27**, 125–138 (2011)
24. Gil, O., Cortés-Cediel, M.E., Cantador, I.: Citizen participation and the rise of digital media platforms in smart governance and smart cities. In: Research Anthology on Citizen Engagement and Activism for Social Change, pp. 1186–1202. IGI Global (2022)
25. Hevner, A.R., March, S.T., Park, J., Ram, S.: Design science in information systems research. MIS Q. 75–105 (2004)
26. Dresch, A., Lacerda, D.P., Antunes, J.A.V.: Design Science Research: A Method for Science and Technology Advancement. Springer, Cham (2015). https://doi.org/10.1007/978-3-319-07374-3_4
27. Lallemand, C., Gronier, G.: Méthodes de design UX: 30 méthodes fondamentales pour concevoir et évaluer les systèmes interactifs. Eyrolles (2015)
28. Davis, F.D.: Perceived usefulness, perceived ease of use, and user acceptance of information technology. Manag. Inf. Syst. **13**, 319–339 (1989)
29. Grimm, P.: Pretesting a questionnaire. Wiley International Encyclopedia of Marketing (2010)

30. Boone, H.N., Boone, D.A.: Analyzing likert data. J. Ext. **50**, 1–5 (2012)
31. Faulkner, L.: Beyond the five-user assumption: benefits of increased sample sizes in usability testing. Behav. Res. Methods Instrum. Comput. **35**, 379–383 (2003). https://doi.org/10.3758/BF03195514
32. Nielsen, J.: Why You Only Need to Test with 5 Users. https://www.nngroup.com/articles/why-you-only-need-to-test-with-5-users/. Accessed 2021 17 June 2021

The Use of Open Government Data to Create Social Value

María Elena López Reyes(✉) and Rikke Magnussen

Aalborg University, A.C Meyers Vænge 15, 2450, Copenhagen SV, Denmark
melr@ikp.aau.dk

Abstract. The current work aims to identify the perspectives from which scholars have studied the link between the citizens' involvement in the use of Open Government Data (OGD) and the creation of social value to solve local issues in cities as the expected result. Recent studies have concentrated on studying the barriers and conditions of using OGD by focusing on specific types and users' motivations. Researchers have found that the critical problem of Open Data initiatives is the lack of utilization. Therefore, to allow more rigorous empirical research to assess if the estimated effects of OGD are measurable, there is a need to investigate the link between the types of users and the potential type of effects, that for this proposal is the creation of social value. The study adopted a systematic literature review to map the most current work addressing the utilization of OGD to create social value within different domains. Forty-six records were identified and characterized into four categories of studies: i) Governance - the interconnection of aspects that allow managing and using OGD; ii) Availability- aspects limiting OGD access and re-use; iii) Adoption - aspects that enable the acceptance or rejection of OGD; and iv) Impact - capacity to solve social problems. This study reinforces the move toward decentralizing data governance and civic services.

Keywords: Open government data · Social value creation · Citizens' involvement

1 Introduction and Background

Over the past decades, there has been an increase in the collaboration between citizens, public institutions, the private sector, and knowledge institutions to facilitate the creation of social value to solve local issues [1]. It has been acknowledged that public services are no longer provided only by governmental agencies but are designed and delivered through coordination across multiple sectors [2]. At the same time, it has become more accepted that as "experts on themselves," citizens take more responsibility for the services they or their dependents receive playing a more proactive role [3]. Align to this trend, the Open Government Data (OGD) movement entered the global political agendas to encourage public organizations to collect and make factual, nonperson-specific data public [4].

Published by Springer Nature Switzerland AG 2022
M. Janssen et al. (Eds.): EGOV 2022, LNCS 13391, pp. 244–257, 2022.
https://doi.org/10.1007/978-3-031-15086-9_16

The Open Data philosophy's central proposition is that data, information, and knowledge become a shared asset in society, allowing anyone to use it to engage and participate in economic, social, political, and cultural projects [4]. Data availability enables the coalition, combination, and enhancement of data through processes and tools [5] that allow the use, reuse, redistribution, and merge of available OGD with other data sources [6]. These processes enable the transformation of data into fact information, insight, interface, new data, or services [7–9].

The goal of the release of OGD is to transform how governments relate to the public by engaging citizens in using the available data [10]. The intention is to enable citizens to transform their community or environment; or help local governments solve challenges by benefiting from their knowledge, ideas, and the ability of people to provide surveillance [6]. The expected effects can be of three kinds. Firstly, it can drive social effects by creating or improving solutions to public service provision and creating social value. Secondly, it can improve governance by raising transparency and accountability, increasing citizen trust, and stimulating citizen participation. And thirdly, it can lead to economic effects by driving economic development [11, 12].

Specifically, using datasets related to public services and facilities can increase social value as they offer citizens the opportunity to enhance social life quality [13]. The use of OGD allows citizens to share information, take part in policing and law enforcement, analyzing and monitoring social issues and government actions, developing social innovation, engaging in public services innovation or improvement, generate wealth through the downstream use of outputs, and more generally, enhance the interaction between government and citizens to solve local problems [10, 12].

Despite the efforts to engage citizens in the use of OGD [14] and the rapid advances in information and communication technology [11], several studies point out that the critical problem of OGD initiatives is the lack of its utilization [6, 12]. There has been a significant focus in the literature on studying the relationship between the utilization of OGD and the social and technical conditions enabling or disabling its use [6, 12, 15, 16]. Scholars have found that the barriers and conditions to using OGD are related to the quality of data such as metadata and readability; legislation on topics such as policy and privacy; challenges related to the user such as lack of knowledge, lack of skills, or lack of interest; barriers related to the infrastructure such as interoperability, availability, and security; and finally economic challenges [6, 12, 15, 16].

More recent studies have concentrated on the barriers and conditions of using OGD by focusing on specific types and users' motivations [12]. For example, Purwanto et al. [9] focused on the individual citizens' drivers and inhibitors for engaging with the use of OGD. However, to allow more rigorous empirical research to assess if the estimated effects of OGD are measurable, there is a need to investigate the link between the types of users and the potential type of effects [12].

In the current paper, we focus on identifying the perspectives from which scholars have studied the link between the citizens' involvement in using OGD and the expected effect of the creation of social value to solve local issues in cities as an expected result. The research question guiding this study is "what perspectives have been used to study citizens' involvement in using OGD when the expected effect is creating social value to solve local issues in cities?"

The article's content has the following structure: The next section describes the methodology, including a systematic literature review [17]; the third section presents the content analysis results. The fourth section discusses the research findings, conclusion, and study's limitations. This review belongs to the European Union's Horizon 2020 innovation program ODECO. The research focus will serve as a building block to broader research on Open Data Ecosystems [18] that seeks to understand how to sustain OGD availability and increase its use to create social value and solve local problems.

2 Method

This section explains the method of the literature study performed to identify the perspectives used by scholars to study citizens' involvement in using OGD. The focus has been on understanding the effect of data used to create social value to solve local issues in cities. The methodological approach followed was a systematic review which helps to appraise and synthesize research evidence [19] and it is more reliable than other traditional reviews as it considers a transparent process to increase methodological rigor [20]. A five-step method described in the following paragraphs and illustrated in Fig. 1 was applied [21].

The first step was to define the review process and the inclusion and exclusion criteria. Considering the goal of this review, the keywords to perform the search were defined, as well as the set of inclusion and exclusion criteria. As this study aimed to identify perspectives to study citizens' involvement in using OGD, the term "open government data" and its variations (e.g., open data, open government, public sector information, public data, public government data, open public data) were used. The inclusion criteria were determined as follows: Papers should be academic journal articles and conference papers available online in full text, which are relevant to the study goal and to answer the research question. Table 1 shows the articles' complete list of inclusion criteria to define the relevance of the studies to be considered. Examples of relevant papers are studies mentioning open data platforms, user needs, social effects, public value cocreation, open government data initiatives implementation, and citizen participation. The exclusion criteria were defined by publications that are not primary studies, date outside the range of dates from 2017 and 2022, and lack an empirical approach to study the use of OGD when the expected outcome is to create social value to solve local issues in cities.

The second step was doing database searches and applying the selected search sting. The search was undertaken in February 2022 using Scopus, and ACM Digital Library. The query string used in the databases was: ("Open Government Data" OR "Open Data" OR "public sector information" OR "public data" OR "public government data" OR "open public data") AND ("Social value creation" OR "Public value creation" OR "Public Service creation" OR "Public Service innovation") AND ("citizen use" OR "citizen engagement" OR "citizen participation" OR "citizen involvement") AND ("local" OR "community" OR "urban" OR "city"). The selection of the keywords was done after reviewing the first outcomes of the search, and to ensure that it covered all the possible variations of the keywords.

Table 1. Inclusion criteria for selecting papers for characterization

Inclusion criteria:	Studies should …
Record standard	1.Be available online in full text as part of an academic journal article or as a conference paper 2.Be studies dating from 2017 to 2022 3.Be primary studies with empirical approaches 4.Include the keywords in the title, abstract, or keywords to ensure that citizens' use of OGD remains central
Citizens' use of OGD	5.Involves citizens in the use of OGD
Open Government Data	6.Include the implementation of Open Government Data initiatives
Social value	7.Include the aim to create social value to solve local issues in cities

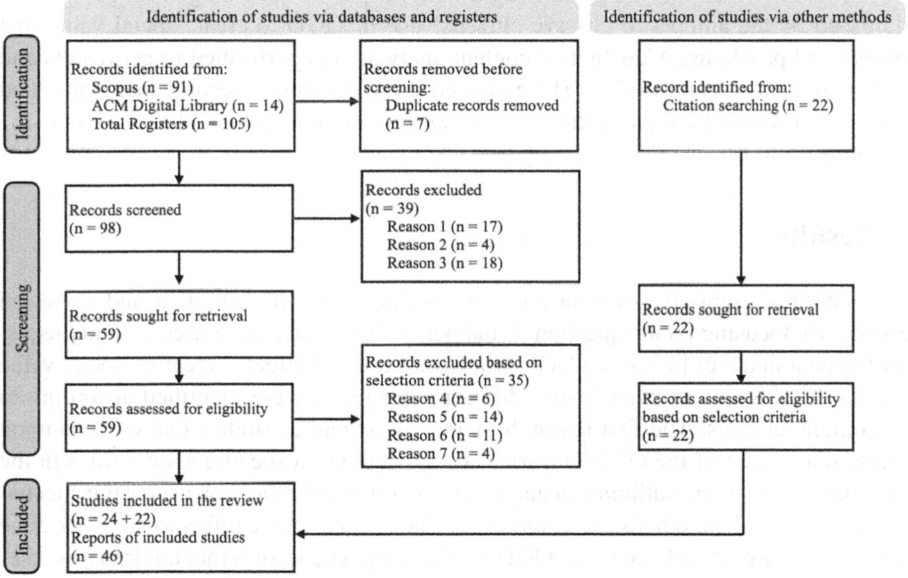

Fig. 1. Systematic mapping review process flow diagram modified from the Preferred Reporting Items for Systematic Reviews (PRISMA) flowchart [17].

This search string allowed the identification of studies with both focus on OGD and the interplay of citizens and government representatives in the creation of social value. The search allowed us to look for the keywords in the article title, abstract, keywords list, and full text. Since OGD is a multidomain field, the journals were not limited to one specific area. Moreover, since the development of the OGD domain in the latest years has significantly increased and transformed, the search was performed by only considering publications from 2017 to 2022 to portray the latest developments and avoid outdated approaches. The query resulted in 91 records in Scopus, and 14 in ACM Digital Library. The searches resulted in a total of 105 records. The third step was the selection of the literature sample. The first step was to look for double items through a manual review of the list of 105 records, which resulted in 98 unique records. Then, a screening was performed to verify the inclusion and exclusion criteria prior defined.

The document type and the availability online were verified. After removing books, book chapters, book reviews, conference reviews lists (exclusion reason 1, 17 records), articles dating out from 2017 to 2022 (exclusion reason 2, 4 records), and records without an empirical approach (exclusion reason 3, 18 records), 59 were assessed for eligibility. The screening of abstracts resulted in 24 eligible articles. A snowballing approach [22] was used to complement the search resulting in 24 additional records. Figure 1 summarizes the literature identification, screening, and inclusion process through the PRISMA flowchart [17].

The last step was analyzing and categorizing the papers according to the perspective addressed by the authors to observe citizens' use of OGD to create social value that solves local problems. A qualitative content analysis was performed to get results and synthesize the reviewed studies. The extracted information was recorded and classified using Excel worksheets. Next, the content was structured to present the findings in the following section.

3 Results

This section presents the content analysis results of the 46 identified and reviewed records. By focusing on the question "what perspectives have been used to study users' involvement in the utilization of OGD when the expected effect is creating social value to solve local issues in cities?" four different categories were identified according to the content analysis. The first research theme encompasses studies that touches upon a particular aspect of the OGD Governance, by studying a specific actor's roles in the open data ecosystem, outlining management recommendations, or proposing mechanisms or evaluation methods for governance. The second theme refers to the work done that observes aspects related to the OGD Availability. The studies that fall into this categorization focus on understanding user needs regarding the specific media to make data available and the effects of different data collection methods and provisions. The third theme encapsulates the research done by taking an angle referring to OGD Adoption, mainly referring to the drivers or motives for using OGD and reflecting on the assessment of its use. Finally, the fourth theme concerns understanding the OGD impact or value, and the research is done to understand the effects or assessment mechanisms to unveil the value of using OGD. The reviewed and categorized articles included in Table 2 are the records that met the inclusion criteria listed in Table 1. The categorization of the identified articles is shown in Table 2.

Table 2. Overview of reviewed articles and identified research perspectives of studying the use of OGD to create social value in cities characterized by four different themes.

Theme	Authors	No. studies
Governance	[23–34]	12
Availability	[35–46]	12
Adoption	[27, 30, 33, 47–54]	11
Impact	[55–65]	11

3.1 Governance

According to the literature, effective development, and implementation of OGD initiatives require structures, policies, actors, and institutions to manage, produce, access, share, exchange, and use different types of data [66]. In that sense, the reviewed articles take a governance perspective on researching the use of OGD to create social value, as they discuss the different roles that actors can play within the open data infrastructures and the interrelations that can influence the data-driven value creation mechanisms [24, 25, 28–30, 34], as well as the effects of different governance models [27, 32]. In some cases, they also consider the expected outcomes like innovation [26] or democracy [23]. The discussion raised by the perspective of this group of research highlights the relevance of the interrelation, and the interdependency between actors, communication tools, and contexts, to succeed in the OGD service delivery and value creation. In this regard, some studies suggest that actors' engagement might be influenced by geographic proximity and the effect of local contexts [27–29].

Most of the studies explored governance by taking the perspective of one of the actors involved and considering how they shape or get shaped by the technological elements of the OGD infrastructure. This was explored by comparing cases to propose recommendations, conceptual frameworks, or models to assist the development of OGD initiatives or programs [23, 26, 27, 30, 31, 34]. For example, some studies offer theoretical models based on empirical case studies to deal with the context interdependence and allow the emergence and development of innovation [26, 32]. Some others offer conceptual models to deepen the understanding of specific actors' roles or democratic processes, such as Calzada [29], who proposed a taxonomy of digital citizenship regimes, or Rujier et al. [23], who developed a Democratic Activity Model of Open Data Use. Another example is the research that focuses on the role of ICT developments and their effects on the coproduction and cocreation of value within the network of stakeholders by offering insights to improve the governance models. For example, Rodríguez [25] focuses on the role of e-participation technologies and the need for introducing collaborative and participative governance models, while Zhang et al. [34] offer reflections on networking computing and its role in creating sustainable value, specifically in the smart transportation systems.

3.2 Availability

Open data availability refers to the different elements that need to be in place so that the public can access data without restrictions that would impede the re-use of information [66]. The studies included in this theme focus on analyzing three different perspectives that would affect the channels through which data is being made available for users to create social value. In the first group, the authors focus on collecting data to make it available [38, 42]. A second group focuses on aspects that affect the accessibility to data [35, 36, 41, 44–46]. Finally, a third group focuses on the users' needs to access it [37, 39, 40, 43].

An emerging issue affecting the data availability and addressed by the first group of the literature identified in this theme is the integration of different data sources. In this perspective, the authors reflect on cases in which the collected data comes from sensors, crowdsourcing, or data collected by citizens [36, 38, 42]. The educational contexts arise as a setting that allows exercising inclusion, addressing the skills gaps in dealing with data, and enabling a greater observation control [38, 42]. The technological resources for automatization and data processing become relevant aspects to continuing to be explored, especially considering citizens' co-production of information [36, 42] and the involvement and exploitation of new data sources [38].

The second group of authors identified in this group addressed the accessibility and reflected on the technical capabilities and channels that affect data provision and integration mediums [41, 44, 46]. For example, Chatfield & Reddicks [41] reflect on how the data portals' capabilities might differ according to the data formats, policies, and resources. All these considerations would also define the channels, which according to Rodríguez et al. [44], should contemplate transparency and citizens' participation influenced by demographic characteristics such as population density or educational level within the city. On its part, Ho and Lee [46] bring in their observations on the problems that arise when there are divergent geographic levels or time horizons within the data collected, which are challenges that public officers face when trying to augment existing data sources. These studies provide empirical evidence and quantitative conclusions from their analysis of open data portals [41, 44] and analytical inputs for data curation and privacy-preserving of the OGD [46].

The third group of authors addressing the users' needs to access to data highlight the display of information as a critical aspect to consider in terms of data availability. According to some of these authors, visualization techniques are being explored to provide citizens with the analytical tools to exploit data [35, 45]. Also, in this direction, the revised literature follows different approaches to investigate user needs, challenges, and conditions for their individual and collective involvement, primarily focusing on the technological channels of interaction [37, 39, 40, 43]. For example, one of the studies explores the accessibility of OGD portals in India by comparing them to portals in other countries [40]. On her part, Alizadeh et al. [37] analyzed participatory tools to allow communities to be part of a deliberative process of public decision-making by using social media as a source for improving the quality of data.

3.3 Adoption

According to the reviewed literature, there is a need to understand how to drive adoption to increase the use of data. In this context, we refer to adoption as the choices an individual makes to accept or reject a particular innovation, and the extent to which that innovation is integrated into the appropriate context [67]. In that sense, the reviewed articles present two clear paths of research. On the one hand, there is an interest in identifying the drivers that can lead to the OGD adoption [27, 30, 33, 48, 52]. In some cases, the adoption of OGD is studied when it is used through e-participation platforms [51, 53], and in other cases when it is used through IoT tools [54]. On the other hand, there is also a focus on assessing the maturity level of the open data ecosystems [49] and the strengths and weaknesses of specific cases [47], which would ultimately influence the adoption of OGD.

Another important aspect to understand the adoption of OGD is identifying the factors and motivators for its use. For example, one of the reviewed studies identified adoption factors for an e-participation tool in Czech cities. The study concluded that the innovativeness of a city or increasing the number of e-participation tools would not necessarily increase the number of adopters. Instead, researchers suggest focusing on contacting current adopters of participation activities to understand the possible adoption process [51]. For example, a study analyzing Romanian and Italian cities through a knowledge management perspective found that the efforts to use open data concentrate on the economy, mobility, and people [47]. However, another study points out that one of the reasons for not using the data is the lack of communication channels with the platform managers. In that sense, one possible research direction could be to focus on first adopters to improve communication with platform managers [27].

3.4 Impact

Even though there has been an increase in the number of OGD initiatives, the impact is still uncertain [60, 62]. We refer to impact as the extent to which data helps "solving problems and meet essential needs of individuals, communities or society at large" [68]. In that sense, most of the articles that fall into this theme take as the main challenge the assessment of the impact that the use of OGD can bring to communities. Several of the reviewed articles focused on assessing the impact of the use of ODG through a specific tool [61, 63, 65], within a specific context [56, 62, 64], or by assessing a specific outcome [58]. For example, Allen et al. [61] examined the impact of citizen e-participation on service performance, while Wilson and Cong [62] focused on assessing the impact of municipal government data in nine cities across the US, and finally, Reddick et al. [58] focused on assessing the performance of the government online budget transparency portals in the US.

Another branch of research under this theme focused on the development of assessment mechanisms to get conclusions about the impact of the use of OGD on creating social value [59, 60]. For example, in their work, Cabitza et al. [60] developed a conceptual model to understand the perceived social value of real-life open data sets in the health care domain. However, the results only provided insights on the perceptions of the users and the results of the study give feedback on the users' preferences regarding the presentation of the information, and not on the benefits perse. Finally, the most recent contribution by Gao and Janssen [59] combined the components of the business model canvas and value creation conceptualization from literature to create the value model canvas. The model creates an overview of the needs in terms of data and capabilities to understand the value generation logic. It is important to mention that within this theme, there has been also a focus on empirically understanding the negative effects of the use of OGD through digital platforms, which is an emerging research direction in the Open Data domain. That is the case of Marjanovic and Cecez-Kecmanovic [55] who analyzed the negative effects of the performance data from Australian schools.

Overall, the research in this category focused on case studies or cross-case analyses using quantitative and qualitative approaches. These are the first attempts to create conceptual frameworks and give recommendations for improving the impact of the use of OGD. The studies suggest that more research is still missing that focuses on public value creation [58] and understanding how the use of different e-governance tools can influence complex problems affecting the involvement of multiple agencies [61]. The researchers also mention the lack of monitoring mechanisms to evaluate the broader effect of the use of OGD [62].

4 Discussion and Conclusion

The current work presents the results of a systematic mapping review comprising 46 articles to address the question "what perspectives have been used to study citizens' involvement in using OGD when the expected effect is creating social value to solve local issues in cities?" This review belongs to broader research on Open Data Ecosystems [18] that has the aim to provide insights that serve as a building block in the understanding of the use and value of OGD on a local level. Through a content analysis, four research perspectives of the most current research on the use of OGD were identified and categorized.

These perspectives evidence the relevance of understanding the different aspects of the interdependence within OGD infrastructure which are Governance, Availability, Adoption, and Impact. Across the studies in all categories, there has also been special attention to understanding the different scales in which the elements can be affected and interrelated, such as national and local, network and individual, platform and ecosystems, and specific tools or technology.

The research included in the Governance theme shows a growing interest in studying the OGD phenomena by focusing on specific interactions, actors' interrelations, and the different elements intertwined in the implementation of OGD efforts, such as individual actors and the outcomes of their interactions. One of the relevant aspects of the Governance perspective is that it evidences the significance of considering the role of technology and how the mechanisms are affected by the rapidly changing digital dynamics and technological advances.

The attention in the research studies belonging to the theme of Availability shows the significance of understanding the lifecycles of OGD. From OGD collection to the mechanisms and tools to make it available until the service delivery by taking care of the interactions and usability. This category of studies reveals an interest in creating models and frameworks for evaluating different aspects of the implementation of an OGD ecosystem, such as the data collection mechanisms, accessibility, and usability.

Regarding the theme of OGD Adoption, the focus on elements, specific geographical contexts, industries, or specific motivations such as transparency, corruption, participation, or decision-making appears to be necessary to create a more empirical body of knowledge regarding the different dimensions of evaluation and assessment for the adoption of OGD. These aspects would ultimately affect the OGD's potential to create public value.

Finally, the focus on the Impact of OGD shows a more strategic perspective on delivering value through OGD. The mechanisms and assessment tools to prove the effectiveness of OGD in creating value appear to be an essential branch of knowledge that requires a broader development and exploration in empirical scenarios. One crucial aspect to consider in this regard is to be aware of the negative impact that the OGD utilization might cause. An emergent direction for research in this category is to focus on specific types of channels to deliver OGD and different sectors to understand and compare results that can show the value and impact of using OGD.

The emerging research directions elucidated through the different perspectives to investigating the use of OGD confirm that the decentralization of civic services requires new perspectives on how to plan, implement, assess, and follow up the OGD initiatives if the intention is to create and sustain the value that is expected to deliver. This study reinforces the move toward decentralizing data governance and civic services by discussing the different perspectives that emerge in the literature when focusing on the citizens' involvement in using OGD to create public value. This review contributes to the gap of a holistic overview of the perspectives on using OGD to create social value. Moreover, to sustain the Availability and value of the OGD, there is a need to address the different barriers holistically by also considering the different domains encountered in implementing OGD initiatives.

The review also considers some limitations as it only covers peer-reviewed journals and conference papers from 2017 to March 2022; this could limit the perspectives present in the literature. Another limitation is the depth of the analysis, as more layers could have been considered, such as methods to study the use of OGD, types of use and types of relationships, and technologies concerning the use of OGD. The identified perspectives could be evaluated further, and future work can be developed to analyze different layers of the perspectives.

References

1. Puerari, E., de Koning, J., von Wirth, T., Karré, P., Mulder, I., Loorbach, D.: Co-creation dynamics in urban living labs. Sustainability **10**(6), 1893 (2018). https://doi.org/10.3390/su10061893
2. Bovaird, T., Loeffler, E.: From engagement to co-production: the contribution of users and communities to outcomes and public value. VOLUNTAS: Int. J. Volunt. Nonprofit Organ. **23**(4), 1119–1138 (2012). https://doi.org/10.1007/s11266-012-9309-6
3. Brandsen, T., Steen, T., Verschuere, B.: Co-Production and Co-Creation; Engaging Citizens in Public Services. Taylor & Francis Group, Milton Park (2018). www.routledge.com

4. Wessels, B., Finn, R., Wadhwa, K., Sveinsdottir, T.: Open data and the knowledge society. In: Open Data and the Knowledge Society. Amsterdam University Press (2017). https://doi.org/10.5117/9789462980181
5. Bichard, J.-A., Knight, G.: Improving public services through open data: public toilets. Proc. Inst. Civ. Eng.- Munic. Eng. **165**(3), 157–165 (2012). https://doi.org/10.1680/muen.12.00017
6. Bachtiar, A., Suhardi, Muhamad, W.: Literature review of open government data. In: 2020 International Conference on Information Technology Systems and Innovation (ICITSI), pp. 329–334 (2020). https://doi.org/10.1109/ICITSI50517.2020.9264960
7. Davies, T.: Open data, democracy and public sector reform (2010). http://www.practicalparticipation.co.uk/odi/report/
8. Susha, I., Grönlund, Å., Janssen, M.: Organizational measures to stimulate user engagement with open data. Transform. Gov.: People Process Policy **9**(2), 181–206 (2015). https://doi.org/10.1108/TG-05-2014-0016
9. Purwanto, A., Zuiderwijk, A., Janssen, M.: Citizen engagement with open government data. Int. J. Electron. Gov. Res. **16**(3), 1–25 (2020). https://doi.org/10.4018/IJEGR.2020070101
10. Hossain, M.A., Dwivedi, Y.K., Rana, N.P.: State-of-the-art in open data research: insights from existing literature and a research agenda. J. Organ. Comput. Electron. Commer. **26**(1–2), 14–40 (2016). https://doi.org/10.1080/10919392.2015.1124007
11. Yuan, Q.: Co-production of public service and information technology: a literature review. In: Proceedings of the 20th Annual International Conference on Digital Government Research, pp. 123–132 (2019). https://doi.org/10.1145/3325112.3325232
12. Safarov, I., Meijer, A., Grimmelikhuijsen, S.: Utilization of open government data: a systematic literature review of types, conditions, effects, and users. Inf. Polity **22**(1), 1–24 (2017). https://doi.org/10.3233/IP-160012
13. Kalampokis, E., Hausenblas, M., Tarabanis, K.: Combining social and government open data for participatory decision-making. In: Tambouris, E., Macintosh, A., de Bruijn, H. (eds.) Electronic Participation, vol. 6847, pp. 36–47. Springer, Cham (2011). https://doi.org/10.1007/978-3-642-23333-3_4
14. Huijboom, N., Van den Broek, T.: Open data: an international comparison of strategies. Eur. J. ePract. **12**(1), 4–16 (2011)
15. de Azambuja, L.: Drivers and barriers for the development of smart sustainable cities: a systematic literature review. In: 14th International Conference on Theory and Practice of Electronic Governance, pp. 422–428 (2021). https://doi.org/10.1145/3494193.3494250
16. Neto, A.J.A., Neves, D.F., Santos, L.C., Junior, M.C.R., do Nascimento, R.P.C.: Open government data usage overview. In: Proceedings of the Euro American Conference on Telematics and Information Systems, pp. 1–8 (2018). https://doi.org/10.1145/3293614.3293619
17. Page, M.J.: The PRISMA 2020 statement: an updated guideline for reporting systematic reviews. PLoS Med. **18**(3) (2021). https://doi.org/10.1080/10630732.2017.1285123
18. van Loenen, B., Zuiderwijk, A., Vancauwenberghe, G., et al.: Towards value-creating and sustainable open data ecosystems: a comparative case study and a research agenda. JeDEM – eJ. eDemocr. Open Gov. **13**, 1–27 (2021). https://doi.org/10.29379/jedem.v13i2.644
19. Grant, M.J., Booth, A.: A typology of reviews: an analysis of 14 review types and associated methodologies. Health Inf. Libr. J. **26**, 91–108 (2009). https://doi.org/10.1111/j.1471-1842.2009.00848.x
20. Tranfield, D., Denyer, D., Smart, P.: Towards a methodology for developing evidence-informed management knowledge by means of systematic review. Br. J. Manag. **14**(3), 207–222 (2003). https://doi.org/10.1111/1467-8551.00375
21. Wolfswinkel, J., Furtmueller, E., Wilderom, C.: Using grounded theory as a method for rigorously reviewing literature. Eur. J. Inf. Syst. **22**(1), 45–55 (2013). https://doi.org/10.1057/ejis.2011.51

22. Wohlin, C.: Guidelines for snowballing in systematic literatures studies and a replication in software engineering. In: Proceedings of the 18th International Conference on Evaluation and Assessment in Software Engineering - EASE 2014, pp. 1–10 (2014). https://doi.org/10.1145/2601248.2601268
23. Ruijer, E., Grimmelikhuijsen, S., Meijer, A.: Open data for democracy: developing a theoretical framework for open data use. Gov. Inf. Q. **34**, 45–52 (2017). https://doi.org/10.1016/j.giq.2017.01.001
24. Ojo, A., Mellouli, S.: Deploying governance networks for societal challenges. Gov. Inf. Q. **35**, 106-S112 (2018). https://doi.org/10.1016/j.giq.2016.04.001
25. Rodríguez Bolívar, M.P.: Analyzing collaborative environments in smart cities. In: Proceedings of the 11th International Conference on Theory and Practice of Electronic Governance (ICEGOV 2018), pp. 489–498 (2018). https://doi.org/10.1145/3209415.3209428
26. Bonina, C., Eaton, B.: Cultivating open government data platform ecosystems through governance: lessons from Buenos Aires, Mexico City, and Montevideo. Gov. Inf. Q. **37**(3), 101479 (2020). https://doi.org/10.1016/j.giq.2020.101479
27. Slobodova, O., Becker, S.: Zooming into the ecosystem: agency and politics around open data platforms in Lyon and Berlin. Front. Sustain. Cities **2**, 20 (2020). https://doi.org/10.3389/frsc.2020.00020
28. Reggi, L., Dawes, S.: Creating open government data ecosystems: network relations among governments, user communities, NGOs and the media. Gov. Inf. Q. **101675** (2022). https://doi.org/10.1016/j.giq.2022.101675
29. Calzada, I.: Emerging digital citizenship regimes: pandemic, algorithmic, liquid, metropolitan, and stateless citizenships. Citizsh. Stud. (2022). https://doi.org/10.1080/13621025.2021.2012312
30. McBride, K., Toots, M., Kalvet, T., Krimmer, R.: Open government data driven co-creation: moving towards citizen-government collaboration. In: Parycek, P., et al. (eds.) Electronic Government. LNCS, vol. 11020, pp. 184–195. Springer, Cham (2018). https://doi.org/10.1007/978-3-319-98690-6_16
31. Rodriguez Müller, A.P., Steen, T.: Behind the scenes of coproduction of smart mobility: evidence from a public values' perspective. In: Lindgren, I., et al. (eds.) Electronic Government. LNCS, vol. 11685, pp. 338–352. Springer, Cham (2019). https://doi.org/10.1007/978-3-030-27325-5_26
32. Hyun Park, C., Longo, J., Johnston, E.W.: Exploring non-state stakeholder and community-led open governance: beyond the three pillars of open government. Public Perform. Manag. Rev. **43**(3), 587–612 (2020). https://doi.org/10.1080/15309576.2019.1677253
33. Seo, H., Myeong, S.: Determinant factors for adoption of government as a platform in South Korea: mediating effects on the perception of intelligent information technology. Sustainability **13**, 10464 (2021). https://doi.org/10.3390/su131810464
34. Zhang, J., Li, S., Wang, Y.: Shaping a smart transportation system for sustainable value co-creation. Inf. Syst. Front. (2021). https://doi.org/10.1007/s10796-021-10139-3
35. Gagliardi, D., Schina, L., Sarcinella, M.L., Mangialardi, G., Niglia, F., Corallo, A.: Information and communication technologies and public participation: interactive maps and value-added for citizens. Gov. Inf. Q. **34**(1), 153–166 (2017). https://doi.org/10.1016/j.giq.2016.09.002
36. Lieven, C.: DIPAS – towards an integrated GIS-based system for civic participation. Proc. Comput. Sci. **112**, 2473–2485 (2017). https://doi.org/10.1016/j.procs.2017.08.182
37. Alizadeh, T., Sarkar, S., Burgoyne, S.: Capturing citizen voice online: enabling smart participatory local government. Cities **95**, 102400 (2019). https://doi.org/10.1016/j.cities.2019.102400

38. Longo, A., Zappatore, M., Bochicchio, M.A.: Apollon: towards a citizen science methodology for urban environmental monitoring. Futur. Gener. Comput. Syst. **112**, 899–912 (2020). https://doi.org/10.1016/j.future.2020.06.041
39. Nikiforova, A., McBride, K.: Open government data portal usability: a user-centred usability analysis of 41 open government data portals. Telematics Inform. **58**, 101539 (2021). https://doi.org/10.1016/j.tele.2020.101539
40. Doctor, G., Joshi, P.: Empowering cities through open data - open government data initiatives in India. In: 14th International Conference on Theory and Practice of Electronic Governance, pp. 352–361 (2021). https://doi.org/10.1145/3494193.3494241
41. Chatfield, A.T., Reddick, C.G.: A longitudinal cross-sector analysis of open data portal service capability: the case of Australian local governments. Gov. Inf. Q. **34**(2), 231–243 (2017). https://doi.org/10.1016/j.giq.2017.02.004
42. Saddiqa, M., Rasmussen, L., Magnussen, R., Larsen, B., Pedersen, J.M.: Bringing open data into Danish schools and its potential impact on school pupils. In: Proceedings of the 15th International Symposium on Open Collaboration, pp. 1–10 (2019). https://doi.org/10.1145/3306446.3340821
43. Lee-Geiller, S.: Conditions influencing e-participation: a cross-country comparative mixed-methods analysis. In: Proceedings of the 13th International Conference on Theory and Practice of Electronic Governance (ICEGOV 2020), pp. 754–761 (2020). https://doi-org.zorac.aub.aau.dk, https://doi.org/10.1145/3428502.3428615
44. Rodríguez Bolívar, M.P., Villamayor Arellano, C.L., Alcaide Muñoz, L.: Demographical attributes explaining different stages of OG development in spanish local governments. In: Viale Pereira, G., et al. (eds.) EGOV 2020. LNCS, vol. 12219, pp. 387–399. Springer, Cham (2020). https://doi.org/10.1007/978-3-030-57599-1_29
45. Changfeng, J., Yanl, Z., Mingyi, D., Xintao, L.: Visualizing spatiotemporal patterns of city service demand through a space-time exploratory approach. Trans. GIS **25**(4), 1766–1783 (2021)
46. Ho, D.H., Lee, Y.: Big data analytics framework for predictive analytics using public data with privacy preserving. In: IEEE International Conference on Big Data, pp. 5395–5405 (2021). https://doi.org/10.1109/BigData52589.2021.9671997
47. Leon, R.-D., Romanelli, M.: Rethinking Romanian and Italian smart cities as knowledge-based communities. In: Lazazzara, A., Ricciardi, F., Za, S. (eds.) Exploring Digital Ecosystems, vol. 33, pp. 11–23. Springer, Cham (2020). https://doi.org/10.1007/978-3-030-23665-6_2
48. Kassen, M.: Open data and e-government–related or competing ecosystems: a paradox of open government and promise of civic engagement in Estonia. Inf. Technol. Dev. **25**, 552–578 (2019). https://doi.org/10.1080/02681102.2017.1412289
49. Rahmatika, M., Krismawati, D., Rahmawati, S.D., Arief, A., Sensuse, D.I., Fadhil Dzulfikar, M.: An open government data maturity model: a case study in BPS-statistics Indonesia. In: 7th International Conference on Information and Communication Technology (ICoICT), pp. 1–7 (2019). https://doi.org/10.1109/ICoICT.2019.8835352
50. Kopackova, H., Komarkova, J., Horak, O.: Enhancing the diffusion of e-participation tools in smart cities. Cities **125**, 103640 (2022). https://doi.org/10.1016/j.cities.2022.103640
51. Kopackova, H., Komarkova, J.: Participatory technologies in smart cities: what citizens want and how to ask them. Telematics Inform. **47**, 101325 (2020). https://doi.org/10.1016/j.tele.2019.101325
52. Currie, M.: Data as performance – showcasing cities through open data maps. Big Data Soc. **7**(1) (2020). https://doi.org/10.1177/2053951720907953
53. Vidiasova, L., Tensina, I.: E-participation social effectiveness: case of "Our Petersburg" portal. In: Chugunov, A., Misnikov, Y., Roshchin, E., Trutnev, D. (eds.) Electronic Governance and

Open Society: Challenges in Eurasia, vol. 947, pp. 308–318. Springer, Cham (2019). https://doi.org/10.1007/978-3-030-13283-5_23
54. Chohan, S.R., Hu, G.: Success factors influencing citizens' adoption of IoT service orchestration for public value creation in smart government. IEEE Access **8**, 208427–208448 (2020). https://doi.org/10.1109/ACCESS.2020.3036054
55. Marjanovic, O., Cecez-Kecmanovic, D.: Open government data platforms – a complex adaptive sociomaterial systems perspective. Inf. Organ. **30**(4), 100323 (2020). https://doi.org/10.1016/j.infoandorg.2020.100323
56. Mutambik, I., Nikiforova, A., Almuqrin, A., Liu, Y.D., Floos, A.Y.M., Omar, T.: Benefits of open government data initiatives in Saudi Arabia and barriers to their implementation. J. Glob. Inf. Manag. **29**(6), 1–22 (2021). https://doi.org/10.4018/JGIM.295975
57. Sangkachan, T.: Open government data: the key to promoting public participation, and fighting against corruption. Thai J. Public Adm. **19**(2), 41–70 (2021)
58. Reddick, C.G., Chatfield, A.T., Puron-Cid, G.: Online budget transparency innovation in government: a case study of the U.S. state governments. In: Proceedings of the 18th Annual International Conference on Digital Government Research (DG.O 2017), pp. 232–241 (2017). https://doi.org/10.1145/3085228.3085271
59. Gao, Y., Janssen, M.: The open data canvas–analyzing value creation from open data. Digit. Gov.: Res. Pract. **3**(1), 1–15 (2022). https://doi-org.zorac.aub.aau.dk, https://doi.org/10.1145/3511102
60. Cabitza, F., Locoro, A., Batini, C.: Making open data more personal through a social value perspective: a methodological approach. Inf. Syst. Front. **22**(1), 131–148 (2018). https://doi.org/10.1007/s10796-018-9854-7
61. Allen, B., Tamindael, L.E., Bickerton, S.H., Cho, W.: Does citizen coproduction lead to better urban services in smart cities projects? An empirical study on e-participation in a mobile big data platform. Gov. Inf. Q. **37**(1), 101412 (2020). https://doi.org/10.1016/j.giq.2019.101412
62. Wilson, B., Cong, C.: Beyond the supply side: use and impact of municipal open data in the U.S. Telematics Inform. **58**, 101526 (2021). https://doi.org/10.1016/j.tele.2020.101526
63. Coutinho, E.D., Freitas, A.S.: Public value through technologies developed with open government data: the Love Serenade Operation case. Revista de Administração Mackenzie **22**(6), 1–26 (2021). https://doi.org/10.1590/1678-6971/eRAMD210079
64. Yuan, Q., Gasco-Hernandez, M.: Open innovation in the public sector: creating public value through civic hackathons. Public Manag. Rev. **23**(4), 523–544 (2021). https://doi.org/10.1080/14719037.2019.1695884
65. Manoharan, A.P., Melitski, J., Holzer, M.: Digital governance: an assessment of performance and best practices. Public Organ. Rev. (2022). https://doi.org/10.1007/s11115-021-00584-8
66. Attard, J., Orlandi, F., Scerri, S., Auer, S.: A systematic review of open government data initiatives. Gov. Inf. Q. **32**(4), 399–418 (2015). https://doi.org/10.1016/j.giq.2015.07.006
67. Straub, E.T.: Understanding technology adoption: theory and future directions for informal learning. Rev. Educ. Res. **79**(2), 625–649 (2009). http://www.jstor.org/stable/40469051
68. Harrison, T.M., Pardo, T.A., Cook, M.: Creating open government ecosystems: a research and development agenda. Future Internet **4**(4), 900–928 (2012). https://doi.org/10.3390/fi4040900

A Methodology for Aligning Categories from Open Government Data Portals to a Comprehensive Set of Categories

Higor Pinto, Raissa Barcellos(✉), Flavia Bernardini, and José Viterbo

Institute of Computing, Fluminense Federal University, Niterói-Rj, Brazil
higor@bcc.ic.uff.br, raissabarcellos@id.uff.br,
{fcbernardini,viterbo}@ic.uff.br

Abstract. Nowadays, we can find Open Government Data Portals (OGDPs) from different governmental organizations. The increasing number of OGDPs brings opportunities for integrating these data. The vast majority of OGDPs distribute the data into different categories, and each portal uses its own set of categories. Therefore, due to the lack of homogeneous guidelines in data management, interconnecting data is flawed. Data integration is crucial in improving the functioning and planning of open government data portals. One possibility for integrating data from different portals is using the categories associated with datasets. Putting similar datasets in the same category can turn data integration easier. We propose a methodology for constructing a Comprehensive Set of Categories (*CSC*) extracted from different OGDPs and aligning different categories to this minimal and comprehensive set based on semantic similarity. We carried out an exploratory analysis on 100 portals of densely populated American cities using the categories collected in these portals in 2017. Our approach allowed us to align more than 80% of the collected portal categories to the minimal set according to more than 3 out of 6 similarity measures, which is promising for open data integration.

Keywords: Open Government Data · Open data categories · Categories alignment · Open data integration

1 Introduction

The increasing demand of modern society for transparency and the greater engagement of the citizen in the issues and problems of democratic governments have produced diverse solutions based on computational systems. In the last decade, cities worldwide have been making data available in open formats through portals available on the internet. Particularly in the USA, there was a great effort and encouragement from the federal government for the development

Published by Springer Nature Switzerland AG 2022
M. Janssen et al. (Eds.): EGOV 2022, LNCS 13391, pp. 258–273, 2022.
https://doi.org/10.1007/978-3-031-15086-9_17

of open cities data portals from 2009 [21]. OGDPs are web portals where governments can make their data available and cataloged. Through these portals, society can interact with the available data and produce helpful information [23]. They can also develop application-based solutions for a wide range of applications. Often, the data in these portals are cataloged by categories or groups. These categories distribute the datasets of a portal into various themes. When searching for the same information in different portals, the user may find it challenging to navigate between the different categories available in the different portals.

We understand some scenarios in integrating data portals that can be useful for different users. For instance, a user may want to survey: (i) the management of schools in his city, (ii) the traffic in his neighborhood, (iii) or even expenses with the public machinery of his state. Defining the ideal datasets for solving a given problem can require many hours of research on different portals. Much more time can still be spent integrating the different datasets, that is, producing relationships between the data [3].

It is worth noting that different public organizations publish datasets by grouping them into categories or topics. The datasets available on these portals cover several different topics or categories [17]. Portals use different categories when publishing datasets. We can also find several categories in the different portals with equivalent semantic meanings. Thus, a user who wants to produce a study between the different cities of his state or country, for example, finds it difficult to navigate between the categories of the different portals.

The portal categories represent the subject domain covered by the portal's datasets. As a domain, we define the different areas where Open Government Data (OGD) can be produced. It is also important to emphasize that the literature presents a divergence in nomenclature when referring to the domain of subjects of the datasets in the portals. In this work, we use the term *category* to name the subjects referring to the datasets of a portal.

In the last years, integrating data using different and unstructured datasets has been a typical task in data lakes [20]. It is also a necessary task when considering datasets from different portals. For instance, we may want to integrate datasets that report public schools' availability, quality, and financial spending in different cities. In this use case, we need to visit the portals of the various cities, download the datasets, and produce the integration of these sets. However, this activity may require formatting and conversion processes for data and file types. Thus, many tools have been developed to facilitate integrating data from different portals. The platforms available for building open data portals offer tools that can assist data integration. We highlight here an extension developed for use in CKAN, the CKAN Harvester [4]. This tool dramatically facilitates the import of datasets from a remote CKAN instance, a municipal portal, to another CKAN instance, a federal portal, where all data from municipal instances can be cataloged. This extension is highly customizable, allowing the user to define tags, groups, users, and default permissions for the imported datasets [4]. However, there is a gap when the terms are not precisely the same.

Yang et al. [25], trying to face this problem, proposed a measure to evaluate the coherence of categories of datasets present in OGDP from Taiwan, compared to the structure of the portal to a standard structure, defined by the authors. It is worth noting that ontologies alignment is a complex process that helps to reduce the semantic gap between different overlapping representations of the same domain. Several different techniques and approaches for aligning ontology have been produced, and we found one particularly relevant to this work.

In this work, we describe processes for the semantic alignment of categories. In this way, we apply an SCM approach to open data portals using NLP techniques. Unlike the work of Hoshiai et al. [6] we do not evaluate the documents related to the categories, in this case, the datasets. However, we produce an alignment between the categories themselves, using semantic similarity between small segments of texts or sentences' everyday activity in the NLP. The documents are the data or catalogs of the portals, and the categories are attributes of these documents.

This work proposes a methodology for semantic alignment of the categories from OGDPs using Natural Language Processing (NLP) techniques, a sub-area of Artificial Intelligence (AI). To this end, it is necessary to produce a comprehensive set of categories or groups and align a given set of categories to the comprehensive set. For achieving our goal, we conducted the following steps: (i) we studied the theoretical reference regarding OGDPs, datasets categorization, Natural Language Processing (NLP), and semantic similarity, present in Sect. 2; (ii) we constructed a methodology for semantic alignment of categories, composed by two algorithms — one for constructing a Comprehensive Set of Categories (CSC) and another for aligning categories of an OGDP to the CSC —, present in Sect. 4; and (iii) we conducted an exploratory analysis in 100 OGDPs for constructing a CSC and aligning the categories of the 100 portals to our discovered CSC, present in Sect. 5. We could observe that our solution could align more than 50% of the 976 categories analyzed. Approximately 30% were aligned to the same category, totaling more than 80% of the analyzed categories. Only approximately 5% of all the 976 categories we analyzed, including categories with words not present in the English language or acronyms. Section 6 concludes our work, also presenting possible future works.

2 OGD, OGDP and OGDPs Categorization

Open data initiatives aim to open all non-personal and noncommercial data, or sufficiently anonymized data, especially all data collected and processed by government organizations — called Open Government Data (OGD). An OGDP, in this context, is a collection of datasets, which can be owned by governments, universities, and other institutions. OGDPs are administrated by authorized users, who are in charge of uploading resources and filling metadata fields. The portal also aims to promote the interlocution between society and government actors to think about the most appropriate use of data for a better society. For open data to reach their full potential, they need an essential feature: interoperability, i.e., the ability of various systems and organizations to work together to interoperate. In this case, this implies the possibility of interoperating different datasets. Guaranteeing categories alignment is one way of allowing interoperability among different OGDPs.

We consider an OGDP as a *Web* portal in our perspective. A *Web* portal is a website that provides information content about a common topic or a specific interest. Typically, *Web* portals can define an ontology for the community, defining terminologies for describing the content and serving as an index for content retrieval. In computer systems context, an ontology is a document or file that formally defines the relationships between the terms that describe a content [1]. The most common type of ontology for *Web* has an associated taxonomy and set of inference rules. Taxonomy defines classes of objects and relations between them. Classes, subclasses and relationships between entities are a very powerful tool for use in the *Web*. A taxonomy can express a large number of relationships between entities, assigning properties to classes and allowing subclasses to inherit those properties [1]. Other ways of categorizing information can be based on domain models or simple category hierarchies. Information Retrieval (IR), on the other hand, has explored models of text representation to lead to the discovery of patterns [12]. In the case of open data portals, in general, the categorization is done by specialists or by the organization providing the data and metadata. Thus, the representation of information can assist in the discovery of patterns. However, acquiring knowledge from experts to evolve in knowledge representation is an arduous task. According to Nikiforova et al. [14], there are many portals where datasets are not related or belong to any category. We can solve this problem by building a recommender mechanism that retrieves keywords from the dataset and then recommends the most appropriate categories to assign to the dataset correctly.

3 Text Pre-processing and Semantic Similarity Between Short Sentences

Pre-processing text is needed to enable the machine to process textual information and structure the language, leaving only relevant information. This pre-processing reduces vocabulary and makes data less sparse, a convenient feature for computational processing. We use two essential steps from NLP in this work: Tokenizing and Removing Stopwords. The tokenization process aims to separate words or sentences into units. Another task widely used in text pre-processing is the removal of stopwords. This task consists of removing the most frequent words, such as articles, prepositions, and others, as they do not bring relevant information to the applied domain. Several stopword lists can be found on the internet for different applications. To calculate the similarity between sentences, we calculate the similarity value for the words in each text segment. Thus, the words of each sentence must be extracted, which is a category in this work. The goal is to calculate the similarity between two categories (short sentences).

We obtain the words of each category by tokenizing, separating each word, and removing the stopwords [12].

Another vital step is Semantic Similarity (SS). Calculating SS is an old problem in NLP and can be calculated between (i) two words, (ii) two concepts, or (iii) two sentences. In our case, for calculating SS between two categories, we need to calculate the similarity between sentences. Indeed, calculating SS between short segments of text is fundamental, given that short segments of text form categories. So, it is not enough to calculate similarities between two words or two concepts, although they are used for calculating similarities between sentences. So, we first describe SS between two words or concepts in what follows. After, we describe SS between short sentences and technologies we used for this end.

SS **between two words** can be, in general, calculated using the conceptual distance between two objects in a given ontology of semantic concepts [15]. These objects represent the words or concepts to be compared. For calculating *SS between two concepts*, there is a set of widely used methods using a lexical database, or ontology, that contains concepts and links between them. The similarity is calculated using the hierarchical structure of words and meanings distributed in tree form. These methods use the distance between the concepts in this tree [15]. One of the most extensive lexical databases used in English is *WordNet* [5]. Wordnet has related concepts of names, verbs, adjectives, and adverbs, grouped into sets of synonyms. These two are pretty similar for our purposes, and so, in what follows, we use words and concepts as synonyms for our purpose.

Measures for calculating SS between two words or concepts are basically divided into two categories: Edge-Counting and Content-Based. Edge-Counting measures calculate the similarity between two concepts C_1 and C_2, determining the path connecting the taxonomy concepts. We use in this work three Edge-Counting measures:

- Path distance [18] sim_{pd}: The conceptual distance, in Eq. 1, between two nodes (words or sentences) C_1 and C_2 is generally proportional to the number of edges that separate the two nodes in the hierarchy, where MAX is the maximum path length between two concepts in the taxonomy, *i.e.*, the longest possible path in the hierarchy; and L is the minimum number of edges between the concepts C_1 and C_2.

$$sim_{pd}(C_1, C_2) = 2 \times MAX - L \tag{1}$$

- Wu and Palmer Similarity [24] sim_{wp}: The similarity measure, in Eq. 2, considers the position of the concepts C_1 and C_2 in the taxonomy related to the position of the concept of greater common specificity C, where N_1 and N_2 is the number of C_1 and C_2 hyperlinks, respectively, for the most common concept C, and H is the number of C hyperlinks for the root of taxonomy. The concept of greater common specificity C is the common parent between the concepts C_1 and C_2 with the minimum number of hyperonymous[1] links. As there can be several parents for each concept, two concepts can share parents in several ways [22].

$$sim_{wp}(C_1, C_2) = \frac{2H}{N_1 + N_2 + 2H} \quad (2)$$

- Leacock and Chodorow Similarity [8] sim_{lch}: The similarity measure , in Eq. 3, was proposed by Leacock and Chodorow [8], where *length* is the shortest path length between the two concepts C_1 and C_2 considering a node count; and D is the maximum depth of the taxonomy.

$$sim_{lch}(C_1, C_2) = -\log \frac{length}{2 * D} \quad (3)$$

Content-Based measures is based on the information content of each concept. The notion of the informational content of a concept C is directly related to the frequency of the term in a given collection of documents, *i.e.*, the frequencies of terms in the taxonomy are estimated using nominal frequencies in some extensive collections of texts. Associating probabilities with concepts in the taxonomy, for each concept C, $p(C)$ is the probability of finding the concept C in the taxonomy, defined as $p(C) = freq(C)/N$, where N is the total number of terms in the taxonomy, $freq(C) = \sum_{n \in words(C)} n$ and $words(C)$ is the set of terms included by C. Several SS use these probabilities informational content of the parents sharing the two terms C_1 and C_2, where $S(C_1, C_2)$ is the set of concepts that include (are parents of) C_1 and C_2. Thus Eq. 4 is the lowest probability of the shared parents of C_1 and C_2 [22], used to calculate the three Content-Based similarity measures used in this work:

$$p_{mis}(C_1, C_2) = min_{C \in S(c1,c2)} p(C) \quad (4)$$

- Resnik Similiraty [19] sim_{res}: This measure, in Eq. 5, is based on the more information two terms share in common, the more similar they are. Information shared by two terms is indicated by the informative content of the term that includes them in the taxonomy [22].

$$sim_{res}(C_1, C_2) = -\ln p_{mis}(C_1, C_2) \quad (5)$$

- Lin Similarity [10] sim_{lin}: This similarity measure, in Eq. 6, uses both the informational content of the parents shared between the two terms and the informational content of the compared terms. It is worth noticing that the previous Resnik Similarity measure depends solely on the informative content of the shared parents, and there are as many possible values for similarity as there are terms of ontology. Using the informative content of the compared

[1] Hyperonymy is the hierarchical semantic relation of one lexical unit to another according to which the extension of the first term, more general, encompasses the extension of the second, more specific. A term is hyperonymous if the meaning of the first includes the second concept.

terms and the shared parent, the number of possible values is quadratic in the number of terms that appear in the ontology, thus increasing the probability of having different values for different pairs of terms. Consequently, the Lin Similarity measure offers a more sensitive similarity measure than the Resnik Similarity measure.

$$sim_{Lin}(C_1, C_2) = \frac{2\ln p_{mis}(C_1, C_2)}{\ln p(C_1) + \ln p(C_2)} \tag{6}$$

- Jiang et al. Similarity [7] sim_{jcn}: The authors firstly present a semantic distance measure, in Eq. 7. Thus, $SS(C_1, C_2)$ is given by Eq. 8. This measure can result in arbitrarily large values, such as the Resnik Similarity measure, although in practice it has a maximum value of $2\ln(N)$, where N is the size of the corpus. In addition, it combines informational content from the shared parent and the compared concepts, as the Lin Similarity measure does. Thus, Jiang et al. Similarity measure seems to combine the properties of the two previous presented similarity measures [22].

$$dist_{jcn}(C_1, C_2) = -2\ln p_{mis}(C_1, C_2) - (\ln p(C_1) + \ln p(C_2)) \tag{7}$$

$$sim_{jcn}(c1, c2) = 1 - dist_{jcn}(c1, c2) \tag{8}$$

***SS* between two sentences**: There are several techniques in literature to calculate SS between longer texts, but only a few studies address calculating SS between small sentences [9], which is our case. Unlike calculating the similarity between long texts, which can be obtained by analyzing the frequency of the words that occur in the two texts, in the similarity of small sentences, the words are almost, if ever, repeated [9]. Thus, other approaches are needed to compare two short text segments.

Given two short text segments, or sentences (the categories in our case), T_1 and T_2, a frequently explored approach is to calculate the similarity between the words in each text segment S_1 and S_2, and then calculate SS of the sentences. We use in this work an evolution of the method for calculating SS between short sentences presented by Mihalcea et al. [13], determining the similarities of the words between the two sentences T_1 and T_2. For each word in the sentence T_1, the greatest similarity of that word is calculated with all the other words of the sentence T_2. The same process is done for T_2. SS is calculated by Eq. 9, where $pS(w, T_i) = \sum_{w \in T_i} maxS(w, T_i)$; and $maxS(w, T_i)$ is the maximum similarity of a word w of the sentence T_j related to all the words in the T_i sentence. It is essential to observe that the method initially proposed by Mihalcea et al. [13] uses the inverse document frequency to balance the sum terms. However, we balance the equation with just the value of the keyword set size for each sentence, given by $|T_1|$ and $|T_2|$. For the applied domain and given the short size of the evaluated sentences, we do not apply content information to calculate semantic similarity between the sentences. In the following section, we present how to calculate the similarity between words.

$$sim(T_1, T_2) = \frac{1}{2}\left(\frac{pS(w, T_2)}{|T_1|} + \frac{pS(w, T_1)}{|T_2|}\right) \tag{9}$$

For calculating SS between the short sentences, we used WordNet and NLTK. Wordnet [5] is a large lexicon database in English. Nouns, verbs, adjectives, and adverbs are grouped into sets of cognitive synonyms, called *synsets*, each expressing a different concept. The *synsets* are interconnected through conceptual, semantic, and lexical relationships. WordNet structure turns it into a useful tool for computational linguistics and NLP. WordNet is similar to a dictionary, as it groups words based on their meanings. However, there are some important distinctions. First, WordNet connects not just word forms but specific word meanings. As a result, words close to each other on the network do not have semantic ambiguity. Second, WordNet labels semantic relations between words, while grouping words in a thesaurus does not follow any explicit pattern [5]. The most frequently coded relationship between *synsets* is the super-subordinate relationship (also called hyperonymy, hyponymy or *is-a* relationship). It links more general *synsets* to more specific ones. Thus, WordNet states that, for instance, the *furniture* category includes *bed*, which in turn includes *bunk*. On the other hand, concepts like *bed* and *bunk* make up the category *furniture* [5].

In this research domain, we do not have the context of predefined words. Thus, we use an algorithm for disambiguating words known as a maximum similarity. This algorithm proposes to use the greatest similarity between the *synsets* of a word pair.

The maximum similarity $argmax_{synset(a)} = \sum_i^n max_{synset(i)}(sim(i, a))$ among all the *synsets* of a word pair. In this way, the similarity between all *synsets* of the two words is calculated and the greatest similarity is the final result.

NLTK (Natural Language Toolkit) [11] is a development platform written in Python, which implements several algorithms, techniques, and methods for NLP tasks. The framework provides easy interfaces to more than 50 lexical resources, such as WordNet, along with a set of word processing libraries for classification, tokenization, *stemming*, *tagging*, analysis, and reasoning semantic. In this work we use the implementation of *WordNet* provided in NLTK [11]. All processes of tokenization and removal of *stop words* were also implemented using the methods available in NLTK [11].

4 Methodology for Aligning Open Data Portals Categories

Considering the sets of categories SC_{NY}, SC_{LA} and SC_{Ch} extracted from the OGDPs of the three most densely populated cities in the United States, namely New York City, Los Angeles and Chicago, which are: SC_{NY} = {Business, City Government, Education, Environment, Health, Housing & Development, Public Safety, Recreation, Social Services, Transportation}; SC_{LA} = {A Livable and Sustainable City, A Prosperous City, A Safe City, A Well Run City};

and SC_{Ch} = {Administration & Finance, Buildings, Community, Education, Environment, Ethics, Events, FOIA, Facilities & Geo. Boundaries, Health and Human Services, Historic Preservation, Parks & Recreation, Public Safety, Sanitation, Service Requests, Transportation}. Intuitively, we can manually produce a generic Comprehensive Subset of Categories CSC = {Business, City Government, Education, Environment, Economic Development, Health, Public Safety, Recreation, Transportation, Uncategorized}, containing the most frequent categories in those portals. A generic alignment from SC_{Ch} to SC_G can be the following set of pairs: {(Administration & Finance $\mapsto$ City Government), (Buildings $\mapsto$ Economic Development), (Community $\mapsto$ Economic Development), (Education $\mapsto$ Education), (Environment $\mapsto$ Environment), (Ethics $\mapsto$ City Government), (Events $\mapsto$ Economic Development), (FOIA $\mapsto$ Uncategorized), (Facilities & Geo. Boundaries $\mapsto$ City Government), (Health and Human Services $\mapsto$ Health), (Historic Preservation $\mapsto$ Education), (Parks & Recreation $\mapsto$ Recreation), (Public Safety $\mapsto$ Public Safety), (Sanitation $\mapsto$ Health), (Service Requests $\mapsto$ City Government), (Transportation $\mapsto$ Transportation)}. In this work, we present two algorithms for automatically carrying out this alignment, considering some specific inputs given by the user. The first algorithm extracts CSC containing the most frequent categories in the selected OGDPs, which basic steps and a deeper analysis were presented in a previous work [16]. The second algorithm aims to align the categories of a given OGDP in this CSC. In what follows, we show examples of the steps using the categories of the sets SC_{NY}, SC_{LA}, and SC_{Ch}.

Constructing the Comprehensive Subset of Categories CSC: Given a set of OGDPs, CSC is obtained through the frequency analysis of the categories present in the set of OGDPs. Algorithm 1 shows the general steps for constructing CSC. The first parameter of this algorithm (SC) is the set of sets of categories $SC = \{SC_1, ..., SC_M\}$ extracted from M different OGDPs, used as reference for constructing CSC. The second parameter (ϕ) coverage parameter used for constructing CSC. The use of these parameters and the presented steps are better described in what follows.

Algorithm 1. Constructing the Comprehensive Subset of Categories CSC.

Require:
$SC = \{SC_1, ..., SC_M\}$: set of categories extracted from M different OGDPs;
ϕ: coverage parameter for constructing CSC

1: Extract SW: set of words extracted from SC;
2: Construct SWF: set of words and their respective frequencies;
3: Construct CSW: set of a comprehensive set of words given *phi*;
4: Construct $SWtoC$: set of words mapped to their respective categories and frequencies;
5: Construct CSC;
6: Return CSC;

Step 1 aims to extract all words w of each category $Cat \in SC$, decomposing each Cat into words, constructing SW. Step 2 aims to count the words frequency of each $w \in SW$. Words frequencies are calculated related to the entire SC. This task constructs a table containing all words and their respective occurrence frequencies as output. Considering the sets SC_{NY}, SC_{LA} and SC_{Ch}, the words and their respective frequencies is given by the set of pairs SW ={(education, 2); (social, 1); (ethics, 1); (environment, 2); (livable, 1); ...}.

Step 3 aims firstly to calculate the coverage of each word $W \in SW$ as the number of portals where a group of words occurs. Considering again the sets SC_{NY}, SC_{LA} and SC_{Ch}, the words and their respective coverage is given by the set of pairs SW ={(education, 66.7%); (social, 66.7%); (ethics, 66.7%); (environment, 100%); (livable, 100%); ...}. For this simple case, the maximum frequency was 2 in SW. In this way, the words with frequency value 1 have coverage of 66.7%; and those with frequency 2 have coverage of 100%. For finally constructing Comprehensive Set of Words CSW, we reversely order SW by frequency, let W_1 be the set made up of the first most frequent word in the ordered SW; W_2, the set made up of the first and second most frequent words in the ordered SW; and W_n, the set of first n most frequent words the ordered SW. We must calculate the number of portals for each of these sets. All the words in the set co-occur. Let T_n be the set of portals where all the words in set W_n occur. So, we define the Coverage Value $Cov(W_N)$ for each $N = 1, ..., n$. We choose the first $W_i, i = 1, ..., n$ for which $Cov(W_i) = \phi$, the second parameter of the algorithm. We want to observe that, considering our toy example, we may choose between the values 66.7% and 100%. If we use $\phi = 66.7\%$, the first set that satisfies the condition is W_1, containing only one word (education). It is not a good choice, as the CSW set has only one word, and consequently, the CSC set will also have only one category. If we use $\phi = 100\%$, the first set to satisfy the condition is the set W_{13} ={education, business, services, livable, transportation}, which is a more comprehensive set of words.

Step 4 aims to construct a structure $SWtoC$ that contains the categories associated with each word $w \in CSW$, as well as the categories frequencies. More specifically, given each $w \in SW$, this step constructs a set of structures mapping each word to the categories it was originated and the frequency the category appears in SC. Considering the set $SC = SC_{NY} \cup SC_{LA} \cup SC_{Ch}$, this step constructs the set $SWtoC$ ={ (education $\mapsto$ [(Education, 2)]); (environment $\mapsto$ [(Environment, 2)]); (health $\mapsto$ [(Health, 1), (Health & Human Services, 1)]); ...}. Thus, in the next step, for each More Comprehensive Word, we can associate the most frequent category in the different portals where the word occurs.

Finally, Step 5 aims to select the most frequent categories of $SWtoC$ to compose CSC. If there is a tie between the frequencies, one of the categories is chosen for the CSC. Considering again the set $SC = SC_{NY} \cup SC_{LA} \cup SC_{Ch}$, CSC = {Education, Health & Human Services, Environment, Transportation, Business, City Government, Public Safety, Housing & Development, Parks & Recreation, Social Services}.

Algorithm for Aligning Categories From an OGDP to the Comprehensive Subset of Categories CSC: Algorthim 2 presents the main steps for aligning categories from an OGDP (given to the algorithm by the first parameter SC_1) to the Comprehensive Subset of Categories CSC (given to the algorithm by the second parameter CSC). The third parameter is a SS measure to calculate SS between a pair of words w_1 and w_2. These measures can be one of the six different measures sim_{pd}, sim_{wp}, sim_{lch}, sim_{res}, sim_{lin} and sim_{jcn} presented in Sect. 3. Step 1 is the same as Step 1 of Algorithm 1, except that the categories to be analyzed is from one specific OGDP, called SC_1, where the index 1, in this case, aims to reinforce the idea of analyzing only one portal at this step of the methodology. The other steps are described next.

Algorithm 2. Constructing the Comprehensive Subset of Categories CSC.

Require:
  SC_1: set of categories extracted from an OGDPs;
  CSC: set of Comprehensive Subset of Categories;
  $sim(w_1, w_2)$: SS measure for calculating SS between a pair of words w_1 and w_2

1: Extract SW: set of words extracted from SC_1;
2: Construct $Align$: map of pairs of categories from SC_1 to CSC;
3: Return $Align$;

Step 2 aims to calculate SS between a pair of categories $Cat \in SC_1$ and $Cat' \in CSC$. Given two categories $Cat \in SC_1$ and $Cat' \in CSC$, $SS(Cat, Cat')$ is firstly calculated by calculating SS between all pairs of words that form the categories using $sim(w_1, w_2)$. This measure is than used for calculating $sim(T_1, T_2)$ according to Eq. 9, where in our case $T_1 \in SC_1$ and $T_2 \in CSC$. The output of this step is a set (map) of alignments $Align$ with pairs of categories of the form $(Cat_i \mapsto Cat'_j)$ associated to a similarity value $SS(Cat_i, Cat_j)$, where the first element Cat_i is the i-th category from SC_1 and the second element Cat'_j is the j-th category from CSC.

As an example, we can calculate SS between the categories *Public Works & Engineering* and *Land Use*. We need to calculate the similarity between the six pairs, resulting in combining all the component words. Using sim_{pd} for calculating SS for each pair of words, we have the following: (public, land, 0.33); (public, use, 0.125); (works, land, 0.33); (works, use, 0.5); (engineering, land, 0.25); and (engineering, use, 0.33). For the first word of T_1 (public), we choose the greatest similarity between the words of T_2, (land or use, which is 0.33; we did the same for the other two words (works – 0.5; engineering – 0.33). For the first word of T_2 (land), we also choose the greatest similarity between the words of T_1 (public, works, or engineering, which is 0.33); we did the same for the other word (use – 0.5). In this way:

$$SS(\text{'Public Works \& Engineering', 'Land Use'}) = \frac{1}{2}\left(\frac{0.33+0.5+0.33}{3} + \frac{0.33+0.5}{2}\right) = 0.4$$

5 Experimental Analysis

We collected manually all categories of 100 OGDPs of the most densely populated cities in the United States. For verifying which were these cities, we used the *Census Bureau's Population Estimates Program.* After this selection, we searched for its OGDP on the internet using the search string containing the name of the city followed by "open data portal"[2]. From these, we collected 976 categories. A total of 1530 words used in the categories of the datasets were processed, from which 507 are different. One striking difference between the portals is the number of categories used to distribute the datasets. There is a wide variation in the number of categories between the different portals: the minimum value found was 3 categories; the highest value found was 70.

We applied Step 1 of our Algorithm 1. Considering that our SC is composed of the categories present in the 100 portals, we executed Step 1 to extract SW. After this, we constructed the sets SWF (set of words and their respective frequencies); CSW (set of a comprehensive set of words given *phi*); $SWtoC$ (set of words mapped to their respective categories and frequencies); and CSC considering SC composed by the categories present in the 100 portals and initially $phi = 100\%$. We could observe that we reached 100% coverage of the portals using the 200 most frequent words. Between the sets of 50, 100, and 150 words, the scope in the portals does not change, being fixed at 98%. In this way, we deeply analyzed the set of the first 50 words through the frequency of occurrence of this set in the various portals. Thus, we constructed the set CSW with C_{24}, containing the first 24 most frequent words in the portals. In this way, CSW = {safety, transportation, services, recreation, development, planning, business, parks, government, education, health, boundaries, community, environment, finance, housing, infrastructure, property, police, culture, land, economy, zoning, budget}.

Given CSW, we continued to execute Steps 4 and 5 from Algorithm 1 to find CSC. We found the following CSC, with the respective frequency of each category in the 100 portals: CSC = {Public Safety (45); Transportation (46);

[2] The 100 densely populated cities with open data portals found were: NYC, Los Angeles, Chicago, Houston, Phoenix, Philadelphia, San Antonio, San Diego, Dallas, San Jose, Austin, Jacksonville, San Francisco, Columbus, Indianapolis, Fort Worth, Charlotte, Seattle, Denver, Washington, Boston, Detroit, Nashville, Portland, Oklahoma City, Las Vegas, Louisville, Baltimore, Tucson, Sacramento, Mesa, Kansas City, Atlanta, Long Beach, Colorado Springs, Raleigh, Miami, Virginia Beach, Omaha, Oakland, Minneapolis, Tulsa, New Orleans, Wichita, Tampa, Aurora, Honolulu, Anaheim, Santa Ana, Riverside, Lexington, St. Louis, Pittsburgh, Saint Paul, Cincinnati, Anchorage, Henderson, Greensboro, Plano, Newark, Orlando, Chula Vista, Jersey City, Durham, Laredo, Madison, Scottsdale, Glendale, Reno, Norfolk, Chesapeake, Fremont, Baton Rouge, Richmond, Boise, San Bernardino, Spokane, Birmingham, Tacoma, Oxnard, Fayetteville, Montgomery, Little Rock, Akron (County of Summit), Grand Rapids, Salt Lake City, Huntsville, Mobile, Tallahassee, Knoxville, Worcester, Tempe, Santa Clarita, Cape Coral, Providence, Chattanooga, Santa Rosa, Sioux Falls, McKinney and ElkGrove.

City Services (4); Community Services (4); Recreation (8); Economic Development (6); Planning (10); Business (15); Parks & Recreation (6); Government (12); Education (19); Health (13); Boundaries (14); Community (4); Community Services (4); Environment (12); Finance (9); Housing (19); Infrastructure (19); Property (7); Police (7); Culture and Recreation (4); Land Base (2); Land Use (2); Land Records (2); Economy (4); Planning & Zoning (4); Zoning (4); Business & Budget (3)}. We can verify in this set that there are similar or repeated categories among the categories of the obtained set. Thus, we can choose only one category among the most frequent of these words to compose CSC. So, we finally achieved CSC ={Public Safety; Community; Transportation; Environment; City Services; Finance; Parks & Recreation; Housing; Economic Development; Infrastructure; Planning; Property; Business; Police; Government; Land Use; Education; Economy; Health; Zoning; Boundaries}.

In order to verify the behavior of our Algorithm 2, we considered aligning back the categories of each of the 100 OGDPs to our CSC. Figure 1 shows the values of SS for all categories collected in SC according to each similarity measure between words presented in Sect. 3: sim_{pd} in Fig. 1(a); sim_{wp} in Fig. 1(b); sim_{lch} in Fig. 1(c); sim_{res} in Fig. 1(d); sim_{jcn} in Fig. 1(e); and sim_{lin} in Fig. 1(f). Each value presented is the highest similarity value obtained in the alignment of a given category. That is, each bar represents the highest similarity value of the alignment of a category of a portal with the most similar category of the Comprehensive Subset, for all categories of all portals. We can observe in these graphs that some measures cannot align all the categories, being the sim_{jcn} the one that stands out in this negative characteristic.

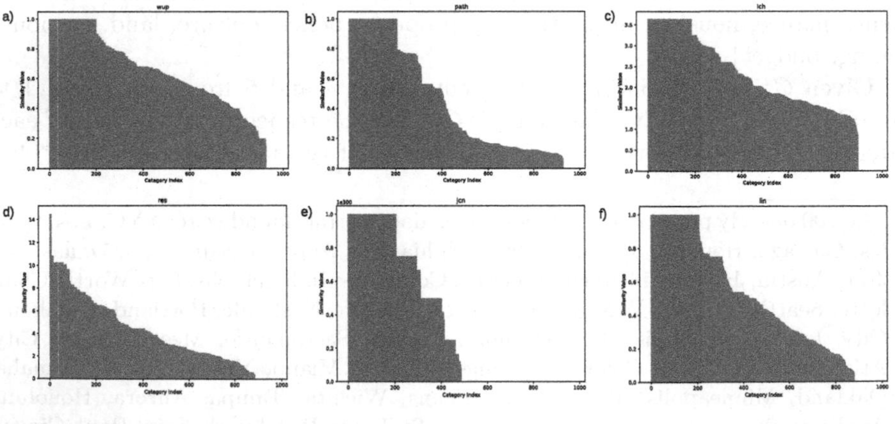

Fig. 1. Absolute SS values between categories (X-axis: Similarity value, Y-axis: Category index.

The alignment result produced by each measure was obtained and compared to calculate the Agreement Value AV, defined as the number of techniques that exhibited the same result for an alignment if the six methods present the same result for a given alignment, $AV = 6$. In the case of an alignment where the six methods present different results, $AV = 1$. In a given alignment, the chosen category by the most significant number of methods is presented as the most similar category. The category chosen for the alignment is the one with the highest AV.

Figure 2 shows AV values when aligning all categories in SC with the CSC. $AV = 6$ indicates that all six SS used measures showed the same result; $AV = 5$ indicates that 5 out of 6 measures had the same result; and so on. $AV = 0$ indicates no possible alignment by any of the techniques used. The vertical axis in this graph shows the numbers of aligned categories. We can observe in this figure that, for most of the categories of the analyzed portals, the methods proposed the same category for alignment; that is, for most of the categories collected in the portals, the six methods agreed in the alignment result. Also, in all cases where it was possible to align the categories, at least two methods proposed the same alignment result. There was no case where the formulations proposed completely different results from each other. On the other hand, there are some cases where the methods fail to assign any category within the CSC. These categories may be described in specific contexts or use acronyms, making the semantic analysis of the text segment used difficult. In these cases, categorization can be done manually, or a category can be created to group all non-aligned categories.

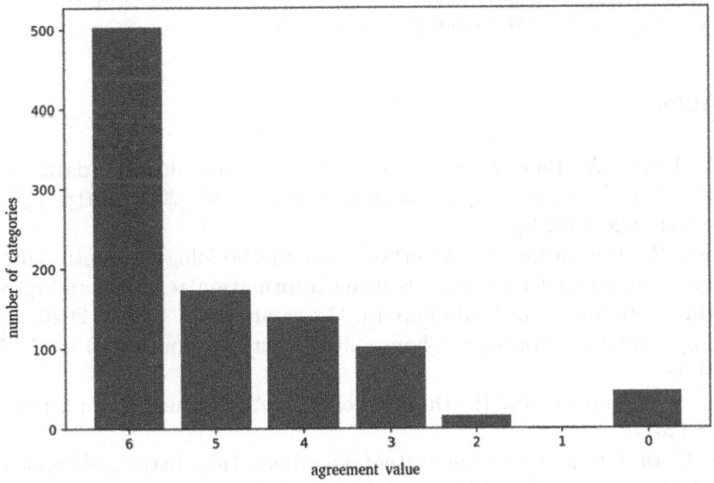

Fig. 2. Number of categories and AV for the 6 used measures. (X-axis: Agreement value, Y-axis: Number of categories)

6 Conclusions and Future Work

In this work, we present a methodology for automatically aligning categories of an OGDP to a Comprehensive Subset of Categories (CSC), also constructed by our methodology. For constructing CSC, we use categories from OGDPs that organize their portals by categories. We conducted an exploratory analysis using categories extracted from 100 portals from densely populated cities located in United Stated. Observing our study, we can see that our automatic category alignment methodology can support the alignment of category sets of OGDPs.

A limitation of this work is that we need perhaps more than one relevant category for a given dataset. At the moment, we only stick to one category per dataset. One future work we plan to conduct is a survey to evaluate the level of complexity that people may find to align categories with a given CSC, as well as to evaluate the Agreement Value between people, in order to compare to the AVs we obtained with the similarity measures we used. We also think it would be interesting to implement our methodology in frameworks that support the construction of OGDPs, such as CKAN Harvester [4]. Implementations like these would allow us to compare the results for recovering similar datasets from different OGDPs using our methodology with tools that use Question and Answering technology, such as the one proposed by [2]. Another interesting future work with this implementation could be evaluating our methodology in different scenarios.

Acknowledgements. This study was financed in part by the Coordenação de Aperfeiçoamento de Pessoal de Nível Superior - Brasil (CAPES) - Finance Code 001. We would also like to thank Mr. Daniel Castellani Ribeiro and the NYU Center for Urban Science and Progress for welcoming us to the center and allowing us to discuss the general ideas that led us to the results in this work.

References

1. Adi, E., Anwar, A., Baig, Z., Zeadally, S.: Machine learning and data analytics for the IOT. Neural Comput. Appl. **32**(20), 16205–16233 (2020). https://doi.org/10.1007/s00521-020-04874-y
2. Barcellos, R., Bernardini, F., Viterbo, J.: A methodology for retrieving datasets from open government data portals using information retrieval and question and answering techniques. In: Viale Pereira, G., et al. (eds.) EGOV 2020. LNCS, vol. 12219, pp. 239–249. Springer, Cham (2020). https://doi.org/10.1007/978-3-030-57599-1_18
3. Bischof, S., Kämpgen, B., Harth, A., Polleres, A., Schneider, P.: Open city data pipeline (2017)
4. CKAN: Ckan data management system documentation. https://docs.ckan.org/en/ckan-1.7.4/harvesting.html. Accessed 20 Jan 2022
5. Fellbaum, C.: WordNet. In: Poli, R., Healy, M., Kameas, A. (eds.) Theory and Applications of Ontology: Computer Applications, pp. 231–243. Springer, Dordrecht (2010). https://doi.org/10.1007/978-90-481-8847-5_10
6. Hoshiai, T., Yamane, Y., Nakamura, D., Tsuda, H.: A semantic category matching approach to ontology alignment. In: EON. Citeseer (2004)
7. Jiang, J.J., Conrath, D.W.: Semantic similarity based on corpus statistics and lexical taxonomy. arXiv preprint cmp-lg/9709008 (1997)
8. Leacock, C., Chodorow, M.: Combining local context and WordNet similarity for word sense identification. WordNet Electron. Lexical Database **49**, 265–283 (1998)

9. Li, Y., McLean, D., Bandar, Z.A., O'Shea, J.D., Crockett, K.: Sentence similarity based on semantic nets and corpus statistics. IEEE Trans. Knowl. Data Eng. **18**(8), 1138–1150 (2006). https://doi.org/10.1109/TKDE.2006.130
10. Lin, D.: Principle-based parsing without overgeneration. In: Proceedings of the 31st Annual Meeting on Association for Computational Linguistics, pp. 112–120. Association for Computational Linguistics (1993)
11. Loper, E., Bird, S.: Natural Language Toolkit. https://www.nltk.org/
12. Manning, C.D., Raghavan, P., Schütze, H.: Introduction to Information Retrieval. Cambridge University Press, Cambridge (2008)
13. Mihalcea, R., Corley, C., Strapparava, C.: Corpus-based and knowledge-based measures of text semantic similarity. In: Proceedings 21st National Conference on AI - Vol. 1, pp. 775–780. AAAI 2006. AAAI Press (2006)
14. Nikiforova, A., Lnenicka, M.: A multi-perspective knowledge-driven approach for analysis of the demand side of the open government data portal. Gov. Inf. Q. **38**(4), 101622 (2021)
15. Pawar, A., Mago, V.: Calculating the similarity between words and sentences using a lexical database and corpus statistics. CoRR (2018)
16. Pinto, H.d.S., Bernardini, F., Viterbo, J.: How cities categorize datasets in their open data portals: An exploratory analysis. In: Proceedings 19th Annual International Conference Digital Government Research - dg.o 2018, pp. 25:1–25:9. ACM, New York, NY, USA (2018)
17. Quarati, A.: Open government data: usage trends and metadata quality. J. Inf. Sci. 01655515211027775 (2021)
18. Rada, R., Mili, H., Bicknell, E., Blettner, M.: Development and application of a metric on semantic nets. IEEE Trans. Syst. Man Cybern. **19**(1), 17–30 (1989)
19. Resnik, P.: Semantic similarity in a taxonomy: an information-based measure and its application to problems of ambiguity in natural language. CoRR (2011)
20. Sawadogo, P., Darmont, J.: On data lake architectures and metadata management. J. Intell. Inf. Syst. **56**(1), 97–120 (2020). https://doi.org/10.1007/s10844-020-00608-7
21. Thorsby, J., Stowers, G.N., Wolslegel, K., Tumbuan, E.: Understanding the content and features of open data portals in American cities. Gov. Inf. Q. **34**(1), 53–61 (2017)
22. Varelas, G., Voutsakis, E., Raftopoulou, P., Petrakis, E.G., Milios, E.E.: Semantic similarity methods in wordnet and their application to information retrieval on the web. In: Proceedings 7th Annual ACM International Workshop on Web Information and Data Management, pp. 10–16. ACM (2005)
23. van der Waal, S., Węcel, K., Ermilov, I., Janev, V., Milošević, U., Wainwright, M.: Lifting open data portals to the data web. In: Auer, S., Bryl, V., Tramp, S. (eds.) Linked Open Data – Creating Knowledge Out of Interlinked Data. LNCS, vol. 8661, pp. 175–195. Springer, Cham (2014). https://doi.org/10.1007/978-3-319-09846-3_9
24. Wu, Z., Palmer, M.: Verbs semantics and lexical selection. In: Proceedings of the 32nd Annual Meeting on Association for Computational Linguistics, pp. 133–138. Association for Computational Linguistics (1994)
25. Yang, H.-C., Lin, C.S., Yu, P.-H.: Toward automatic assessment of the categorization structure of open data portals. In: Wang, L., Uesugi, S., Ting, I.-H., Okuhara, K., Wang, K. (eds.) MISNC 2015. CCIS, vol. 540, pp. 372–380. Springer, Heidelberg (2015). https://doi.org/10.1007/978-3-662-48319-0_30

Why Should You Believe in Open Data? – A Document Study Examining Persuasion Rhetoric of OGD Benefits

Karin Ahlin[1](✉) and Jonathan Crusoe[2,3]

[1] Service Research Centre, Karlstad University, Universitetsgatan 2, 651 88 Karlstad, Sweden
karin.ahlin@kau.se

[2] Faculty of Librarianship, Information, Education and IT, Swedish School of Library and Information Science, University of Borås, 503 32 Borås, Sweden
jonathan.crusoe@hb.se

[3] Swedish Center for Digital Innovation, Department of Applied IT, University of Gothenburg, 405 30 Gothenburg, Sweden
jonathan.crusoe@ait.gu.se

Abstract. The rhetoric related to benefits of Open Government Data (OGD) seems to lack anchor in practice affecting practitioners and empirical evidence restraining academia. This rhetoric could be hard to see for those already persuaded. As such, the rhetoric could contain inconsistencies that are based more on myths than facts, contributing to the slow pace of OGD development. OGD is sometimes based on dogmatic rhetoric that is overly simplistic, which hides significant benefits and blocks potential audiences from seeing the practical applications of OGD. The purpose of the present study was to analyse the persuasiveness of present OGD arguments from a rhetorical perspective to identify rhetorical patterns. We conducted desktop research, investigating the rhetoric of eight websites emphasising OGD benefits. Our findings include four common patterns of the rhetoric involving persuasion and dissuasion. The rhetoric contains paradoxes of promises and discoveries, which we categorised as the grand quest, promised opportunities, tribal solidarity, and the silver bullet patterns. A further finding was two mythical paradoxes: (1) promises versus discovery and (2) proving while arguing.

Keywords: Open government data · Rhetoric · Persuasion · Dissuasion · Mythical paradox

1 Introduction

Open government data (OGD) is data available to everyone, without restrictions in terms of copyright, costs, and patents [1]. OGD builds on an "open

Published by Springer Nature Switzerland AG 2022
M. Janssen et al. (Eds.): EGOV 2022, LNCS 13391, pp. 274–287, 2022.
https://doi.org/10.1007/978-3-031-15086-9_18

to everyone" vision, often emphasised by politicians and other governing actors [e.g., 7,23,29]. Further highlighted are the benefits of OGD, with repeated messages about opening up data for transparency, accountability, cost savings, and economic growth [e.g., 17,35]. The focus on these benefits is intentional, as a part of persuasion, aiming to change people's minds and behaviours to support OGD [11,12]. [9] explains that persuasion is an important activity within OGD. For example, public organisations looking to acquire resources to publish OGD might need success stories to persuade others of its benefits [41]. Persuasion is an ongoing activity, varying in intensity [11]. [19] framed the OGD persuasion as part of a revolution, declaring: *"Like all revolutions, it is being driven by a powerful set of arguments, forwarded by passionate believers in the benefits of new ways of knowing and acting in the world and an alliance of vested interests who gain from its unfolding"* (p. 113). Hence, the act of persuasion involves roles such as **sender** and **audience**; that is, the sender intends an argument to be compelling to a particular audience. For OGD, the sender often holds a role as an enthusiast or sometimes a politician. The audience can be managers in public organisations, or OGD enthusiasts like students at universities or hobby programmers. Therefore, activists and politicians attempt to construct arguments that will persuade this broader audience. Several arguments for OGD have been identified in practice [e.g., 14,25,31], and some academics have also provided arguments [e.g., 2,5]. However, the persuasion has involved myths and motivations [e.g., 15,17,39], not focusing on the reality for practitioners or providing enough theoretical back-up for academia. [30] noted that the benefits of OGD are proclaimed rather than empirically proven. Practitioners are left without tools to persuade managers and managers are left without tools to persuade decision-makers, etc. This chain restrains the possible benefits that OGD practitioners can produce, adding to their burden to continue OGD. In academia, theorising OGD benefits has not attracted much interest, which adds to the mainstream argumentation. Thereby, the arguments themselves could be part of the low pace of publishing and using OGD [3], which would be difficult to see for those already persuaded to believe in OGD.

Therefore, the purpose of this study is to analyse the persuasiveness of present OGD arguments from a rhetorical perspective to identify rhetorical patterns. The study focuses on how the arguments can persuade and dissuade an audience where the objective is to highlight the value of studying rhetoric within the OGD community. In this study, 'persuade' means convincing the audience to believe in OGD, while 'dissuade' means convincing them to not believe in OGD. The findings could explain why anyone would be generally inclined or not to participate in OGD, but also help OGD senders to develop better arguments. Therefore, this study is guided by the following research question: What are the rhetorical patterns among OGD practitioners' arguments, in the form of persuasion and dissuasion, drawing on the benefits of OGD?

2 Background

Senders tend to argue for OGD based on perceived societal needs or problems, which the release and use of OGD could cure or improve upon society [9]. The problems include dysfunctional democracies, walled data gardens that are only accessible to a small elite, wasted potential of untapped data, and obscure governments [24,25,33,34]. The improvements that have been suggested to address these problems are to show political, social, economic, operational, and technical benefits [17] where the core is to maximise the value of OGD and minimise wasted work and storage for said OGD. Through persuasion, a persuaded audience gains purpose and reason to work with OGD [9]. OGD is driven by a powerful set of arguments, often presented by passionate believers in the benefits of OGD [19]. The arguments are based on statements used to gain legitimacy for believing or not in OGD without a determinable basis of facts or evidence are myths [17]. Therefore, the arguments of OGD could be myth-driven rather than evidence-driven. On the other hand, an audience might see risks and dangers in OGD and resist or refuse to believe in it [4,38,42]. Propensities in OGD arguments emerge repeatedly, although the arguments do not seem to reflect what is happening in practice. To approach this phenomenon further, we describe fundamental parts of rhetoric.

2.1 Rhetoric

Rhetoric is the study and practice of persuasion. People need each other and work in collaboration. Because of the need for collaborators to agree on common goals, people need to be able to influence each other. Hence, much interaction requires persuasion [20]. Persuasion consists of arguments. An argument is a set of evidence (datum) to support a claim and an effort to support certain views with reasons [18,40]. Rhetoric occurs when a sender provides a speech or a written text for an audience in response to an occasion where their interpretations are based on their presuppositions [20].

Rhetorical analysis studies persuasion in order to understand how people have been and can be persuaded, which can help us become better judges and advocates by analysing the effectiveness of the arguments. This analysis can study calls to character (ethos), emotions (pathos), and reasoning (logos), but also rhythm, structure, and style [36]. Our research is based on Toulmin's argument mode, enhanced by Longaker and Walkers' argument analysis [20].

Toulmin explained that an argument attempts to answer an **issue** by providing **datum** towards a **claim**. The leap from datum and a claim is supported by a **warrant**, which explains how the datum leads to the claim and is captured as a general statement. A warrant certifies all arguments of the appropriate type similar to a law. It is supported by **backing**, which explains why, in general, a certain warrant should be accepted as having authority [36]. A sender can draw on warrants whose acceptability is taken for granted (warrant-using) or attempt to establish a new warrant by applying it to a number of cases (warrant-establishing). In the former, the conclusion is commonly accepted and understood, while in the latter the warrant is novel and original. Warrant-establishing is common in scientific papers [36]. In addition, **qualifiers** indicate the strength conferred by a warrant (such as can, could, and might), while a **rebuttal** indicates circumstances when the general authority of a warrant would not apply [36]. Toulmin's model focused on logos, which abates ethos and pathos, so we have included Longaker and Walkers' argument analysis. Their argument analysis studies the establishing of ethos, connections to an audience's pathos, and asking who is the audience and what the sender wants the audience to believe, feel, and do [20]. Toulmin's model is summarised in Fig. 1. The next section explains how his model and Longaker and Walkers' argument analysis were used.

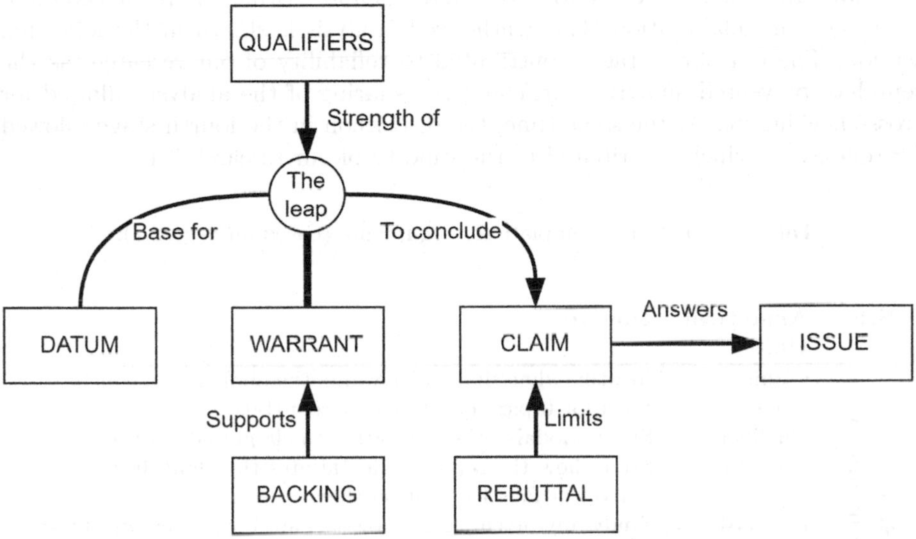

Fig. 1. A representation of Toulmin's model.

3 Research Approach

The method for this research followed a general qualitative methodology [22] analysing documents [6] and was conducted in four stages: (1) identify documents, (2) create an analysis template, (3) individual analysis, and (4) collaborative analysis. The first stage was to use desktop research focusing on identifying existing websites based on OGD benefits. For this purpose, we chose eight websites to analyse as documents. The *criteria* for the websites, besides arguing OGD benefits, were a combination of public and business organisations, and interest groups. Their headquarters are located in Sweden, Europe, and worldwide. Further criteria were variations in the communication styles and preferable different perspectives on the benefits, which contributed to triangulation in our research [8]. The second stage was to create an inductive analysis template based on the Toulmin model, enhanced by Longaker and Walkers' argument analysis;

Table 1. The template was applied in a top- down fashion with possible iterations between the analytical units, where some units were based on previous units. The third stage was the individual analysis, using inductive analysis based on the previously created template. The template was used in three steps: (1) the argumentation, (2) the audience, and (3) analysis of the parts for persuasion and dissuasion. The first step was descriptive and gap-filling; the second step was interpretive and derivative; and the third step was analytical. This analysis was performed for each website. The fourth stage was to jointly discuss the individual analysis, comparing our findings and writing the persuasion and dissuasion in collaboration. The synthesised analysis is shown in the following section. The last three stages contributed to reliability of our research, as the template prevented analytical drift and the sharing of the analysis allowed for cross-checking [8]. At the same time, the discussion in the fourth stage allowed for reflexivity, which contributed to the validity of our research [21].

Table 1. Analytical template for arguments (based on Sect. 2.1).

Steps	Analytical Unit	How-to
Step 1. Argumentation	Claim	Identify what the sender wants the audience to conclude.
	Issue	Look for topics, questions, or rebuttals.
	Qualifier	Study modal verbs in relation to claim and warrants.
	Rebuttal	Study how the sender differentiates the claim from alternatives or fails to mention them.
	Establish Ethos	Study any attempts on how to gain legitimacy and trust, such as presentation of logos and statements of expertise.
	Datum	Identify evidence or statements used to support the claim.
	Warrant	Identify general statements and determine if they are warrant-using or warrant-establishing.
	Backing	Identify statements that support the warrant.
	Connection to pathos	Study how the sender uses humour, values, and statements to emotionally connect to an audience.
Step 2. Audience	Who?	Scrutinise the argument to construct an idea of the intended audience.
	Asked to believe	Identify warrants and statements an audience needs to accept on face value and condense them into a belief.
	Asked to feel	Compare the connection to pathos with the above; what feelings are the sender attempting to rise?
	Asked to do	Study the claim and warrants; if so, how does the sender want an audience to change their behaviours or act?
Step 3. Analysis	Persuasion	Analyse why an audience should be persuaded by the argument by bringing the above together.
	Dissuasion	Analyse why an audience should be dissuaded by the argument by bringing the above together.

4 Findings and Analysis

Table 2 presents an overview of the analysed arguments. The following subsection presents the identified rhetorical patterns.

Table 2. Overview of OGD arguments.

Sender	Medium	Type	Audience	Structure	Approach
[7]	Webpage	Text, video	Governments, enthusiasts	Tool kit	Encourage
[27]	Blog post	Text, GIFs	Beginners	Ten bullet points	Humour
[29]	Webpage	Text	Beginners	Two-tier	Encourage
[37]	Document	Text	Governments	Body text	Encourage
[32]	Blog posts	Text	Governments, enthusiasts	Counter-rebuttals	Motivate
[35]	Article	Text	Governments, enthusiasts	Two-tier	Encourage
[26]	Webpage	Text	Governments, enthusiasts	Body text	Enthuse
[23]	Webpage	Text	Governments, enthusiasts	Two-tier	Encourage

4.1 Rhetorical Patterns

The findings show that senders of OGD arguments for benefits use and combine four rhetorical patterns: (1) the grand quest, (2) promised opportunities, (3) tribal solidarity, and (4) the silver bullet. The pattern related to the grand quest can be explained by framing OGD as a big adventure and the promised opportunities adds in various directions, such as just promises or even prophesies. Rhetoric pattern related to the tribal solidarity looks upon the community aspect of OGD and rhetoric related to the silver bullet frames various or individual patterns of the benefits related to OGD. Each pattern is presented with a description, some empirical examples, and the reasons we see for persuasion and dissuasion. Table 3 presents the patterns' occurrences and variations in the analysed OGD arguments, which is further detailed through the subsection.

Table 3. Rhetorical patterns in analysed OGD arguments.

Sender	Grand quest	Promised opportunities	Tribal solidarity	Silver bullet
[7]	Challenge	Promises	Partnership	Scattered
[27]	N/A	Prophesy	Everyone	Social, Economic
[29]	Untapped	Promises	Support	Social, Economic
[37]	Untapped	Mixture	Initiative	Social, Economic
[32]	Resistance	Solutions	Alliances	N/A
[35]	Progress	Promises	Community	Social, Economic
[26]	Untapped	Mixture	N/A	Scattered
[23]	Progress	Mixture	N/A	Scattered

The grand quest pattern frames OGD as a challenge or resistance to overcome, untapped potential to unlock, or progress towards benefits. It contains challenges, treasures, and possible rewards at the end. The grand quest argues for OGD as another type of journey, where there will be new challenges in relation to what the audience previously has experienced. Still, the texts emphasise the journey as being worth it, as the discovered results are more valuable than the efforts. For example, *"[...] OGD still remains an uncharted territory. Much untapped potential could be unleashed if government data are turned into OGD."* [37, p. 4], *"Open data, especially open government data, is a tremendous resource that is as yet largely untapped. [...] At the same time it is impossible to predict precisely how and where value will be created in the future. The nature of innovation is that developments often comes from unlikely places."* [29, p. 1,3], and

> *"Releasing Open Data is not easy. It requires time and resources and it can also be a challenge to make sure the fine line between transparency and privacy isn't compromised. So if it is so challenging and requires money, then the question is : Is it worth it? Take a moment to watch this video about the potential of open data [Video:* https://youtu.be/bwX5MAZ6zKI*] This is just the tip of the iceberg, there is much more to this."* [7, p. 9].

The pattern is persuasive for an audience that seeks to overcome challenges for rewards or discover hidden rewards in uncharted territory (it appeals to an audience's spirit of adventure), while it dissuades an audience for the same reasons. It asks the audience to believe that there will be a reward once the grand quest is completed, but an adventure can include risks and dangers, which could stop the adventure in its tracks. **The promised opportunities** pattern frames OGD as a deliverable, a certain possibility for benefits, or promise. If an audience invests time and resources, the pattern explicitly or implicitly promises that the audience will gain, unlock, or enable certain categories of benefits. It is sometimes woven into the grand quest pattern as the final destination. Three good examples of this pattern are:

> *"From a social perspective, open data enhances participation, collaboration, and enables the inclusion of marginalised groups. It enables citizens to make better-informed decisions but more importantly, empowers citizens to contribute to policies that are better designed to their needs and to a more engaging relationship with their governments. [...] As discussed, there are benefits to open data, including its impact on economic growth and society. The benefits of open data create substantial value to society as a whole and impact your daily life."* [35, p. 7], and

> *"In addition to increasing government transparency and public awareness of government programmes and activities, opening up data can also help generate insights into how to improve government performance. Increased data transparency provides the basis for public participation and collaboration in the creation of innovative, value-added services."* [37, p. 4].

The promised opportunities pattern persuades by presenting the audience with the possible benefits of OGD. This gives the audience an idea of what OGD could do for them. However, it dissuades an audience by framing benefits in general terms and failing to disclose the data leading to the benefits. The pattern potentially oversells OGD.

The tribal solidarity invites the audience to an OGD community, which has open boundaries. For example, *"**Be more open** To find out more about how we can help your organisation become more open, get in touch."* [29, p. 8],

> *"Interested in learning more about the benefits and value of using open data? Explore the EDP's news archive, feature articles, and use cases! Aware of open data examples? Tell us your story and share them with us via mail, and follow us on Twitter, Facebook, or LinkedIn to stay up to date!"* [35, p. 8], and

> *"**C. I Don't Know Who To Talk To About It** [...] Often, strong open data movements start with actors both inside and out of government. If you're having trouble identifying allies in one sector, look for champions and co-leads in the other. Community groups with overlapping interest may include a local chapter of US PIRG, the League of Women Voters, FOI advocates, Code for America, tech meetups, and more."* [32, part 3, p. 11].

The tribal solidarity persuades by showing the audience that others are involved in OGD who can help and support the audience. It can dissuade the audience as it sometimes constructs an "us versus them" thinking, implies social commitments to others, and alienates the audience.

The silver-bullet pattern presents OGD as a solution to many problems, relating to the promised opportunities pattern. Examples are...

> *"In the computer world there is something called Linus' Law, which states: "given enough eyeballs, all bugs (problems) are shallow." and one can draw parallels from it for almost everything. There can also be long-term or unanticipated benefits to opening data."* [7, p. 14] and

> *"The publication of data is driven by the belief that it brings enormous benefits to citizens, businesses, and public administrations, while at the same time enabling stronger co-operation across Europe. Open data can bring benefits in various fields, such as health, food security, education, climate, intelligent transport systems, and smart cities"* [13, p. 2].

The silver bullet pattern draws on sweeping generalisations to persuade an audience that can be attracted by benefits, such as efficiency or transparency. The dissuasion reflects that the argument does not take into account the fact that it is hard to relate to the benefits with specific data or easy to identify rebuttals. At the extreme extent, the generalisations make the benefits sound too good to be true.

5 Discussion

This paper's findings show that an OGD argument reasons as follows: *"public organisations possess vast vaults of restrained data that, if made open, could (or will) lead to certain benefits. Therefore, the audience should believe in OGD"*. The warrantal leap is from the could (or will) to should, where the benefits are assumed to be an accepted common good. When this reasoning lacks basis in facts or evidence, it can help to produce myths [17]. This section discusses patterns in the OGD argumentation for benefits, mythical paradoxes in the argumentation, the value of studying rhetoric within the OGD community, and implications for practice and academia.

5.1 Patterns in the OGD Argumentation

OGD builds on an "open to everyone" vision, which is often emphasised by politicians and other governing actors [e.g., 7,23,29]. Most of the literature has argued for OGD as a grand quest involving more than the organisation's IT department. Even though the OGD commonly is viewed as a grand quest, the argument does differ. Some arguments focus solely on the OGD as resource [29], while others attribute it to a journey [23]. The resource variation emphasises OGD as an untapped resource, regardless of the content. The argument is not aligned to a specific audience and leaves the audience to align it to their specific context. The perspective of journey varies from challenge to progress [7,23]. both of which should appeal to different types of audiences. The challenge might appeal to public organisations that need to choose to invest their scarce resources on various assigned tasks, whereas progress could favour entrepreneurs.

All texts argue for OGD as a resource with promising opportunities of yielding benefits in the future. A common way to give promises is by emphasising what will happen when OGD is published [7]. Another way is by claiming opportunities when OGD is in use as a service [23]. The promises can be viewed as pure promises or as prophecies, where the latter adds less credibility to the argument. Still, the promises can have low credibility as the publishing rate is relatively low and thereby the real benefits. Arguing for OGD as the foundation for services approaches not just the resource, but also the work of others, such as extraction or development [10].

The pattern of tribal solidarity varies among the texts. Some of the analysed OGD arguments do not present tribal solidarity in their arguments, such as [23,29]. The answer to why a resource from public organisations is viewed as part of some tribal solidarity could be the inclusiveness related to the resource itself [1], the "open to everyone" vision [e.g., 7,23,29]. Still, it differs from the role of public organisations focusing on its stipulated domain and not being a natural way to collaborate. Besides this situation, the tribal solidarity differs from including everyone [31] to following someone's initiative [37]. The initiative charity could also include support by reaching out [28] or even creating alliances [32].

The silver bullet pattern includes two variations, the scattered, like [23] and the social-economic [31]. Both variations are general and could apply to an audience on a management level, which is not the intended audience for the text. The scattered silver bullet approach, solving all types of problems, give the audience a misleading view of a specific dataset and how it can be used. Reducing the silver bullet to socio-economic perspectives aligns with public organisations' boundaries and does not focus on what benefits OGD can yield as a resource.

5.2 Mythical Paradoxes in the OGD Argumentation

Promises Versus Discovery. The analysed OGD arguments tend to fluctuate between coulds and shoulds, possibilities and certainties, and discoveries and promises. The findings present a paradox in the OGD argumentation, which is stretched among the grand quest, promised opportunities, and silver bullet patterns. When the first pattern is used with one or both of the latter patterns, they can create a contradiction between discovery and promises of OGD benefits. Several of the arguments contain an idea of an adventurous journey or exploration of uncharted territory. Those arguments attract an audience that wants to be adventurers and frontier entrepreneurs, but excludes an audience that needs to show stability and safe and stable progress. We believe that this thread within the OGD arguments could be one reason for why the OGD movement is stagnating [3]. It would help to explain the myths encountered by previous OGD research [15,17] since the adventurers are on a journey towards a higher vision and the quest could be considered more important than the facts. The collective acceptance of a grand quest pattern could be further motivated by the tribal solidarity pattern. This thread can be further enhanced by arguments based on a dichotomy of promised benefits and discovery. This dichotomy creates a paradox in the argumentation where the sender promises an adventure of discovery, while also promising concrete benefits at the end of this adventure. The journey is framed as challenging with risks, but also safe and certain. Consequently, the adventure could be understood as not being an adventure. It is a path towards something specific, which means it cannot be a discovery. This paradox is expressed in OGD arguments as a contradiction between warrant and backing, which makes a leap from datum to claim difficult (as OGD arguments are backed with promises about benefits that cannot be known). The result is that an audience needs to follow OGD with a degree of blind faith.

Proving While Arguing. Another paradox relates to the promised opportunities and silver bullet patterns. It is like using warrants at the same time as you are establishing them (similar to arguing based on deduction by proving it through induction). In this context, the sender argues on two levels: (1) to prove certain OGD leads to certain benefits and that certain OGD leads to certain benefits and (2) to prove that the audience should believe in OGD. When the sender argues based on certain benefits (such as political, social, and economic), it reuses warrants about assumed common goods, which could be sought after by the audience. On the other hand, the sender still needs to prove that OGD could lead to these benefits, while the benefits might not have previously been realised. The sender needs to establish new warrants for the audience. This paradox creates a situation where a sender might express promised opportunities, but also declares how OGD can solve several previous problems. The paradox tends to be expressed as sweeping generalisations from a few specific cases to a general warrant [20] combined with fluctuations in qualifiers.

5.3 A Rhetorical Perspective on OGD

The paper's findings show that OGD senders face a daunting challenge. Senders need to use and establish warrants for a broad audience and convince the audience that OGD, as something new, can lead to already familiar benefits (such as transparency, economic growth, and innovations), while being uncertain about its possibilities. This leading also involves the introduction of a new leap from datum to claim, which is a task that is often found in academic literature [36]. While practitioners can see many possible OGD benefits [17,30] identified that many OGD benefits are only proclaimed and have not been empirically tested. Similarly, [16] called for more research about economic benefits. This research gap most likely means that OGD practitioners need to rely on myths rather than facts to persuade an audience [15,17]. As such, a rhetorical analysis of OGD arguments revealed a practical challenge, where future OGD research can help improve the OGD arguments. This has helped us to see how OGD practitioners and OGD researchers can become better advocates of OGD.

5.4 Implications

Practitioners can use the results to further detail their rhetoric related to benefits and specify it to their intended audience. One angle is to contextualise the benefits related to the domain specific content. Another angle is understand the specific audience and their boundaries, such as the difference between public organisations and entrepreneurs, or knowledge level; namely, beginners versus OGD specialists.

Researchers can use the results to motivate studies that further understanding variations on OGD benefits and elaborate on them from factors such as audience and OGD content. By adding this knowledge, practitioners can feel more secure about publishing OGD. Further, our use of rhetoric related to OGD can inspire use related to other software implementations, such as larger ERP installations.

6 Conclusion

We found several patterns when investigating the rhetorical patterns among OGD practitioners, in the form of persuasion and dissuasion, related to the benefits of OGD. The patterns are the grand quest, promised opportunities, tribal solidarity, and silver bullet. The grand quest declares OGD as a journey, either focusing on OGD as a resource or contextual parts. Promised opportunities mean that there are opportunities with OGD, either just as promises or as prophecies. Another pattern is tribal solidarity, which ranges from including everyone to following others' initiatives. This pattern can relate to OGD as being accessible and used by everyone and that the benefits have to be shared among domain-specific contexts. The silver bullet approach adds to the rhetoric on what OGD can solve, viewed as everything in a scattered or socio-economic perspective. Besides the pattern, we see few persuasive benefits and dissuasion while aligning audience and OGD benefits. The two major contributions of this paper are the mythical paradoxes of (1) promises versus discovery and (2) proving while arguing.

6.1 Limitations and Future Research

The foundation for this study is eight texts focusing on OGD and its benefits. Although the sampling is divided among contexts, an increase in the number of texts changes the findings. Besides increasing the number of analysed arguments, an interesting avenue for future research on the same path is to divide the text among contexts, such as public transportation or health. Another angle is to use the results and analyse OGD benefits from a bottom-up perspective in the contexts mentioned earlier, adding detailed knowledge on the benefits that OGD delivers.

References

1. Ayers, D.: Evolving the link. IEEE Internet Comput. **11**(3), 96–95 (2007)
2. Ayre, L.B., Craner, J.: Open data: what it is and why you should care. Public Libr. Q. **36**(2), 173–184 (2017)
3. Open Data Barometer: Open data barometer (2018). https://opendatabarometer.org/
4. Barry, E., Bannister, F.: Barriers to open data release: a view from the top. Inf. Polity **19**(1–2), 129–152 (2014)
5. Boulton, G.: Why open data? Leaders Activating Research Networks (LEARN) (2017)
6. Bowen, G.A.: Document analysis as a qualitative research method. Qual. Res. J. **9**(2), 27–40 (2009)
7. Code Aotearoa: Open data tool kit (2021). https://codeforaotearoa.github.io/
8. Creswell, J.W., Creswell, J.D.: Research Design: Qualitative, Quantitative, and Mixed Methods Approaches. Sage Publications, Thousand Oaks (2017)
9. Crusoe, J.: Open government data as a reform and ecosystem: a conceptual framework for evolution and health. Ph.D. thesis, LiU-Tryck (2021)
10. Crusoe, J., Ahlin, K.: Users' activities for using open government data-a process framework. Transforming Gov.: People Process Policy **13**(3–4), 213–236 (2019)
11. Crusoe, J., Simonofski, A., Clarinval, A.: Towards a framework for open data publishers: a comparison study between Sweden and Belgium. In: Viale Pereira, G., et al. (eds.) EGOV 2020. LNCS, vol. 12219, pp. 262–274. Springer, Cham (2020). https://doi.org/10.1007/978-3-030-57599-1_20

12. Duhaney, D., Munteanu, F., Davis, L., Philpott, A., Scott, A., et al.: Open data leaders network digest (2016)
13. European Data Portal: Catalogues – European Data Portal (2021). https://www.europeandataportal.eu/data/catalogues?locale=en&country=se&page=1
14. Frick, A., Ainali, J.: Öppna data – en guide för beslutsfattare (2017). https://internetstiftelsen.se/kunskap/rapporter-och-guider/oppna-data-guide-for-beslutsfattare/
15. Hellberg, A.S., Hedström, K.: The story of the sixth myth of open data and open government. Transforming Gov.: People Process Policy **9**(1), 35–51 (2015)
16. Hossain, M.A., Dwivedi, Y.K., Rana, N.P.: State-of-the-art in open data research: insights from existing literature and a research agenda. J. Organ. Comput. Electron. Commer. **26**(1–2), 14–40 (2016)
17. Janssen, M., Charalabidis, Y., Zuiderwijk, A.: Benefits, adoption barriers and myths of open data and open government. Inf. Syst. Manag. **29**(4), 258–268 (2012)
18. Kelley, D.: The Art of Reasoning: An Introduction to Logic and Critical Thinking. WW Norton & Company, New York (2013)
19. Kitchin, R.: The Data Revolution: Big Data, Open Data, Data Infrastructures and Their Consequences. Sage, Thousand Oaks (2014)
20. Longaker, M.G., Walker, J.: Rhetorical Analysis: A Brief Guide for Writers. Pearson Longman, London (2011)
21. Mays, N., Pope, C.: Assessing quality in qualitative research. BMJ **320**(7226), 50–52 (2000)
22. Myers, M.D.: Qualitative Research in Business and Management. Sage Publications Limited, Thousand Oaks (2013)
23. Myndigheten för digital förvaltning: Öppna och delade data (2021). https://www.digg.se/utveckling-av-digital-forvaltning/oppna-och-delade-data
24. Open Data Charter: Principles (2015). https://opendatacharter.net/principles/
25. Open Data Handbook: What is open data? (2015). https://opendatahandbook.org/guide/en/what-is-open-data/D
26. Open Data Handbook: Why open data? (2015). https://opendatahandbook.org/guide/en/why-open-data/
27. Open Data Institute: What is 'open data' and why should we care? (2017). https://theodi.org/article/what-is-open-data-and-why-should-we-care/D
28. Open Knowledge Foundation: What is open? (2020). https://okfn.org/opendata/
29. Open Knowledge Foundation: Why open data? (2021). https://okfn.org/opendata/why-open-data/
30. Safarov, I., Meijer, A., Grimmelikhuijsen, S.: Utilization of open government data: a systematic literature review of types, conditions, effects and users. Inf. Polity **22**(1), 1–24 (2017)
31. Scott, A.: What is 'open data' and why should we care? – the odi (2020). https://theodi.org/article/what-is-open-data-and-why-should-we-care/
32. Sunlight Foundation: Tag archive: why open data (2013). https://sunlightfoundation.com/taxonomy/term/why-open-data/
33. Sunlight Foundation: Ten principles for opening up government information (2014). https://sunlightfoundation.com/policy/documents/ten-open-data-principles/
34. Tauberer, J., Lessig, L.: The 8 principles of open government data (2007). https://opengovdata.org/
35. The European Data Portal: The benefits and value of open data (2020). https://data.europa.eu/en/highlights/benefits-and-value-open-data
36. Toulmin, S.E.: The Uses of Argument. Cambridge University Press, Cambridge (2003)

37. Ubaldi, B.: Open government data – towards empirical analysis of open government data initiatives (2013). https://doi.org/10.1787/5k46bj4f03s7-en. https://www.oecd-ilibrary.org/governance/open-government-data_5k46bj4f03s7-en
38. Wang, F., Zhao, A., Zhao, H., Chu, J.: Building a holistic taxonomy model for OGD-related risks: based on a lifecycle analysis. Data Intell. **1**(4), 309–332 (2019)
39. Welch, E.W., Feeney, M.K., Park, C.H.: Determinants of data sharing in US city governments. Gov. Inf. Q. **33**(3), 393–403 (2016)
40. Weston, A.: A Rulebook for Arguments, 4th edn. Hackett Pub, Indianapolis (2009)
41. Yang, T.M., Lo, J., Shiang, J.: To open or not to open? Determinants of open government data. J. Inf. Sci. **41**(5), 596–612 (2015)
42. Zuiderwijk, A., Janssen, M.: The negative effects of open government data-investigating the dark side of open data. In: Puron-Cid, G., Robertson, S., Zhang, J., Gil-Garcia, J.R. (eds.) Proceedings of the 15th Annual International Conference on Digital Government Research, pp. 147–152. Association for Computing Machinery (2014)

AI, Bots and Data Analytics

Discretion, Automated Decision-Making and Public Values: Background and Test of an Approach for Unpacking Human and Technological Agency

Agneta Ranerup[1](✉) and Lupita Svensson[2]

[1] Department of Applied Information Technology, University of Gothenburg, Gothenburg, Sweden
agneta.ranerup@ait.gu.se
[2] School of Social Work, Lund University, Lund, Sweden

Abstract. This study aims to develop a theoretical and analytical approach for studying discretion, automated decision-making (ADM) and the consequential public values. This is achieved through our proposed approach, an overview of literature and an empirical test. The context of our empirical test is decisions made about economic support in social work. The research questions are as follows: 1) What are the relevant components in a theoretical and analytical approach with this specific aim? 2) How does human, non-human and joint, 'hybrid', agency influence digital discretion and the consequential public values in social work? 3) What are the usefulness and prospective problems with the approach? Our approach enhances the understanding of the ground for discretion in ADM, which is seen as an emergent routine in the form of knowledge about process, and the details of human and non-human actors involved in relation to consequential public values. To develop its usefulness, the approach should primarily be applied in multiple case studies of 'in-between' contexts, such as social work, to generate a theory of the role of human and non-human agency in the consequential public values of ADM.

Keywords: Discretion · Automated decision-making · Public values · Social work

1 Introduction

How does automated decision-making (ADM) influence the discretion or right of civil servants to decide more independently and the consequential public values, such as transparency and fairness [8]? In general, the concept of discretion refers to the right of civil servants to make decisions with a certain degree of autonomy but within the limits of available laws [24]. Recently, their situation has changed due to the ability to make decisions through various forms of ADM [40]. ADM exists in the form of decision support or tools provided in the form of information technology (IT), which helps civil

Published by Springer Nature Switzerland AG 2022
M. Janssen et al. (Eds.): EGOV 2022, LNCS 13391, pp. 291–306, 2022.
https://doi.org/10.1007/978-3-031-15086-9_19

servants find and evaluate information or provide suggestions about what to decide [18]. The technology might even, depending on the available laws in a country [32], provide what can be characterised as 'a decision' [40]. ADM can be practiced through various forms of IT, of which robotic process automation (RPA) is a relatively simple category [17]. An RPA function, or a software 'robot', can analyse structured data in the form of, for example, information provided by clients based on its algorithms or programme. In this manner, it can perform simple, repetitive tasks, such as suggesting an outcome of such a process ('a decision') [17]. A more complex form of ADM uses artificial intelligence (AI) with a more independent capacity to develop its' algorithm [39].

The influence of IT on discretion has been studied through various themes and concepts. A first theme is studies that suggest new concepts to be used in research. Busch and Henriksen [8] coined the concept of digital discretion to denote the new situation in view of the role of different types of IT. In contrast, Bullock [6] and Young et al. [39] coined the concept of artificial discretion upheld by AI in various forms of ADM in the public sector, in contrast to the concept of human discretion upheld by civil servants. A second theme is studies of the positive and not-so-positive effects of IT on discretion [4, 29]; the latter is often denominated as the curtailment thesis. In these studies, various degrees of consideration about the details of the studied context, humans and technologies appear. The third theme is a small but growing number of studies with a close view of the appearing technologies and their influence on civil servant discretion [29, 31]. Inspired by the actor-network theory [10] and the oft-cited review of algorithm studies by Kitchin [21], Ranerup and Henriksen [31] (first published online in December 2020) simply opted for an approach of 'unpacking' human and technological agency. They did so in a qualitative study of civil servants and clients in social work and their use of IT therein in decisions about social assistance ('economic support for people in need'). They focused on evaluating the effects of discretion and IT in terms of public values [8].

Recently, Glaser, Pollock, and D'Adderio [16] and D'Adderio [11] proposed close studies of humans and technologies in the form of the 'full socio-technical assemblage' (i.e. a configuration of human and non-human actors) in conjunction with decision processes or routines that involve algorithms. As a result of a quantitative study of ADM and discretion, de Boer and Raaphorst [4] suggested further research in the form of close studies of IT and performed tasks to better explain their effect on civil servants' discretion. Thus, close studies of human and non-human actors in decision processes, with a focus on discretion and ADM, are timely and potentially relevant. Thus, the following question arises: how would an approach for studies about discretion, ADM and the consequential public values with a close view of the repertoire of involved technologies and humans look like?

2 Context, Aim and Research Questions

A larger aim of this study is to propose and test an approach for analysing human, non-human and joint ('hybrid') agency [10, 21] in digital discretion in ADM and the consequential public values. This is achieved through inspiration obtained from authors such as Glaser et al. [16] and D'Adderio [11], but with a focus on ADM and discretion in decision processes or routines rather than on algorithms. Thus, the gap addressed is to provide a theoretical and analytical approach to produce more qualified knowledge about discretion, ADM and the consequential public values [2, 8] in public administration. This is in contrast to high-level, distant studies [4] or studies of more unprecise contexts.

The context used in our empirical test is social work, especially regarding decisions about social assistance. In their systematic literature review of discretion and IT [8], denominated as digital discretion, Busch and Henriksen summarised the situation regarding different contexts: Researchers agree on how complex and sensitive environments make it difficult to use IT in decision-making, whereas in structured mass-transactions, even ADM is possible. The most promising avenue for further research, they argued, is the 'in-between' contexts, such as social work, where certain aspects of decision-making or discretionary practices can be taken over by IT.

The arrangements and legal framing for such economic support might vary, but they are often provided at a minimum level and sometimes with requirements of activities to enhance self-support [15]. In Sweden, civil servants at the municipal level make decisions about providing social assistance to cover expenses for food, housing, etc., based on on-paper applications. Applications for social assistance are increasingly submitted by IT ('e-applications') instead of paper and, in a small albeit rising number of municipalities, include decision support by RPA [32].

The research questions are as follows:

- What are the relevant components of a theoretical and analytical approach with this specific aim?
- How does human, non-human and joint 'hybrid' agency influence digital discretion and the consequential public values in social work?
- What are the usefulness and prospective problems with the proposed approach?

The remainder of this paper is organised as follows. First, the method is outlined. This is followed by our proposed approach and the literature background. After that, we find an account of human and non-human agency in our case study of ADM in social work serving as a test of our approach. This is followed by a discussion about the consequential public values, the value of our approach, conclusions and further research.

3 Methodology

In this study, we further develop and test an approach for studying digital discretion, ADM and public values. To strengthen our approach, a narrative literature review is performed by combining the concept of discretion or digital discretion with other relevant concepts (i.e. IT, civil servants, clients, algorithms, ADM and public values). This is also done by testing the usefulness of our approach through a case study of social work and a concluding critical discussion. The empirical case is the municipality of Trelleborg in the south of Sweden (~45,000 inhabitants), which is the first municipality to use ADM in decisions related to social assistance in 2017.

The empirical data are based on 11 interviews conducted with managers, caseworkers and politicians in the municipality between 2017 and 2019 [31] and four new interviews conducted in June–August 2020 and November 2021. Questions are asked to get the interviewees to talk about the case management process, the IT used, what the involved humans did and the result in terms of public values. Internal reports documenting the activities from the perspective of the municipal labour market agency and external reports about the new method of working are also used.

The collected data are used in a symmetric account [10] and analysis (Sects. 5.2 and 5.3) of the application process for social assistance, with the intention of unpacking [21] the 'assemblage' of the types of human and non-human actors involved. In a straightforward manner, we try to 'follow the actors' [10] involved in the process. As a second step, in a deductive manner shown in Sect. 5.3, we apply a few of the categories of IT use and purposes related to the repertoire of public values chosen from a repertoire suggested by Busch and Henriksen [8] on this account (Table 1). Finally, in Sect. 6, we conduct a critical discussion of our approach.

4 Our Approach and Its' Background

Our original simple idea for studying digital discretion and the involved human and technological actors [31] was, as noted in the Introduction, inspired by Kitchin [21] and ANT [10]. However, Glaser et al. [16] outlined a perspective to be used in studies of algorithms. They suggested what they characterised as a socio-material, performative perspective involving an 'assemblage' of human and non-human actors: the last type, both in the form of algorithms and IT, being part of an emergent 'routine'. In addition, the time dimension was addressed by formulating three 'bibliographical moments': addressing and resolving performance struggles, inscribing and layering programmes of action and translating algorithms to other contexts. In this manner, they could take into account, for example, the theories and goals behind the algorithms; the roles of human actors, such as users and designers and the features of the involved technologies during the course of time. D'Adderio [11] also suggested using the concept of 'assemblage' but with a stronger emphasis on the issue of studying more persistent routines of different types that might be in the form of processes for making decisions. The important aspects of routines include the accomplishment of particular tasks, particular sequences in which actions are performed, the recurrent nature of action patterns and simple regulation in the form of, for example, standard operation procedures performed by involved managers and employees [14]. Recently, Alshallaqi [1] proposed using a 'socio-materiality' perspective on discretion, albeit differentiating between 'users' (social) and 'technology' (material) agency. Compared to these studies, our general approach is simpler (Fig. 1): It says that discretion and ADM should be studied by analysing the agency of a broad repertoire or an 'assemblage' of human and non-human actors, including joint or 'hybrid' activities, in a specific context with known qualities and tasks. The focus is on a case management process or a routine [11, 16] for decision-making in, for example, social assistance with all forms of IT instead of RPA alone. This unravels the influence of the layout of a concrete form of digital discretion on public values [8]. To strengthen the background for our approach, we will now describe recent research related to the concept of discretion combined with 1) technologies, 2) algorithms, 3) humans, 4) contexts and tasks and 5) public values being part of our approach.

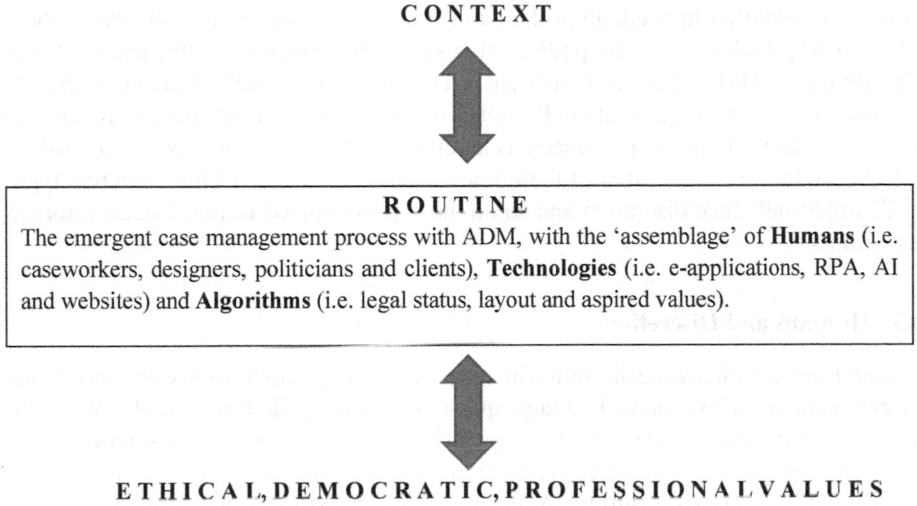
CONTEXT
ROUTINE
The emergent case management process with ADM, with the 'assemblage' of **Humans** (i.e. caseworkers, designers, politicians and clients), **Technologies** (i.e. e-applications, RPA, AI and websites) and **Algorithms** (i.e. legal status, layout and aspired values).
ETHICAL, DEMOCRATIC, PROFESSIONAL VALUES

Fig. 1. Relationship between theoretical concepts in our approach

4.1 Technologies and Discretion

In their systematic literature review of digital discretion, Busch and Henriksen [8] described the technologies that appeared in the included empirical studies, such as telephones, databases, websites, case management systems and automated systems. They noticed that technology 'has certain inherent capabilities affording certain actions, [but] street-level bureaucrats do not necessarily make use of them. Various technologies are adopted in street-level bureaucracies influencing discretionary practices differently' [8, p. 15]. However, they argued that the IT that supports automation limits discretion. As noted by these authors, IT is sometimes not described in any detail but might be decisive for discretion. Qualitative studies of social work have highlighted that what was denominated as decision-making tools, through their design and theoretical background, influenced caseworkers' decision-making [18]. Nordensjö et al. [27] indicated that discretion and the social worker–client relationship is negatively influenced by IT policies and their use. They argued that future work should investigate whether this is balanced by gains in accountability and lawfulness.

In contrast, Bullock [6] discussed how AI influences discretion, emphasising that its' role might differ in various contexts. Ranerup and Henriksen [31], in a more pragmatic study, analysed IT and its' interaction with humans in a case study of decisions about social assistance and discretion. They found a repertoire of IT-like e-applications, case management systems and RPA, all of which played important roles.

4.2 Algorithms and Discretion

Algorithms in public-sector decision-making is a growing area of research. However, their agency might vary in ADM due to the design and degree of control by humans [28]. In terms of children in need, algorithms might have a prominent role in advice about who should get what type of help [26]. Other studies have focused on the legal status of algorithms in ADM and issues about transparency regarding details in their design [19]. Alternatively, the more general public values of efficiency, fairness and transparency in decision-making might be influenced as an effect of the design and use of algorithms [5]. (For a detailed description of these issues, see the Sect. 4.5.) Thus, different types of IT might influence discretion and so do the aspects related to non-human actors as algorithms.

4.3 Humans and Discretion

Research about humans and discretion includes many categories, the most common being caseworkers or civil servants. In a large quantitative survey, de Boer and Raaphorst [4] investigated the experiences of ADM by civil servants in relation to discretion. They concluded that civil servants perceived that they became more legal and accommodative in their enforcement style through ADM. However, ADM led to less perceived discretion, and it is, therefore, important to provide more details in concrete contexts. Busch et al. [9], in turn, analysed attitudes toward digitalisation in relation to discretion. They found positive attitudes to be greater when professional aspects are promoted, whereas professional discretion is considered necessary for more complex tasks. With examples from policing, social welfare and online moderation, Enarsson et al. [12] analysed the issue of 'humans in the loop' as a complement to ADM. The difficulties in what they denominated as 'hybrid' decision-making, when algorithms and humans are combined, were emphasised.

Zouridis et al. [40] and Lindgren et al. [23], in turn, highlighted the enlarged role of IT developers in the design of discretion. This is because they are important in designing and implementing ADM as well as the information used as a ground for decision-making. IT developers are also important stakeholders in local contexts [23]. Ranerup and Henriksen [30] showed how local politicians played an active role in the context of social work promoting the use of ADM, including the aspired effects in terms of efficiency and effectiveness.

Although discretion is a concept with the main emphasis on civil servants, clients and citizens, at large, are *de facto* involved in various ways [31]. Bernhard and Wihlborg [3] studied the issue of digital discretion and clients in the form of how professionals are related to the former when RPA is used in state administration. Caseworkers developed strategies for supporting clients to become active in the now digital application and case management processes. Thus, discretion and ADM are relevant from the perspective of caseworkers, but future studies should involve other groups.

4.4 Context, Tasks and Discretion

Bullock [6] discussed the strength of AI and humans in ADM for different tasks and contexts: 'Tasks that are low in complexity and uncertainty are the likeliest candidates for automation by AI, whereas tasks high in complexity and uncertainty should remain under the purview of human discretion' [p. 759]. In turn, Zouridis et al. emphasised large execute organisations that have become system-level bureaucracies, mentioning 'internal revenue services, departments for work and pensions and social security agencies' [40, p. 314]. They argued that ADM is often used to handle easy cases, whereas the harder, more difficult cases still require human intervention. However, studies of specific contexts of, for example, social work have concluded that discretion is not an 'all-or-nothing' phenomenon but a result of 'gradations of power that exist in the relationship between managers and professional workers' [13, p. 881].

In addition, in a case study of a court, Busch [7] specifically focused on IT and found that technology has no unilateral effect on discretion. Contextual factors, such as social complexity in a case, skills of caseworkers, need for face-to-face contact and the IT in use, are important. Thus, the context and tasks are proposed as influencing ADM and discretion. More nuanced studies of the 'in-between' contexts, such as social work, are required to improve the current understanding of discretion [8].

4.5 Public Values and Discretion

The concept of public values is seen as a response to new public management logics [2], since it includes other values than the economic value typically credited to the digitalisation of processes and systems in the commercial sector. It can be applied in studies of design and use in digitalisation, in general, and in ADM, in particular. There is a repertoire of frameworks that expresses dimensions or aspects of public values. For example, Bannister and Conolly [2] differentiated among duty-, service- and socially oriented values. Selten and Meijer [33], in turn, analysed values related to efficiency and effectiveness ('sigma values'), fairness and transparency ('theta values') or aspects of being adaptive and robust ('lambda values').

The more specific issue of public values and ADM has been addressed in a few studies. Against the background of three cases of ADM, Kuziemski and Misuraca [22] discussed the public sector predicament to protect citizens from potential algorithmic harms that are at odds with the temptation to improve efficiency in case management.

As a result of their systematic literature review of digital discretion and public values, Busch and Henriksen [8] distilled 16 categories of IT use and purposes related to the four dimensions of public values proposed by Kernaghan [20]: ethical, democratic, professional and people values (also developed by MacCarthaigh [25]). In short, ethical values provide a guide to what are 'good' actions, and representative values are integrity, fairness, loyalty and honesty. Democratic values refer to good connections between the opinions of people and the actions of public administration. Representative values are rule of law, accountability and representativeness. Professional values or professionalism mark civil servants as professional persons. Representative values are effectiveness, efficiency, service, leadership, excellence, innovation and quality.

Table 1. Digital discretion parameters (adapted from [8]).

Societal problem	Leads to	Purpose of IT	Desired effects
Ethical public service values			
Wrong decisions due to different interpretations of rules and personal factors	Unfair and random decision-making	Enforce adherence to rules and procedures	Fair and uniform decision-making
Democratic public service values			
Erroneous assessments of cases	Wrong decisions	Allow citizens/clients to participate in decision-making processes	Empower citizens/clients
Professional public service values			
Discretion is costly and inefficient	High public expenditures and reduced efficiency	Faster decision-making	Reduced costs
Erroneous and inefficient decision-making	Reorganisation of public services	Change work processes	Increased efficiency and improved quality of decision-making

Peoples' values refer to respect for people in different contexts and with different needs. Representative values are caring, fairness, tolerance, compassion, courage, and humanity. The purpose of using IT from the perspective of ethical values is about avoiding unethical actions and corruption to reveal the reasoning behind decisions. From the perspective of professional values, it can be about increasing efficiency by using IT for faster decision-making (Table 1) [8].

In a study of ADM in decisions about social assistance, Ranerup and Henriksen [31] applied 9 out of the 16 categories of IT use and purpose. The aim was to test Kitchin's [21] idea of uncovering the full 'assemblage' of actors. Nevertheless, compared to Busch and Henriksen [8], the fewer categories of IT use and purposes being related to the public values the result led to more simplifications being seen as necessary. This is even more so in the present study, since we want to improve the granularity of our approach for analysing ADM in our unpacking of human and non-human actors, as described above (Fig. 1), and in the research overview in this chapter. Therefore, we address the ethical, democratic and professional values through a limited number (four) of categories of IT use and purposes in relation to these (Table 1). Our chosen categories represent a selection of what we consider as core values and purposes related to the desired effects of fair and uniform decision-making, empowerment of citizens and efficiency, as well as quality of discretion.

5 Empirical Test of the Approach

5.1 Context and Background

The Social Services Act (2001:453) implemented in Sweden states that the provided support shall 'strengthen economic and social security, equal opportunities and active participation in society' (Sect. 1). Social assistance is considered a short-time minimum support where an individual's responsibilities and activities are emphasised and decisions are handled in case management at the municipal level.

The municipality of Trelleborg introduced a new work model regarding social assistance and reorganisation, meaning that a Labour Market Board rather than a Social Board would handle these issues [34]. The application process was streamlined to provide quick service, and e-applications were introduced in 2015. These changes were made based on a larger programme to improve the efficiency and effectiveness of the case management of social assistance. The goal was to help people in need to become self-supporting (for a full view of aspired intentions, see [30]). In 2016, ADM by RPA was introduced in a few areas of public administration, and in early spring of 2017, it started to be used in simple decisions about social assistance.

5.2 Human and Non-human Actors in the Application Process

Clients. Clients can apply for social assistance on paper or through a device for e-applications on the municipal website. Here, they need to log in using a personal Bank ID. In 2020, up to 85% of the applications were submitted through this device (Personal communication, Manager no. 1, 25 June 2020).

Municipal Website. The device for e-applications asks for information about family members, income and personal expenses, such as rent, childcare and home insurance. The design process is described as follows:

> We had a communication plan, we had meetings. The IT function was involved and caseworkers from the section that formally handle the decision […] A group of citizens was selected to participate in the tests and provide their reactions […] Basically, these are the ones that must understand, not us. (Manager no. 1, 26 September 2017)

Clients. The clients provide the requested information. If they are unable to complete the application and need assistance, they can go to a help desk at the City Hall. From the beginning, no paper documentation was needed in the new applications. However, since May 2019, a formal contract for housing and rent is being requested. In addition, the submitted applications are regularly checked. A manager explained,

> Normally, we check every tenth application. Then these clients must send in their documents, which is why the decision process might take longer than normal. (Manager no. 2, September 26 2017).

Municipal Website. The application is registered in the internal case management system and in the personal account *My Pages.* A few times for a next-day appointment with a caseworker working with labour market issues is suggested.

Clients. The clients can choose the appointment time. A client attends meetings with a caseworker working on labour market issues and answers the caseworkers' questions and discusses alternatives.

Caseworker Who Works With Labour Market Issues. A plan for further activities is put together and continuously evaluated, with the aim of finding a job, education or other activities related to becoming self-supporting. A caseworker described what happened,

> First, we must determine if the applicant tried to obtain work. […]. We try to keep this part as brief as possible. Second, we try to focus on how to get a job. We base this part on the individual citizens´ competences, plans, and needs. (Caseworker who works with labour market issues, 29 November 2017).

A manager continued, 'What I wanted to say is that the plan is a joint product [i.e., actively involving clients and caseworkers]' (Manager no. 1, 12 August 2019). The caseworker continuously registers in the case management system if the applicant is found to be active to become self-supporting.

Municipal Website: The plan about becoming self-supporting was originally provided on paper, but from the autumn of 2020, it has become part of the client account *My Pages.* This has been a complex process due to GDPR and the fact that the plan is individual, whereas the application is made in a way that it can include several people. The case management system holds the information provided by clients, the caseworker working with labour market issues and the actual RPA device itself. The algorithm used by the RPA can, during the spring of 2017, handle rather simple positive decisions. The RPA is made to log into the information in the internal case management system, copy the information and make the required checks formulated by its program or algorithm.

> This system does what our instructions says it should do. Everything comes from the regulations that we have […] It is about building a system based on different variables: Income; yes or no. Rent; yes or no. So it is very logical (Manager no. 2, 26 September 2017).

The RPA solution and programming are provided by a large company Valcon.

> We have written what we want and they have worked with this. And then we have had days when they visit us and actually do the work. And then the caseworkers are available for advice. (Manager no. 1, 9 October 2018).

Additional information about social benefits that the clients receive, such as unemployment benefits, pensions and student allowances, is provided by a national platform for information on social benefits.

Clients, Caseworkers, Algorithms and Technologies: The final stage of the decision about social assistance is made by the RPA and its algorithm for approximately 25% of the (digital) applications and partially so for 75% of the applications in 2019 [37]. However, '[N]o negative decisions are made by the RPA alone' (Manager no. 4, 3 November 2021). Negative decisions are made possible as part of the RPA regarding some cases in June 2020 (e.g. partially negative decisions when the approved rent can be 4,000 Skr but not the sum of 5,000 Skr applied for). Very difficult decisions are handled by a caseworker, and communication with clients is offered through telephone and e-mail. A caseworker described his situation,

> No we haven´t lost anything. A caseworker stands behind the application.[…] We have not lost our right to decide, but on the contrary improved our capacity to make judgements about what is reasonable costs. […] Because we can say that it not reasonable to have an electricity bill for 2000 Skr when last month it was 500 Skr (Caseworker, 29 November 2017).

In the municipality, this decision involving caseworkers, algorithms and technologies is seen as legally binding. This is because the meeting between the client and the caseworker working with labour market issues is seen as a central component and a ground for the decision in 'full' ADM. However, caseworkers check most decisions to safeguard their quality (Manager no. 4, 3 November 2021). The time spent on the administrative case management of the applications has, according to the consultants, gone down by up to 85% [38]. The decision is submitted to *My Pages* on the municipal website. Since 2015, most applicants have been receiving their decisions after one day [34].

Municipal Website: The personal account *My Pages* shows the decisions with provided motivations, which have been further developed over the years.

> So we have improved the openness about how the text about the decisions are formulated. And the rules behind when the robot should choose a certain message. […] It is mainly the caseworkers that have worked with this. […] And we have asked the help desk about when people come with a negative decision, what is it that they don´t understand? […] And the new law about public agencies in May has much to say about that we should communicate in a way that is easy to understand. (Manager no. 1, 9 October 2018.)

Small improvements have the intention '[T]o help the applicants to do right when they apply, so that they don't get a negative decision due to this' (Manager no. 4, 3 November 2021). This helps the applicants and caseworkers, making the process quicker and less resource-consuming.

There is a strive to build up internal competence about RPA in the municipality:

> We have a RPA-developer in the municipality and will probably get one more […] to safeguard that they make the adjustments that we need. And it is of course not AI but it does only exactly that we tell it to do and it is closely connected to our e-service (Manager no. 4, 3 November 2021).

Furthermore, since July 2019, the platform contains a device for filing appeals against negative decisions.

Clients: The clients can log into their accounts and see the decisions and motivations. They participate in agreed-upon activities with the aim of becoming self-supporting. If needed, they can submit a renewed application and continuously attend meetings with caseworkers dedicated to providing support. During the last few years, these activities have been further simplified in terms of all steps in the e-service process, as well as to provide support from teams with a focus on defined parts of the labour market. Activities have been initiated about sharing these services with a nearby municipality [35, 36]. The clients in this adjacent municipality are handled in a separate section of the internal case management system. These arrangements include help to become self-supporting and activation plans.

5.3 Analysis of Public Values in the Application Process

One selected instance of ethical public service values [8] in our study is about using IT to enforce adherence to rules and procedures, with the desired effect of *fair and uniform decision-making* (Table 1). The involved caseworkers use ADM as a decision support [18] or in a limited number of instances for the full decision with additional check-ups. The IT, algorithms and explanations for decisions are continuously developed [29], but internal competence related to RPA is strived for. Appeals against decisions can be made by a new IT device. What has been considered fair and uniform decision-making has demanded that paper documentation of housing and rents be provided. Many more complex decisions are still not fully made by the ADM. In contrast, the data included in the applications are those provided by clients (sometimes with the help of caseworkers at the help desk), and not collected in a more abstract manner from information about a large number of clients to provide input to an AI device [26]. We see a repertoire of types of IT and what they can be used for in the role of supporting humans to act in line with the laws and regulations rather than replacing them.

One selected instance of a democratic public service value applied is about using IT to allow clients to participate in decision-making to *become empowered and avoid wrong decisions*. As emphasised by Ranerup and Henriksen [31], client participation and empowerment are enabled through the available e-services and the help desk. However, the recent high uptake of e-applications also means that social assistance in this manner becomes more of a regular type of public service. In addition, the plan about how to become more self-supporting has recently become part of the digital infrastructure that can be easily accessed by clients. The explanations for decisions have, as mentioned, been continuously developed through caseworkers who have direct contact with applicants and know their needs and questions. However, this is a more indirect study of citizen empowerment and accountability enabled by the layout of digital discretion [27], which is also primarily a concept focusing on civil servants. Caseworkers sometimes make 'unwelcome' decisions regarding economic support or required activities from the clients' side. Digital discretion in line with a democratic public service value does not remove this obligation from civil servants.

Instances of professional public service values applied are about using IT to *accomplish reduced costs* as well as *increased efficiency and improved quality*. The streamlining and design of the case management process or routine has, from the perspective of politicians and designers alike, had the aim of accomplishing a faster process. However, in this way, the risk of 'costly discretion' was noticeably counteracted to a significant extent before ADM was introduced in 2017. An open issue is, thus, about the actual effect of ADM in terms of faster decisions, in contrast to other forms of reorganisation and streamlining of case management processes [30]. The instance of democratic public service values about allowing clients to participate in the form of, for example, checking applications, plans and decisions through the digital infrastructure *(My Pages)*, is also in line with this value, since caseworkers' time to handle questions by phone and otherwise might be saved. However, whether or not this happens needs to be further studied.

A reorganisation of the process or routine, including new roles for caseworkers with an emphasis on decisions about applications or providing support, has occurred. The process has also changed through IT and streamlining. Regarding the desired effect of improved quality in the routine, in general, and decision-making, in particular, the IT and algorithms have continuously been developed by designers and caseworkers [29]. However, the activities required to enable clients to become self-supporting have also been developed. In particular, in an analysis of digital discretion, one must take into account the 'state of the art' of the full repertoire of IT, its design and use, but also how the time that is saved by ADM is spent. In the area of social assistance, such activities are important examples.

6 Conclusions, Limitations and Further Studies

This paper outlines and tests an approach for close studies of the 'assemblage' of human and non-human actors in the analyses of ADM, discretion and the consequential public values in decision processes or routines [11, 14, 16, 21]. Section 4 outlined our approach and its components using related research. How, then, does human, non-human and joint, 'hybrid' agency influence digital discretion and the consequential public values in social work? Section 5 presented our test and analysis of the test result We conclude that the *joint capacity* of an 'assemblage' of continuously developed human and non-human actors is decisive for the *de facto* discretion in ADM, as shown by our case. However, the decision as such might also be made by a 'hybrid' in situations where ADM by involved actors is seen as critical in the final decision. This is because the meetings between caseworkers working with labour market issues and clients in our empirical case are defined as central for the outcome. An instance of relatively 'full ADM' can, thus, be based on the appearances of 'humans in the loop' [12].

Regarding ethical values, there might be a repertoire of components in the 'assemblage' of an emerging infrastructure for a case management routine that can be of help in fair and uniform decision-making [5]. Regarding democratic values, clients might be empowered by the participation enabled by different types of IT, but the discretion of civil servants is preserved in the form of their capacity to make 'complex' decisions and their obligation to play an active role in more or less appreciated decisions and activities. Regarding professional values, ADM and discretion might also be influenced by the reorganisation of the process as a whole (in our case, for example, the full repertoire of IT and its actual use in the case management process and the support provided). An important conclusion is, therefore, that studying digital discretion as a routine [11, 16] also enlightens the changes influencing decision-making in the remaining non-digital parts, as well as the situation of civil servants and clients herein, the latter with an option to remain non-users. Last, due to our approach and the result of our empirical test, we conclude that ADM and (digital) discretion are influenced by the continuous redesign of non-human actors (i.e. e-applications, further developed algorithms, infrastructure for offering access to decisions and explanations and plans), as well as other more human or organisational parts of the routine (i.e. meetings and forms of support).

Thus, what are the usefulness and prospective problems with the approach? Ironically, in our case, we detected an instance of a later phase in Glaser et al.'s approach [16]: 'Translating algorithm to other contexts' in the form of an arrangement for handling a case management process of a nearby municipality. Our approach has rightly not been about analysing phases in a development process, as in Glaser et al.'s [16] study, but about capturing important historical facts behind the routine for case management. However, our approach of uncovering the 'full assemblage' of actors, including notes about history, might be questioned for containing data about different points in time. However, the significant advantage is that the case management routine [11, 16] is at the centre of attention. This supports the value of detailed studies of actors and actions [1], in contrast to more distant or undefined situations [4].

Our case study shows the ways in which ethical, democratic and professional values [8] are influenced by the repertoire of IT in the routine, its design and use related to digital discretion. However, multiple forms of agency and public values must be accounted for. There is a need to focus on a few categories of IT use and purposes related to public values (Table 1). In the present study, we selected four out of a total of 16 categories [8]. This study is limited to one case of social services. Further studies should apply the approach to several cases in, for example, social services and their arrangements in the 'assemblage' of actors [11, 16]. This will enable evaluations of the detailed configurations of actors in the routines, comparisons and the creation of typologies of design related to the digital discretion parameters, as described above. Of course, the simpler and more complex contexts [6, p. 40] regarding the organisation of discretion, in contrast to the 'in-between' level of social services, are also relevant for further studies [8]. However, the account and analysis of 'ín-between' contexts might contain content to enable a result in terms of theorising the identified components of the 'assemblage' that influence digital discretion and the resulting values.

Acknowledgements. Ethical approval has been received from the Swedish Ethical Review Authority Dno. 2020-02097.

Funding. This work was supported by the Swedish Research Council for Health, Working Life and Welfare (FORTE) Grant no. 2019-00710.

References

1. Alshallaqi, M.: The complexities of digitalization and street-level discretion: a socio-materiality perspective. Public Manag. Rev. (2022). https://doi.org/10.1080/14719037.2022.2042726
2. Bannister, F., Connolly, R.: ICT, public values and transformative government: a framework and programme for research. Gov. Inf. Q. **31**(1), 119–128 (2014)
3. Bernhard, I., Wihlborg, E.: Bringing all clients into the system – professional digital discretion to enhance inclusion when services are automated. Inf. Polity 1–17 (2021)
4. de Boer, N., Raaphorst, N.: Automation and discretion: explaining the effect of automation on how street-level bureaucrats enforce. Public Manag. Rev. (2021).https://doi.org/10.1080/14719037.2021.1937684
5. Borry, E.L., Getha-Taylor, H.: Automation in the public sector: efficiency at the expense of equity? Public Integr. **21**(1), 6–21 (2019)
6. Bullock, J.B.: Artificial intelligences, discretion, and bureaucracy. Am. Rev. Public Adm. **49**(7), 751–761 (2019)
7. Busch, P.A.: The role of contextual factors in the influence of ICT on street-level discretion. In: Proceedings of the 50th Hawaii International Conference on System Sciences. IEEE (2017). http://hdl.handle.net/10125/41514
8. Busch, P.A., Henriksen, H.Z.: Digital discretion: a systematic literature review of ICT and street-level discretion. Inf. Polity **1**, 1–26 (2018)
9. Busch, P., Henriksen, H.Z., Sæbø, Ø.: Opportunities and challenges of digitized discretionary practices: a public sector worker perspective. Gov. Inf. Q. **35**(4), 547–556 (2018)
10. Callon, M.: Some elements of a sociology of translation: domestication of the scallops and the fishermen in St. Brieuc Bay. In: Law, J. (ed.), Power, Action and Belief: A New Sociology of Knowledge (pp. 196–233). Routledge (1986)
11. D´ Adderio, L.: Materiality and routine dynamics. In: Feldman, M.S. et al. (eds.) Cambridge Handbook of Routine Dynamics, pp. 85–99. Cambridge University Press (2022)
12. Enarsson, T., Enqvist, L., Naarttijärvi, M.: Approaching the human in the loop – legal perspectives on hybrid human/algorithmic decision-making in three contexts. Inf. Commun. Technol. Law (2022). https://doi.org/10.1080/13600834.2021.1958860
13. Evans, T., Harris, J.: Street-level bureaucracy, social work and the (exaggerated) death of discretion. Br. J. Soc. Work. **34**, 871–895 (2004)
14. Feldman, M.S., Pentland, B.T., D´Adderio, L., Dittrich, K., Rerup, C., Seidl, D.: What is routine dynamics? In: Feldman, M.S. et al. (eds.) Cambridge Handbook of Routine Dynamics, pp. 1–18. Cambridge University Press (2022)
15. Gjersøe, H.M.: Providing help or restrictions? Frontline workers´ understanding of behavioral conditionality for health-related social insurance and social assistance benefits in a joined-up governance context. Eur. J. Soc. Work (2021). https://doi.org/10.1080/13691457.2021.1934412
16. Glaser, V.L., Pollock, N., D´ Adderio, L.: The biography of an algorithm: performing algorithmic technologies in organizations. Organ. Theory **2**, 1–2 (2021)
17. Houy C, Hamberg M, Fettke, P.: Robotic Process Automation in public administration, Digitalisierung von Staat und Verwaltung. Lecture Notes in Informatics (LNI), Bonn, pp. 62–74 (2019)
18. Høybye-Mortensen, M.: Decision-making tools and their influence on caseworkers' room for discretion. Br. J. Soc. Work. **45**, 600–615 (2015)
19. Kaun, A.: Suing the algorithm: the mundanization of automated decision-making in public services through litigation. Inf. Commun. Soc. (2021). https://doi.org/10.1080/1369118X.2021.1924827

20. Kernaghan, K.: Integrating values in public service: the values statement as the centerpiece. Public Adm. Rev. **63**(6), 711–719 (2003)
21. Kitchin, R.: Thinking critically about and researching algorithms. Inf. Commun. Soc. **20**(1), 14–29 (2017)
22. Kuziemski, M., Misuraca, G.: AI governance in the public sector: three tales from the frontiers of automated decision-making in democratic settings. Telecommun. Policy (2020). https://doi.org/10.1016/j.telpol.2020.101976
23. Lindgren, I., Åkesson, M., Tomsen, M., Toll, D.: Organizing for robotic process automation in local government: observations from two case studies of robotic process automation implementation in Swedish municipalities. In: Juell-Skielse, G., et al. (eds.) Service Automation in the Public Sector, pp. 189–203. Springer, Cham (2022). https://doi.org/10.1007/978-3-030-92644-1_10
24. Lipsky, M.: Street-level Bureaucracy: Dilemmas of the Individual in Public Services (30th anniversary ed.). Russell Sage Foundation, New York (2010)
25. MacCarthaigh, M.: Public service values. Institute of Public Administration, Dublin (2008)
26. Meilvang, M.L., Dahler, A.M.: Decision support and algorithmic support: the construction of algorithms and professional discretion in social work. Eur. J. Soc. Work. https://doi.org/10.1080/13691457.2022.2063806
27. Nordensjö, K., Scaramuzzino, G., Ulmestig, R.: The social worker-client relationship in the digital era: a configurative literature review. Eur. J. Soc. Work **25**, 1–3 (2021)
28. Peeters, R.: The agency of algorithms: understanding human-algorithm interaction in administrative decision-making. Inf. Polity **1**, 1–16 (2020)
29. Petersen, A.C.M.: Discretion and public digitalisation. A happy marriage or ugly divorce? Ph.D. Dissertation. IT-University of Copenhagen (2021)
30. Ranerup, A., Henriksen, H.Z.: Value positions viewed through the lens of automated decision-making: the case of social services. Gov. Inf. Q. **36**(4), 101377 (2019)
31. Ranerup, A., Henriksen, H.Z.: Digital discretion: unpacking human and technological agency in automated decision making in Sweden's social services. Soc. Sci. Comput. Rev. **40**(2), 445–461 (2022). https://doi.org/10.1177/0894439320980434
32. Ranerup, A., Svensson, L.: Actors and intensions in dissemination of robotic process automation in social work. In: Juell-Skielse, G., Lindgren, I., Åkesson, M. (eds.) Service Automation in the Public Sector, pp. 129–145. Springer, Cham (2022). https://doi.org/10.1007/978-3-030-92644-1_7
33. Selten, F., Meijer, A.: Managing algorithms for public value. Int. J. Public Adm. Digit. Age **8**(1), 1–6 (2021)
34. Trelleborg Municipality: Report 2015 - Labor Market Agency. [Årsanalys 2015 – Arbetsmarknadsnämnden.] Trelleborg (2016)
35. Trelleborg municipality: Activity plan [Verksamhetsplan 2020]. Trelleborg (2019)
36. Trelleborg municipality: Activity plan [Verksamhetsplan 2021]. Trelleborg (2020a)
37. Trelleborg municipality (2020b). Yearly report [Årsanalys 2019]. Trelleborg (2020b)
38. Valcon: With digitalization you can do more. Trelleborg Robotics Event, 6 October 2017. [Om du digitaliserar så hinner du mer.]. Valcon (2017)
39. Young, M.M., Bullock, J.B., Lecy, J.D.: Artificial discretion as a tool of governance: a framework for understanding the impact of artificial intelligences on public administration. Perspect. Public Manag. Gov. **2**(4), 301–313 (2019)
40. Zouridis, S., van Eck, M., Bovens, M.: Automated discretion. In: Evans, T., Hupe, P. (eds.) Discretion and the Quest for Controlled Freedom, pp. 313–329. Palgrave Macmillan, Cham (2020)

Dismantling Digital Cages: Examining Design Practices for Public Algorithmic Systems

Sem Nouws(✉), Marijn Janssen, and Roel Dobbe

Delft University of Technology, Delft, The Netherlands
{s.j.j.nouws,m.f.w.h.a.janssen,r.i.j.dobbe}@tudelft.nl

Abstract. Algorithmic systems used in public administration can create or reinforce *digital cages*. A digital cage refers to algorithmic systems or information architectures that create their own reality through formalization, frequently resulting in incorrect automated decisions with severe impact on citizens. Although much research has identified how algorithmic artefacts can contribute to digital cages and their unintended consequences, the emergence of digital cages from human actions and institutions is poorly understood. Embracing a broader lens on how technology, human activity, and institutions shape each other, this paper explores what design practices in public organizations can result in the emergence of digital cages. Using Orlikowski's structurational model of technology, we found four design practices in observations and interviews conducted at a consortium of public organizations. This study shows that design processes of public algorithmic systems (1) are often narrowly focused on technical artefacts, (2) disregard the normative basis for these systems, (3) depend on involved actors' awareness of socio-technics in public algorithmic systems, (4) and are approached as linear rather than iterative. These four practices indicate that institutions and human actions in design processes can contribute to the emergence of digital cages, but also that institutional – opposed to technical – possibilities to address their unintended consequences are often ignored. Further research is needed to examine how design processes in public organizations can evolve into socio-technical processes, can become more democratic, and how power asymmetries in the design process can be mitigated.

Keywords: Public algorithmic system · Digital cage · Design process · Structuration

1 Introduction

Algorithmic systems used in public administration can have a detrimental impact on citizens. The predictive, structuring, and learning capacities of algorithmic applications are used to, for example, allocate social services, assess livability of neighborhoods, or for predictive policing [35]. However, practice shows that incorrect decisions are made by or based on these systems. For example, Ranchordas & Scarcella [24] discuss two cases in the USA and the Netherlands in which risk indication models were used to

Published by Springer Nature Switzerland AG 2022
M. Janssen et al. (Eds.): EGOV 2022, LNCS 13391, pp. 307–322, 2022.
https://doi.org/10.1007/978-3-031-15086-9_20

predict cases of fraud. In both cases, many citizens were falsely accused of fraud, had to pay back received benefits, and were not able to rectify the incorrect decisions. This caused high debts, and mental and physical health problems for the affected citizens. Following Peeters & Widlak [23], we consider these incorrect decisions and their impact as unintended consequences of digital cages. A *digital cage* refers to the rigidity of algorithms and information architectures that results in automation creating its own reality.

Research on the digital cage and its consequences has increased in recent years. Harms produced by public algorithmic systems have been extensively described. For example, studies show that algorithmic decision-making is often discriminatory (e.g., [26, 30]), that systems make incorrect decisions (e.g., [23]), that both citizens and users lose agency when these systems are used (e.g., [22, 31]), and that algorithmic systems are inscrutable (e.g., [1, 14, 29]). These findings urge public organizations to search for instruments to ensure safe, explainable and accountable algorithms.

Whereas most research is focused on the effects of algorithmic systems on citizens, the ways in which digital cages emerge are poorly understood. Digital cages and their unintended consequences result from the implementation of digital and analytical technologies in public administration (assuming that these cages do not intentionally emerge from political or strategic motives). Several authors have studied practices that may partly explain the emergence of digital cages. For example, the increase of chain decisions [34], the emphasis on technocratic governance [13], or the search for a complete view on citizens [4] can explain the materialization of algorithmic systems with severe impacts on citizens. Other scholars look at the development of AI systems in general, for example, the way in which vagueness is often wrongly addressed by developers and therewith results in citizen harms [5]. Finally, some authors specifically examine the dynamics between actors in public organizations. For example, Van der Voort et al. [25] analyzed the interactions between data-analysts and policy-makers. These authors all provide leads to approach digital cages from a socio-technical perspective. However, this perspective has not been used to study the specific case of emerging digital cages in public algorithmic systems. This impedes initiatives of public organizations to prevent, mitigate, or correct these cages.

Hence, the goal of this paper is to gain insight into what design practices of public algorithmic systems can contribute to the emergence of digital cages and their consequences. We study this emergence by using the structurational model of technology of Orlikowski [20] as an analytical lens. We use this model to empirically analyze design practices in public organizations based on observations and interviews. The analysis indicates four practices that can be related to the emergence of digital cages. We will close this paper by presenting the implications of these design practices.

2 Motivation and Background

To study unintended consequences of public algorithmic systems, Peeters & Widlak [23] demonstrated the usefulness of the digital cage as analytical concept. As the concept will be central in this paper, we will elaborate on it in this section. Thereafter, we show that the scope of digital cage research should be broadened by using the structurational model of technology and that practice can also use such a perspective.

2.1 Digital Cages

The use of algorithmic systems in public administration alters the bureaucratic organizations that they are situated in. The emergence of these systems has triggered refinements of Weber's [32] notion of bureaucracy (e.g., [15, 36]) as they change the nature of formalization in bureaucracy. For example, algorithmic decision-making based on code is less flexible compared to the deliberative practice of a legal system based on speech and written word [10]. Furthermore, algorithmic formalization results in what Janssen & Kuk [13] characterize as *technocratic governance*: "assuming that complex societal problems can be deconstructed into neatly defined, structured and well-scoped problems that can be solved algorithmically and in which political realities play no role" (p. 372).

Although Weber's notion of bureaucracy is not fully applicable to public administration in the current information society, bureaucracies using algorithmic and information systems do produce the digital equivalent of Weber's *iron cage:* the *digital cage.* The iron cage represents the continuous rationalization of society – through rules and procedures – over which individuals have no control. In the digital cage, these rules and procedures are (partly) replaced algorithmic and information systems. Peeters & Widlak [23] define the digital cage as "a highly disciplining infrastructure that rationalizes the execution of tasks through information architecture and algorithms instead of Weberian rules and procedures" (p. 182). Both civil servants and dependent technical or social systems are disciplined by the digital cage. Civil servants see their street-level discretion curtailed [34], their agency limited [22], and their behavior changed as their daily routines are governed by the cage [13]. Algorithmic systems can discipline other systems such as laws or other automated decision-making systems. For example, they can dictate the interpretation of a law and one small error in the algorithmic system can result in an accumulation of errors in systems that depend on the algorithm's outcome [34].

Adverse effects of digital cages are the exclusion of citizens and the obscuration of the decision-making process, which is another similarity to Weber's bureaucracy. His conception of the iron cage has often been compared to the excluding and disorienting implications of iron cages in Franz Kafka's work (e.g., [11]). Like iron cages, digital cages can create Kafkaesque situations in which citizens are caught up in a digital bureaucratic system without knowing how to solve their problems. For example, Peeters & Widlak [23] describe the case of a woman whose car was incorrectly registered. The registration ultimately led to large and erroneous tax debts at different public organizations. The woman was not informed about the incorrect registration. Moreover, she could not find out who made the mistake or which organization could correct the registration [33].

These adverse effects, which can be considered as unintended consequences of digital cages, are often studied from a deterministic perspective. The goal to make decision-making more fair, accurate, and efficient through algorithmic systems often backfires. This was the case for the two risk indication models mentioned in the introduction. Tax offices wanted to make detecting fraud more efficient and accurate but created situations in which the fraud cases detected by their algorithmic system did not resemble reality [24]. To the best of our knowledge, such cases are mostly studied from the deterministic perspective discussed above. In other words, research emphasizes the way in which the digital cages – its technology – disciplines human agents and other systems. However, that ignores the way in which these digital cages – and therefore their unintended consequences – emerge. In order to prevent, mitigate, or correct the unintended consequences of digital cages, a broader perspective is needed that also includes human actions and the influence of institutions – i.e., social rules that structure the behavior of human agents [12] – on the emergence of these cages.

2.2 The Structuration Model of Technology and the Digital Cage

The structurational model of technology by Orlikowski [20] – based on Giddens' structuration theory [6–8] – is a framework that can show the shortcomings of a deterministic perspective on digital cages. The model is based on the idea that socio-technical systems comprise three components: a technical artefact, human agents, and institutions. Orlikowski describes four important interactions between these components. Firstly, technology mediates human action. Secondly, the use of technology can reinforce or transform institutions. Thirdly, technology is the product of human action. Finally, institutions structure human actions. This combination of interactions makes full control over the complete trajectory of outcomes impossible. Therefore, unintended consequences can emerge (see Orlikowski [20] for an elaboration on the model).

Since public algorithmic systems are socio-technical systems, they can be studied with the structuration model of technology. In these systems, the technical artefact is a machine-based application (cf. [19]) – either rule-based or case-based – situated in an information architecture. Human agents are involved in or affected by the system as the application automates, supports, or augments (parts of) decision-making in public administration. Finally, the public algorithmic system includes institutions that form the basis for an algorithmic system, institutions that constrain and structure the usage of algorithmic system, and institutions that organize the design process of such systems. Without the human agents and institutions, the information architecture does not work. Therefore, the disciplining nature of digital cages cannot only arise from the information architecture.

Research on digital cages has mostly focused on two types of interactions described by the structurational model. First, descriptions of how the digital cage disciplines users and dependent systems focus on how technology mediates human action. For example, the reduction of street-level discretion by the system. Second, research showing the changes of algorithm use to public administration emphasize the reinforcement or transformation of institutions by technology. This can be observed in the technocratic governance that arises because of using public algorithmic systems. The way in which human actions – structured by institutions or not – contribute to digital cages is underexplored. Therefore, this research focuses on influence of human action and institutions on the emergence of digital cages and their unintended consequences.

2.3 The Design Process of Public Algorithmic Systems

In practice, the design process of public algorithmic systems also shows ignorance of the third and fourth interactions in the structurational model. This is problematic as human actions and institutions are steering the design process. After all, the *design process* is a set of deliberative actions – performed by agents who are not directly affected by the system – to shape or change the public AI systems in reaction to a question, a problem statement, or emergent behavior of the system.

The emergence of public algorithmic systems confronts public organizations with the shortcomings of their current design and policy-making processes. The democratic basis of design processes is often obscure, the political debate in design processes is underdeveloped, and the design process emphasizes technological fixes [17, 18]. Similarly, Van Zoonen [27] observes that the "transition to data-driven social policy almost completely takes place out of political and social view" (p. 3) and that the design process is in an institutional void.

Considering the flaws in current design processes, this research focuses on the influence of current design practices – i.e., a specific constellation of human action and institutions in the design process – on the emergence of digital cages and their unintended consequences. When considering human action, one can examine both the design and use mode of systems. These are analytical lenses to distinguish between two general classes of activities [20]. In the design mode, the system is intentionally created by designing actors. The system is also changed when users operate the system. This article focuses mostly on the design mode, as this is the part that public organizations mostly focus on. However, the two modes cannot fully be examined separately. Therefore, this article will sometimes also refer to the usage of public algorithmic systems.

3 Research Methods

We identified design practices that may result in digital cages and their unintended consequences by using an explorative case study. We analyzed how institutions and human actions in those organizations influence the structure of technical artefacts. Public organizations are considered as designing actors of public algorithmic systems. An explorative case study research was performed to study current design processes in public organizations through the structurational model of technology.

The explorative research was conducted at a consortium of Dutch public organizations that collaboratively realized policy instruments for public control on the development and use of algorithms. They developed an algorithm register, procurement conditions, a governance framework for development and use, and guidelines for objection procedures in government. The consortium consisted of several Dutch public organizations – five municipalities, three provinces, and three executive agencies – that were supported by the Ministry of Internal Affairs. The consortium was selected as a useful case, since the development of the instruments also asked for a reflection on the design process of algorithms. Furthermore, the participating organizations represented the majority of public organization types in the Netherlands; the consortium, therefore, also provided insight in differences between organizational design processes.

Since the consortium had just started with brainstorming about the policy instruments, the explorative research started with observations of the biweekly meetings of the core team members of the consortium. In these meetings, the project leaders shared the progress of the instruments and shared insights from within their own organizations. In total, 10 meetings, taking place from March to December 2020, were used for observations. The participants of the meetings differed, but the 5 core team members – representing two municipalities and two provinces – were consistently involved in the meetings. The observations were documented in a logbook. Documents shared during the meetings were also included in the logbook.

To test and complement the insights of the observations, semi-structured interviews of 90 min were conducted with the four project leaders after the observations. Four of the five core members – i.e., one lead developer and three policy makers involved in compliance; representing two municipalities and one province – were interviewed. The core team members were the project leaders of the instruments, and therefore had a full overview of the progress of the consortium. The interviewees were first asked to describe and reflect on the design process within their own organizations. Thereafter, they were asked to evaluate the policy instruments of the consortium. The topic guide of the interviews was based on the Institutional Analysis and Development (IAD) framework by Elinor Ostrom [21]. This analytical framework provides 11 important variables that need to be considered when looking at human action and the emergence of institutions.

We coded the observatory records and interviews transcripts thematically. The coding was focused on isolating the human actions and institutions in the design process. The IAD framework was used for the isolation of the factors. Thereafter, the relationships and interactions between the different human actions and institutions were derived from the records and transcripts by using the structurational model of technology [20].

4 Results: Observed Design Practices

This section discusses the design practices within public organizations following from institutions and human actions. The explorative study identifies four design practices: (1) a narrow focus on technology; (2) disregard of the normative basis for algorithmic systems; (3) designers are unaware of socio-technical components and interactions; and (4) caught in linear design processes. The four practices will be discussed here.

4.1 Narrow Focus on Technology

The silo structure of public organizations results in a narrow focus on technology. The observations and interviews showed that generally three organizational elements – each with its own jargon name – are involved in the design process: the *business*, *ICT*, and *compliance.* The domain-specific departments, which public organizations call "the business", commission a public algorithmic system which they will use in executing their tasks. Next, the algorithmic system is developed by an "ICT" function or department, or by an external party. Finally, "compliance" functions or departments ensure that the algorithmic systems are in line with rules and regulations. Three interactions arise in the horizontal relationship between the three organizational elements.

First, when algorithmic systems are developed internally, the system is developed by ICT or data-analytics departments – which are considered facilitative elements in the organization. In theory, the business should be in the lead in defining the goal and boundaries of a system in a policy. However, they largely depend on the knowledge of ICT to create the information architecture for their executive tasks. The business has to be told about what is technically possible and what is not. Due to this great dependence on technical knowledge, ICT naturally becomes the lead in designing public algorithmic systems. Often, the business and ICT work together, however, the strong position of ICT creates an imbalance in this collaboration.

Second, the algorithmic system is usually developed by a private or external party, since most public organizations do not have the capacity to develop these systems. Concerning algorithm development an interviewee stated: "It is also the starting point of the government. People say we do not want to disrupt markets. We are the coordinator, we outsource what we can outsource [to external parties]... Well, that is also the direction that the government has taken in recent years. [trans.]" The external party controls the development of the technical artefact. The consortium developed procurement conditions to strengthen the position of public organizations in this dependent relationship. However, the conditions do not change the fact that the public domain is partly designed by private parties and that they make part of the political trade-offs. One interviewee stated: "...when a product is outsourced, there are conditions that a developer needs to adhere to. That also includes ... policy goals or policy principles... But, the translation to an algorithm, the technical translation. They fully trust the developer to do the translation properly. [trans.]".

Third, compliance departments that ensure non-technical aspects of systems– such as safety and security, privacy, and ethics – are often viewed as burdensome in the design process. Compliance officers increasingly have a say in developing and using public algorithmic systems, especially privacy officers after the introduction of the GDPR. However, these actors often have few means and a relatively weak position to intervene in the design process. They tend to be informed late, making it harder to stop a project with high sunk costs. One interviewee stated about their position as compliance department: "The tricky thing is, we cannot control the money. The money is at 'the business', we cannot stop them. [trans.]" Another interviewee indicated how this leads to being considered as a burden: "... as compliance you are considered as hindering. Whereas if we would be involved early on, there are lots of possibilities to ensure compliance with frameworks and guidelines. At present, we are considered burdensome at the end of a project and, well, there is a continuous battle between innovation and formulating compliance frameworks and guidelines within the organization. [trans.]".

The three interactions result in a strong and reinforced position for techno-focused actors (e.g., engineers, data-analysts) throughout the design process of public algorithmic systems. Interviewees also provided examples of the leading role of ICT. For example, ICT provides products for several domain departments that are strictly separated. ICT is naturally put in a position in which they become aware of possible connections between different departments. One interviewee stated concerning the interactions between departments and their role as developer: "The product owners [i.e., domain department] mostly do not know each other, they do not actively exchange [about their projects and insights]. Encouraging and facilitating these exchanges, using insights more broadly within the organization, and educating product owners is really our role. [trans.]" Technology seems to become a vehicle for making public organizations work more comprehensive; however, not in an interdisciplinary way. ICT is the leading force – with its specific perspective. The assignment of this role is not a deliberate choice but a gradual and natural process.

The central position of ICT results in an emphasis on the technical artefact in public algorithmic systems. Other departments consider ICT as a facilitative element to which the development of public algorithmic systems is 'thrown over the fence'. In this way, the development attains a sense of neutrality that also disguises the central role of ICT in the design process. Naturally, the technical artefact attains most attention, neglecting institutional and agential components of public algorithmic systems. Compliance departments cannot correct this due to their weak position.

4.2 Disregarding the Normative Basis for Public Algorithmic Systems

Vertical disconnections in public organization's structure and culture impedes addressing normative aspects in the design process. Most of the time, public algorithmic systems must aim to promote public values and not infringe them, but such high-level statements leave room for interpretation. Civil servants seem to specify these norms in an ad hoc manner.

Missing channels of vertical communication create distance between the political decision-making level and the operational levels. Various interviewees stated that public administration is traditionally well-equipped to formulate policies and attune them to the political debate; this is a familiar practice within public organizations. However, the translation of the work done on public algorithmic systems – on the operational level –to the political debate on the decision-making level often falls short. The awareness of political trade-offs in public algorithmic systems and the feeling of agency to make these trade-offs is often low at the operational level. For example, the consortium often discussed the need for using values in the design process; however, they did not acknowledge that those values can be in conflict.

The lack of vertical communication also follows from a lack of clarity, concreteness, and direction on normativity given by the decision-making level. This seems to emerge from the (political) discourse associated to public algorithmic systems, which is still based on the premise that technology is neutral (see also [13, 25]). AI is still seen as a technology with great benefits for public organizations – although it is unclear what the actual affordances are. The limitations of the technology are increasingly recognized, but tend to be considered as something that can be resolved by developers. Moreover, the political debate is mostly reactive. Decision-makers react to incidents such as the introduction of the GDPR (explaining the emphasis on privacy) and recently the child benefit scandal *(Toeslagenaffaire)* in the Netherlands (resulting in a push for more transparency). Because of this reactive practice, politicians or decision-makers have not provided univocal and holistic normative or evaluative frameworks for public algorithmic systems.

Furthermore, the consortium considered the lack of awareness of algorithmic system use among citizens as one of the flaws in the current public debate. Citizens usually do not know whether and how systems were involved in making decisions that do affect them. To overcome this information asymmetry, the consortium developed an algorithm register. However, when writing this article, it is unclear whether this register will provide meaningful insight into the workings of the systems – including their interaction with policy, laws and regulations – and will support a public debate on algorithms used. Discussions within the consortium showed that the register can be used for a wide variety of goals and publics, for example, as internal archive for algorithms or as repository for citizens that want to appeal decisions. Furthermore, the effectiveness of the register depends on the status it is given by the public organization. The final form of the register will determine its support to the public debate.

The normative flaw in the design process makes it unclear for designers what values are applicable for specific public algorithmic systems and how trade-offs between these values have to be made. The lack of a public debate also hinders the formulation of such a normative framework. Currently, the design process is insufficiently embedded in political processes and deliberation about design choices is missing as these choices are not acknowledge as political choices. As engineers make these design choices, the narrow focus on technology is strengthened even more.

4.3 Designers are Unaware of Socio-technical Components and Interactions

All interviewees pointed out the importance of involved actors' approaches to the design process. Interviewees argued that, in the current situation, a project is approached more comprehensive or interdisciplinary when designers are involved that are aware of the socio-technics of the systems. One interviewee explained the dynamics within a project in which the awareness was high: "The specific people involved in this project were already thinking about these [socio-technical] themes. So, not just developing an application, but to think, okay, why do I program these choices in this model? [trans.]".

However, most employees in public organizations have little awareness of the different socio-technical components (and their interactions) of public algorithmic systems. They consider algorithmic systems as mere automation: a simple and objective tool for executive tasks. They are unaware of the fact that a public algorithmic system is an integral part of policies and regulations. In other words, they are unfamiliar with the fact that an algorithm can also influence the interpretation of those policies and regulations. Furthermore, the lack of awareness was observed in the difficulty of demarcating system boundaries. Interviewees stated that product owners (i.e., the business) are not always aware what is affected by an application and that they often do not recognize the products they use as algorithmic systems.

Whereas the first two design practices show the influence of institutions on the emergence of a focus on the technical artefact, this third design practice shows the importance of human actions in designing or using the system. The narrow focus on technology and lack of normative debate will not be resolved if the awareness of socio-technical components of public algorithmic systems is not increased. Increasing awareness is possible. Interviewees gave examples of regulations (e.g., GDPR), political events and, incidents that increased the urgency to deal with privacy and transparency. However, these are also exemplary for the reactive practice discussed in Sect. 4.2.

4.4 Caught in a Linear Design Process

The final design practice relates to how public organization standardize the design process. The common linear conception of design processes conflicts with the idiosyncratic nature of those processes; public organizations consider and structure design processes chronologically or sequentially (cf. waterfall). Governance documents or procedures often contain schemes with one-way arrows between discrete design process steps. Furthermore, in discussing the practical reorganization of design processes, the consortium tended to abstract the process to a series of subsequent steps.

Similarly, public organizations experience difficulties because they make sharp distinctions between the development and the use of algorithmic systems. The responsibility for design and use tends to be assigned to different teams and functions. However, the consortium often discussed the difficulties of transferring systems from the development phase to the use phase. Organizations try to overcome this divide between the two phases by, for example, letting designers interact with street-level bureaucrats that will use the system. However, these interactions are mostly about training the users instead of involving practice and practitioners in earlier design stages.

Although most actors still considered the design process to be linear, a shift in thinking could be observed in the consortium and its participating organizations. Two municipalities were experimenting with new design practices. One municipality developed complex algorithmic systems in an iterative and lean fashion, so-called agile-scrum sprints. The other municipality experimented with interdisciplinary teams in which all important actors were involved from the start of the design process. Nevertheless, in talking about a governance framework, the consortium often came to the conclusion that a linear abstraction of processes is needed to make it "workable". One interviewee stated that their team is constantly asked for new iterations of developed or implemented systems. In that case, the "business" asks to add new (technical) features to the system. In other words, implicitly there are already some iterative processes occurring; however, this brings difficulties. The iterations are mostly approached from a technical perspective and an overview of what iterations are commonly made within a project is absent. These ad-hoc iterations may obscure a clear overview of the project. For example, the goal of the algorithmic system may be lost out of sight.

More importantly, the design process misses correction and detection mechanisms of flaws in algorithmic systems. Public organizations are familiar with correction mechanisms, such as due process and objection procedures, or court cases. The consortium also tried to improve these procedures by enhancing the information position of civil servants that need to handle the objection to a decision made by or with the support of algorithms. However, traditional correction mechanisms mostly focus on individual cases. Failures ingrained in the algorithmic systems may be corrected for an individual, but there is no process yet to determine whether an individual incorrect or undesired outcome necessitates redesign on a system-level. Such system-level corrections also require detection of failures or changes in a system. The consortium was often confronted with the need to define a substantial or significant change in a public algorithmic systems. For example, determining the magnitude of changes in a system that must result in the alteration of a description in the algorithm register. However, the consortium was unable to operationalize a substantial change in algorithmic systems.

Public organizations have created design processes that do not align with how public algorithmic systems are developed in reality. This is mostly because the starting point of the design process – i.e., linearity – conflicts with the nature of development – i.e., iterative. Public organizations lack the swiftness to react to changes in systems and their perspective focuses on the internal organization – external forces changing the system are overlooked. Moreover, it is hard for public organizations to change their ways of designing, as it means that other processes within the organization have to be changed as well. Changing the design process is a complex operation.

As a final observation, we examine the efforts of the consortium to enhance the design process using their four policy instruments. Their approach focused on instruments has its advantages. For example, the instruments helped to raise awareness within public organizations for the need for transparency in using algorithmic systems. However, the instruments have their limitations. The instruments clearly show that the current organization of the design process is the starting point for reforms. The consortium sustains a fragmented and narrow perspective on designing public algorithmic systems – e.g., singular impact assessments for different effects or an algorithm register that only gives insight what type of system is used. The instruments do not show a deliberate approach to deal with structuration – i.e., they ignore the interactions between the socio-technical components and apply instruments to very specific aspects of the design process.

5 Discussion

The four design practices show that institutions and human actions in the design process have distinctive influence on the development of public algorithmic systems. In this section, we extrapolate those design practices to the emergence of digital cages. The four practices indicate (1) that institutions and human actions in design processes need to be considered when examining the emergence of digital cages and their unintended consequences. We will elaborate on the implications of all four practices.

First, the narrow focus on technology obstructs considering the role of other socio-technical components in the emergence of digital cages. Section 4.1 shows that technology and engineers – although considered facilitative – have gained a strong position in the design process, reinforcing the false assumption that algorithms are neutral or objective. Similar to practice, research focuses on technology in automated decision-making [28]. The pivotal role of technology in design processes results in a focus on formalizing processes in public administration through algorithms (with emphasis on, for example, optimizing accuracy). This formalization is the, now strengthened, driving force behind digital cages. By prioritizing the technical artefact, the possibilities of public organizations to address digital cages and their unintended consequences are reduced; designers ignore institutions and human actions as ways to address digital cages. For example, institutions that protect the discretion of civil servants, tend to be unexplored by public organizations. Actors that could provide those perspectives lack the means to intervene.

Second, the unclear normative basis inhibits anticipating to and assessing possible unintended consequences within the design process. The digital cage is inherently normative, as it emerges from political and ideological choices about the level of formalization, the relationship between citizen and government, and the role of technology in executing public services. Dencik et al. [4] show how austerity policies have resulted in automated assessments of citizens based on risks; thereby shifting responsibilities to citizens and obstructing the engagement in scrutinizing government decisions. The flaws in the public debate could result in difficulties at the side of both citizens as the public organization. Since citizens are unable to participate in the debate, several perspectives, needs, and interests are currently not involved in the design process. These perspectives, when included, could provide crucial or critical insights on the emergence of specific unintended consequences. Similarly, the lack of public debate can also impede deliberation on the assessment of unintended consequences. In the design process, (un)intended consequences of public algorithmic systems should be assessed on their impact and whether and how this impact should be prevented or mitigated. Finally, there is the possibility that a digital cage is intentionally or strategically implemented, making the consequences less unintended. The lack of public debate may result in withholding information about the rationales behind public algorithmic systems and digital cages.

Third, since a narrow focus on technology is undesirable, designers need to have awareness of socio-technical interactions within public algorithmic systems. When public organizations do not acknowledge that their public algorithmic systems can evolve into digital cages, they will not feel the urge to (re)design their systems to tackle the unintended consequences of digital cages. Similarly, designers that are unaware of the socio-technical nature of their systems and the digital cage, are unaware of the influence of human actions and institutions on digital cages and therefore cannot adequately address their unintended consequences. Furthermore, the lack of awareness may result in resistance to compliance activities in the design process. The first design practice already showed a need for situating systems in their social and institutional context. However, the importance of awareness shows that it is not only about changing the organizational structure. The culture or shared meanings within organizations, formed by the accumulation of human actions, also has to change.

Finally, organizing the design process linearly conflicts with the emergent nature of digital cages. In a linear process, unintended consequences will quickly appear for those who are harmed. However, those that need to correct the consequences will only acknowledge the detrimental impact of digital cages in late stages of developing and using the algorithmic system. For example, correction mechanisms are based on individual cases and therefore do not provide insight in more systemic failures or do not provide citizens with a voice to reveal problems in public algorithmic systems [33]. More sensitivity and response to the emergence of material harms for citizens is needed. Those should be picked up and acknowledged earlier and lead to corrective – i.e., redesign – and compensating actions – to alleviate harm. Public organizations are familiar with that sensitivity in or control on their processes, because citizens – the locus in public administration – need protection. However, guaranteeing the generation of public value and the possibility for public control on the process often conflicts with facilitating an innovative environment – i.e., providing flexibility and room for experimentation [16]. That flexibility is also needed when dealing with unintended consequences, as they cannot always be predicted or can be overlooked. Still, this does not necessarily mean that one cannot have control over the design process. One could, for example, think of dissent channels to give citizens a voice [5]. This asks for new institutional environments for the design process.

Our observations provide only few indications that public organizations are changing their design practices to address digital cages more effectively. We observed that instruments sustain the current rationale behind design processes. For example, public organizations obtain broader perspectives, but only on specific topics such as transparency. Moreover, policy makers clearly consider the political debate as an activity for politicians, but they also do not provide politicians with possibilities to enhance the communication between politicians and designer. Finally, the instruments are based on the common linear way of thinking about design. Still, the instruments are useful tools to create awareness about socio-technics within public organizations.

However, this explorative research to identify design practices contributing to the emergence of digital cages in public algorithmic systems has its limitations. Only a select group of public organizations was observed and interviewed. And although the organizations represented a diverse set of public organizations, they were all situated in the Netherlands and therefore in Dutch governmental practices. Furthermore, the participants of the consortium were already thinking about how to address harms of public algorithmic systems. They may not fully represent public organizations that lack the capacity to contemplate on their use of algorithmic systems – for reasons of, for example, being too small (e.g., small municipalities that outsource algorithm development). Finally, the research focused on discussions of policy-makers about the design process; actual design processes were not observed.

Hence, more research on the organization of the design process is needed. First, public organizations should obtain a broader perspective in the design process, but it is poorly understood how that can be achieved. Socio-technical design research provides some substantive starting points, such as making the design process integral [2], interdisciplinary [3], political [2], and iterative [20]; but it is unclear what these concepts entail for the design process of public algorithmic systems. Similarly, public organizations are faced with the challenge to change their organizational culture. Research could show how the deterministic and objectivistic perspective on technology can be replaced by a broader and situated view on technology. Finally, the need for a broader perspective also implies that public organizations have to reflect on their dependency on external developers. Therefore, more research is needed on the extent to which external parties make or influence critical design choices for the public domain.

Second, the need for flexibility in public design processes justifies more research. Studies on achieving flexibility could use unintended consequences as a starting point and examine processes to anticipate and react to these consequences. In this respect, an interesting avenue for research could be to examine the extent to which public organizations validate their algorithmic systems and what the value of validation could be. Next, research could show how flexibility can be combined with public control on design processes and the implementation of checks and balances in the design process.

Third, the role of the designer in the emergence of digital cages needs to be analyzed alongside the role of the designer. This research mostly focused on designers, but, users' actions are as important in the emergence of digital cages. For example, discretion is not only curtailed by the technical artefact, it is also affected by how users interact with or react to technology. More insight is needed in the role of users in the development of digital cages. This research seems to indicate that considering the role of the users has to go further than user experience, user participation, or user training.

Finally, more research is needed on integrating public debates in design processes and vice versa. Regarding this topic, most literature points towards participation. However, there is much more to it (see, for example, [9]). The public debate comprises more complex forms of deliberation and democracy. Moreover, normativity asks for mapping the values that are touched upon in digital cages and how trade-offs between these values can be made in a democratic way.

6 Conclusions

The increasing use of public algorithmic systems can reinforce the emergence of digital cages. Although digital cages are familiar symptoms of algorithms used in public administration, there is a lack of knowledge in the design practices that result in the emergence of digital cages. Therefore, the goal of this paper was to provide insight in these design practices in order to support the prevention, mitigation, or correction of detrimental impact, following from digital cages, on citizens.

The diagnosis of the design process, presented in this article, shows that the current organization of design processes in public organizations ignores the fact that specific human actions and institutions contribute to the emergence of digital cages. Four practices that impede addressing digital cages were identified. Firstly, design processes emphasize technical aspects and effects of public algorithmic systems. Thereby, causes for digital cages in institutional or social parts of these systems are ignored. Secondly, politics are hidden in the design process and the discourse on public algorithmic systems remains narrow. Public deliberation on the normative impact of digital cages is missing. Thirdly, the consideration of socio-technics in design processes heavily depends on the awareness of designers. Finally, public organizations struggle with facilitating corrective iterations during a system's life-cycle. Design processes do not have the flexibility to deal with the complexity of a socio-technical design process and are only partly able to adequately react to unintended consequences.

In order to address digital cages, the design process of public algorithmic systems needs to be altered. However, public organization public organizations only show little attempts to reflect on their design practices. The instruments they implement to rearrange design processes continue the current organization of those processes. In other words, the techno-centric and sequential way of thinking is maintained, and the publicness and the impact on citizens of algorithmic systems is still neglected. However, the interviewees also showed the motivation to start such reflections. In order to support public organizations in their reflection on design processes, more research is needed to practices of anticipation and reaction to unintended consequences, the implementation of flexibility and checks and balances in the design process, and how design processes can become more democratic.

References

1. Burrell, J.: How the machine 'thinks': understanding opacity in machine learning algorithms. Big Data Soc. **3**(1), 1–12 (2016)
2. Clegg, C.W.: Sociotechnical principles for system design. Appl. Ergon. **31**, 463–477 (2000)
3. De Bruijn, H., Herder, P.M.: System and actor perspectives on sociotechnical systems. IEEE Trans. Syst. Man Cybern. – Part A: Syst. Hum. **39**(5), 981–992 (2009)

4. Dencik, l., Redden, J., Hintz, A., Warne, H.: The 'golden view': data-driven governance in the scoring society. Internet Policy Rev. **8**(2), 1–24 (2019)
5. Dobbe, R., Krendl Gilber, T., Mintz, Y.: Hard choices in artificial intelligence. Artif. Intell. **300**, 103555 (2021)
6. Giddens, A.: New Rules of Sociological Method. Basic Books, New York (1976)
7. Giddens, A.: Central Problems in Social Theory: Action, Structure and Contradiction in Social Analysis. University of California Press, Berkeley (1979)
8. Giddens, A.: The Constitution of Society: Outline of the Theory of Structure. University of California Press, Berkeley (1984)
9. Himmelreich, J.: Against "Democratizing AI". AI Soc. (2022). https://doi.org/10.1007/s00146-021-01357-z
10. Hildebrandt, M.: Law for Computer Scientists. Oxford University Press, Oxford (2019)
11. Hodson, R., Martin, A.W., Lopez, S.H., Roscigno, V.J.: Rules don't apply: Kafka's insights on bureaucracy. Organization **20**(2), 256–278 (2012)
12. Hodgson, G.H.: What are institutions? J. Econ. Issues **40**(1), 1–25 (2006)
13. Janssen, M., Kuk, G.: The challenges and limits of big data algorithms in technocratic governance. Gov. Inf. Q. **33**, 371–377 (2016)
14. Kroll, J.A.: The fallacy of inscrutability. Philos. Trans. A **376**, 20180084 (2018)
15. Lorenz, L., Meijer, A., Schuppan, T.: The algocracy as a new ideal type for government organizations: predictive policing in Berlin as an empirical case. Inf. Polity **26**, 71–86 (2021)
16. Meijer, A., Thaens, M.: The dark side of public innovation. Public Perform. Manag. Rev. **44**(1), 136–154 (2021)
17. Mulligan, D.K., Bamberger, K.A.: Saving governance-by-design. Calif. Law Rev. **106**(3), 697–784 (2018)
18. Mulligan, D.K., Bamberger, K.A.: Procurement as policy: administrative process for machine learning. Berkeley Technol. Law J. **34**(3), 773–851 (2019)
19. OECD: Recommendation of the Council on Artificial Intelligence. OECD/LEGAL/0449 (2021)
20. Orlikowski, W.J.: The duality of technology: rethinking the concept of technology in organisations. Organ. Sci. **3**(3), 398–427 (1992)
21. Ostrom, E.: Understanding Institutional Diversity. Princeton University Press, Princeton (2005)
22. Peeters, R.: The agency of algorithms: understanding human-algorithm interaction in administrative decision-making. Inf. Polity **25**, 507–522 (2020)
23. Peeters, R., Widlak, A.: The digital cage: administrative exclusion through information architecture – the case of Dutch civil registry's master data management system. Gov. Inf. Q. **35**, 175–183 (2018)
24. Ranchordas, S., Scarcella, L.: Automated government for vulnerable citizens. William Mary Bill Rights J. (2021)
25. Van der Voort, H.G., Klievink, A.J., Arnaboldi, M., Meijer, A.J.: Rationality and politics of algorithms. Will the promise of big data survive the dynamics of public decision making? Gov. Inf. Q. **36**, 27–38 (2019)
26. Van Schie, G., Smit, A., Coombs, N.L.: Racing through the Dutch governmental data assemblage: a postcolonial data studies approach. Global Perspect. **1**(1) (2020)
27. Van Zoonen, L.: Data governance and citizen participation in the digital welfare state. Data Policy **2**(10), 1–17 (2020)
28. Vydra, S., Klievink, B.: Techno-optimism and policy-pessimism in the public sector big data. Gov. Inf. Q. **36**, 101383 (2019)
29. Wachter, S., Mittelstadt, B., Russell, C.: Counterfactual explanations without opening the black box: automated decisions and the GDPR. Harvard J. Law Technol. **31**(2), 841–887 (2018)

30. Wachter, S., Mittelstadt, B., Russell, C.: Why fairness cannot be automated: bridging the gap between EU non-discrimination law and AI. Comput. Law Secur. Rev. **41**, 105567 (2020)
31. Wagner, B.: Liable, but not in control? ensuring meaningful human agency in automated decision-making systems. Policy Internet **11**(1), 104–122 (2019)
32. Weber, M.: Economy and Society. University of California Press, Berkeley (1978). Translated by G. Roth and C. Wittich, Original work published in 1925
33. Widlak, A., Peeters, R.: Administrative errors and the burden of correction and consequence: how information technology exacerbates the consequences of bureaucratic mistakes for citizens. Int. J. Electron. Gov. **12**(1), 40–56 (2020)
34. Zouridis, S., Bovens, M., Van Eck, M.: Digital discretion. In: Evans, T., Hupe, P. (eds.) Discretion and the Quest for Controlled Freedom. Palgrave/MacMillan (2019)
35. Zuiderwijk, A., Chen, Y., Salem, F.: Implications of the use of artificial intelligence in public governance: a systematic literature review and a research agenda. Gov. Inf. Q. **38**(3), 101577 (2021)
36. Zuurmond, A.: From bureaucracy to infocracy: are democratic institutions lagging behind? In: Snellen, I.T.M., van de Donk, W.B.H.J. (eds.) Public Administration in an Information Age: A Handbook. IOS Press, Amsterdam (1998)

Artificial Intelligence and Blockchain Technologies in the Public Sector: A Research Projects Perspective

Evangelos Kalampokis[1,2(✉)], Nikos Karacapilidis[3], Dimitris Tsakalidis[4], and Konstantinos Tarabanis[1,2]

[1] Centre for Research and Technology - Hellas, 6th km. Charilaou-Thermi RD, Thessaloniki, Greece
{ekal,kat}@uom.edu.gr
[2] University of Macedonia, Egnatia 156, 54636 Thessaloniki, Greece
[3] IMIS Lab, MEAD, University of Patras, Patras, Greece
karacap@upatras.gr
[4] Novelcore, Patras, Greece
tsakalidis@novelcore.eu

Abstract. Artificial Intelligence (AI) and blockchain are two of the most prominent technologies having the potential to streamline public sector. The objective of this paper is to reveal the latest developments and trends regarding the utilization and deployment of these technologies in the public sector, as this is reflected through nineteen recently funded Horizon 2020 research projects. This study is based on a well-known literature review method that enables a concept-centric analysis of the accumulated knowledge in the field under consideration. Through a detailed consideration of these projects and their pilot case implementations, a series of insights about recent research development and applications in the public sector are extracted and discussed. The findings of this study are further justified or challenged by referring to recent review articles that investigate the use of AI and blockchain in the public sector.

Keywords: Artificial Intelligence · Blockchain · Digital government · H2020 · Research projects

1 Introduction

During the last decade, various emerging technologies have been adopted by electronic government (e-Government) in order to facilitate both the achievement and the advancement of its goals [29]. Emerging technologies is a dynamic concept comprising a continuously growing list of ICTs that reshape human action and interaction. Representative examples of such technologies that have been applied and tested in the public sector include blockchain [5,8,9,35], artificial intelligence [2,6,16,23,25,32,34], semantic technologies [7,15,17,22] and

Published by Springer Nature Switzerland AG 2022
M. Janssen et al. (Eds.): EGOV 2022, LNCS 13391, pp. 323–335, 2022.
https://doi.org/10.1007/978-3-031-15086-9_21

Internet of Things (IoT) [11,33]. From an organization science point-of-view, emerging technologies do much more than automate and inform, thus posing a series of challenges that distinguish them from prior technologies [27]. This is mainly due to the following key factors: (i) emerging technologies become increasingly "intelligent", in that they lead to developments that could someday mimic or possibly outperform humans in a great diversity of skilled and cognitive acts; (ii) they enable new forms of data analytics that significantly enhance public sector's ability in tracking, deciphering, and influencing the behaviors of individuals and groups; (iii) they enable new approaches to innovation and collaboration within and across organizations, which foster the co-creation of new knowledge and accelerate the development of novel services and processes [1,19]; (iv) they demonstrate a rapid diffusion and adoption rate, which in turn transforms the way things get done and leads to the creation of novel business models [3].

As a consequence, a series of recently published research articles and working papers elaborate diverse issues related to the implementation and adoption of emerging technologies in the public sector. For instance, [13] discusses the deployment of a creative mix of emerging technologies and innovation in the public sector and provides perspectives on the nature of smart governments; [18] identifies the challenges involved in implementing and adopting IoT and AI in the public sector, and accordingly proposes a comprehensive research framework for smart government transformation; [21] aims to provide an understanding of the awareness aspect of emerging technologies; [14] discusses how the use of emerging information technologies can support participatory urbanism, particularly among low-income and underserved populations; [12] proposes a comprehensive digital government success model that attempts to integrate implementation and adoption perspectives; [22] presents an overview of applied Semantic Web technologies in the open government data domain that increase openness and transparency of government; [28] elucidates the implications of various governance choices in each level of governance and provides a primer for researchers and policy practitioners on the design of blockchain-based systems in the public sector; finally, based on the analysis of data collected in 20 countries, [29] offers insights from strategies and practical examples concerning how governments attempt to integrate AI and blockchain technologies in the public sector.

In this context, the aim of this paper is to reveal the latest developments and trends regarding the utilization and deployment of two emerging technologies, namely Artificial Intelligence (AI) and blockchain in the public sector, as this is reflected through recently funded research projects. In particular, we focus on projects that were funded by the European Union during the last H2020 work programme, i.e. from 2018 to 2020, thus being active from 2019 to 2024. To the best of our knowledge, this is the first attempt to gain such insights from a research projects perspective, which may reveal useful information about the utilization and deployment of these technologies in real-life settings.

The remainder of this paper is organized as follows: Sect. 2 presents the research design that was followed in order to achieve the objectives of this study. Section 3 presents the findings of this study, which are further justified or challenged in Sect. 4, by referring to research results from the related literature on the use of AI and blockchain in the public sector. Finally, Sect. 5 outlines concluding remarks, comments on the boundaries and limitations of this study and sketches future research directions.

2 Research Design

This paper is based on the research method proposed by Webster and Watson for conducting a systematic literature review in the field of Information Systems [30]. This method provides guidelines on (i) setting the boundaries of the work, (ii) identifying the source material, (iii) structuring the review, and (iv) identifying critical gaps.

e-Government is part of the European Agenda since the beginning of the century [26]. The European Commission started to systematically fund e-Government research within the 5th (1998–2002), the 6th (2003–2006), and the 7th (2007–2013) Framework Programmes. This trend continued in the latest Framework Programme, namely Horizon 2020 (H2020), which was active for seven years, from 2014 to 2020. In particular, three distinct Work Programmes were published, covering three periods inside H2020, namely 2014–2015, 2016–2017 and 2018–2020.

In this study, we have thoroughly considered nineteen (19) research projects that are related to the use of ICTs in the public sector and were funded through the calls of the last period of the H2020 framework programme (i.e., 2018–2020). The corresponding calls were included in Societal Challenge 6 (SC6) "Europe in a changing world - inclusive, innovative and reflective societies". Two out of the three SC6's calls were related to the public sector, namely "Socioeconomic and cultural transformations in the context of the fourth industrial revolution" and "Governance for the future". The research projects considered in this study were funded through the following three topics, under which eight (8) calls for proposals were issued between 2018 and 2020:

- DT-TRANSFORMATIONS-02-2018-2019-2020: Transformative impact of disruptive technologies in public services. This topic focuses on public administrations' and policy makers' *"use of disruptive technologies (such as artificial intelligence and big data analytics, block chain, Internet of Things, virtual and augmented reality, simulations or gamification)"*;
- DT-GOVERNANCE-05-2018-2019-2020: New forms of delivering public goods and inclusive public services. This topic refers to *"the transformative impact of new technologies"* in the public sector;
- DT-GOVERNANCE-12-2019-2020: Pilot on using the European cloud infrastructure for public administrations. This topic refers to public administrations' use of *"open and big data, in particular as facilitated by high-performance computing (HPC) capabilities offered by the European Cloud Initiative"*.

We adopt pilot cases as the level of analysis, and we investigate how they apply the ICTs in a specific context. This may include the use of ICTs to streamline digital public service provision in a specific country or to augment the quality of decision making in a specific citizen group.

To ensure the accumulation of a relatively complete census of relevant literature, we have not only identified the research projects, but also elicited the details about the use of AI and blockchain in the pilot cases of each specific project. The Community Research and Development Information Service (CORDIS), which is the European Commission's primary portal for disseminating information about EU-funded research projects and their results, was searched for projects that have been funded under the above mentioned calls. The nineteen (19) research projects identified officially started within the 2018–2021 period and, as of the time of writing this article, most of them are active.

The websites of these projects were also scrutinized to identify deliverables that describe the application and exploitation of emerging technologies in their pilot cases. It is noted that for projects that are still in their early implementation stages, only limited content was available in the CORDIS portal; in these cases, additional information was sought and collected by directly contacting the project coordinators and/or associated partners. Table 1 provides a detailed list of the projects considered in this study.

Table 1. The H2020 projects reviewed in this study.

Acronym	Topic	Duration
Qualichain	DT-TRANSFORMATIONS-02	2019–21
URBANAGE	DT-TRANSFORMATIONS-02	2021–24
ETAPAS	DT-TRANSFORMATIONS-02	2020–23
IMPULSE	DT-TRANSFORMATIONS-02	2021–24
URBANITE	DT-TRANSFORMATIONS-02	2020–23
HECAT	DT-TRANSFORMATIONS-02	2020-23
TOKEN	DT-TRANSFORMATIONS-02	2020–22
CO3	DT-TRANSFORMATIONS-02	2019–21
ACROSS	DT-GOVERNANCE-05	2021–24
inGOV	DT-GOVERNANCE-05	2021–23
GLASS	DT-GOVERNANCE-05	2021–23
INTERLINK	DT-GOVERNANCE-05	2021–23
mGov4EU	DT-GOVERNANCE-05	2021–23
DE4A	DT-GOVERNANCE-05	2020–22
DUET	DT-GOVERNANCE-12	2019–22
PolicyCLOUD	DT-GOVERNANCE-12	2019–22
IntelComp	DT-GOVERNANCE-12	2021–23
AI4PublicPolicy	DT-GOVERNANCE-12	2021–23
DECIDO	DT-GOVERNANCE-12	2021–23

According to the adopted research method, a review should be concept-centric. A concept-centric analysis, in contrast to the author-centric approach, helps others to make sense of the accumulated knowledge in the field under consideration. As a result, the most important concepts that will facilitate the analysis and synthesis of the identified content need to be specified. The *EU research projects* and the respective *pilot cases* are in the centre of this study. The research projects considered include a set of pilot cases that aim to demonstrate the applicability of the proposed solutions in real world settings and evaluate their results. Moreover, a research project has a *scope* that could be either *public service provision* or *policy/decision making*. Finally, we consider each pilot case being involved with a government activity. By adopting Core Public Service Vocabulary Application Profile (CPSV-AP)[1], our study classifies these activities according to the *Type* property of a public service, which refers to the purpose of a government activity. According to CPSV-AP v.2.2, the *Type* property is populated using the classification of the functions of government (COFOG) glossary, which was developed by the Organisation for Economic Co-operation and Development and published by the United Nations Statistical Division as a standard for the classification of the purposes of government activities.

3 Results

In total, we identified 74 pilot cases, resulting in an average of 4.4 pilots per project. This average value is similar in both public service provision and policy/decision making categories. It is worthy mentioning that 47 pilots are included in public service provision projects, while 27 in policy/decision making ones. In addition, it is mentioned that although most of the projects comprise several pilot cases addressing different problem areas, four (4) projects focus on a single problem area. These include *public education* (Qualichain), *urban planning* (URBANAGE), *urban mobility* (URBANITE), and *labour market* (HECAT).

3.1 Public Service Provision

We examined the reasons of employing AI and blockchain in the identified public services. A specific technology can be employed in multiple public services for the same reason. Table 2 depicts the different uses of AI in public service provision. The specific tasks supported by the use of the technology are presented along with the respective public services. These include the provision of personalised recommendations, the verification of copies or mobile photos of official documents through image recognition, and citizens authentication through facial recognition.

Table 3 summarises the use of blockchain in public service provision. The validation of evidences (e.g., official documents, information, etc.) that are requested

[1] https://joinup.ec.europa.eu/collection/semantic-interoperability-community-semic/solution/core-public-service-vocabulary-application-profile/releases.

Table 2. Artificial Intelligence use in public services.

Aim of the technology use	Public Services
Provision of personalised recommendations	Students gets personalised recommendation on courses
Verification of photos/copies of official documents	Issuance of eID
Facial recognition to authenticate citizens	Issuance of eID

during the execution of a public service is the most common reason for using blockchain technologies. In this case, a public agency issues an evidence as a verifiable credential in a digital form, which is cryptographically signed by the issuer agency. The citizen stores the verifiable credential along with a cryptographic proof in a digital wallet. If the citizen, at a later stage, invokes the execution of a public service that requires the specific evidence as an input, she shares the digital verifiable credential with the responsible public agency, which then verifies and uses the evidence.

Other reasons for using blockchain technologies include the creation of immutable time stamps, the development of a digital wallet that could replace the transfer of social benefits, the trusted distributed ownership of information, the recording of transactions, and user authentication. In particular, recording the date and time of an event, known as time stamping, is important in many scenarios in the public sector, e.g., in order to leave proof of the moment when a citizen or a business triggers the execution of a public service. In the case of competitive processes, such as public procurement, trust and transparency are also important for all parties involved; blockchain provides the means to create immutable and trustful time stamps.

The public sector provides numerous benefits to people in need. Many of these benefits are focused on specific citizens' needs such as food, health, and housing, and thus they can be only exchanged in specific authorised locations. For example, food stamps can be used only in authorised retailers. Blockchain enables the public to create tokens, while digital wallets enable users to exchange these tokens easily. Tokens can be used to distribute social benefits to citizens in need, while citizens can exchange these tokens with actual products or services from authorised providers.

3.2 Policy/Decision Making Projects

The pilots included in the policy/decision making projects aim at addressing one or more policy objectives in various policy areas such as public order and safety and environmental protection. As shown in Table 4, the most prominent uses of Artificial Intelligence technologies in policy/decision making include predictive analytics, computational simulation models, explainable AI, risk factor

Table 3. Blockchain use in public services.

Aim of the technology use	Public services
Validation of evidences (e.g., official documents, information, etc.)	Citizens apply for a job in the public sector Companies participate in a public procurement process Citizens issue social security number Citizens request a diploma recognition SMEs apply for public funding Education institutions issue qualification component to citizens
Creation of immutable time stamps	Companies participate in a public procurement process
Distribution of social benefits	Social distribution of quality food excess
Document transactions	Suppliers of data trace the use of data made by third parties
Trusted distributed ownership of information	Local authorities dynamically grant access to a city
Trusted and verified parties can manage their identities	Local authorities dynamically grant access to a city

prediction and clustering. In particular, predictive analytics scenarios include the forecasting of energy consumption in the "Energy management and optimization" pilot in AI4PublicPolicy. Examples of computational simulation models include (i) the transport planning case in URBANITE, which exploits an agent-based modelling approach for trip chains analysis in order to find out the outcomes of interventions with the traffic network, e.g., by building a tunnel, and (ii) the models and algorithms of the traffic assignment problem of the digital twill developed in DUET. Risk factor prediction cases include the calculation of predictive risk of fires during evacuation procedures in the "Prevention and protection against forest fires" pilot in DECIDO, or the calculation of the traffic jam factor of a road in a specific time slot in URBANITE. Finally, clustering cases include the grouping of clients upon similar energy usage in the "Energy management and optimization" pilot in AI4PublicPolicy.

Natural language processing technologies such as opinion mining and sentiment analysis, named entity recognition, and topic modeling are employed to analyse user generated content in Social Media. In particular, in a pilot case of the PolicyCloud project, opinion mining techniques were applied on Twitter data to identify radicalisation efforts and link those efforts to particular terrorist groups or attacks.

Moreover, the exploitation of visual analytics for business intelligence has been reported in many cases as AI solutions. These dashboards aim at aggregating diverse data from multiple sources and enable policy makers monitor the real time picture of a situation, thus gaining a complete understanding of a certain

Table 4. Artificial Intelligence use in policy making.

Aim of the technology use	Policy objective
Predictive analytics	Prevention and protection against forest fires Emergency policies related to floods and weather alerts Address unemployment Energy management and optimization
Simulation computational models	Support and improve sustainable mobility (including bike mobility, public transport, etc.)
Risk factors prediction	Support and improve sustainable mobility (including bike mobility, public transport, etc.) Prevention and protection against forest fires
Clustering	Energy Management and Optimization
Keyword extraction/named entity recognition	Policies against radicalisation
Opinion mining/sentiment analysis	Policies against radicalisation Improve investments in agri-food promotion

topic. Example cases include the visualisation of signals received via a municipality call centre regarding numerous topics (PolicyCloud), a dashboard that monitors wine sales price on specialized websites and generates alarm systems when prices fall below a minimum price (PolicyCloud), a dashboard regarding the forest fire risk management that exploits data provided by the Finnish Meteorological Institute, the European Forest Fire Information System and meteorological data from Copernicus climate data (DECIDO), and a dashboard offering map layers, charts and graphs that summarise the status of bike mobility in the city (URBANITE). These dashboards allow decision makers and policy makers to have, in a single view, the overall and relevant information they need to gain insights about a specific topic.

4 Discussion

In this section, we attempt to further justify (or challenge) the results reported above. To this aim, we refer to research results pointed out in the related literature, focusing on recent review articles elaborating and commenting on the use of the technologies under consideration in the public sector.

4.1 Artificial Intelligence

With respect to AI technologies, a systematic literature review of 26 papers focusing on the implications of their use in public governance appears in [34]. As identified, the potential benefits of AI use in government span nine categories, namely (i) efficiency and performance benefits, (ii) risk identification and monitoring benefits, (iii) economic benefits, (iv) data and information processing benefits, (v) service benefits, (vi) benefits for society at large, (vii) decision-making benefits, (viii) engagement and interaction benefits, and (ix) sustainability benefits.

In particular, for the decision-making benefits category, it is argued that Machine Learning could support government decision-makers and lead to better and more accurate decision-making; AI is expected to reduce administrative burden and Big Data Algorithmic Systems can enable automatic decision making within public institutions [20]. Undoubtedly, the above nine categories cover both the public service provision and the policy-making/decision-making scopes distinguished in our study, and justify the balanced allocation of projects in the corresponding categories. Moreover, the diverse list of challenges identified in [34], covering (i) data challenges, (ii) organizational and managerial challenges, (iii) skills challenges, (iv) interpretation challenges, (v) ethical and legitimacy challenges, (vi) political, legal, and policy challenges, (vii) social and societal challenges, and (viii) economic challenges, justify the broad use of AI technologies in the public sector.

The aforementioned diversity in terms of benefits of AI use and challenges is also made clear in [25] and [10], where it is clearly highlighted that the public sector is increasing the utilization of Artificial Intelligence in its services. Finally, very interesting results that are in full accordance with the findings of our work are discussed in [31], a study that is based on a quantitative and qualitative analysis of 189 articles to review the current literature on AI in the public sector. As reported, the current state of research is heterogeneous and thematically and methodologically unbalanced; many studies focus on governance and administration, while more specific application areas receive less attention; studies to date focus in detail on changes to existing government structures, while the creation of entirely new structures due to new AI technologies is given less consideration.

4.2 Blockchain and Distributed Ledgers

As far as blockchain technologies are concerned, two perspectives for the related architectures and applications in the public sector have been distinguished in [35], namely the perspective of *governance by BC*, in which public organizations adopt blockchain technologies for their own processes (like service provisioning) and that of *governance of BC*, which determines how blockchain technologies should look like, how to adapt to changes and should ensure that public values and societal needs are fulfilled. All projects considered in our study fall in the former perspective. The fact that blockchain technologies are mentioned only in public service provision projects is justified by the primary expectation of blockchain, which is to facilitate direct interaction between citizens, providing administration without a governmental administrator and tailoring services provided by governments; all these fall out of the policy/decision making scope.

The above fact is also justified by a systematic literature review of blockchain-based applications [5], arguing that the adoption of blockchain technology in the public sector concerns particularly the utilisation of a secure, distributed, open, and inexpensive database technology to reduce cost and bureaucracy, increase efficiency and authenticate many types of persistent documents; while blockchain applications in the public sector include document verification, e-residency approaches, development of more reliable and transparent taxation mechanisms, development of more robust regulatory compliance frameworks, and land management. All these fall in the public service provision scope. Similar results and indications are reported in [24], concluding that most of the current cases of blockchain technologies in the public domain have been applied to services, improving transactional and registry functionality, while in all cases interoperability can be enhanced.

The majority of the pilot cases of the projects considered in our study deal with the aforementioned verification-related issues and applications. However, there are also cases that build on blockchain technology to develop public services for not well explored so far purposes; these concern the immutable time stamping, the development of digital wallets, the distributed ownership of information, the distribution of social benefits related to food, health and housing, as well as the user identification and authentication. In turn, this justifies the ever increasing adoption and applicability of blockchain technology nowadays; it is also in accordance with the research presented in [4], which aimed to identify the relevance of the New Public Governance (NPG) paradigm to the design of public blockchain solutions, and concluded that blockchain-based public service delivery has so far only partly met the various expectations associated with NPG.

5 Conclusion

Given the lack of a comprehensive overview of applications of emerging technologies in the public sector, the concept-centric approach proposed in this paper aims to analyze and compile relevant findings from nineteen recently funded Horizon 2020 research projects to provide an integrative overview of the utilization and deployment of such applications in real-life pilots. To the best of our knowledge, this paper is the first attempt to contribute to the theoretical body of knowledge on the use of two emerging technologies, namely AI and blockchain, in the public sector from a research projects perspective. Specifically, the particular study contributes by identifying how these technologies contribute towards the achievement of the e-Government vision and objectives set by the EU, and which e-Government pilot cases these technologies enable.

Acknowledgements. This publication has been produced in the context of the European Union's Horizon 2020 Projects inGov and GLASS, which are co-funded by the European Commission under the Grant Agreement IDs: 962563 and 959879, respectively.

References

1. Androutsopoulou, A., Karacapilidis, N., Loukis, E., Charalabidis, Y.: Towards an integrated and inclusive platform for open innovation in the public sector. In: Katsikas, S.K., Zorkadis, V. (eds.) e-Democracy 2017. CCIS, vol. 792, pp. 228–243. Springer, Cham (2017). https://doi.org/10.1007/978-3-319-71117-1_16
2. Androutsopoulou, A., Karacapilidis, N., Loukis, E., Charalabidis, Y.: Transforming the communication between citizens and government through AI-guided chatbots. Gov. Inf. Q. **36**(2), 358–367 (2019). https://doi.org/10.1016/j.giq.2018.10.001
3. Bailey, D., Faraj, S., Hinds, P., von Krogh, G., Leonardi, P.: Special issue of organization science: emerging technologies and organizing. Organ. Sci. **30**(3), 642–646 (2019). https://doi.org/10.1287/orsc.2019.1299
4. Brinkmann, M.: The realities of blockchain-based new public governance: an explorative analysis of blockchain implementations in Europe. Digit. Gov. Res. Pract. **2**(3), 1–14 (2021). https://doi.org/10.1145/3462332
5. Casino, F., Dasaklis, T.K., Patsakis, C.: A systematic literature review of blockchain-based applications: current status, classification and open issues. Telematics Inform. **36**, 55–81 (2019). https://doi.org/10.1016/j.tele.2018.11.006
6. Chen, T., Guo, W., Gao, X., Liang, Z.: AI-based self-service technology in public service delivery: user experience and influencing factors. Gov. Inf. Q. **38**(4), 101520 (2021). https://doi.org/10.1016/j.giq.2020.101520
7. Clark, S.D., Lomax, N.: Linguistic and semantic factors in government e-petitions: a comparison between the united kingdom and the United States of America. Gov. Inf. Q. **37**(4), 101523 (2020). https://doi.org/10.1016/j.giq.2020.101523
8. Clavin, J., et al.: Blockchains for government: use cases and challenges. Digit. Gov. Res. Pract. **1**(3), 1–21 (2020). https://doi.org/10.1145/3427097
9. Domalis, G., Karacapilidis, N., Tsakalidis, D., Giannaros, A.: A trustable and interoperable decentralized solution for citizen-centric and cross-border eGovernance: a conceptual approach. In: Scholl, H.J., Gil-Garcia, J.R., Janssen, M., Kalampokis, E., Lindgren, I., Rodríguez Bolívar, M.P. (eds.) EGOV 2021. LNCS, vol. 12850, pp. 259–270. Springer, Cham (2021). https://doi.org/10.1007/978-3-030-84789-0_19
10. Dreyling, R., Jackson, E., Tammet, T., Labanava, A., Pappel, I.: Social, legal, and technical considerations for machine learning and artificial intelligence systems in government. In: Proceedings of the 23rd International Conference on Enterprise Information Systems, ICEIS, vol. 1, pp. 701–708. INSTICC, SciTePress (2021). https://doi.org/10.5220/0010452907010708
11. El-Haddadeh, R., Weerakkody, V., Osmani, M., Thakker, D., Kapoor, K.K.: Examining citizens' perceived value of internet of things technologies in facilitating public sector services engagement. Gov. Inf. Q. **36**(2), 310–320 (2019). https://doi.org/10.1016/j.giq.2018.09.009
12. Gil-Garcia, J.R., Flores-Zúñiga, M.A.: Towards a comprehensive understanding of digital government success: integrating implementation and adoption factors. Gov. Inf. Q. **37**(4), 101518 (2020). https://doi.org/10.1016/j.giq.2020.101518
13. Gil-Garcia, J.R., Helbig, N., Ojo, A.: Being smart: emerging technologies and innovation in the public sector. Gov. Inf. Q. **31**, I1–I8 (2014). https://doi.org/10.1016/j.giq.2014.09.001. iCEGOV 2012 Supplement
14. Giusti, L., Schladow, A., Boghani, A., Pomeroy, S., Wallen, N., Casalegno, F.: Designing a platform for participatory urbanism: transforming dialogue into action in underserved communities. In: Kotzé, P., Marsden, G., Lindgaard, G., Wesson, J., Winckler, M. (eds.) INTERACT 2013. LNCS, vol. 8117, pp. 796–803. Springer, Heidelberg (2013). https://doi.org/10.1007/978-3-642-40483-2_57

15. Kalampokis, E., Karamanou, A., Tarabanis, K.: Interoperability conflicts in linked open statistical data. Information **10**(8), 249 (2019). https://doi.org/10.3390/info10080249
16. Kalampokis, E., Karamanou, A., Tarabanis, K.: Applying explainable artificial intelligence techniques on linked open government data. In: Scholl, H.J., Gil-Garcia, J.R., Janssen, M., Kalampokis, E., Lindgren, I., Rodríguez Bolívar, M.P. (eds.) EGOV 2021. LNCS, vol. 12850, pp. 247–258. Springer, Cham (2021). https://doi.org/10.1007/978-3-030-84789-0_18
17. Kalampokis, E., Tambouris, E., Tarabanis, K.: A classification scheme for open government data: towards linking decentralised data. Int. J. Web Eng. Technol. **6**(3), 266–285 (2011). https://doi.org/10.1504/IJWET.2011.040725
18. Kankanhalli, A., Charalabidis, Y., Mellouli, S.: IoT and AI for smart government: a research agenda. Gov. Inf. Q. **36**(2), 304–309 (2019). https://doi.org/10.1016/j.giq.2019.02.003
19. Karacapilidis, N., Loukis, E., Dimopoulos, S.: A web-based system for supporting structured collaboration in the public sector. In: Traunmüller, R. (ed.) EGOV 2004. LNCS, vol. 3183, pp. 218–225. Springer, Heidelberg (2004). https://doi.org/10.1007/978-3-540-30078-6_36
20. Long, C.K., Agrawal, R., Trung, H.Q., Pham, H.V.: A big data framework for e-government in industry 4.0. Open Comput. Sci. **11**(1), 461–479 (2021). https://doi.org/10.1515/comp-2020-0191
21. McKenna, H.P.: Rethinking learning in the smart city: innovating through involvement, inclusivity, and interactivities with emerging technologies. In: Gil-Garcia, J.R., Pardo, T.A., Nam, T. (eds.) Smarter as the New Urban Agenda. PAIT, vol. 11, pp. 87–107. Springer, Cham (2016). https://doi.org/10.1007/978-3-319-17620-8_5
22. Milić, P., Veljković, N., Stoimenov, L.: Semantic technologies in e-government: toward openness and transparency. In: Rodríguez Bolívar, M.P. (ed.) Smart Technologies for Smart Governments. PAIT, vol. 24, pp. 55–66. Springer, Cham (2018). https://doi.org/10.1007/978-3-319-58577-2_4
23. Petsis, S., Karamanou, A., Kalampokis, E., Tarabanis, K.: Forecasting and explaining emergency department visits in a public hospital. J. Intell. Inf. Syst. 1–22 (2022). https://doi.org/10.1007/s10844-022-00716-6
24. Sarantis, D., Alexopoulos, C., Charalabidis, Y., Lachana, Z., Loutsaris, M.: Blockchain in digital government: research needs identification. In: Themistocleous, M., Papadaki, M., Kamal, M.M. (eds.) EMCIS 2020. LNBIP, vol. 402, pp. 188–204. Springer, Cham (2020). https://doi.org/10.1007/978-3-030-63396-7_13
25. de Sousa, W.G., de Melo, E.R.P., Bermejo, P.H.D.S., Farias, R.A.S., Gomes, A.O.: How and where is artificial intelligence in the public sector going? A literature review and research agenda. Gov. Inf. Q. **36**(4), 101392 (2019). https://doi.org/10.1016/j.giq.2019.07.004
26. Strejcek, G., Theil, M.: Technology push, legislation pull? E-government in the European Union. Decis. Support Syst. **34**(3), 305–313 (2003). https://doi.org/10.1016/S0167-9236(02)00123-9. Digital Government: Technologies and Practices
27. Sun, T.Q., Medaglia, R.: Mapping the challenges of artificial intelligence in the public sector: evidence from public healthcare. Gov. Inf. Q. **36**(2), 368–383 (2019). https://doi.org/10.1016/j.giq.2018.09.008
28. Tan, E., Mahula, S., Crompvoets, J.: Blockchain governance in the public sector: a conceptual framework for public management. Gov. Inf. Q. **39**(1), 101625 (2022). https://doi.org/10.1016/j.giq.2021.101625

29. Ubaldi, B., et al.: State of the art in the use of emerging technologies in the public sector. OECD Working Papers on Public Governance No. 31 (2019). https://doi.org/10.1787/932780bc-en
30. Webster, J., Watson, R.T.: Analyzing the past to prepare for the future: writing a literature review. MIS Q. **26**(2), xiii–xxiii (2002)
31. Wirtz, B.W., Langer, P.F., Fenner, C.: Artificial intelligence in the public sector - a research agenda. Int. J. Public Adm. **44**(13), 1103–1128 (2021). https://doi.org/10.1080/01900692.2021.1947319
32. Wirtz, B.W., Weyerer, J.C., Geyer, C.: Artificial intelligence and the public sector - applications and challenges. Int. J. Public Adm. **42**(7), 596–615 (2019). https://doi.org/10.1080/01900692.2018.1498103
33. Wirtz, B.W., Weyerer, J.C., Schichtel, F.T.: An integrative public IoT framework for smart government. Gov. Inf. Q. **36**(2), 333–345 (2019). https://doi.org/10.1016/j.giq.2018.07.001
34. Zuiderwijk, A., Chen, Y.C., Salem, F.: Implications of the use of artificial intelligence in public governance: a systematic literature review and a research agenda. Gov. Inf. Q. **38**, 101577 (2021). https://doi.org/10.1016/j.giq.2021.101577
35. Ølnes, S., Ubacht, J., Janssen, M.: Blockchain in government: benefits and implications of distributed ledger technology for information sharing. Gov. Inf. Q. **34**(3), 355–364 (2017). https://doi.org/10.1016/j.giq.2017.09.007

Adoption of Robotic Process Automation in the Public Sector: A Survey Study in Sweden

Gustaf Juell-Skielse[1](✉), Evrim Oya Güner[2], and Shengnan Han[2]

[1] University of Borås, 501 90 Borås, Sweden
gustaf.juell-skielse@hb.se

[2] Stockholm University, 164 07 Kista, Sweden

Abstract. The public sector has increased its use of robotic process automation (RPA) in administration, decision making and citizen services. Available studies mostly focused on the specific cases of using RPA in public organizations. Thus, we lack the helicopter view of the adoption of RPA in a country. In this paper, we present the results of a national survey of RPA adoption in the public sector in Sweden. The results show that the awareness of RPA is high in the Swedish public sector although the level of adoption is still modest. Also, there are notable differences in the level of adoption between central and local government. The study goes beyond the limitations of case studies, and contribute new knowledge of RRA adoption, benefits, routine capability and governance on a national level. The knowledge and insights can serve as a reference for other countries and public administrative models.

Keywords: Robotic process automation · Public sector · Information technology adoption · Survey · Routine capability · Benefit

1 Introduction

Robotic process automation (RPA) has emerged as an important technology for reducing repetitive and manual labor in administrative and standardized tasks [1, 2]. In recent years, the public sector has increased its use of robotic process automation (RPA) in administration, decision making and citizen services [3]. Available studies mostly focused on the specific cases of using RPA in public organizations [4]. Although the findings from these studies provide deep understanding of the RPA adoption by the case organizations in the public sector, we still lack a general helicopter view of how RPA is adopted in the public sector, its perceived benefits, and an understanding of RPA governance in public sector organizations. To fill this knowledge gap, we investigated the benefits and implications of RPA use in the Swedish public sector, with particular attention on RPA penetration, impact on routine capabilities, RPA governance, and distribution of responsibilities between administrators and IT personnel. A survey was e-mailed to 525 Swedish public sector organizations, and we received 217 usable responses. The results show that Swedish public sector organizations are aware that RPA can improve

Published by Springer Nature Switzerland AG 2022
M. Janssen et al. (Eds.): EGOV 2022, LNCS 13391, pp. 336–352, 2022.
https://doi.org/10.1007/978-3-031-15086-9_22

routine administrative tasks and capabilities, although the level of adoption is moderate. This paper contributes to the knowledge regarding RPA use in public organizations in Sweden. The paper demonstrates the RPA general penetration in public sector, as well the insights of RPA benefits and impacts on improving routine capabilities in pubic organizations. The paper also depicts the governance structure of RPA. The knowledge and insights can serve as a reference for other countries and public administrative models.

The remainder of this paper is structured accordingly. Section 2 presents a theoretical background to RPA, including governance, organizational benefits and routine capability. Section 3 describes the research method and the context. The results are presented in Sect. 4. Section 5 discusses the findings, limitations and future research. Section 6 concludes the paper.

2 Theoretical Background

Robotic Process Automation (RPA) is becoming established and "...can now be considered a mature technology which seems to have passed a hype without enduring a large dip in expectations." [2, p. 130]. Willcocks et al. define RPA as the automation of service tasks by configuring software that controls robots to perform the work previously done by humans [1]. Similarly, Penttinen et al. [5] and Dias et al. [6] describe RPA as a process automation technology configured to perform work by interacting with information systems through existing user interfaces [5–7]. Also, RPA can be combined with artificial intelligence to increase its ability to capture and process information, so called cognitive RPA [8, 9]. RPA is considered as lightweight IT since it is non-invasive [10] and easy to configure such that less programming skills are needed for its implementation [1, 11].

2.1 Level of Adoption

Public organizations have started to adopt RPA technology. By adoption we mean that an organization accepts and starts to use a technology [12]. Several cases of RPA implementation in public organizations have been reported in literature. Dias et al. [6] examined how organizations transform knowledge work when adopting artificial intelligence. The result is based on a case study of a Finnish government shared services center that implemented AI-centric robotic process automation. Houy et al. [8] report on a cognitive automation application of RPA for determining issue date of trade tax notices provided by municipalities using different notice layouts. The application was developed and tested as a prototype. Ranerup and Henriksen [13], reporting on a case from municipal social services, found that the adoption of RPA contributed to several public sector value positions: professionalism, efficiency, and service. On the other hand, Gustafsson [14] calls attention to conflicts and tensions in relation with the introduction of RPA in public organizations. Having results from three case studies conducted in Swedish municipalities, Gustafsson [14] shows how RPA integration in public services can potentially create tensions in the areas of governance (i.e., policies and legislations), public administration (i.e., organization and management), technical infrastructure and data (issues of privacy and security). Güner et al. [4] survey eight cases of RPA in public sector organizations. These cases include examples of RPA adoption for automating a variety of work practices and processes. For instance, at higher education institutions, RPA is adopted to automate payroll processes in HR practices [15] and to automate examination result manual data entries [16]. In both cases, automated processes involve high volumes of manual data entries. Local governments adopt RPA to automate administrative processes, case handling practices [17] and decision-making processes in social assistance practices [18, 19]. Although these cases show that public organizations have begun to adopt RPA technology, they do not provide a comprehensive picture of the level of adoption, which makes it difficult to understand how widespread the use of RPA technology is in a wider public context.

2.2 Benefits of RPA Adoption

Previous literature shows that there are several benefits associated with implementing RPA, including time savings, error reduction and cost savings [20–24]. For example, the cost of RPA software licenses range between 1/3 and 1/5 of Full Time Equivalent (FTE) costs [24–26]. Although the degree of FTE savings varies depending on the business context and the process type, a study by Wewerka and Reichert [27] shows that FTE savings can be calculated using simple variables (i.e., number of cases, processing time, and daily working time of the employee) with concrete measures. Wewerka and Reichert [27] found that successful RPA projects decrease FTE costs independent of the context. Kedziora and Kiviranta [23] show the impact of RPA on FTE savings in different industries. In some cases, Return on Investment (ROI) from RPA projects can be up to 200% within one year [28]. Time savings or reduced time is another benefit of RPA [20–22, 29]. Although some studies report that a human employee can complete tasks faster than the bots [30], RPA implementation usually increases the process speed [16, 20, 24, 27, 28, 31, 32]. As a result of increasing the process speed and reducing the task completion time, RPA implementation frees employees from repetitive and tedious work, giving them more time to perform value added critical tasks [33–35]. Another benefit of RPA is error reduction. Many data intensive processes (i.e., finance, accounting, insurance, healthcare, and telecommunication applications) are prone to human errors. RPA eliminates human errors and improves the accuracy and quality of the processes [6, 21, 22, 24, 36]. For example, a case study [16] showed that a task performed by an RPA bot was free of errors. The literature also shows that the increased accuracy leads to accountability, which is important for decision-making [5, 13, 36, 37].

In addition, some of the benefits of RPA such as accessibility, scalability, and improved compliance can be attributed directly to its technological features. According to Lacity and Willcocks [7], RPA is designed to meet security, scalability, auditability, compliance requirements, and aspects of work that support continuity of service [38]. RPA software saves the logs of each activity, which are performed based on pre-defined rules. The configuration of the bots to follow regulations allows processes to be audited easily [7, 39, 40]. A case study [32] showed that RPA provides transparency in actions and decisions and supports the compliance with regulations.

Table 1. Summary of benefits found in literature.

Benefit category	Description and motivation	Benefit	Reference/source
Reduce cost of case management	Cost reduction, i.e., based on ROI, FTE, working hours, task volume, and completion time	Cost reduction	[5, 13, 20, 21, 22, 23, 24, 30, 32, 33, 34]
		FTE savings	[23, 24, 27, 31]
		Scalability	[20, 21, 27, 31, 32]
Free up time for civil servants	Free up employees' time and increase productivity, i.e., accuracy of practices in a fast and consistent manner	Reduced time	[6, 16, 20–22, 27, 29–32, 34, 36]
		Free up employees' time	[6, 20, 23, 24, 28, 29, 34, 36, 41]
Improve the working environment	Provide a working environment where employees develop new skills, perform more value-added tasks, share knowledge, and collaborate	Skills development	[6, 8, 24, 41]
		Perform value-added task	[20, 24, 29, 34, 36]
		Knowledge sharing	[6]
Increase citizen service	Increased citizen service through improved service accessibility, and simpler and faster decision-making processes	Faster processing	[13, 16, 20, 24, 27, 28, 30–32, 34]
		24/7 access to services	[13, 22, 27, 28, 30]
		Service continuity	[32, 38]
Increase legal certainty in case handling	Error reduction and increased quality in case handling by elimination of human errors, decisions according to pre-defined rules, data quality checks, process compliance	Error reduction	[16, 22, 29, 30, 32, 36]
		Increased compliance	[7, 27, 28, 30–32, 34]
		Increased accuracy	[6, 13, 21, 22, 24, 32, 34, 36]

A recent study of RPA professionals found that the main expected benefits of RPA adoption were consistent improvements in speed, availability, compliance, and quality [27]. Additionally, benefits for public organizations are usually aligned with the pre-defined benefits for RPA use and adoption. For example, Ranerup and Henriksen [13] found that automated decision-making was part of digitalization initiatives when the main benefits for adoption were clear before RPA implementation. Accordingly, automated decision-making with RPA significantly reduced the response time for social assistance applications and improved the efficiency of the social services. As a result, time savings were achieved processing applications, costs were reduced, and accountability was increased [13]. Also, RPA adoption reduced response times and the administrative workload of employees in the short term and increased the quality of social work in the long term [41]. In addition, RPA provides a cost-effective automation solution with a short implementation time [5, 42]. The benefits identified in the literature were placed into five benefit categories adapted to the perspective of public administration: free up time for employees, reduce cost for administration, improve working environment, increase customer service, and increase legal certainty, see Table 1.

2.3 Technology as Routine Capability

Swanson [43] proposes an overarching perspective – "technology as routine capability" – for the study of the interplay between technology, routines, capabilities, and practices. This perspective theorizes that routine is integral to technology itself and that capabilities are associated with device-enabled (or technology-enabled) routines by which human practices are advanced.

Technology as routine capability makes routine the linchpin in the analysis. Routines are patterns of action of people as well as machines. Swanson [43] argues that devices (technologies) are employed only through routines (device as routine component). The affordance offered by devices is largely received through routines (affordance built-in routine performance). Practice entails a family of routines executed in coordination and in a certain social order (routine as practice component). Since routine is integral to technology itself, the capability generated by the new routines will advance human practice (technology as routine capability built in practice). Therefore, practice is theorized as constituted from routines and capabilities. Practices can be advanced at three levels: individual, organizational, and social [43]. The individual level is concerned with the human practice, which is improved by the new routine capabilities provided by technology. The organizational level is about gaining new or improved existing routine capabilities of the organization through technology. The social level is about the whole society, including industries, professional services, professions, and other units of the society that are advanced by the new routine capabilities.

Swanson [43] links capabilities with practices and argues that "technology as routine capability serves to advance human practice". Advancing human practice occurs in a variety of contexts with regards to improvement such as "its economics, social acceptance, or politics" [43, p. 1011]. Improvement covers, e.g., "simplifying it or otherwise reducing its costs, for instance, or finding new outlets for it, expanding its presence, or increasing its appeal, making it more enjoyable, or obtaining favored social treatment for it, or improving its reputation" [43, p. 1011].

Considering that people and organizations constantly seek to improve their practices and therefore their routines, it can be concluded that advancing human practice drives change in technology [43]. The new technology, in turn, promotes human practice and unites new routines and devices to provide new capabilities. In addition, Swanson claims that this perspective of technology as routine capability serves as "a new theoretical and meta-analytic framework that allows insights from multiple studies to accumulate in a way that both illuminates and motivates further research on technological change" [43, p. 1008].

2.4 RPA Governance

IT has come to play a more strategic role in digitalizing public services. The governance of IT is becoming an integral part of public governance that define and implement processes, structures, and relational mechanisms that enable both business- and IT people to execute their responsibilities in support of effective and qualitative public services and the creation of more public value from IT enabled investments [c.f. 44]. Research on RPA governance is limited, but RPA is considered a lightweight IT with a higher level of end-user involvement in configuration and implementation [1]. This perspective implies a hybrid governance model [45] that involves both business and IT functions. Forrester [46] suggests that organizations establish centers of excellence for RPA governance, with business roles, such as process owners and subject matter experts, and IT roles, such as developers. Hence, it is expected that business personnel, such as administrators, are actively involved in RPA governance in the public sector.

3 Method

The survey reported here was mailed to 525 public sector organizations in Sweden – 235 selected government agencies and all 290 municipalities. 31 government agencies were not included because they were either currently inactive (e.g., Oljekrisnämnden) or too small to have their own e-mail address (e.g., Riksvärderingsnämnden). Also, the Swedish Courts, were treated as one authority.

The questionnaire,, see Appendix, included 20 questions related to the following areas: level of adoption, routine capability, benefits, and RPA governance (distribution of responsibilities between administrators and IT personnel). Between December 2019 and May 2020, invitations to participate were e-mailed to the selected organizations and the e-mail included a link to the online survey. The survey used three question formats: Likert scales, multiple responses, and open responses. The online survey format was chosen to simplify survey distribution, enable different answering patterns and simplify data analysis [47].

After the survey data were collected, we performed a thematic analysis of the data. The analysis included six steps: familiarization with data, generating initial codes, searching for themes among codes, reviewing themes, defining and naming themes, and producing the final report [48]. To ensure reliability and validity of the results, the team performed the analysis jointly. The consensus and agreements in interpretations were achieved through team discussions and meetings.

3.1 Research Context

This research is situated in the context of Swedish public administration rooted in the Nordic social model of European countries [49, 50]. The Nordic model is unique as it combines high levels of social protection expenditures and universal welfare provisions with high levels of employment and low levels of poverty by emphasizing equity and efficiency [51]. Also, Sweden is ambitious in implementing automated decision making. The Swedish National Audit Office [52] has recently evaluated the use of automated decision-making in 13 of the largest Swedish government agencies. These 13 agencies make 148 million decisions annually (e.g., parental benefit, income taxation, and driving licenses). 138 million of these decisions are included in automated decision processes and 121 million are fully automated. Automation has shortened lead-times for decision-making without increasing costs for processing. In addition, automated decision-making has improved some aspects of legal certainty leading to cases are treated more equally.

4 Results

Of the 525 public organizations (290 municipalities and 235 government agencies) that were sent an invitation to participate, 217 responded (response rate of 41%): 90 from government agencies and 127 from municipalities. The respondents had different roles in their organizations: 53% were involved in IT; 21% were administrators such as case handling officers and accountants; 21% worked with digitalization and other strategic staff functions such as organizational development and legal issues; and 4% did not specify their roles.

4.1 Level of Adoption

The level of adoption of robotic process automation is illustrated in Fig. 1. Nine government agencies and 40 municipalities (23% of the total number of respondents) had already implemented and used robotic process automation, 22 government agencies and 63 municipalities planned to implement RPA (39% of the total number of respondents), and 59 government agencies and 24 municipalities (38% of the total number of respondents) had no plans to implement RPA.

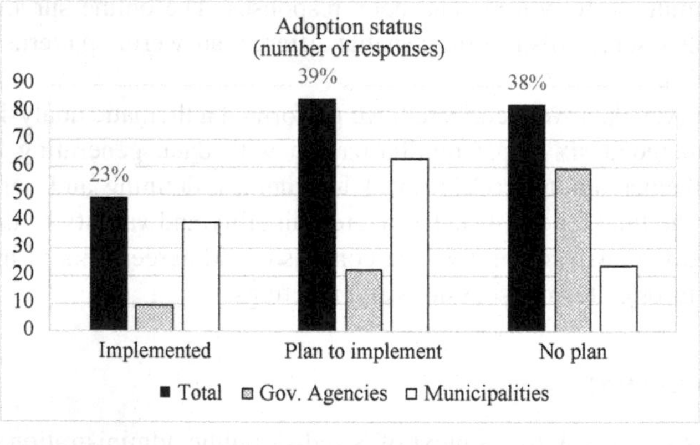

Fig. 1. Adoption status.

Over a third (38%) of the respondents – 24 municipalities and 59 government agencies – did not have plans to implement robotic process automation (Fig. 1). The motives for not implementing RPA can be roughly divided into two categories: business and technical. Business motives are related to organizational benefits and business process characteristics, whereas technical motives are related to IT policies and legacy systems. The business motives for not implementing RPA differ somewhat. Some respondents showed an interest in RPA but had not developed any plans for adopting RPA. Some respondents did not find that RPA provides sufficient value in relation to other digitization initiatives or that their business processes or decision-making are suitable for automation using RPA. The main technical motive for not implementing RPA is that organizations preferred to integrate systems at the Application Program Interface (API) level rather than using RPA. In addition, some organizations require software suppliers to provide open APIs when sourcing new systems and that they focus on transforming processes to become fully digitally integrated. In addition, organizations believe that RPA integration threatens to cement outdated information systems by automating simple and short-lived processes and that RPA will increase IT maintenance costs.

4.2 Routine Capability

New Routines
Respondents who had implemented RPA in their organizations acknowledged that new routines have been built: (1) automated processes, e.g., administration processes and financial processes (reporting support for social assistance services and payroll management); (2) PRA speeds up the processing of routine tasks and minimizes the risk of errors which give more time to humans to make quality decisions; (3) RPA replacing manual routines as new routines in public services; and (4) management of RPA and the bots create new routines that will require new job descriptions and positions.

Respondents who plan to implement RPA indicated that the organizations have positive expectations of implementing RPA such as automating different processes that consist of manual repetitive tasks. However, to implement RPA in the organizations, they need to develop new management and RPA implementation methods, they need to prioritize processes that can be automated by RPA, and they need to train and educate employees in the use of the RPA solutions.

New Capabilities (RPA as New Capabilities Advancing Practice)
We identified ten routine capabilities related to RPA implementation: (1) reduce costs in administration and provide public services; (2) provide quality analysis and add value to their services to better meet the citizens' individual needs; (3) free up time for the employees; (4) reduce human errors and avoid human emotions in the employees' work; (5) provide more time for employees to develop new skills; (6) produce more confident decisions after RPA through an analysis of a case; (7) make work more process oriented; (8) develop new e-services that complement RPA; (9) improve digital capabilities of the employees and increase organizational digital maturity; and (10) use RPA to simplify and integrate different systems. From the perspective of routine capabilities, such applications change the routines in an improvisational way and advance the practices. In addition, the organizations point out that new management practices and change management programs are necessary for the implementation of RPA.

Handling of Complaints Caused by RPA

Since the use and implementation of RPA is in the early stage, very few complaints are related to RPA implementation. The survey indicates that most of the organizations handle the complaints the same way as other complaints received in the public services. For example, the complaints are received through a customer center and then forwarded to the digitization councils. Some respondents noted that the use of RPA is only changing the internal work processes and citizens may not notice the changes. Thus, the complaints related to the use of RPA in public services are not an issue at the moment.

4.3 Benefits Fulfilment of RPA Adoption

The result shows that organizations that have already implemented RPA and organizations that plan to implement RPA want to free up time for administrators (Table 2). Other benefits are considered less important. The means for benefits for the organizations that implemented RPA are significantly lower than the means for importance ($P < 0.01$; paired t-test assuming two-tailed distribution) for the benefits free up time for administrators and reduce cost of case management. For the remaining three benefits, it was not possible to determine whether the benefits' importance and fulfilment were significantly different.

Table 2. Importance of benefits for RPA for public organizations that have implemented and plan to implement RPA. Benefits fulfilment for public organizations that have implemented RPA: 1 – lowest and 5 – highest.

Goal	Importance of Goal Implemented (1-5)		Goal Fulfilment Implemented (1-5)		Importance of Goal Planned (1-5)	
	Mean	Median	Mean	Median	Mean	Median
Free up time for administrators *	4,6	5	4,1	4	4,5	5
Reduce cost of case management *	3,6	4	3,0	3	3,7	4
Improve the working environment	3,3	3	3,1	3	3,4	3
Increase citizen service	3,6	4	3,2	3	3,5	4
Increase legal certainty in case handling	3,8	4	3,6	3	3,7	4

*Means significantly lower ($P < 1\%$) for benefits fulfilment than benefits importance for organizations who have implemented RPA.

In addition, the respondents had the possibility to provide free-text descriptions of the benefits. Most free-text responses were variations of the benefits in Table 3. However, we identified a handful of new benefits: build knowledge, support digitalization in general, increase quality of information, and perform technical integration. Building knowledge relates to organizations learning to effectively use RPA. RPA is becoming an integral part of technologies for digitalization of public organizations in general. Increasing quality of information is related to the benefit increase legal certainty in case handling but applies to administration in general. Also, RPA is a tool for technical integration of government information systems.

4.4 RPA Governance

The majority of agencies used or planned to use standard software (e.g., Ui-Path, Blue Prism, and Automation Anywhere) when adopting RPA (Table 3). Also, almost half of the agencies use or plan to use consultants to configure the software (45% for implemented and 54% for planned), while 16% of implemented and 31% of plan to configure the software internally. In addition, only a few agencies have developed (8%) or plan to develop (13%) their own software for RPA.

Table 3. Overview of how the agencies govern or plan to govern RPA software.

How do you implement RPA software?	Implemented (n = 49)	Plan to implement (n = 85)
We develop software for RPA internally	8%	13%
We buy standard software for RPA	82%	76%
We set-up and configure the RPA software internally	16%	31%
We use consultants to set-up and configure the RPA software	45%	54%

Administrators were involved, to various degree, in IT-related tasks when public organizations adopt RPA (Table 4). A five-step scale was used to measure involvement: 1 (not involved) and 5 (involved to a high degree). Administrative staff were highly involved in managing requirements and setting up robots, but they were rarely involved in the actual purchasing of the RPA software.

Table 4. IT-related tasks performed or planned to be performed by administrators in conjunction with the adoption of RPA: 1 – not involved and 5 – involved to a high degree.

IT-related tasks performed by administrators	Implemented (1-5)		Planned (1-5)	
	Mean	Median	Mean	Median
Set-up of robots *	3,9	4	3,2	3
Requirements Management *	3,8	4	3,3	3
Test	3,4	4	2,9	3
Implementation *	3,1	3	2,5	2
Purchase of software for RPA	2,1	1	1,8	1

*Significantly higher means ($P < 0.05$) for organizations that have implemented RPA compared to organizations that plan to implement RPA.

There is a statistically significant difference ($P < 0.05$) in the expectations of administrators to participate in the management of requirements, set-up, and implementation of robots of the public organizations that plan to implement RPA and the experience of the public organizations that have implemented RPA. Public organizations that had implemented RPA responded that administrators were more involved in these three tasks than expected.

5 Discussion

This paper studies the current adoption and implementation of RPA in Swedish public organizations. The results show that the awareness of RPA is high in the Swedish public sector though the level of adoption is still modest. Also, there are notable differences in the level of adoption between central and local government. The reasons for this discrepancy seem to be that many government agencies do not find RPA to be suitable for automating their processes or decision-making and that RPA threatens to increase dependency on outdated information systems. The results indicate that Swedish public organizations use standard software for RPA, have positive experiences and expectations of using RPA, and are aware of the advantages and benefits of implementing RPA. RPA improves the current routines (e.g., administrative, and decision-making processes), which results in better performance of civil servants because RPA frees them from repetitive work, which gives them more time to do valuable work, including personalizing services for citizens. The organizations that do not plan to adopt RPA are mainly hindered by economic and technical reasons.

The study also finds that RPA generates routine capability for public organizations which produce benefit, such as free up work time for valuable tasks, improving working environments, reducing errors in handling cases, and increase personalized citizen service. However, the results show that the benefits of freeing up time for administrators and reducing costs of case management are lower than expected. The reasons for these results are unclear but could be related to the fact that public organizations need to also build knowledge for how to appropriately use RPA assets and how to manage their impact on organizational performance [53]. Clearly, the administrative personnel are heavily involved in the set-up and implementation of the software robots which demonstrate the common governance structure of RPA. Which indicates that organizations that plan to implement RPA underestimate the involvement of administrative staff in managing requirements, set-up, and implementation of the robots as compared to the experience from organizations that have implemented RPA. That is, public organizations planning to implement RPA need to better prepare administrative staff to use lightweight IT, such as RPA, and increase the requirements on administrative staff to be actively involved in IT-related work.

The study provides a first overview of RPA adoption in the public sector on the country level. Moreover, it provides a case of RPA in the context of the Nordic administrative model with a strong emphasis on equity and efficiency [49, 51]. In this context, the use of RPA could potentially help to improve efficiency and legal certainty in case handling and support digitalization by providing means of lightweight IT [11].

The knowledge and insights can serve as a reference for other countries and public administrative models. We present five guidelines that would help towards a broader adoption of RPA in Sweden and in general. First, the adoption of RPA in public sector is necessary to improve the quality of public administration and service quality to citizens. Standard RPA solutions can be easily adopted and added to organizational IT infrastructure since RPA is a lightweight IT. Second, there are challenges to identify which process to be automated. In Sweden, public organizations automate various processes, for example, internal administration process, decisions of social assistance, school students' healthcare management, and income support process. Public organizations need to analyze their routines and organizational needs before they select which process to automate. Third, the identified benefits serve as a framework for public organizations to formulate goals for RPA and for evaluating its usefulness, however, the benefits may not occur equally in all cases of RPA adoption. Fourth, public organizations must prepare public administrators for participating in the management, set-up, and implementation of software robots. Therefore, public organizations need to build knowledge about the appropriate use of RPA assets and how to manage the RPA assets, so they improve their performance. Fifth, public organizations need to build a new RPA governance structure to manage RPA operations and to facilitate the collaboration between the IT organization and the administrative staff.

6 Conclusion and Future Work

We conclude that the awareness of RPA is high in the Swedish public sector but that the level of adoption is still modest. One possible limitation is that data collection was primarily carried out before the COVID-19 pandemic fully hit Sweden. There might be a quick shift towards automating routines in public administration because of the pandemic, which is not shown in our data [54]. We anticipate that the number of organizations without plans should decrease significantly. Another limitation of the study is that the data do not completely capture the Swedish public sector, but it is expected that most Swedish government agencies and municipalities will be invited to participate as data collection continues. Hence, we expect to establish a more complete understanding of the status of RPA adoption in the Swedish public sector. It would also be interesting to extend the survey to include other sectors and compare the results with other countries. Also, the use of RPA in the public sector could provide an interesting case of lightweight IT to overcome the challenges of outdated systems that hinder digitalization.

Appendix. Survey RPA Adoption Swedish Public Administration

(The survey was translated to English from Swedish. The survey was conducted in Swedish.)

<u>RPA was described accordingly in the survey:</u> *By RPA is meant that work processes are automated using software robots. Repetitive tasks are automated by the software robots mimicking how people perform the tasks. Normally this is done by the robot communicating with different computer systems via the user interfaces.*

1. Which statement is true for your organization? a) We are a municipality b) We are a government agency.
2. Which statement is true for your organization? a) We have implemented and use RPA in our business. b) We plan to implement RPA in our business. c) We do not plan to implement RPA in our business. (a - Respondents directed to answer questions 3 – 13, b - Respondents directed to answer questions 3 – 6 and 15 – 20; c - Respondent directed to answer questions 3 – 6 and 14)

3–6. Background information about demographics and respondent's role.

7. Were new work routines created during or after the implementation of RPA? a) Yes, examples: ____________ b) No
8. Do these new work routines mean that your organization also gains new capabilities, for example, in the form of more time for critical decisions, increased flexibility, or more support in decision-making? a) Yes, examples: ____________ b) No
9. Has the implementation of RPA led to complaints from residents/citizens? a) Yes, examples: ____________ b) No
10. How was the RPA software acquired? More than one answer is possible. a) We developed it internally b) We bought a standard software (e.g., UiPath, Blue Prism, and Automation Anywhere) c) We adapted and configured the software internally d) We hired external consultants to customize and configure the software
11. How involved are/were business staff, e.g., administrators, in the introduction of RPA? Rate all, from low (1) to high (5). a) Purchase of software b) Test of RPA software c) Identify requirements d) Set-up of software for specific work processes e) Implementation of software
12. What are the expected benefits of implementing RPA? Rate all, from low (1) to high (5). a) Free up time for administrators b) Increase citizen service c) Increased legal certainty in case handling d) Reduce cost of case management e) Improve the working environment f) Other: ____________
13. How well did you achieve the benefits of RPA? Rate all, from low (1) to high (5). a) Free up time for administrators b) Increase citizen service c) Increased legal certainty in case handling d) Reduce cost of case management e) Improve the working environment
14. Why do you plan not to implement RPA? Free-text answer: ____________
15. Will new work routines be created during or after the introduction of RPA? If so, give examples of new work routines that will be created. a) Yes, examples: ____________ b) No
16. Do these new work routines mean that your organization also will gain new capabilities, for example, in the form of more time for critical decisions, increased flexibility, or more support in decision-making? If yes, feel free to describe with examples how your routine capability has increased because of RPA. a) Yes, examples: ____________ b) No
17. Can the introduction of RPA lead to complaints from residents/citizens? If so, how do you plan to handle these complaints? a) Yes, examples: ____________ b) No
18. How do you plan to acquire the RPA software? More than one answer is possible. a) We will develop it internally b) We will buy standard software (e.g., UiPath, Blue

Prism, and Automation Anywhere) c) We will adapt and configure the software internally d) We will hire external consultants to customize and configure the software

19. How involved will business personnel be, e.g., administrators, be in the introduction of RPA? Rate all, from low (1) to high (5). a) Purchase of software b) Test of RPA software c) Identify requirements d) Set up software for specific work processes e) Implementation of software
20. What are the expected benefits of implementing RPA? Rate all, from low (1) to high (5). a) Free up time for administrators b) Increase citizen service c) Increased legal certainty in case handling d) Reduce cost of case management e) Improve the working environment f) Other: ________

References

1. Willcocks, L.P., Lacity, M., Craig, A.: The IT function and robotic process automation. The Outsourcing Unit Working Research Paper Series (15/5). London School of Economics Outsourcing Unit Working Papers (2015)
2. Kregel, I., Koch, J., Plattfaut, R.: Beyond the hype: robotic process automation's public perception over time. J. Organ. Comput. Electron. Commer. **31**(2), 130–150 (2021)
3. Ivančić, L., Suša Vugec, D., Bosilj Vukšić, V.: Robotic process automation: systematic literature review. In: Di Ciccio, C., et al. (eds.) BPM 2019. LNBIP, vol. 361, pp. 280–295. Springer, Cham (2019). https://doi.org/10.1007/978-3-030-30429-4_19
4. Güner, E.O., Han, S., Juell-Skielse, G.: Enhancing routine capability through robotic process automation in the public sector: a case survey. In: Juell-Skielse, G., Lindgren, I., Åkesson, M. (eds.) Service Automation in the Public Sector, Concepts, Empirical Examples and Challenges, pp. 169–188. Springer, Cham (2022). https://doi.org/10.1007/978-3-030-92644-1_9
5. Penttinen, E., Kasslin, H., Asatiani, A.: How to choose between robotic process automation and back-end system automation? In: 28th European Conference on Information Systems, Portsmouth, UK (2018)
6. Dias, M., Pan, S., Tim, Y.: Knowledge embodiment of human and machine interactions: Robotic process automation at the Finland government. In: 27th European Conference on Information Systems (ECIS), Stockholm, Uppsala, Sweden, June 8–14, (2019)
7. Lacity, M.C., Willcocks, L.P.: Robotic process automation: the next transformation lever for shared services. The Outsourcing Unit Working Research Paper Series (16/01), London School of Economics (2016)
8. Houy, C., Hamberg, M., Fettke, P.: Robotic Process Automation in Public Administrations. Digitalisierung von Staat und Verwaltung (2019)
9. Juell-Skielse, G., Balasuriya, P., Güner, E.O., Han, S.: Cognitive robotic process automation: concept and impact on dynamic IT capabilities in public organizations. In: Juell-Skielse, G., Lindgren, I., Åkesson, M. (eds.) Service Automation in the Public Sector. PROIS, pp. 65–88. Springer, Cham (2022). https://doi.org/10.1007/978-3-030-92644-1_4
10. Hofmann, P., Samp, C., Urbach, N.: Robotic process automation. Electron. Mark. **30**(1), 99–106 (2019). https://doi.org/10.1007/s12525-019-00365-8
11. Bygstad, B.: Generative innovation: a comparison of lightweight and heavyweight IT. J. Inf. Technol. **32**(2), 180–193 (2016)
12. Salahshour Rad, M., Nilashi, M., Dahlan, H.M.: Information technology adoption: a review of the literature and classification. Univ. Access Inf. Soc. **17**(2), 361–390 (2018)

13. Ranerup, A., Henriksen, H.Z.: Value positions viewed through the lens of automated decision making: the case of social services. Gov. Inf. Q. **36**(4) (2019)
14. Gustafsson, M.S.: Integration of RPA in public services: a tension approach to the case of income support in Sweden. In: Juell-Skielse, G., Lindgren, I., Åkesson, M. (eds.) Service Automation in the Public Sector. PROIS, pp. 109–127. Springer, Cham (2022). https://doi.org/10.1007/978-3-030-92644-1_6
15. Denagama Vitharanage, I.M., Bandara, W., Syed, R., Toman, D.: An empirically supported conceptualization of robotic process automation (RPA) benefits. In: 28th European Conference on Information Systems (ECIS 2020), Marrakesh, Morocco, 15–17 June 2020 (2020)
16. Patil, S., Mane, V., Patil, P.: Social innovation in education system by using Robotic Process Automation (RPA). Int. J. Innov. Technol. Explor. Eng. **8**(11), 3757–3760 (2019)
17. Lindgren, I.: Exploring the use of robotic process automation in local government. In: EGOV-CeDEM-ePart 2020, pp. 249–258 (2020)
18. Ranerup, A.: Translating robotic process automation in social work: aspirational changes and the role of technology. In: 11th Scandinavian Conference on Information Systems (SCIS 2020), Sundsvall, Sweden, 9–11 August 2020 (2020)
19. Ranerup, A., Henriksen, H.Z.: Digital discretion: unpacking human and technological agency in automated decision making in Sweden's social services. Soc. Sci. Comput. Rev. 1–17 (2020)
20. Ratia, M., Myllärniemi, J., Helander, N.: Robotic process automation-creating value by digitalizing work in the private healthcare? In: Proceedings of the 22nd International Academic Mindtrek Conference, pp. 222–227 (2018)
21. Geyer-Klingeberg, J., Nakladal, J., Baldauf, F., Veit, F.: Process mining and robotic process automation: a perfect match. In: BPM (Dissertation/Demos/Industry), pp. 124–131 (2018)
22. Jimenez-Ramirez, A., Reijers, H.A., Barba, I., Del Valle, C.: A method to improve the early stages of the robotic process automation lifecycle. In: Giorgini, P., Weber, B. (eds.) CAiSE 2019. LNCS, vol. 11483, pp. 446–461. Springer, Cham (2019). https://doi.org/10.1007/978-3-030-21290-2_28
23. Kedziora, D., Kiviranta, H.M.: Digital business value creation with Robotic Process Automation (RPA) in northern and central Europe. Management **13**(2), 161–174 (2018)
24. Naga Lakshmi, M.V.N., Vijayakumar, T., Sai Sricharan, Y.V.N.: Robotic process automation, an enabler for shared services transformation. Int. J. Innov. Technol. Explor. Eng. **8**(6), 1882–1890 (2019)
25. Enríquez, J.G., Jiménez-Ramírez, A., Domínguez-Mayo, F.J., García-García, J.A.: Robotic process automation: a scientific and industrial systematic mapping study. IEEE Access **8**, 39113–39129 (2020). https://doi.org/10.1109/ACCESS.2020.2974934
26. Capgemini: Robotic process automation-Robots conquer business processes in back offices (2016). https://www.capgemini.com/consulting-de/wp-content/uploads/sites/32/2017/08/robotic-process-automationstudy.pdf
27. Wewerka, J., Reichert, M.: Towards quantifying the effects of robotic process automation. In: International Workshop on Frontiers of Process Aware Systems (FoPAS 2020), in Conjunction with EDOC 2020, Eindhoven, The Netherlands (2020)
28. Lacity, M.C., Willcocks, L.P., Craig, A.: Robotic Process Automation: Mature Capabilities in the Energy Sector. The Outsourcing Unit Working Research Paper Series (15/06). The London School of Economics and Political Science, London, UK (2015)
29. Hallikainen, P., Bekkhus, R., Pan, S.L.: How OpusCapita used internal RPA capabilities to offer services to clients. MIS Q. Exec. **17**, 41–52 (2018)
30. Aguirre, S., Rodriguez, A.: Automation of a business process using robotic process automation (RPA): a case study. In: Figueroa-García, J.C., López-Santana, E.R., Villa-Ramírez, J.L., Ferro-Escobar, R. (eds.) WEA 2017. CCIS, vol. 742, pp. 65–71. Springer, Cham (2017). https://doi.org/10.1007/978-3-319-66963-2_7

31. Lacity, M.C., Willcocks, L.P., Craig, A.: Robotic process automation at Telefónica O2. The Outsourcing Unit Working Research Paper Series (15/02). The London School of Economics and Political Science, London, UK (2015)
32. Schmitz, M., Dietze, C., Czarnecki, C.: Enabling digital transformation through robotic process automation at Deutsche Telekom. In: Urbach, N., Röglinger, M. (eds.) Digitalization Cases: How Organizations Rethink Their Business for the Digital Age, Management for Professionals, pp. 15–33. Springer, Cham (2019). https://doi.org/10.1007/978-3-319-95273-4_2
33. Bhatnagar, N.: Role of robotic process automation in pharmaceutical industries. In: Hassanien, A.E., Azar, A.T., Gaber, T., Bhatnagar, R., F. Tolba, M. (eds.) AMLTA 2019. AISC, vol. 921, pp. 497–504. Springer, Cham (2020). https://doi.org/10.1007/978-3-030-14118-9_50
34. Suri, V.K., Elia, M., van Hillegersberg, J.: Software bots - the next frontier for shared services and functional excellence. In: Oshri, I., Kotlarsky, J., Willcocks, L.P. (eds.) Global Sourcing 2017. LNBIP, vol. 306, pp. 81–94. Springer, Cham (2017). https://doi.org/10.1007/978-3-319-70305-3_5
35. Leno, V., Dumas, M., Maggi, F.M., La Rosa, M.: Multi-perspective process model discovery for robotic process automation. In: CEUR Workshop Proceedings, pp. 37–45 (2018)
36. Fernandez, D., Aman, A.: Impacts of robotic process automation on global accounting services. Asian J. Account. Gov. **9**, 123–132 (2018)
37. Šimek, D., Šperka, R.: How robot/human orchestration can help in an HR department: a case study from a pilot implementation. Organizacija **52**, 204–217 (2019)
38. Torkhani, R., Laval, J., Malek, H., Moalla, N.: Intelligent framework for business process automation and re-engineering. In: 2018 International Conference on Intelligent Systems (IS), pp. 624–629. IEEE (2018)
39. Syed, R., et al.: Robotic Process Automation: contemporary themes and challenges. Comput. Ind. **115** (2020)
40. Lacity, M.C., Willcocks, L.P.: A new approach to automating services. MIT Sloan Manag. Rev. **58**(1), 41 (2016)
41. Nauwerck, G., Cajander, Å.: Automatic for the people: implementing robotic process automation in social work. In: 17th European Conference on Computer-Supported Cooperative Work (2019)
42. Cewe, C., Koch, D., Mertens, R.: Minimal effort requirements engineering for robotic process automation with test driven development and screen recording. In: Teniente, E., Weidlich, M. (eds.) BPM 2017. LNBIP, vol. 308, pp. 642–648. Springer, Cham (2018). https://doi.org/10.1007/978-3-319-74030-0_51
43. Swanson, E.B.: Technology as routine capability. MIS Q. **43**(3), 1007–1024 (2019)
44. Van Grembergen, W., De Haes, S.: Enterprise Governance of Information Technology: Achieving Strategic Alignment and Value. Springer, New York (2009). https://doi.org/10.1007/978-0-387-84882-2
45. Weill, P., Ross, J.: A matrixed approach to designing IT governance. MIT Sloan Manag. Rev. **46**(2), 26–34 (2005)
46. Forrester Research: Building a Center of Expertise to Support Robotic Automation (2014). https://neoops.com/wp-content/uploads/2014/03/Forrester-RA-COE.pdf. Accessed 18 Mar 2022
47. Evans, J.R., Mathur, A.: The value of online surveys. Internet Res. **15**(2), 195–219 (2005)
48. Braun, V., Clarke, V.: Using thematic analysis in psychology. Qual. Res. Psychol. **3**(2), 77–101 (2006)
49. Premfors, R.: Reshaping the democratic state: Swedish experiences in a comparative perspective. Public Adm. **76**(1), 141–159 (1998)
50. Greve, B.: What characterise the Nordic welfare state model? J. Soc. Sci. **3**(2), 43–51 (2007)

51. Sapir, A.: Globalization and the reform of European social models. JCMS: J. Common Mark. Stud. **44**(2), 369–390 (2006)
52. Swedish National Audit Office: Automatiserat beslutsfattande i statsförvaltningen – effektivt, men kontroll och uppföljning brister. Riksrevisionen 2020:22, Sweden (2020)
53. Soh, C., Markus, M.L.: How IT creates business value: a process theory synthesis. In: International Conference on Information Systems, p. 4 (1995)
54. Yang, G.Z., et al.: Combating COVID-19—The role of robotics in managing public health and infectious diseases. Sci. Robot. **5**(40) (2020)

Why is it Difficult to Implement Robotic Process Automation?
Empirical Cases from Swedish Municipalities

Ida Lindgren(✉), Björn Johansson, Fredrik Söderström, and Daniel Toll

Department of Management and Engineering; Information Systems, Linköping University, 581 83 Linköping, Sweden

{ida.lindgren,bjorn.se.johansson,fredrik.soderstrom,daniel.toll}@liu.se

Abstract. Swedish municipalities have been urged by policy makers to implement automation technologies to make administrative work more cost-efficient. As a response, a large set of municipalities have attempted to implement Robotic Process Automation (RPA) solutions with the intention to speed up administrative processes. However, although RPA has been promoted for several years, implementation has been limited and slow. This paper explores challenges related to RPA implementation experienced by three Swedish municipalities. We use an extensive interpretive case study as our empirical foundation, generated in collaboration with three Swedish municipalities, complemented with interviews with RPA consultants. Through interpretive analysis, we generate challenges along four themes. Our analysis shows that RPA implementation requires that different organizational sub-units and stakeholders cooperate. Challenges arise from: initiating RPA top-down without bottom-up support; insufficient process- and IT-competence; dependence on individual enthusiasts and external RPA consultants; and subsequent difficulties in finding the right processes to automate. Our study contributes with empirical illustrations of how RPA implementation is made difficult by current organizational structures and resources. We confirm and further contribute to previous findings by pointing to multiple dimensions in which challenges can arise.

Keywords: Automation · Public sector · Municipality level · Robotic process automation · Case study

1 Introduction

The Swedish welfare system is currently being challenged by increasing costs and problems in recruiting personnel that can provide services to citizens. This affects municipalities in particular, as these organizations are responsible for delivering welfare services to citizens on the local government level [5]. Simply put, there is a general concern that the municipalities, in a near future, will fail to provide quality service to citizens if costs are not cut [20]. For almost a decade, Swedish policymakers have therefore promoted

Published by Springer Nature Switzerland AG 2022
M. Janssen et al. (Eds.): EGOV 2022, LNCS 13391, pp. 353–368, 2022.
https://doi.org/10.1007/978-3-031-15086-9_23

automation technologies as a means for municipalities to increase quality and cut costs in administrative work related to public service provision. The promotion has mainly been made through a set of influential policy documents (e.g., [20–22]). Interestingly, Robotic Process Automation (RPA) is explicitly mentioned in these documents as being a simple, cost-effective, and suitable technology for automation. Consequently, these policy documents, in combination with extensive media coverage of an RPA success story in a Swedish municipality (Trelleborg), seems to have created a pressure and a general feeling amongst those responsible for digitalization in the municipalities of 'having' to consider the use of RPA [23, 24]. Accordingly, RPA has been attributed a role of being a success factor, especially in local government (cf. [8]).

RPA refers to software that can be programmed to perform structured work tasks [17] by imitating a human user's interactions in one or several systems [11, 31], for example transfer of data between different systems and platforms [1]. RPA is sometimes referred to as being 'lightweight' IT [3], as it can transfer data across IT systems through the user interfaces of the systems, thus being non-invasive [16]. This is in contrast to so-called 'heavyweight' IT, as traditionally delivered by the IT department, including extensive systems and advanced system integration [4]. RPA can thus quickly integrate systems that would otherwise require considerable resources if integrated through traditional back-end (heavyweight) integration. Therefore, suppliers of RPA-solutions market the technology as being easy to use and state that little IT competence is needed to implement these systems [26].

Although RPA has been promoted for several years, most Swedish municipalities are still in the starting blocks of this implementation; the slow implementation rate has attracted the attention of scholars interested in e-government and social work [23]. Recent studies show that the municipalities struggle both to (1) identify what processes are suitable for automation, and (2) identify suitable ways to organize for automation [25, 30]. For example, there are legal frameworks that require that human case workers are involved in case work [23, 24], making automation possible only for a limited set of tasks. In addition, RPA potentially challenges existing governance structures in the municipalities, especially the traditional role of the IT-department [13]. All in all, RPA implementation in local government has turned out to be far more challenging than envisioned by both policy makers and the municipalities [2, 13, 30] and scholars call for more research on this topic [7, 18, 19, 28].

We have identified a clear gap between what is expected from the municipalities' RPA implementation and how their RPA implementation plays out in practice. In this paper, we aim to address this gap by investigating what challenges Swedish municipalities experience when attempting to implement RPA in their organizations. We use extensive case study data as our empirical foundation, generated in collaboration with three Swedish municipalities and representatives of RPA consultancy firms. Based on interpretive analysis of our case study material, we generate a set of different challenges experienced by the case study organizations. These empirical findings contribute with important insights for both e-government research and practice.

The paper is organized as follows. In Sect. 2, we outline previous work on this topic. In Sect. 3, we present our interpretive case study, in which we have studied RPA implementation in three municipalities. In Sect. 4, we present a set of challenges that we have identified in the material. In Sects. 5, we relate and discuss the identified challenges to previous research on this topic. Lastly, in Sect. 6, we conclude our findings and discuss the implications and limitations of our work, as well as possibilities for future research.

2 Previous Research

In the Swedish context, local government is comprised of 290 municipalities responsible for a large and diverse set of public service towards citizen (e.g., social services, care for children and the elderly, public schools, libraries, emergency services, and building permissions). Simply put, a Swedish municipality is a self-governed and politically steered organization typically comprised of multiple administrations responsible for different service areas (e.g., education, health services, urban planning). The administrations are directed by politically elected steering committees, with separate budgets, governed by different legal frameworks [5].

An already identified challenge for municipalities pursuing automation with RPA is how to organize RPA initiatives [13]. In the general information systems literature, different scholars point to different solutions and organizational strategies. For example, some suggest that RPA should be implemented using a centralized top-down approach, whereas others propose a de-centralized, bottom-up, approach where the business layer autonomously develops RPA [31]. Also, others suggest that RPA implementations should be organized using a centralized center of excellence that can function as a combination of centralized and de-centralized development [15]. Central in these approaches is that RPA implementation challenges the traditional relationship between the core business functions of the organization and its support functions; especially the traditional IT-department [31].

No matter what approach is used, RPA initiatives require that detailed domain knowledge about business processes is combined with extensive IT competence, as typically found in the IT-department [16, 31]. Implementing RPA in a large and diverse organization, such as a municipality, thus requires collaboration across administrations and competences, integration of data from various systems, and adhering to multiple and sometimes conflicting legal frameworks [13, 25] In other words, RPA implementation in Swedish municipalities requires interoperability along multiple dimensions, e.g. Cultural-Legal-Organizational-Semantic-Technical interoperability [6]. Interoperability has been confirmed as being a significant challenge in e-government [9], as digitalization efforts typically require collaboration and funding structures that cut across administrations, putting high demands on their abilities to interoperate [6]. In this paper we thus interpret interoperability as the ability of different sub-systems of the larger organization, such as the municipality's administrations and support functions, to collaborate and work together by utilizing resources and competences across their organizational boundaries.

3 Research Approach and Data Collection

The analysis presented in this paper is part of an ongoing research project that seeks to (1) map current implementations and use of RPA for automated case handling in local government, and (2) develop an analytical tool that can be used by researchers and practitioners to decide if, and to what degree, a specific case handling process can (and should) be automated [12]. The project builds on principles of engaged scholarship [27] and is made up by a set of case studies, conducted based on a qualitative and interpretive approach [14, 29].

The material presented in this paper builds on data generated during 2020–2021; see Table 1. In this paper, the 'cases' refer to a set of municipalities' work to organize for and implement RPA in their organizations. The data presented here was predominantly generated through semi-structured interviews. The municipalities were chosen based on maximum variation sampling. We have sought to include municipalities that work with RPA-related projects in different phases, e.g., during planning, design and implementation, and post-implementation. Two of the included municipalities – here called North and East – had carried out pilot projects and then implemented a handful of RPA solutions in their respective organization at the time of data generation (phase: *design and implementation*). The last municipality – here called West – had implemented over 20 RPA solutions in their organization at the time of data generation (phase: *post-implementation*). In each organization, we interviewed employees that represent different stakeholder groups (in relation to RPA implementation) to explore their views on and experiences of automation and RPA (e.g., digitalization directors, digitalization strategists, business process developers, IT-technicians, case workers). To complement the perspectives of the municipalities, we have also interviewed RPA-experts representing three consultancy firms that supply RPA solutions.

Table 1. Overview of data generation

Municipality	Org. size	RPA implementations	Data generation
Municipality North	40 000 citizens 3 000 employees	~5	13 interviews with mainly personnel at executive level
Municipality East	165 000 citizens 8 000 employees	~5	21 interviews (18 respondents) with managers, directors, leaders, business developers
Municipality West	150 000 citizens 11 000 employees	20+	6 interviews (8 respondents) with digitalization manager, IT-personnel, managers, case worker
RPA consultants	8 interviews with RPA-experts from 3 consultancy firms		

In line with the interpretivist (hermeneutic) tradition [10], we have continuously discussed, analyzed, and synthesized the data generated from the above interviews with the purpose of finding e.g., patterns, commonalities, contradictions, and tensions in the material (both within and across the included organizations). This approach enables a deep understanding of the phenomena at hand and allows for multiple perspectives and interpretations of the material [14]. The material is very rich and for this paper, we have delimited our account of these three organizations' experiences of implementing RPA to a set of challenges that emerged in our abductive analysis of the material.

4 Findings – Challenges Related to RPA Implementation in Municipalities

RPA implementation affects a large set of stakeholders. We have created a simplified overview of these stakeholders, all with different and sometimes conflicting interests in relation to RPA (see Fig. 1).

To support digitalization projects such as RPA implementation, the municipalities included in our study have all formed some kind of strategic *digitalization group* responsible for innovation and implementation projects related to IT. The responsibilities of these groups are to pave way for increased digitalization in the municipalities, function as a center of excellence of sorts, and function as a driver of digitalization and automation, e.g., through organizing educational and inspirational activities, in which representatives of the administrations are encouraged to work with automation. They are also expected to compose, or contribute to, digitalization strategies for their respective municipalities. In two of the municipalities, the digitalization group belongs to the IT-department (North, West). In one of the municipalities (East), the digitalization group is a stand-alone group positioned directly under the City Council (the highest level of management in the municipality).

The main responsibility of the IT-department, which plays an important role in RPA implementation, is to control and maintain the existing IT-systems and IT-infrastructure in the municipality. In the three municipalities, the *IT-personnel* can support procurement and implementation of IT in the organization, but they have very limited resources for new developments and adjusting procured systems. For these tasks, they are highly reliant on external, commercial, RPA consultants. These companies have been contracted through public procurement processes. These companies perform the actual programming and implementation of the RPA solutions in collaboration with those working in the administrations.

Lastly, and most importantly, RPA implementation involves operational staff working in various administrations of the municipality. This group includes professionals on various management levels, business developers, and civil servants working in processes where automation can be relevant. Considering the broad spectrum of services included in the municipalities' responsibilities, these can be e.g., financial assistants, human relation specialists, engineers, home care staff, janitors, and more. The important point is that this group includes people with a large variety of different professions, and different degree of education and IT-competence.

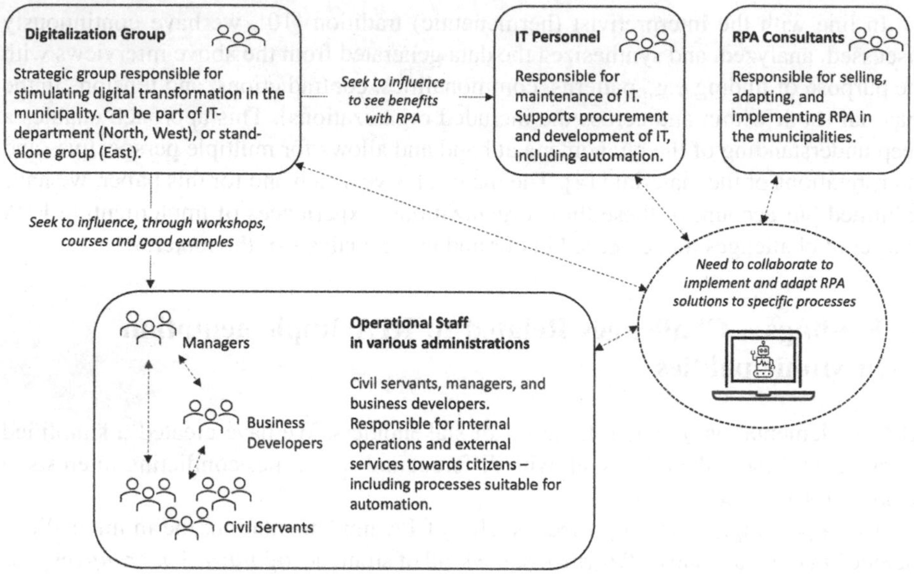

Fig. 1. Overview of stakeholders involved in RPA implementation in the municipalities

Our respondents, across the three municipalities, are in agreement that, in order to successfully implement RPA in the municipalities, all of these groups need to collaborate. However, they all testify that this collaboration is made difficult due to several interlinked challenges, as addressed below. All three municipalities have tried out RPA in the pilot format first. They have then tried, but so far failed, to scale up this implementation. Only one of the included municipalities (West) has succeeded in implementing more than a handful RPA-applications in the municipality. Still, not even that municipality has implemented as many RPA-applications as first planned for. In our interviews with employees across multiple professions and administrations within the three municipalities, we have identified challenges that have hindered further implementation of RPA in these organizations. These challenges are of various kinds, sizes, and degree of severity, and are partly echoed by the RPA consultants that we have interviewed (although they have a more limited view of RPA implementation in municipalities). Here we present the most salient challenges in relation to four interlinked themes; 1) initiating RPA top-down without bottom-up support; 2) lacking sufficient process- and IT-competence; 3) dependence on individual enthusiasts and external RPA consultants; and, 4) difficulties in finding the right processes to automate.

4.1 Initiating RPA Top-Down Without Bottom-up Support

The initial initiative to automate work was politically and strategically driven in all three municipalities. In other words, this was an initiative driven top-down; "*it comes from above, from the management of the city, politicians and so on, that "everything that can be automated, shall be automated"*" (MW, HR specialist, 2021-05-27). The digitalization groups have then become carriers of this initiative and responsible for promoting automation. However, they have been given very limited budgets and mandate for this task. The underlying idea is that each administration should pay for RPA implementation in their respective parts of the municipality, as each administration has its own, annual budget with resources set aside for IT. However, the funds for developing new IT and digitalization projects are typically very limited, or not included, in these budgets. Additionally, current financial structures within the municipalities make shared IT-investments across administrations difficult.

Although the initiative to use RPA is driven from the top, our respondents are in agreement that in order to succeed, initiatives to implement RPA in specific processes must come from the bottom of the organization – from the operational staff – and be linked to concrete problems experienced in operational work. A business process developer in the digitalization group in Municipality North states that "*if we as an IT and digitization department come up with a project and say that "Now you are going to do this", or "Now we are going to do this for you", then we have immediate problems with the issue of ownership and also the purpose and need for a project. So, we are quite careful to look for needs that exist in the operational work to step in and help and manage projects (...) based on the expertise we have around robotics or other automation solutions that we have*". (MN, Business Process Analyst, 2021-05-18). Similarly, one of the responsible IT-technicians in Municipality West states that the operational staff "*are the experts of their own organizations. I mean, we neither want, nor can, nor should, be experts on everybody's processes*" (MW, Digitalization Group Member, 2021-05-28). An important part of the digitalization groups' responsibilities has thus been to promote automation to employees in the administrations, who are then expected to gain an interest in RPA.

The three municipalities have tried different approaches to inform employees in the administrations about automation and RPA to encourage RPA uptake. In two of the municipalities (North, East), the digitalization groups have run RPA pilots, in cooperation with one or two administrations, hoping that these pilots can provide 'good examples' of automation that can later be showcased across administrations to encourage further RPA uptake. In parallel, they have promoted automation and RPA in various internal forums, as a way of educating operational staff about RPA and its potential merits. In both municipalities, RPA uptake has been slow. Despite RPA having been promoted internally for several years, only a handful of finished RPA solutions had been implemented at the time of data collection (2021).

In contrast, Municipality West adopted a more hands-on approach and offered a six-week implementation sprint for free to each administration. Each administration then got help by employees in the digitalization group to identify a suitable process to automate and were then put into contact with an external RPA consultancy firm that adjusted and implemented the RPA solution with them. Many, but not all, administrations in Municipality West accepted this offer. With this approach, Municipality West implemented slightly over 20 RPA solutions during a two-year period. But even so, RPA implementation did not take off as expected throughout the organization in general. All in all, our respondents working in the digitalization groups at the three municipalities report that they have found it difficult to spark an interest in RPA in their municipalities.

The top-down push of RPA implementation has also created unclear relationships between the digitalization group and the 'regular' IT-personnel. Somewhat simplified, the digitalization groups push RPA and automation as a new thing and try to get the operational staff's attention. At the same time, RPA implementation is dependent on the IT-personnel's input, as the RPA solution must eventually be handled and maintained as part of the municipality's general IT-infrastructure. The IT-personnel, however, see RPA as just another way of integrating systems (i.e., nothing 'new'). Also, they regard RPA as an inferior method for integrating systems, and push for other, more robust solutions (e.g., system integration platforms, API). Here, conflicts arise concerning who is responsible for what, why, and how. An IT-personnel in Municipality North describes the relationship between the digitalization group and the IT-personnel in the following way: "*But automation, we have been doing that using IT for 10–15 years, it is nothing new at all. So, we have worked with automation since yes, in the 2000s, we have automated things, it should be easy to do things. But when the municipality started talking about automatization, they did not talk automation, they talked "robotization", that was the focus. Then it* [the robotization] *does not end up in IT, it ended up in the Digitalization unit. So, it's a bit outside of IT. And this* [digitalization] *unit, there are people there who like new technology and stuff like that, who actually have no idea about IT and how to run IT, and how to maintain IT. So, they run a little fast, I think, so that they throw in robots, and then they just think "Now you can fix the rest" "What! fix the rest?" "You have to take care of it" roughly. There is usually no budget, it's just that someone should solve the problems they have created.*"(MN, IT-personnel, 2021-06-18).

The self-governed administrations, with a mandate and budget to procure and install IT-systems on their own, in combination with unclear mandates of the digitalization groups and IT-personnel, creates a challenging IT-infrastructure overall. One of the respondents states that the IT-personnel "*has no power whatsoever to influence what IT-systems an administration buys. And that leads to us having a more complicated build* [IT-ecosystem] *than we could have and wish we had*" (MW, Digitalization Group Member, 2021-05-28).

In short, different views on RPA and unclear mandates and relationships between the various administrations and support functions in the municipalities make RPA a slow endeavor.

4.2 Lacking Sufficient Process- and IT-Competence

When the work to implement RPA in the municipalities started, it soon became clear that employees in the municipalities generally lack sufficient process- and IT-competence needed to implement RPA. Respondents from all three municipalities describe that working with automation and RPA implementation has made salient that operational staff in the administrations are not used to view their work from a process perspective. Hence, they are not used to modelling processes, which is needed when wanting to apply robotic process automation, as described by the digitalization director in Municipality East: "*in our municipality, the general understanding of processes is low (…) so, when one has dialogues with the administrations, one quickly realizes that, first and foremost, to find those persons who understand the operational processes, is really difficult*" (MW, Digitalization Director, 2021-05-28). Not being used to structure and describe the daily work in terms of processes has slowed down the implementation of RPA – those stakeholders with technical skills to develop RPA solutions cannot program RPA solutions without the input from those stakeholders knowledgeable about the work to be automated. These, in turn, cannot model their work without input on what to document and how, from those responsible for the RPA implementation. The competence needed for successful RPA implementation is thus distributed across multiple stakeholders that need to collaborate in various and new ways.

When asked why the level of IT-competence is low, one of the digitalization directors stated that "*…basically, the municipality does not perceive IT as part of its core business activities, one gets to hear that many times - "why should we spend money on these things [IT]? Why not have more teachers?" – that's stated about once a week. And that leads to the municipality not building competence around IT or IT-development, so they have not been able to drive and formulate demands in systems procurements that are sensible…*" (MW, Digitalization Director, 2021-05-28). The respondents also describe that this view on IT also contributes to insufficient funding being budgeted for IT and digitalization efforts.

4.3 Dependence on Individual Enthusiasts and External RPA Consultants

As a consequence of the circumstances described above, RPA implementation in the municipalities has become dependent on a few RPA-enthusiasts who manage to maneuver this complicated landscape. These enthusiasts are typically operational staff that are interested in technology and digitalization and who want to see changes made in the current work procedures. They are quite easily identified in our material as they are typically the ones who have been responsible for the process modelling and coordination of involved stakeholders, including being the contact person towards the external RPA consultancy firm. Typically, these enthusiasts have also ended up being responsible for the maintenance of the RPA once it is implemented and operational. This means that these persons have been heavily involved and learned a lot during the development and implementation process, about current work procedures, related regulations, and RPA technology. After RPA implementation, much of the important know-how is isolated to these persons only. One of these enthusiasts states that "*if I were to run a round this afternoon and get hit* [by a car] *and won't be able to work for a half year, then nobody will be able to take care of it* [the RPA] *– he's in my head. (…) they haven't started on any routines or checklists or similar either, because I have that in my head. (…) I haven't felt that the organization has been ready for me to let go, I might have too much feeling of responsibility*" (MW, Case Worker, 2021-06-16).

Hence, as long as these enthusiasts stay on in the organization, they become an important link between all of the stakeholder groups, but the municipalities risk losing important knowledge and know-how if these persons quit their jobs. A related problem is that these enthusiasts are found in separate parts of the municipality, and there are no given or natural venues for these persons to meet and share their knowledge with each other and other interested employees. One of the directors of digitalization states that "*my vision, initially, when we started, was that the different administrations would be able to learn from each other. And I feel, it's perhaps a failure from my side, that we have not come that far that I can say that they learn from each other*" (MW, Digitalization Director, 2021-05-28).

There is also a strong dependence on the external RPA consultancy firms throughout the development and implementation processes. For some RPA implementations, this dependence remains also when the RPA solutions have been implemented, as described by one of our respondents: "*we are dependent on* [the external company] *(…) there are no adjustments we can do ourselves*" (MW, Manager, 2021-06-21).

4.4 Difficulties in Finding Suitable Processes to Automate Using RPA

All municipalities testify of difficulties in finding suitable processes to automate. This is related to the competence and collaboration issues presented so far, but it also relates to more concrete problems related to legal-, semantic, and technical issues.

In the municipality setting, RPA is perceived as a technology that can collect, integrate, and manage information in a way that can prepare for the human case worker's decision. According to the RPA literature (e.g., [31]), this technology is best suited for simple and rule-based processes, that are preferably repetitive and of high volume. As a general observation, all municipalities involved in our study have applied RPA to more complex processes than is recommended. A possible reason for this is that the digitalization groups have marketed RPA internally as a technology that can help civil servants solve bottle necks in administrative processes. Hence, the operational staff seems to have chosen to automate tasks with bottle necks in their administrative routines. Some of the processes chosen, however, suffer from bottle necks due to adhering to complicated legal frameworks, rather than due to high volumes of cases (as is assumed). Respondents from all three municipalities express that they have realized late in the implementation process, that they have chosen too complicated processes to automate using RPA. Still, they have proceeded to implement RPA solutions for these processes, causing delays and exceeding the budget.

Technically, RPA can also be used to make formal decisions in cases that have clear-cut decision grounds, but this use of RPA is not yet allowed according to regulations steering public service provision on the municipality level in Sweden. Current regulations demand that decisions are made by humans that can be held accountable for the decisions. However, automated decision-making is allowed on the state level; automated decision-making is therefore expected to be allowed on the local level in the future. Automation furthermore requires combinations of data from various registries. There are extensive legal frameworks concerning what data can be handled and combined for various purposes and services. The investigated municipalities have all experienced problems concerning interpreting the legal frameworks concerning what data can be shared across administrations and departments within the municipality, and what data they can extract and use from national registries. Sometimes there are contradictions that need to be dealt with by consulting legal experts, as expressed by a case worker in Municipality West: "*we have the Swedish Local Government Act, which says one thing, and we have the Administrative Procedure Act, which says something else*" (MW, Case Worker, 2021-06-16).

The need for human involvement in the case handling processes has to do with accountability. A fear amongst operational and legal staff in the municipalities is that critical knowledge in the municipality will be lost when automating, as described by a legal specialist in Municipality East "*what I fear is that one will not know why, why something* [in the automated procedure] *is the way it is and cannot explain to a manager or to a co-worker, so one has to, simultaneously, one cannot lose too much competence out there because one has digitalized so much that one barely need to think for oneself*" (ME, Legal specialist, 2020-11-13). The legal issues thus concern both the process and the employees' ability to explain and be held accountable for the output of the process. In Municipality West, the issue of accountability has been solved for some RPA solutions by distributing a sub-set of incoming cases to human case workers, while the RPA solution handles the majority of the cases. Through this set-up, process knowledge is kept in the organization and the case worker can also perform quality controls of the RPA solution's output.

The push to automate work has exposed difficulties for various professions to understand each other's vocabularies and perspectives. Those knowledgeable in how to automate find it difficult to explain automation in terms that the operational staff can understand. Likewise, the operational staff finds it difficult to explain their work, the regulations steering their work, and the multitude of exceptions to these regulations, in a way that the IT-personnel and others can grasp. Our respondents report that misunderstandings are frequent and that even choices of certain words can create confusion and conflict. For example, one of the RPA consultants explain that "*one thing that has gained attention is that they chose to call it "robots" initially, and "digital co-workers". That became charged. It* [RPA] *isn't a big difference in relation to the automation they've had previously – when you change a system or create an integration. Then, the purpose is also to automate and do something in a more efficient way. That, they've done for a very long time. But, when one says that a "robot" will do something, take over tasks, that spurs debates that robots take over our jobs, and so on*" (RPA consultant, Senior Project Manager, 2020-06-15). These semantic issues also affect their ability to agree on what processes to automate.

Turning to some of the technical issues that have arisen, the very reason for choosing RPA is that some of the municipalities' existing systems cannot be integrated in a more robust way, using e.g., API. RPA is thus described as being a kind of "*duct tape*" that can be used to integrate the systems, as explained by a data architect in Municipality East: "*There are some use cases where I don't really see any other alternative, and in those cases, it is an exceptionally good solution. It is good that the alternative exists, but often there are, in my opinion, better solutions, and in those cases I think those should be used.*" (ME, Data Architect, 2020-12-09). One reason for this statement is that the RPA implementations have proven to be highly sensitive to changes being made in the systems the RPA is operating in. "*RPA is stupid. Yes, it really is, because if you have programmed him* [the RPA] *to go from here to there, and to there, and then you'll put up a stop on the way, well, then he just stands there staring. Well. So, even the slightest hiccup for the system on the way, well, then he cannot go further. (...) He only does exactly what he's been told to do.*" (MW, Case Worker, 2021-06-16). For example, for some of the RPA implementations in Municipality West, the robots have not been technically compatible with the desktop versions of their enterprise systems, forcing them to connect the RPA to online versions of the systems. Also, the robots cannot work in the systems at the same time as human case workers are active in the systems, creating a need to schedule the times when the RPA solutions are active in the systems.

5 Discussion

Swedish municipalities are asked by policy makers to implement RPA to improve administrative processes. Our analysis shows that RPA implementation is difficult for multiple reasons. The municipalities included in our study lack sufficient competence to work successfully with RPA, creating dependencies on those few employees that can manage this technology implementation. RPA has potential to integrate data and processes across administrations in the municipalities, but current work practices make cooperation across administrations difficult. Previous research on general RPA use has illustrated that RPA implementation provokes existing organizational structures, especially the IT-department's traditional focus on maintenance and robust IT-infrastructures [15, 31]. Also, previous studies have illustrated that RPA implementation is more difficult than envisioned by politicians and policy makers [2, 24, 30]. Our current empirical work confirms these previous findings.

As seen in the account above, the initial push to implement RPA came from the policy level (e.g., [20–22]). In turn, the digitalization group in each municipality was charged with the task of promoting RPA implementation locally. The digitalization groups, however, did not have enough knowledge and insight into the concrete work practices and problems experienced in the administrations; consequently, they could not facilitate the match between problems and solutions. Instead, the digitalization groups tried to educate employees in the administrations about RPA so that these employees could see the potential uses of RPA for their particular administration. Hence, this is a clear example of a top-down initiative. At the same time, there is consensus amongst our respondents that successful RPA implementation requires bottom-up approaches. By forming digitalization groups, such as the center of excellence promoted by [15], with the expressed purpose to promote innovation and horizontal digitalization initiatives, the municipalities have all tried to encourage a move from vertical administration-based ways of approaching digitalization to a shared horizontal digitization strategy. It is questionable if this strategy for promoting organizational interoperability has yet succeeded, given the challenges experienced on multiple dimensions.

RPA is about interconnecting and sharing data and information across systems [16]. This makes legal interoperability, as well as technical interoperability, extremely important (cf. [6]). How to share data and information in accordance to existing legal frameworks, as well as how to do this technically, are central themes when choosing a process to automate and when setting up the actual RPA solutions. A core issue is whether or not information can be shared across administrations adhering to different legal frameworks. When sharing data across administrations, semantic interoperability also becomes important, to ensure that information is not lost when data is transferred from one system to another. However, the semantic interoperability of current RPA systems requires data to be structured and well-defined [1]. Therefore, to ensure a precise and understandable meaning during information exchange [9], the semantic interoperability in an RPA context also relates to the different professions' knowledge and vocabularies. The same term can have different meanings in different legal frameworks and call for professional discretion [18]. These features create a further need for closer collaboration between stakeholders in the municipality that are not used to working together.

Furthermore, in each administration and support function, different competences are promoted and valued [25]. Our respondents agree that RPA implementation requires collaboration across administrations and support functions. The administrations are however described as stovepipes and most respondents testify that shared initiatives are still difficult. As previously illustrated by Erlingsson and Wänström [5], the administrations function as independent organizations. The digitalization groups are working to create new venues for different stakeholder groups to meet and share their respective knowledge and perspective; hence encouraging organizational interoperability (cf. [6]). However, the municipalities' journey towards organizational-wide digitalization and automation initiatives has only just begun; calling for further research on this topic.

From our interviews, it is clear that a handful of enthusiastic individuals in each municipality are responsible for most of the RPA-related work, as also illustrated by Lindgren et al. [13]. These enthusiasts are typically employees with a personal interest in digitalization and business development, working together with external consultants hired to help the organization to implement RPA. Through the implementation process, they have learned about process modelling, and studied legal frameworks and current work practices in order to translate these into RPA solutions. They typically function as hubs of loosely formed networks of people needed to implement RPA. At best, enthusiasts like these can mediate communication between various administrations and stakeholders by interpreting and translating information, work practices, and legal frameworks in various ways. At worst, however, these enthusiasts represent limited interests and create undue dependencies on individuals. In other words, there is cause for concern when a small number of people is given the power to influence the work practices of public organizations in this manner.

It is quite clear that the challenges illustrated in our analysis are interrelated. All three municipalities testify that it is difficult to identify suitable processes for RPA implementation. This is in part due to insufficient cooperation between affected stakeholders, but also due to inexperience of process modeling and IT development. These challenges, in turn, are related to a dependence on individual enthusiasts and external RPA consultancy firms for making RPA implementation happen. Put together, RPA implementation is currently difficult to implement in Swedish municipalities. Although RPA is described as lightweight IT in the literature, the knowledge requirements and the need for collaboration between different administrations and support functions, make RPA solutions heavyweight in terms of needed technical skills and competence (cf. [4]).

6 Conclusion, Limitations, and Future Research

Swedish municipalities are currently encouraged by policy makers to implement RPA to support administrative work. RPA implementation is driven top-down, facilitated by newly formed digitalization groups meant to function as centers of excellence. In our interpretive analysis of three Swedish municipalities' work to implement RPA, we identify challenges related to the top-down push of RPA implementation, with little bottom-up support and insufficient collaboration between affected stakeholders. We also identify interrelated challenges concerning insufficient process- and IT-competence; difficulties in identifying the right processes to automate; as well as overreliance on individual enthusiasts and external RPA consultancy firms for making RPA implementation happen. These findings confirm previous studies on RPA use in general and previously illustrated digitalization challenges in the public sector. So, what is new? Our findings illustrate that many of the challenges that e-government research has illustrated throughout the years are still prevalent in e-government practice. We contribute with empirical and contextualized illustrations of some of these challenges. More work needs to be put into the systematic study of the source of the challenges identified here and potential solutions. Furthermore, more efforts should be put into bridging the gap between e-government research and practice.

Our study is limited to three Swedish municipalities, including interviews with representatives from a smaller set of companies selling RPA solutions to the municipalities. In order to gain more depth in our understanding of RPA implementation in government, future research could expand the scope of investigation to additional levels of government and additional national contexts. Our work presented here is also highly descriptive; by adding theoretical perspectives to our material in future work, we hope to be able to come up with more prescriptive conclusions, complementing the empirical illustrations made here. For example, the municipalities, as well as RPA-suppliers and consultancy firms, emphasize the need for holistic and horizontal approaches to RPA implementation. Further research is needed to inform how the municipalities can organize innovation initiatives of this kind.

Acknowledgements. This research is funded by AFA Insurance (AFA Försäkring), project 190200.

References

1. Aguirre, S., Rodriguez, A.: Automation of a business process using robotic process automation (RPA): a case study. In: Figueroa-García, J.C., López-Santana, E.R., Villa-Ramírez, J.L., Ferro-Escobar, R. (eds.) WEA 2017. CCIS, vol. 742, pp. 65–71. Springer, Cham (2017). https://doi.org/10.1007/978-3-319-66963-2_7
2. Borry, E.L., Getha-Taylor, H.: Automation in the public sector: efficiency at the expense of equity? Public Integr. **21**(1), 6–21 (2019)
3. Bygstad, B.: The Coming of Lightweight IT. ECIS 2015 Completed Research Papers. Paper 22 (2015)
4. Bygstad, B.: Generative innovation: a comparison of lightweight and heavy-weight IT. J. Inf. Technol. **32**(2), 180–193 (2017)
5. Erlingsson, G.Ó., Wänström, J.: Politik och förvaltning i svenska kommuner. Studentlitteratur, Lund (2021)
6. European Commission: Proposal for a European Interoperability Framework for Smart Cities and Communities (EIF4SCC) (2021). https://doi.org/10.2799/545570
7. Germundsson, N.: Promoting the digital future: the construction of digital automation in Swedish policy discourse on social assistance. Crit. Policy Stud. 1–19 (2022)
8. Gil-García, J.R., Pardo, T.A.: E-government success factors: mapping practical tools to theoretical foundations. Gov. Inf. Q. **22**(2), 187–216 (2005)
9. Guijarro, L.: Semantic interoperability in eGovernment initiatives. Comput. Stand. Interf. **31**(1), 174–180 (2009)

10. Klein, H.K., Myers, M.D.: A set of principles for conducting and evaluating interpretive field studies in information systems. MIS Q. **23**(1), 67–93 (1999)
11. Lacity, M.C., Willcocks, L.P.: Robotic process automation at telefónica O2. MIS Q. Exec. **15**(1), 21–35 (2016)
12. Lindgren, I.: Exploring the use of robotic process automation in local government. Ongoing Research Paper. In: CEUR-Proceedings from EGOV-CeDEM-ePart, pp. 249–258 (2020)
13. Lindgren, I., Åkesson, M., Thomsen, M., Toll, D.: Organizing for robotic process automation in local government: observations from two case studies of robotic process automation implementation in Swedish municipalities. In: Juell-Skielse, G., Lindgren, I., Åkesson, M. (eds.) Service Automation in the Public Sector. PROIS, pp. 189–203. Springer, Cham (2022). https://doi.org/10.1007/978-3-030-92644-1_10
14. Myers, M.D.: Qualitative research in information systems. MIS Q. 241–243 (1997)
15. Noppen, P., Beerepoot, I., van de Weerd, I., Jonker, M., Reijers, H.A.: How to keep RPA maintainable? In: Fahland, D., Ghidini, C., Becker, J., Dumas, M. (eds.) BPM 2020. LNCS, vol. 12168, pp. 453–470. Springer, Cham (2020). https://doi.org/10.1007/978-3-030-58666-9_26
16. Osmundsen, K., Iden, J., Bygstad, B.: Organizing robotic process automation: balancing loose and tight coupling. In: Proceedings of the Annual Hawaii International Conference on System Sciences, 2019-January, pp. 6918–6926 (2019)
17. Penttinen, E., Kasslin, H., Asatiani, A.: How to choose between robotic process automation and back-end system automation? In European Conference on Information Systems, vol. 15 (2018)
18. Ranerup, A., Henriksen, H.Z.: Digital discretion: unpacking human and technological agency in automated decision making in Sweden's social services. Soc. Sci. Comput. Rev. 1–17 (2020)
19. Ranerup, A., Henriksen, H.Z.: Value positions viewed through the lens of automated decision-making: the case of social services. Gov. Inf. Q. **36**(4), 101377 (2019)
20. SALAR: Automatiserad ärendehantering (2018a). www.skr.se
21. SALAR: Automatisering av arbete (2018b). https://skr.se/tjanster/merfranskr/rapporterochskrifter/publikationer/automatiseringavarbete.27511.html
22. SOU: Automatiserade beslut: färre regler ger tydligare reglering (Vol. 75). E-Delegationen (2014)
23. Svensson, L.: Automatisering-till nytta eller fördärv? Socialvetenskaplig Tidskrift **3**(4), 341–362 (2019)
24. Svensson, L.: "Tekniken är den enkla biten": Om att implementera digital automatisering i handläggningen av försörjningsstöd. Lund University (2019b)
25. Toll, D., Lindgren, I., Melin, U.: Process automation as enabler of prioritized values in local government – a stakeholder analysis. In: Scholl, H.J., Gil-Garcia, J.R., Janssen, M., Kalampokis, E., Lindgren, I., Rodríguez Bolívar, M.P. (eds.) EGOV 2021. LNCS, vol. 12850, pp. 288–300. Springer, Cham (2021). https://doi.org/10.1007/978-3-030-84789-0_21
26. Toll, D., Söderström, F.: What is this "RPA" they are selling? In: Virkar, S., et al. (eds.) EGOV-CeDEM-ePart 2020, pp. 365–370 (2020)
27. van de Ven, A.H.: Engaged Scholarship: A Guide for Organizational and Social Research. Oxford University Press On Demand (2007)
28. Veale, M., Brass, I.: Administration by Algorithm? Public Management Meets Public Sector Machine Learning, pp. 1–30 (2019)

29. Walsham, G.: Interpretive case studies in IS research: nature and method. Eur. J. Inf. Syst. **4**, 74–81 (1995)
30. Wihlborg, E., Larsson, H., Hedström, K.: The computer says no! - A case study on automated decision-making in public authorities. In: Proceedings of the Annual Hawaii International Conference on System Sciences, 2016-March, pp. 2903–2912 (2016)
31. Wilcocks, L., Lacity, M.: The IT Function and Robotic Process Automation. The Outsourcing Unit Working Research Paper Series (2015)

Automated Topic Categorisation of Citizens' Contributions: Reducing Manual Labelling Efforts Through Active Learning

Julia Romberg(✉) and Tobias Escher

Heinrich Heine University, Düsseldorf, Germany
{julia.romberg,tobias.escher}@hhu.de

Abstract. Political authorities in democratic countries regularly consult the public on specific issues but subsequently evaluating the contributions requires substantial human resources, often leading to inefficiencies and delays in the decision-making process. Among the solutions proposed is to support human analysts by thematically grouping the contributions through automated means. While supervised machine learning would naturally lend itself to the task of classifying citizens' proposal according to certain predefined topics, the amount of training data required is often prohibitive given the idiosyncratic nature of most public participation processes. One potential solution to minimise the amount of training data is the use of active learning. While this semi-supervised procedure has proliferated in recent years, these promising approaches have never been applied to the evaluation of participation contributions. Therefore we utilise data from online participation processes in three German cities, provide classification baselines and subsequently assess how different active learning strategies can reduce manual labelling efforts while maintaining a good model performance. Our results show not only that supervised machine learning models can reliably classify topic categories for public participation contributions, but that active learning significantly reduces the amount of training data required. This has important implications for the practice of public participation because it dramatically cuts the time required for evaluation from which in particular processes with a larger number of contributions benefit.

Keywords: Topic classification · Public participation · Active learning · Natural language processing

1 Introduction

Democratic authorities are regularly using public participation to consult and involve citizens in order to inform political decisions and increase public support

The original version of this chapter was revised: this chapter was previously published non-open access. The correction to this chapter is available at https://doi.org/10.1007/978-3-031-15086-9_37

M. Janssen et al. (Eds.): EGOV 2022, LNCS 13391, pp. 369–385, 2022.
https://doi.org/10.1007/978-3-031-15086-9_24

[8]. While their function and effectiveness is open to debate [19], they enjoy considerable popularity among the public that regularly contributes hundreds or even thousands of proposals to such consultations. As a consequence, policy-makers and their administrations regularly face the problem of how to make sense of the diversity of statements that the public provides while at the same time maintaining the high standards of transparency and due process required for such important democratic processes. Usually this requires human analysts to read each contribution, detect duplicates, identify common themes, and categorise contributions accordingly before preparing conclusions from the input. This is a time consuming effort that often leads to inefficiencies and delays in the decision-making process [2,7,23].

While human assessment should not be abandoned, given the relevance of citizens‘ input to the democratic decision-making, technical solutions have long been proposed as a means to reduce the workload of human evaluators [18]. Here we focus on approaches to support analysts by using Natural Language Processing (NLP) techniques to categorise disparate contributions into groups that share certain thematic properties. As we review below, both supervised as well as unsupervised machine learning strategies have been applied to this task with mixed results. Given that categorisation of citizen contributions generally follows certain pre-defined goals such as sorting according to particular topics or administrative responsibilities, categorisation schemes are not arbitrary but constructed before the participation process. As a consequence, we assume that supervised machine learning approaches like classification are better suited to the task than completely unsupervised procedures that aim to detect latent structures in the data. However, these supervised procedures require manually labelled training data, calling into questions any efficiency gains that motivated automation in the first place. This demand would not constitute a barrier if models could be pre-trained and subsequently applied. Yet, regularly public participation processes are distinct and require tailored categorisation schemes. This idiosyncratic nature means models need to be customised for each process, requiring substantial amounts of training data.

A potential solution to minimise the amount of data is the use of active learning, a semi-supervised procedure that (to the best of our knowledge) has been applied to the evaluation of participation contributions only once [20]. While since that study almost 15 years ago, active learning strategies (and NLP in general) have advanced, these promising technologies have not been applied to the analysis of citizen participation. Therefore we systematically assess how different active learning strategies can reduce manual labelling efforts while maintaining a good model performance. To this end we study data from online participation processes in three German cities that consulted citizens on improvements for cycling. Specifically, we investigate different supervised machine learning models in order to establish what classification quality can be achieved without active learning (RQ1). We use this as a baseline to investigate how much manual labelling effort can be saved through active learning (RQ2). However, given that our focus is on enabling a practical application of these models, we also test how time-efficient the different categorisation approaches are to assess whether these could be used in realistic scenarios (RQ3).

We start by discussing previous NLP approaches to structuring contributions thematically (2) before introducing our dataset (3) and the active learning techniques applied (4). We evaluate the results of different query strategies and classifiers (5) and discuss their implications for practical application (6). Finally, the concluding section summarises the results and outlines avenues for further research (7).

2 Approaches to Thematically Structure Contributions

Organising citizens' contributions thematically is a basic step in the evaluation of public participation processes and so far two machine learning strategies have been proposed to support this task. These are unsupervised approaches, mainly topic modeling, on the one hand, and supervised classification algorithms on the other.

Unsupervised machine learning algorithms cluster similar content by discovering hidden patterns in the data. As these rely on unlabelled datasets, they require no previous manual coding which makes them attractive to use. Several such algorithms have been applied in previous work, including k-means and k-medoids clustering [23,25], non-negative matrix factorization [2], associative networks [24] and correlation explanation topic modeling [5]. By far the most popular is topic modeling with Latent Dirichlet Allocation (LDA) (see for example [2,10,11,15,16]).

Much of the work mentioned above shows that the detection of meaningful topics by unsupervised learning is subject to major limitations. To start with, for algorithms such as LDA and k-means the number of topic clusters to be identified must be specified in advance. This risks that the number of topics is somewhat arbitrary. What is more, while an approximate number of topics can be found with strategies such as experimenting with different values using human judgment or statistical measures, this requires considerable manual analysis effort [10,23]. An even more serious limitation are the topic clusters that emerge. Even with an appropriate number of topics to be found, there is still no guarantee that the algorithms will return those topics that are required by the user.

However, human evaluators of participation processes generally already have a good idea of what categories they are interested in. The reason is that such processes are initiated in order to consult the public on a specific topic such as a proposed infrastructure project or a legal text. Therefore, even before the process begins, there are a number of categories on which the analysts expect input and this pre-defined categorisation scheme can then later be refined when contributions are reviewed. As a consequence, we argue that it is more suitable to benefit from this prior knowledge in order to provide clusters of interest rather than to rely on latent structures that might not be relevant to the user. This is exactly the function of supervised machine learning which we therefore consider more appropriate to support categorising contributions thematically [1,4,6,13,14].

Given a set of labelled training data, supervised models are trained to classify citizen contributions into categories that have been previously defined by the user. Most works relied on conventional approaches such as support vector machines, but more recent works also included neural networks and transformer models like BERT. Some promising results have been obtained, but only under the condition that a sufficient amount of previously (usually manually) categorised data is available for training the models. This may be true in certain cases, such as in the use case described by Kim et al. [13] who used a categorisation by administrative unit for a city platform that is available to citizens in the long term. Once trained, the model can support officials by being used to automatically classify new requests that are constantly coming in.

However, many participation processes are singular events that have a specific objective and only run for a short period of time. Therefore, regularly analysts have to adapt the thematic categories of the evaluation to the respective process. This usually makes the transfer of trained models impossible. Rather, the classification models must be trained anew for each process with appropriate data, which requires to label (at least part of) the contributions from the process under consideration. This additional human labelling effort must not be underestimated as the previously introduced studies show that relied on training datasets consisting of several thousand data points. Yet, as is not least documented by our dataset, many of the consultation processes, e.g. in municipalities, do not even generate these large numbers of contributions. While hundreds or a few thousands of contributions pose substantial burden to administration to evaluate, fully supervised machine learning may not remedy the situation when analysts would still have to code a large share of the dataset in order to train a classifier. As a consequence, supervised machine learning might not offer an efficiency benefit for a whole range of practical applications in the area of public participation.

In order to provide a feasible solution also for processes with a lower number of contributions, Purpura et al. [20] motivated a human-in-the-loop approach. *Active learning* aims to reduce the amount of required training data by selecting a minimal subset that provides the greatest performance gain in training a classification model. The algorithm works in close collaboration with the user, who gradually categorises small parts of the dataset until the model performs satisfactorily. The authors were able to confirm that active learning can reduce manual labelling efforts while maintaining a high model performance. Nevertheless, depending on the number of categories (17 or 39), still more than 600 respectively more than 800 sentences had to be labelled manually until an accuracy of 70% was reached - a score which is comparable to the results of many of the works on supervised classification introduced above. In summary, it was thus evident that the use of active learning is promising, but the approaches still need to be improved.

Since the study of Purpura et al., the research on NLP and on active learning has evolved. Our goal is to apply state-of-the-art methods to citizen contributions and to evaluate to what extent the advanced methods can further reduce the amount of training data needed. In addition, we also assess the runtime of these models as another potential barrier for practical application.

3 The Cycling Dialogues Datasets

In this paper we focus on contributions collected from citizens in three nearly identical participation processes in the German municipalities of Bonn, Ehrenfeld (a district of Cologne) and Moers. In each city, the authorities consulted the public in order to identify planning measures that would improve the situation for cyclists. To do so, from September to October 2017 citizens were invited to propose measures for particular locations using a map-based online participation platform. Before the process, the local traffic planning authorities of the three cities that initiated these consultations developed a set of eight categories, representing different aspects for improvement such as cycle path quality or lighting. These would subsequently be used in order to process the proposals from citizens.

Initially, each contribution was assigned to a single (primary) category by the citizens when submitting the contribution. This assignment was checked by the moderators of the online platform and adjusted if necessary. After the online participation phase, an analyst went through the contributions from all three processes again and checked the categorisation. In rare cases this led to reassignment of primary categories. What is more, for those contributions whose content would qualify for more than one category, in addition to the primary category further secondary categories where assigned. The share of multi-labelled contributions regarding the eight main categories amounts to 10% in Bonn and Moers, and 15% in Ehrenfeld. Among these, only few contributions had more than two labels assigned (Bonn: 21, Ehrenfeld: 10, Moers: 3).

We use this categorisation as the basis for our study and investigate how to accurately and efficiently predict the correct label(s) for each contribution. While one could certainly insist that this body of data lacks intersubjectivity, it represents a scenario that regularly occurs in practical applications as individual analysts code large parts or even the entire contributions on their own. Nevertheless, although the categorisation is ultimately based on one individual analyst and may contain a somewhat subjective bias on his part, it is by no means arbitrary because it also incorporates the judgement of different people (citizen and moderators). We thus argue that it is certainly sufficient for most of the use cases where this categorisation is the starting point of further processing of contributions. More important for our study is that the labels reflect a consistent assignment [20] which is certainly the case as all were reviewed by a single person.

The coded dataset comprises a total of 3,139 contributions. *Cycling Dialogue Bonn* has received the most contributions with 2,314, whereas *Cycling Dialogue Ehrenfeld* and *Cycling Dialogue Moers* account for 366 and 459 unique contributions respectively. The contributions contain an average of 4.83 (Bonn), 4.66 (Ehrenfeld) and 4.78 (Moers) sentences. Table 1 gives insights into the thematic priorities within the eight categories. Cycling traffic management and cycle path

Table 1. Overview of datasets and distribution of topic categories by single labels and multiple labels respectively.

Categories	Primary labels						Primary & secondary labels					
	Bonn		Ehrenfeld		Moers		Bonn		Ehrenfeld		Moers	
Cycling traffic management	1,020	(44.1%)	195	(53.3%)	222	(48.4%)	1,056	(45.6%)	204	(55.7%)	229	(49.9%)
Signage	150	(6.5%)	16	(4.4%)	19	(4.1%)	182	(7.9%)	20	(5.5%)	27	(5.9%)
Obstacles	319	(13.8%)	35	(9.6%)	31	(6.8%)	364	(15.7%)	45	(12.3%)	33	(7.2%)
Cycle path quality	449	(19.4%)	58	(15.8%)	111	(24.2%)	519	(22.4%)	71	(19.4%)	118	(25.7%)
Traffic lights	178	(7.7%)	34	(9.3%)	47	(10.2%)	197	(8.5%)	39	(10.7%)	51	(11.1%)
Lighting	37	(1.6%)	1	(0.3%)	10	(2.2%)	47	(2.0%)	2	(0.5%)	15	(3.3%)
Bicycle parking	108	(4.7%)	22	(0.6%)	9	(2.0%)	112	(4.8%)	26	(7.1%)	9	(2.0%)
Misc	53	(2.3%)	5	(1.4%)	10	(2.2%)	84	(3.6%)	25	(6.8%)	27	(5.9%)
Total documents	2,314		366		459		2,314		366		459	

quality attracted the most interest in all datasets, followed by either obstacles or traffic lights. The (larger) differences in the amount of contributions as well as the (smaller) difference in the distribution of categories can be attributed to both contextual factors such as city size or local infrastructure, and individual-level factors such as the participating stakeholders.

A noteworthy characteristic of the datasets is that some categories are only rarely represented. For example, lighting occurs only twice in Ehrenfeld and bicycle parking occurs only 9 times in Moers. Although this is likely to make classification more difficult, such uneven distributions by topic are not at all the exception in citizen comments, making the results of the evaluation with regard to the rarely occurring classes of great interest.

In contrast to the work of Purpura et al. [20], here we categorise entire contributions rather than individual sentences within these. This is motivated by the fact that this is also the approach chosen by practitioners in the field of citizen participation (see for example [2,23]). What is more, in our dataset the contributions contain just about five sentences on average and thus are relatively short in comparison to the average length of 41.55 sentences reported by Purpura et al. [20].

4 Methodology

In the following, we introduce the concept of active learning and describe the techniques selected to be part of our study. These are various specific strategies for selecting the data points to be labelled as well as suitable classification algorithms.

We consider two types of classification problems, both of which will be addressed in the evaluation. On the one hand, we want to identify the thematic focus, i.e. the primary category, of the contributions. To do this, we solve a *single-label classification problem* in which a decision function is learned that maps each input vector to exactly one class. Second, we are interested to see to what extent all associated topics of a contribution can be recognised. In such a *multi-label classification problem*, the input vectors can be mapped to one or more classes.

4.1 Active Learning

The goal of active learning is to quickly learn a good decision function for classifying data points to save manual labelling effort. Optimally, the subset of data to be labelled should be minimal while the prediction accuracy is maximised. Being an interactive process, the human expert is sequentially consulted by the computer to (in our case) categorise samples of contributions whose labelling can be of most use in training the model.

In each iteration of the process, the k most informative data points are selected using some query strategy. Subsequently, these samples are manually labelled and added to the pool of so far labelled data points (i.e. from earlier iteration rounds). The classification model is then retrained with all labelled samples and evaluated. If the classification performance is sufficient (according to some stopping criterion), the active learning process terminates.

Specific to each active learning approach is therefore on the one hand the choice of *query strategy* and on the other hand the choice of *classifier*.

4.2 Query Strategies

Active learning attempts to find a minimal training dataset that simultaneously maximises the classification performance. Therefore, the challenge is to select those data points whose labelling provides the greatest benefit for training of the classifier in each iteration. Query strategies attempt to find an approximate solution to this problem and here we investigate four different query strategies.

Random Sampling (RS) is a query strategy that randomly selects data points from a pool of unlabelled samples. In this very basic strategy, there is no prioritisation of samples regarding their value for the training. While we can anticipate that this naive approach will not yield the best results, we are interested in seeing what improvements the more targeted strategies can achieve in comparison.

Query by Committee (QBC) [22] is a query strategy in which the disagreement between a committee of classifiers serves as a measure of information gain. To this end, the classifiers, previously trained on already labelled samples, categorise each unlabelled sample and subsequently the predictions are used to calculate a disagreement score (e.g. 0 if all predictions match). The unlabelled samples are then ranked in descending order based on their disagreement scores, and the top-k (i.e. those that the committee was least confident about) are forwarded to the human annotator.

In our experiments, we use a committee of three classifiers and define the disagreement score of a sample as the number of distinct class predictions minus one. We follow the course of action by Purpura et al. [20], but dispense with the specifications for hierarchical schemas.[1] If assignment to more than one category is allowed, we sum up the class-wise disagreement scores.

[1] We also forgo the computationally expensive additional clustering that has been suggested as an extension because of runtime considerations.

Minimum Expected Entropy (MEE) [12] is a query strategy that tries to minimise the prediction uncertainty of unlabelled data points by selecting those with the largest expected uncertainty to be labelled first. The prediction uncertainty of a data point is estimated with the entropy measure. Given a discrete random variable X, $\mathcal{H}(X)$ takes a value between 0 and 1 depending on the probability distribution over the variable's possible values (e.g. the prediction outcome of the current classification model for the different categories C):

$$\mathcal{H}(X) = -\sum_{c \in C} P(X = c) \log_2 P(X = c)$$

Contrastive Active Learning (CAL) [17] is a recent approach to improve querying by selecting so-called contrastive samples. These are samples that are close to each other in the feature space (e.g. share a similar vocabulary), but for which the current classification model's predictions are very different. Similar samples are found using the k-nearest neighbour algorithm and the difference in prediction probabilities is measured using the Kullback-Leibler divergence. The authors could show that CAL can perform equivalently or even better than a range of query strategies such as entropy for several tasks, including topic classification.

4.3 Classifier

In addition to the choice of a suitable query strategy, the choice of the classifier is crucial for the success of active learning. We therefore compare different classifiers, including both classical and state-of-the-art approaches. Following the setup from [20], we consider *support vector machines* (SVM), the *maximum entropy classifier* (MaxEnt), and the *naive Bayes classifier* (NB), some of which are known to perform well across a range of classification tasks. We also test an ensemble classifier that combines SVM, MaxEnt and NB. The textual contributions were transformed into tf-idf-weighted term vectors to obtain a machine-readable format. Non-word tokens were excluded, the words were lower-cased and lemmatised. To further reduce the dimensionality of the feature vectors, we also removed less discriminative words, i.e. words that occurred only once or in more than 80% of the contributions in the respective dataset. We furthermore include *BERT* (Bidirectional Encoder Representations from Transformers) in the comparison, one of the most popular transformer models. Within the last few years, transformer models have contributed significantly to the improvement of results in various NLP applications, and more recently they have also been considered for use in active learning [9]. In this work, we initialise BERT with the case-sensitive gbert-base model[2], a pre-trained language model for German, and encode the textual contributions accordingly.

[2] Model available at https://huggingface.co/deepset/gbert-base.

5 Evaluation

We address three research questions, starting by investigating how well the automated topic classification of citizen contributions already works. Keeping this knowledge of the potential and limitations of topic classification in mind, we turn our attention to the savings in manual labelling efforts through the use of active learning. Finally, we analyse the runtime of the approaches and thus consider a second key aspect for their practical applicability.

We answer the questions for public participation processes on cycling in the cities of Bonn, Ehrenfeld and Moers. This allows us to make a direct comparison between three thematically similar processes that differ, however, in the number of citizen ideas collected and the distribution along the categories. In order to obtain reliable results, especially with the small datasets, the experiments were realised with a 5-fold cross-validation of 80%−20% splits for training and testing the classification model. The model score will be reported as the average outcome of the five runs and the standard deviation will be indicated. We measure category-wise performance with the F_1 score, the harmonic mean of model precision and recall for the respective class. For assessing model performance on a global level, we compute the proportion of correct predictions using *accuracy* for single-label classifications and *micro-averaged* F_1 for multi-label classifications. Micro-averaged F_1 is a common measure, and for single-label scenarios, it is equivalent to accuracy.

5.1 RQ1: What Classification Quality Can Be Achieved Without Active Learning?

First of all, we are interested in how well topic classification can work on our datasets in general. Table 2 shows the results for each of the five classifiers presented above, for single-label and for multi-label classification respectively. To improve the model fit on the datasets, we tuned hyperparameters in each cross-validation split (see Appendix A for more details).

The results are encouraging: the primary thematic focus of citizens' contributions could be correctly predicted in 75% to 80% of the cases, depending on the dataset. If all related topic categories were to be found, similarly good outcomes were achieved with between 72% and 80% of the predicted labels matching the human annotation. As expected, BERT can improve the accuracy respectively the micro-averaged F_1 score, in our setting by up to 0.11 compared to MaxEnt, the best performing among the other models. The effects are particularly remarkable for rarely occurring categories, such as bicycle parking in Moers, where only seven to eight matching contributions were available for training the model (the remaining contributions were part of the test set). This clearly emphasises the strengths of the pre-trained language model, which stores previously learned knowledge about semantic relationships between words. Comparing the results for the different classification tasks, i.e. single-labelling and multi-labelling, shows that most classifiers perform similarly well in both appli-

Table 2. Results of single-label and multi-label topic classification.

			Single-Label Classification								
			Cycling traffic management	Signage	Obstacles	Cycle path quality	Traffic lights	Lighting	Bicycle parking	Misc	Accuracy
F_1	*Bonn*	SVM	0.75(0.02)	0.45(0.14)	0.65(0.07)	0.71(0.03)	0.73(0.04)	0.74(0.11)	0.82(0.10)	0.03(0.07)	0.71(0.02)
		MaxEnt	0.76(0.02)	0.44(0.10)	0.65(0.08)	0.72(0.02)	0.72(0.03)	0.77(0.11)	0.84(0.07)	**0.12**(0.13)	0.71(0.02)
		NB	0.68(0.02)	0.05(0.05)	0.39(0.14)	0.57(0.02)	0.30(0.06)	0.00(0.00)	0.15(0.09)	0.00(0.00)	0.56(0.02)
		Ensemble	0.76(0.01)	0.44(0.12)	0.66(0.08)	0.71(0.02)	0.73(0.03)	0.73(0.09)	0.83(0.08)	0.03(0.07)	0.71(0.02)
		BERT	**0.80**(0.03)	**0.58**(0.06)	**0.71**(0.04)	**0.75**(0.04)	**0.80**(0.03)	**0.81**(0.10)	**0.90**(0.04)	0.06(0.13)	**0.76**(0.02)
	Ehrenfeld	SVM	0.76(0.04)	0.10(0.22)	0.66(0.13)	0.34(0.18)	0.68(0.05)	0.00(0.00)*	0.62(0.19)	0.00(0.00)	0.66(0.04)
		MaxEnt	0.75(0.05)	0.20(0.18)	**0.68**(0.11)	0.40(0.21)	0.69(0.07)	0.00(0.00)*	**0.84**(0.12)	0.00(0.00)	0.67(0.03)
		NB	0.66(0.04)	0.00(0.00)	0.19(0.25)	0.06(0.08)	0.04(0.10)	0.00(0.00)*	0.00(0.00)	0.00(0.00)	0.49(0.05)
		Ensemble	0.77(0.03)	0.10(0.22)	0.65(0.14)	0.36(0.18)	0.68(0.05)	0.00(0.00)*	0.78(0.08)	0.00(0.00)	0.68(0.04)
		BERT	**0.83**(0.02)	**0.36**(0.25)	0.66(0.14)	**0.63**(0.10)	**0.73**(0.09)	0.00(0.00)*	**0.84**(0.10)	0.00(0.00)	**0.75**(0.03)
	Moers	SVM	0.78(0.05)	0.25(0.23)	0.46(0.15)	0.66(0.10)	0.74(0.24)	0.33(0.31)	0.27(0.37)	0.00(0.00)	0.70(0.05)
		MaxEnt	0.78(0.04)	0.31(0.17)	0.37(0.13)	0.67(0.09)	0.78(0.07)	0.59(0.38)	0.67(0.41)	0.00(0.00)	0.71(0.03)
		NB	0.72(0.03)	0.00(0.00)	0.00(0.00)	0.67(0.03)	0.44(0.14)	0.00(0.00)	0.00(0.00)	0.00(0.00)	0.62(0.03)
		Ensemble	0.77(0.05)	0.25(0.23)	0.40(0.21)	0.67(0.09)	0.74(0.24)	0.37(0.34)	0.13(0.30)	0.00(0.00)	0.70(0.05)
		BERT	**0.84**(0.03)	**0.52**(0.17)	**0.59**(0.09)	**0.81**(0.10)	**0.91**(0.08)	**0.70**(0.45)	**0.73**(0.43)	0.00(0.00)	**0.80**(0.03)

			Multi-Label Classification								
			Cycling traffic management	Signage	Obstacles	Cycle path quality	Traffic lights	Lighting	Bicycle parking	Misc	Micro-avg F_1
F_1	*Bonn*	SVM	0.77(0.02)	0.45(0.10)	0.66(0.03)	0.70(0.01)	0.76(0.05)	0.67(0.23)	0.79(0.07)	0.18(0.14)	0.71(0.01)
		MaxEnt	0.75(0.01)	0.46(0.06)	0.64(0.01)	0.69(0.02)	0.76(0.04)	0.79(0.14)	0.80(0.09)	0.28(0.14)	0.70(0.01)
		NB	0.65(0.01)	0.15(0.05)	0.37(0.05)	0.65(0.02)	0.37(0.06)	0.04(0.09)	0.19(0.12)	0.17(0.13)	0.52(0.01)
		Ensemble	0.75(0.02)	0.45(0.10)	0.64(0.04)	0.69(0.05)	0.73(0.09)	0.59(0.25)	0.76(0.11)	0.24(0.17)	0.69(0.02)
		BERT	**0.81**(0.01)	**0.48**(0.17)	**0.71**(0.02)	**0.78**(0.03)	**0.78**(0.03)	**0.83**(0.09)	**0.89**(0.04)	**0.39**(0.07)	**0.77**(0.01)
	Ehrenfeld	SVM	0.45(0.41)	0.00(0.00)	0.39(0.17)	0.29(0.19)	0.45(0.34)	0.00(0.00)	0.54(0.32)	0.20(0.17)	0.43(0.26)
		MaxEnt	0.73(0.04)	0.25(0.25)	0.50(0.12)	0.45(0.06)	0.68(0.08)	0.18(0.25)	0.62(0.29)	0.15(0.14)	0.61(0.04)
		NB	0.77(0.05)	0.00(0.00)	0.21(0.16)	0.26(0.09)	0.17(0.12)	0.00(0.00)	0.11(0.16)	0.24(0.18)	0.49(0.02)
		Ensemble	0.74(0.02)	0.08(0.18)	0.28(0.27)	0.23(0.16)	0.55(0.19)	0.00(0.00)	0.33(0.41)	0.06(0.13)	0.56(0.07)
		BERT	**0.82**(0.03)	**0.33**(0.21)	**0.65**(0.11)	**0.57**(0.13)	**0.76**(0.07)	**0.20**(0.45)	**0.77**(0.20)	**0.24**(0.15)	**0.72**(0.02)
	Moers	SVM	0.78(0.02)	0.30(0.20)	0.25(0.16)	0.69(0.11)	0.82(0.10)	0.46(0.36)	0.33(0.47)	0.00(0.00)	0.69(0.04)
		MaxEnt	0.79(0.07)	0.23(0.13)	0.29(0.09)	0.68(0.09)	0.82(0.07)	**0.63**(0.18)	0.67(0.41)	0.00(0.00)	0.70(0.04)
		NB	0.75(0.06)	0.05(0.11)	0.08(0.11)	0.62(0.09)	0.49(0.07)	0.00(0.00)	0.00(0.00)	**0.13**(0.12)	0.58(0.03)
		Ensemble	0.78(0.04)	0.24(0.14)	0.28(0.18)	0.71(0.03)	0.81(0.09)	0.58(0.35)	0.40(0.55)	0.11(0.25)	0.70(0.04)
		BERT	**0.88**(0.05)	**0.41**(0.34)	**0.56**(0.24)	**0.82**(0.06)	**0.93**(0.03)	0.55(0.16)	**1.00**(0.00)	0.00(0.00)	**0.80**(0.04)

cations. This suggests that predicting all associated labels of a contribution is by no means more difficult than the recognition of the primary topic.

All models had problems with recognising contributions that were grouped in the misc category, which is not surprising due to the missing thematic coherence of the content. It should also be noted that in Ehrenfeld the category lighting occurs too infrequently to allow evaluation in the single-label case.

5.2 RQ2: How Much Manual Labelling Effort Can Be Saved Through Active Learning?

It is evident from the results for RQ1 that even smaller datasets have the potential to provide enough information to train good topic classification models. With the application of active learning, we are now taking a closer look at this potential.

In our experiments, the active learning process (implemented using the small-text library [21]) is initialised with 20 randomly drawn samples (i.e. contribu-

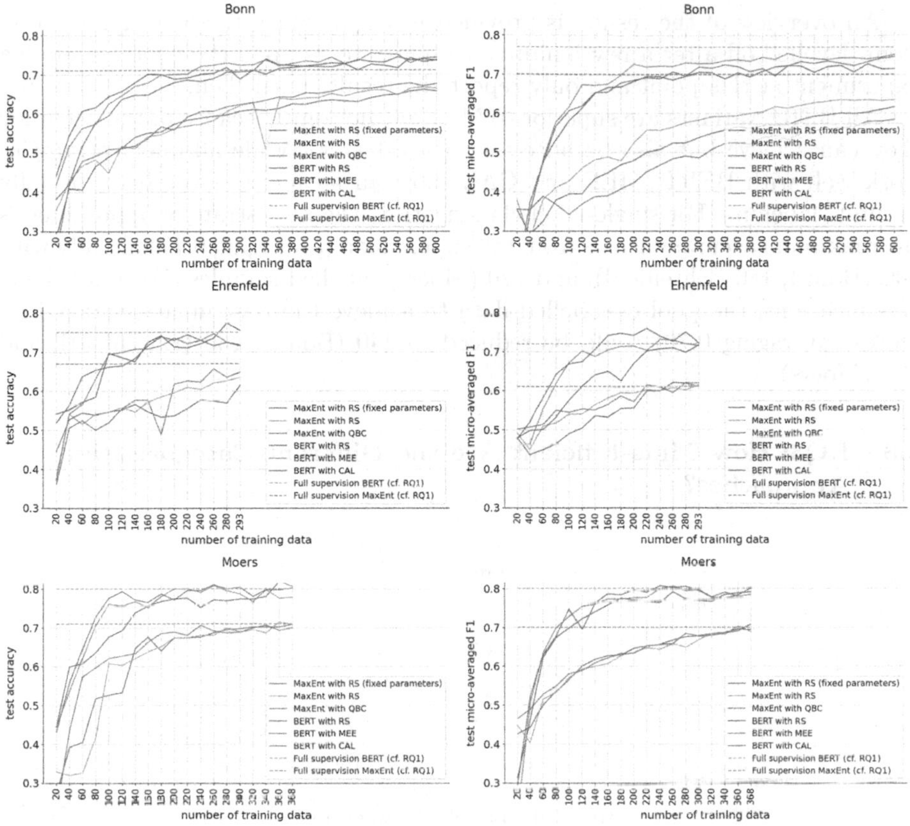

(a) Single-Label Classification (b) Multi-Label Classification

Fig. 1. Accuracy respectively micro-averaged F_1 scores for active learning per iteration.

tions). Then, in each active learning loop, 20 unlabelled samples are retrieved with the respective query strategy and added to the pool of labelled data. We compare the two best performing classifiers from RQ1 and first evaluate them with RS to have a baseline. QBC and MEE follow a similar strategy of selecting samples (by disagreement of a committee and uncertainty in prediction, respectively). With respect to the work of [20], we combine MaxEnt with QBC. A combination of BERT and QBC, on the other hand, was rejected because of runtime considerations since in addition to the costly transformer model, three further models would have to be trained per active learning iteration. Instead, we use the well-known MEE query strategy with BERT. Furthermore, we explore whether the recently developed query strategy CAL can further improve active learning with BERT. To keep model training time low, hyperparameter tuning for BERT is limited to selecting the best model from 10 training epochs. For MaxEnt, we compare a gridsearch-optimised model against one with fixed hyperparameters.

An overview of the results is provided in Fig. 1. Since the learning curve in Bonn levelled off after a few hundred samples, we stopped the time-consuming experiment at this point and only report the results until then.

All BERT variants are superior to MaxEnt, not only because of the accuracy they can achieve but also because they learn faster. While all query strategies work well with BERT, MEE and CAL show an advantage over RS especially in multi-labelling. For single-label classification, the best strategy approximates the maximum accuracy scores from full supervision (averaging 0.77) already with 500 (Bonn), 180 (Ehrenfeld), and 120 (Moers) labelled samples. For multi-label classifications, the pool of labelled data to achieve the best micro-averaged F_1 scores (averaging 0.76) could be reduced to 440 (Bonn), 160 (Ehrenfeld), and 200 (Moers).

5.3 RQ3: How Time-Efficient Are the Different Categorisation Approaches?

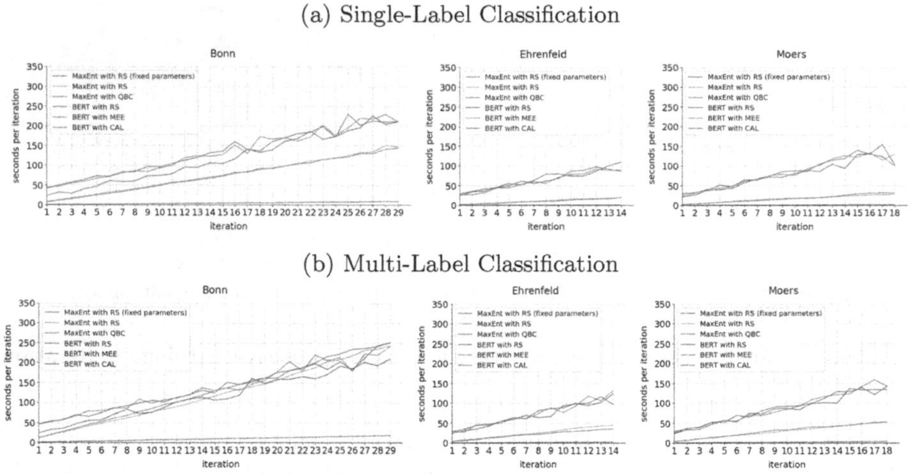

Fig. 2. Time duration of active learning iterations in seconds.

Not only the quality of the results but also the runtime is relevant if such an approach is to be developed for use by practitioners. Figure 2 reports how long the individual iterations, i.e. loops, of active learning take. This reflects the time a user has to wait between coding sessions. BERT-based experiments were run on Google Colab with Tesla P100-PCIE-16GB GPU and 2.2 GHz Intel Xeon CPU processor. The other classifiers were evaluated on a local machine with 1.8 GHz Intel Core i7-8565U CPU processor.

Encouragingly in terms of applicability, no iteration in the observation interval lasts longer than five minutes. Taking into account the findings from RQ2, to achieve these results on average a human analyst would have to wait less than three minutes (Bonn) or even less than one minute (Ehrenfeld, Moers) between the coding sessions. At the same time, however, we can observe that BERT is more computationally intensive than MaxEnt, even though we severely limited hyperparameter tuning in our experiments.

6 Discussion

Based on the evaluation summarised above we can now answer the research questions and discuss their implications.

For the first research question (RQ1), the results show that supervised machine learning can predict the correct label(s) on average for about 77% of the cases. We believe that this accuracy is already sufficient for most of the practical use cases because this categorisation is only the starting point of further manual processing of contributions. During this further processing possible misclassification would be detected and could easily be corrected. A number of issues are particularly noteworthy about this level of accuracy. First of all, the classification works equally well for single and multi-labelling. What is more, BERT as a current state-of-the-art approach offers the best results - not only because it achieves higher accuracy, but also because it works more reliably for categories with few contributions than the other classifiers evaluated. Finally, we test the models on three different datasets that vary in size and we can show that these results can be achieved also on datasets that contain only a few hundred contributions.

These results already show that automated classification through supervised models could be useful in supporting human evaluation of contributions. However, as discussed in the introduction, the main barrier to its practical application is that full supervision requires the manual labelling of large parts of the data. In our evaluation, this accuracy was achieved through coding a share of 80% of the entire dataset, an approach also pursued in several studies that focused on maximising the accuracy of approaches but neglected the drawback of manual labelling effort (e.g. [4]).

To address this shortcoming, as a second research question (RQ2) we investigated the potential of different active learning strategies to reduce manual labelling efforts. Our results show conclusive evidence that active learning can indeed obtain a similar performance while requiring only a fraction of the data to be manually coded. For the three datasets it was sufficient to manually label about 20% (Bonn), 50% (Ehrenfeld), and 30% (Moers) to achieve about the same level of accuracy as with full supervision. Naturally, these efficiency-improvements grow with the size of the dataset. Active learning significantly reduces manual labelling efforts and outperforms the previously used approaches for topic classification of participation contributions [20].

However, this would only offer a useful support for practice if these models can be realistically computed in common administrative settings. Therefore we also investigated the time-efficiency of the different categorisation approaches (RQ3). As it turns out, all of these require only a few minutes per iteration to compute. However, it should be noted that these time benchmarks depend on specific hardware (e.g. GPU and processor). The implications for practical use will need to be investigated in future work.

To put these figures in perspective and estimate the efficiency gains, we optimistically assume that it would take a human 30 s to code a single contribution. Using the dataset of Bonn and the results of the single-labelling experiments, fully manual coding of the entire 2,314 contributions would thus require 19 h and 17 min of labour. In contrast, training a machine learning model with active learning requires the labelling of only 500 data points (about 22% of the corpus) to achieve a performance that would be comparable to a model with full supervision in training. This would amount to 4 h and 10 min of manual coding time with machine assistance. We might add a human analyst's waiting time in between manual annotation sessions that is required in the active learning process for the computation of the next set of samples to be labelled. However, this only increases total time by 1 h (on average about 150 s for the 24 iterations). What is more, this time can be used to carry out other tasks or to provide the necessary breaks in coding session to the human analyst. This means the time required to label the whole dataset with active learning amounts to 5 h 10 min in contrast to more than 19 h.

Even if we take into account that the machine learning model would produce a number of misclassifications (based on the results from RQ1 we assume this to be the case for about one in four samples, i.e. 580) which would require manual correction once each result is processed by the human analysts, with about 4 h and 50 min of additional work this still amounts to a substantial reduction in time required: Instead of more than 19 h, it would take just 10 h (including one hour of waiting time). Relying on the same assumptions the total time required is reduced by 20% in Ehrenfeld and 50% in Moers through active learning. While the actual efficiency gains will depend on a number of factors (size of corpus, coding time per data point, computing time per iteration, amount of training data required, model accuracy), we believe that in any realistic scenario active learning will always represent a significant reduction in time required from human analysts.

In sum, our results show not only that supervised machine learning models can reliably classify topic categories for public participation contributions, but also that by utilising active learning this can be achieved with manually labelling only a comparatively small part of the data. This has important implications for the practice of public participation because once implemented, these models substantially cut the time required for manual coding.

7 Conclusion and Future Work

Public consultations are popular instruments in democratic policy-making but the subsequent evaluation of the (written) contributions requires considerable human resources. While supervised machine learning offers a way to support analysts in thematically grouping citizen ideas, often the amount of training data required is prohibitive given the idiosyncratic nature of most public participation processes. One possible solution to minimise the manual labelling effort is the use of active learning. However, the merits of this semi-supervised method for evaluating participation data have received little attention so far.

In this study, we researched the application of active learning based on online participation processes in three German cities. We first explored the capabilities of automated topic classification in general. Building on this, we investigated how much manual labelling effort can be saved through active learning and how time-efficient the different approaches are. Our results show that supervised machine learning models can reliably classify topic categories for public participation contributions. When combined with active learning, the amount of training data required can be significantly reduced while keeping algorithmic runtime low. These findings can be of great benefit to the practice of public participation, as they significantly reduce the time required for the thematic pre-sorting of submissions to participation processes.

Despite these exciting findings, some questions remain unanswered that need to be addressed in future work. So far, the coding of our dataset reflects primarily the assessment of a single analyst. Although this is a realistic application scenario, future research should attempt to evaluate predictions based on labels with (higher) intercoder reliability. It could well be that the actual model accuracy is even higher if misclassifications in the training data are avoided. Furthermore, we limited hyperparameter tuning for BERT to reduce computation time. For real-world implementation, we strongly recommend fine-tuning the BERT model to increase model accuracy if a higher runtime is acceptable. Similarly, we would like to evaluate other transformer architectures as well as further query strategies, in particular those specifically designed for deep neural network models (e.g. [3]).

Likewise, we need to address possible limitations of our approaches, such as applicability to long texts and runtime dependency on the GPU. Finally, classes with few contributions deserve a more thorough investigation, examining how effectively they can be found through the various query strategies in active learning and what impact a failure of detection has on the utility in practical application. Eventually, our long-term goal is to make these approaches available as software to make their use feasible for practitioners.[3]

Acknowledgements. This publication is based on research in the project CIMT/Partizipationsnutzen, which is funded by the Federal Ministry of Education and Research of Germany as part of its Social-Ecological Research funding priority, funding no. 01UU1904. Responsibility for the content of this publication lies with the author.

Appendix A: Hyperparameter Tuning

For SVM, we apply a gridsearch over the hyperparameters $C \in [0.1, 1, 10, 100]$, $\gamma \in [1, 0.1, 0.01, 0.001]$, and with either the RBF or the linear kernel. For MaxEnt, we search for $C \in [10, 100, 1000]$ in combination with the L1 or the L2 norm for penalty. In the Ensemble classifier, we reduce the number of hyperparameter combinations to keep the duration of the experiments within reasonable limits and thus do not consider $C \in [0.1]$ and $\gamma \in [0.01, 0.001]$ for SVM.

[3] The datasets and the code that was used to run the experiments are available at https://github.com/juliaromberg/egov-2022.

BERT is trained using the AdamW optimizer with a learning rate of $2e-5$ and $\epsilon = 1e{-}8$. Training runs for 10 epochs, from which the best model is selected using a validation set. In the non-active setup we tested batch sizes of 2, 4 and 8. We found that a batch size of 2 gave the best results (RQ1) and for this reason, we opted for this batch size in the active learning experiments (RQ2).

References

1. Aitamurto, T., Chen, K., Cherif, A., Galli, J.S., Santana, L.: Civic CrowdAnalytics: making sense of crowdsourced civic input with big data tools. In: Proceedings of the 20th International Academic Mindtrek Conference, AcademicMindtrek 2016, pp. 86–94. Association for Computing Machinery, New York (2016)
2. Arana-Catania, M., et al.: Citizen participation and machine learning for a better democracy. Digit. Gov. Res. Pract. **2**(3), 1–22 (2021)
3. Ash, J.T., Chicheng, Z., Akshay, K., John, L., Alekh, A.: Deep batch active learning by diverse, uncertain gradient lower BoundsDeep batch active learning by diverse, uncertain gradient lower bounds. In: International Conference on Learning Representations 2020 (ICLR 2020) (2020)
4. Balta, D., Kuhn, P., Sellami, M., Kulus, D., Lieven, C., Krcmar, H.: How to streamline AI application in government? A case study on citizen participation in Germany. In: Lindgren, I., et al. (eds.) EGOV 2019. LNCS, vol. 11685, pp. 233–247. Springer, Cham (2019). https://doi.org/10.1007/978-3-030-27325-5_18
5. Cai, G., Sun, F., Sha, Y.: Interactive visualization for topic model curation. In: Proceedings of the ACM IUI 2018 Workshop on Exploratory Search and Interactive Data Analytics (2018)
6. Cardie, C., Farina, C., Aijaz, A., Rawding, M., Purpura, S.: A study in rule-specific issue categorization for e-rulemaking. In: Proceedings of the 9th International Conference on Digital Government Research, pp. 244–253 (2008)
7. Chen, K., Aitamurto, T.: Barriers for crowd's impact in crowdsourced policymaking: civic data overload and filter hierarchy. Int. Public Manag. J. **22**(1), 99–126 (2019)
8. Dryzek, J.S., et al.: The crisis of democracy and the science of deliberation. Science **363**(6432), 1144–1146 (2019)
9. Ein-Dor, L., et al.: Active learning for BERT: an empirical study. In: Proceedings of the 2020 Conference on Empirical Methods in Natural Language Processing (EMNLP), pp. 7949–7962. Association for Computational Linguistics (2020)
10. Hagen, L.: Content analysis of e-petitions with topic modeling: how to train and evaluate LDA models? Inf. Process. Manag. **54**(6), 1292–1307 (2018)
11. Hagen, L., Uzuner, Ö., Kotfila, C., Harrison, T.M., Lamanna, D.: Understanding citizens' direct policy suggestions to the federal government: a natural language processing and topic modeling approach. In: 2015 48th Hawaii International Conference on System Sciences, pp. 2134–2143 (2015)
12. Holub, A., Perona, P., Burl, M.C.: Entropy-based active learning for object recognition. In: 2008 IEEE Computer Society Conference on Computer Vision and Pattern Recognition Workshops, pp. 1–8 (2008)
13. Kim, B., Yoo, M., Park, K.C., Lee, K.R., Kim, J.H.: A value of civic voices for smart city: a big data analysis of civic queries posed by Seoul citizens. Cities **108**, 102941 (2021)

14. Kwon, N., Shulman, S.W., Hovy, E.: Multidimensional text analysis for eRulemaking. In: Proceedings of the 2006 International Conference on Digital Government Research, dg.o 2006, pp. 157–166. Digital Government Society of North America (2006)
15. Levy, K.E.C., Franklin, M.: Driving regulation: using topic models to examine political contention in the U.S. trucking industry. Soc. Sci. Comput. Rev. **32**(2), 182–194 (2014)
16. Ma, B., Zhang, N., Liu, G., Li, L., Yuan, H.: Semantic search for public opinions on urban affairs: a probabilistic topic modeling-based approach. Inf. Process. Manag. **52**(3), 430–445 (2016)
17. Margatina, K., Vernikos, G., Barrault, L., Aletras, N.: Active learning by acquiring contrastive examples. In: Proceedings of the 2021 Conference on Empirical Methods in Natural Language Processing, pp. 650–663. Association for Computational Linguistics, Punta Cana (2021)
18. OECD: Promise and Problems of E-Democracy. OECD (2003)
19. Parry, G., Moyser, G.: More participation, more democracy? In: Beetham, D. (ed.) Defining and Measuring Democracy. Sage, London (1994)
20. Purpura, S., Cardie, C., Simons, J.: Active learning for e-rulemaking: public comment categorization. In: Proceedings of the 9th International Conference on Digital Government Research, pp. 234–243 (2008)
21. Schröder, C., Müller, L., Niekler, A., Potthast, M.: Small-text: active learning for text classification in Python (2021)
22. Seung, H.S., Opper, M., Sompolinsky, H.: Query by committee. In: Proceedings of the Fifth Annual Workshop on Computational Learning Theory, pp. 287–294 (1992)
23. Simonofski, A., Fink, J., Burnay, C.: Supporting policy-making with social media and e-participation platforms data: a policy analytics framework. Gov. Inf. Q. **38**(3), 101590 (2021)
24. Teufl, P., Payer, U., Parycek, P.: Automated analysis of e-participation data by utilizing associative networks, spreading activation and unsupervised learning. In: Macintosh, A., Tambouris, E. (eds.) ePart 2009. LNCS, vol. 5694, pp. 139–150. Springer, Heidelberg (2009). https://doi.org/10.1007/978-3-642-03781-8_13
25. Yang, H., Callan, J.: OntoCop: constructing ontologies for public comments. IEEE Intell. Syst. **24**(5), 70–75 (2009)

Taking Stock of the Situation

The Situational Context of Bureaucratic Encounters

Søren Skaarup(✉)

IT University of Copenhagen, Copenhagen, Denmark
skaa@itu.dk

Abstract. This paper contributes to e-government research by presenting a conceptual framework of the key-features of the situational context that informs citizens approaches to bureaucratic encounters with government (BEs). The framework is developed through a qualitative hermeneutic approach involving several different literatures. The framework identifies five basic features of the citizen's situation that may affect how citizens approach BE's: 1) Consequences: the possible outcomes of the situation 2) Vulnerability: how well equipped is the citizen to deal with the possible outcomes. 3) Familiarity: how much can the citizen draw on previous experiences with similar situations. 4) Complexity: how complex does the citizen perceive her situation to be. 5) Urgency: what time-constraints are there on the citizen getting the issues resolved.

The framework can be a useful tool for analysing citizens' strategies concerning the bureaucratic encounters and their use of self-service systems and the effects thereof for both citizens and authorities. In addition, the framework can be used by researchers and practitioners alike to analyse self-service-systems and multi-channel strategies and service designs to identify how they take the different features of the situation into account.

Keywords: Citizen–government interaction · Digitalization · Theory-building · Digital services · Situation

Submitted to the EGOV 2022 Conference

1 Introduction and Background

Citizens increasingly conduct their business with government online [1]. Understanding citizens' strategies and behaviors for these encounters is important to improve the quality of service, to optimize efficiency and effectiveness and to ensure an accessible, inclusive, and fair access to government and government services for all citizens.

Citizens encounter government in a wide range of contexts and for a wide range of reasons. In this paper, the focus is on "bureaucratic encounters" (BE) [2, 3]. This is where most people have direct experience with government. Much work on bureaucratic encounters focus on face-to-face encounters. However, as Nass and Moon have shown [4, 5], people unwittingly apply social and human attributes to interactive systems such as self-service systems. Thus, interactions with self-service systems may qualify as

Published by Springer Nature Switzerland AG 2022
M. Janssen et al. (Eds.): EGOV 2022, LNCS 13391, pp. 386–401, 2022.
https://doi.org/10.1007/978-3-031-15086-9_25

encounters with proxies for humans and the organizations they represent. In this paper, "Encounters" therefore covers all types of "bureaucratic" interactions between citizens and authorities, no matter what channels are used.

When citizens engage with government to seek information, to apply for a benefit or a service or to fulfill some obligation, they do so in a wider context, or "situation".

The situation is the circumstances or events in the citizen's life that gives rise to the need for engaging with the authority or which constitutes the context for this engagement when the BE is initiated by the authority. The situation is the context for the BE, it includes the citizens expectations for the BE and the possible consequences of the BE but does not include the BE itself. An understanding of the "situation" is a key element in understanding approaches to bureaucratic encounters [6–9], alongside citizens' needs and goals for the encounter [10] and the skills and resources they are able to bring to the encounter [11].

Citizens' strategies and behaviors in relation to these encounters have in the e-government literature, primarily been studied from a channel choice[1] perspective [9, 11–13]. In the e-government literature [6–9, 11–17] as well as in the medium-theory literature [18], focus has often been on the nature of tasks citizens have to go through and particularly on their complexity and ambiguity, and on how that affects citizens choices and behaviors in relation to their BEs. The "situation" has achieved less attention and the literature has not arrived at a unified set of features that characterize the situation.

Ebbers, Jansen & Pieterson [6] identifies: Urgency (time pressure), need for closure (need to complete task), and the task at hand (the nature of the problem or the interaction). Ebbers, Pieterson & Noordman [7] includes availability/channel constraints and emotions (which are not very well defined). They also talk of the "contextual situation" without further unfolding this concept. Pieterson & Ebbers [8] also include "importance" (the personal relevance of the matter to the citizen). Lindgren et al. [14] highlights Goodsell's use of the "lateral dimension" as part of the scope of the encounter. This is the impact the service the encounter is about may have on the citizen's life. Lindgren et al. [14] argues that this concept is understudied and under-theorized. In general, I will argue in this paper, that this goes for many of the concepts applied to characterize the situation, they are fuzzy, underdeveloped, and under-studied, empirically as well as theoretically.

Expanding on this previous work I will propose a revised framework for describing the "situation" as an important part of the background for citizens choices and strategies in relation to their bureaucratic encounters.

This paper addresses the need for citizen-centred research as well as native theory development within e-government studies, which has been stated repeatedly in the literature [16, 19–22]. It also addresses the need for more theoretical work to fully understand citizens strategies and behaviors for the BE, for reviews and revisions of existing Channel Choice models and for the development of new models [13].

[1] As Pieterson [9] has pointed out, "choice" implies an essentially rational and conscious selection between options, and this oversimplifies the issue. Pieterson and most later authors in the field, use the term "behaviour" instead. I use the terms behaviour and "approaches". Nevertheless, the name of the subfield of e-government research is known under the name Channel-choice, so I will use the that as a label for the literature involved.

The paper contributes to the e-government literature by presenting a conceptual framework of aspects of the situation that are important for citizens and their approaches to bureaucratic encounters. Scholars can use this framework to investigate the effects for citizens of applying different technologies in the BE. Practitioners can use the framework in the design of self-service systems, the organizational designs of BE service delivery, and in the design of multichannel strategies.

The rest of the paper is structured as follows: Sect. 2 outlines the method applied for the literature review. In Sect. 3 I review the literature and construct the conceptual framework. Section 3 falls in three parts. Section 3.1 reviews and discuss how the literature construes the features of the task. Section 3.2 does the same for the situation. In Sect. 3.3 the conceptual framework is created. Section 4 contains a brief discussion, suggestions for application of the framework and future research and a discussion of the limitations of the study.

2 Method

The framework presented here is an artefact developed through a "hermeneutic literature review" [23], based on the principles of the hermeneutic circle [24], synthesising theory and findings from previous research.

The selection and search of these literatures is based on a set of initial assumptions (Table 1) founded in previous literature readings, supplemented by experiences from my career as a civil servant serving citizens at the frontlines.

Table 1. Initial assumptions

	Assumption	Inspired by
1	The trigger for initiating a bureaucratic encounter are circumstances or events in the citizens life that gives rise to the need for a service, benefit or permit from government, or the need to fulfil some obligation with government	Katz et al. 1975 [2], Goodsell 2018 [3], Hassenfeld [26]
2	The circumstances and needs that gives rise to the BE may affect the citizen's approach to the encounter as well as her abilities to handle it	Pieterson 2009 [9], Madsen & Kræmmergaard 2015 [15]
3	Citizens are rarely experts in the rules, regulations, and procedures of relevance for the encounter	Lindgren, et al. 2019 [14]
4	A fundamental condition for the BE is the power-asymmetry between the citizen and the authority	Järvinnen, Larsen og Mortensen [27], Mik-Meyer & Villadsen [29], Lenk 2002 [30]

The review-process included the five steps outlined by Boell & Cecez-Kecmanovic [23]:

1) **Reading:** Based on the initial assumptions and following the example set by Rose et al. [25], I draw on five different literatures which can shed light on the situational context for citizens' bureaucratic encounters: 1) the e-government literature – in particular the channel choice literature– this is the literature my contribution is aimed at and it constitutes the largest part of the literature reviewed. 2) The private sector service encounter literature, 3) The medium theory literature 4) The public administration literature 5) Sociological literature with a focus on the asymmetries of power in citizen-authority encounters. Each field of research contributed with perspectives on" the situation" which could be relevant for the framework..
2) **Identifying ideas and concepts** of relevance for the research objective and evaluating how they might relate to the emerging conceptual framework. Focus here was on ideas and concepts that described features of "the situation".
3) **Critically assessing the literature** to identify what could be considered foundational features of the situation.
4) **Developing and revising the framework** as additional concepts and ideas are identified and evaluated. The framework began with considerably more elements and more overlap between concepts. Narrowing it down was a question of identifying what could be consider basic features.
5) **Searching** based on references and new perspectives found in the literature consulted so far.

These steps were applied iteratively and not necessarily in the order presented here. Searching, reading, analysing, and framework development were closely interconnected.

During this iterative process of searching, reading, and analysis, I synthesised the framework through a series of revisions and elaborations. The process stopped when saturation was reached, and no further dimensions for the framework were identified [23].

An interpretive, hermeneutic approach will always and unavoidably rely on the researcher's pre-understanding. What is important is to make these pre-understandings explicit, as has been done here with the initial assumption.

The initial assumptions have also served as a point of departure for seeking alternative perspectives on the encounter that are not usually represented in the e-government literature. At the same time, the selection of literature has been limited by these assumptions. Other literatures, such as the service-design and digital-design literatures, could have provided additional insights. However, the intention of this study has not been to conduct an exhaustive survey of all relevant literatures but, through a limited search of selected literatures, to provide a framework that provides a more basic understanding of the role of the situational context for the BE.

3 Conceptual Framework

The result of the literature review is a conceptual framework intended to serve as a foundation and reference point for further investigation [31]. The framework identifies the key aspects of the situation that may influence citizens' approaches to the BE. Table 2 presents this framework.

Table 2. The situation framework

Feature	Description	References
Consequences	Consequences have to do with the possible outcomes: Will the citizen get or loose a benefit? Will her application for a permit denied or approved? Has she filed out her tax-papers correctly, or will she get a fine? Will she be treated well, or will she be treated badly? What matters here is the citizens perception of the possible outcomes and their likelihood more than what is formally possible or likely	[3, 8, 51, 52]
Vulnerability	Vulnerability has to do with the citizen's perception of how well equipped she is to deal with the possible effects of undesirable outcomes, be they substantive (such as not receiving a benefit) or affective (lack of respect, recognition, stigmatisation, etc.)	[26, 28, 29, 37, 53]
Familiarity	Is this a familiar situation, a situation the citizen has been in before, where she can draw on experience and a basic mental map of what is going to happen (or perhaps draw on the experience of someone close to him)? Or is it unfamiliar territory?	[11]
Complexity	Does the citizen perceive the situation as more or less complex	[6, 7, 36, 38]
Urgency (time)	How important is it for the citizen to get the issues resolved within a specific time frame	[6, 9]

In this section of the paper, I first report my review of the selected literature and then establish the framework based on this reading. The first part of the review (Sect. 3.1) focus on what the literature has to say about the influence of the task and its characteristics on the choice of channels, the second part (Sect. 3.2) on the features of the situation and its characteristics on channel choice. Finally, in Sect. 3.3, the framework is established.

3.1 The Task and Its Characteristics

In the channel choice literature [6–9, 13, 38] (see [15] for an overview). The situation is one among several dimensions that affect citizens choice of channel(s) for the BE. Other dimensions that are frequently included are channel characteristics/channel related factors, task characteristics. Personal characteristics (age, education, gender), and habits.

The first attempts to explain medium-strategies and -choices by their context focused on the characteristics of the task(s) to be performed and came from medium theory [18], claiming that particular media would be chosen for particular types of tasks. As the subsequent critique of this approach showed (see [32] and [33]), there is no straightforward task-medium fit. Tasks cannot simply be classified according to objective criteria, and people choose different mediations for different tasks, as they are perceived in the situation [8]. Perceptions of the task and the situation are closely interrelated. In addition, people are generally pragmatic in their evaluations of different elements of a service and may prefer some types of service for some tasks or some stages of a task and other types of service for other tasks or stages [34].

The channel choice literature has generally agreed that complexity and ambiguity are the key features of a task in the context of channel choice What constitutes complexity and ambiguity has not, however, been quite settled.

Complexity

Pieterson & Van Dijk [38] define complexity objectively as the number of interrelated steps necessary to complete a task. Ebbers, Pieterson & Noordman [7] expands it to also encompass the degree of uncertainty about tasks, inputs processes and outcomes. [6] further elaborates by adding the amount of information that has to be transferred.

A conceptualization of complexity as the number of steps necessary to complete a task or the amount of information to be transferred while easy to operationalize, renders complexity a criterion divorced from both the citizen involved (and her skills, resources, and experiences) and the situational context and any influence that may have on the citizen's perceptions of complexity. The inclusion of the degree of uncertainty about the task inputs, process, and outcomes, greatly expands the concept from something essentially countable to something essentially experiential, however it is the objective definition that has generally been applied in the empirical studies reviewed.

Backlund [36] defines the complexity of a system as "*the effort (as it is perceived) that is required to understand and cope with the system*". Here complexity is in the eye of the beholder and her perception may change over time, or with the situation.

The level of cognitive load, the effort required, and the perceived complexity will arguably always depend to some degree on the individual doing the cognition and on how many cognitive resources she can bring to the task, as well as on the circumstances and demands of the situation. Complexity arises then both from the citizens subjective experiences with and perceptions of her life-situation, and from the way the authorities and services involved are organized, designed, and practiced. Potential tasks and steps may arise both from the wider situation and from the way the organizational context. Many aspects of the situation may lead to it being perceived as complex and this may vary considerable from person to person and may even change during the encounter.

Ambiguity

Daft & Lengel [18] define ambiguity as the degree to which multiple conflicting interpretations of the information exist. They see the reduction of uncertainty and ambiguity (which they call "equivocality") as two important aspects of communication. When the problem is uncertainty, we know what kind of questions to ask and what information we need, and more information may help. When the problem is ambiguity, we are not sure what questions to ask (we don't know what we don't know), what information to seek, or how to interpret the information we have, and any new data may increase uncertainty, rather than reducing it. Citizens bureaucratic encounters with government will often be characterized by low domain-skills [11]. Citizens lack the experience and "mental map" to help them confidently translate their situation into the way services etc. are organized, and to plan, ask questions, evaluate information, and navigate the encounter. This may contribute to a sense of ambiguity.

In Daft and Lengel's definition of ambiguity it arises from the knowledge of competing interpretations. This entails that citizen will have to be aware of such competing interpretations. However, it may also be the mere *possibility* of conflicting interpretations that gives rise to a sense of ambiguity. The citizen may only be aware of one interpretation (her own) but at the same time have a feeling that this may not be the only possible one or indeed the correct one.

Ebbers, Pieterson & Nordmann [7] adopts Daft & Lengel's definition but also talk about "problem ambiguity", which they describe as not feeling sure of how to interpret the information one gets about what to do. The "problem" here seems to be solving the concrete tasks involved in the BE. Problem ambiguity could also be applied to the more basic issue of translating the circumstances of the citizen's situation into a "problem" or set of problems which fits categorization of the world seen from the authority's perspective [37]. This could be a major source of situational ambiguity.

Ambiguity then arises primarily from how the citizen's frame of reference for the encounter matches what the authority presents. It is not an independent feature of the situation in the same way as complexity is. Reducing ambiguity may require some degree of interaction and exchange of views and perspectives, in order to "*overcome different frames of reference or clarify ambiguous issues and change understanding in a timely manner*" [18:560], what Kock [40] calls schema alignment.

Ambiguity is always a possibility [33], but if it does not surface in the situation, it has no effect in that particular case. However, when it does, it may even contribute to a feeling of the situation being biased against the citizen or potentially unfair, due to a sense of lack of control over the situation. [41].

3.2 The Situation and its Characteristics

While the characteristics of "the task" have been extensively studied in the literature, the characteristics of the situation are considerably less developed, theoretically as well as empirically. The channel choice literature identifies, as we have seen, urgency, need for closure, the task at hand, emotions, and importance. And, from the public administration literature, we get the "lateral scope" or potential consequences of the encounter. In this section I will discuss these aspects of the situation, as well as the additional – and foundational – aspect of the power-asymmetries between the citizen and the authorities as well as the role of the citizen's familiarity with the situation.

Urgency and the Need for Closure

Pieterson [9] as well as Ebbers et al. [6], see urgency only as a matter of time; how quickly does the matter that gives rise to the BE have to be resolved.

Ebbers, Pieterson and Nordmann [42:192] (quoting Kruglanksi [39]) defines need for closure as "*a definite answer on some topic, any answer as opposed to confusion and ambiguity*". Ebbers et al. [6], describes it as a need to reduce uncertainty by finishing the task as soon as possible. This makes the difference between this and urgency somewhat fuzzy.

In the literature, urgency is a matter of time-constraints and the need for closure is a feeling of the importance of getting the issues definitively resolved. Where urgency can be considered a feature of the situation. The need for closure is a need [10] which must arguably derive from some other – more fundamental - feature of the situation.

The Task at Hand

"The task at hand" is in the literature described in terms of the nature of the problem/interaction: is it difficult, important, or complex to solve/perform? [6]. In this construal, it is not clear why this should be a separate aspect of the situation and could not be covered by complexity (see above) and importance (see below).

Availability/Channel Constraints

Availability/channel constraints has to do with the limitations and possibilities of choice of channel. This includes the availability of the channel at the particular time and place where the citizen has to choose, the distance to the channel (for physical contact points) and wait times (contact speed) [35]. Availability and constraints are a product both of situational factors – like time or location and of the organizational design of the service – like opening hours, office locations, and wait-times.

Emotions

Ebbers, Pieterson and Nordmann [7], describe emotions important in consumer behavior. They distinguish between negative emotions; anger, fear, sadness and shame and positive emotions: contentment, happiness, pride, and love. Citizens' emotions are somehow connected to the different channel's they may use for the BE, but this connection is not entirely clear. The concept and role of emotions are generally underdeveloped in the channel choice literature.

The role of emotions has received considerable attention in the private sector service literature. Drawing on appraisal theory, Chase & Dasu [43, 44] describe how emotions are both input to and output of the encounter. They argue that what emotions are involved depend on whether the encounter has the potential to improve the situation or make it worse, is associated with a potential penalty or a reward, whether is a significant situation or not, whether the possible consequences can be difficult to cope with or not, on how much influence the individual has over the encounter and its outcome and on the perceived likelihood of all of the above. All of this are aspects of the situation and of its possible consequences. As with need for closure, rather than being a fundamental feature of the situation, emotions must derive from some more fundamental aspects of the situation.

Importance

Pieterson & Ebbers [8] describe importance as the personal relevance of the matter to the citizen. It drives a need for closure. Again, the importance must follow from some more fundamental feature – what it is in the situation that makes it important.

The Lateral Dimension – The Potential Impact of the Encounter

Goodsell [3] talks about the scope of the encounter in two dimensions – a horizontal dimensions – the time it takes before the issues are solved, and a lateral dimension, the potential impact that getting or not getting the service, benefit etc., which the encounter may have on the citizen's life.

Lindgren et al. [14] argue that the lateral dimension is understudied and undertheorized. In general, this appears to be the case for many of the concepts applied in the channel choice literature to characterize the situation, they are fuzzy, underdeveloped, and under-studied, empirically as well as theoretically, and it is not entirely clear that they are all basic features of the situation.

Issues of Power, Problems, and Identities

To understand the nature of the situation, it is important to remember that BE occurs in situations often characterized by a clear asymmetry of power [28, 29] and that the outcome of the BE may have serious consequences for the citizen, not only substantially (getting a benefit or a service or not) but also with regards to the citizens sense of self [37]. The BE is often the locus of a transformation, of citizens "troubles" into "problems" that the authority can recognize and address and of identities [45]. As Lipsky puts it in the context of encounters with street level bureaucrats: *"People come to street level bureaucrats as unique individuals with different life experiences, personalities, and current circumstances. In the encounters … they are transformed into clients*" [46:59]."*Clients tend to experience their needs as individual problems and their demands as individual expressions of expectations and grievances. They often expect treatment appropriate to individuals. Street level bureaucrats experience clients' problems as calls for categories of action and their demands are perceived as components of aggregates.*" [46]:60. In this transformation, certain aspects of the citizen and her situation are selected as relevant and others as irrelevant [29]. The situation surrounding a BE may thus entail some degree of personal vulnerability for the citizen [26:9].

Familiarity

Skaarup 2020 [11], argues that citizens often find themselves lacking domain skills when they engage in bureaucratic encounters with government. They have insufficient experience with and knowledge of the service, the authority, the channels and most importantly, the situation they are facing. They may never have been in this situation before or have been a considerable time ago and lack the metal map that may allow them to confidently do things in their own. This establishes familiarity as a key feature of the situation. Both uncertainty and ambiguity are in part products of unfamiliarity. And unfamiliarity may create or add to a sense of the complexity of the situation.

3.3 Establishing the Conceptual Framework

Based on the reading of the selected literature outlined above, I have constructed a conceptual framework which aims to identify the basic features of the situation of importance for citizens approaches to their bureaucratic encounters with government.

1 Consequences

The need for closure, emotions, importance, and the lateral dimension all appears to address the same underlying aspects of the situation. The all have to do with what is at stake for the citizen. If much is at stake, it may be important to get things resolved - to get closure, and that may give rise to emotions.

The question then becomes what it means that "something is at stake". Both Godsell's lateral dimension and "importance" has to do with consequences, what happens if I get/do not get what I need or want? Consequences in turn depends both on the possible outcomes and on the citizen's situated vulnerability in the face of those outcomes.

The possible outcomes and vulnerability may vary independently - for a vulnerable citizen the same consequences may appear more serious than for a less vulnerable citizen. Therefore, in this framework, I will limit "consequences" to the possible outcomes of the BE, independent of the effect those consequence may have for the citizen: Do I get or loose a benefit? Is my application for a permit denied or approved? Have I filed my taxes correctly, or will I get a fine or have to pay back-taxes? Will I be treated well, or will I be treated badly? What matters here is the citizens perception of the possible outcomes and their likelihood[2], more than what is formally possible or likely. These perceptions are shaped both by the citizen's experiences with the situation as well as by her perceptions of the laws and regulations that determines the possible outcomes and her expectations of how the process will unfold and how any caseworkers she may encounter may treat her.

2 Vulnerability

Vulnerability has to do with the citizen's perceptions of how well equipped she is to deal with the possible effects of undesirable outcomes, be they substantive (such as not receiving a benefit) or affective (lack of respect or recognition, stigmatization, etc.). Heimer [48] argues that vulnerability is an expression of the amount of risk incurred by engaging in a particular action. However, this seems to conflate risk (the likelihood that something happens combined with the consequences of it happening) [66] and vulnerability, which I would argue should be kept separate. Vulnerability may be alleviated by institutional safety nets and the citizens access to resources (this may be her own resources or the resources of others that she can draw upon). If the citizen has few resources and if the possible consequences of the outcome have a considerable effect on her life and or sense of self, then that will affect her approach to the encounter. The degree of vulnerability may be a more long-term feature of the citizen's life (e.g., if she is homeless) or it may be tied to the specific situation (e.g., if she has just lost her job, or must cope with a death in the family) – such situations, in particular if they are new and unfamiliar to the citizen, may make the citizen less resourceful and more vulnerable than usual. If little is at stake – the consequences of failing are small and the importance of e.g., lack of skills or other resources may be smaller. If much is at stake, everything counts and even smaller issues in other parts of the wider framework may take on a greater importance.

3 Familiarity

Previous experience with the situation, the service, the authority in question or the channel/systems used may combine to reduce both the perceived complexity and the

[2] Likelihood is here not meant in a statistical sense. As Loewenstein et al. [47] argues, in our ordinary lives we do not deal in statistical probabilities but with "risk-as-feelings".

perceived consequences and vulnerability. Familiarity may reduce the uncertainty about the possible consequences and the sense of vulnerability may be decreased if previous experience shows that the consequences are usually manageable, and the citizen has been able cope well with them.

4 Complexity

The situation itself may introduce complexity, a complexity that may be exacerbated by unfamiliarity, by insufficient skills, and a complexity which may feed ambiguity. The organization, design and implementation of the services involved in the BE may increase or decrease this complexity. It may be difficult in practice to separate the situation-induced complexity from the complexity arising from the way the authority and services presents themselves. However, I have kept complexity as a situational factor, as it is important to profile the sources of complexity that does not arise from the authority but from the citizens life and situation.

5 Urgency

I distinguish between constraints created by the design and organizational setup of the service(s) involved in the BE – such as opening hours, wait times and geographical locations of offices, and the constraints introduced by the citizens situation. The only situational constraint that is entirely citizen related in the literature is how important it is for the citizen to solve her problem quickly, possible within a deadline given – not by the authorities – but by circumstances in the citizens life such as for example getting a new passport before she has to travel. In this framework this constraint will be labeled "urgency", to differentiate it from the constraints introduced by the institutional setup.

Summing up

Citizens approach the bureaucratic encounter within the context of a situation in their lives that affects their behaviours and choices. At one end of the spectrum, the situation may be unfamiliar and appear complex, the potential consequences may be considerable, the citizen may be vulnerable in the situation, and it may be important to have it resolved within a specific time frame. At the other end of the spectrum, the citizen may have been in the same situation before, perhaps recently, she may perceive the complexity of the situation as low, the potential consequences are negligible or she has the resources to handle them whatever they are, and she is not in a hurry to have the issue resolved. Where on this spectrum the situation falls (and there may be many ways of combining the different aspects of the framework), may have significant influence on how the individual citizen approach the bureaucratic encounter, what emotions are involved, what channels she will use and in what order, what help and assistance she might need and so on.

4 Discussion and Conclusion

This paper set out to establish a conceptual framework for describing and analysing the situation that gives rise to the need for engaging in bureaucratic encounters with government. Through an analysis of several literatures, I have constructed a framework at an analytical level that allows it to be applied to and adequately characterize the key features of the situation that influences citizens approaches to the BE. This is of course a considerable simplification of the multitude of circumstances and experiences that characterizes citizens' real-life situations. The framework is a shorthand, a tool for analysis, and not a substitute for studying and understanding citizens real-life situations in more detail and on their own terms.

The framework is, in essence, technology neutral. Consequences and vulnerability are not determined by technology or citizens experience with technology but by laws, rules and regulation and the circumstances of the citizens life-situation. The importance of the citizens familiarity with the situation may be alleviated by the design of services and citizen-facing IT-systems to the extent that they help citizens analyse and understand their situation better, but the degree of familiarity, as a circumstance of the situation is not dependent on the technology and designs applied. The importance of the time-constraints that may exist in the situation may be reduced if the service is easily and readily available and the issues can be resolved quickly. But the time-constraint itself is not created by technology or the design of services.

It is well-described in the channel choice literature that citizens may choose different channels for different services or tasks or for different parts of a service or task. The framework constructed here indicates that channel-behaviour may be driven in part by features of the situation. However, the circumstances of the situation are only one of several sets of factors that may influence citizens' behaviour in the face of bureaucratic encounters. Other factors are the skills and resources the citizen bring to the encounter, the needs and goals citizens have for the encounter, previous experiences that citizens may draw upon, what constitutes socially sanctioned and appropriate behaviour in the situation, and how the service and IT-systems involved are organized, designed, implemented, and practiced. All of this may in various ways influence the citizen's perception of the aspects of the situation outlined in the framework. And all of these factors must be taken into account when deciding to what extent and how services could and should be digitalized.

Understanding the features of the situation that affects citizens approaches to bureaucratic encounters is important for the design of all types of services, regardless of the degree of digitalization involved.

4.1 Suggestions for Application and Further Research

The framework provides a valuable tool for e-government researchers to study channel-behaviour and e-government adoption and for studying the authorities' strategies and choices in designing systems and services. The framework could also serve as a tool for practitioners in designing and evaluating systems, services, and strategies.

The framework contributes to the e-government field in addressing the need for citizen-centred research [20, 21, 49], and in engaging other theoretical fields to advance e-government theory building [50, 51]. To bring the field further forward, I propose a research agenda for the e-government community with the following research questions:

- Does the framework have ecological validity, can it be used to adequately describe citizens' real-life perceptions of the influence of their situations for their approaches to bureaucratic encounters?
- How do the features of the situation interact with each other, with citizen's need and goals for the bureaucratic encounter, with their skills and resources and with the way the citizens perceive the organization of the authorities and the design of their services? This could be explored both theoretically and empirically.
- How and to what extent can the design and organisation of services contribute to the reduction of situational complexity (which goes beyond the complexity of the services in themselves), to addressing issues arising from low familiarity and to address issues arising from high vulnerability.
- In what types of bureaucratic encounters/with what types of services are issues of familiarity, complexity, and vulnerability particularly salient and do this disproportionately effect particular groups of citizens.
- What effects can improvements in the way the authorities takes the aspects of the situation into account when designing and organizing services have for citizen's perceptions of service-quality, for the job-satisfaction of front-line staff, for the creation of public value and for the efficiency and effectiveness of the service delivery.

Apart from answering these specific questions, such research could also contribute to further refinement and elaboration of the framework through its application to empirical data.

Practitioners could apply the framework as a tool in the design of services and systems. They could, for example for investigating the importance of the different aspects of the situation for a given target groups, different services, or different ways of implementing services, to inform the designing a new service/system, as input to a multi-channel service design, or for evaluating existing systems and services. While the design of systems and services will always have to be based on an authoritative interpretation of the law, and on procedures established by law or other binding regulations, a good design will have to take into account that citizens will often only have a vague and maybe erroneous idea of what the law actually says, what substantive consequences may actually be possible and even to some extent how vulnerable this makes them. Thus, it is important for designers to take the features of the situation into account.

4.2 Limitations and Concluding Comments

Most of the literature cited is based on the U.S. context, and the researcher's own experiences are from a Danish public sector context. However, the concepts of consequences, vulnerability, familiarity, complexity, and urgency are, I would argue, universal. They may play out differently and have different consequences for citizens choices and strategies dependent on the cultural and institutional context. This is an important point with the framework. It does not say what individual citizens will do for particular encounters with particular bureaucracies in particular cultures, but what situational factors may influence the choices and strategies.

While I have investigated a range of literatures in this paper, my aim has not been an exhaustive investigation of them all, but through an interpretive, hermeneutic approach to identify salient and important perspectives on the situational context for citizens' approaches to the bureaucratic encounter. Through this, I hope to have provided a framework for a more holistic investigation and understanding of citizens perspectives. The real test of the usefulness of this framework will be its application on empirical data and in practical settings, and I hope such applications will contribute to the improvement and elaboration of the framework.

References

1. European Commission: Digital Economy and Society Index (DESI) Report on Digital Public Services (2019). https://ec.europa.eu/digital-single-market/en/desi
2. Katz, D., Gutek, B., Kahn, R.L., Barton, E.: Bureaucratic Encounters. University of Michigan Survey Reserarch Center, Ann Arbor (1975)
3. Goodsell, C.T.: The New Case for Bureaucracy. SAGE, London (2018)
4. Nass, C., Fogg, B.J., Moon, Y.: Can computers be teammates? Int. J. Hum. Comput. Stud. **45**(6), 669–678 (1996). https://doi.org/10.1006/ijhc.1996.0073
5. Nass, C., Moon, Y.: Machines and mindlessness: social responses to computers. J. Soc. Issues **56**(1), 81–103 (2000). https://doi.org/10.1111/0022-4537.00153
6. Ebbers, W., Jansen, M., Pieterson, W., van de Wijngaert, L.: Facts and feelings: the role of rational and irrational factors in citizens' channel choices. Gov. Inf. Q. **33** (2016). https://doi.org/10.1016/j.giq.2016.06.001
7. Ebbers, W.E., Pieterson, W.J., Noordman, H.N.: Electronic government: rethinking channel management strategies. Gov. Inf. Q. **25**(2), 181–201 (2008). https://doi.org/10.1016/j.giq.2006.11.003
8. Pieterson, W., Ebbers, W.E.: Channel choice evolution: an empirical analysis of shifting channel behavior across demographics and tasks. Gov. Inf. Q. **37**, 101478 (2020). https://doi.org/10.1016/j.giq.2020.101478
9. Pieterson, W.: Channel Choice - Citizens' Channel Behavior and Public Service Channel Strategy. University of Twente (2009)
10. Skaarup, S.: Beyond substantive goals – a framework for understanding citizens need and goals in bureaucratic encounters. In: Scholl, H.J., Gil-Garcia, J.R., Janssen, M., Kalampokis, E., Lindgren, I., Rodríguez Bolívar, M.P. (eds.) EGOV 2021. LNCS, vol. 12850, pp. 86–102. Springer, Cham (2021). https://doi.org/10.1007/978-3-030-84789-0_7
11. Skaarup, S.: The role of domain-skills in bureaucratic service encounters. In: Viale Pereira, G., et al. (eds.) EGOV 2020. LNCS, vol. 12219, pp. 179–196. Springer, Cham (2020). https://doi.org/10.1007/978-3-030-57599-1_14
12. Reddick, C.G., Turner, M.: Channel choice and public service delivery in Canada: comparing e-government to traditional service delivery. Gov. Inf. Q. **29**(1), 1–11 (2012). https://doi.org/10.1016/j.giq.2011.03.005
13. Ebbers, W.E., Jansen, M.G.M., van Deursen, A.J.A.M.: Impact of the digital divide on e-government: expanding from channel choice to channel usage. Gov. Inf. Q. **33**(4), 685–692 (2016). https://doi.org/10.1016/j.giq.2016.08.007
14. Lindgren, I., Madsen, C.Ø., Hofmann, S., Melin, U.: Close encounters of the digital kind: a research agenda for the digitalization of public services. Gov. Inf. Q. **36**(3), 427–436 (2019). https://doi.org/10.1016/j.giq.2019.03.002

15. Madsen, C.Ø., Kræmmergaard, P.: Channel choice: a literature review. In: Tambouris, E., et al. (eds.) EGOV 2015. LNCS, vol. 9248, pp. 3–18. Springer, Cham (2015). https://doi.org/10.1007/978-3-319-22479-4_1
16. Madsen, C., Hofmann, S.: Multichannel Management in the Public Sector: A Literature Review, pp. 20–35 (2019)
17. Mundy, D., Umer, Q., Foster, A.: Examining the potential for channel shift in the UK through multiple lenses. Electron. J. e-Gov. **9**(2), 203–213 (2011)
18. Daft, R.L., Lengel, R.H.: Organizational information requirements, media richness and structural design. Manag. Sci. **32**(5), 554–571 (1986). https://doi.org/10.1287/mnsc.32.5.554
19. Reddick, C.G.: Citizen-initiated contacts with government: comparing phones and websites. J. E-Gov. **2**(1), 27–53 (2005). https://doi.org/10.1300/J399v02n01_03
20. Scott, M., DeLone, W.H., Golden, W.: Understanding net benefits: a citizen-based perspective on e-Government success. In: 30th International Conference on Information Systems (ICIS 2009), vol. Paper 86, pp. 1–11. AIS, Phoenix, Arizona (2009). http://aisel.aisnet.org/icis2009/86/
21. Meijer, A.J., Bekkers, V.: A metatheory of e-government: creating some order in a fragmented research field. Gov. Inf. Q. **32**(3), 237–245 (2015). https://doi.org/10.1016/j.giq.2015.04.006
22. Kolsaker, A., Lee-Kelley, L.: Citizens' attitudes towards e-government: a UK study. Int. J. Public Sect. Manag. **21**(7), 723–738 (2008)
23. Boell, S.K., Cecez-Kecmanovic, D.: A hermeneutic approach for conducting literature reviews and literature searches. Commun. Assoc. Inf. Syst. **34**(1), 257–286 (2014). https://doi.org/10.17705/1cais.03412
24. Gadamer, H.G.: Hermeneutics and social science. Philos. Soc. Crit. **2**(4), 307–316 (1975). https://doi.org/10.1177/019145377500200402
25. Rose, J., Persson, J.S., Heeager, L.T., Irani, Z.: Managing e-Government: value positions and relationships. Inf. Syst. J. **25**(5), 531–571 (2015). https://doi.org/10.1111/isj.12052
26. Hassenfeld, Y.: Human Services as Complex Organizations. SAGE, London (2009)
27. Järvinen, M., Mik-Meyer, N.: At skabe en klient: institutionelle identiteter i socialt arbejde. Reitzel, Copenhagen (2013)
28. Järvinen, M., Larsen, J.E. and Mortensen, N. (ed.): Det magtfulde Møde mellem System og Klient. Århus, Århus Universitetsforlag (2005)
29. Mik-Meyer, N., Villadsen, K.: Magtens Former - Sociologiske Perspektiver på Statens Møde med borgerne. København, Hans Reitzels Forlag (2007)
30. Lenk, K.: Electronic service delivery-a driver of public sector modernisation. Inf. Polity **7**(2–3), 87–96 (2002). https://doi.org/10.3233/ip-2002-0009
31. Jabareen, Y.: Building a conceptual framework: philosophy, definitions, and procedure. Int. J. Qual. Methods **8**(4), 49–62 (2009). https://doi.org/10.1177/160940690900800406
32. D'Arcy, J., Kock, N.: Unraveling the e-collaboration paradox - evidence of compensatory adaption to low media naturalness (2003)
33. Kock, N.: Media richness or media naturalness? – The evolution of our biological communication apparatus and its influence on our behavior towards e-communication tools. IEEE Trans. Prof. Commun. **48**(2) (2005)
34. Howard, M., Worboys, C.: Self-Service - a contradiction in terms or customer led choice. J. Consum. Behav. **2**(4), 382–392 (2003)
35. Pieterson, W., van Dijk, J.: Channel choice determinants; an exploration of the factors that determine the choice of a service channel in citizen initiated contacts. In: 8th Annual International Conference on Digital Government Research (DG.O 2007), vol. 228. Digital Government Research Center (2007)
36. Backlund, A.: The concept of complexity in organisations and information systems. Kybernetes **31**, 30–43 (2002). https://doi.org/10.1108/03684920210414907

37. Gubrium, J.F., Järvinen, M.: Turning Troubles into Problems: Clientization in Human Services. Routledge, London (2013)
38. Skaarup, S.: The Mediation of Authority. Syddansk Universitet. Det Samfundsvidenskabelige Fakultet (2017)
39. Kruglanski, A.W., Webster, D.M., Klem, A.: Motivated resistance and openness to persuasion in the presence or absence of prior information. J. Pers. Soc. Psychol. **65**, 861–876 (1993)
40. Kock, N.: The Psychobiological model: towards a new theory of computer-mediated communication based on Darwinian evolution. Organ. Sci. **15**(3), 327–348 (2004)
41. Curley, S.P., Yates, F.J., Abrams, R.A.: Psychological sources of ambiguity avoidance. Organ. Behav. Hum. Decis. Process. **38**, 230–356 (1986)
42. Ebbers, W.E., Pieterson, W.J., Noordman, H.N.: Electronic Government: Rethinking Channel Management Strategies
43. Chase, R.B., Dasu, S.: Psychology of the experience - the missing link in service science. Paper at Cambridge Service Science, Management and Engineering Symposium, 14–15 July 2007 (2007)
44. Dasu, S., Chase, R.B.: Designing the soft side of customer service. MIT Sloan Manag. Rev. **52**(1), 33–39 (2010)
45. Margaretha Järvinen og Nanna Mik-Meyer: At skabe en klient. Institutionelle identiteter i socialt arbejde. Reitzel (2003)
46. Lipsky, M.: Street-Level Bureaucracy - Dilemmas of the Individual in Public Service. Russell Sage, New York (2010 [1980])
47. Loewenstein, G., Weber, E., Hsee, C., Welch, N.: Risk as feelings. Psychol. Bull. **127**, 267–286 (2001). https://doi.org/10.1037/0033-2909.127.2.267
48. Heimer, C.A.: Solving the problem of trust. In: Cook, K.S. (ed.): Trust in Society, pp. 40–88. Russell Sage, New York (2001)
49. Bertot, J.C., Jaeger, P.T.: The E-Government paradox: better customer service doesn't necessarily cost less. Gov. Inf. Q. **25**(2), 149–154 (2008). https://doi.org/10.1016/j.giq.2007.10.002
50. Richard, H., Bailur, S.: Analyzing e-government research: perspectives, philosophies, theories, methods, and practice. Gov. Inf. Q. **24**(2), 243–265 (2007)
51. Bannister, F., Connolly, R.: The great theory hunt: does e-government really have a problem? Gov. Inf. Q. **32**(1), 1–11 (2015). https://doi.org/10.1016/j.giq.2014.10.003
52. Dahler-Larsen, P.: At fremstille kvalitative data.pdf. Odense Universitetsforlag, Odense (2002)
53. Dey, I.: Grounding Grounded theory: Guidelines for Qualitative Inquiry. Emerald Publishing Group, Bingely (1999)

Adapting a Faceted Search Task Model for the Development of a Domain-Specific Council Information Search Engine

Thomas Schoegje[1](✉), Arjen de Vries[2], and Toine Pieters[1]

[1] Utrecht University, Utrecht, The Netherlands
{t.schoegje,t.pieters}@uu.nl
[2] Radboud University, Nijmegen, The Netherlands
arjen@acm.org

Abstract. Domain specialists such as council members may benefit from specialised search functionality, but it is unclear how to formalise the search requirements when developing a search system. We adapt a faceted task model for the purpose of characterising the tasks of a target user group. We first identify which task facets council members use to describe their tasks, then characterise council member tasks based on those facets. Finally, we discuss the design implications of these tasks for the development of a search engine.

Based on two studies at the same municipality we identified a set of task facets and used these to characterise the tasks of council members. By coding how council members describe their tasks we identified five task facets: the task objective, topic aspect, information source, retrieval unit, and task specificity. We then performed a third study at a second municipality where we found our results were consistent.

We then discuss design implications of these tasks because the task model has implications for 1) how information should be modelled, and 2) how information can be presented in context, and it provides implicit suggestions for 3) how users want to interact with information.

Our work is a step towards better understanding the search requirements of target user groups within an organisation. A task model enables organisations developing search systems to better prioritise where they should invest in new technology.

Keywords: Task analysis · User studies · Information seeking behaviour · Information needs · Domain analysis

1 Introduction

Users and information needs at the municipality of Utrecht are diverse. Some of these user groups have complex information needs [28], which may require specialised search functionality before search satisfaction can be achieved [12]. If organisations do not identify these specialised requirements they risk investing in search solutions that are unsatisfactory, which must then be replaced

M. Janssen et al. (Eds.): EGOV 2022, LNCS 13391, pp. 402–418, 2022.
https://doi.org/10.1007/978-3-031-15086-9_26

within a few years. We investigated the needs of council members as a target user group because they perform complex intellectual tasks [28] and are therefore likely to benefit from specialised search functionality. Our main research goal was to extend an existing (search) task model from the information seeking and retrieval literature to adapt it for the purpose of identifying council member search requirements. We applied this design approach to develop an e-government search application that supports council member search tasks.

We found that existing task models are not designed for the purpose of representing domain-specific information needs. To address this, we adapted an existing task model based on users' descriptions of their tasks, which includes a domain-specific topic facet that describes how tasks relate to information subsets in that domain. Below we discuss how the adapted task model can inform the design of a search engine, as the interface should clearly reflect where users can perform each of their tasks; what information is necessary for each task; and how users want to interact with this information.

We first contextualise the tasks by describing the information seeking of council members, which we do by describing the users, information sources and channels involved. We then identify council member tasks and relate these to the available information systems. This reveals tasks that are not adequately supported by those systems. We then discuss the design implications of the task model for better support of those tasks, by extending the information model and creating a better interface. We end by discussing how the proposed system is more suitable to council tasks than the pre-existing system.

We performed our analysis at two Dutch municipalities with consistent findings, suggesting that the search functionality for council members in similar contexts can be standardised.

2 Related Work

Developing useful search tools for target user groups requires an understanding of how and why they search. Users start searching for information as a part of performing some broader (work) task [15]. In professional settings work tasks often follow from the professional's responsibilities [7,17,21], which in turn follow from their role within the organisation [20]. If we can model the situational context of information tasks, we can assess whether a search engine is able to aid the user in their goals [13] and therefore whether useful for the user in task completion [2,35].

We introduce several domain-independent task models from the information seeking and retrieval literature as complementary perspectives at the basis of the current work. We start with the broadest model and ending with the narrowest, and then introduce increasingly domain-specific models.

2.1 Domain Independent Task Models

Different research purposes have resulted in different kinds of conceptual models, with characteristics such as 1) how much is modelled (broad or narrow), 2) whether a process or static situation is modelled, 3) whether something directly observable or something more theoretical is modelled (concrete or abstract) and 4) how much the model generalises beyond domains (general or specific) [15,16].

Ingwersen and Järvelin argue that all information seeking and searching is performed by actors, who interpret information and their tasks through their own perspectives. Therefore, they propose a model of information seeking from the cognitive perspective [15]. This broad and abstract framework contains five main components, where the interrelation between these components (over time) provide important context for each individual component. The five components are 1) the information seeker/user, 2) the interface, 3) the IT systems underlying the interface, 4) the information objects in those systems and 5) their social/organisational/cultural context. They note that work tasks may originate from the organisational context, but they may also originate from e.g. newly found information. In this model, work tasks arise as a result of interactions between the actor and the other components. Work tasks are directed from components towards the actor, and search tasks are directed from the actor towards other components.

Taylor proposed that all information acquisition and use in a professional setting is performed in a contextual environment [32], and defined such contextual factors. Byström et al. extended this work [6] to represent the context of Workplace Information Environments. These describe important variables grouped in four categories: 1) sets of people, 2) work tasks, 3) settings and 4) task resolutions. They note that one's profession leads to work activities, which in turn necessitate (work) tasks.

Byström and Hansen present a narrower conceptual model focusing on what work tasks, information seeking tasks and search tasks are, and how they are interrelated [5]. In their definition, an information seeking task includes all steps a user takes to gather information, including interpersonal ones. Information seeking can consist of several information search tasks, which are search episodes with their own search goal. A search task performed within a search engine or database is also known as a retrieval task. Rather than focusing on tasks from an individual's perspective, Byström considers how to characterise the tasks of a user groups, and the social practices that will affect task performance [7].

Li and Belkin reviewed the literature on information tasks and proposed a narrower model [21]. They characterised tasks with independent facets that affect the information behaviour and the subtasks that a given task produces. This framework has been used to describe tasks and create simulated tasks [14,30]. An extension included the information level of results as a facet [8].

Byström and Hansen show that we can describe an information need in three levels of increasing context [5]. At the lowest level there is a topical description and query, similar to traditional laboratory experiments [15]. The second level includes a situational description, which is the context of the task at hand. The faceted task framework is a step towards gathering research on this area [21]. The third level is all the contextual factors that affect the search, such as the four categories of the workplace information environment [6] and the five components of the cognitive framework [15].

These models have some overlap, but also different strengths. Ingwersen and Järvelin's model is useful for a cognitive user centered perspective. The model by Byström et al. model for the workplace information environment is valuable for investigating work practices in the workplace. Byström and Hansen's task level model is good at describing tasks from a process perspective. Li and Belkin's model is a powerful tool for describing information behaviour. These models all generalise beyond domains, which gives them explanatory power in a wide range of settings. We find however, that there is a trade-off between a model's ability to generalise beyond domains, and its expressive power within a narrower domain. Li and Belkin were unable to add task topic as a facet because without a domain a list of topics would be unlimited [21]. Byström and Hansen noted the importance of finding a better way to characterise context- and situation-aware descriptions based on real-life data [5]. Ingwersen and Järvelin noted that our increased understanding of tasks had not yet translated to better design criteria for information (retrieval) systems. To address these concerns we now turn to increasingly domain-specific task models.

2.2 Domain Specific Task Models

The above models are applicable during information seeking and retrieval in most domains. We now focus on smaller domains, which allows us to introduce task descriptions that capture increasingly more situational and contextual context.

The classic example to model the user's goal is the web search taxonomy of query intents [4,24]. Within enterprise search there may exist a similar taxonomy of search tasks [27], and between search tasks there seem to be recurring sequences of task types [27]. User interfaces can better support the search experience when they are designed to reflect the typical flow of the users' tasks. When we consider tasks within professional search domains we find complex tasks with similar characteristics [36,37]. When we focus on the tasks within a single organisation we can introduces an element of the organisations' objectives [17], but these are still far removed from the users' immediate goals.

There are also examples of search task studies outside of a professional/work setting, which often analyse all users of a system collectively [31,34], or focus on supporting specific tasks [10,33].

Taylor provided a contextual description of the information use environment of American legislators [32]. This information use environment describes the people, problems, setting and problem resolutions. Legislative culture is described as verbal, non-hierarchical, time-constrained and as having the political party as a major centralising force. An observational study of knowledge workers at a municipal administration identified four main types of work tasks that involved search tasks [28]. Working on legislative processes includes complex information seeking tasks [22,28], possibly because knowledge creation (such as the creation of legislation) is cognitively complex [19]. Complex tasks are more likely to require specialised search functionality.

The present study approach focuses more specifically on one target user group, and adapting an existing task model for the purpose of search design. This approach contrasts with previous work for similar user groups (e.g. [11,18], http://zoek.openraadsinformatie.nl), which typically focus on the data- or technology-driven innovations.

3 Council Member Information Seeking

Council members in the Netherlands have three main responsibilities:

1. Prescribing guidelines for new legislation
2. Verifying whether the municipal workers have adequately translated the council's decisions to concrete policy
3. Representing the citizens' interests while forming legislation guidelines

These are the same responsibilities that Taylor identified for American legislators [32]. Work responsibilities form the highest level of motivation for work tasks and subsequent search tasks [7]. The first and second responsibilities lead to active tasks, whereas the third occurs passively during the other tasks. In performing the first responsibility the council is informed by experts, debates solutions, and decides on new policy over a series of meetings. Members aim to create solutions and arguments that extend or modify existing policies. Members then try to persuade others to support their solutions during meetings. Most of these solutions and knowledge are created during the preparation for domain-specific commission meetings. When the council is not unanimous on a solution, members refine and prepare their proposals before a final discussion in a council meeting. In this article we investigate the sub-tasks of preparing for council meetings, because all council work is oriented around these meetings. Users complained that the previous system was not satisfactory for performing the search tasks within this work task, and hence specialised search functionality may be valuable. A critical challenge is that council members must often extend existing policies, that were created before the members joined the council. It is thus crucial that they understand the existing policy and how it was formed.

3.1 Council Members and Supporting User Groups

Multiple user groups support council members during their tasks. Because of space limitations we only briefly and informally introduce these in Table 1. Here we characterise them using their knowledge types [15]. Domain knowledge can be declarative (what is it about) and procedural (how to do it). Search knowledge can also be declarative (where will I be successful) procedural (how do I search effectively). Professional searchers typically have a high domain and search knowledge, and are thorough when searching [1,20,26]. Table 1 is based on observations of search behaviour and interviews at two municipalities.

Council members become professional searchers with domain expertise over time, but the election cycle leads to the replacement of experts with inexperienced members. A notable difference from typical professional search domains is

Table 1. Characterising the knowledge of council members and supporting groups

User	*Domain knowledge*		*Search knowledge*		Thoroughness
	Declarative	Procedural	Decl.	Proc.	
Council member	Experience dependent		Diverse	Diverse	Time-limited
Faction staff	Experience dependent		Diverse	Diverse	Thorough
Adviser	High	High	Unknown	Unknown	Unknown
Search expert	Low	Low	High	High	Thorough
Public servants	High	High	Unknown	Unknown	Thorough

that council members are not trained to search effectively, unlike other experts [1,25]. Many are unfamiliar with Boolean operators and strategies for effective query formulation. Council members may therefore benefit from search training and/or a search interface that supports them in expressing complex queries.

3.2 Information Sources

Due to space limitations, we will only briefly contextualise the information systems we observed during interviews and interactive search sessions at two municipalities. The two primary information sources were web search engines (mainly Google) and an internal system called iBabs. iBabs is an app used for planning meetings and archiving the official policy documents used during these meetings. A copy of the public data can be accessed at http://api.openraadsinformatie.nl/ (accessed May 2022).

Information seeking on a new topic typically began with performing a web search to find general background information (from indexed news outlets or information published on the municipality's homepage for example). This was followed up by searching in iBabs. This archival system provides an internal search engine that allows users to (re)find known documents by filtering facets such as the date and title of the meeting. This type of functionality is less useful for non-specific needs. This is consistent with findings at a Finnish municipality, which showed that the organisation's internal systems tended to perform well for specific tasks (such as re-finding a known document), but less well for more amorphous tasks (such as exploring a topic) [29].

As we may expect from previous literature [29], the other prominent internal information sources and channels included e-mail (personal or collective faction inboxes) and human sources (colleagues, party-neutral advisers and a temporarily appointed clerk whose main responsibility was to search for information). Some larger political parties created internal solutions to share information (e.g. documenting plans in the cloud), although their main information advantage appears to be in having council members with more experience. Experienced council members remember older events and documents, which is a significant benefit given the difficulties in exploring archived information.

4 Methodology

In the first of two analyses we used a codebook to analyse interview data to identify what tasks facets council members used to describe their tasks. In the second analysis we summarised the council member tasks we identified in the interview data and an observational study and characterised them based on the facets we previously identified.

The two analyses were based on interview data from three studies. Both analyses were initially performed on the interview data that resulted from two studies performed at the municipality of Utrecht, and then a third study was conducted at the municipality Hollands Kroon to test if the results could be reproduced with a similar user group in a different organisation.

The municipality of Utrecht is one of the largest and oldest municipalities in the country, whereas municipality Hollands Kroon is of average size and was formed less than 10 years ago as a fusion of smaller municipalities. Selecting municipalities of such different sizes and histories allows us to determine whether the work tasks we identify are organisation-dependent, or whether council member tasks are similar across organisations.

4.1 Participants

Each study included a sample of council members that were diverse in terms of experience (years in council), demography (gender, age) and the political parties that they represent (size, ideology). This sample was selected by council clerks.

4.2 Data Collection

The first study was a series of six one-hour interviews performed to construct a customer journey for preparing a council meeting. These semi-structured interviews were not limited to search-related questions, but aimed to identify all work tasks. The study aimed to map out relevant information channels and sources; relevant user groups; communication channels; the triggers that move users to actions; and noted which steps went well and which did not. We only report the aspects relevant to the present research scope.

During the second study these same participants (except for one replacement) performed simulated search tasks in an interactive session. These simulated tasks were recreations of real council tasks in a laboratory setting where we asked users to search for pre-defined topics. Each participant in the session had an observer who asked them unstructured questions about their information seeking. This setup allowed us to observe more instrumental search tasks (i.e. tasks that were not explicit user goals, but necessary sub-steps).

The third study at municipality Hollands Kroon consisted of five semi-structured interviews designed to first identify the work tasks performed in preparation of a council meeting. For each work task we focused on the search tasks involved, and we concluded by asking for (recent) examples of each search task.

4.3 Analysis 1: Identifying Task Facets

We first identified which task facets characterised tasks in the domain. We analysed the task facets that users used to describe their tasks by developing a codebook based on the interview data. Coding is a qualitative method used to analyse interview data by annotating (potentially overlapping) fragments of interviews with codes by theme. It allows the researcher to identify concepts and relations between concepts [9]. The development of a codebook is an iterative process that occurs over multiple studies. With every study analysed, one tries to improve the codebook until it explains all new data from new studies. New codes are found in two main ways. Data-driven codes emerge to represent themes and recurring concepts in the data. Theory-driven codes are added when the data reflects themes from the relevant literature. In our case the theory driven codes include the task facets. We focused on analysing the task-related themes and generate the codebook on data from of Utrecht. We then apply the codebook to the data from Hollands Kroon to test whether its completeness for describing tasks performed in this new context.

4.4 Analysis 2: Characterising Council Member Tasks

We characterised the work tasks that users described and showed us during the studies at Utrecht using the task facets we identified using the codebook. We then compared the tasks identified to those we found at Hollands Kroon to identify whether our list of tasks is exhaustive.

5 Results 1: Identifying Task Facets

By applying the codebook to the data from the first study we found four task-related codes: the task objective, information sources, topic aspect and task specificity. We applied the codebook to the second study at of Utrecht to find further evidence for the previous codes and the retrieval unit as a new code.

The task objective is a description from the users' perspective. The information sources are the systems they mentioned, implying which underlying datasets are necessary for the task. The topic aspect represents different types of declarative domain knowledge. Consider the example topic 'the sound leak in Tivoli'. Over time users may be interested in different aspects of this, such as the background of the issue; how the council has dealt with this topic in the past; and what aldermen have previously promised to do about the issue. We found a limited set of topic aspects that are important for many topics. These aspects are reflected in the interview data when users implicitly switch their definition of what a topic's 'context' is. These topic aspects are closely related to the four kinds of information that Taylor identified among American legislators [32]. The only difference is that we found a distinction between background information and policy information, which Taylor grouped as one information type.

The retrieval unit code reflects that users do not always seek documents, but can instead seek, for example, a fact or (the contact details of) a person [23]. It

Table 2. The work tasks identified at of Utrecht, described using the task facets council members use to describe their tasks

Task ID	Task objective	Topic aspect	Information sources	Retrieval unit
WT1	*Understand the agenda item*	Background information	Google	Facts
WT2	*Evaluate existing or proposed policy*	Policy	iBabs, Google	Document
WT3	*Analyse previous council decisions*	Decision history	iBabs	Document(s), timeline
WT4	*Understand political positions*	Political context	iBabs, Google	Statement
WT5	*Create an argument*	Mixed	iBabs, Google	Mixed
WT6	*Create or defend a perspective*	Mixed	iBabs, Google	Mixed
WT7	*Evaluate progress on policy execution*	Administrative context	BMT	Statement

Table 3. The search tasks identified at of Utrecht, and the work tasks during which they occur

Task identifier	Search task	Associated WTs
ST1	Find news articles, municipality publications and other substantive public documents	WT1, WT2, WT6
ST2	Find reports and other (internally generated) substantive documents	WT1, WT2
ST3	Find the aldermens' commitments (formal agreements to the council)	WT7
ST4	Find agenda items and corresponding transcripts where this topic was previously discussed	WT3
ST5	Find documents that were key in the previous discussion of this topic	WT3
ST6	Find documents containing the current policy	WT4
ST7	Find previous statements from aldermen or colleagues	WT4, WT2, WT6
ST8	Find public articles containing political standpoints	WT4
ST9	Find sources supporting an argument	WT5
S10	Find the alderman responsible for this topic	WT3, WT4, WT2

Table 4. Characterising the search tasks identified in Table 3 using the task facets. Many tasks can be either amorphous (am) or specific (spec). These are joined in the Table for formatting.

Task ID	Topic aspect	Info sources	Retrieval unit	Task specificity
ST1	Topic background	Google	Document	Am or Spec
ST2	Topic background	iBabs	Document	Am or Spec
ST3	Decision history	BMT	Statement	Am or Spec
ST4	Decision history	iBabs	Timeline	Am or Spec
ST5	Decision history	iBabs	Document(s)	Am or Spec
ST6	Policy	iBabs/Web	Document	Am or Spec
ST7	Political context	iBabs	Statement	Am or Spec
ST8	Political context	Google	Mixed	Am or Spec
ST9	Mixed	Mixed	Mixed	Mixed
ST10	Administrative context	Google	Mixed	Specific

is related to the information level facet but captures more of the user's goal. The final facet is the task specificity, which indicates how specific the information is that users are looking for in a search task.

5.1 Generalisation of Codebook

We applied the codebook developed at of Utrecht to the data from Hollands Kroon. The codebook was able to explain all task-related themes. This suggested that the codes we used for task facets were stable (also known as theoretical saturation) and can properly represent tasks in this domain.

Five task codes were found based on how council members characterised their tasks: the task objective, the information sources, the topic aspect, the retrieval unit and the task specificity. We adopt these five codes as the task facets to describe the domain-specific task context.

6 Results 2: Council Member Tasks

Table 2 introduces the work tasks found at Utrecht. Tables 3 and 4 respectively describe and characterise the search tasks identified.

6.1 Generalisation of Tasks

To test whether the list of council member tasks is exhaustive we performed a study at Hollands Kroon and compared the findings to those at Utrecht. At Hollands Kroon we found work tasks WT1-6 from Table 2, but not WT7: evaluating the progress on alderman's commitments. This may be because the municipality is smaller, making it easier to keep track of such commitments.

At Hollands Kroon we found all search tasks except ST3 and ST8. ST3 is less significant in this municipality because WT7 is less significant. It is unclear why users here search for fewer public articles containing political standpoints (ST8). Perhaps the municipality has a smaller profile in the news because it is smaller. There is a slight difference in how users search for previously discussed topics (ST4), as the municipality Hollands Kroon does not maintain transcripts of each meeting. Their council is only provided with the video recordings of meetings. Because these are not searchable, this search task is not well supported. This is because Hollands Kroon has less resources.

The council tasks identified at municipality of Utrecht are a superset of those found at municipality Hollands Kroon. We therefore expect our that our list of council member tasks within the Netherlands is fairly exhaustive.

7 Supporting Specialised Council Task Functionality

When comparing tasks identified with the existing systems (see Table 5) we found that 1) filter-based search functionality is insufficient for non-specific tasks and 2) there is no support for investigating different topic aspects. We discuss how to design a more suitable domain-specific search engine based on the task model. We specifically consider how the interface should enable each of these tasks, what information is necessary for each of these tasks and how users want to interact it. We introduce the domain-specific search engine we developed in cooperation with Spinque, publicly available at https://ureka.utrecht.nl/app/.

7.1 Linking Tasks to Information Subsets

The task topic aspect indicates which datasets and document genres are relevant for a given task, informing how information in the domain should be modelled.

Within council information we found that tasks related to the topic background aspect should search within public web sources. Tasks involving the political context aspect involve searching the political statements made during meetings (i.e. segments of the council meeting minutes). A search engine that supports the policy aspect should enable searching all council documents. Tasks involving the decision history aspect involve the specific document genre council proposals, and finding the meetings that discuss these proposals.

The retrieval unit facet indicates how these document genres should be indexed: users search for the official council proposal documents in some tasks, but only look for segments of the meeting minutes in other tasks. Identifying the relevant document genres and retrieval units can indicate how the information model that the search engine is based on should be extended (e.g. by extracting political statements from meeting minutes).

7.2 Interface Design Implications

Work tasks reflect user goals and inform how the user approaches the system. Hence it should be clear to the user where he should go for any given work task.

Information is ideally presented in a useful context, which depends on the topic aspects we identified. The format and presentation of individual results depends on the retrieval units we identified.

Based on these guidelines we designed a different view (page) in the interface for each topic aspect, as shown in Figs. 1, 2, 3 and 4. We developed search verticals for existing policy, political context and administrative context. The decision history of council proposals was added as a contextual view when clicking a search result. We did not include functionality for the background information topic aspect, as interviews indicated that web search is satisfactory for this.

The search tasks reflect how users want to interact with the information within these views. The current model does not capture these requirements explicitly, but is a step in that direction. The task specificity facet indicates whether users will need filtering functionality (with high precision) or explorative functionality (with high recall). For example, when users search for statements by specific people (ST7) there is an implied requirement for filtering statements by the speaker. We could investigate the concrete requirements (e.g. on what information features does the user want to filter) by asking users about example tasks or by observing users perform the tasks in questions. Future work may include a search task facet that captures which filters should be included for specific tasks, and which dimensions are of interest in amorphous tasks.

7.3 Comparing the Proposed Improvements

In this paper we focus on the design process that resulted in a new search system, rather than individual improvements for specific tasks. As a result, the new system introduces many changes (e.g. the interface, result ranking, the datasets included) and it is both unfeasible and not our goal to evaluate the impact of each variable we changed. To show the value of our design approach we instead compare the proposed system to the existing system. We compare systems based on their ability to facilitate user tasks, because the best search system is the one that is most useful for the user's goals [3,35].

Table 5. A comparison of the existing and proposed search systems. We summarise the tasks by their facets, because tasks with the same facets require the same functionality.

Requirement	iBabs	Proposed
TA: Background info	Web search	Web search
TA: Existing policy	Filtering	Vertical in Fig. 1
TA: Political context	None	Vertical in Fig. 2
TA: Administrative context	None	Vertical in Fig. 3
TA: Decision history	None	Result page in Fig. 4
Retrieval unit	Document/meeting	TA dependent (Figures)
Specific search tasks	Filters	Filters on the same features
Amorphous search tasks	None	Timeline of decision history

Fig. 1. Vertical for the Policy topic aspect.

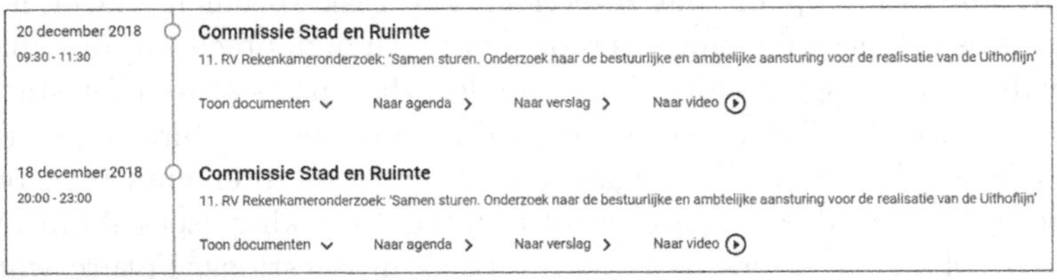

Fig. 2. Vertical for the Polical Context topic aspect.

Fig. 3. Vertical for the Administrative Context topic aspect.

Fig. 4. Search result view for political documents (Decision History topic aspect).

Table 5 summarizes the tasks that users want to perform (based on our previous results), and how both systems support these tasks. Because our design approach led to a better understanding of the target user group's requirements, we were able to develop more useful functionalities. This can aid developers and organisations in prioritising the importance of different functionalities. An enthusiastic response by its users and the interest of other local municipalities suggests that our approach was successful at specifying the user search requirements.

8 Conclusion

A target user group may require specialised search functionality to perform their work effectively. In this paper we investigate how to model the search requirements by extending the faceted task model with facets that capture domain-specific information. Comparing these tasks to the existing systems allows us to find initial design implications for improving the search experience, because it illustrates 1) how each task relates to subsets of information in the domain and 2) how users want to interface with this information.

We characterised council members as professional searchers who have not had time to specialise in their domain, and have not had any search literacy training. We found that council members information seeking usually begins with a web search to identify background information, using news sites and municipal websites. They then access internal council information systems to inform themselves about different topic aspects.

We found that existing task classifications were generic by design, and unable to represent domain-specific aspects of tasks. We extended this work by identifying the five task facets that council members used to characterise their tasks, and discussing how these can be used to represent domain-specific tasks. We found the task objective, the topic aspect, the information sources, the retrieval unit and the task specificity. We discussed how tasks have implications for how the information should be modelled, and how the interface should facilitate them.

We used the topic aspect to determine which datasets and document genres are important for which tasks (similar to search verticals). We used the retrieval unit to determine how to index (segments) of documents. For the interface design we used the task aspect of work tasks to present information in a useful context, resulting in different a different interface views for different topic aspects. The retrieval unit informed how individual search results should be presented. The search task specificity is a first step towards understanding how users want to interact with the information. Once we identify task specificity, we can investigate what type of filters are beneficial for a (high precision) specific task, or what dimensions users want to explore in (high recall) explorative tasks.

We found the same task facets and the same tasks at two municipalities. If the task model generalises to municipalities in similar contexts, then the search functionality we developed could be standardised across Dutch municipalities.

References

1. Anderson, M.J.: A comparative analysis of information search and evaluation behavior of professional and non-professional financial analysts. Acc. Organ. Soc. **13**(5), 431–446 (1988)

2. Belkin, N.J.: On the evaluation of interactive information retrieval systems. The Janus Faced Scholar (2010)
3. Belkin, N.J.: People, interacting with information. SIGIR **49**(2), 13–27 (2015)
4. Broder, A.Z.: A taxonomy of web search. SIGIR Forum **36**(2), 3–10 (2002)
5. Byström, K., Hansen, P.: Conceptual framework for tasks in information studies. J. Am. Soc. Inf. Sci. Technol. **56**(10), 1050–1061 (2005)
6. Byström, K., Heinström, J., Ruthven, I.: Information at Work: Information Management in the Workplace. Facet Publishing (2019)
7. Byström, K., Kumpulainen, S.: Vertical and horizontal relationships amongst task-based information needs. Inf. Process. Manag. **57**(2), 102065 (2020). https://doi.org/10.1016/j.ipm.2019.102065
8. Cole, M.J., Hendahewa, C., Belkin, N.J., Shah, C.: User activity patterns during information search. ACM Trans. Inf. Syst. **33**(1), 1:1-1:39 (2015)
9. DeCuir-Gunby, J.T., Marshall, P.L., McCulloch, A.W.: Developing and using a codebook for the analysis of interview data: an example from a professional development research project. Field Methods **23**(2), 136–155 (2011)
10. Donato, D., Bonchi, F., Chi, T., Maarek, Y.S.: Do you want to take notes? Identifying research missions in Yahoo! search pad. In: Proceedings of the 19th International Conference on World Wide Web, WWW 2010, pp. 321–330. ACM, Raleigh, NC (2010)
11. Erjavec, T., et al.: The ParlaMint corpora of parliamentary proceedings. Lang. Resour. Eval. 1–34 (2022). https://doi.org/10.1007/s10579-021-09574-0
12. Findwise: Enterprise search and findability survey 2015. Technical report, Findwise (2015). https://findwise.com/en/enterprise-search-and-findability-survey-2015
13. Hansen, P., Järvelin, A., Eriksson, G., Karlgren, J.: A use case framework for information access evaluation. In: Paltoglou, G., Loizides, F., Hansen, P. (eds.) Professional Search in the Modern World. LNCS, vol. 8830, pp. 6–22. Springer, Cham (2014). https://doi.org/10.1007/978-3-319-12511-4_2
14. Hienert, D., Mitsui, M., Mayr, P., Shah, C., Belkin, N.J.: The role of the task topic in web search of different task types. In: Proceedings of the 2018 Conference on Human Information Interaction and Retrieval, CHIIR 2018, pp. 72–81. ACM, New Brunswick, NJ (2018)
15. Ingwersen, P., Järvelin, K.: The Turn - Integration of Information Seeking and Retrieval in Context, The Kluwer International Series on Information Retrieval, vol. 18. Springer, Dordrecht (2005). https://doi.org/10.1007/1-4020-3851-8
16. Järvelin, K., Wilson, T.D.: On conceptual models for information seeking and retrieval research. Inf. Res. **9**(1), 9-1 (2003)
17. Jonasen, T.: Automatic indexing in e-government: improved access to administrative documents for professional users? Ph.D. thesis, Aalborg Universitet (2012)
18. Kaptein, R., Marx, M.: Focused retrieval and result aggregation with political data. Inf. Retr. **13**(5), 412–433 (2010). https://doi.org/10.1007/s10791-010-9130-z
19. Kelly, D., Arguello, J., Edwards, A., Wu, W.: Development and evaluation of search tasks for IIR experiments using a cognitive complexity framework. In: Proceedings of the 2015 International Conference on The Theory of Information Retrieval, ICTIR 2015, pp. 101–110. ACM, Northampton, MA (2015)
20. Leckie, G.J., Pettigrew, K.E., Sylvain, C.: Modeling the information seeking of professionals: a general model derived from research on engineers, health care professionals, and lawyers. In: The Library Quarterly, vol. 66, no. 2, pp. 161–193. University of Chicago Press, Chicago, IL (1996)
21. Li, Y., Belkin, N.J.: A faceted approach to conceptualizing tasks in information seeking. Inf. Process. Manag. **44**(6), 1822–1837 (2008)

22. Marcella, R., Baxter, G., Davies, S., Toornstra, D.: The information needs and information-seeking behaviour of the users of the European parliamentary documentation centre: a customer knowledge study. J. Documentation **63**(6), 920–934 (2007)
23. Ramirez, G., de Vries, A.P.: Relevant contextual features in XML retrieval. In: Proceedings of the 1st International Conference on Information Interaction in Context, IIiX 2006, pp. 56–65. ACM, Copenhagen, Denmark (2006)
24. Rose, D.E., Levinson, D.: Understanding user goals in web search. In: Feldman, S.I., Uretsky, M., Najork, M., Wills, C.E. (eds.) WWW 2004, New York, USA, 17–20 May 2004, pp. 13–19. ACM (2004)
25. Russell-Rose, T., Chamberlain, J.: Expert search strategies: the information retrieval practices of healthcare information professionals. JMIR Med. Inform. **5**(4), e33 (2017)
26. Russell-Rose, T., Chamberlain, J., Azzopardi, L.: Information retrieval in the workplace: a comparison of professional search practices. Inf. Process. Manag. **54**(6), 1042–1057 (2018). https://doi.org/10.1016/j.ipm.2018.07.003
27. Russell-Rose, T., Tate, T.: Designing the Search Experience - the Information Architecture of Discovery. Morgan Kaufmann (2012)
28. Saastamoinen, M., Järvelin, K.: Queries in authentic work tasks: the effects of task type and complexity. J. Documentation **72**(6), 1114–1133 (2016)
29. Saastamoinen, M., Kumpulainen, S.: Expected and materialised information source use by municipal officials: intertwining with task complexity. Inf. Res. **19**(4) (2014)
30. Singh, J., Anand, A.: Designing search tasks for archive search. In: Proceedings of the 2017 Conference on Conference Human Information Interaction and Retrieval, CHIIR 2017, pp. 361–364. ACM, Oslo, Norway (2017)
31. Sohn, T., Li, K.A., Griswold, W.G., Hollan, J.D.: A diary study of mobile information needs. In: Proceedings of the 2008 Conference on Human Factors in Computing Systems, CHI 2008, pp. 433–442. ACM, Florence, Italy (2008)
32. Taylor, R.S.: Information use environments. Prog. Commun. Sci. **10**(217), 55 (1991)
33. Teevan, J., Collins-Thompson, K., White, R.W., Dumais, S.T., Kim, Y.: Slow search: information retrieval without time constraints. In: Symposium on Human-Computer Interaction and Information Retrieval, HCIR 2013, pp. 1:1–1:10. ACM, Vancouver, BC, Canada (2013)
34. Trippas, J.R., et al.: Learning about work tasks to inform intelligent assistant design. In: CHIIR 2019, pp. 5–14. ACM, Glasgow, Scotland (2019)
35. Vakkari, P.: The usefulness of search results: a systematization of types and predictors. In: O'Brien, H.L., Freund, L., Arapakis, I., Hoeber, O., Lopatovska, I. (eds.) CHIIR 2020: Conference on Human Information Interaction and Retrieval, Vancouver, BC, Canada, 14–18, March 2020, pp. 243–252. ACM (2020). https://doi.org/10.1145/3343413.3377955
36. Vassilakaki, E., Garoufallou, E., Johnson, F., Hartley, R.J.: Users' information search behavior in a professional search environment: In: Paltoglou, G., Loizides, F., Hansen, P. (eds.) Professional Search in the Modern World. LNCS, vol. 8830, pp. 23–44. Springer, Cham (2014). https://doi.org/10.1007/978-3-319-12511-4_3
37. Verberne, S., He, J., Wiggers, G., Russell-Rose, T., Kruschwitz, U., de Vries, A.P.: Information search in a professional context - exploring a collection of professional search tasks. CoRR abs/1905.04577 (2019)

Letting Your Data Imagination Run Away with You. Promises and Perspectives of a Public Sector Data Analytics Implementation

David Jamieson[1,2(✉)], Rob Wilson[1,2], and Victoria Pagan[1,2]

[1] Newcastle Business School, Northumbria University, Newcastle upon Tyne, UK
david.a.jamieson@northumbria.ac.uk
[2] Newcastle University, Newcastle upon Tyne, UK

Abstract. Public service organizations are encouraged to believe that data analytics can transform services and organizations. Spurred on by these claims – or promises - this paper examines the implementation of a public sector-focused Office of Data Analytics in the Northeast of England. We explore the promises of data analytics and what basis these might have. Comprising of a single case study, we apply a critical lens – informed by Beer's (2008) data gaze - to the implementation and find that there were challenges to the application of data analysis within complex societal environments. This challenge was juxtaposed with an unnerving belief – stemming from public policy and strategy - in the promises that adopting and implementing data analytics and a data platform can bring to the public sector. As a result, we present an assessment of a public sector data platform implementation where realities emerge that dismiss the promises and imaginaries that are often promoted – whilst highlighting previously cautioned "myths" and "impossibilities".

Keywords: Data analytics · Big data · Data imaginary · Digital government

1 Introduction

The benefits of applying data analytics have been well-documented (Mayer-Schönberger and Cukier 2013; Barbosa et al. 2018; Wang and Wang 2020). Commentators are keen to highlight the successes that have been brought about by data analytics projects (see Eaton and Bertoncin 2018). Such stories of success have inevitably begun to be filtered to the public sector (Joseph and Johnson 2013; Wang et *al.* 2015). Access to swathes of vital data has created a point of convergence between suppliers looking to provide insight tools, and policymakers who believe that efficiencies can be made in publicly delivered services. Data analytics for public sector organizations, offers several promises: assistance with the allocation of their resources, increasing impact, a way to restructure services accordingly in response to early indicators, and a reduction in more expensive, upstream interventions (Kim, Trimi and Chung 2014).

Published by Springer Nature Switzerland AG 2022
M. Janssen et al. (Eds.): EGOV 2022, LNCS 13391, pp. 419–431, 2022.
https://doi.org/10.1007/978-3-031-15086-9_27

Predicated on this, the Mayor's Office of Data Analytics (MODA) in New York City established a civic intelligence center, which allowed New York City to:

"*...aggregate and analyze data from across City agencies, to more effectively address crime, public safety, and quality of life issues...the Office uses analytics tools to prioritize risk more strategically, deliver services more efficiently, enforce laws more effectively, and increase transparency*" (NYC Analytics 2019).

Using MODA as its template, in late-2016 a Government Innovation Team (GIT), worked with a number of UK regions to help them join up, analyze and act upon data at a city or regional scale. Its purpose, like MODA, was to improve public services and tackle challenging policy problems. The Office of Data Analytics (ODA) methodology (Nesta 2016; Eaton and Bertoncin 2018), established as a result of this work, specifically focused on combining data from multiple different organizations and sources. The primary objective was to emulate MODA and act upon data insights to enable more effective public sector interventions.

Within this paper, we explore the establishment of a regionalized ODA located in the Northeast of England (NE-ODA), its origins, and its appointment of a third-party Data Analytics Organization (DAO). We also explore the outcomes of the NE-ODA initiative against the promises that are offered by data analytics in order "to see what was promised as well as the actual data solutions that are then deployed on the ground" (Beer 2018, p. 33). To do so, we frame the NE-ODA using Beer's Data Gaze (2018) to explore the following research questions:

- What are the promises offered by the data gaze when applied to public sector analytics?
- How do these promises translate into application in public sector data analytics realities?
- What alternative perspectives do we have on analyzing the underlying intentions and objectives of public sector data analytics initiatives?

2 The Allure of Data Analytics for Public Services

From the 1950s the debates on the application of computers by the state was primarily focused on the use of data in governance (6. 2004) The more recent history of the application of data to solve the perceived problems of government is long and tangled moving from centralized data collection to more localized approaches and points between (see Wilson et al. 2011). In one of the more recent turns the United Kingdom government released "Seizing the opportunity" a strategy for UK "data capability" (HM Government 2013). The strategy highlighted that the benefits of data analytics in the improvement of wider society and the economy. The strategy specified that, "the ability to handle and analyze data is essential for the UK's competitive advantage and business transformation" (HM Government 2013, p. 5).

In February 2017, a policy paper - "Government Transformation Strategy: better use of data" - stated that data has the "ability to make easy data-driven decisions" and "is becoming vital to the way that we all live and work. This should be the way that government provides services." (Government Digital Service 2017). The policy continues to suggest that when the government makes effective use of data, this leads to better policy and the delivery of better, more tailored services for users. Data can be used in real-time by front-line staff to ensure the person they are serving receives the best possible support to meet their needs. Joseph and Johnson (2013) suggest that government services can be greatly improved by big data and data analytics, increase government efficiency and effectiveness and is the ultimate evolutionary stage of e-government. Kitchin (2014, p. 115) proposes that this is reflective of "discourses around efficient government and value for money, citizenship and empowerment, fairness and anti-crime, security and safety" and that they that "appeal to the notion that common problems and issues are being addressed through shared logic and principles". Similarly, Kitchin (2014), also highlights that data does not exist independently of ideas, techniques, technologies, systems, people, and contexts, regardless of them being presented in this manner. This data assemblage is "composed of many apparatuses and elements that are thoroughly entwined and develop and mutate over time and space" (Kitchin 2014, p. 24). Here, Kitchin identities that data, how it came to be produced and how it is used, are co-terminus and mutually constituted (Kitchin 2014, p. 25).

In a climate of neo-liberalism and political uncertainty, data and data technologies have become viewed as essential to the success of public service delivery (Henman 2019). As our romanticism with all things tech abides our many sensibilities, who – or what – will be used to understand the governance and intentions of public sector data analytics initiatives where the outputs are private sector focused?

3 Promises into Practice

As a conceptual framing to help address the assemblage of data analytics and public services, Beer's Data Gaze (2018) allows us the following considerations and components as to what is promoted: envisioning the power of data analytics; perpetuating and applying a rationality of speed; technical infrastructures and tools used to deliver the vision of data analytics; and professionals operating within the data analytics industry. The rationale for its selection is predicated by previous "myths' (Janssen *et* al. 2012) and "impossibilities" (Jamieson *et* al. 2019) of the use of data within the public sector and the unheeded guidance that this literature base provides.

From this, we can summarize that the Data Gaze can be described as the visions, the technical infrastructures, and practices assigned to the process of data analytics and data analytics organizations. Equally, as expressed by Boyd and Crawford (2012), there is a mythological interplay between the technological, analytical, and mythological aspects associated with (big) data. Taken from Foucault's clinical gaze from The Birth of the Clinic (Foucault 2012), the Data Gaze is a concept that targets an understanding of the connections, structures, and performances of power within data analytics (Beer 2018, p. 7). Beer's focus of the Data Gaze is to obtain an improved understanding of an industry that has emerged alongside - contributed to - new events of data production and manipulation. The Data Gaze, Beer (2018) suggests, stretches far into our lives, makes it routine and structurally significant in ordering the social world. As such, we are now in a world where the importance of data and the ability and desire to interpret it are now embedded in our day-to-day lives (Kitchin 2014). Beer comments (2018) that because of this emergence, there is a need to explore how data-led processes spread, how data-informed knowledge is legitimated, and how this industry approaches and frames data. Specifically, Beer asks who possesses, and who has been given, the power to speak with our data whilst creating and expanding "an inescapable gaze" replete with "unending scrutiny" (Beer 2018). The phraseology here is interchangeable with Janssen et al. (2012) and Jamieson et al. (2019).

Referring to Schrock and Shaffer (2017), Beer suggests that there is a need to understand the visions, infrastructures, and practices - including organizations, software packages and individuals (Beer 2018) - that facilitate what - and by whom - is said with our data. Notions of value are often woven into these uses and understandings of data as well as the visions and promises that are attached to them. These visions and claims are wrapped up in a "veneer of knowing" which aims to draw people into a data rationality. This results in the need to interpret, make sense of, and make comprehensible, data. This in turn has then led to the emerging, "from the shadows" of new types of knowledge and expertise where those that are data informed, along with their software packages and comprehension of data (Becker 2007), are held aloft. These "new prophets of capital" (Aschoff 2015), are now, as a direct consequence of their significance in society due to their participation and perpetuation within the Data Gaze, an inevitable force - and the standard repertoire of business (Bucher 2018). Kitchin (2014) suggests that this is the result of a discursive regime and atmosphere which remakes the world in a particular vision, reshaping it so all those with a vested interest necessitate the affective response.

Beer (2018) terms this salesman-like approach of data analytics as the "data imaginary". This imaginary, positioning key organizational issues or inefficiencies, leverages data analytics as the must-have solution. The role of the data imaginary, Beer argues, is to "shove back" the "data frontier" - the limits of understanding or resistance to data analytics - and persuade, enact, and produce notions and ideals relating to data analytics. Beer's data imaginary consists of six themes - or "promises" - which emphasize a particular property or feature (Beer 2018, p. 21) within data analytics and data analytics organizations, and their approach. To this extent, in the following section, we explore further the individual "promises" of the Data Gaze. We do so as a precursor to study a deployment involving several public sector organizations to examine the utility of looking through such theoretical lenses in the prosecution of data analytics projects in the public sector.

The 'data imaginary', according to Beer (2018) is an active part of the assemblage of human actors, code, software and algorithms that shape the circulation and integration of new forms of data. Consisting of six aspects (or promises) which combine to extend the reach of data analytics and a particular type of data informed rationality (Beer 2018).

We adopt the Data Gaze (Beer 2018) to explore and frame the implementation of NE-ODA and the emergent power that data analytics practice and organizations perpetuate. We have done so using the following methodology.

4 Methodology and Approach

This paper uses a single case study approach. The case study focuses on the analysis of the implementation of the "Data Office" and the associated promises used to establish it. The focus of the Data Office was to address the social harms caused by alcohol to young people - those aged between 0 and 25 - across six neighboring municipalities in England. Data collection was achieved through a combination of participant observation, interviews, and observations within the establishment of the project and undertaking of the necessary tasks including the acquisition, interpretation, and visualization of the data. The analysis in this paper draws on this combination of a longitudinal ethnographic approach commencing with the initial meetings to provide a specification of the data analytics platform. To carry out the analysis we used a multi-perspective approach in the form of the account of the data analytics platform and blending the views of stakeholders its development. These concepts were used as the basis of a thematic analysis (Miles and Huberman 2002) to draw out the key themes over the duration of the project applying the theoretical concepts of the 'data gaze' to explore the visions and promises of the project and its processes and products. A key reason for selecting a case study approach is that that the lead author of this paper was the data scientist leading the project on behalf of the Data Analytics Organization (DAO) responsible for delivering the implementation. The selection of a case study approach – and the direct involvement of the author – seeks only to explain or interpret this single historical episode as an apparatus through which future implementations can be interpreted.

5 Findings

Our research findings set out below plot the development of the case, from its commencement with the initial framing of the NE-ODA concept following the procurement of a commercial organization to award the contract in response to procurement response in February 2017, through to its full implementation in June 2017 and subsequent evaluation in October 2017. This is presented in three phases describing the 'imaginary' promises and realities of the use of the data and the technical tools which allows for an assessment of the narrative to explore rationale, relationships, attitudes, beliefs, and intentions of those stakeholders who were engaged with the shaping, delivery and analysis of the NE-ODA project.

5.1 Implementation: Stage 1 - Background and Rationale of the NE-ODA

As previously highlighted, the original inspiration for the creation of the ODA initiative was that of the Mayor's Office of Data Analytics (MODA) in New York City. MODA as civic an intelligence center sourced data from different city organizations and overlaid and plotted them on the same maps. The benefits, as observed by Copeland (2015), were financial savings through data sharing, increased joined up working across departments and agencies, and spreading of skills in data-driven management of public services. The Government Innovation Team (GIT) working with several UK regions to help them join up, analyze, and act upon data at a city or regional scale to improve public services and tackle challenging policy problems. The Office of Data Analytics (ODA) methodology which they established (Office of Data Analytics 2016), specifically focused on combining data from multiple different organizations and sources. The primary objective was to act upon data insights to enable more effective interventions.

There was a recognition by the GIT that due to the pressure experienced by public services at the time, local authorities are required to do more and better with less money, and with fewer resources. The GIT also recognized that public sector bodies had begun to respond to these limitations by using their own data to become more efficient and effective. As a result, there was the belief that significant benefits would be possible if organizations collaborate with their data to address issues at a larger scale (Eaton and Bertoncin 2018). Furthermore, the GIT methodology for the ODA consisted of the following considerations and tasks (Office of Data Analytics 2016):

1. Enable coordinated services/scaling of shared services. Suggesting that "public sector data often resembles a jigsaw: everyone has their piece of the puzzle, but no one can see the whole picture" the ODA methodology pieces together disparate datasets so it's possible to see how problems, opportunities and demand transcend geographic boundaries or change over time, and "intelligently design services to proactively address emerging issues" (Office of Data Analytics 2016).
2. Target resources toward cases of greatest need, risk, and importance. Highlighting the geospatial considerations of different datasets on a single map, or "creating an algorithm to prioritize cases", the methodology believed that data could help focus efforts when and where they are needed most. This contrasts with "less effective, but common public service practice such as treating cases chronologically" (Office of Data Analytics 2016).
3. Predict future instances of a problem to enable prevention or early intervention. Nesta (2016) suggested that by modelling past cases and learning about the factors that correlate with higher risk, predictive data analytics can be applied to help spot problems at an earlier stage when they are cheaper and simpler to resolve. The methodology also suggests that this technique may also "perhaps predict where the next incidents are most likely to happen" (Office of Data Analytics 2016).

Regions were invited by Nesta to bid to pilot the idea of an ODA to explore the feasibility of the US model in the UK in line with broader movement around devolved governance in England. The NE of England then the subject of conversations around a Northeast devolution with a regional Mayor being proposed with a range of cross-cutting responsibilities around several issues such as public health and transport. This appeared to be good fit as a location with an emerging place agenda in which to test the ODA initiative. After several discussions between local authorities and representatives from Nesta the decision was made to explore a long-standing public health-related issue in the Northeast of England – alcohol related harms.

The initiative was devised to highlight the perceived power and modernity of data analytics and how it might improve, and impact upon, a localized and specific, socio-economic issue. Established as a pilot project, the membership of the NE-ODA consisted of six municipalities within the Northeast of England. Using the data supplied by its members, the NE-ODA was to assist in the development of a data visualization platform which would then be used to help usher in shared discussions regarding the socio-economic issue. It was hoped that the data outputs from the platform would allow for collaborative practice across the municipalities and inform commissioning and resource allocation. This would then lead to localized and targeted interventions. The data visualization platform used the latest technologies and techniques and was created by an appointed local Data Analytics Organization (DAO). It would come to include predictive analytics and machine learning algorithms to assist the NE-ODA with their decision making: all the features data analytics has come to promise.

The focus of the pilot, the subject of this case study research, was to provide a mechanism to share best practice through the provision of a boundary object that enabled conversations regarding a specific subject matter affecting all municipalities. The intended outcome of the information sharing was to facilitate analysis, and understand patterns and relationships related to alcohol harms across all the municipalities. Any findings would then lead to the potential redesign, redeployment, or recommissioning of services to prevent future harm. The ambition was to visualize the data in such a way as to aid better region-wide policy discussions on factors related specifically to alcohol harms. It looked to achieve this by sharing the geographic and anonymized health and social service data related to alcohol harms of each the municipal organizations and a procured, private sector, Data Analytics Organization (DAO).

5.2 Implementation: Stage 2 – Selection of the Data Analytics Organization

The procurement exercise to appoint the DAO commenced in February 2017 and concluded in March 2017. The DAO was awarded to a North-East data analytics organization that had previously completed successful engagements with other public sector organizations providing business intelligence solutions and data analysis services. The response of the DAO was predicated by the following requirements:

1. Experience/ability to use data aggregation, transposition, and data visualization tools to facilitate analysis and problem solving.
2. Ability to acquire further open data to enrich the specific model around alcohol harms in the Northeast.
3. An understanding of data protection legislation and a secure hosting infrastructure.
4. We require that the final information product will be provided at no cost as open source in perpetuity for the partner organizations and/or another organization to scale up.
5. At the end of the project, we require that knowledge of how to use and refresh data in the product will be transferred to the partner organizations through a workshop. Occasional attendance at and presentations at project workshops, writing of blogs as subject matter experts.
6. Suppliers will be required to sign up to a partner information sharing protocol as data processor.

In response, to satisfy the data protection requirement, the DAO proposed that the project was to be delivered using a Cloud-based architecture supplied via Amazon Web Services and would be located within a UK-based data center. The response also suggested that the DAO had "experience of data aggregation, transposing data and visualizing data as part of daily operations and client-led projects". The delivered product would be a "data visualization platform, which utilized machine learning to establish deeper and predictive analysis of the underlying data". The use and application of the Hadoop ecosystem was suggested as means to ensure open-source provisioning but also to harness the modern, technological components used by big data. It is this aspect to which we turn our attention as we believe this helps us further support a data imaginary proposed by the DAO.

Whilst the exact technical functionalities are outside the scope of this paper, the proposal of the DAO heavily referenced the open-source Hadoop architecture of Hive, Hadoop, Mahout and Zeppelin. Potentially presented in response to the open-source requirement of the project, Beer (2018, p. 87) suggests that the use of the Hadoop infrastructure is reflective of the codified clinic and that this "infrastructure implies the pursuit of the next model and the always pressing advancement of capacities and components" - another example of the speediness promised through the data imaginary.

5.3 Implementation: Stage 3 – Outputs of the DAO for the NE-ODA

The work of the DAO commenced in April 2017 and completed at the end of July 2017. During this time, the DAO proceeded to establish their suggested data stores and Cloud-based technologies to ingest data provided by the municipal authorities. Inevitably, there were several challenges that occurred because of the activities of the DAO and attempting to align them to the requirements of the ODA. These observations are explored and discussed as follows.

Initially, it was assumed that all six municipalities were to be engaged with the NE-ODA. Additionally, that the scope of each the datasets that were to be provided by each municipality - including format, volume, and subject areas - had been established. However, this was not to be the case. Over the course of the project, only three of the municipalities would agree to supply any datasets - with one engaging entirely to supply any requested data. Furthermore, upon commencement of the project, the "problem statement" that the NE-ODA was established to address was, as has been discussed, that of alcohol-related harms. However, during the project, the exact "problem statement" went through several iterations. It was discussed that the subject of alcohol-related harms was not a "problem" experienced throughout all municipalities. In addition, the "low-hanging fruit" of alcohol-related harm - that of harm caused by the Night-Time Economy (NTE) such as pubs, clubs and associated public disorder crimes and related data - was to be excluded. This ensured that the previously supplied data was now redundant.

The final "problem statement" of the NE-ODA was to focus on alcohol-related harm relating to young people - that is those aged between 0 - and 18 - or 25, depending on the municipality and their perspective - which itself caused issues that led to a disparity in the data sets that were to be supplied. Additionally, where there was once a data processing agreement to supply or provide access of anonymized information from health and social care, and police and rehabilitation of offender's datasets, and public health departments, this was now rendered invalid. It was left to the DAO to determine what the cause of alcohol-related harm might be in absence of Subject Matter Experts and datasets. This conflict appears to impact as to how the data was represented, what data sources were required and, ultimately, accepted by all involved parties within the NE-ODA. However, given the need of the DAO to produce insights and the variety of data provided, this caused issues in attempting to extract something of meaning from the data provided - even more so given the external nature of the analytics organization undertaking the work. This was only established once the project was underway.

5.4 Single Reality or Multiple Imaginaries? Viewing the NE-ODA Through the Data Gaze

We now turn our attention to a comparison of the promises and realities of the imaginary of the NE-ODA applying the aspects of the imaginary outlined in the Data Gaze in the Table 1:

Table 1. NE-ODA reality and multiple data imaginaries

Promise	ODA/NE-ODA promise	Reality
Speedy	Statement of promise in the form of real-time data visualizations powered by data analytics to improve the delivery of public services	Data provided to NE-ODA was neither contemporary or real-time therefore preventing the notion that the lag between data and knowledge could be reduced and the promise of speed was not realised in NE-ODA. This was due in part to the unclear framing of the problem but also the reluctance to share data
Accessibility	The provision of an open-source data visualization tool making use of geospatial data and maps	The outputs produced by DAO were of limited application, but they were accessible. However, despite the suggestion to use the Hadoop eco-system, the final data visualization platform was delivered using Microsoft Power BI which then incurred licensing costs which were not sustainable beyond the original project lifecycle
Revealing	Acquisition and extension of provided data sets with open data as means to provide additional "joined-upness" of data	Significantly, the ODA pilot work appears to move from the original promise which was 'what do we want to ask the data?' to a re-framing 'what do we want the data to tell us?'. This shift led to a loss of focus on what the NE-ODA proposed to address meant the promise to produce insight beyond what the partners had already was significantly reduced
Panoramic	Sharing of data across all involved organization to encourage improved interventions and understanding of a shared problem and see the "whole problem"	Partners in the project had a mutual reluctance to share data - both internally amongst the local authorities - but also with the DAO due to concerns with data protection and information sharing. As has been observed by Gamage (2016) public sector entities do not share data - potentially due to the risk of breaching privacy laws and regulations; or the possibility of damaging the organization's reputation
Prophetic	Enable the prediction of future problems in order to provide intervention - or the early intervention of service delivery. The use of predictive analytics can be used for preventative purposes	The lack of data from all partners, meant that the joining of data, despite from the same time period, was not possible. Furthermore, the limited time frame of the data - in order to comply with privacy - meant that the ability to apply the appropriate algorithmic techniques was not possible

(*continued*)

Table 1. (*continued*)

Promise	ODA/NE-ODA promise	Reality
Smart	The very latest tools and techniques should be used - specifically those that are used for big analytics to deal with the variance and volume of the data	The promise of applied tools such as the Hadoop ecosystem and machine learning were not achieved. This was in part due to the common problems such as heterogeneity and incoherence of data, allied to a lack of granularity in the data provided by the municipalities. The end visualization was not smart, but instead used traditional data visualization

Table 1 allows us to see the clear gap between the promises of data analytics made in the broader programme and in the initiation of the NE-ODA compared to the challenges that emerged through the reality of attempting to apply data to addressing the complex problems of alcohol harms across a heterogeneous group of public sector partners. It is important to note that many of the realities described here are not specific to this case but rather a wider set of realities in the burgeoning field of data (open, big and otherwise in government). Work on societal issues such as the activity undertaken by the NE-ODA on alcohol harms, implies multi-agency working whether that be intra- or inter-agency. As has been seen, despite the proximity of the municipalities, not all twelve were engaged within the project whilst those that did, did not supply the same sets or volume of data. As such, the ability to provide not only an equitable approach to the NE-ODA, coupled with a shared question, but more importantly a shared interpretation of the data, most likely led to the lack of progress in the ways it was promised.

Schintler and Kulkarni (2014) suggest that a typical approach to address public policy is that problems need to be identified and conceptualized to be addressed. This may be a result of the faith in the ability of analytics to deliver the anticipated success using the available data sets. It was also perceived that everyone had a vested interest and shared the same experiences and perspective in relation to the issues that required investigation. However, as the ODA progressed this did not appear to be the case for instance those local municipality areas with active night-time economies versus those without. We also recognize the limitations of using a single case study and how that generalization is applied within the broader subject of public sector analytics. This is pertinent in light of the other ODAs set up as part of a wider programme across the UK. Interestingly, other ODA's were reported as having greater success (Eaton and Bertoncin 2018) than the case selected within this paper. However, whilst we have omitted detailing the other Data Offices, we believe the plurality of actors and perspectives within them that significantly exacerbated the challenges of meeting the promises outlined at the start. The NE-ODA had specific characteristics including spatial cross-boundary issues as a significant part of the, that is not as prevalent with other implementations (in that other ODA's has been primarily based on a single municipality or locality).

6 Findings

Based on this evidence we would argue that our case study demonstrates the utility of applying of the conceptual lenses of the 'Data Gaze' to reflecting on the complex challenges of implementing data analytics programmes in the public sector. It allows us to identify and foreground the key challenges faced by the stakeholders because of the promises and realities of data analytics in this case study. Finally, we can distinguish between the problems of collective data myopia and data hyperopia across the aspects of the imaginary data gaze which ensued during the progress of the project as the relationship between promises (of the future) and realities (of the contemporary activity) moved further apart.

This case also highlights the need for a constructive unifying narrative of how the application of data and analytical capacities might bring some insight to addressing the processes of aspiration and need for collaborative responses to societal issues. This, we believe includes the requirement to explicitly acknowledge the sorts of frames (as described by Beer in the Data Gaze) implicit in the applications of data to complex which as we saw in this case acted as 'blinkers' or 'goggles' to a deeper understanding the potential benefits of an Office of Data Analytics. Considerations that might have been made include an evaluation of available data sources (as suggested by Erickson et al. 2013) before embarking on public sector data analytics projects. A data catalogue of all stakeholders would help understand what data sources were readily available or may need to be made available and what issues could be addressed with it. This would help in the readjustment of the scope of the data analytics work and improve the focus. Furthermore, the activities reported upon within this paper were partially problematic because of the top-down approach of addressing public policy and issues (Sivarajah et al. 2015). The absence of the citizen or community within this process leaves out a key source of insight when exploring complex issues such as alcohol harms. Sivarajah et al. (2015) suggest that forums such as e-participation could be leveraged as way to improve policy-based decision making in local government that is participatory and inclusive. In addition, we suggest that this would require a conscious interpretative turn where the aims would be to shape spaces and occasions that are truly supportive of the use of data in conversations of local governance where the dynamic sharing and use of the breadth of data that relates to people, places and transactions becomes a normal part of the improvement of services and participation in the wider civic realm (Cornford et *al.* 2013; Lips 2019).

Despite the increasing prevalence of data analytics, it remains to be understood if a true measure of an implementation – successful or otherwise - exists. In this research, we uncover a means from which practitioners can explore the perceived promises of data analytics and assess the appropriateness for their own organization. Our case within this paper highlights the rationales within which data analytics projects are undertaken, but also how the issues of visibility of these rationales come to be. This is even more relevant in complex environments, such as those addressed by NE-ODA, where complex issues are simplified by data analytics implementations. As such, the intentions – both from those of the wider data analytics disciple and internal motivations can be assessed and understood and, within the context of the public sector, demonstrated in the service delivery. From this perspective, practitioners can both query and pre-evaluate analytics projects prior to their commencement. In summary, our findings can help guide practitioners in approaching the implementation of data analytics projects and how the romanticism of data analytics – and other challenges to the implementation of data analytics in general (see Sivarajah et *al.* 2017) might be better considered in the first instance.

Finally, previous studies on data analytics have tended to focus on either the potential value of data analytics or on the potential issues of the processes involved with undertaking data analytics. The work of Boyd and Crawford (2012) suggests that the discussion of Big Data and data analytics leads to both utopian and dystopian rhetoric. Our study suggests that the limitations of such perspectives instead providing a focus on the imagined promises both of data in abstract and in context and the ways in which this frames a combination of myopic and hyperopic responses of the stakeholders to the process. This suggests that the consideration of such intentions and realities is essential in determining under what basis such projects can be deemed successful or not. Additionally, whilst adopting a critical framing, our research contributes to the current understanding by providing an evaluative framework for the assessment of data analytics projects within the public sector. Our research is a cautionary tale where even in a case where the 'template' for successful innovation of a NE version of ODA was seemingly clear, in the form of MODA, the promises were not realized.

References

6 P: E-governance: Styles of Political Judgment in the Information Age Polity. Palgrave MacMillan, Basingstoke (2004)

Aschoff, N.: The New Prophets of Capital. Verso Books (2015)

Barbosa, M.W. et al.: Managing supply chain resources with Big Data Analytics: a systematic review. Int. J. Logist. Res. Appl. 177–200 (2018)

Becker, A.: Electronic Commerce: Concepts, Methodologies, Tools, and Applications: Concepts, Methodologies, Tools, and Applications. IGI Global (2007)

Beer, D.: The Data Gaze: Capitalism, Power and Perception. SAGE (2018)

Boyd, D., Crawford, K.: Critical questions for big data: provocations for a cultural, technological, and scholarly phenomenon. Inf. Commun. Soc. **15**(5), 662–679 (2012)

Bucher, T.: If...Then: Algorithmic Power and Politics. Oxford University Press (2018)

Cornford, J., Wilson, R., Baines, S., Richardson, R.: Local Governance in the new information ecology: the challenge of building interpretative communities. Public Money Manag. **33**(3), 201–208 (2013)

Copeland, E.: Big Data in The Big Apple: the lessons London can learn from New York's data-driven approach to smart cities. Capital City Foundation (2015). http://eddiecopeland.me/wp-content/uploads/2015/11/Big-Data-in-the-Big-Apple-Report.pdf

Eaton, M., Bertoncin, C.: State of Offices of Data Analytics (ODA) in the UK (2018). https://media.nesta.org.uk/documents/State_of_Offices_of_Data_Analytics_ODA_in_the_UK_WEB_v5.pdf

Foucault, M.: The Birth of the Clinic. Routledge (2012)

Gamage, P.: New development: leveraging "big data" analytics in the public sector. Public Money Manag. **36**(5), 385–390 (2016)

Government Digital Service: Government Transformation Strategy: better use of data, gov.uk. GOV.UK (2017). https://www.gov.uk/government/publications/government-transformation-strategy-2017-to-2020/government-transformation-strategy-better-use-of-data. Accessed 28 Mar 2020

HM Government: Seizing the data opportunity: a strategy for UK data capability (2013). https://assets.publishing.service.gov.uk/government/uploads/system/uploads/attachment_data/file/254136/bis-13-1250-strategy-for-uk-data-capability-v4.pdf

Henman, P.: Of algorithms, apps and advice: digital social policy and service delivery. J. Asian Public Policy **12**, 71–89 (2019). https://doi.org/10.1080/17516234.2018.1495885

Huberman, A., Miles, M.: The Qualitative Researcher's Companion (2002)

Jamieson, D., Wilson, R., Martin, M.: The (im) possibilities of Open Data? Public Money Manag. (2019). http://nrl.northumbria.ac.uk/38265/

Janssen, M., Charalabidis, Y., Zuiderwijk, A.: Benefits, adoption barriers and myths of open data and open government. Inf. Syst. Manag. **29**(4), 258–268 (2012)

Joseph, R.C., Johnson, N.A.: Big data and transformational government. IT Prof. **15**(6), 43–48 (2013)

Kim, G.-H., Trimi, S., Chung, J.-H.: Big-data applications in the government sector. Commun. ACM **57**(3), 78–85 (2014)

Kitchin, R.: The Data Revolution: Big Data, Open Data, Data Infrastructures and Their Consequences. SAGE (2014)

Lips, M.: Digital Government: Managing Public Sector Reform in the Digital Era. Routledge (2019)

Mayer-Schönberger, V., Cukier, K.: Big Data: A Revolution that Will Transform How We Live, Work, and Think. Houghton Mifflin Harcourt (2013)

NYC Analytics (2019). https://www1.nyc.gov/site/analytics/index.page. Accessed 8 Mar 2022

Offices of Data Analytics (2016). nesta.org.uk. https://www.nesta.org.uk/project/offices-of data-analytics/. Accessed 2 Mar 2022

Schintler, L.A., Kulkarni, R.: Big data for policy analysis: the good, the bad, and the ugly. Rev. Policy Res. **31**(4), 343–348 (2014)

Schrock, A., Shaffer, G.: Data ideologies of an interested public: a study of grassroots open government data intermediaries. Big Data Soc. **4**(1) (2017)

Sivarajah, U., et al.: The role of e-participation and open data in evidence-based policy decision making in local government. J. Organiz. Comput. Electron. Commerce (26)

Sivarajah, U., Kamal, M.M., Irani, Z., Weerakkody, V.: Critical analysis of Big Data challenges and analytical methods. J. Bus. Res. (70), 263–286 (2017)

Wang, W.Y.C., Wang, Y.: Analytics in the era of big data: the digital transformations and value creation in industrial marketing. Ind. Mark. Manag. **86**, 12–15 (2020)

Wang, Y., Kung, L., Ting, C., Byrd, T.A.: Beyond a technical perspective: understanding big data capabilities in health care. In: 2015 48th Hawaii International Conference on System Sciences, pp. 3044–3053 (2015)

Wilson, R., Cornford, J., Baines, S., Mawson, J.: New development: information for localism? Policy sense-making for local governance. Public Money Manag. **31**(4), 295–300 (2011)

Leveraging Government Data Using Unsupervised and Supervised Machine Learning for Firms' Investment Policy-Making in Economic Crises

Loukis Euripidis(✉) and Kyriakou Niki

University of the Aegean, Samos, Greece
{eloukis,nkyr}@aegean.gr

Abstract. In market-based economies economic crises of different geographical scopes and durations are often appearing, and are resulting in economic recessions, which have quite negative consequences for the economy and the society. Governments respond by undertaking large-scale economic stimulation programs, spending vast amounts of financial resources (with orders of magnitude between 3–6% of GDP), in order to mitigate these negative consequences. It is of critical importance to make effective use of these huge financial resources, in order to have high positive impact on the economy and the society in these tough crisis periods. This necessitates careful and rational design and implementation of these large and costly economic stimulation programs. Since one of the most important consequences of economic crises is the decrease of firms' investments, the above economic stimulation programs include investment support actions, which aim to mitigate these crisis-induced firms' investment decreases, and include a wide range of interventions for this reason, such as investment incentives, subsidies, low-interest loans as well as relevant tax rebates. In this paper is presented an integrated methodology for leveraging government data from economic crisis periods, using on one hand Unsupervised Machine Learning techniques, and on the other hand Supervised Machine Learning ones, in order to provide support for the rational design and implementation of firms' investment support actions in economic crises. A first application of the proposed methodology is presented, based on existing data from the Greek Ministry of Finance and the Statistical Authority concerning 363 firms for the economic crisis period 2009–2014, which gave interesting and encouraging results.

Keywords: Economic crisis · Recession · Stimulation packages · Artificial Intelligence · Machine learning · Supervised learning · Unsupervised learning

1 Introduction

In market-based economies economic crises of different geographical scope and durations are often appearing, and are resulting in economic recessions, which have quite

M. Janssen et al. (Eds.): EGOV 2022, LNCS 13391, pp. 432–448, 2022.
https://doi.org/10.1007/978-3-031-15086-9_28

negative consequences for the economy and the society [1–6]. During the last century numerous economic crises have appeared [2]. A decade ago, we experienced the severe 2007 Global Financial Crisis, while recently we experienced an economic crisis caused by the COVID-19 pandemic [7], and currently the Ukraine war, and the big increases in the prices of oil, gas, wheat and other goods it gives rise to, is expected to spark another economic crisis.

As the negative consequences of economic crises are often severe, governments undertake large-scale economic stimulation programs, and spend vast amounts of financial resources, having orders of magnitude between 3–6% of GDP, in order to mitigate these consequences (such as the recent American Recovery and Reinvestment Act (ARRA) in the United States and the European Economic Recovery Plan (EERP) in the European Union) [8–12]. These increase considerably national debts and cause big macro-economic problems in the post-crisis periods. Therefore, it is of critical importance to design and implement carefully and rationally these large and costly economic stimulation programs, in order to use these huge financial resources effectively, and have high positive impact on the economy and the society in these tough crisis periods. For this purpose, considerable research has been conducted for the assessment of the effects of such economic stimulation programs, which have been designed and implemented for addressing previous economic crises, such as the 2007 Global Financial Crisis, in order to draw useful conclusions, insights and knowledge that can be used for addressing future crises [11, 12]. However, there is a lack of research concerning the use and leveraging of the extensive firm-level data from crisis periods that government agencies possess for this highly important purpose: for the support of the rational design and implementation of these large-scale economic stimulation programs, in order to increase their effectiveness and positive economic and social impact. It is therefore a big challenge, of critical economic and social importance, to extract from these extensive government firm-level data from crisis periods as much as possible insight and knowledge, which can be useful in the future for optimizing these economic stimulation programs and using more effectively their huge financial resources.

As many crises have appeared in the last decades, while the economic stability periods have become shorter, governments gradually realize that they have to learn more about how to manage not only normal economic stability periods, but also tough economic crisis periods as well. It is therefore imperative to increase their knowledge about the multiple types of consequences of these economic crises, as well as the possible interventions that can be undertaken in order to mitigate these consequences, and also ways to make these interventions more effective. For these purposes quite useful can be both the macro-economic, and also the micro-economic data as well, which are collected by government agencies during economic crises periods. It is necessary to leverage these valuable data as much as possible, by making the most intensive possible exploitation of them, by using highly sophisticated techniques, especially from the Artificial Intelligence (AI) domain, such as Unsupervised and Supervised Machine Learning techniques, in order to maximize the extraction of useful insights and knowledge from these data, and also to make reliable predictions based on them. These are going to enable governments to design and implement better and more focused and effective programs as well as specific actions for mitigating the negative consequences of economic crises for the economy and the society.

This paper contributes to filling the abovementioned research gap, focusing on one of the most critical components of these economic stimulation programs for addressing economic crises: the firms' investment support actions (which are highly important for their post-crisis competitiveness). In particular, it presents an integrated methodology for leveraging firm-level government data from economic crisis periods, using AI techniques, on one hand Unsupervised Machine Learning techniques, and on the other hand Supervised Machine Learning ones [13–17], in order to provide support for the rational design and implementation by government of firms' investment support actions during economic crises. It includes initially the use of Clustering Analysis techniques (Unsupervised Machine Learning), in order to investigate if we can distinguish some typologies of firms with respect to the impact of economic crisis on the main types of investments they make. If this happens, the proposed methodology includes the use of Analysis of Variance (ANOVA) next, in order to understand better the main characteristics of these typologies of firms (e.g. with respect to personnel, ICT use, processes, strategic directions, innovation, exports, etc.). Finally, it includes the use of Prediction techniques (Supervised Machine Learning) in order to develop prediction models for firm's investment resilience in economic crisis based on the abovementioned individual characteristics of them. Also, a first application of the proposed methodology is presented, based on existing data from the Greek Ministry of Finance and the Statistical Authority concerning 363 firms for the economic crisis period 2009–2014, which gave encouraging and interesting results.

Our research contributes to the growing body of knowledge concerning the use of Artificial Intelligence (AI) in government (briefly reviewed in Sect. 2.2), by developing a composite integrated methodology of AI exploitation, which includes of combination of Unsupervised and Supervised Learning techniques, for the design and implementation of policies, programs and actions concerning one of the most severe and difficult problems that governments face: the economic crises.

In the following Sect. 2 the background of our methodology is outlined, while in Sect. 3 the methodology is described, followed by the abovementioned application of it in Sect. 4. The final Sect. 5 summarizes conclusions and proposes directions for future research.

2 Background

2.1 Economic Stimulation Programs

According to relevant literature [1–6] the economic crises usually result in contractions of economic activity, leading to economic recessions, which have two main categories of negative effects on firms: a) decrease of firms' production, procurement, and personnel employment (which increases unemployment, poverty and social exclusion); and b) decrease of the different types of investments they make (e.g. in equipment, buildings, training of personnel, R&D, innovation, etc.). Though the former category of negative effects of the economic crises on firms is more widely and extensively debated, due to their painful short-term consequences, such as the increase of unemployment, and therefore poverty and marginalization, the latter category has equally or even more detrimental medium- or long-term consequences; the most important of them are firm's technological backwardness and obsolescence, loss of important development opportunities, and finally lower competitiveness and growth.

So, governments, in order to mitigate these negative consequences of economic crises, which can give rise to social unrest and political extremism, undertake large-scale economic stimulation programs, spending huge amounts of financial resources [8–12]. These programs vary in size (e.g. the stimulus program of the EU for addressing the recent 2007 Global Financial Crisis amounted to 5% of GDP in the EU [8], while the corresponding program of China was much bigger, reaching an estimated 12.5% of its GDP [10]) as well as in composition (i.e. in the specific actions they include). In general, they include two main categories of actions: i) demand-side oriented ones (aiming to stimulate domestic consumption by citizens, e.g. unemployment assistance, nutritional aid, health and welfare payments, tax cuts, etc.); and ii) supply-side oriented ones (public infrastructure investments, as well as private investment incentives, subsidies, low-interest loans, relevant tax rebates, etc., usually promoting 'green growth', adopting new technologies, innovation, etc.) [10]. The shares of these two categories of actions in the economic stimulation programs vary among countries, but all of them place great emphasis in the mitigating firms' investment decrease during economic crises, through various kinds of actions, such as investment incentives, low-interest loans, subsidies, relevant tax rebates, etc. However, it is widely recognized that these actions should be highly focused on the firms that really need support of their investments (in general, or for specific types of investment, such as the 'soft investments' (e.g. in personnel training, marketing/advertisement) or 'innovation investment' (e.g. in R&D, processes innovation, products/services innovation, etc.).

Our research aims to leverage existing firm-level data from crisis periods possessed by government, by performing highly sophisticated processing of them, using AI techniques, in order to support the design and implementation of this particular highly important supply-side oriented firms' investment support actions in economic crises.

2.2 Artificial Intelligence in Government

Even though AI existed for several decades, its 'real life' exploitation was limited; however recently there has been a high interest in the 'real life' application of AI techniques, initially by private sector firms, for a number of reasons: a) availability of large amounts of data, which enable a more effective training of AI algorithms (and finally the extraction of more reliable models and rules); b) advances in computing power and reduction of its cost; c) substantial improvements of AI algorithms [13–17]. The first AI use initiatives in the private sector have revealed the great potential of AI techniques to offer important benefits, such as improvements in productivity, increase of sale revenue and growth, better decision-making as well as substantial innovations in internal processes, products and services [18].

These first success stories of high beneficial application of AI in the private sector have generated high levels of interest to use AI techniques in the public sector as well, in order to exploit better the huge amounts of data possessed by government agencies, on one hand for supporting decision-making and policy-making, and on the other hand for automating or supporting substantially more sophisticated mental tasks than the simpler routine ones automated or supported by the traditional operational IS of government agencies [21–27]. According to the study described in [26] AI has great potential to support and improve the core government functions:

i) Policy-Making (by enabling/supporting the detection of social issues more quickly, the improvement of public policy decisions, the estimation of potential effects of policy, the monitoring of the implementation of policy as well as the evaluation of existing policy, and the enhancement of citizens' participation in policy making);
ii) Public Services Delivery (by enabling/supporting the improvement of the information services of the organization, as well as the delivery of public service to businesses and citizens, and also the development of new innovative public services);
iii) Internal Management (by enabling/supporting the improvement of the allocation of human resources, the recruitment services of the public organizations, their financial management, the detection of fraud and/or corruption, the maintenance of equipment, the public procurement processes and also organizational (cyber)security).

Using the above typology of AI exploitation in government as an analysis framework, a sample of 250 cases of government use of AI across the European Union were analyzed; it was concluded that AI is used mainly to support the improvement of public service delivery, followed by the enhancement of internal management, but only in a limited number of cases AI was used for the support (directly or indirectly) of policy and decision making.

Some research has been conducted on the development of ways/methodologies of exploiting AI in different public sector thematic domains, for various kinds of problems and tasks, for instance in education, for the prediction of applicants for teacher positions who will be more effective and successful, in order to support making the optimal recruitment decisions [28]; in social policy, for the prediction of higher risk youth concerning criminal activity, in order to target prevention interventions [29]; in restaurant hygiene inspections, for harnessing the social media on-line reviews in order to identify restaurant likely to be severe offenders, for optimizing inspections [30]; in public security, for predictive police patrolling, in order to use more effectively scarce human resources [31], and for the automated analysis and classification of crime reports [32]; in public transportation management in order to predict high crime risk transportation areas [33]; in environmental management and planning for the prediction of ground water levels [34]; in healthcare, for supporting diseases' diagnosis and treatment planning [35].

However, it is widely recognized that only a small part of the great potential of AI use in government has been discovered and exploited; so further research is required in order to exploit this potential to a larger extent: for the development of new innovative ways and methodologies (including combinations of AI techniques, and possibly advanced statistical techniques), for exploiting the potential of AI in different public sector thematic domains, for various kinds of problems and tasks, with main focus on the most severe problems of modern societies and economies. In this direction our research makes a useful contribution, by developing and making a first application of an integrated methodology for leveraging government data from economic crisis periods, using a combination of Unsupervised and Supervised Machine Learning techniques, and also Statistical techniques, in order to provide support for the rational design and implementation of firms' investment policies in economic crises.

2.3 Firm Performance Determinants

Previous economic and management science research has investigated the main elements of a firm that determine its performance. Economic research has concluded that the main production factors of a firm that determine its output and performance are:

a) its capital (meant as the different kinds of production equipment it uses), discriminating between non-computer capital and computer capital,
b) its labor (meant as numbers of personnel of various educational levels and specializations), discriminating between non-computer labor and computer labor,

   while recently there is an increasing recognition of the importance also of firm's 'organizational capital' (meant as processes and structures adopted by the firm) as well as 'human capital' (meant as the skills and knowledge of firm's personnel) for its output and performance [36–39].

At the same time management science research has developed several conceptualizations of the main elements of a firm that determine its performance; the most widely recognized and used one is definitely the 'Leavitt's Diamond' framework [40]. According to it the most important elements of a firm that determine its performance are:

a) its task (= the strategies of the firm, as well as the administrative and production processes it follows for implementing these strategies),
b) its people (= the skills of firm's human resources of the firm),
c) its technology (= the technologies used for implementing the above administrative and production processes),
d) its structure (= the organization of the firm in departments, and the communication and coordination patterns them).

An extension of it has been developed subsequently, which analyses the above 'task' element into the 'strategy' and 'processes' elements [41]. We remark that this 'Leavitt's Diamond' framework includes a wider set of firm's elements that determine its performance in comparison with the abovementioned economic framework. Furthermore, there are similarities between these two frameworks: some of the above five main elements of a firm that determine its performance correspond at least to some extent to those determined by economic research. In particular, the 'technology' corresponds to 'capital' (non-computer and computer one), the 'people' correspond to 'labor' and 'human capital', while the 'structure and the 'processes' part of the 'task' correspond to 'organizational capital'.

We can expect that firm's characteristics concerning the above five main elements (strategy, processes, people, technology and structure) will determine to a considerable extent firm's performance during not only normal economic stability periods, but also economic crisis periods as well; these characteristics are expected to determine firm's ability to cope with the difficult economic crisis conditions, minimizing the decrease of sales revenue and profits due to the crisis, and therefore increasing the availability of financial resources for making investments, and also to identify, design and implement successfully highly valuable investments for handling the difficult crisis context.

3 The Proposed Methodology

The proposed methodology uses firm-level data possessed by government from economic crisis periods concerning:

i) the extent of decrease during the economic crisis period of the main types of firm's investments, such as 'basic investments' (e.g. in production equipment, buildings, etc.), 'soft investments' (e.g. in personnel training, marketing/advertisement) and 'innovation investment' (e.g. in R&D, processes innovation, products/services innovation, etc.) (variables INVD1, INVD2, …, INVDN);
ii) various firm characteristics concerning the abovementioned five main elements of a firm that determine its performance, such as personnel, ICT use, processes, strategic directions, innovation, exports, etc. (variables CH1, CH2, …, CHM).

These data are usually collected annually by Ministry of Finance – Taxation Authorities and Statistical Authorities, as firms have legal obligation to provide them, and also there are sanctions in case of not providing these data, or providing inaccurate data; therefore these data possessed by government are of high quality: they are complete and highly reliable, so they are appropriate to be used for extracting insight and knowledge from them, and also for estimating prediction models.

These data undergo advanced processing, which consists of three stages (Fig. 1):

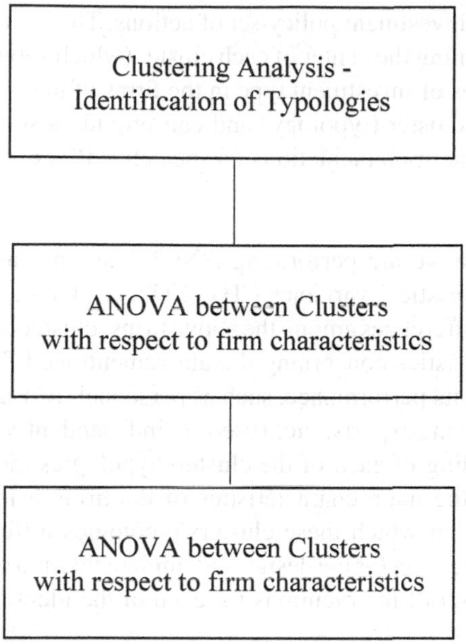

Fig. 1. Structure-stages of the proposed methodology

a) In the first stage we are using Clustering Techniques (Unsupervised Learning) in order to investigate whether we can distinguish some discrete clusters/typologies of firms with respect to the impact of the economic crisis on the main types of investments.

   For this purpose, we are using the abovementioned investment decrease variables INVD1, INVD2, …, INVDN (which measure the extent of decrease of the main types of investments made by each particular firm) for performing Clustering Analysis [13–17]:

   - initially we perform Hierarchical Clustering, in order to determine the number of clusters (based on the 'gaps' of the dendrogram);
   - then using this number of clusters we perform K-means Clustering, in order to determine for each of the firms of our dataset to which if the clusters it belongs (cluster membership);
   - based on the cluster memberships of these firms we calculate the center of each cluster (= averages of the above investment decrease variables over all the firms of the cluster);
   - and finally perform Analysis of Variance (ANOVA) between the clusters with respect to these investment decrease variables, in order to identify the variables (i.e. types of investment) in which these clusters differ most.

   If more than one clusters are identified this indicates that an 'one size fits all' investment policy/set of actions for mitigating the crisis-induced decrease of firms' investments is not the most appropriate approach; it is necessary for each firms' cluster/typology to design and implement a different more focused and specialized investment policy/set of actions. The results of the above Cluster Analysis concerning the center of each cluster (which show the extent of decrease of the main types of investment type in the firms of the cluster) enable an understanding of the cluster (typology) and can provide a sound basis and direction for the design and implementation of a specialized/focused investment policy/set for these firms.

b) In the second stage we are performing ANOVA among the clusters with respect to the firm characteristics' variables CH1, CH2, …, CHM, in order to investigate whether there are differences among the above firms' clusters/typologies with respect to various characteristics concerning the abovementioned five main elements of a firm that determine its performance, such as personnel, ICT use, processes, strategic directions, innovation, exports, etc. (used as independent variables). This enables a better understanding of each of the clusters/typologies identified in the previous stage, concerning the main characteristics of the firms it includes, as well as the firm characteristics in which these clusters/typologies differ most; so, it provides further basis and direction for the design and implementation of a specialized/focused investment policy/set of interventions for each of the identified clusters/typologies of firms.
c) In the third stage we are using Prediction Techniques (Supervised Learning) in order to construct prediction models for an overall index of investment decrease in economic crisis INVD, which is equal to the average of the INVD1, INVD2, …, INVDN variables, using as predictors the abovementioned the firm characteristics' variables CH1, CH2, …, CHM. For this purpose, we can use the existing Supervised Learning algorithms for predicting continuous dependent variables, such as Generalized Linear Modelling, Deep Learning, Decision Trees, Random Forests, Gradient Boosted Trees, Support Vector Machines, etc. [13–17], and select the one that exhibits the highest performance (the lowest absolute error). It is necessary these predictions to be as 'explainable' as possible, so in this direction we have to exploit the research that has been conducted on 'Explainable Artificial Intelligence' [42].

This third stage enables predicting for an individual firm the extent of investment decrease in economic crisis, which can be viewed as its 'investment resilience in economic crisis', based on its particular characteristics, such as personnel, ICT use, processes, strategic directions, innovation, exports, etc. This capability can be very useful for the more effective implementation of investment policies, interventions and programs during economic crisis. In particular, this enables the prediction of this 'investment resilience in economic crisis' for all firms applying for various interventions/programs of investment incentives, subsidies, low-interest loans, tax rebated, etc. implemented in the beginning of future economic crises; this prediction can be taken into account as an additional selection criterion, favoring firms that are predicted to exhibit lower investment resilience, and therefore larger decrease of investments, in economic crisis, so that these interventions/programs can be more focused on such firms, and therefore be more focused and effective.

The first and the second stage of the proposed methodology provide support for gaining a better and deeper understanding of the impact of the particular economic crisis on the main types of investments that firms make, so they provide a sound base for the 'evidence-based' design of appropriate effective firms' investment support policies/actions (and possibly a set of different specialized/focused policies/actions for different groups/clusters of firms, instead of a single 'one size fits all' investment policy/actions that might be less effective). The third stage of our methodology supports relevant internal operations of the government agencies, which are responsible for the implementation of these firms' investment support policies, enabling the effective implementation of them, by focusing on the firms that are expected to have the largest decrease in the investments, so they will be most in need of investment support by government. Therefore, the proposed methodology supports and improves two out of the three core government functions that according to [26] (as mentioned in more detail in Sect. 2.2) AI has a great potential to support and improve: policy-making and internal operations/management (which according to this study are the least exploited types of AI use in the governments of the member states of the European Union).

4 Application

A first application of the proposed methodology has been made, using data for 363 firms for the period 2009–2014 from the Ministry of Finance – Taxation Authorities and the Statistical Authority of Greece. These firms cover a wide range of sectors and sizes: 40.2% of them were from manufacturing sectors, 9.4% from constructions, and 50.4% from services sectors; also, 52.6% of them were small, 36.1% medium and 11.3% large ones. In particular, we used data concerning the following variables:

- extent of decrease of firm's investments in production equipment, buildings, personnel training, marketing/advertisement, R&D, processes innovation and products/services innovation (variables INVD1, INVD2, …, INVD7 – five levels ordinal variables: 1 = 'negligible'; 2 = 'small decrease'; 3 = 'moderate decrease'; 4 = 'large decrease'; 5 = 'very large decrease'),
- strategic orientations: extent of adoption by the firm of the main strategies described in relevant strategic management literature [43]: cost leadership, differentiation and innovation (variables STRAT_CL, STRAT_DIF, STRAT-INNOV five levels ordinal variables: 1 = 'not at all'; 2 = 'to a small extent'; 3 = 'to a moderate extent'; 4 = 'to a large extent'; 5 = 'to a very large extent'), introduction of process and product innovations by the firm in the last three years (INNOV_PROC, INNOV_PRS – binary variables), introduction of innovations by the firm in the production or service delivery processes, in the sales, shipment or warehouse management processes, and in the support processes (e.g. equipment maintenance processes) in the last three years (INN_PRSD, INN_SSWM, INN_SUPP – binary variables), percentage of 2014 firm's sales revenue coming from new products/services introduced during the last three years (NEW_PS – continuous variable), percentage of 2014 firm's sales revenue coming from products/services introduced before 2012 but significantly improved during the last three years (IMPR_PS – continuous variable), existence of Research &

Development in the firm (R&D – binary variable) and percentage of exports in firm's sales revenue in 2014 (EXP_P – continuous variable),

- processes: use of 'organic' structural forms of work organization in the firm, such as teamwork and job rotation [44, 45] in the last three years (ORG – binary variable),
- personnel: number of firm's employees at the end of 2014 (EMPL – continuous variable), shares of firm's employees having tertiary education, vocational/technical education, high school education, elementary school education (EMPL_TERT, EMPL – VOCT, EMPL_HIGH, EMPL_ELEM – continuous variables), shares of firm's employees using for their work computers, firm's intranet (internal network), Internet (EMPL_COM, EMPL – INTRA, EMPL_INTER – continuous variables) and share of specialized ICT personnel in firm's workforce (EMPL_ICT – continuous variable),
- technology: extent of use of ERP, CRM, SCM, Business Intelligence/Analytics, Collaboration Support systems in the firm (ERP, CRM, SCM, BIBA, CS - five levels ordinal variables: 1 = 'not at all'; 2 = 'to a small extent'; 3 = 'to a moderate extent; 4 = 'to a large extent'; 5 = 'to a very large extent'), conduct of e-sales of products/services (E-SAL – binary variable), extent of use of social media by the firm for sales promotion, collection of customers' opinions, comments and complaints, collections of ideas for improvements and innovations in firm's products/services, finding personnel, supporting the internal exchange of information and co-operation among firm's employees, supporting the external exchange of information and co-operation with other firm (e.g. suppliers, partners, customers, etc.) (SM_SPRO, SM_OPCO, SM_IMINN, SM_PERS, SM_INTCO, SM_EXTCO – three levels ordinal variables: 1 = 'not at all', 2 = 'to a small extent', 3 = 'to a large extent'), use of cloud computing by the firm (CLOUD – binary variable), extent of use of cloud IaaS, PaaS and SaaS services by the firm (CL_IAAS, CL_PAAS, CL_SAAS - five levels ordinal variables: 1 = 'not at all'; 2 = 'to a small extent'; 3 = 'to a moderate extent'; 4 = 'to a large extent'; 5 = 'to a very large extent')
- general firm information: sector (SECT – binary variable: 1 = 'manufacturing or constructions', 2 = 'services'), level of firm's comparative performance in comparison with the other competitor firms in terms of profitability, sales revenue, market share and return on investment (ROI) (COMP_PROF, COMP_SALR, COMP_MS, COMP_ROI - five levels ordinal variables: 1 = 'much lower than the average'; 2 = 'lower than the average'; 3 = 'about at the average'; 4 = 'higher than the average'; 5 = 'much higher than the average').

4.1 Cluster Analysis

Initially, using the investment decrease variables INVD1, INVD2, …, INVD7 we performed Hierarchical Clustering in order to determine the number of clusters – firms' typologies with respect to investment decrease during the economic crisis. Based on the 'gaps' of the dendrogram we can distinguish three clusters of firms. Then we performed K-means Clustering, setting the number of clusters equal to three, in order to determine for each of our dataset the cluster it belongs to (cluster membership), and then calculate the centers of the three clusters with respect to the abovementioned investment decrease variables, which are shown in the second, third and fourth column of Table 1.

Table 1. Center of clusters – ANOVA results

Variable	Cluster 1	Cluster 2	Cluster 3	F-ANOVA	Sig
INVD1	3.85	2.99	1.70	145.927	0.000
INVD2	3.84	2.88	1.40	138.873	0.000
INVD3	3.68	2.87	1.34	236.410	0.000
INVD4	4.16	3.16	1.69	183.856	0.000
INVD5	4.25	2.47	1.22	380.962	0.000
INVD6	3.92	2.38	1.23	444.162	0.000
INVD7	3.72	2.39	1.23	291.181	0.000

We remark that the firms of the first cluster had medium to large decrease (being closer to the latter) in their basic investments in production equipment and buildings, in their soft investment in personnel training, as well as in their investment in products/services innovation and process innovation, and large to very large decrease in their soft investment in marketing/advertisement, as well as in R&D. Therefore in these firms the economic crisis haD severe negative impact on their investment, especially in their soft investment in marketing/advertisement and in R&D.

The second cluster of firms had slightly lower than moderate decrease in their basic investments in production equipment and buldings, and in their soft investments in personnel training, but only small to moderate (closer to the former) decrease in their innovation oriented investments in R&D, products/services innovation and process innovation; also, they had slightly higher than moderate decrease in their marketing/advertisement investment. The firms of this second cluster exhibited a quite different behaviour during the economic crisis with respect to their investment than the ones of the first cluster: they maintain the level of investment in innovation, in order to cope with the difficult economic conditions of the crisis (decrease in products/services demand, and therefore in sales revenue) through innovation (innovative products/services, and also innovation in internal processes in order to reduce operating costs). At the same time they make less than moderate reductions in the remaining types of investment, with the only exception of the marketing/advertisement ones.

Finally, the third cluster of firms had negligible to small decrease in all the examined types of investments, being closer to negligible decrease in their innovation-oriented investments in R&D, products/services innovation and process innovation, as well as in their investments in buildings and personnel training, and closer to small decrease in their production equipment and in their marketing/advertisement investments. These firms use innovation as a central strategy for coping with the difficult economic conditions of the crisis, while at the same time they maintain to a good extent they levels of the other types of investment. The above results indicate that we are far from having a homogeneous effect of the economic crisis on the Greek firms, and we can distinguish some discrete typologies of firms with respect to the impact of the crisis on their investment; so in relevant firms' investment policies, interventions and programs more emphasis should be placed on the first cluster/typology firms, in order to mitigate their technological backwardness and obsolescence, and even survival, risks.

Furthermore, we performed ANOVA among these three clusters with respect to the above investment decrease variables, and the results are shown in the fifth and sixth columns of Table 1. We can see that there are statistically significant differences among the three clusters in all seven investment decrease variables. Therefore, the three clusters differ in the decrease they had during the economic crisis in all the examined types of investment; the F-values shown in the sixth column of Table 1 indicate that the highest differences among the three clusters are in the extent of decrease they had in the innovation-oriented investments (in R&D, products/services innovation and process innovation), followed by the personnel training investments.

4.2 Analysis of Variance of Clusters with Respect to Firms' Characteristics

We next performed ANOVA among the three clusters with respect to firms' main characteristics concerning strategic orientations, processes, personnel, technology and comparative performance, which are described in Sect. 4. We found that the three clusters differ mostly (based on the value and the significance of the F) in comparative performance (variables COMP_PROF, COMP_SALR, COMP_MS and COMP_ROI), existence of Research & Development (variable R&D), employment of personnel having tertiary education and vocational/technical education (variables EMPL_TERT, EMPL – VOCT), process innovation (variables INN_PROC, INN_PRSD, INN_SSWM, INN_SUPP), use of cloud (variable CLOUD) and also use of Business Intelligence/Analytics and Collaboration Support systems (variables BIBA and CS). These enable an even better understanding of these three firms' clusters/typologies, and provides further support and direction for the design of investment policies, interventions and programs in economic crisis periods (including incentives, subsidies and support for the employment of tertiary education and vocational/technical education personnel, for making process innovations, as well as use cloud services, business intelligence/analytics and collaboration support systems).

4.3 Prediction of Investment Decrease in Economic Crisis

Finally we construct prediction models for the overall index of investment decrease in economic crisis INVD, which is equal to the average of the INVD1, INVD2, …, INVD7 investment decrease variables, using as predictors the abovementioned firms' main characteristics described in Sect. 4 (concerning strategic orientations, processes, personnel, technology and comparative performance), with six Supervised Learning algorithms for predicting continuous dependent variables: Generalized Linear Modelling, Deep Learning, Decision Trees, Random Forests, Gradient Boosted Trees, Support Vector Machines [8–12]. In Fig. 2 we can see the prediction performance (mean absolute prediction error) of these algorithms. We can see that the Random Forest algorithm exhibits the lowest mean absolute error (0.788). This is a satisfactory prediction performance, given the small size of the dataset we have used (data from 363 firms), so using a larger dataset (this is feasible, as governments have such data for quite large numbers of firms) can result in a smaller mean absolute error, and therefore an even more accurate firm-level prediction of investment decrease during economic crisis.

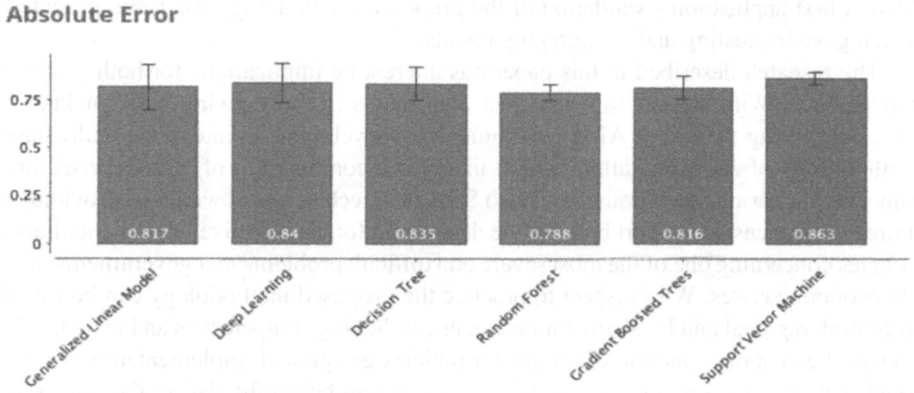

Fig. 2. Mean absolute prediction errors of the six prediction algorithms

In Table 2 we can see the top 10 predictors in terms of weight of the above best performing Random Forest algorithm, which have the highest influence on the predictions it produces of the firm-level investment decrease during economic, providing some level of 'explainability' of the predictions.

Table 2. Most influential predictors (having highest weights)

Predictor variable	Weight
EMPL_ICT	0.291
EMPL_VOCT	0.116
IMPR_PS_P	0.109
SM_EXTCO	0.108
SM_OPCO	0.100
E_SAL	0.085
EMPL_HIGH	0.075
CL_PAAS	0.071
SM_PERS	0.069
CL_IAAS	0.052

5 Conclusions

In the previous sections has been presented an integrated methodology for leveraging government data from economic crisis periods, using on one hand Unsupervised Machine

Learning techniques (clustering analysis), and on the other hand Supervised Machine Learning ones (prediction algorithms), in order to provide support for the rational design and implementation of firms' investment policies/actions for economic crisis periods. Also, a first application - validation of the proposed methodology has been presented, which gave interesting and encouraging results.

The research described in this paper has interesting implications for both research and practice. With respect to research it contributes to the growing body of knowledge concerning the use of AI in government, by developing an integrated multi-stage methodology of AI exploitation, which includes a combination of Unsupervised and Supervised Learning techniques, and also Statistical techniques as well, and providing a more comprehensive support both for the design and for the effective implementation of policies concerning one of the most severe and difficult problems that governments face: the economic crises. With respect to practice the proposed methodology can be useful to central, regional and local government agencies having competences and responsibilities in the area of economic development policies design and implementation, for the tough periods of economic recessionary crises. It can be useful also to the numerous consulting firms undertaking studies and government support in the above areas.

Future research is required towards: i) further application of the proposed methodology using larger datasets, in other national contexts experiencing economic crises of different intensities; ii) investigation of the prediction performance of other algorithms, and especially Deep Learning ones; iii) analysis of the legal aspects of the practical application of the proposed methodology, and especially with respect to the EU GDPR.

References

1. Keeley, B., Love, P.: From Crisis to Recovery - The Causes, Course and Consequences of the Great Recession. OECD Publishing, Paris (2010)
2. Knoop, T.A.: Recessions and Depressions: Understanding Business Cycles, 2nd edn. Praeger Santa Barbara, California (2015)
3. Allen, R.E.: Financial Crises and Recession in the Global Economy, 4th edn. Edward Elgar Publications, Cheltenham (2016)
4. Santana, M., Valle, R., Galanb, J.L.: Turnaround strategies for companies in crisis: watchout the causes of decline before firing people. Bus. Res. Q. **20**(3), 206–211 (2017)
5. Izsak, K., Markianidou, P., Lukach, R., Wastyn, A.: The impact of the crisis on research and innovation policies. European Commission, DG Research, Brussels (2013)
6. Arvanitis, S., Woerter, M.: Firm characteristics and the cyclicality of R&D investments. Ind. Corp. Chang. **23**(5), 1141–1169 (2014)
7. Baldwin, R., Di Mauro, B.W.: Mitigating the COVID Economic Crisis: Act Fast and Do Whatever it Takes. Center of Economic Policy Research Press, London (2020)
8. European Commission, Directorate-General for Economic and Financial Affairs: Economic Crisis in Europe: Causes, Consequences and Responses. Office for Official Publications of the European Communities, Luxembourg (2009)
9. Khatiwada, S.: Stimulus Packages to Counter Global Economic Crisis: A review. International Institute for Labour Studies, Geneva (2009)
10. Kalinowski, T.: Crisis management and the diversity of capitalism: fiscal stimulus packages and the East Asian (neo-)developmental state. Econ. Soc. **44**(2), 244–270 (2015)
11. Coenen, G., Straub, R., Trabandt, M.: Gauging the Effects of Fiscal Stimulus Packages in the Euro Area. Working Paper 1483, European Central Bank, Frankfurt am Main, Germany

12. Taylor, J.: Fiscal Stimulus Programs During the Great Recession. Economics Working Paper 18117, Hoover Institution, Stanford, CA (2018)
13. Russell, S., Norvig, P.: Artificial Intelligence: A Modern Approach, 3rd edn. Pearson, Essex (2020)
14. Tan, P.N., Steinbach, M., Karpatne, A., Kumar, V.: Introduction to Data Mining, 2nd edn. Pearson Education, Upper Saddle River (2019)
15. Witten, I.H., Frank, E., Hall, M.A., Pal, C.J.: Data Mining - Practical Machine Learning Tools and Techniques. Morgan Kaufmann, Amsterdam, London (2017)
16. Blum, A., Hopcroft, J., Kannan, R.: Foundations of Data Science. Cambridge University Press, Cambridge (2020)
17. Siegel, E.: Predictive Analytics. Wiley, New Jersey (2013)
18. Craglia, M. (ed.): Artificial Intelligence - A European Perspective, EUR 29425 EN. EU Publications Office, Luxembourg (2018)
19. Duan, Y., Edwards, J.S., Dwivedi, Y.K.: Artificial intelligence for decision making in the era of Big Data – evolution, challenges and research agenda. Int. J. Inf. Manag. **48**, 63–71 (2019)
20. OECD: Artificial Intelligence in Society. OECD Publishing, Paris (2019)
21. Eggers, W.D., Schatsky, D., Viechnicki, P.: AI-Augmented Government. Using Cognitive Technologies to Redesign Public Sector Work. Deloitte University Press (2017)
22. Desouza, K. C.: Delivering Artificial Intelligence in Government: Challenges and Opportunities. IBM Center for the Business of Government, Washington D.C. (2018)
23. DeSousa, W.G., DeMelo, E.R.P., De Souza Bermejo, P.H., Sous Farias, R.A., Gomes, A.O.: How and where is artificial intelligence in the public sector going? A literature review and research agenda. Gov. Inf. Q. **36**(4), 101392 (2019)
24. Misuraca, G., van Noordt, C.: AI Watch-Artificial Intelligence in Public Services. Publications Office of the European Union, Luxembourg (2020)
25. Medaglia, R., Gil-Garcia, R., Pardo, T.A.: Artificial intelligence in government: taking stock and moving forward. Soc. Sci. Comput. Rev. (2021, in-press)
26. Van Noordt, C., Misuraca, G.: Artificial intelligence for the public sector: results of landscaping the use of AI in government across the European Union. Gov. Inf. Q. (2022, in-press)
27. Manzoni, M., Medaglia, R., Tangi, L., Van Noordt, C., Vaccari, L., Gattwinkel, D.: AI Watch. Road to the Adoption of Artificial Intelligence by the Public Sector. Publications Office of the European Union, Luxembourg (2022)
28. Rockoff, J.E., Jacob, B.A., Kane, T.J., Staiger, D.O.: Can you recognize an effective teacher when you recruit one? Educ. Finance Policy **6**(1), 43–74 (2010)
29. Chandler, D., Levitt, S.D., List, J.A.: Predicting and preventing shootings among at-risk youth. Am. Econ. Rev. **101**(3), 288–292 (2011)
30. Kang, J.S., Kuznetsova, P., Luca, M., Choi, Y.: Where not to eat? Improving public policy by predicting hygiene inspections using online reviews. In: Proceedings of Empirical Methods in Natural Language Processing Conference 2013, pp. 1443–1448 (2013)
31. Camacho-Collados, M., Liberatore, F.: A decision support system for predictive police patrolling. Decis. Supp. Syst. **75**, 25–37 (2015)
32. Ku, C.H., Leroy, G.: A decision support system: automated crime report analysis and classification for e-government. Gov. Inf. Q. **31**(4), 534–544 (2014)
33. Kouziokas, G.N.: The application of artificial intelligence in public administration for forecasting high crime risk transportation areas in urban environment. Transp. Res. Proc. **24**, 467–473 (2017)
34. Kouziokas, G., Chatzigeorgiou, A., Perakis, K.: Artificial intelligence and regression analysis in predicting ground water levels in public administration. Eur. Water Publ. **57**, 361–366 (2017)

35. Sun, T.Q., Medaglia, R.: Mapping the challenges of Artificial Intelligence in the public sector: evidence from public healthcare. Gov. Inf. Q. **36**(2), 368–383 (2019)
36. Brynjolfsson, E., Hitt, L.: Paradox lost? Firm-level evidence on the returns to information systems. Manag. Sci. **42**(4), 541–558 (1996)
37. Pilat, D.: The ICT productivity paradox: insights from micro data. OECD Econ. Stud. **2004**(1), 38–65 (2005)
38. Arvanitis, S.: Computerization, workplace organization, skilled labour and firm productivity: evidence for the Swiss business sector. Econ. Innov. New Technol. **14**(4), 225–249 (2005)
39. Arvanitis, S., Loukis, E.: Information and communication technologies, human capital, workplace organization and labour productivity: a comparative study based on firm-level data for Greece and Switzerland. Inf. Econ. Policy **21**(1), 43–61 (2009)
40. Leavitt, H.J.: Applied organization change in industry: structural, technical, and human approaches. In: Cooper, S., Leavitt, H.J., Shelly, K. (eds.) New Perspectives in Organizational Research, pp. 55–71. Wiley, Chichester (1964)
41. Scott-Morton, M.S.: The Corporation of the 1990s. Oxford University Press, New York (1991)
42. Meske, C., Bunde, E., Schneider, J., Gersch, M.: Explainable artificial intelligence: objectives, stakeholders, and future research opportunities. Inf. Syst. Manag. **39**(1), 53–63 (2022)
43. Whittington, R., Regner, P., Angwin, D., Johnson, G., Scholes, K.: Exploring Strategy, 12th edn. Pearson Education Limited, Harlow (2020)
44. Donaldson, L.: The Contingency Theory of Organization. Sage Publications, London (2001)
45. Jones, G.R.: Organizational Theory, Design, and Change, 7th edn. Pearson Education Limited, London (2013)

Smart Cities

On the Way to Smarter Cities: What Goals and Values Swiss Municipalities Prioritize

Flurina Wäspi(✉), Alperen Bektas, Amir Sahi, Anja Wüst, and Stephan Haller

Business School, Bern University of Applied Sciences, Brückenstrasse 73, CH-3005 Bern, Switzerland
flurina.waespi@bfh.ch

Abstract. Smart cities have become a trending topic in transdisciplinary discourses and academic research over recent decades. In the context of modern governmental institutions striving to create public value for the benefit of their inhabitants, smart cities play a pivotal role. While aspiring to encourage the transformation towards smart cities, it is essential to carry out strategy development and accompanying monitoring processes using key performance indicators (KPIs). Even though smart cities have received much attention by scholars, the link between public value and smart city strategy development and monitoring is empirically under-researched. This study, therefore, investigates 280 Swiss municipalities – public actors on the frontline – to determine where they set smart city goals, the relevance they assign to selected KPIs to measure progress, and what this reveals about underlying public values. The results indicate that Swiss municipalities prioritize action fields regarding sustainable city development, energy efficiency, public transport, and traffic management. While only a minority already uses KPIs to measure progress, a majority plans to use them in the future. Our analysis, linking the prioritized action fields, corresponding KPIs and public value types, suggests that the public value currently generated by municipalities is located primarily in the social and stewardship dimension, but that in the future, environmental and political public value could move into the foreground.

Keywords: Smart city · Smart governance · Public value · Digitalization · Strategy development · Strategy monitoring · Public sector transformation · Key performance indicators

1 Introduction

For over a decade now, the concept of smart cities has been enticing public and private actors with the idea of exploiting information and communication technologies (ICTs) for (public) good, offering a plethora of promises to improve quality of life, efficiency of city and municipal activities and services as well as overall competitiveness, while coincidently ensuring the fulfilment of economic, social, environmental and cultural needs

Published by Springer Nature Switzerland AG 2022
M. Janssen et al. (Eds.): EGOV 2022, LNCS 13391, pp. 451–468, 2022.
https://doi.org/10.1007/978-3-031-15086-9_29

of present and future generations [25]. In recent years and in the context of the ongoing climate crisis, hopes are increasingly focused on reaching sustainability goals (e.g., reducing CO2 emissions) by using digital technologies. Although research suggests that the link between smart city projects and sustainability might not be as straightforward as desired [1, 36] – sometimes even leading to unwanted negative ecological side-effects [39] – we are assuming in this paper that a transformation towards smarter cities is overall desirable. That then triggers the question pertinent of how a city or municipality may operationalize its development and transformation towards a smart city. As Meijer puts it, employing technology "is never entirely a matter of engineering but of strategic, political and value-laden choices" [29]. To address strategy first: In addition to the development of a strategy, a complementary monitoring process based on key performance indicators (KPIs) is needed to monitor and guide progress [3]. Otherwise, it is impossible to determine whether the goals outlined in a strategy are anywhere close to being achieved, or whether changing circumstances require an adaptation of the strategy. Strategy monitoring is particularly important in the public sector, whose representatives are expected to be guided by the overall goal of creating public value. The concept of public value depicts the value that an organization (public or private) provides to society [33].

This leads us to consider the second half of the above statement by Meijer – that employing technology is just as much a matter of values. On a conceptual level, the literature proposes a reciprocal and beneficial relationship between smart cities and public value. When aimed at improving transparency, accountability and citizen participation, the use of ICTs is said to lead to an increase in public value generated by governments [6]. In similar vein, Cosgrave et al. state that "adopting the PVM [Public Value Management] paradigm could support the successful delivery of smart cities, predominantly through the ability to understand value beyond the optimization of systems" [13].

Much research has been undertaken regarding the implementation of smart city projects and the state (maturity level) of smart cities all over the world, and the literature is ripe with conceptual discussions on the creation of public value. The empirical application of the public value concept is however quite sparse and dominated by case studies [20]. And while there is a theoretical connection made between the smart city concept and the creation of public value, the link between public value and strategic smart city goals and corresponding KPIs – two essential components of the implementation of smart cities – is empirically under-researched. To the best of our knowledge, no dataset that would allow us to investigate this link exists. Based on an own survey among 280 Swiss municipalities, we thus seek to answer the following research questions:

1. In which smart city fields of action do municipalities set goals to generate public value?
2. On the way to implementing their goals, what key performance indicators (KPIs) are of relevance to municipalities?
3. What kind of public value do municipalities seek to generate?

The structure of the paper is organized as follows: In the following chapter we conduct a literature review and present its findings relevant to the research questions, particularly introducing the concept of smart cities and the Smart City Wheel, as well as discussing the creation of public value. Building on the literature, Sect. 2.4 proposes a conceptual framework outlining the sequential steps of how public value (as a result of government action) can be understood. The model thus provides another structure for conceptually linking strategic goals in specific action areas, KPIs, and public value generation. Chapter 4 discusses the methodology used to carry out the survey. Chapter 5 presents the core results of the study in terms of the overarching research questions. Chapter 6 discusses the overall findings, limitations faced during the study, and points to future research opportunities.

2 Literature Review

In the following sections, we discuss the smart city concept, and how the breadth of it brings about the challenge of establishing a smart city strategy and corresponding strategy monitoring. Whatever its design, scholars suggest that the overall goal of a smart city should be the creation of public value [14, 33]. Neuroni et al., for example, state that "a smart city is a city that can capture, model and increase public value creation" [33]. This leads us to investigate more in detail the question of how value is created in the public sector, and how the concept of public value is understood in the context of this study. Based on the literature review, we then go on to develop a conceptual framework illustrating the links between strategic goal setting, monitoring and public value creation in smart cities.

2.1 More than Technology – The Concept of Smart Cities

Digital technologies and digitalization processes are ever evolving, and governmental organisations, including cities and municipalities, have acquired an increasing awareness of possibilities to grow "smarter". There is, however, no uniform understanding of what the smart city concept entails. In broad terms, smart cities are expected to innovate on the solving and mitigating of the plethora of environmental, economic, and social challanges any city must deal with, making use of the information and communication technologies of the 21st century [33]. One well-known definition was recommended by the International Telecommunication Union ITU, stating that "a smart sustainable city is an innovative city that uses information and communication technologies (ICTs) and other means to improve quality of life, efficiency of urban operation and services and competitiveness, while ensuring that it meets the needs of present and future generations with respect to economic, social, environmental, as well as cultural aspects" [25]. Similarly, Anttiroiko and Komninos state that smart cities are essentially about "the power of new technologies, most notably the Internet, in empowering citizens and organizations to create urban innovations and collaborative solutions that make cities more efficient, inclusive and sustainable" [2]. These definitions illustrate that a modern understanding of a smart city goes much beyond the marketing and technology world in which the term was originally coined – namely by the multinationals IBM and Cisco imagining more intelligent future cities thanks to the use of their ICT tools [40].

As Zuccardi Merli and Bonollo put it, the "smart" in smart city is no longer only connected to technological advances and the mere presence or use of digital infrastructure; but increasingly also requires some form of active citizen participation. This in turn assigns a bigger role to human, social and relational forms of capital that a city can and should draw on to succeed as a smart city [40]. We rediscover this position in a visual contribution by Boyd Cohen [11, 12]: With the Smart City Wheel, six key dimensions and corresponding action fields are suggested, ranging from Smart Energy to Smart Government, all of them said to be essential for a holistic smart city strategy [12]. As a comprehensive framework covering many aspects relevant to society, the Smart City Wheel has become widely accepted, and is being used in academia and by practitioners alike (Fig. 1).

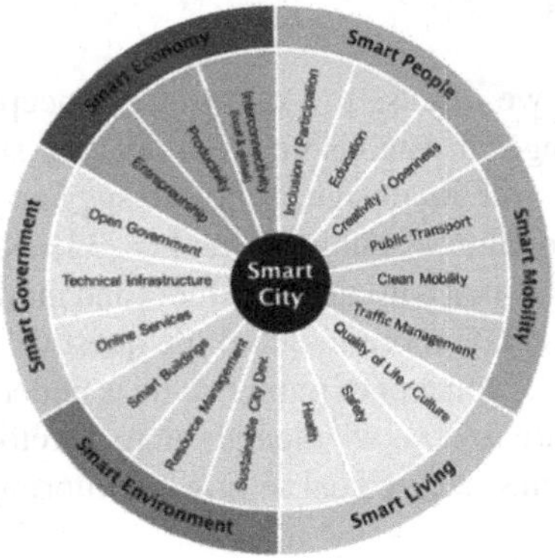

Fig. 1. Smart city wheel with its six dimensions and related action fields (Adapted from Cohen [12])

For the Swiss context, the Swiss Federal Office of Energy provides a useful description of the Smart City Wheel dimensions, on which we also rely on (see Appendix A, Table 1).

2.2 Components of Smart City Strategies – Governance and Progress Monitoring

The breadth of the smart city concept as illustrated above is making the need for a form of governance with stakeholder involvement apparent. Public governance and participatory government are concepts that come to mind [40]. It is suggested that participatory government needs to be accompanied by some form of reporting on the actions of the local government – so that a local government or municipality may be able to learn where and how to improve a strategy, make better decisions on the distribution of resources, and ensure an adequate level of accountability towards stakeholders external to the administration (e.g. citizens) [40]. Zuccardi Merli and Bonollo stress the importance of external accountability, which is said to be especially important for a smart city, because "(…) in order to develop involvement of the stakeholders in its smart projects, the local government must provide prompt and transparent communications about the performance achieved" [40]. To be able to report on achievements, a smart city strategy should thus be accompanied by a comprehensive monitoring process based on key performance indicators [3, 15].

On a European level, different indicator frameworks exist. For an overview, the EU project CITYkeys serves as a good basis: CITYkeys developed and validated, with the aid of cities, key performance indicators and data collection procedures for the common and transparent monitoring as well as the comparability of smart city solutions across European cities [9]. In Switzerland, especially the indicator frameworks Energiestadt (56 energy related indicators), the Circle Indicateur (37 sustainable development related indicators) and City Statistics (31 sustainable development related indicators) are well known. As an overarching indicator framework addressing all smart city areas, the Smart City Wheel comes with an indicator set of 62 indicators developed by the creator of the Smart City Wheel Boyd Cohen [11]. For a smart city strategy monitoring to be manageable with reasonable effort, the process should ideally be supported by tools or a platform, as well as internal processes allowing for continuous monitoring [16]. For Switzerland – estimated to have reached an overall maturity level of "minimum smart city" [26] – recent research has illustrated the municipalities current strategy development and monitoring practices still hinge on cumbersome and error prone paper- or Excel-based approaches [38 forthcoming]. On a European level, good practice examples can be found in the bigger Austrian cities, and especially Vienna: Having launched their Smart City Wien Initiative in 2011 already, the city has concretized this initiative with a comprehensive strategy and monitoring framework (Smart City Wien Framework Strategy SCWR), planning ahead until 2050 [22, 23].

2.3 Value Creation in the Public Sector

For the private sector, an assessment of value added or created is relatively straightforward. For instance, a company can carry out a cost-benefit analysis to evaluate the added value of an investment. It can then abandon or pursue the investments based on the assessment results. That assessment is a bit more challenging in the public sector – a context shaped by the presence of a multitude of stakeholders with heterogeneous needs and preferences that aren't done justice by the limited perspective of cost-benefit type analysis, customer-orientation or the application of rational choice models only [30]. This is where the concept of public value comes in. It provides a different way of thinking about the performance of governmental strategies and actions (e.g., investments). The public value concept was first introduced by Moore in his seminal work *Creating Public Value: Strategic Management in Government* [31] and has since been referred to, interpreted, and extended in many other influential studies thereafter. Moore states that public organizations make decisions (e.g., investment decisions or actions) that are inevitably political. Therefore, decision-makers must determine how best to make such decisions. They need to look after all the public stakeholder's interests. According to Moore's description, public value refers to the value that an organization or an activity contributes to the society. In other words, public value is the product of municipally produced[1] benefits for all the stakeholders of society (e.g., individuals, firms). Establishing public value to be the primary performance objective, a new vision of management was

[1] We used the term municipally produced since the paper focuses on the generation of public value through municipal decisions. It can be generalized as governmentally produced [19] for the city or state-level contexts.

thus created, adding to (or replacing) the traditional bureaucratic view of public administration and its successor, the new public management framework (NPM) that was focused on efficiency and economic key figures (citizens as customers) [6]. As an important distinction, the public value approach conceives the public interest neither definitively as it is politically defined/expressed in the law (traditional public administration) nor as represented by the aggregation of individual interest (new public management), but as a result of a continuous dialogue about shared values [6]. In the various definitions of public value reiterated in the literature, authors usually highlight this contextuality of the concept: what the public values are can change and vary according to the specific technological, political and economic circumstances and the problem at hand [7, 8, 21, 30]. As Bolivar [6] puts it, the concept of public value thus provides "a useful way of thinking about the goals and performances of public policy but focusing on the meaning it has for people, rather than what a public sector decision-maker might presume is best for them, and encompasses not only outputs but also outcomes (...)" [6]. This is thus also true for smart city strategies – the public value a strategy seeks to generate will be adapted to the environment and the challenges it holds for a city or a region. This points to a major challenge of the public value concept: While the benefit of a public value-oriented approach in the operations of public institutions might be mostly undisputed today, to describe what public value is, and measure whether and how it is achieved, is a much more complex issue.

As stated in the introduction, this article aims to contribute to the smart city literature by empirically applying the public value concept (outside of a case study): Determining where municipalities set their smart city goals, we deduct on what this tells us about the kind of public value they are aiming to generate. However, we do not measure their actual output or impact achieved over time. It would thus be beyond the scope of this article to go into detail on the possibilities for measuring public value, but we refer to Bolivar [6] for a comparison of existing frameworks. Regarding the first element – what public value is or can be – a first realization from the literature is that there is no single approach to classifying public value that has found broad acceptance. Scholars even speak of an "identification problem", caused by a lack of agreement between and among scholars and public-sector representatives on how public values may be identified [18, 24]. In a similar vein, Huijbregts et al. argue that due to the complexity and the variety of policy issues the public sector is dealing with, there might not be a universal way to identify public values [24]. According to Bozeman, public values can be either identified with a) intuition, b) elections, polling, public opinion surveys or similar approaches, and c) by consulting the scholarly literature [32]. For the purpose of this paper, we follow the seven generic types of public value proposed by Harrison et al. [19] to capture possible results of government action (Table 1). Harrison et al. advise against considering public value as an aggregate indicator of government outcomes, arguing that this "misses the variety of interests and possible benefits across many stakeholders", because the logic of public value was precisely building upon the link between government action and multiple types of public value that could occur [19].

While the first four types are said to be related to substantive private interests of individuals or groups, the last three are connected to more intrinsic, or societal/democratic

Table 1. Types of public value according to Harrison et al. [19]

Types of public value	Description
Economic	Impacts on current or future income, asset values, liabilities, entitlements, or other aspects of wealth or risks to any of the above
Political	Impacts on a person's or group's influence on government actions or policy, on their role in political affairs, influence in political parties, or prospects for public office
Social	Impacts on family or community relationships, social mobility, status, and identity
Strategic	Impacts on a person's or group's economic or political advantage or opportunities, goals, and resources for innovation or planning
Quality of life	Impacts on individual and houschold health, security, satisfaction, and general well-being
Ideological	Impacts on beliefs, moral, or ethical commitments, alignment of government actions or policies or social outcomes with beliefs, moral, or ethical positions
Stewardship	Impacts on the public's view of government officials as faithful stewards or guardians of the value of the government in terms of public trust, integrity, and legitimacy

outcomes [19]. According to Harrison et al., there are different value generating mechanisms behind the production of those value types. They propose a list of seven value generators consisting of efficiency, effectiveness, enablement, intrinsic enhancements, transparency, participation, and collaboration [19, 35]. Harrison et al. provide the example of a governmental agency releasing information on an acute environmental problem to citizens. The value generator in this case is transparency, and the value created can be social value (enabling the citizen to act upon this information for his or her benefit) or stewardship value (as the citizen gains greater trust in the government to provide clarification on important matters) [19].

2.4 The Relationship Between Smart City Strategies and Public Value

Based on the literature, this section presents a conceptual framework (Fig. 2) depicting the overall process of public value creation in smart cities, from strategy development to the potential type of public value created. It is similar to others discussed in previous studies [34]. We follow that framework in the next chapters to examine the public value types that Swiss municipalities strive to create through their prioritized action fields as well as KPI choices.

Strategy development was specified as the initial step of the framework. Governmental organizations, municipalities in the scope of this paper, should develop smart city strategies to plan how to overcome existing challenges or improve in-house practices, creating public value in the process. For this, they need first to identify action fields in

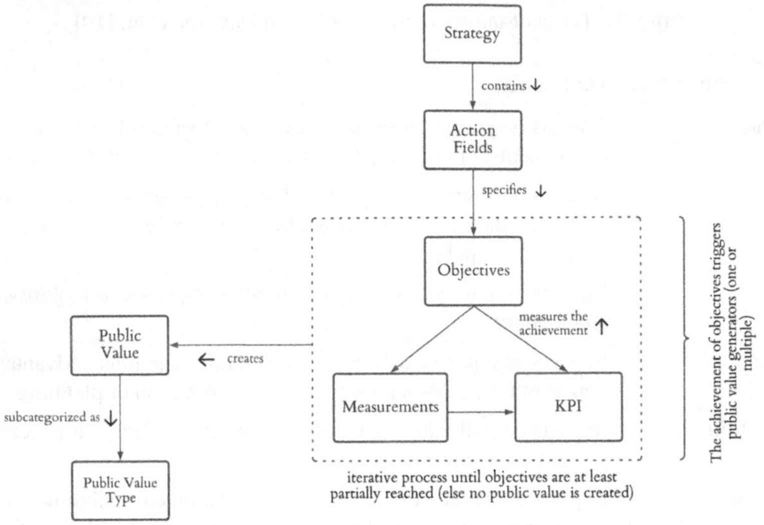

Fig. 2. Conceptual framework covering the steps from strategy development to public value generation

which improvements can enhance the well-being of public stakeholders. Specific objectives (targets) should be ex-ante specified for each action field. That is, for each action field, municipalities (or cities) should measure the current practice and situation (i.e., actual state) and define objectives to be achieved (i.e., desired state). To measure the actual state as well as the achievement of the desired state, they need to designate key performance indicators (KPIs) to the chosen action fields. Thus, they can iteratively measure the improvements in action fields and monitor the achievement of their objectives. The achievement of objectives can be seen as public value generators, as illustrated in the dashed box in Fig. 2. An improvement in a specific action field leads up to one or multiple public value generators such as effectiveness, transparency, participation, efficiency, and intrinsic enhancements. Public value generators are involved in the iterative process of the conceptual framework, and they are somewhat abstracted since the core focus of the paper is on the public value types. Nevertheless, their occurrences are measured via KPIs. For instance, as discussed in the results chapter, voter turnout is one of the most frequently used KPIs by Swiss municipalities. An improvement in that KPI leads to the participation type of public value generators. Successful (partial) completion of the iterative process, which means the achievement of objectives, leads to the creation of a type of public value. For instance, the social type of public value can be obtained because of an improvement in a KPI measuring collaboration among public stakeholders. In the same vein, stewardship type of public value can be obtained due to the improvement in a KPI measuring transparency. To sum up, the presented framework consists of potential steps of public value creation in smart cities. In the following chapters, we discuss an application of the model with Swiss municipalities through the survey that we carry out to learn their prioritized action fields as well as the importance attached to selected KPIs.

3 Data and Methods

This chapter consists of two sections addressing issues related to study design (i.e., constructing the questionnaire) and the methodology used throughout the paper. It also provides rationale regarding the selection of the municipality level we investigated and insights about the data collection procedure.

3.1 Study Design

The methodological design of the study consists of a survey among Swiss municipality officials, with the primary aim of investigating the fields of action municipalities set smart city goals in (research question 1), and the key performance indicators they considered important for their progress monitoring (research question 2). For the first research question, the respondents were asked to select among a list of potential action fields drawn from the Smart City Wheel (Fig. 1). For the second research question and based on the previous selection of relevant action fields, the survey asked to indicate among a list of corresponding key performance indicators, which indicators the respondent's municipality was a) already measuring, and b) they thought would be worthwhile measuring in the future. For the survey, the original Smart City Wheel indicator catalogue was adapted to the Swiss municipal context, resulting in a list of 30 potential indicators (Appendix B, Table 6). Additional information was collected on the respondent's personal information and key figures of the municipality they represented. Some introductory questions on general challenges related to the strategy development and monitoring process in the respective municipality – including whether there were even any strategies in place or not – were also asked.

Based on the literature, where we discussed the complexity and contextuality of the public value concept, we decided that a quantitative setting did not lend itself well to asking individuals directly for an evaluation of the public values their municipality was committed to. To answer our third research question, we therefore used the actions fields in which municipalities set strategic goals and the associated smart city indicators as a proxy. In other words, we revealed their public value preferences based on their ongoing actions, which is similar to the well-established revealed preferences theory frequently used in economics and finance research [4]. Connecting the indicators to the public value dimensions proposed by Harrison et al. [19] we arrived at an evaluation grid enabling us to deduct on what public values municipalities prioritize on their way to smarter cities (Appendix B, Table 6).

For our research, we focus on Switzerland, and specifically the level of municipalities. In Switzerland, there exist (at the time of writing) 2148 political municipalities distributed across 26 cantons, ranging from the smallest Zumdorf (canton of Uri) with less than 5 inhabitants, to the biggest Zurich (canton of Zurich) with over than 420'000 inhabitants [5]. From an international perspective, their size might seem very small on the map – but as the lowest administrative unit in Switzerland, municipalities possess numerous political powers. In Switzerland, the political organization of the municipal level is the responsibility of the cantons, which explains why municipalities differ from canton to canton, in terms of size but also in terms of their areas of responsibility and their administrative and political structure [5].

In general, however, the most important task of municipalities in Switzerland is regarded to be their self-organization in the form of public administration and municipal authorities, including the areas of basic municipal infrastructure such as water supply, wastewater and local roads, and waste disposal [28]. Practically all Swiss municipalities also deal with construction, spacial planning and the approval of building applications [28]. Furthermore, 9 out of 10 municipalities assume competences regarding school and social welfare, and the provision of services in the areas of culture, sports and environmental protection [28]. Referring back to the Smart City Wheel and its action areas (Fig. 1), it is apparent that Swiss municipalities are directly and immediately involved in core smart city concerns. In sum, this makes the Swiss municipalities a prime case for studying questions of public value generation in relation to smart city strategies. To answer the research questions and add to the case-study dominated public value literature, a quantitative approach was chosen.

3.2 Data Collection and Analysis

The online survey was carried out between February 22 and March 10, 2022, among a broad sample of municipalities and targeting municipality officials dealing with digitalization, innovation, and smart city projects and/or actively engaged in strategy development and monitoring. The sample consisted of 1795 municipalities – addressing 83% of Swiss municipalities with the total number of municipalities in Switzerland being 2148 at the time of writing – distributed across the German and the French-speaking part of Switzerland and with varying characteristics such as population size and degree of urbanization. As the sample was not randomly selected, there is the potential of a selection bias, for one because the municipalities from the Canton of Ticino (i.e., the only Italian-speaking Canton of Switzerland) were not included, and those from the Romandie (i.e., the French-speaking region of Switzerland) are statistically underrepresented by about 14%. Using the survey tool *Qualtrics*, we sent out an invitation to answer the online survey, including no incentive.

A reminder was sent out one week later to encourage participation in the survey. A total of 280 respondents participated in our survey, making for a cooperation rate of 15.5%. The raw data was cleaned and analyzed using the software packages of the R programming language as well as properties of Qualtrics. Cross-tabulation (i.e., contingency table) analysis was carried out to examine descriptive statistics of categorical variables including their relationships, as suggested in Wildemuth [37]. The analysis was enhanced by chi-square test, as carried out in many other studies [e.g., 27]. Chi-square test was mainly employed to examine whether there is a significant difference between three municipality types (i.e., small, medium, and large) in terms of the attached importance on different smart-city action fields. The test is commonly used in the literature to test the relationship between two categorical variables [17].

4 Results

The proportion of the population size of the responding municipalities is illustrated in Fig. 3. As shown, more than half of them have fewer than three thousand inhabitants. Only about 4.5% of them have more than thirty thousand inhabitants - those we can consider as highly urbanized municipalities. To facilitate the analysis of municipalities in this paper, we recoded the municipalities according to their size, ending up with three categories of municipalities: Small (≤3000), medium (3001–10'000) and large (>10'000). The primary rationale to shrink the number of categories was to have enough sample size for each of them to be used further in the statistical tests as well as cross-tabulations. Below, these categories are illustrated in similar color shadings.

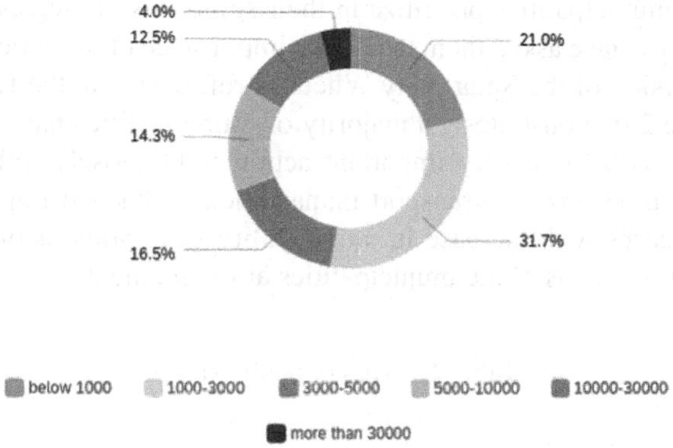

Fig. 3. Population size of responding municipalities

Concerning strategy development, the results have revealed that almost half of the responding municipalities already have strategy development experience i.e., they have already developed a strategy. We have followed up with a question on the type of strategies they have already carried out, the majority indicating having developed strategies concerning municipal development, digitalization, legislature, and spatial development. We have cross-tabulated the municipality size and the strategy development experience to examine their relationship (Fig. 4).

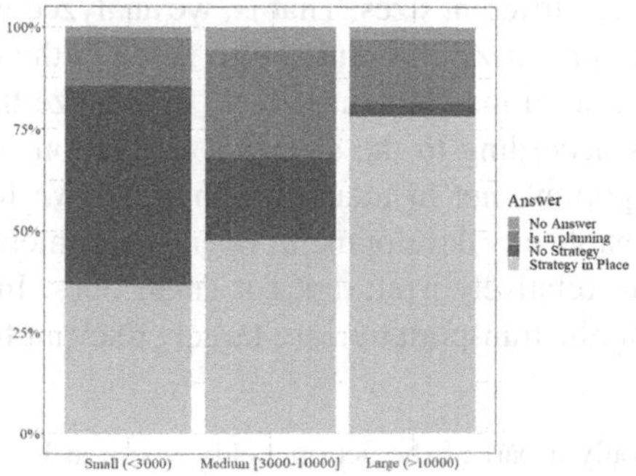

Fig. 4. Municipalities according to strategy development experience

As shown, more than three quarter of large municipalities have already developed a strategy, which is far above the proportion of the overall sample (45.7%). That proportion is about 45% for medium-sized municipalities and about 40% for small ones. That shows us that with increasing population size, the intention and experience of strategy development increases as well. That is in line with the previous research stating that increasing population size poses new challenges for the large municipalities; thus, they are more likely to invest resources (e.g., time, labor, finance) to develop and monitor strategies to overcome these challenges [38].

One of the primary goals of the present study is to learn about the action fields in which municipalities set smart city goals. In other words, it is intended to examine the action fields that Swiss municipalities prioritize in their smart city strategies to create public value. Therefore, we have asked them to rate the importance of the action fields included in the adapted version of the Smart City Wheel as referenced in the Literature Review (Fig. 1). As Table 2 demonstrates[2], a majority of municipalities has stated sustainable city development as being a very important action field, closely followed by energy efficiency, public transport and transport management. Attached importance on these action fields increases with increase in municipality size. Some action fields such as tourism are not at the focus of the municipalities at the moment[3].

Table 2. Types of public value

Very important				
Action field	Average	Small	Medium	Large
Sustainable city development	51.7%	42.8%	61.2%	61.5%
Energy efficiency	49.7%	38.4%	62.5%	65.5%
Public transport	49.4%	39.6%	57.1%	69.2%
Traffic management	40.6%	30.7%	50.0%	61.4%

Regarding the action fields, we proceeded to carry out a statistical test to examine whether the distribution of the importance of the action fields is heterogeneous among municipalities with different sizes. That is, we analyzed whether large, medium, and small municipalities prioritize different action fields in their strategy development towards smart cities. We used the chi-square test[4] to analyze the association between municipality categories according to the size and evaluation of an action field (very important, partially important, not in focus, no answer). We found that action fields like productivity, sustainable city development, open government are concerns for large municipalities. They are relatively irrelevant for small ones. In the same vein, inclusion/participation and public transportation are largely relevant for the middle and large municipalities.

[2] Table 2 demonstrates only a part of the action fields whom at least 40% of the responding municipalities stated very important. We provide a table with the whole set of action fields in the Appendix.

[3] A table providing "not in focus at the moment" proportions of all action fields is provided in Appendix D.

[4] For the chi-square table see Appendix E, Table 9.

To the action fields, specific key performance indicators (KPIs) are attached for performance monitoring purposes. In a following question, the municipalities were asked which of the KPIs they have already used/plan to use/are not interested in to monitor the achievement of their goals. The KPIs are displayed to a municipality according to the action fields that it states very important or partially important. As is apparent in Table 3[5], almost two third of the municipalities already monitor the number of social assistance rate. Voter turnout and unemployment rate are other popular KPIs which are already being monitored by the majority. The monitoring proportion soars up with the increasing population size significantly.

Table 3. KPIs that a majority of municipalities has stated to be "already monitoring"

Already monitoring				
KPI	Average	Small	Medium	Large
Social assistance rate	63.9%	52.8%	62.8%	85.0%
Civic engagement: voter turnout	53.8%	43.1%	58.4%	61.9%
Unemployment rate	50.0%	38.4%	48.5%	75.0%

Next, Table 4 demonstrates the popular KPIs that the absolute majority of the municipalities stated as "would be relevant in the future". It is worthy to note that three of them are related to energy. That shows us that many municipalities have already acknowledged the importance of managing limited resources such as energy and plan to orientate themselves in the future accordingly.

Table 4. Top KPIs municipalities have stated "would be relevant in the future"

Would be relevant in the future				
KPI	Average	Small	Medium	Large
Percentage of house with smart metering systems	59.8%	59.0%	60.5%	68.4%
Total household energy consumption per capita	59.5%	61.1%	64.7%	47.8%
Proportion of government services via the internet	57.0%	57.8%	58.3%	52.1%
Percentage of total energy from renewable sources	55.7%	56.7%	58.9%	47.6%
Proportion of total population with digital literacy skills	52.3%	53.9%	50.0%	58.3%
Annual number of journeys by public transport per capita	50.7%	52.1%	52.3%	47.6%

[5] Table 3 illustrates the KPIs that the absolute majority (more than 50%) already monitors. The rest of the KPIs are provided in Appendix C.

5 Discussion

In the present paper, we have focused on three research questions: (1) In which smart city fields of action do municipalities set goals to generate public value, (2) on the way to implementing their goals, what key performance indicators (KPIs) are of relevance to municipalities and (3) what kind of public value municipalities seek to generate. Regarding the first question, we have found that municipalities currently declare to prioritize goal setting in areas related to Smart Environment (Sustainable City Development, Energy Efficiency) and Smart Mobility (Public Transport and Transport Management). Considering recent initiatives in environmental policy and developments such as the rise of the green party in Switzerland since the last parliamentary elections in 2019, it makes sense that these are topics high on the municipalities' agenda. It is interesting to note however, that not all Action Fields of Smart Environment enjoy the same popularity: when it comes to Environmental Protection, the municipalities report to be less engaged. It might be that the municipalities consider this to be a topic where higher levels of government are in charge of goal setting and municipalities are more in the role of the executioner.

When we now consider the key performance indicators municipalities report to measure, we see a different picture: the KPIs an overall majority of all municipalities has stated to be already monitoring, are neither related to Environment nor Mobility, but rather Smart People (civic engagement), Smart Economy (unemployment rate) and Smart Living (social assistance rate). Thus, we observe a disparity between where municipalities self-report to set goals, and where they report to measure their performance. It is a gap, municipalities seem willing to close: While only an average of 18% already monitors KPIs in Smart Environment, an average of 45% is striving to do so in the future. In general, we can see that municipalities think that most indicators are more relevant than they currently treat them – for 22 out of 30 indicators, the average values for "would be relevant in the future" are higher than for the "already measuring" question. Considering the previously displayed Table 4 (Top KPIs Municipalities have stated "would be relevant in the Future"), the difference is especially striking for the KPI measuring the share of the population with digital literacy skills (from 1.56% of municipalities already monitoring the KPI to 52% wanting to monitor it). Taken together with the high rating for future measurements of "Proportion of Government Services via the Internet", Smart Government seems to be another smart city area municipalities want to place more attention on in the future.

Based on the evaluation of KPIs we proceeded to analyze our third research question: the public value municipalities seem to be striving to generate. For this, we started with the public value dimensions framework provided by Harrison et al. [19]. Looking at the fields of action and KPIs relevant for Swiss municipalities, we realized that the framework was not a perfect fit – there was no dimension to reflect the importance municipalities accorded to Smart Environment topics. We would have had to somewhat awkwardly associate environmental topics with either the quality of life or the ideological dimension. Considering that the dimensions were developed in 2011 – at a time where the climate crisis and its consequences was not yet in global focus – we thought it justified to update the dimensions system and add an "environmental" dimension. On the other hand, we found it difficult to associate the "ideological" dimension with indicators from the Smart City Wheel, which is why we excluded this dimension from analysis (for an overview of public value types and assigned KPIs see the Appendix C, Table 7). One could argue that certain indicators such as the monitoring of greenhouse gas emissions, could also have been sorted in the ideological dimension, if interpreted as a more of a signal of public administrations to demonstrate to citizens the alignment of government actions with the (by large parts of the population) perceived urgency of the climate issue. With regard to our third research question, we find that based on what municipalities are already monitoring, the social and stewardship public value types seem to be predominantly produced (Fig. 5). If we consider what municipalities would like to monitor in the future, greater importance of the environmental and political value dimension can be predicted.

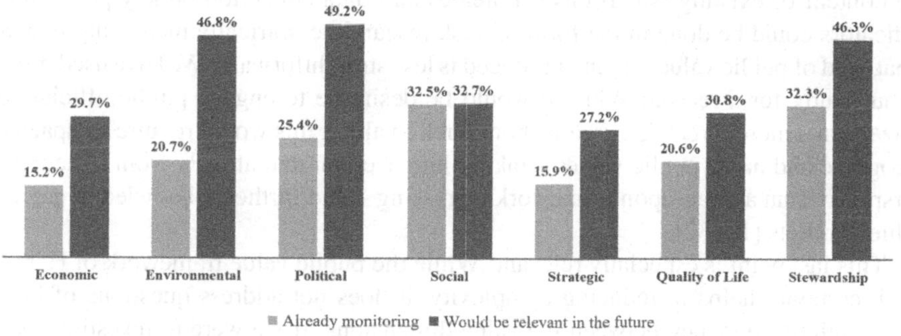

Fig. 5. Dimensions of public value and average monitoring

6 Conclusion and Outlook

With this study, we contribute to the smart city and public value theory and research in the following ways: We connect the concepts of smart city goals and key performance indicators to the issue of public value creation. In line with this conceptual integration, we propose a theoretical framework for understanding public value creation in smart cities. Based on our framework, public value is empirically investigated by conceptualizing it as something that can be understood by analyzing the relevance of goals and indicators to public actors. By using quantitative research methods, we contribute to filling a gap in research regarding the empirical application of the public value concept, a research area largely dominated by case studies.

In summary, our results indicate that Swiss municipalities prioritize action fields regarding sustainable city development, energy efficiency, public transport, and traffic management. The importance awarded to these action fields gradually increases with municipality size, as the cross-tabulation analysis reveals. We have demonstrated that there is a heterogeneity among municipalities in terms of their priorities and preferences. Our analysis linking the prioritized action fields, corresponding KPIs and public value types, suggests that the public value currently generated by municipalities might be located primarily in the social and stewardship dimension, but that in the future, environmental and political public value could move into the foreground.

Concerning limitations, one might argue that the Swiss case is too specific. In many regards, Switzerland is a special case because of its direct democratic system and general wealth. While Swiss municipalities may not be directly representative in terms of their small size, they make for a comparable case in terms of their struggle for and difficulty in the allocation of financial and human resources. Having to navigate a complex field of tasks with limited resources, Swiss municipalities are comparable in an international context. As a main caveat, however, we identify that our results are stemming from municipality representatives self-reporting on their municipalities' goals and actions – comparing the actual output of municipalities' strategy work to what they have reported to (want) to be doing should be the object of further research. While mapping and analyzing the content of existing (smart city) strategies and data collection on key performance indicators could be done in the form of desk research, empirically measuring how and what kind of public value is being produced is less straightforward. We have used proxies in our study for a reason: While it would be desirable to engage public officials and citizens in a more direct discussion about public values, this would require a capacity to recognize and name public values – taking into account that already from a theoretical perspective, an agreed-upon framework is missing – and further acknowledge potential value conflicts [10, 32].

This last point is especially relevant: While the public value framework of Harrison et al. certainly helps in reducing complexity, it does not address questions of hierarchy or interdependency between the value dimensions. If we were to investigate more closely the added "environmental public value"-dimension, this would be a crucial point, because certain policy measures in Smart Environment might not be in line with immediate economic or even social interests. In general, and for municipalities especially, reconciling competing interests with very limited resources is a main challenge. Bearing in mind the context-specificness of public value, questions of how the creation of one type of public value could lead to the destruction of another, and how this bargaining process might unravel at the municipal level, seem worthy of further scholarly attention.

Acknowledgements. This research is part of the activities of the Inoville 4.0 project, which is financially supported by the Swiss Innovation Agency (Innosuisse).

Appendix

Link to the Appendix: https://drive.switch.ch/index.php/s/G3rYSBMNP289BVl.

References

1. Aichholzer, G., Kubicek, H., Torres, L.: Evaluating e-participation. Frameworks, Practice, Evidence. Springer, Cham (2015). https://doi.org/10.1007/978-3-319-25403-6
2. Anttiroiko, A.-V., Komninos, N.: Smart public services: using smart city and service ontologies in integrative service design. In: Rodriguez Bolivar, M. (eds) Setting Foundations for the Creation of Public Value in Smart Cities. Public Administration and Information Technology, vol. 35, pp. 17–47 (2019). https://doi.org/10.1007/978-3-319-98953-2_2

3. Bektas, A. and Haller, S.: InoVille 4.0 – Eine plattform für strategische governance in smart cities und smart municipalities. In: TOGI Symposium (2021)
4. Beshears, J., Choi, J.J., Laibson, D., Madrian, B.C.: How are preferences revealed? J. Public Econ. **92**(8–9), 1787–1794 (2008)
5. BFS. Die 2148 Gemeinden der Schweiz am 1.1.2022 (2022). https://www.bfs.admin.ch/bfs/de/home/statistiken/kataloge-datenbanken/karten.assetdetail.20604220.html. Accessed 9 Mar 2022
6. Bolivar, M.P.R. (ed.): Setting Foundations for the Creation of Public Value in Smart Cities. Public Administration and Information Technology Series, vol. 35. Springer, Cham (2019). https://doi.org/10.1007/978-3-319-98953-2
7. Brown, P.R., Cherney, L., Warner, S.: Understanding public value – why does it matter? Int. J. Public Adm. **44**(10), 803–807 (2021)
8. Charles, M.B., Martin de Jong, W., Ryan, N.: Public values in western Europe: a temporal perspective. Am. Rev. Public Adm. **41**(1), 75–91 (2011)
9. CITYkeys. The Project (2015). http://www.citykeys-project.eu/. Accessed 15 Mar 2022
10. Coffey, B.: Environmental challenges for public value theory and practice. Int. J. Public Adm. **44**(10), 818–825 (2021)
11. Cohen, B.: The smartest cities in the world 2015: methodology. Fast Company **11**(20), 2014 (2014)
12. Cohen, B.: Blockchain cities and the smart cities wheel. Medium (2018)
13. Cosgrave, E., Tryfonas, T., Crick, T.: The smart city from a public value perspective (2014)
14. Dameri, R.P.: Smart City Definition, Goals and Performance. Progress in IS, pp. 1–22. Springer, Cham (2017). https://doi.org/10.1007/978-3-319-45766-6_1
15. Flury von Arx, R., Stephan, H., Juen, S.: Smartcity-Monitoring der kommunalen Entwicklung (2019). https://www.societybyte.swiss/2019/02/08/smartcity-monitoring-der-kommunalen-entwicklung/. Accessed 29 Mar 2021
16. Flury von Arx, R., Juen, S.: Swiss Smart City-Monitoring-System SSCMS. Ein Monitoring-System für smarte Schweizer Städte und Gemeinden. Schlussbericht zum Vorprojekt und Projektskizze Hauptprojekt. ARGE Kommunales Monitoring (2020)
17. Franke, T.M., Ho, T., Christie, C.A.: The chi-square test. Am. J. Eval. **33**(3), 448–458 (2012)
18. Fukumoto, E., Bozeman, B.: Public values theory: what is missing? Am. Rev. Public Adm. **49**(6), 635–648 (2019)
19. Harrison, T., Pardo, T., Cresswell, A., Cook, M.: Delivering public value through open government. Center for technology in government (2011)
20. Hartley, J., Alford, J., Knies, E., Douglas, S.: Towards an empirical research agenda for public value theory. Public Manag. Rev. **19**(5), 670–685 (2017)
21. Hartley, J., Sancino, A., Bennister, M., Resodihardjo, S.L.: Leadership for public value: political astuteness as a conceptual link. Public Adm. **97**(2), 239–249 (2019)
22. Homeier, I., et al.: SMART City Indikatoren und MONITORing für Smart City Zielsetzungen am Beispiel der "Smart City Wien Rahmenstrategie" (SMART. MONITOR). Bundesministerium für Verkehr, Innovation und Technologie, Wien (2017)
23. Homeier, I., Pangerl, E., Tollmann, J., Daskalow, K.: Monitoringbericht. Smart City Wien Rahmenstrategie (2017)
24. Huijbregts, R., George, B., Bekkers, V.: Public values assessment as a practice: integration of evidence and research agenda. Public Manag. Rev. **24**(6), 1–20 (2021)
25. ITU-T. Overview of Key Performance Indicators in Smart Sustainable Cities. Recommendation ITU-T Y.4900/L.1600. Series Y: Global Information Infrastructure, Internet Protocol Aspects and Next Generation Networks, Internet of Things and Smart Cities. ITU-T, Geneva (2016)

26. Jaekel, M.: Smart City wird Realität. Wegweiser für neue Urbanitäten in der Digitalmoderne/Michael Jaekel. Springer Vieweg, Wiesbaden (2015). https://doi.org/10.1007/978-3-658-04455-8
27. Jenkins, V., Fallowfield, L., Saul, J.: Information needs of patients with cancer: results from a large study in UK cancer centres. Br. J. Cancer **84**(1), 48–51 (2001)
28. Ladner, A., Haus, A.: Aufgabenerbringung der Gemeinden in der Schweiz: Organisation, Zuständigkeiten und Auswirkungen. Cahier de l'IDHEAP 319. IDHEAP, Lausane (2021)
29. Meijer, A.: Datapolis: a public governance perspective on "smart cities." Perspect Public Manag. Gov. **1**(3), 195–206 (2018)
30. Meynhardt, T.: Public value inside: what is public value creation? Int. J. Public Adm. **32**(3–4), 192–219 (2009)
31. Moore, M. H.: Creating Public Value. Strategic Management in Government. Harvard University Press (1997)
32. Nabatchi, T.: Putting the "Public" back in public values research: designing participation to identify and respond to values. Public Admin Rev. **72**(5), 699–708 (2012)
33. Neuroni, A.C., Haller, S., van Winden, W., Carabias-Hütter, V., Yildirim, O.: Public value creation in a smart city context: an analysis framework. In: Rodriguez Bolivar, M.P. (ed.) Setting Foundations for the Creation of Public Value in Smart Cities. PAIT, vol. 35, pp. 49–76. Springer, Cham (2019). https://doi.org/10.1007/978-3-319-98953-2_3
34. Pereira, G.V., Macadar, M.A., Luciano, E.M., Testa, M.G.: Delivering public value through open government data initiatives in a Smart City context. Inf. Syst. Front. **19**(2), 213–229 (2016). https://doi.org/10.1007/s10796-016-9673-7
35. Public Value and Public Administration. Georgetown University Press (2015)
36. Tomor, Z., Meijer, A., Michels, A., Geertman, S.: Smart governance for sustainable cities: findings from a systematic literature review. J. Urban Technol. **26**(4), 3–27 (2019)
37. Wildemuth, B.M.: Applications of Social Research Methods to Questions in Information and Library Science, 2nd edn. Pearson Education, Oxford (2016)
38. Wüst, A., Bektas, A., Wenger, N., Haller, S.: A smart government platform to promote strategy development in municipalities. Manuscript submitted for publication
39. Yigitcanlar, T., Lee, S.H.: Korean ubiquitous-eco-city: a smart-sustainable urban form or a branding hoax? Technol. Forecast. Soc. Chang. **89**, 100–114 (2014)
40. Zuccardi Merli, M., Bonollo, E.: Performance measurement in the smart cities. In: Dameri, R.P., Rosenthal-Sabroux, C. (eds.) Smart City. PI, pp. 139–155. Springer, Cham (2014). https://doi.org/10.1007/978-3-319-06160-3_7

Coping with the Opportunities and Challenges of Smart Policing: A Research Model

Muhammad Afzal(✉) and Panos Panagiotopoulos

Queen Mary University of London, London, UK
{m.afzal,p.panagiotopoulos}@qmul.ac.uk

Abstract. The paper aims to examine how police managers cope with the threats and opportunities associated with the implementation of smart policing applications. Smart policing has reshaped the practices of police managers by offering opportunities to improve decisions with data-driven approaches. These new approaches change the traditional ways in which police managers exercise discretion. Using the theoretical lens of coping theory, we develop the foundations for a research model to explain how smart policing stimulates problem-focused and emotion-focused strategies depending on managers' perceptions of control and discretion. Future empirical studies using the model can inform more broadly on our understanding of how public sector employees respond to data-driven technologies and automated decision-making.

Keywords: Coping strategies · Discretion · Automated decision-making

1 Introduction

Developments in computational power and machine learning techniques have changed expectations in the public sector [1–5]. Police organisations have focused on data-driven technologies that serve as decision support systems under the umbrella term of smart policing [6, 7]. Smart policing can facilitate day-to-day operational decisions and help police organisations improve operational efficacy, decision quality and supervision of police officers' routines.

These developments have triggered a shift from street-level policing to system-level policing, where face-to-face interactions between police officers and the public are being replaced by digital systems and algorithmic management [2, 8, 9]. Automated decision making considerably influences the discretionary practices of police officers, who are increasingly asked to make decisions based on data insights rather than their experience and professional knowledge. This reinforces pressures toward standardisation, formalisation and centralisation in public organisations [2, 6, 9].

These changes tend to replace administrative discretion exercised by police officers with "digital discretion". Smart policing applications and the evolution of digital discretion offer great opportunities as well as pose several risks by having both enabling and constraining effects on the freedom of street-level bureaucrats like police officers to

Published by Springer Nature Switzerland AG 2022
M. Janssen et al. (Eds.): EGOV 2022, LNCS 13391, pp. 469–478, 2022.
https://doi.org/10.1007/978-3-031-15086-9_30

exercise discretion [10]. Advantages include better organisational performance in terms of the improved and consistent exercise of decision making through increased scalability, decreased costs, and reduced information asymmetries [1, 2, 6, 9]. Conversely, smart policing may deprive police officers of their traditional discretion or ability to make decisions based on experience, deteriorate professional norms and standards, negatively affect public service motivation and cause unintended outcomes like increased workloads [9–14].

Previous research has focused on configuring digital practices in public services [15] and the impacts and outcomes of technologies on service quality [16]. These research streams have concluded that case officers act as mediators between digital systems and clients in decision making automation [17] and that humans and algorithms augment each other while sharing responsibilities in new ways [18]. Less attention has been given to unpacking the internal processes and interactions taking place when data-driven applications are implemented in the public sector [15]. Scholars in this research stream have focused on postulating how digital evolution can have both enabling and constraining effects on street-level bureaucrats [10]. Still, little is known about how street-level bureaucrats cope with the pressures and tensions, opportunities and threats arising out of smart policing applications and the new nature of discretion in smart policing [7, 9, 10, 20]. For instance, de Boer and Raaphorst [21] found that automated decision-making rendered street-level bureaucrats more legalistic in their enforcement style, but higher facilitative and accommodative enforcement styles necessitated a higher perception of discretion. Busch, Henriksen and Sæbø [12] examined how judges and caseworkers in Norway cope with digitised discretionary practices.

These studies support the case for new research on the intricacies between street-level bureaucrats' perception of discretion in the implementation of smart policing applications. This study attempts to address these intricacies by exploring the following research questions:

(1) What strategies do police managers adopt to cope with the perceived threats and opportunities associated with smart policing applications?
(2) How does police officers' perception of discretion affect how they cope with smart policing applications?

We use the theoretical lens of coping theory to develop our understanding of how smart policing applications stimulate coping strategies depending on police officers' perception of discretion and control [22]. The theory of coping is chosen for three reasons. First, it focuses on how individuals deal with disruptive events that derive from their interaction with the environment, which allows examination of the event (smart policing applications) and the users (police officers' responses). Second, it enables identification of the critical elements explaining individual appraisal of the event and resultant complex responses [23]. Third, it provides a robust foundation for understanding user behaviour in information systems associated with organisational change [23–26]. We introduce coping theory in the context of smart policing in Sect. 2 and develop a research model to explore our research questions in Sect. 3. The paper concludes with a discussion on the potential for in public management and policing.

2 Conceptual Background

Coping is defined as "constantly changing cognitive and behavioural efforts exerted to manage specific external and/or internal demands that are appraised as taxing or exceeding the resources of the person" [22]. Internal demands relate to personal desires or obligations (e.g., need for achievement), while external demands are imposed by the external environment (e.g., social pressures). Such demands can be considered disruptive events if they exceed one's resources to manage them [27]. Coping is associated with both negative and positive situations requiring respective adaptation. The coping process comprises four steps: an incident or situation, appraisal, coping strategies and outcomes [22, 28].

Beaudry and Pinsonneault [29] developed a coping model of user adaptation based on coping theory to investigate behaviours before, during, and after an IT event. The model postulates that the perception of an IT event triggers adaptive behaviours based on two critical subprocesses. The primary appraisal consists of assessing the potential consequences and the personal relevance of the event. A relevant primary appraisal may be perceived as a threat or opportunity [26]. The secondary appraisal involves the assessment of personal, social, psychological, emotional and physical resources like sense of confidence and self-efficacy and control over the situation [22]. It determines an individual sense of control over the situation and influences the selection between two main coping strategies: problem-focused coping and emotion-focused coping [22, 26].

Problem-focused strategies attempt to address the problem or situation instrumentally. For example, a user can try to switch to an alternative application after using a non-satisfactory one. Emotion-focused strategies aim to regulate an individual's emotions in response to the situation. Although previous research has found mixed effects, a higher sense of control leads to adaptation of problem-focused strategies while a lower sense of control leads to adaptation of emotion-focused strategies [23]. For example, an individual who perceives the IT-related event as an opportunity and senses a high degree of control over the technology implementation environment is more likely to adapt work processes to maximise advantages offered by the IT – this refers to a benefits maximising strategy as a type of problem-focused coping [26, 29]. On the contrary, an individual who perceives the IT-related event as a threat and senses a low degree of control over the technology implementation environment is more likely to resort to behaviours like distancing, avoidance or withdrawal – this refers to a self-preservation strategy as a type of emotion-focused coping [26, 29].

These affective reactions more strongly determine post-adoptive behaviours for continuous use of digital systems and organisational performance benefits than measuring cognitive beliefs or intentions to use [30]. Empirical studies have confirmed the insights offered by the coping model of user adaptation in the contexts of digital banking, resource planning systems and administrative software packages [27, 31].

Despite the importance attached to the appraisal process in shaping user behaviours, the model by Beaudry and Pinsonneault [29] does not explicitly explore the factors determining the appraisal event [26]. The information systems adoption literature has highlighted factors that determine user control, such as performance expectancy, effort expectancy, social influence, and facilitating conditions [32]. Fadel and Brown [26] found health managers' performance and effort expectancy to be significantly associated with the appraisal process in the case of electronic medical systems.

Instead of adoption-related constructs, we introduce perceived discretion as a determinant of the appraisal process [10, 14]. Police officers, like other street-level bureaucrats, exercise considerable discretion in the performance of their work routines. However, the introduction of smart policing applications is likely to affect their expectation of exercising discretion [2, 9, 10]. In the next section, we develop our research model based on coping theory in the context of a study with police managers in Pakistan.

3 Research Model and Study Context

The individuals of interest in this research are operational police managers in the Punjab Police Department region of Pakistan. The environmental change is the introduction of a smart policing application, namely, the Police Station Record Management System (PSRMS) across the region's entire network of police departments. The system supports operational police managers in making decisions based on a number of data streams available. The decisions that police managers make with the new system relate to hotspot policing, wherein they can reallocate existing resources, monitor the performance of police officers, assign tasks to police officers regarding the arrest of accused at large, and monitor case closure rates and performance of street-level police officers.

In the context of this study and with respect to hypothesis development, police managers make a series of appraisals about the system's impact on their working practices.

A primary appraisal consists of assessing threats and opportunities related to internal and external demands of PSRMS. The subsequent secondary appraisal will correspond to their perceived control over the use of PSRMS, which will eventually determine the coping strategies police managers employ in the use of PSRMS.

We operationalise these series of appraisals and their respective hypotheses based on coping theory as shown in the research model presented in Fig. 1.

3.1 Primary and Secondary Appraisals

Primary appraisal is the initial awareness and assessment of the potential consequences of personal and professional relevance for the new information systems implementation [29]. Smart policing applications, like PSRMS, are multifaceted, offering opportunities and posing threats. PSRMS is an integrated digital platform providing operational police managers with access to vast amounts of crime and personnel data that may assist them in their daily work routines. The data offer opportunities to enhance efficiency and public trust by enhancing situational awareness, improving risk assessments and increasing visibility in troubled areas [33, 34]. Police managers using the data-driven outputs of the system may plan and coordinate policing activities, assign new tasks to street-level officers, monitor the performance of street-level officers (case closure rates, arrest of wanted persons etc.) and rethink and reshape policing objectives and quality of interventions. The embedded opportunity of hotspot policing allows police managers access to the latest geospatial crime data enabling them to reallocate resources towards

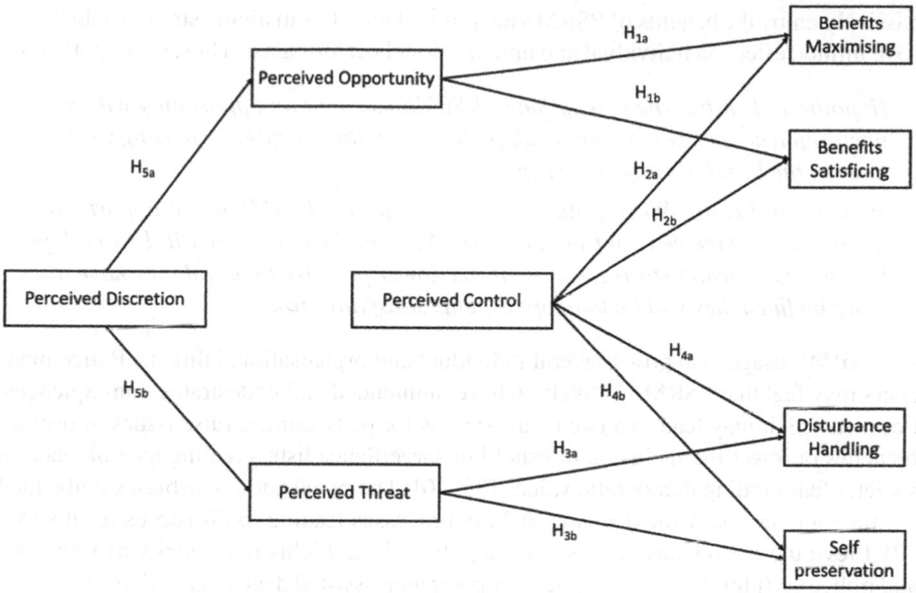

Fig. 1. Research model

dynamic crime hotspots for increasing police visibility and crime prevention [7]. The accessibility to big data may also be seen as an opportunity for experimenting and developing new skills and routines [35–37].

According to the coping model of user adaptation [29], the perceived opportunity fosters either the adoption of benefits maximising or benefits satisficing strategies depending on the level of control users exercise [29, 31]. The secondary appraisal has three main components: work, self and technology. Control over work refers to the degree to which police managers feel they have sufficient autonomy to modify and adapt their tasks to PSRMS and the sufficiency of resources to implement the usage of PSRMS in their police establishment [38]. Control over the self refers to whether police managers feel they have the sufficient capability to address any problems arising from the use of PSRMS in their police establishment and the degree of ease with which they can implement the usage of PSRMS in their police establishment [22]. Control over technology refers to how much influence the police managers have over the features and functionalities of PSRMS during its usage or development [29, 39]. In this case, if users have a high degree of control, their adaptation efforts will mainly be problem-focused to take full advantage of the opportunities offered by PSRMS. For instance, they will be focused on modifying operational processes, developing new behavioural standards and aspirations and engaging in productive activities [29]. These benefit-maximising strategies will likely improve performance by reducing errors, making faster and quality decisions, higher case closure rates, increased arrest of wanted criminals etc.

On the other hand, if users have a lower perception of control, their adaptation efforts will be minimal since they neither feel the need to reduce tensions associated with PSRMS nor can they do much to exploit the benefits of the PSRMS [29]. They passively enjoy the benefits of PSRMS adapting a benefits-satisficing strategy which will have limited effect on individual and organisational performance. Thus, we hypothesise:

Hypothesis 1 (a-b): The perception of PSRMS usage as an opportunity will positively influence police managers' adaptation of (a) the benefits maximising strategy and (b) the benefits satisficing strategy.

Hypothesis 2 (a-b): When police managers appraise PSRMS as an opportunity, (a) the more perceived control they have, the more inclined they will be to adopt benefits maximising strategies and (b) the lower perceived control they have, the more inclined they will be to adopt benefits satisfying strategy.

PSRMS usage also poses several individual and organisational threats. Police managers may feel that PSRMS is likely to have unintended and undesirable consequences. For instance, it may lead to a rise in arrest rates for petty crimes, raise issues of privacy breaches or lower the inclusion threshold in surveillance lists, creating an ambience of societal fear eroding democratic values [33, 40]. The racial and other biases embedded within data may skew the decision-making processes leading to disastrous results [41, 42]. Previous research has also shown that police officer highly rate their own experience and police craft for decision making over computer-assisted decisions [34]. Some police officers may even think that sitting in front of a computer is an analyst's job. This will threaten their professional norm and create a sense of an increase in workload.

According to the coping model of user adaptation [29], the perceived threat fosters the adoption of cautious behaviours like disturbance handling and self-preservation strategies depending on the secondary appraisal [29, 31]. When PSRMS is perceived as a threat and police managers feel that they have some control over the situation, they are likely to adopt a mix of problem-focused and emotion-focused strategies to manage the situation and restore emotional stability respectively [29]. They will try to find positive aspects of the situation and grow and improve them. This is called a disturbance handling strategy and will likely increase individual efficiency and organisational performance. On the other hand, if PSRMS is perceived as a threat but police managers feel they have minimal control, they will be focused on reducing tensions emanating from PSRMS. They will adapt self-preservation strategies like avoidance, self-deception, selective attention, and distancing [29]. It may restore their emotional stability but will have little impact on individual efficiency and organisational performance. Thus, we hypothesise:

Hypothesis 3 (a-b): The perception of PSRMS usage as a threat will positively influence the police managers' adaptation of the (a) disturbance handling strategy and (b) self-preservation strategy.

Hypothesis 4 (a-b): When police managers appraise PSRMS as a threat, (a) the more perceived control they have, the more inclined they will be to adopt disturbance handling strategies and (b) the lower perceived control they have, the more inclined they will be to adopt self-preservation strategy.

3.2 Discretion and Control

Street-level bureaucrats and managers exercise a high degree of discretion and autonomy from the central authorities for determining the nature, amount and quality of benefits and sanctions provided to the public [14]. This discretion and autonomy are inherent in their job descriptions. They play an essential role in developing patterns of routines, devices, and strategies for effectively addressing the uncertainties, ambiguities and complexities of organisational goals, individual circumstances, and work pressures. Lipsky's [14] discretion theory has been widely applied in social work, policing, education, and healthcare. It has been influential in unravelling the routines, practices and processes developed during policy implementation and the factors shaping them.

The introduction of smart policing applications provides central authorities with a tool to control the discretion of operational managers through the standardisation of work processes and outputs [2, 9, 10]. Police officers, like other street-level officers, enjoy considerable discretion in their routine duties, especially for making arrests. But the use of PSRMS is likely to replace their discretion with digital discretion. It may direct them to make arrests in trivial or petty cases, like family disputes, where the police officer's experience dictates them to avoid arrest. Moreover, police officers use their discretion to ignore some matters. At the same time, PSRMS will flag all kinds of issues forcing them to deal with matters considered less important according to their police craft. In short, the evolution of smart policing tools is likely to create uncertainties and work pressures for police managers, devouring them of their discretion [10]. This will affect their perception of opportunities and threats related to PSRMS. If police managers perceive that PSRMS is likely to reduce their discretion, they will feel work pressures and uncertainties, negatively affecting their perception of opportunities associated with PSRMS. Thus, we hypothesise:

Hypothesis 5(a-b): Police managers' perception of discretion will (a) positively influence their perception of PSRMS related opportunities and (b) negatively influence their perception of PSRMS related threats.

4 Conclusion

The empirical research in progress aims to validate an operationalised version of the model presented in Fig. 1 with a suitable questionnaire instrument. The findings of the study will contribute to our understanding of emerging behavioural patterns of public sector managers in the adaptation of digital applications and tools. It will also reveal the role street-level discretion plays in the evolution of different behavioural patterns and highlight new research avenues for public management scholars. In the context of smart policing, we develop the theoretical foundations for a balanced investigation to uncover which coping strategies correspond to user assessments of the new system as threat and opportunity (research question 1). Key to this coping explanation is the perception of discretion for police managers that engage with the data-driven and algorithmic features of new applications that present fundamental changes to their established decision-making practices (research question 2).

Coping theory provides a useful theoretical foundation for examining various user responses or adaptation strategies that emerge during the implementation of smart policing applications. Since the theory does not specify any attributes of a disruptive event that may shape the user behaviour, we focus on the importance frontline discretion as a critical driver of user adaptation strategies. This makes our potential contribution two-fold. First, we extend coping theory to the domain of policing. Second, we contribute to the discretion literature by unpacking how discretion plays out amidst digital technologies. We introduce discretion-as-perceived as an antecedent of coping behaviours thereby developing a link between discretion theory and the coping framework. There are two competing hypotheses explaining the impact of digital evolution on discretion-as-perceived: the curtailment hypothesis and the enablement hypothesis [10]. The curtailment hypothesis argues that the implementation of digital technologies tends to diminish the discretion of street-level bureaucrats or frontline public servants who experience less leeway to make decisions [2]. On the contrary, the enablement hypothesis treats digital technologies as one of the various contextual factors that shape discretion [10]. According to this view, such technologies do not provide the whole picture to managers and further obscure the informal dimensions of use of frontline discretion. This study tends to incorporate both theoretical positions and examines how discretion-as-perceived in the context of smart policing applications impacts the opportunities and challenges associated with them and drives various street-level behaviours to exploit opportunities and deal with challenges.

More broadly, the study will increase our understanding of how public sector employees respond to data-driven technologies that aims to provide automated decision-making support.

References

1. Young, M.M., Bullock, J.B., Lecy, J.D.: Artificial discretion as a tool of governance: a framework for understanding the impact of artificial intelligence on public administration. Perspect. Public Manag. and Governance **2**, 301–313 (2019)
2. Bovens, M., Zouridis, S.: From street-level to system-level bureaucracies: how information and communication technology is transforming administrative discretion and constitutional control. Public Adm. Rev. **62**, 174–184 (2002)
3. Veale, M., Brass, I.: Administration by algorithm? Public management meets public sector machine learning. In: Yeung, K., Lodge, M. (eds.) Algorithmic Regulation Oxford University Press (2019)
4. Barth, T.J., Arnold, E.: Artificial intelligence and administrative discretion: implications for public administration. Am. Rev. Public Adm. **29**, 332–351 (1999)
5. Bullock, J.B.: Artificial intelligence, discretion, and bureaucracy. Am. Rev. Public Adm. **49**, 751–761 (2019)
6. Meijer, A., Lorenz, L., Wessels, M.: Algorithmization of bureaucratic organizations: using a practice lens to study how context shapes predictive policing systems. Public Adm. Rev. **81**, 837–846 (2021)
7. Afzal, M., Panagiotopoulos, P.: Smart policing: a critical review of the literature. In: Viale Pereira, G., et al. (eds.) EGOV 2020. LNCS, vol. 12219, pp. 59–70. Springer, Cham (2020). https://doi.org/10.1007/978-3-030-57599-1_5
8. Egbert, S.: Predictive policing and the platformization of police work. Surveill. Soc. **17**, 83–88 (2019)
9. Busch, P.A., Henriksen, H.Z.: Digital discretion: a systematic literature review of ICT and street-level discretion. Inf. Polity **23**, 3–28 (2018)
10. Buffat, A.: Street-level bureaucracy and e-government. Public Manag. Rev. **17**, 149–161 (2015)
11. Maynard-Moody, S., Musheno, M.: State agent or citizen agent: two narratives of discretion. J. Public Adm. Res. Theory **10**, 329–358 (2000)

12. Busch, P.A., Henriksen, H.Z., Sæbø, Ø.: Opportunities and challenges of digitized discretionary practices: a public service worker perspective. Gov. Inf. Q. **35**, 547–556 (2018)
13. Thomann, E., van Engen, N., Tummers, L.: The Necessity of Discretion: A Behavioral Evaluation of Bottom-Up Implementation Theory. Journal of Public Administration Research and Theory **28**, 583–601 (2018)
14. Lipsky, M.: Street-Level Bureaucracy: Dilemmas of the Individual in Public Service. Russell Sage Foundation, New York (2010)
15. Andersson, C., Hallin, A., Ivory, C.: Unpacking the digitalisation of public services: configuring work during automation in local government. Gov. Inf. Q. **39**, 101662 (2022)
16. Vial, G.: Understanding digital transformation: a review and a research agenda. J. Strateg. Inf. Syst. **28**, 118–144 (2019)
17. Wihlborg, E., Larsson, H., Hedstrom, K.: "The computer says no!" -- a case study on automated decision-making in public authorities. In: Proceedings of the 49th Hawaii International Conference on System Sciences (HICSS-49), pp. 2903–2912. IEEE, Kauai, HI, USA (Year)
18. Grønsund, T., Aanestad, M.: Augmenting the algorithm: emerging human-in-the-loop work configurations. J. Strateg. Inf. Syst. **29**, 101614 (2020)
19. Mazmanian, M., Cohn, M., Dourish, P.: Dynamic reconfiguration in planetary exploration. MIS Q. **38**, 831–848 (2014)
20. Hupe, P., Hupe, P., Hill, M., Buffat, A.: Understanding Street-Level Bureaucracy. Policy Press, Bristol (2015)
21. de Boer, N., Raaphorst, N.: Automation and discretion: explaining the effect of automation on how street-level bureaucrats enforce. Public Manag. Rev. 1–21 (2021)
22. Lazarus, R.S., Folkman, S.: Stress, Appraisal, and Coping. Springer, New York (1984)
23. Folkman, S., Moskowitz, J.T.: Coping: pitfalls and promise. Annu. Rev. Psychol. **55**, 745–774 (2004)
24. Folkman, S.: Stress: appraisal and coping. In: Gellman, M.D., Turner, J.R. (eds.) Encyclopedia of Behavioral Medicine, pp. 1913–1915. Springer, New York, New York, NY (2013). https://doi.org/10.1007/978-1-4419-1005-9_215
25. De Guinea, A.O., Webster, J.: An investigation of information systems use patterns: technological events as triggers, the effect of time, and consequences for performance. Mis Quart. 1165–1188 (2013)
26. Fadel, K.J., Brown, S.A.: Information systems appraisal and coping: the role of user perceptions. Commun Assoc Inf Syst, 26, 6 (2010)
27. Bhattacherjee, A., Davis, C.J., Connolly, A.J., Hikmet, N.: User response to mandatory IT use: a coping theory perspective. Eur. J. Inf. Syst. **27**, 395–414 (2018)
28. Folkman, S.F., Lazarus, R.S.: If it changes it must be a process: study of emotion and coping during three stages of a college examination. J. Pers. Soc. Psychol. **48**, 150–170 (1985)
29. Beaudry, A., Pinsonneault, A.: Understanding user responses to information technology: a coping model of user adaptation. MIS Q. **29**, 493–524 (2005)
30. Bhattacherjee, A., Perols, J., Sanford, C.: Information technology continuance: a theoretic extension and empirical test. J. Comput. Inf. Syst. **49**, 17–26 (2008)
31. Elie-Dit-Cosaque, C.M., Straub, D.W.: Opening the black box of system usage: user adaptation to disruptive IT. Eur. J. Inf. Syst. **20**, 589–607 (2011)
32. Venkatesh, V., Morris, M.G., Davis, G.B., Davis, F.D.: User acceptance of information technology: toward a unified view. MIS Q. **27**, 425–478 (2003)
33. Brayne, S.: Big data surveillance: the case of policing. Am. Sociol. Rev. **82**, 977–1008 (2017)
34. Ratcliffe, J.H., Taylor, R.B., Fisher, R.: Conflicts and congruencies between predictive policing and the patrol officer's craft. Policing and Society 1–17 (2019)
35. Barlette, Y., Jaouen, A., Baillette, P.: Bring your own device (BYOD) as reversed IT adoption: insights into managers' coping strategies. Int. J. Inf. Manag. **56**, 102212 (2021)

36. Bowling, B., Iyer, S.: Automated policing: the case of body-worn video. Int. J. Law Context **15**, 140–161 (2019)
37. Carter, J.G., Grommon, E.: Officer perceptions of the impact of mobile broadband technology on police operations. Polic. Soc. **27**, 847–864 (2017)
38. Shaw, J.B., Barrett-Power, E.: A conceptual framework for assessing organization, work group, and individual effectiveness during and after downsizing. Hum. Relat. **50**, 109–127 (1997)
39. Orlikowski, W.J.: Improvising organizational transformation over time: a situated change perspective. Inf. Syst. Res. **7**, 63–92 (1996)
40. Wiig, A.: Secure the city, revitalize the zone: smart urbanization in Camden, New Jersey. Environ. Plann. C Polit. Space **36**, 403–422 (2018)
41. Moses, L.B., Chan, J.: Algorithmic prediction in policing: assumptions, evaluation, and accountability. Polic. Soc. **28**, 806–822 (2018)
42. Hannah-Moffat, K.: Algorithmic risk governance: big data analytics, race and information activism in criminal justice debates. Theor. Criminol. **23**, 453–470 (2019)
43. Kelloway, E.K.: Structural equation modelling in perspective. J. Organ. Behav. **16**, 215–224 (1995)
44. Hair, J.F., Hult, G.T.M., Ringle, C.M., Sarstedt, M.: A primer on partial least squares structural equation modeling (PLS-SEM). SAGE, Los Angeles (2022)
45. Avkiran, N.K., Ringle, C.M. (eds.): Partial Least Squares Structural Equation Modeling. ISORMS, vol. 267. Springer, Cham (2018). https://doi.org/10.1007/978-3-319-71691-6
46. Ringle, C.M., Wende, S., Becker, J.-M.: SmartPLS 3. SmartPLS GmbH (2015). http://www.smartpls.com

Supporting Smart Mobility in Smart Cities Through Autonomous Driving Buses: A Comparative Analysis

Christopher Latz, Veronika Vasileva, and Maria A. Wimmer(✉)

University of Koblenz, Universitätsstrasse 1, 56070 Koblenz, Germany
{latz,vvasileva,wimmer}@uni-koblenz.de

Abstract. As more and more people are moving to bigger cities, housing is becoming less and less available and cities are becoming more congested due to the high number of people and their cars. This leads to increased traffic, congestion, air pollution and degradation of quality of life. One approach to deal with this problem is to operate autonomously driving buses through artificial intelligence and internet of things. This paper compares four projects with autonomous driving buses. The aim is to find out, what added value such projects bring to smart cities. Findings indicate that well-implemented autonomous buses can reduce air and noise pollution, reduce congestion, and improve safety. In the paper, we identify enablers and challenges for autonomous driving from the four cases. While artificial intelligence and internet of things pose the biggest challenges in terms of scalability and interoperability, these disruptive technologies are also the biggest enablers, as these make the deployment of autonomous driving buses possible in the first place. The new data from the internet of things open up new possibilities for planning and operating autonomous busses.

Keywords: Smart city · Smart mobility · Autonomous bus · Artificial intelligence · Internet of things

1 Introduction

In recent years, more and more cities want and need to develop and transform themselves into a smart city through modernization in various areas and by applying new concepts of citizen involvement in order to expand their potential. This is one of the mission objectives of the Horizon Europe program, which started in 2021[1]. Expectations are that a city becomes more attractive and livable for citizens, businesses and other stakeholders. This is a particular problem in urban cities, where space is limited, and where the population continues to grow as people move into the cities [1]. The main consequence

[1] https://ec.europa.eu/info/research-and-innovation/funding/funding-opportunities/funding-programmes-and-open-calls/horizon-europe/missions-horizon-europe_en (last access: June 5, 2022).

Published by Springer Nature Switzerland AG 2022
M. Janssen et al. (Eds.): EGOV 2022, LNCS 13391, pp. 479–496, 2022.
https://doi.org/10.1007/978-3-031-15086-9_31

of this trend is that cities become congested, due to the high number of people, and also higher number of cars, as almost every citizen owns a car. This has great disadvantages for health, the environment and stress levels.

One approach to minimize this challenge is smart mobility. This concept, as e.g. proposed by Giffinger et al., is mainly used in regions with high population density to provide a sustainable, clean and efficient solution for all citizens and the city overall[2] [2, 3]. Autonomous public transport systems are one solution approach in the field [4]. In such a system, the transport vehicles such as a bus or tram are characterized by the use of computerized systems to make driving decisions. No human is used for driving, braking, accelerating, and observing the road. This is achieved through the use of artificial intelligence (AI), which is trained with data, receives input data from various sensors in the vehicle and on the road, and makes driving decisions based on this data. Solutions of autonomous driving are supplemented by Internet of Things (IoT) sensors that can continuously record and share data [5, 6]. However, AI and IoT are still new technologies with limited practical experience, and questions of AI safety and scalability across an entire city remain unanswered. Whether autonomous driving is a realistic solution for a smart city is therefore open [7].

While AI can act as an enabler and can greatly increase autonomy through automated decision making, AI is also a challenge. Key concerns and open questions are e.g. the minimum reliability requirements of a system when human life is completely entrusted to it, and whether this disruptive technology even has the potential to function on a large scale. This paper aims to investigate these issues and puts forward the following research questions (RQs) to identify the potentials of autonomous driving buses along a comparative analysis of four cases:

RQ 1: What value do autonomous driving buses contribute to smart city?
RQ 2: What are enablers and challenges for autonomous driving buses in smart city?

In order to answer these research questions, four projects in the field of autonomously driving buses were identified. The projects are located in Switzerland, Germany, and Italy and thus allow a good comparison, as they operate under similar conditions. The structure of this paper is as follows: Sect. 2 presents the theoretical foundation and outlines significant concepts of smart city and mobility for this paper. Section 3 outlines the selected autonomous driving bus projects and the selection criteria. The comparative analysis of the smart mobility projects is explained in Sect. 4, including the development of the comparison framework that is based on the criteria of Benevolo et al. In Sect. 5, enablers and challenges of autonomous driving are discussed along four literatures studied. Section 6 finally concludes the paper and gives an outlook on future research needs about autonomous public transportation systems.

[2] Ibid. A sustainable and climate neutral smart city is also part of the mission objectives of the Horizon Europe program.

2 Theoretical Foundations

The theoretical background is based on scientific literature and was conducted along systematic literature review based on Webster and Watson [8] and vom Brocke et al. [9]. The research included conceptualizing the topic on autonomous buses in the field of smart mobility as part of the concept of smart cities, and elaborating a basic understanding of Artificial Intelligence (AI) and Internet of Things (IoT). Based on this approach, a total of 81 scientific papers were read, of which 30 were used for the work.

2.1 Smart City

The term smart city evolved primarily in 1998, where various smart city approaches were initialized. The aim was to innovate the city by dealing with urban challenges with alternative concepts [10]. Since then, different scholars developed smart city concepts, resulting in multiple models and a multitude of definitions of smart cities. There is no uniform understanding or definition and no one is universally acknowledged [11].

Giffinger et al. define Smart City as *"a city well performing in a forward-looking way in these six characteristics, built on the 'smart' combination of endowments and activities of self-decisive, independent and aware citizens"* [3]. This definition puts focus on the citizen, on the innovation of the city as well as on the application of the smart city dimensions. Another definition by Harrison et al. describes a smart city as *"connecting the physical infrastructure, the IT infrastructure, the social infrastructure, and the business infrastructure to leverage the collective intelligence of the city"* [12]. This definition adds the social and the business determinants as well as the IT infrastructure. These are mandatory for creating public value from the services of a city.

These definitions emphasize a similar understanding of the term smart city, although they address different aspects. Overall, smart city combines the exploration and usage of information and communication technology (ICT), in particular disruptive technologies such as IoT [13], for improving *"the quality of the city life for all stakeholders"* [14]. This implies to create better living conditions and to integrate citizens in decision making processes of the city. Hence, creating a sustainable economic development of the city is a crucial intended achievement [14]. Therefore, the term "smarter" aggregates characteristics like more efficient, sustainable, livable, and equitable.

The concept of smart city is complex. Giffinger et al. identifies the following six dimensions: Smart People, Smart Economy, Smart Governance, Smart Mobility, Smart Environment and Smart Living [3]. Each dimension has its own definition. Since this paper focuses on smart mobility, only this definition is elaborated further.

2.2 Smart Mobility

Because Smart Mobility is in its early stages of development, the term is not uniquely defined in literature. Allam et al. define smart mobility as a broad term, which emphasizes infusing technologies into urban infrastructure and the effect on how people interact with the urban environment (cited in [15]). According to Yigitcanlar (cited in [15]), smart mobility is substantial for a smart city plan. Moreover, smart mobility is associated with intelligent transportation systems. These systems are specialized to collect, store and process data and to provide knowledge, performance and assessment of the policies and initiatives, which are integrated in smart mobility [15]. Urban areas also benefit from the connection to innovative ideas facilitated by IoT [2].

The general understanding of smart mobility is a form of transportation, which is efficient, sustainable, and inclusive. Hence, further definitions of the term smart transportation evolved. The importance of smart mobility relates to different aspects, such as improving the efficiency of traveling, and reducing crashes caused by humans, and reducing pollution [16, 17]. This implies that autonomous driving is reached by the deployment of the newest technologies, where people, institutions and technologies are integrated and interconnected [18].

According to Giffinger et al., the six dimensions of smart city are interconnected and influence each other. Thus, smart mobility can have a strong impact on smart environment, where the goals are to reduce pollution, preserve and protect natural conditions, and use resources sustainably [3]. This connection becomes particularly clear in Sect. 0, which describes the project See-Meile, which is in a green district in Berlin to protect nature and the environment, and to make it more liveable.

2.3 Disruptive Technologies AI and IoT

Disruptive technologies have the potential to make the government in a city act more effective and efficient [19] by dramatically changing the processes and operations in a particular area of the public sector [20]. Disruptive technologies are, alongside the use of established ICT, a new and important part of Government 3.0 [21]. According to Pereira et al., AI and IoT are particularly suitable for making automatic decisions based on collected data [22].

Artificial Intelligence (AI) is defined by Li and Du as "a variety of human intelligent behaviors, such as perception, memory, emotion, judgment, reasoning, proof, recognition, understanding, communication, design, thinking, learning, forgetting, creating, and so on, which can be realized artificially by machine, system, or network" [23]. AI therefore stands for many intelligent behaviors that adapt human behavior, become adaptive and can act autonomously [24]. It imitates intelligent human thinking but is many times faster in weighing and calculating many variables, because a computer has more computing power than a human brain [25]. A critical influencing factor for AI is learning through Machine Learning (ML). With ML, algorithms make it possible to learn by patterns and regularities of examples and can be applied to unknown data to predict relevant results under the right conditions [26]. The chance and possibility for automated decision making arises from the increasing amount of data collected by IoT capable devices [26]. Through increasing intelligence of systems and computers, it is possible to make a computer learn and adapt and make automatic decisions based on provided data [27]. This disruptive technology can, under certain conditions, be used in autonomous vehicles and enrich the public transport network [25]. The advantages of AI in autonomous vehicles are the speed of data processing and the uninterrupted attention of the system.

According to Porru et al., **Internet of Things** (IoT) refers to networked telematics, which is employed to improve the quality of the public transportation services. IoT technologies enable an easy and effective collection of data. The information flow network includes the things and devices [2]. According to Pereira, the combination of IoT and other disruptive technologies make it possible to achieve more effective public services. This combination allows an improvement of all services in the city, e.g., digital government and automated decision making [22].

In the next section, we introduce four cases of autonomously driving buses that embark on AI and IoT in different smart mobility initiatives.

3 Introduction to Four Cases of Autonomously Driving Buses

This section outlines four selected smart mobility projects with autonomous driving buses in the cities of Sitten, Berlin, Hamburg, and Turin. The projects are from Europe and were chosen because of relevant information available online. The research was performed in summer 2021. The projects are described along their objective, their disruptive technologies, and how (and which) stakeholders are involved. The information on the autonomous bus projects was collected via publicly accessible web sources.

Project PostAuto in Sitten, Switzerland. The objective of the project PostAuto, initiated in 2014, in Sitten is to create a smart and sustainable mobility by using autonomously driving shuttles[3]. The goal is to achieve a diversification of mobility offerings by covering the needs of the passengers. Nevertheless, a clear objective is to expand and not to replace the public transportation. The project tries to fill identified gaps of the transportation system, for example, where normal buses cannot drive safely, like on narrow roads. Two autonomously driving smart shuttles were tested in Sitten as a part of the mobility laboratory. A route of 1,5 km was chosen for the test phase. The bus drives fully electrically, with a maximum speed of 20 km/h and a charging time of 5–8 h. In total, the vehicle is capable to transport 11 passengers, including barrier free access[4]. During the test phase, an attendant was present in the bus to monitor the transportation of the passengers and to interfere in case of emergency. In the bus, an emergency button can be effected that causes the bus to stop immediately.

The stakeholders involved in this project are the subsidiary of swiss post, the start-up company BestMile[5], Navya as the developer of the shuttles, Siemens Mobility AG providing support to the project, and the citizens of Sitten as service users.

Sensors and cameras are used to determine the exact position to support decision making for the navigation of the shuttles. Furthermore, novel infrared cameras are used to increase safety in driving operations. The cameras are mounted on a lightening tower and are able to detect vehicles entering the traffic observation circle from a distance of 50 m. Additionally, IoT technology is used to connect the status and schedule information of the shuttle bus to a mobile app for the citizens. Through this app, interested citizens

[3] https://www.swissinfo.ch/ger/pilotprojekt_autonom-fahrende-postautos-in-sitten/41848488 (last retrieved 30.07.2021).

[4] https://www.postauto.ch/de/projekt-uvrier (last retrieved 30.07.2021).

[5] https://press.zf.com/press/de/releases/release_32320.html (last access: June 5, 2022).

can see the current position of the shuttle, possible fault massages concerning the bus service, and also have a booking option to order the shuttle service.

Project See-Meile in Berlin, Germany. The objectives of the project "See-Meile" are to contribute to an efficient and sustainable urban transportation and to gain findings and experience for making the city smarter. Innovative technology of automated driving shall be tested on a real route with mixed traffic. Also, technology shall be brought closer to the citizens to become familiar with the technology and to adapt to it[6].

A highly automated minibus is tested on the public roads in the green district Alt-Tegel, Berlin. The area covers forests and offers a good quality of life. The minibus drives a total distance of 600 m and accommodates 6 passengers at a time. Citizens could use the service on weekdays. On the weekends, the usage was free of charge.

The main seven stakeholders are: The city of Berlin is the coordinator of the research project. Their aims are to promote projects with the focus on innovative transport technologies to enable better planning and organization of mobility and automated connective driving in the future. Another stakeholder is the Berliner Verkehrsbetriebe with the aim to improve the comfortability, punctuality, and environmental sustainability and to reduce costs[7]. Easy mile operates as the manufacturer and deliverer of the driverless minibus shuttle[8]. The company aims at providing the latest technologies of autonomous driving for passengers and thereby improving the public transport system. Zentrum Technik und Gesellschaft from TU Berlin is a competence center of interdisciplinary research[9], which conducts research on the acceptance of the autonomous minibus by the citizens. The district office Reinickendorf of Berlin creates the frame for testing the autonomous minibus on public roads under real conditions[10].

Different disruptive technologies are used to drive the autonomous vehicle. The company easy mile uses on-board machine learning and deep learning to adapt the vehicle's behavior and to improve the driving capabilities without human attendance. For example, this means adaptation to distinguish lampposts and pedestrians. Additionally, the minibuses use radars, cameras, and sensors with real time data to get a 360° view of the surrounding. Also, they have implemented a vehicle agnostic software.

Project Heat in Hamburg, Germany. The Hamburg Electric Autonomous Transportation (HEAT) project is an electric autonomous bus in Hamburg's port district. The project started in 2017 and is scheduled to be implemented by 2021, with increasing demands on the bus from year to year. In total, the bus can transport up to seven people over a test distance of 1.8 km with a maximum speed of 25 km/h[11].

---

6 https://www.emo-berlin.de/de/projekte/see-meile/ (last access: June 5, 2022).

7 Berliner Verkehrsbetriebe: https://www.bvg.de/de (last access: June 5, 2022).

8 https://www.easymile.com/ (last access: June 5, 2022).

9 https://www.tu-berlin.de/ztg/menue/startseite_ztg/ (last access: June 5, 2022).

10 https://www.berlin.de/ba-reinickendorf/aktuelles/pressemitteilungen/2019/pressemitteilung.838170.php (last access: June 5, 2022).

11 https://www.hamburg.de/pressearchiv-fhh/10120472/2017-12-20-bwvi-projekt-heat/ (last access: June 5, 2022).

The objective of the project is to provide a sustainable and reliable solution for public transport. It is a pilot project of the main responsible stakeholder, the HOCHBAHN Hamburg AG, to demonstrate that by the year 2021 fully automated, autonomously driving minibuses can be used safely in urban road traffic[12]. As this is primarily a pilot project with lighthouse character, the objectives are mainly to gain experience with the handling of autonomous vehicles, to derive requirements for this transport technology, to develop the technology and increase the acceptance of the technology, as well as to clarify whether autonomous vehicles are suitable for public transport at all.

The main stakeholders in this project are Hamburg's HOCHBAHN AG, which acts as the operator and has been responsible for the bus and rail network in Hamburg for over 100 years. The project is further accompanied by the Deutsches Zentrum für Luft- und Raumfahrt, which determines user requirements and provides guidance for the design of vehicles and transport services. It evaluates the passenger acceptance. The Behörde für Verkehr und Mobilitätswende handles transportation planning through the Landesbetrieb Straßen, Brücken und Gewässer (LSBG) and implements and operates the necessary road infrastructure systems for an autonomous project. The LSBG operates also another project in Hamburg, the Teststrecke für das automatisierte und vernetzte Fahren (TAVF) project[13]. A defined stretch of Hamburg's city center will be equipped with special devices and sensors to test and enable the autonomous operation of cars in this area.

The used disruptive technologies include AI and IoT. The AI on board the bus takes care of the control of the bus and the evaluation of received and perceived data. The responsibilities of this AI are to distinguish passers-by from traffic lights and to make the right decisions. IoT is applied because the bus is equipped with a lot of technology that perceives its environment and communicates with it. There are three critical areas for the successful implementation of the project. Firstly, the components of the bus including sensors technology such as radar lidar and cameras, as well as very accurate maps of the route. Secondly, the control center technology for external monitoring that checks that everything is okay with the bus, so there is a permanent connection, monitoring and perception. The last critical component is the track. Special active and passive sensors must be installed with which the bus can communicate for driving information. This is the responsibility of the LSGB with the TAVF project.

Project Olli in Turin, Italy. Olli is an autonomously driving minibus from the company LocalMotors. This company manufactures the buses on up to 80% 3D printed parts and sells and operates them in interested cities. Turin won a challenge and was chosen as the city because of its very good conditions. The bus was operated and tested in the period January to May 2020 on the campus of the International Training Centre of the International Labour Organization (ITCILO). The bus can transport a maximum of 12 passengers at a speed of 25 kmh. The range is 50 km[14].

---

12 https://www.hochbahn.de/de/projekte/das-projekt-heat (last access: June 5, 2022).

13 https://tavf.hamburg/ (last access: June 5, 2022).

14 https://localmotors.com/mobility-and-innovation-the-deployment-of-the-olli-autonomous-shuttle-starts-in-turin/ (last access: June 5, 2022).

The main objective of the project is to test whether the vision of a global solution is feasible to implement a shift in mobility to self-driving transport vehicles. Sustainability is a key factor, as the impact on the environment is lower due to the use of electrical energy. The buses need to be easy to use for everyone, also for people with disabilities. The ultimate goal is to take the responsibility away from the driver of the bus, i.e., from the human being, and to transfer it to the machine.

In this project, a collaboration of different stakeholders takes place in order to realize it. Local Motors acts as provider, operator, and developer of the electric and self-driving bus Olli. Reale Mutua is one of the main sponsors and supports the development and acts as insurer, providing third party insurance for potential damage by the self-driving car. ITCILO is a hub for technological innovation, skills development and future entrepreneurship, and Olli is a driving force to kick-start change in sustainable mobility. Furthermore, feedback is collected and evaluated here about the project.

The used disruptive technologies in the projects are AI and IoT. These two technologies are strongly interlinked in this project. A cloud-based AI in the bus Olli, IBM Watson, is used via IoT.This is adapted and learns about road behaviour.[15]

In the next section, we introduce the framework for comparing the four cases and the enablers and challenges identified in the cases.

4 Comparative Analysis of Cases

The comparative analysis is built on the review of relevant scientific literature [8, 9], which was applied in Sect. 2. Based on this approach, a total of 81 scientific papers were read, of which 30 were used for the work. For the comparative analysis, the taxonomy put forward by Benevolo et al. [17] built the basis to develop a conceptual framework to guide the data analysis of the four autonomous bus projects.

4.1 Comparative Analysis Framework

The taxonomy of Benevolo et al. was chosen as the conceptual framework guiding the data analysis for the research [17]. The authors identified the six most important benefits of smart mobility (i.e. reducing air pollution, reducing traffic congestion, increasing people's safety, reducing noise pollution, improving transfer speed and reducing transfer costs) along with the measure of the intensity of the information and communication technologies (ICT) used [17], and they identified various actors in the literature and in different projects. This resulted in a taxonomy with three main columns: (i) smart mobility actors, who are the main agents moving the smart initiatives, (ii) the use and intensity of ICT used in the initiatives, and (iii) the benefits of the cases on the smart mobility goals mentioned above [17].

---

[15] https://www.sustainable-bus.com/smart-mobility/olli-debuts-in-italy-turin-deploys-the-3d-printed-driverless-shuttle/, https://www.ibm.com/blogs/industries/olli-ai-and-iot-autonomous-bus/, https://www.ibm.com/watson (last access: June 5, 2022).

The taxonomy is applied to evaluate the projects according to their characteristics and technologies to achieve the objectives. To adjust the framework to autonomous driving buses, eight criteria were added to indicate relevant involved agents (i), which are derived from literature review on smart mobility (see Sect. 2.2): *Electric vehicles* criterion requires the use of electric vehicles in transport operations. This reduces pollution and noise and lowers transfer costs for citizens. The second criterion is *Vehicles with automated driving* and uses the disruptive technologies AI and IoT to drive computer-controlled. The accurate calculations and fast responses of AI can reduce congestion and increase traffic safety. *Open to public* reviews accessibility of the autonomously driving buses to the public, whether registration is required or not. If this point is given, all objectives of smart mobility are covered, because this is the primary goal of smart mobility. *Area-wide transport network* checks whether a wide road network is possible for autonomously driving buses or whether these are bound to a specific route – aiming to avoid congestion, increase transfer speed and safety. *Street sensors* are used to check whether the streets of the city are equipped with the appropriate sensors for autonomously driving buses. The sensors increase safety and transfer speed. *Integrated ticket system* enables tickets to be purchased online/mobile, saving time when entering the bus and reducing costs, as no physical receipt is needed anymore. In addition, *Information service for citizen* as app provides information to the citizen, such as timetable, arrival, loading status of the bus, etc. This can help avoid congestion and increase travel speed, as citizens can select the appropriate buses in advance and access the data live. *Monitoring by administration* indicates that the autonomously driving buses are monitored by a human authority. This enables fast reaction and intervention in case of emergency, and it increases safety and can contribute to noise reduction. The resulting framework is shown in Table 1.

The adopted ICT (column (ii) of Benevolo et al.'s framework) by each initiative and in each category of agents is rated 0, 0.5 or 1 points. 0 stands for not implemented, 0.5 for partial and 1 for full implementation. The value is multiplied by the benefits according to Benevolo et al. (iii), which are indicated with 'x' if realized by the respective agent, with each benefit having a multiplier of 1. Thus, the multiplier per category can be a maximum of 6. Each row in Table 1 shows in the last column the points of the project for the agent. Finally, all values for each project are summed up.

Points for each project along each agent were awarded by the first two authors of the paper in a two-stage process. First, the two authors evaluated the cases individually on the basis of each criterion and assigned points. In the second step, the results were compared, discussed, and reflected by the two authors in order to achieve a result that was as objective as possible. The third author finally acted as reviewer. Each category was applied to each project. In this process, the intensive knowledge about the four projects, which was acquired in the course of this work, was of particular importance.

5 Comparative Analysis of Cases

Table 1 shows the results of the analysis of the different influencing agents of autonomous driving buses in relation to the objectives of smart mobility. The last column indicates the points awarded to each individual project in each category. The last rows visualize the score of each benefit by project and so indicates strengths and weaknesses.

A closer look at the various benefits of smart mobility in Table 1 reveals that the PostAuto fulfils all the benefits. It received a point in the first category by using a completely electrical minibus. For the second agent it also received a point for driving completely autonomous with the help of different sensors. PostAuto offers free access for everyone and therefore scored a point in the third category. A special feature of the PostAuto is that it has no fixed route network and can choose its route for passengers as required. This feature was awarded a point in the fourth category. The minibus uses only its own sensors in the bus and no road sensors, so it received only half a point. The use of the bus is supported by a comprehensive app, which allows citizens to buy tickets and access status information about the bus. As a result, the project received one point each in categories six and eight. In the test phase, until it demonstrated its reliability, the minibus was controlled and monitored by an employee, who was always on board, but not by a central monitoring office. Therefore, the project receives half a point for agent seven. The only slight weaknesses are in increased safety (4,5/5), reduction of noise pollution (2,5/3) and improving transfer speed (3,5/4). This is due to the fact that the PostAuto project does not make use of road sensors, which could communicate with the vehicle and exchange data on the roads and traffic situation. This could increase speed and safety. Furthermore, monitoring is only carried out by a staff member on the bus, who intervenes in emergency and there is no central monitoring. However, the bus itself is equipped with very good sensors for safe traffic and has already been tested extensively since 2016. Furthermore, it is accessible to the public and offers an app for information retrieval and ticket booking. Overall with PostAuto, the city of Sitten is pursuing a serious and sustainable path for the development of its city and its citizens.

Another good project, but with other strengths and weaknesses, is HEAT. Particularly noteworthy here is the use of road sensors to support the autonomously driving bus to include more data for automatic decision making. The LSBG, which is one of the main stakeholders of HEAT, also handles another project in Hamburg, the "Test track for automated and connected driving"[16]. The projects complement and interact with each other, generating synergies. As a result, the bus is already being tested in the real road network among other vehicles.

[16] https://tavf.hamburg/ (last access: June 5, 2022).

Table 1. Evaluating the benefits of the four autonomous driving buses

Assessments									
		Adopted ICTs	Benefits in Smart Mobility						
Categories / Agents	Project	0, 0,5 or 1 point	Reduction of pollution	Reduction of congestion	Increased safe-ty	Reduction noise pollution	Improving transfer speed	Reducing transfer costs	Points
Electric vehicles	PostAuto	1	X			X		X	3/3
	See-Meile	1							3/3
	HEAT	1							3/3
	Olli	1							3/3
Vehicles with automated driving	PostAuto	1		X	X				2/2
	See-Meile	1							2/2
	HEAT	1							2/2
	Olli	1							2/2
Open to public	PostAuto	1	X	X	X	X		X	5/5
	See-Meile	1							5/5
	HEAT	0,5							2,5/5
	Olli	0,5							2,5/5
Area-wide transport net-work	PostAuto	1		X	X		X		3/3
	See-Meile	0,5							1,5/3
	HEAT	0,5							1,5/3
	Olli	0							0/3
Street sensors	PostAuto	0,5			X		X		1/2
	See-Meile	0,5							1/2
	HEAT	1							2/2
	Olli	0							0/2
Integrated ticket system	PostAuto	1					X	X	2/2
	See-Meile	1							2/2
	HEAT	1							2/2
	Olli	1							2/2
Monitoring by administration	PostAuto	0,5			X	X			1/2
	See-Meile	0,5							1/2
	HEAT	1							2/2
	Olli	0							0/2
Information service for citizen (app)	PostAuto	1		X			X		2/2
	See-Meile	0							0/2
	HEAT	1							2/2
	Olli	0							0/2
Score of each project for each benefit	PostAuto		2/2	4/4	4/5	2,5/3	3,5/4	3/3	
	See-Meile		2/2	2,5/4	3,5/5	2,5/3	2/4	3/3	
	HEAT		1,5/2	3/4	4/5	2,5/3	3,5/4	2,5/3	
	Olli		1,5/2	1,5/4	1,5/5	1,5/3	1/4	2,5/3	

This collaboration between projects and stakeholders shows that the city of Hamburg is striving to expand the area of smart mobility and further transforms it towards the smart city. The project is supported and funded by the Federal Ministry for the Environment, Nature Conservation and Nuclear Safety, which in turn reinforces the lighthouse character for Germany. The project, as it is still in the testing phase, is behind its capabilities and has slight weaknesses in reduction of pollution (1,5/2), congestion avoidance (3/4) and safety (4/5). This is due to the fact that public access is currently only possible in advance with registration and the route network is fixed on two routes. Thus, not many citizens can use the service and the streets remain full of private cars. However, the safety provided by the bus is very high, as it uses the road sensors for communication, an employee is always present and there is central monitoring by a control centre.

The Olli project operates on a university campus to the exclusion of the public. The barrier-free and free access to the bus is positive, but there is no support from road sensors, on-board personnel, or central monitoring. It is questionable whether the project can be successfully implemented in a street environment.

Table 2 summarizes the scoring of the different projects in a compact and clear manner. This allows a qualitative comparison of the projects based on the points they scored. It is striking that PostAuto and HEAT scored at least 80% of the points and are therefore already good autonomous driving projects in their current form. The HEAT project in particular, which is a lighthouse project in Hamburg, is achieving this goal well, as is the PostAuto in Sitten.

Table 2. Evaluation results of the autonomous bus projects

Score/Project	PostAuto	See-Meile	HEAT	Olli
Points	19/21	15,5/21	17/21	9,5/21
Percentage	90,4%	73,8%	80,95%	45,2%

The next sections investigates enablers and challenges of autonomous driving buses.

6 Enablers and Challenges of Autonomous Driving Buses

Based on the knowledge gained about the four autonomous bus projects and the findings of the intensive literature research, enablers and challenges for the use of these projects were sought. For this purpose, intensive literature research was conducted in the field of disruptive technologies such as AI and IoT in the area of autonomous driving and smart mobility following [8, 9]. Keyword search was carried out in the literature for enablers and challenges in the context of autonomous driving. In a second step, this was expanded to include the keywords AI and IoT. These criteria were used to ensure that thematically relevant and specific literature was selected that was highly significant for the topic of this paper. Literature of Davidsson et al. [6], Porru et al. [2], Yaqoob et al. [29], and Campbell et al. [30] turned out to be significant sources for the identification of enablers and challenges in the field of autonomous driving.

The findings from the literature analysis on enablers and challenges are presented in Table 3. Along each key literature, the enablers and challenges are spotted in columns three and four. The goal was to identify the most important enablers and challenges for the type of technology/project in order to facilitate the planning of future projects. As a final step, the identified enablers and challenges were put into context with the selected projects to determine whether and how these are implemented or addressed in practice. The application of the identified enablers and challenges is indicated in green rows if the autonomous bus projects full comply with the identified enablers/are fully affected by the challenges listed by the authors. Yellow rows represent partial agreement/being affected. Red for not being affected at all did not occur in the context of this evaluation.

Interestingly, literature focuses more on challenges than on enablers. According to Davidsson et al. [6] and Porru et al. [2], the challenges for the IoT in smart mobility and public transport lie primarily in the use of data. Davidsson et al. stress the integrity and security of the data, which must be protected from external access and influence. Furthermore, the data must be systematically collected so that it can be used. This concerns citizens when they want to access information about the public transport network, but also the use for planning, creating business models and the scalability of the public transport system to larger scales [6]. Porru et al. have a similar view, as their challenge is to define standard metrics for route evaluation, dynamic optimal routes, and planning. For these challenges, Porru et al. also consider data collection and management as important challenges [2]. Both papers see correct planning and operation as the main enabler or opportunity. IoT allows unplanned situations to be better managed and maintenance to be improved. Real-time monitoring and transmission of data is a key enabler for autonomous driving. Furthermore, the new data stream collected by the IoT enables better planning of road networks and detection of traffic congestion, thus contributing significantly to the realization of autonomous driving buses [2, 6].

With regard to the use of AI in autonomous driving vehicles, Yaqoob et al. identify precisely this technology as a challenge as well [29]. They acknowledge the potential of this disruptive technology but point out the challenges of not having sufficient real-time data analysis solutions. Furthermore, they mention the often very complex datasets of heterogeneous types. This challenges interoperability, i.e. data that cannot be used in other ecosystems of smart city. Standards would need to be defined for the collection and management of data.

The convergence of edge computing and AI is cited as an enabler. This is an interesting concept, as the data collected should be processed and interpreted on the spot by AI [29]. The biggest challenge is also the biggest enabler according to Yaqoob et al. This contrasts with other scientific sources and the Olli project, where the autonomous driving bus performs its calculations via IBM Watson[17], a cloud AI[18]. Deep learning solutions is listed as another enabler. Deep learning is a subarea of machine learning and is an essential component of an AI that learns and continues to develop[19]. This is particularly important in road traffic, as new situations are constantly arising and the autonomous bus cannot only drive according to pre-programmed decisions [29].

[17] https://www.ibm.com//watson (last access: June 5, 2022).

[18] https://www.ibm.com/blogs/internet-of-things/olli-ai/ (last access: June 5, 2022).

[19] https://datasolut.com/machine-learning-vs-deep-learning/ (last access: June 5, 2022).

Table 3. Enabler and challenges of autonomous driving identified in literature

Authors	Disruptive technology	Enablers/ Opportunities	Challenges
Davidsson et al. (2016) [6]	Internet of Things in public transport	**Operations:** Manage unplanned situations; Self-driving vehicles; Maintenance **Planning**: Collection of traveler/vehicle/traffic data **Travelling**: Real-time delay/vehicle information; Ticket-buying support	Business models Privacy and integrity issues Security Interoperability Scalability Usability Data collection Deployment
Full compliance of cases		PostAuto, HEAT	PostAuto, See-Meile, HEAT, Olli
Partial matches of cases		See-Meile, Olli	
Porru et al. (2020) [2]	Smart Mobility / Public transport with focus on Internet of Things	**Planning**: opportunities of interest to strategic transport planners **Operations**: opportunities of interest to operators	Definition of standard metrics for route evaluation Dynamic optimal route Planning and programming public investments in transport Data collection & management
Full compliance of cases		PostAuto, HEAT	PostAuto, See-Meile, HEAT, Olli
Partial matches of cases		See-Meile, Olli	
Yaqoob et al. (2020) [29]	Artificial Intelligence for autonomous driving cars	Convergence of edge computing and AI Data fusion and deep learning-based solutions	AI for autonomous driving cars Lack of real-time data analysis solutions Complex heterogeneous datasets
Full compliance of cases		See-Meile, HEAT, Olli	
Partial matches of cases		PostAuto	PostAuto, See-Meile, HEAT, Olli
Campbell et al. (2010) [30]	Autonomous driving in general	Vehicle safety systems Intelligent highway and roadway infrastructure Fully autonomous driving	System integration Prediction and trust Learning Interaction with other agents Scaling up
Full compliance of cases		HEAT	PostAuto, See-Meile, HEAT, Olli
Partial matches of cases		PostAuto, See-Meile, Olli	

Campbell et al. also indicate prediction and trust as a challenge [30], i.e. trust in the autonomous vehicle to recognize and calculate all variables in good time and to make the correct decision. AI must not have any lapses and make mistakes. Along this, Learning and Interaction with other agents are further challenges that come into play. The system must continue to develop and adapt and must also be able to cope with new and unfamiliar situations. The challenge of scalability is also mentioned here [30]. All four projects are carried out on a small scale and are still being tested and trialed, as scaling to a large city traffic is very difficult and probably brings more risks than benefits at this point in time. Finally, Campbell et al. indicate car safety systems and intelligent road networks and infrastructure as important enablers [30]. Both are being implemented in the project HEAT[20], for example, through numerous camera and proximity sensors in the bus, as well as IoT-enabled sensors in the street to enable a constant flow, exchange, and collection of information.

Noticeably all projects make use of AI and IoT. Project HEAT, through its collaboration with TAVF, is taking full advantage of the possibility of using road sensors to increase safety. Furthermore, all projects are also almost completely affected by the challenges. Due to their early development and test phase, all four projects face challenges in the areas of scalability, data collection, definition of standards and system integration. This indicates that the projects are still in the early stage of development and are aware of their potentials as well as of their challenges.

7 Conclusion and Outlook

The analysis of the different agents of the autonomous bus projects in the context of the benefits of smart mobility has shown that projects like the PostAuto and HEAT can generate added value for the citizens of a city and contribute to the context of a smart city. Furthermore, the findings of the paper have shown that autonomous buses are not only good projects in terms of smart mobility, but also in terms of smart environment. The use of electric buses can reduce noise and air pollution, which helps to keep the city natural, cleaner, and therefore more livable and healthier for the citizens. They also increase safety in the transport network through the combined use of AI and IoT. Furthermore, the data collected through the use of IoT sensors in the road and in the vehicles will result in new applications such as the planning of new route networks and more effective deployment of new bus routes. This leads to a reduction in costs and increased transport speed for the citizens. At the same time, the deployment of an effective autonomous bus network can avoid congestion, as fewer citizens use their cars. This results in a quality-of-life improvement for the citizen on a social level and a sustainable solution is implemented for the city. This answers the first research question.

To answer the second research question, the literature review on enablers and challenges in the context of autonomous buses and the disruptive technologies of AI and IoT has revealed that the scalability of IoT and AI is increasingly seen as a problem. According to the literature, these are technologies with great potential for autonomous driving, but it is still challenging to implement them on a large scale for large cities in large numbers. Another identified challenge, which is connected to scalability, is data. Data is about the collection, analysis, management, storage type and use of data. Each city and company employ different approaches and choose their own standards and formats. However, a uniform standard for data and frameworks for the implementation of autonomously driving buses must be applied in order to ensure interoperability and scalability.

Another critical challenge is trust in AI. This is about the ability to make the right decisions in critical situations, to react to new circumstances and to learn. If this cannot be guaranteed without errors, the realization of autonomously driving buses is not possible.

[20] https://www.hochbahn.de/de/projekte/das-projekt-heat (last access: June 5, 2022).

Proper data management is therefore critical. Hence, the concept of data governance would lend itself to the unified control, maintenance, management, and protection of data against manipulation, which can lead to negative consequences in machine learning processes. Just as AI and IoT are seen as major challenges, these are also major enablers for autonomous driving. Their use can greatly improve the planning and organization of the road network and public transport by providing a new stream of real-time data. This can also be used to increase the safety of the vehicles by transmitting current status information, adjusting maintenance intervals and alerting to unforeseen events. At the same time, machine learning enables a learning process that makes the vehicle safer with each ride. Furthermore, the government is of course an enabler through a transparent and open information policy on autonomous driving buses.

As an outlook for future research, the interoperability and scalability of the disruptive technologies AI and IoT used in autonomous driving buses is of great importance. This paper has shown that the analyzed projects can become a central foundation for a future autonomous public transport system, but only if a uniform data management and transfer of the findings to other means of public transport is possible. The more autonomous vehicles are deployed, the better an autonomous transport system will work. Hence, frameworks and standards need to be developed in this field to facilitate implementation and deployment by cities.

Literature review has also revealed a serious gap about security in autonomous vehicles which is receiving too little attention. Especially in a future, where buses will be driven and controlled exclusively digitally, the risk of significant damage through digital intrusion and malware is high. AI decisions are based on data. If this data is influenced, biased and incorrect decisions can be made. At this point, secure data processing, for example through data governance, must be ensured. If the appropriate security for autonomous vehicles cannot be guaranteed, this is hardly a vital option.

Finally, the comparative analysis has shown valuable insights into projects such as PostAuto and HEAT, which fulfil the benefits of smart mobility according to Benevolo et al. However, this is only a special consideration of the benefits of smart mobility. In a smart city, other areas also play an important role, which can benefit from the services and advantages of autonomously driving buses. The Smart Sustainable City Framework by De Azambuja, Pereira and Krimmer can be used to identify further values in the areas of social, economic, governance and urban infrastructure [28]. This is subject of further research.

References

1. Falconer, G., Mitchell, S.: Smart city framework: a systematic process for enabling smart+connected communities. CISCO Internet Bus. Solut. Gr. 1–11 (2012)
2. Porru, S., Misso, F.E., Pani, F.E., Repetto, C.: Smart mobility and public transport: opportunities and challenges in rural and urban areas. J. Traffic Transp. Eng. **7**(1), 88–97 (2020). https://doi.org/10.1016/j.jtte.2019.10.002
3. Giffinger, R., Fertner, C., Kalasek, R., Milanovic, N.P.: Smart cities: ranking of European medium-sized cities, Vienna (2007). http://www.smartcity-ranking.eu/download/city_ranking_final.pdf. Accessed 5 June 2022

4. Fayazi, S.A., Vahidi, A.: Vehicle-in-the-loop (VIL) verification of a smart city intersection control scheme for autonomous vehicles. In: Conference on Control Technology and Applications, pp. 1575–1580 (2017). https://doi.org/10.1109/CCTA.2017.8062681
5. Fleetwood, J.: Public health, ethics, and autonomous vehicles. Am. J. Public Health **107**(4), 532–537 (2017). https://doi.org/10.2105/AJPH.2016.303628
6. Davidsson, P., Hajinasab, B., Holmgren, J., Jevinger, Å., Persson, J.A.: The fourth wave of digitalization and public transport: opportunities and challenges. Sustainability **8**(12), 1248 (2016). https://doi.org/10.3390/su8121248
7. Keller, P.: Autonomous vehicles, artificial intelligence, and the law. J. Robot. Artif. Intell. Law **1**(2), 101–110 (2018)
8. Webster, J., Watson, R.T.: Analyzing the past to prepare for the future: writing a literature review. MIS Q. Manag. Inf. Syst. **26**(2), xiii–xxiii (2002)
9. vom Brocke, J., Simons, A., Riemer, K., Niehaves, B., Plattfaut, R., Cleven, A.: Standing on the shoulders of giants: challenges and recommendations of literature search in information systems research. Commun. Assoc. Inf. Syst. **37**(9), 205–224 (2015). https://doi.org/10.17705/1cais.03709
10. Anthopoulos, L.G.: Defining smart city architecture for sustainability. In: Electronic Government and Electronic Participation Conference, pp. 140–147 (2015). https://doi.org/10.3233/978-1-61499-570-8-140
11. Cocchia, A.: Smart and digital city: a systematic literature review. In: Dameri, R.P., Rosenthal-Sabroux, C. (eds.) Smart City. PI, pp. 13–43. Springer, Cham (2014). https://doi.org/10.1007/978-3-319-06160-3_2
12. Harrison, C., et al.: Foundations for smarter cities. IBM J. Res. Dev. **54**(4), 1–16 (2010). https://doi.org/10.1147/JRD.2010.2048257
13. Costa, C., Santos, M.Y.: BASIS: a big data architecture for smart cities. In: Proceedings of 2016 SAI Computing Conference, pp. 1247–1256 (2016). https://doi.org/10.1109/SAI.2016.7556139
14. Dameri, R.P., Benevolo, C.: Governing smart cities: an empirical analysis. Soc. Sci. Comput. Rev. **34**(6), 693–707 (2016). https://doi.org/10.1177/0894439315611093
15. Bazzan, A.L.C., Klügl, F.: Introduction to intelligent systems in traffic and transportation. Synth. Lect. Artif. Intell. Mach. Lear. **7**, 1–37 (2013)
16. Bıyık, C., et al.: Smart mobility adoption: a review of the literature. J. Open Innov. Technol. Mark. Complex. **7**(146), 1–20 (2021). https://doi.org/10.3390/joitmc7020146
17. Rovenský, J., Payer, J., Herold, M.: Smart mobility in smart city - action taxonomy, ICT intensity and public benefits. In: Rovenský, J., Payer, J., Herold, M. (eds.) Dictionary of Rheumatology, pp. 327–340. Springer, Cham (2016). https://doi.org/10.1007/978-3-319-21335-4_20
18. Yigitcanlar, T., Kamruzzaman, M.: Smart cities and mobility: does the smartness of Australian cities lead to sustainable commuting patterns? J. Urban Technol. **26**(2), 21–46 (2019). https://doi.org/10.1080/10630732.2018.1476794
19. Cordella, A., Bonina, C.M.: A public value perspective for ICT enabled public sector reforms: a theoretical reflection. Gov. Inf. Q. **29**(4), 512–520 (2012). https://doi.org/10.1016/j.giq.2012.03.004
20. Kostoff, R.N., Boylan, R., Simons, G.R.: Disruptive technology roadmaps. Technol. Forecast. Soc. Change **71**(1–2), 141–159 (2004). https://doi.org/10.1016/S0040-1625(03)00048-9
21. Ronzhyn, A., et al.: Scientific foundations training and entrepreneurship activities in the domain of ICT- enabled governance report for electronic governance research and practice worldwide (2018)
22. Pereira, G.V., Wimmer, M., Ronzhyn, A.: Research needs for disruptive technologies in smart cities. In: ICEGOV 2020: Proceedings of the 13th International Conference on Theory and

Practice of Electronic Governance, pp. 620–627 (2020). https://doi.org/10.1145/3428502.3428594
23. Li, D., Du, Y.: Artificial Intelligence with Uncertainty, 2nd edn. CRC Press, Bejing (2017)
24. High-level expert group on artificial intelligence, a definition of AI: main capabilities and disciplines. Eur. Comm. 7 (2019)
25. Schwarting, W., Alonso-Mora, J., Rus, D.: Planning and decision-making for autonomous vehicles. Annu. Rev. Control. Robot. Auton. Syst. **1**, 187–210 (2018). https://doi.org/10.1146/annurev-control-060117-105157
26. Murphy, K.P.: Machine Learning - A Probabilistic Perspective. MIT Press (2012). https://doi.org/10.1038/217994a0
27. Davenport, T.H., Harris, J.G.: Automated decision making comes of age. MIT Sloan Manag. Rev. **46**(4), 83–89 (2005)
28. De Azambuja, L.S., Pereira, G.V., Krimmer, R.: Clearing the existing fog over the smart sustainable city concept: highlighting the importance of governance. In: Proceedings of ICEGOV 2020, pp. 628–637 (2020). https://doi.org/10.1145/3428502.3428595
29. Yaqoob, I., Khan, L.U., Kazmi, S.M.A., Imran, M., Guizani, N., Hong, C.S.: Autonomous driving cars in smart cities: recent advances, requirements, and challenges. IEEE Netw. **34**(1), 174–181 (2020). https://doi.org/10.1109/MNET.2019.1900120
30. Campbell, M., Egerstedt, M., How, J.P., Murray, R.M.: Autonomous driving in urban environments: approaches, lessons and challenges. Philos. Trans. R. Soc. Math. Phys. Eng. Sci. **368**(1928), 4649–4672 (2010). https://doi.org/10.1098/rsta.2010.0110

E-government Evaluation

AI Systems for Occupational Safety and Health: From Ethical Concerns to Limited Legal Solutions

Sophie Weerts[1], Dana Naous[1](✉), Maéva El Bouchikhi[1,2], and Christine Clavien[2]

[1] University of Lausanne, Lausanne, Switzerland
{sophie.weerts,dana.naous,maeva.elbouchikhi}@unil.ch
[2] University of Geneva, Geneva, Switzerland
Christine.clavien@unige.ch

Abstract. Digital technologies in the workplace have undergone a remarkable evolution in recent years. Biosensors and wearables that enable data collection and analysis, through artificial intelligence (AI) systems became widespread in the working environment, whether private or public. These systems are heavily criticised in the media and in academia, for being used in aggressive algorithmic management contexts. However, they can also be deployed for more legitimate purposes such as occupational safety and health (OSH). Public authorities may promote them as tools for achieving public policy goals of OSH, and public employers may use them for improving employees' health. Despite these positive aspects, we argue that the deployment of AI systems for OSH raises important issues regarding dual use, chilling effects and employment discrimination. We exemplify how these ethical concerns are raised in three realistic scenarios and elaborate on the legal responses to these issues based on European law. Our analysis highlights blind spots in which laws do not provide clear answers to relevant ethical concerns. We conclude that other avenues should be investigated to help determine whether it is legally and socially acceptable to deploy AI systems and eventually promote such tools as means to achieve the OSH public policy.

Keywords: AI · Occupational health and safety · Law · Ethics · Public sector

1 Introduction

The use of new digital technologies in the workplace has undergone a remarkable evolution in recent years, especially since the outbreak of the Covid-19 crisis [1, 2]. Artificial intelligence (AI) systems, the internet of things (IoT), mobile devices, big data applications and advanced robotics are among the components of the new digital technologies enabling this evolution. The high degree of interconnectivity made possible by these digital technologies is conducive to what is called 'algorithmic management', when algorithmic software has the power to 'assign, optimise, and evaluate human jobs through algorithms and tracked data' [3, 4]. The increased use of digital technologies

Published by Springer Nature Switzerland AG 2022
M. Janssen et al. (Eds.): EGOV 2022, LNCS 13391, pp. 499–514, 2022.
https://doi.org/10.1007/978-3-031-15086-9_32

has adverse effects repeatedly denounced by media. Specifically, digital intrusion in the workplace becomes an important topic (e.g., Uber monitoring surveillance system [5]; Amazon's AI recruitment tool biased against women [6, 7]).

Scholars have highlighted the transformative impact of such technological deployment in the workplace [2, 8–10]. Digital technology in the workplace notably reshapes employment relationships, calling into question traditional work cultures related to the place and nature of work, the type of surveillance, and more broadly, the organisation and management of the work activities [11, 12]. Despite these disruptive aspects, new digital technologies may also be deployed for positive purposes such as occupational safety and health (OSH), which can also be a legal obligation for employers. Examples include the development of protective clothing like smart personal equipment [13, 14], AI devices for the well-being of employees in office jobs including smart watches in corporate wellness programmes [15], or emotion-sensing technologies for stress detection [16]. But, whenever biosensors connected through AI systems are deployed in the workplace, it does not remove concerns regarding privacy [17] or a blurring effect between using technology for OSH purposes and employee evaluations [18].

The aim of this paper is to address the question of how to guarantee that AI systems for OSH are deployed in a human-centric approach, meaning with the goal of improving welfare and freedom. Considering that law is one of the key requirements to achieve such a goal, there is a need to identify the main concerns raised by the use of digital technologies for OSH purposes and to determine the adequacy of legal requirements to address these concerns. While this concerns both the private and public sector, the latter is subject to more stringent legal requirements for its decisions, which must directly respect human rights and principles of good administration. The paper also informs policymakers of the risks related to the promotion of digital solutions for occupational health when they are mainly focused on the risks related to the increasing deployment of AI and digital technologies regarding the algorithmic management [19–23].

The paper is structured as follows: First, we begin with a background on OSH and how AI systems can contribute to such a public purpose. Next, we present our approach to explore this complex problem from a dual point of view: law and ethics. We then outline the European legal framework and elaborate on three scenarios regarding the deployment of IoT for the purpose of OSH, highlighting the major ethical issues. In light of these scenarios, we discuss the possible legal responses to the identified ethical challenges, thereby pinpointing important blind spots that need to be addressed. Considering the states' direct obligations to respect, protect, and fulfil human rights, we conclude that it is important to encourage the public sector, in its leadership role, to assess the potential impact on these human rights and set up necessary safeguards before favouring the deployment of an AI system for an occupational health public policy purpose.

2 Background

2.1 Maintaining the Safety and Health of Employees

'Occupational accidents and diseases create a human and economic burden' [24] and lead to a political response with the recognition of individual workers' rights [25], enshrined in international human rights law[1]. In 1950, the International Labour Organization (ILO) and the World Health Organization (WHO) adopted a common definition of OSH, considering 'its ultimate goal as the promotion and maintenance of the highest degree of physical, mental and social well-being of workers in all occupations' [26]. The concept of well-being in occupation was also defined as 'relate(d) to all aspects of working life, from the quality and safety of the physical environment, the climate at work and work organization'. The measures taken to ensure well-being in the workplace shall then be consistent with those of OSH 'to make sure workers are safe, healthy, satisfied and engaged at work'. In this perspective, OSH deals with the 'anticipation, recognition, evaluation and control of hazards arising in or from the workplace that could impair the health and well-being of workers, taking into account the possible impact on the surrounding communities and the general environment' [27].

The protection and promotion of safety and health involves the development of national public policy. To assist States in developing such a policy, the ILO has adopted a series of conventions, recommendations and guides [27].[2] From this perspective, employers have a duty to protect workers from and prevent occupational hazards, but also to inform workers on how to protect their health and that of others, to train their workers, and to compensate them for injuries and illnesses [27]. In the European Union context, based on article 153(2) TFEU, the directive 89/391/EEC of June 12, 1989, addresses measures to encourage improvements in the safety and health of workers at work. Its scope of application concerns the private and public sectors. The employer's obligations are part of a preventive approach [28]. In this respect, the directive requires that States take measures to ensure that the employer assesses the risks, evaluates those that cannot be avoided, combats them at the source, adapts the work to the individual or develops a coherent prevention policy covering technology, working conditions, social relations and the influence of health-related factors. In addition, when the employer introduces new technologies, they must be subject to consultation with the workers and/or their representatives about the consequences of the choice of equipment, working conditions and environment on the safety and health of the workers. The preventive approach promoted to achieve OSH involves an assessment of the risks that rise in the course of work, which may be related to the use of a new technology.

2.2 AI Systems for Occupational Safety and Health

Data-driven health initiatives are gaining interest among employers to improve OSH through monitoring and tracking employees in the workplace [29]. These initiatives rely on the deployment of AI systems that are a combination of software and hardware

[1] Several international texts expressed their commitment for the protection of safety and health of the workers: the 1948 Universal Declaration of Human Rights (art. 23); the 1966 Covenant on Social, Economic and Cultural Rights (art. 7); and the European Social Charter, adopted in 1961 and revised in 1996 (right to safe and healthy working conditions (art. 3), right to health protection (art. 11), obligation to improve work conditions and environment (art. 22).

[2] The ILO Convention, 1981 (No. 155) and its Recommendation (No. 164); the ILO Convention, 1985 (No. 161) and its Recommendation (No. 171); and the ILO Promotional Framework for Occupational Safety and Health Convention (No. 187) and Recommendation (No. 197).

that enable data capture and analysis to achieve a certain outcome. Among the building blocks of AI systems is the IoT technology. IoT enables access to various types of data in a cyber-physical system. Combined with machine learning algorithms, IoT applications form AI systems that allow the collection and analysis of physical data in the aim of providing actionable insights. With the rapid development of ubiquitous IoT devices, IoT initiatives are being used for self-quantifying and digital monitoring to detect and prevent health issues and to mitigate health risks [30].

In fact, organisations employ these technologies to collect data related to health, fitness, location and emotions [31, 32]. Wearable technology is most prominently used for such purposes. It includes smart accessories (e.g., smart watches and smart glasses) and smart clothing (e.g., smart shirts and smart shoes) that can record physiological and environmental parameters in real-time, perform analysis to the data, and provide insights to the users in the form of nudges or interventions [33]. Moreover, sensor networks can be placed in different places and are commonly used to detect ambient conditions such as temperature, air quality or occupancy [34, 35]. IoT is used in the workplace for physical health monitoring, either through addressing physical inactivity/sedentary behaviour or poor postures that cause musculoskeletal disorders [36].

In addition, AI systems employing IoT enable emotional health monitoring through detecting occupational stress or burnouts that can affect the health of employees and compromise the quality of work in the long run. This can be achieved through the measurement of biomedical data including heart rate and body temperature for an estimation of emotional levels, most commonly through wearables [37, 38] or facial and speech recognition techniques [39]. These systems assess the employee's state and provide suggestions for healthier habits based on the analysed data. Moreover, environmental monitoring is another use case for IoT employing sensors (e.g., temperature and humidity) for detecting abnormalities and optimal ambient conditions [40, 41].

Risks associated with the deployment of such technologies in the workplace are then the continuous personal and contextual data collection [42] and its tracking effect [43], information or hidden insights about the employee [44] and the potential bias [45, 46].

3 Research Approach

Considering that the development and deployment of technologies raises new questions for society, we adopt a transdisciplinary ethical and legal approach. From a law perspective, since we were interested in questions related to what ought to be [47] and in the novelty of such digital deployment, we decided to focus on leading institutions in the field of regulation of new technologies and protection of individuals, namely the European Union and the Council of Europe. We collected legal sources through official publication websites of both organisations (EUR-Lex and HUDOC). We used several keywords (occupational health, artificial intelligence, worker's right to data protection, data protection law) for collecting authoritative texts produced by legislators (legislation) and judges (case-law) [48]. The legal analysis was conducted by two authors.

For the ethical analysis, we collected data on experts' perceptions on OSH digital solutions during a workshop that took place in December 2021, including ten stakeholders with various expertise (technology, medicine, public administration, politics and ethics). Participants had more than five years of experience within their respective field. During the discussion, we presented to participants three scenarios describing the deployment of IoT and AI systems for a typical OSH purpose. We have built these scenarios based on a review of literature on existing solutions for OSH in office settings. The objective of the workshop was to discuss the acceptability, benefits and ethical issues or risks that could be associated to the deployment of these solutions in the workplace. We took the necessary measures to safeguard the confidentiality of participants' inputs. A preliminary data screening of the discussion[3] was operated by two authors. Our examination was based on the four ethics principles – respect to human autonomy, prevention of harm, fairness and predictability – identified and defined by the Ad hoc Committee on Artificial Intelligence (CAHAI) [19]. This analysis helped us to highlight specific concerns raised by the deployment of the new technologies for OSH purposes. In a second stage, we used the technique of subsumption applied in legal interpretation: we linked the four main concerns that we have identified to existing legal rules in order to assess whether those rules provide satisfactory responses. In the case of failure, it means that we have identified blind spots in which laws do not provide clear or satisfying answers to relevant ethical concerns.

4 Legal Framework About AI Systems in the Workplace

The discussion on new technologies has largely focused on the erosion of privacy produced by the indiscriminate processing of data. The technology sophistication goes and will go beyond the question of data privacy and there is a political will to regulate AI systems and their use in the workplace. These two fields need to be investigated.

4.1 Regarding Privacy

The surveillance inherent in the employment relationship cannot neglect the employees' right to privacy. Various institutional sources show that workers' data should be treated with caution. First, the European Court of Human Rights ruled that article 8 protects the employee in the performance of his professional duties, thus establishing a limit to the principle of surveillance in employment relationships.[4] It also recognised that between employer and employee's rights, the States have the obligation to balance the interests.[5]

[3] In addition to the workshop, we conducted a series of individual interviews with a diversified panel of stakeholders. A detailed qualitative analysis is undergoing and will be published in a separate paper.

[4] ECtHR, Niemietz v. Germany, n°13710/88, 16 December 1992, §§33–34. The Court ruled that 'respect for private life comprised to a certain degree the right to establish and develop relationships with others. There was no reason of principle why the notion of 'private life' should be taken to exclude professional or business activities, since it is in the course of their working lives that the majority of people had a significant opportunity of developing such relationships. To deny the protection of Art. 8 on the ground that the measure complained of related only to professional activities could lead to an inequality of treatment, in that such protection would remain available to a person whose professional and non-professional activities could not be distinguished'.

[5] ECtHR, Copland v.UK, n°62617/00, 3 April 2007.

If the intrusion is aimed at remedying an employee's behaviour that is detrimental to the employer, the intrusion can be justified through proportionality.[6] The legal nature of the employer also has a consequence on the nature of the obligations of the state.[7] In the case of public organisations, the European Court of Human Rights also ruled that the public actor is directly bound by the conditions for public interference with an individual right, namely the requirement of a legal basis, the public interest and the principle of proportionality.[8]

Moreover, and in accordance with Convention 108 +, any personal data processing by public sector authorities should respect the right to private life and comply with the 'three tests' of the principle of proportionality: lawfulness, legitimacy and necessity. The lawfulness test implies checking not only if there is a legal basis but also that such a legal basis is 'sufficiently clear and foreseeable'. In the M.M. case, the Court indicated that: 'the greater the scope of the recording system, and thus the greater the amount and sensitivity of data held and available for disclosure, the more important the content of the safeguards to be applied at the various crucial stages in the subsequent processing to date'.[9] The test of legitimacy implies that personal data undergoing automatic processing must be collected for explicit, specified and legitimate purposes, such as national security, public safety and economic well-being. Finally, the test of necessity includes five requirements: minimization of the amount of data collected; accuracy and updating of data; limiting the data process and storage to what is necessary to fulfil the purpose for which they are recorded, limiting the use of data to the purpose for which they are recorded; and transparency of data processing procedures.

All these requirements for data processing are also enshrined in the General Data Protection Regulation (Regulation (EU) 2016/679, GDPR). In the context of employment, the collection and processing of sensitive data for OSH is possible[10]. The GDPR also authorises member states to specifically regulate the processing of data. National legislations can cover the 'recruitment, performance of employment contracts, management, planning and organization of work, equality and diversity in the workplace, health and safety at work, protection of employer's or customer's property and for the purposes of the exercise and enjoyment of social benefits in the course of employment or after the termination of the employment relationship'[11]. Nevertheless, member states must include in their national provisions suitable and specific measures to safeguard the data subject's human dignity, legitimate interests and fundamental rights, with particular regard to the transparency of processing, the transfer of personal data within a group of undertakings, or a group of enterprises engaged in a joint economic activity and monitoring systems in the workplace.

---

[6] ECtHR, Lopez Ribalda and Others v. Spain (GC), n°1874/13 and 8567/13, 17 October 2019, §§ 118, 123.

[7] ECtHR, Bărbulescu v. Romania (GC), n°61496/08, 5 September 2017, §108.

[8] ECtHR, Libert, 22 February 2018, n°588/13; Renfe c. Espagne (déc.), n°35216/97, 8 September 1997 and Copland (mentioned above, §§ 43–44).

[9] ECtHR, M.M. v. UK, 13 November 2012, n°24029/07, §200.

[10] GDPR, art. 9.2(h).

[11] See also recital 155.

Finally, the ILO recommendation No. 171 of 1985 provides that OSH services should record data on workers' health in confidential medical files. Persons working in the service should only have access to these records if they are relevant to the performance of their own duties. If the information collected includes personal information covered by medical confidentiality, access should be limited to medical staff. It is also provided that personal data relating to health assessment may only be communicated to third parties with the informed consent of the worker concerned. The ILO adopted in 1997 a set of practical guidelines on the protection of workers' personal data and in its 2008 position paper, it recalled that 'provisions must be adopted to protect the privacy of workers and to ensure that health monitoring is not used for discriminatory purposes or in any other way prejudicial to the interests of workers' [27].

4.2 Future Legal Developments Regarding AI Systems

New digital innovation generates new risks. In the context of the European Union, the legislator wants to maintain the balance between the protection of fundamental rights and the economy. For this purpose, a legislative proposal on AI systems is under discussion. It already offers some insights about how employers could tackle legal issues. At this stage, only the explanatory comments announced to pursue 'consistency with the EU Charter of Fundamental Rights and the existing secondary Union legislation on data protection, consumer protection, non-discrimination and gender equality'. The proposal is presented to complement the current legal framework with 'a set of harmonized rules applicable to the design, development and use of certain high-risk AI systems and restrictions on certain uses of remote biometric identification systems.' It also completes existing Union law on non-discrimination with specific requirements that aim to minimise the risk of algorithmic discrimination, in relation to the design and the quality of data sets used within the AI systems.

Moreover, safety and health are seen as possible outcomes of AI systems. Those are viewed as potential solutions to the problem of work-related health. Nevertheless, annex III for high-risk AI systems includes systems that involve 'employment, workers management and access to self-employment', those operating for recruitment purposes and within 'contractual relationships, for task allocation and monitoring and evaluating performance and behaviour of persons in such relationships.[12] At this stage of the legislative discussion, it is not clear if AI systems for OSH would be considered. They are not expressly listed, but they could be indirectly helpful to define the task allocation in the workers management.

5 Ethical Considerations of AI Systems for OSH

5.1 Scenarios

For the workshop discussion, we presented three scenarios describing the deployment of digital technologies for promoting the health of employees and improving their working conditions. Each scenario describes a different context of implementation of a different

[12] Annex III; recital 36.

device or technology that collects employees' health-related data and output reports. The scenarios vary with respect to what type of health data are collected (posture on a chair, step count, voice tone, etc.), how the device is proposed to employees (consultation, information or opt-out options), how the data is managed (e.g., sent to external companies or not) and processed (e.g., results anonymised or not), and who receives the report (employees, occupational physician or human resources).

Scenario 1: Smart Chairs for Monitoring Sedentary Behaviour
The first scenario discusses the use of smart chairs to avoid chronic illnesses resulting from employees' posture while working. These smart chairs detect poor neck, head and back postures and a red light switches on whenever its user rests in this posture for several minutes. They also produce a light sound as a nudge to inform users when they remain seated for a prolonged period. The smart chairs are designed with a programme that stores data about users' posture and sitting time and generates individual reports including health advice.

Scenario 2: Steps Contest in a Corporate Wellness Programme
The second scenario discusses a steps contest initiative within a corporate wellness programme that aims to motivate employees to engage in more physical activity for the benefit of their health. Employees' steps are monitored by smartwatches provided by the company to all employees willing to participate. The smartwatches monitor users' steps, speed of motion, heart rate, body temperature and blood pressure. On a comprehensive app user interface, participants can access personalised reports of their step performance, general activity and physical health metrics and rankings.

Scenario 3: Stress Monitoring and Management
The third scenario discusses the use of sensor networks in order to assess employees' satisfaction with the flexible work policy and stress levels related to their working conditions and workload. Computers used by the employees are equipped with sensors capturing speech tone and speed (disregarding content). Information collected by the sensors are processed by deep learning algorithms, which output an assessment of individual stress levels and emotional state. These algorithms produce real-time signals and recommendations to employees (such as "It may be the right moment for a break"). Also, reports of overall stress levels are sent periodically to the employees who are encouraged to share them with their direct supervisors as a basis for discussing their satisfaction with the working conditions and workload.

5.2 Ethical Considerations

Based on the inputs provided by the stakeholders' discussion, we identified a series of ethical concerns emerging in the three scenarios. One major issue that we identified is *trust* in the technology and in its intended and actual use by the employer. A linked topic is the question of ensuring that the technology is the right answer to the right problem. For instance, is the smart chair an appropriate response to employees' back pain or shouldn't other organisational changes (working schedule or changes of working tasks) be made to meet the same aim more efficiently? Additionally, what is the employer's real intention in deploying such a technology? Indeed, despite the fact that the three scenarios represent cases of monitoring for health improvement, it cannot be ignored that these tools and the data they collect could be used for other purposes. Moreover, these tools are also intended to be nudging mechanisms. Is such an incentive to behave in a certain way likely to have negative consequences for workers who refuse to comply? For example, in the smart chair scenario, can employees be held responsible for back pain they could have avoided? Could they be deprived of social protection? In light of the AI ethical principles developed by the CAHAI, these elements mainly reflect the requirement of fairness and, secondarily, that of preventing (indirect) harm.

A second major issue encountered in the three scenarios is the tension between employee choice and employer power. In fact, even if consent from employees is required for deploying the technology, the consent provided may not be freely obtained, and therefore ill-founded. Indeed, in some working environments, employees may feel pressured to comply in order to avoid discrimination or other forms of sanctions resulting from their refusal to opt into the new system. In addition, financial incentives may influence employees' judgment (e.g., the provision of smartwatches in the second scenario), which may be seen as a form of indirect pressure to participate since a reward is involved, thus intensifying the power imbalance within the organisation. All these elements raise the issue of respecting the employees' *autonomy* in the employment relationship (respect for human autonomy).

A further important concern is the risk of *discrimination*. This is mainly associated with the use of special devices and algorithmic decision-making. In fact, the main question is how to guarantee the accuracy of the devices in collecting the data and the algorithmic correctness. Biased source data or algorithms implemented in the AI system might generate discriminatory downstream decisions. This issue is particularly worrisome in the case of systems implemented for OSH purposes; the collected data often include health information, location and behaviour. These types of data can easily be reused to assess employees' working capacities and capabilities, which are key factors used for deciding to promote or fire employees. Here again, these issues echo the principles of fairness and prevention of harm.

Privacy is also a central concern when it comes to collecting and processing personal data. In the three scenarios, the employer owns the systems used in the workplace, but data generated is managed and processed by third parties in most cases. Thus, the worker has no or limited control over the data collection, use and sharing, which creates a problem for privacy. Moreover, privacy risk increases with extensive data collection. This concern is particularly relevant when sensitive health data are collected.

Another issue is employer *surveillance*. This issue is also connected to the topic of the intended purpose or use of the system deployed. As mentioned earlier, even though the technology may be implemented for OSH, it may provide data relevant for monitoring work performance or other business relevant factors. If workers are aware of such forms of dual uses, it can create a chilling effect, and influence their behaviour. Workers who know that they are monitored might change their working pace or methods in order to approach social conformity. Surveillance becomes an even more problematic issue when it is extended to employee's homes. Flexible work policy and remote working creates new challenges which are illustrated in our second and third scenarios. When a wearable device for health monitoring is proposed to employees, it means that they will be monitored all day and the data collected corresponds with their physical activity and health status at work and in their private life. When a system is deployed in an at-home setting, private interactions at home are also monitored. These are only two examples of surveillance that trespass the privacy of others (i.e., extrinsic privacy). All these elements regarding privacy and employer surveillance further underline the principles of prevention of harm and fairness.

6 Discussion

Our overview of the extended legal framework that applies to OSH digital solutions provides a range of information regarding the obligations of employers when they purpose to collect data on their employees. Our ethical analysis, based on inputs from the workshop discussion and on the application of a four principles framework helped us to identify ethical issues and group them in relevant categories. In this section, we will assess the adequacy of the legal framework for addressing four main issues that we have identified.

The *trust* concern is about the digital solution and its user (the employer). To ensure that the benefits and costs are balanced with fairness, European law contains the proportionality principle which involves determining whether the means is adequate to achieve the desired end. This principle is also at the foundation of public decisions of liberal and democratic states. For public employers, it means verifying the effectiveness of digital devices to address the public health problem. The legitimacy principle is also useful to address the question of an unintended use of the device which could, by ricochet, violate the data purpose principle of the GDPR.[13] Respecting the intended use of the device is also expressed in the AIA proposal.[14]

The *trust* concern is also a question of information. From this perspective, it is linked to the explicability principle. In terms of legal requirements, it can be addressed with the right to information which is a fundamental right for workers and a common requirement of several pieces of legislation. The OSH directive provides a general obligation to the employer for ensuring 'information and instructions (…) in the event of introduction of any new technology' (art.12).[15] Employers must also inform and consult employees and/or their representatives[16]. The GDPR requires that any data process shall be operated in respect of the transparency principle.[17] The AIA proposal should reinforce

[13] Art. 6 GDPR concerning the lawfulness of the processing; See also art. 9 GDPR concerning the processing of special categories of personal data such as health data; See art. 88 in the context of processing in the context of employment; See recital 50 of the GPDR on the initial link between the purposes for which the data have been collected and the purposes of the intended further processing.

[14] The intended purpose principle, as defined in art.3(12), is mentioned 37 in the AIA proposal and is at the core of the regulation. Requirements (recital (43) and assessment of the risks are assessed at the light of the intended purpose of the system (Recital (42)) and new conformity assessment occurs when the intended purpose of the system changes (recital 66).

[15] Art. 12. 1 OSH Directive.

[16] Art. 6.3 (c) OSHA directive.

[17] Art. 12 GDPR.

this transparency principle.[18] Nevertheless, in the AIA proposal, such an obligation is limited to the AI providers, not the users, and in the case of high-risk AI systems in which OSH initiatives do not seem engaged.

The *autonomy* concern echoes the human autonomy principle. Once more, several legal regulations also enshrine such an ethical principle. From human rights law, it is embedded in the right to personal life. If technology has an individual impact, it must be analysed as limiting the individual autonomy. In such a case, public employers shall respect the principle of proportionality and proceed to the three tests of lawfulness, legitimacy and necessity. In the GDPR, the autonomy concern is related to the consent requirement. On this point, both the European data protection authority and legal scholars [49, 50] agree that, in the working environment, consent could not be considered free and informed. For this, a legal basis for the processing of data is necessary. The field of OSH is precisely a legitimate purpose.[19]

Regarding the *discrimination* concerns, it appears at two levels: in the data set and through the outcomes of the device. At these two levels, the use of a digital solution can generate unfairness practices. To begin, the quality of the data set is of particular importance (i.e., relevance, representativity, completeness and correctness). The AIA should directly address this question of bias in the data set. It will be an obligation for providers who will have to process special categories of data such as health or biometric in a way that ensures the detection, correction and erasure of bias in notably high-risk AI systems[20]. Nevertheless, public employers as users of AI systems are also directly obliged to respect the principle of equality between individuals. If they use a system that leads to discrimination, they can subsequently be held liable for the damage that results from this discrimination. Regarding the discrimination risk as a result of the outcomes of the devices, it echoes the problem of a chilling effect, which happens when 'people might feel inclined to adapt their behaviour to a certain norm'. Technology is likely to influence individuals to change their behaviour without them even being aware of it. In this perspective, technology can be viewed as problematic regarding the right to individual self-determination. At this stage, there is no legal guarantee that employees will be protected against such a phenomenon, despite it being viewed as one of the major concerns in the 2020 report of the CAHAI [19].

The last concern is employee *privacy*, which was related to the blurring effect between professional and personal life. In law, the protection of privacy is guaranteed under the right to the protection of personal data. At an operational level, it means that employers must minimise data collection, limiting it to health purposes, and finally destroy such data. However, compliance with the minimisation and purpose requirement may be particularly challenging to achieve if the device cannot discriminate between data produced by other users - for example, family members - who would also have access to these tools within the family. Moreover, such digital solutions are generally developed by business enterprises that continue to play a role in the data storage and analysis. In such a situation, public employers must also respect their obligations towards such stakeholders. Finally, if the digital device targets the recognition of micro-expressions,

[18] Art. 13.3 AIA proposal.
[19] Art. 9. 2 (h) GDPR; art. 6 OSH directive.
[20] Recital 44 AIA proposal.

voice tone, heart rate and temperature to assess or even predict our behaviour, mental state and emotions, it must be considered as an intrusive tool that collects biometric data and, in the future, should fall under annex III of the AIA.[21] Moreover, at this stage, there is a legal gap. As mentioned by the CAHAI report, biometric data used for an aim other than recognition, such as categorization (for example, for the purpose of determining insurance premium based on statistical prevalence health problems), profiling, or assessing a person's behaviour, might not fall under the GDPR definition. The GDPR only considers automating the processing of data, but not regarding behaviour prediction based on data processing.

This general legal assessment of the ethical concerns shows that the European law does not offer an answer to all the problems identified by our ethical analysis. Nevertheless, it is worth noting that the components of the principle of proportionality appear several times and can be mobilised as preliminary test before deploying OSH digital solutions.

7 Conclusion: Proposal for Social and Human Rights Assessment

This paper discusses the question of how to guarantee a deployment of AI systems for OSH in the public sector in a human-centric approach. In this context, we focused on OSH digital tools. Even if deployed for good purposes, the use of those systems does not exclude complex ethical issues. First, we have shown that AI systems are not deployed in a legal vacuum. They have to meet initial requirements. However, they may generate problems that are sometimes not directly identifiable or have not been taken into account from a legal point of view. To map these problems, we used an inductive approach which helped us to identify a series of ethical concerns regarding the implementation of AI systems for OSH. Further we examined whether the law imposes duties and rights in such situations. We found that legal answers were sometimes insufficient, leaving room for manoeuvre for the user of the AI system and risks for the employees. Therefore, such a conclusion forces us to ask what solution could be promoted to ensure that the use of this type of digital tool is firmly anchored in the respect of the weakest party (the employee) and in the protection and promotion of his or her health.

Other avenues should still be explored considering the AI systems' rapid deployment. From a practical point of view, one may wonder whether the logic of subsumption followed in Sects. 5 and 6 is not already an initial way of proceeding to assess the appropriateness of deploying an AI system. It makes it possible to link an empirical assessment to a legal analysis, including the various proportionality tests. The data protection impact assessment (DPIA), imposed by the GDPR, is a practical tool to assess the privacy risks for data processing technologies (including AI systems), where the realisation of data processing principles is controlled with respect to dedicated safeguards within the deployment of new technologies [51]. This type of assessment is one compliance tool to law, which could help in demonstrating accountability. However, as we have seen, the GDPR does not cover all risks related to technological innovations

[21] The CAHAI report underlines that there is no sound scientific evidence corroborating that a person's inner emotions or mental state can be accurately 'read' from a person's face, heart rate, tone or temperature.

and its DPIA is therefore limited in scope. In line with [52], we believe that an ethical impact assessment could complement the DPIA of new technologies imposed by law to ensure the adequate examination of ethical considerations of different stakeholders before and during the deployment of new technologies. To address that, in [53, 54], the authors call for social and human impact assessment, and in [55] developed a gold standard for discrimination assessment. We, therefore, suggest a more inclusive approach to the assessment, that includes a social and human rights impact assessment with stakeholders that should focus on methods and procedures for identifying ethical concerns and respecting public values. Such an approach would be necessary to mitigate risks and address the identified concerns within a continuously evolving digital sphere. To this end, it therefore requires further research. Finally, in the framework of OSH public policy, all these proposals should also be examined as solutions for preliminary assessment of AI systems' deployment.

Acknowledgements. This research is funded by the Swiss National Science Foundation (grant no. 187429) within the Swiss National Research Programme (NRP77) on "Digital Transformation".

References

1. Lodovici, S., et al.: Teleworking and digital work on workers and society. Special focus on survaillance and monitoring, as well as on mental health of workers. European Parliament (2021)
2. Moore, P., Piwek, L.: Regulating wellbeing in the brave new quantified workplace. Empl. Relat. **39**, 308–316 (2017)
3. Lee, M.K., Kusbit, D., Metsky, E., Dabbish, L.: Working with machines: the impact of algorithmic and data-driven management on human workers (2015)
4. Kaoosji, S.: Worker and community organizing to challenge amazon's algorithmic threat. In: Alimahomed-Wilson, Ellen, J.R. (eds.) The Cost of Free Shipping, pp. 194–206. Pluto Press (2020)
5. de Chant, T.: Uber asked contractor to allow video surveillance in employee homes, bedrooms: employee contract lets company install video cameras in personal spaces. Ars Technica (2021)
6. Dastin, T.: Amazon scraps secret AI recruiting tool that showed bias against women. Reuters (2018)
7. Manokha, I.: New means of workplace surveillance. Monthly Review, vol. 70 (2019)
8. Ajunwa, I., Crawford, K., Schultz, J.: Limitless Worker Surveillance. Calif. Law Rev. **105**, 735–776 (2017)
9. Aloisi, A., Gramano, E.: Artificial intelligence is watching you at work. digital surveillance, employee monitoring, and regulatory issues in the EU context. Spec. Issue Comp. Labor Law Policy J. **41**, 95–122 (2019)
10. Hendrickx, F.: From digits to robots: the privacy-autonomy nexus in new labor law machinery. Comp. Lab. Law Policy J. **40**, 365–388 (2019)
11. Aloisi, A., De Stefano, V.: Essential jobs, remote work and digital surveillance: addressing the COVID-19 pandemic panopticon. Int. Lab. Rev. **161**, 289–314 (2022)
12. Aloisi, A., Gramano, E.: Artificial intelligence is watching you at work: digital surveillance, employee monitoring, and regulatory issues in the EU Context. Comp. Lab. L. Pol'y J. **41**, 95 (2019)

13. Thierbach, M.: Smart personal protective equipment: intelligent protection for the future. European Agency for Safety and Health at Work (2020)
14. Kim, S., et al.: Potential of exoskeleton technologies to enhance safety, health, and performance in construction: industry perspectives and future research directions. IISE Trans. Occup. Ergon. Hum. Factors **7**, 185–191 (2019)
15. Burke, R., Richardsen, A.: Corporate Wellness Programs. Edward Elgar Publishing, Cheltenham (2014)
16. Whelan, E., McDuff, D., Gleasure, R., Vom Brocke, J.: How emotion-sensing technology can reshape the workplace. MIT Sloan Manag. Rev. **59**(3), 7–10 (2018)
17. Collins, P.M., Marassi, S.: Is that lawful?: Data privacy and fitness trackers in the workplace. Int. J. Comp. Lab. Law **37**, 65–94 (2021)
18. Akhtar, P., Moore, P.: The psychosocial impacts of technological change in contemporary workplaces, and trade union responses. Int. J. Lab. Res. **8**, 101–131 (2016)
19. CAHAI - Ad hoc Committee on Artificial Intelligence: Towards a Regulation of AI Systems: Global perspectives on the development of a legal framework on Artificial Intelligence (AI) systems based on the Council of Europe's standards on human rights, democracy and the rule of law. Ad Hoc Committee on Artificial Intelligence, Council of Europe (2020)
20. Independent High-Level Expert Group on Artificial Intelligence: Ethics guidelines for trustworthy AI, Publications Office, 2019. European Commission (2019)
21. Vaele, M., Borgesius, F.Z.: Demystifying the draft EU artificial intelligence Act analysing the good, the bad, and the unclear elements of the proposed approach. Comput. Law Rev. Int. **22**(4), 97–112 (2021)
22. Ebers, M., Hoch, V.R.S., Rosenkranz, F., Ruschemeier, H., Steinrötter, B.: The european commission's proposal for an artificial intelligence act—a critical assessment by members of the robotics and AI law society (RAILS). Multi. Sci. J. **4**, 589–603 (2021)
23. Tan, Z.M., Aggarwal, N., Cowls, J., Morley, J., Taddeo, M., Floridi, L.: The ethical debate about the gig economy: a review and critical analysis. Technol. Soc. **65**, 101594 (2021)
24. ILO: Builidinf a preventive safety and health culture. A guide to the Occupational Safety and Health Convention, 1981 (n°155), its guide Protocole and the Promotional Framework for Occupational Safety and Health Convention, 2006 (n°187). (2013)
25. Abrams, H.K.: A short history of occupational health. J. Public Health Policy **22**, 34–80 (2001)
26. Organisation, I.L.: ILO standards-related activities in the area of occupational safety and health: an in-depth study for discussion with a view to the elaboration of a plan of action for such activities. In: Office, L. (ed.), Geneva (2003)
27. Alli, B.O.: Fundamental Principles of Occupational Health and Safety. International Labour Organization, Geneva (2008)
28. Raworth, P.: Regional harmonization of occupational health rules: the European example. Am. J. Law Med. **21**, 7–44 (1995)
29. Charitsis, V.: Survival of the (data) fit: Self-surveillance, corporate wellness, and the platformization of healthcare. Surveill. Soc. **17**, 139–144 (2019)
30. Yassaee, M., Mettler, T., Winter, R.: Principles for the design of digital occupational health systems. Elsevier (2019)
31. Manokha, I.: The implications of digital employee monitoring and people analytics for power relations in the workplace. Surveill. Soc. **18**, 540–554 (2020)
32. Giddens, L., Leidner, D., Gonzalez, E.: The role of Fitbits in corporate wellness programs: does step count matter?. In: Proceedings of the 2017 Hawaii International Conference on System Sciences, pp. 3627–3635, Hawaii (2017)
33. Fdez-Arroyabe, P., Fernández, D.S., Andrés, J.B.: Work environment and healthcare: a biometeorological approach based on wearables. In: Dey, N., Ashour, A.S., James Fong, S., Bhatt,

C. (eds.) Wearable and Implantable Medical Devices, vol. 7, pp. 141–161. Academic Press (2020)
34. Afolaranmi, S.O., Ramis Ferrer, B., Martinez Lastra, J.L.: Technology review: prototyping platforms for monitoring ambient conditions. Int. J. Environ. Health Res. **28**, 253–279 (2018)
35. Saini, J., Dutta, M., Marques, G.: A comprehensive review on indoor air quality monitoring systems for enhanced public health. Sustain. Environ. Res. **30**, 6 (2020)
36. Gorm, N., Shklovski, I.: Sharing steps in the workplace: changing privacy concerns over time. In: Proceedings of the 2016 CHI Conference on Human Factors in Computing Systems, pp. 4315–4319, San Jose (2016)
37. Han, L., Zhang, Q., Chen, X., Zhan, Q., Yang, T., Zhao, Z.: Detecting work-related stress with a wearable device. Comput. Ind. **90**, 42–49 (2017)
38. Stepanovic, S., Mozgovoy, V., Mettler, T.: Designing visualizations for workplace stress management: results of a pilot study at a swiss municipality. In: Lindgren, I., et al. (eds.) EGOV 2019. LNCS, vol. 11685, pp. 94–104. Springer, Cham (2019). https://doi.org/10.1007/978-3-030-27325-5_8
39. Fugini, M., et al.: WorkingAge: providing occupational safety through pervasive sensing and data driven behavior modeling. In: Proceedings of the 30th European Safety and Reliability Conference, pp. 1–8, Venice (2020)
40. Nižetić, S., Pivac, N., Zanki, V., Papadopoulos, A.M.: Application of smart wearable sensors in office buildings for modelling of occupants' metabolic responses. Energy Buildings **226**, 110399 (2020)
41. van der Valk, S., Myers, T., Atkinson, I., Mohring, K.: Sensor networks in workplaces: correlating comfort and productivity. In: Proceedings of the 10th International Conference on Intelligent Sensors, Sensor Networks and Information Processing (ISSNIP), pp. 1–6. IEEE (2015)
42. Souza, M., Miyagawa, T., Melo, P., Maciel, F.: Wellness programs: wearable technologies supporting healthy habits and corporate costs reduction. In: Stephanidis, C. (ed.) HCI 2017. CCIS, vol. 714, pp. 293–300. Springer, Cham (2017). https://doi.org/10.1007/978-3-319-58753-0_44
43. Hall, K., Oesterle, S., Watkowski, L., Liebel, S.: A literature review on the risks and potentials of tracking and monitoring eHealth technologies in the context of occupational health management (2022)
44. Gaur, B., Shukla, V.K., Verma, A.: Strengthening people analytics through wearable IOT device for real-time data collection. In: Proceedings of the 2019 International Conference on Automation, Computational and Technology Management, pp. 555–560. IEEE, London (2019)
45. Feuerriegel, S., Dolata, M., Schwabe, G.: Fair AI: challenges and opportunities. Bus. Inf. Syst. Eng. **62**, 379–384 (2020)
46. Siau, K., Wang, W.: Building trust in artificial intelligence, machine learning, and robotics. Cutter Bus. Technol. J. **31**, 47–53 (2018)
47. Tyler, T.R.: Methodology in legal research. Utrecht L. Rev. **13**, 130 (2017)
48. Langbroek, P.M., Van Den Bos, K., Simon Thomas, M., Milo, J.M., van Rossum, W.M.: Methodology of legal research: challenges and opportunities. Utrecht Law Rev. **13**, 1–8 (2017)
49. WP29: Opinion 2/2017 on data processing at work. In: Party, A.D.P.W. (ed.) (2017)
50. Brassart Olsen, C.: To track or not to track? Employees' data privacy in the age of corporate wellness, mobile health, and GDPR. Int. Data Priv. Law **10**, 236–252 (2020)
51. Wagner, I., Boiten, E.: Privacy risk assessment: from art to science, by metrics. In: Garcia-Alfaro, J., Herrera-Joancomartí, J., Livraga, G., Rios, R. (eds.) DPM/CBT -2018. LNCS, vol. 11025, pp. 225–241. Springer, Cham (2018). https://doi.org/10.1007/978-3-030-00305-0_17

52. Wright, D., Mordini, E.: Privacy and ethical impact assessment. In: Wright, D., De Hert, P. (eds.) Privacy impact assessment, pp. 397–418. Springer Netherlands, Dordrecht (2012). https://doi.org/10.1007/978-94-007-2543-0_19
53. Jasanoff, S.: The ethics of invention: technology and the human future. W.W. Norton & Company, New York (2016)
54. Metcalf, J., Moss, E., Watkins, E., Singh, R., Elish, M.C.: Algorithmic impact assessments and accountability: the co-construction of impacts. In: ACM Conference on Fairness, Accountability, and Transparency (FAccT '21). ACM, Canada (2021)
55. Wachter, S., Mittelstadt, B., Russell, C.: Why fairness cannot be automated: bridging the gap between EU non-discrimination law and AI. Comput. Law Secur. Rev. **41**, 72 (2021)

Business-to-Government Data Sharing for Public Interests in the European Union: Results of a Public Consultation

Iryna Susha(✉), Jakob Schiele, and Koen Frenken

Copernicus Institute of Sustainable Development, Utrecht University, Princetonlaan 8a, 3584 CB Utrecht, The Netherlands
i.susha@uu.nl

Abstract. Lately governments and companies began experimenting with voluntary data sharing of business data for addressing public problems (so-called Data Collaboratives). This early practice revealed a number of challenges impeding business-to-government (B2G) data sharing and thus limiting the potential of data to provide answers and guide policies and action. One of the key challenges is the lack of a clear regulatory framework for B2G data sharing. To tackle this issue, the European Commission is taking regulatory action and preparing the Data Act which aims to spell out the rules and conditions for B2G data sharing for public interest. These developments, however, are met with resistance. While there is a strong push from the public sector for more private sector data, the private sector is less enthusiastic about the prospective mandatory B2G data sharing. In our study we zoom in on this issue in more detail and pose the following research question: How do public and private sector actors in the European Union view the prospect of mandatory B2G data sharing for public interest? To answer this question, we analyze the open dataset of responses to the public consultation of the European Commission. We find statistically significant results of business opposition to regulatory action and to mandating B2G data sharing, particularly among telecom and finance sectors. We also conclude that opposition to mandatory data sharing varies depending on the public interest purpose and is lowest among businesses with regards to emergencies and highest with regard to education, inclusion, and statistics.

Keywords: Data Sharing · Business-to-Government · e-Consultation · European Union

1 Introduction

In recent years we have witnessed the rise of the so-called 'data for good' movement. This movement pursues the use of data for societal benefit and its normative orientation is that data should serve public interest. This narrative became widespread especially in the context of grand societal challenges and so-called wicked problems. Data is seen as a crucial piece of the puzzle in enabling evidence-based decisions (Choi et al. 2021) and

Published by Springer Nature Switzerland AG 2022
M. Janssen et al. (Eds.): EGOV 2022, LNCS 13391, pp. 515–529, 2022.
https://doi.org/10.1007/978-3-031-15086-9_33

data-driven innovation. Much of the data that can potentially be useful for addressing societal challenges is held by the private sector (Noveck 2015). Unlocking this data from behind the corporate walls is challenging.

Lately governments and companies, often in partnerships with NGOs and research organizations, began experimenting with voluntary data sharing of business data for addressing public problems. These partnerships, termed "data collaboratives" (Susha et al. 2017), created momentum for collaborative problem-solving of grand challenges, however, this early practice also revealed a number of challenges impeding business-to-government (B2G) data sharing and thus limiting the potential of data to provide answers and guide policies and action. The key problem is that, while businesses are willing to provide data on an occasional basis, they lack incentives to scale up such 'data philanthropy' and expect to receive gains in some form from these collaborations (European Commission 2020). Other barriers concern the lack of clear regulatory framework for B2G data sharing.

To tackle the latter issue, the EU is taking regulatory action and preparing the Data Act which aims to spell out the rules and conditions for B2G data sharing for public interest. The Data Act is the key pillar of the European Strategy for Data and, among other things, aims to create the means for public sector bodies to access and use data held by the private sector that is necessary for specific public interest purposes[1] and mandate such sharing in specific situations.

These developments, however, are met with resistance. While there is a strong push from the public sector for more private sector data, the private sector is less enthusiastic about the prospective mandatory B2G data sharing. The preliminary analysis of the public consultation by the European Commission showed that when it comes to making B2G data sharing mandatory, the preferences of public and private sectors vary. 91% of public authorities consider that regulatory action (EU or national) on B2G data sharing is needed, while this is the opinion of just 38% of business actors (European Commission 2021). Furthermore, there appears to be disagreement between public and private sector respondents regarding in which key areas B2G data sharing should be made mandatory (Ibid.). We find these initial results intriguing and in our study we zoom in on the following research question: *How do public and private sector actors in the EU view the prospect of mandatory B2G data sharing for public interest?* To answer this question, we analyze the open dataset of responses to the public consultation of the EC using regression analysis.

The phenomenon of mandatory B2G data sharing for public interest is a recent one and research on this topic is limited to a handful of grey literature publications. Current academic knowledge about mandatory B2G data sharing is limited to situations of compliance, such as financial reporting (Troshani et al. 2018), and the literature on B2G data sharing for public interest is limited to the situations of voluntary data sharing (Susha et al. 2019; Rukanova et al. 2020). Thus, our research aims to fill a literature void on mandatory B2G data sharing for public interest.

The paper is structured as follows: in Sect. 2 a review of relevant literature on B2G data sharing is presented, followed by the description of our research method in Sect. 3.

[1] Data Act Press Release, https://digital-strategy.ec.europa.eu/en/policies/data-act.

In Sect. 4 we present the results of our analysis which are discussed in Sect. 5 in view of implications and significance for research. We conclude the paper with key points in Sect. 6.

2 Modalities of B2G Data Sharing for Public Interest

To date B2G data sharing for public interest has been mainly realized by means of voluntary data sharing arrangements. In research two such approaches to voluntary data sharing are discussed: data donorship, also known as data philanthropy (George et al. 2020, 2022), and data collaboratives (Susha et al. 2017; Klievink et al. 2018), seen as more collaborative initiatives to share data based on mutual interests of government and business (Micheli 2022). Research on data philanthropy views this phenomenon as a subtype of corporate philanthropy and focuses on understanding the benefits to donor firms themselves (Awasthi and George 2019; George et al. 2022). For instance, George et al. (2020) argue that data philanthropy is beneficial to firms and can improve organizational effectiveness but it requires high level of control of the complementary assets (e.g. data expertise). This thesis on the relations between private interest and public value is elaborated in critical literature on digital platforms which questions the common good motives of platform companies (Van Dijck et al. 2018).

Research on data collaboratives views private sector data sharing from a more collective standpoint and strives to identify outcomes at both organizational and societal level (Susha and Gil-Garcia 2019; Susha et al. 2019). Literature on data collaboratives makes a point that the interests and positions of public and private sector actors differ and might even clash in public-private collaborations (Klievink et al. 2018). While the public sector is driven by the realization of public sector values (Bannister 2014), the rationale of the private sector remains largely economic and market-driven. Although in principle altruistic motives underlie data partnerships, research shows that companies can often seek to achieve indirect benefits as a bonus of collaborations (Micheli 2022; Susha et al. 2019). Therefore, some arguments have been put forward that B2G data sharing needs to be mutually beneficial and aim for a win-win arrangement (European Commission 2020). Rukanova et al. (2020) for instance demonstrated how win-wins can be realized by leveraging government leadership and aligning the needs and interests of the different parties. In a similar vein, Susha et al. (2019) conceptualized three different partnerships models wherein self-interest of actors and the societal interest at stake can configure differently. Klievink et al. (2018) demonstrated the success of a data partnership through the mechanisms of collaborative governance and the critical role of trust in public-private relations. Broader literature on inter-organizational collaboration supports this thesis, for instances, as theorized in the work of Porter and Kramer (2019) on shared value or in the framework of collaborative value creation in cross-sector partnerships (Austin and Seitanidi 2012).

There are other less explored modalities of B2G data sharing, such as public procurement of data and tender obligations mandating the supplier of a given service to share their data with a government authority (Micheli 2022). Research on the procurement of private sector data is, to the best of our knowledge, hard to come across. Regarding the latter, the city of Barcelona is becoming a frontrunner in this direction, taking action to introduce the so-called data sovereignty clauses in procurement contracts which would enable the city to access data 'about the city' from private sector providers (Monge et al. 2022). Mandatory B2G data sharing for public interest has not received much attention in the literature yet. However, there has emerged a broader narrative on data sovereignty (Hummel et al. 2021) and the need to give back control of data to citizens. Issues of power dynamics between public and private actors (Micheli 2022) and in relation to the citizens (Mercille 2021) have also been brought to the surface. In a qualitative study of 12 European cities Micheli (2022) found that public bodies often lack the means to set the terms of how data is shared, thus it is not assured the information they get will be useful to their public interest purposes. In this respect the public actors have the role of passive 'recipients' of data (Ibid.) and have to deal with a take-it-or-leave it situation. This dependence on the private sector for data produces emerging negative effects, such as for instance it introduces inequalities between public bodies that were able to access business data and innovate and those that were not (Ibid.).

Having said that, we know little about the interplay between the aforesaid modalities of data sharing, how the actors settle for a particular data sharing mode, and which approach should be favored in any given situation. Vigorito (2022), for instance, makes a point that there is potential for combining voluntary and mandatory modes into a 'hybrid' approach, but how this should be done remains for further exploration. Furthermore, existing research paints a rich picture of drivers and barriers for data sharing between government and business in general (Sayogo and Pardo 2013; Klievink et al. 2016; Susha et al. 2019). Yet, a more nuanced and actor-specific investigation of how public versus private actors experience and view B2G data sharing is needed. The research by Micheli (2022) exploring the experiences and views of local administrations on B2G data sharing is a step in this direction. Our study aims to add to this knowledge by investigating the views of public and private actors regarding the prospect of mandatory B2G data sharing for public interest in the EU.

3 Methodology

To analyze how public and private actors in the EU view the prospect of mandatory B2G data sharing for public interest, we look at survey data collected by the European Commission in a public consultation on the Data Act regarding B2G data sharing. In an online questionnaire, the Commission asked respondents to answer 158 questions and to provide some general information about the respondents. This resulted in an extensive database, including quantitative and qualitative data on 449 respondents, which is publicly accessible on the Commission website[2]. For each respondent, we extracted their answers to eight questions about B2G data sharing, as well as some background information on the respondents (type, size, country, sector).

The main relevant question on B2G data sharing for public interest in the EU is question 3 of the survey ("Should the EU take additional action so that public sector bodies can access and re-use private sector data, when this data is needed for them to carry out their tasks in the public interest purpose?"). The answer to this question

[2] https://ec.europa.eu/info/law/better-regulation/have-your-say/initiatives/13045-Data-Act-&-amended-rules-on-the-legal-protection-of-databases/public-consultation_en.

best captures an actor's general attitude towards regulating B2G data sharing. We only consider respondents who are either favorable ("EU level action is needed") or opposing ("No action is needed"), discarding 15 respondents who express an ambivalent position ("Action at the Member State level only is needed") and 113 respondents who did not provide any response. As our main dependent variable, we created a dummy variable *General* which takes on 1 for respondents who generally oppose regulatory action and 0 for respondents who are generally in favor of regulatory action.

We further consider questions 15–21, which have the same structure as question 3, but are specific to a particular public interest in which data sharing should be mandated ("In which of the following areas do you think that, for specific use-cases with a clear public interest, B2G data sharing should be compulsory, with appropriate safeguards?"). Here, possible responses are binary ("Yes, it should be compulsory" and "No, it should not be compulsory"), again discarding respondents who did not leave a response. We created, similar to the dependent variable *General*, seven dummy variables as dependent variables, which take on 1 for respondents indicating opposition to compulsory data sharing for a specific public interest, and 0 for respondents indicating no opposition to compulsory data sharing for that interest. The seven dummy variables related to the seven public interests are:

Emergency:	"Data (e.g. mobility data from Telecom operators, loss data from insurance companies) for emergencies and crisis management, prevention and resilience";
Statistics:	"Data (e.g. price data from supermarkets) for official statistics";
Environment:	"Data (e.g. emissions data from manufacturing plants) for protecting the environment";
Health:	"Data (e.g. fuel consumption data from transport operators) for a healthier society";
Education:	"Data for better public education services";
Inclusion:	"Data (e.g. employment data from companies) for a socially inclusive society";
Policy:	"Data for evidence-based public service delivery and policy-making".

The background information on the respondents include actor type (*Type*) which distinguishes between (A) "Business Association" (n = 122), (B) "Company/Business organisation" (n = 105), (C) "Public authority" (n = 100), (D) "EU Citizen" (n = 56), (E) "NGO (Non-governmental organisation)" (n = 21), (F) "Academic/Research Institution" (n = 17), (G) "Consumer Organisation" (n = 6), (H) "Non-EU Citizen" (n = 2), (I) "Trade Union" (n = 2) and (J) "Other" (n = 18). As we were mainly interested in differences between government and business actors, we created the dummy variables *Business* (grouping together (A) and (B)) and *Public* (equal to (C)). For the large number of citizens, we created a third dummy *Citizen* (grouping (D) and (H)). All other actor types are used as reference category in the regression analysis.

Organization size (*Size*) is an ordinal variable including "Large (250 or more)" (n = 171), "Medium (<250 employees)" (n = 77), "Small (<50 employees)" (n = 74) and "Micro (<10 employees)" (n = 69), with 58 NAs. As these 58 non-responses coincided with the user type citizen, we decided to group them together with Micro, as a citizen can be regarded as representing a single person. We use as dummy variables *Large, Medium* and *Small*, with *Micro* as reference category.

For the respondent's country (*Country*), a total of 32 countries were mentioned, including some non-EU countries. However, many of these had very low numbers of observations. Therefore, we created dummy variables only for countries with 10 or more respondents to question 3 (on which the main dependent variable *General* is based). This leads to ten country dummies: *Belgium* (n = 44), *Finland* (n = 13), *France* (n = 35), *Germany* (n = 60), *Hungary* (n = 11), *Italy* (n = 18), *Lithuania* (n = 13), *Netherlands* (n = 16), *Poland* (n = 10) and *Spain* (n = 49). All the other countries serve as the reference category.

Similarly, for business sector (*Sector*) we created dummy variables only for sectors with 10 or more respondents. These are: "Agriculture, forestry and fishing" (*Agri*, n = 10), "Automotive, including suppliers, manufacturing, retail, service and maintenance and related after-market services" (*Auto*, n = 13), "Finance, insurance and re-insurance (other than motor insurance)" (*Finance*, n = 19), "IT" (*IT*, n = 42), "Legal advice; market research" (*Legal*, n = 11), "Media, publishing, broadcasting and related services including advertising" (*Media*, n = 10), and "Telecommunications, including suppliers" (*Telecom*, n = 10). All other sectors serve as a reference category.

Below, we present descriptive statistics, as well as the results from eight binary regression models, all using the same list of dummies as independent variables (*Type, Size, Country* & *Sector*), but different dependent variables (*General, Emergency, Statistics, Environment, Health, Education, Inclusion* and *Policy*). Variance Inflation Factors (VIF) were calculated for all regression models, indicating that there is no multicollinearity (values all well below 10). The analysis was done in Rstudio version 4.0.3 (R Core Team 2020), where for data manipulation the package dplyr (Wickham et al. 2021) was used next to the base version and VIF using the package car (Fox and Weisberg 2019).

4 Results

Table 1 shows the descriptive statistics for all variables. Looking first at all respondents, we see that 29% opposes regulation in general, while this percentage tends to be higher for specific public interests. In particular, there is strong opposition against mandatory data sharing for inclusion, which involves sharing of employment data. Apparently, many actors do not feel that mandatory sharing of such data is justified.

Turning to specific categories of respondents, it is clear that the main differences in opinion lie between the *Type* of actors. The majority of *Business* actors oppose B2G data sharing regulation, while the large majority of *Citizen* and *Public* actors are in favor. This pattern is repeated when looking at specific interests, where the share of opposing businesses is generally even larger. In relative terms, businesses seem most open to data sharing for emergency and environmental purposes.

Regarding *Size*, we do not discern clear patterns. *Country* responses are generally also rather close, with only *Belgium* and *Spain* as outliers. Sectoral differences are more pronounced with respondents from data-intensive sectors like *Telecom*, *Finance* and *Media* mostly opposing. Respondents from *Legal* services are most strongly in favor, which may reflect that new regulations provide them with more business.

While the descriptive statistics indicate some patterns, one cannot conclude from percentages alone that some types of respondents would oppose B2G data sharing regulation more than others. To reach more conclusive answers, we run logistic regressions,

Table 1. Percentage of respondents opposing B2G data sharing regulation

Variable	% opposed							
	General	*Emerg*	*Stat*	*Env*	*Health*	*Educ*	*Inclus*	*Policy*
All	29.0	30.2	37.7	26.7	34.4	35.4	47.1	37.0
Business	54.4	54.1	75.2	55.7	58.7	66.3	80.0	68.1
Citizen	10.0	18.0	25.5	13.2	35.3	33.3	42.2	32.6
Public	1.3	5.8	3.3	1.2	6.3	6.6	9.5	4.8
Other	13.9	16.2	20.5	7.8	13.8	9.3	18.1	12.1
Large	31.1	26.1	30.6	21.9	25.9	30.4	40.8	32.1
Medium	27.5	24.0	31.4	22.5	29.2	23.8	36.2	27.1
Small	39.1	40.4	52.3	37.2	42.1	44.1	59.5	47.6
Other	21.7	33.7	42.8	29.7	43.6	42.7	54.1	43.6
Belgium	50.0	62.8	74.3	55.3	56.8	69.0	80.0	70.3
Finland	23.1	7.1	46.7	30.8	30.8	45.5	57.1	33.3
France	25.7	37.0	40.9	32.0	41.7	38.9	57.9	44.0
Germany	38.3	33.0	41.2	30.2	37.3	38.1	53.5	36.0
Hungary	18.2	8.3	7.7	0.0	7.7	16.7	18.2	25.0
Italy	16.7	17.7	52.9	11.1	17.7	26.7	18.8	28.6
Lithuania	23.1	17.7	5.9	10.5	31.3	22.2	22.2	17.7
Netherlands	31.3	58.3	58.3	38.5	41.7	45.5	58.3	46.2
Poland	20.0	33.3	20.0	22.2	44.4	22.2	22.2	28.6
Spain	8.2	7.3	7.7	5.9	12.2	14.6	17.4	16.3
Other	32.6	32.6	47.1	34.0	44.6	43.1	59.1	41.6
Agriculture	30.0	33.3	30.0	12.5	33.3	10.0	50.0	30.0
Automotive	30.8	44.4	91.7	55.6	46.7	63.6	92.9	75.0
Finance	73.7	40.0	66.7	25.0	25.0	33.3	54.6	72.7
IT	35.7	53.7	74.3	50.0	61.1	64.7	68.6	68.6
Legal	18.2	12.5	50.0	20.0	55.6	37.5	66.7	33.3
Media	60.0	66.7	75.0	50.0	66.7	55.6	71.4	75.0
Telecom	80.0	80.0	83.3	80.0	66.7	66.7	83.3	80.0
Other	19.9	20.2	24.1	18.5	25.5	27.1	35.7	24.6

including all variables. In this way, we can assess whether certain types of respondents significantly more often oppose, while controlling for all other factors.

Table 2 shows the results of the binary logit regression models and Table 3 shows the corresponding odds ratios for the significant effects ($p < 0.1$). Note that we only include

Table 2. Regression results

Regression model		Model 1	Model 2	Model 3	Model 4	Model 5	Model 6	Model 7	Model 8
DVs: opposed to sharing in		general	emergencies	statistics	environment	health	education	inclusion	policy
Independent Variables									
Type	Business	2.068 ***	1.855 ***	3.704 ***	3.035 ***	2.586 ***	3.362 ***	3.494 ***	3.066 ***
	Citizen	-0.320	-0.204	-0.207	0.226	0.907	1.516 *	0.938	1.028
	Public	-2.795 **	-0.537	-0.524	-1.211	-0.290	0.233	0.066	-0.406
Size	Large	0.098	-0.774	-1.456 **	-0.937 *	-0.858	-0.419	-0.801	-0.601
	Medium	-0.412	-1.340 **	-2.523 ***	-1.366 **	-1.344 **	-1.413 **	-1.942 ***	-1.425 **
	Small	0.027	-0.711	-1.800 **	-0.990	-0.799	-1.073	-1.024	-0.975
Country	Belgium	-0.168	0.978 *	0.771	0.243	-0.000	0.798	0.531	0.701
	Finland	-0.164	-1.550	0.488	-0.004	-0.344	0.890	0.459	
	France	-1.705 ***	-0.320	-1.681 **	-0.844	-0.798	-0.662	-0.647	-0.706
	Germany	-0.015	0.530	0.122	-0.137	-0.198	0.384	0.200	-0.105
	Hungary	-1.017	-1.726	-2.113 *	-16.292	-2.071 *	-0.848	-1.720 *	0.018
	Italy	-1.551 *	-0.672 *	0.605	-1.726 *	-1.637 **	-0.700	-0.765	-0.389
	Lithuania	1.073	0.306	-2.139	-0.139	0.663	0.446	-0.094	0.360
	Netherlands	-1.028	1.141	0.425	0.070	-0.080	0.643	0.120	0.395
	Poland	-0.287		-0.046					
	Spain	-1.193	-1.129 *	-1.885 **	-1.224	-1.112 *	-0.461	-0.809	-0.242
Sector	Agriculture	1.206		1.034			-1.878		0.835
	Automotive	-0.701	-0.176	2.159 *	0.238	-0.379	0.067	1.568	1.017
	Finance	2.118 ***	0.083					-0.504	1.480 *
	IT	-0.057	1.028	2.418 ***	0.809 *	0.853 *	1.180 **	0.647	1.463 ***
	Legal	0.264		2.672 ***	0.459				
	Media	0.832							
	Telecom	2.167 **	2.168 **						
AIC		294.69	303.14	235.42	255.48	305.91	260.72	269.71	277.09
Observations		321	308	297	300	288	257	272	281

*Significance codes: * $p < 0.1$; ** $p < 0.05$; *** $p < 0.01$*

Table 3. Odds ratios

Regression model		Model 1	Model 2	Model 3	Model 4	Model 5	Model 6	Model 7	Model 8
DVs: opposed to sharing in		general	emergencies	statistics	environment	health	education	inclusion	policy
Independent Variables									
Type	Business	7.90	6.39	40.64	20.81	13.28	28.87	32.93	21.46
	Citizen						4.55		
	Public	0.06							
Size	Large			0.23	0.39				
	Medium		0.26	0.08	0.25	0.26	0.24	0.14	0.24
	Small			0.16					
Country	Belgium		2.66						
	Germany								
	Spain		0.32	0.15		0.32			
	Finland								
	France	0.18		0.18					
	Hungary			0.12		0.12		0.17	
	Italy	0.21	0.51		0.17	0.19			
	Lithuania								
	Netherlands								
	Poland								
Sector	Agriculture								
	Automotive			8.66					
	Finance	8.31							4.39
	IT			11.23	2.24	2.34	3.25		4.32
	Legal			14.47					
	Media								
	Telecom	8.73	8.74						

dummy variables in the regressions with 10 or more observations, which implies that in Models 2–8 some coefficients are missing.

Model 1 with *General* as dependent variable shows the results for the answers to the general question regarding regulation. We observe a highly significant positive effect of *Business* (coef = 2.068, $p < 0.01$). In terms of the odds ratio, business actors are 7.9 times more likely to oppose regulatory action on B2G data sharing. Inversely, *Public* has a negative effect on opposition (coef = −2.795, $p < 0.05$), with public authorities being 16.7 times less likely to oppose B2G data sharing regulation. This confirms the strongly diverging interests and positions held by business actors and public authorities regarding data sharing (Klievink et al. 2018).

Size did not show any significant effect in *Model 1*, so there does not seem to be a discernible difference in attitudes towards general data sharing related to organization size. Looking at *Country* effects, *France* stands out as having a highly significant negative effect on opposition (coef = −1.705, $p < 0.01$) and Italy also has a negative effect, albeit less significant (coef = −1.551, $p < 0.1$). Actors residing in France are 5.6 times less likely and those in *Italy* 4.8 times less likely to oppose data sharing regulation. This fits with the notion of 'varieties of capitalism' which characterizes these countries as a Mediterranean variety, marked by "histories of extensive state intervention" (Hall and Soskice 2001, p. 21). Lastly, respondents from *Finance* (coef = 2.118, $p < 0.001$) and *Telecom* (coef = 2.167, $p < 0.05$) tend to oppose regulation. Finance actors are 8.3 times more likely to oppose data sharing regulation and telecom actors 8.7 times more likely to oppose. In summary, the strongest opposition to regulatory action on B2G data sharing in general can be found in business actors, and specifically, in the finance & insurance and telecommunications sectors.

Looking at the results for specific public interests in Model 2–8, it becomes clear that business actors' strong opposition to compulsory data sharing is consistent across the different subject areas, although it is the least strong in *Emergencies*, and strongest for *Statistics*, followed by *Inclusion* and *Education*.

The coefficients for *Size* show that across the subject areas, *Medium* sized organizations tend to be least opposing regulation. In some areas, *France* and *Italy* again appear as having a negative effect on opposition, but overall a clear country pattern is missing. Finally, we see that the *IT* sector seems to oppose mandatory data sharing for most public interests. This may reflect the data-intensive nature of the IT industry, with the data as a primary resource for their operations and innovations.

5 Discussion

Our research provides convincing **empirical evidence of the divide** in views of government and business on the prospect of mandatory B2G data sharing for public interest in the EU. Our analysis of the results of the public consultation on the Data Act shows that the majority of business actors oppose regulatory action on B2G data sharing for public interest.

The **stronghold of opposition** to mandatory B2G data sharing has been identified to be in the telecom and finance sectors. Interestingly, these sectors already have a track record of 'success stories' in voluntary data sharing collaborations with the government.

Telecom data has been named as one of the most sought-after types of data by government authorities, according to research by Micheli (2022). At the same time, telecom data has high value as a proprietary resource that contains insights about business processes and customer preferences (Taylor 2016). Nonetheless, telecom companies have been rather active lately in the practice of voluntary data sharing through data philanthropy or data collaborative initiatives. In 2017 the GSMA established the Data for Social Good initiative in which 16 world leading mobile network operators joined to leverage their big data capabilities in order to address humanitarian crises. During the Covid-19 pandemic the GSMA was approached by the European Commission with a request to share anonymized and aggregate mobile positioning data in order to study and respond to the pandemic. As a result, 17 mobile operators shared the data with the EC covering 22 EU member states and Norway which was seen as an initiative of "unprecedented nature" (Vespe et al. 2021). Other 'success stories' of voluntary data sharing of telecom data in the times of the pandemic can be found in a special issue of *Data & Policy* (Benjamins et al. 2022). The guest editors of the special issue (two of whom are representatives of the mobile industry) reflected on these practices and formulated two key challenges: financing to ensure long-term supply of data and building capacities and digital skills among government organizations (Ibid.). An interesting case is described by Agren et al. (2021) when an initially non-profit offering of a data analytics product (Crowd Insights) by Telia to the Public Health Agency of Sweden was turned into a commercial contract as the pandemic continued. There is evidence of the same strategy in the research by Micheli (2022) where businesses approach government organizations with a free offering which they afterwards transform into a commercial product. Telecom data thus presents an instance where high commercial value and high potential for societal impact collide.

Our second observation is that **resistance to data sharing varies depending on the public interest purpose**. Our findings show that sharing data for emergencies was met with least opposition from the business side, whereas such public interest purposes, as statistics, inclusion, and education received most resistance. Overall, companies around the world have been engaging in emergency-related activities as part of corporate social responsibility. Research shows that such involvement is based on both ethical/moral motives and instrumental motives (business profitability, continuity) (Johnson et al. 2011). At the same time, the strongest 'pull' for data on the side of the public sector is for data for statistical purposes, emergencies, and environment (European Commission 2021). Our findings point to a **mismatch in terms of demand in the public sector and the willingness to disclose** on the business sector side. In the case of official statistics, so far statistics agencies have experimented with accessing private sector data via voluntary data sharing arrangements with companies; a variety of data sharing models to this end are proposed (Klein et al. 2016; Klein and Verhulst 2017). According to OECD, challenges in these B2G data sharing partnerships for statistics include competitive risks, lack of incentives and turning it into a viable business model, and reputational and ethical risks (Klein et al. 2016). Next to statistics, our findings also point to low levels of enthusiasm among business about mandatory data sharing for education purposes. At the same time, there are rising concerns about the datafication of education and the reliance on private technology providers. Olazp et al. (2022) describe the process of "digital colonization" by digital platforms of the education sector and warn about the changing power dynamics between the incumbent service providers and the platforms where the latter control the data and become unique providers of critical, data-driven value.

Our research demonstrated that when it comes to B2G data sharing private interest and public value are in conflict. Van Dijk et al. (2018) argue that government has a role to play in safeguarding the public value by acting as a regulator, enforcer, or stimulant of public value. At the time of writing, on 23 February 2022, the EC published the text of the proposal for the Data Act, having considered input from stakeholder consultations, including the said public consultation. The proposal mandates the sharing of business data with government in situations of "exceptional need" thus adopting a narrow approach to public interest and favoring more the position of business. The proposal is yet to go through the legislative process of adoption. However, our research shows that the future of B2G data sharing in the EU will be situated in a highly rivalrous landscape where the interests and views of the public and private sectors are extremely divided.

In our future research we aim to enrich the quantitative analysis presented in this paper with insights from qualitative analysis of submissions which accompanied the public consultation responses. This will enable us to shed more light on the underlying arguments of actors in support of or in opposition to mandatory B2G data sharing in the EU.

6 Conclusions

In our research we focused on the state of B2G data sharing in the EU, and namely on the forthcoming EU Data Act and the prospect of mandatory B2G data sharing for public interest. Our analysis focused on the responses to the public consultation with the aim to answer the question: *How do public and private sector actors in the EU view the prospect of mandatory B2G data sharing for public interest?* We produced descriptive statistics of the results, together with eight binary regression models. We found statistically significant results of business opposition to regulatory action and to mandating B2G data sharing, particularly among telecom and finance sectors. We also concluded that opposition to mandatory data sharing varies depending on the public interest purpose and is lowest among businesses with regards to emergencies and highest with regard to education, inclusion, and statistics. We found that there is a mismatch in terms of the needs articulated by the public sector respondents and the willingness to disclose on the side of the private sector. Our findings paint a picture of divergent positions on B2G data sharing for public interest in the EU and call on future research to take a more critical stance on data and the role of the public sector in the data economy.

Studies of public-private relations in digital government research have overly focused on collaboration and finding synergies thereby following a more 'optimistic' curve. Our study exposes the clashing interests and the power struggle in positions of business and government on data and public interest. Our study also adds to a handful of quantitative studies on B2G data sharing (e.g. George et al. 2022). Research on B2G data sharing is heavily based on case studies, and even more so, on case studies of successful collaborations offering anecdotal evidence of mutually beneficial data sharing arrangements. We call on the research community to give due attention to the conflictual nature of information sharing and scrutinize the tensions and even ‘failures’ in business-government collaborations.

The limitations of our study are in part related to the sample. Whereas the overall sample size is reasonably good, some sectors and countries had to be excluded from the regression analysis due to clearly insufficient observations ($n < 10$). Moreover, some remaining dummies still had a quite low number of observations ($n < 20$). This could be ameliorated in future research by using a larger dataset. Nevertheless, our main conclusions remain robust, as they follow from strongly significant effects based on large numbers of observations. In our research we did not discuss in more depth the citizen perspective which we call on future studies to investigate. Citizens have a stake in the B2G data sharing as data subjects and it is important to compare their views against those of the government and business.

References

Choi, Y., Gil-Garcia, J., Burke, G.B., Costello, J., Werthmuller, D., Aranay, O.: Towards data-driven decision-making in government: identifying opportunities and challenges for data use and analytics. In: Proceedings of the 54th Hawaii International Conference on System Sciences (2021)

Noveck, B.: Data collaboratives: sharing public data in private hands for social good. Forbes (2015). www.forbes.com/sites/bethsimonenoveck/2015/09/24/private-data-sharing-for-public-good/-28dab08b65bb. Accessed 10 May 2016

Susha, I., Janssen, M., Verhulst, S.: Data collaboratives as a new frontier of cross-sector partnerships in the age of open data: taxonomy development. In: Proceedings of the 50th Hawaii International Conference on System Sciences (2017)

European Commission: Towards a European strategy for B2G data sharing for the public interest. Final report of the high-level expert group on business-to-government data sharing (2020). https://ec.europa.eu/newsroom/dae/document.cfm?doc_id=64954. Accessed 17 Mar 2021

European Commission: Public consultation on data act and amended rules on the legal protection of databases. Summary report of the public consultation (2021). https://ec.europa.eu/info/law/better-regulation/. Accessed 17 Mar 2021

Troshani, I., Janssen, M., Lymer, A., Parker, L.D.: Digital transformation of business-to-government reporting: an institutional work perspective. Int. J. Account. Inf. Syst. **31**, 17–36 (2018)

Susha, I., Rukanova, B.D., Ramon Gil-Garcia, J., Hua Tan, Y., Gasco, M.: Identifying mechanisms for achieving voluntary data sharing in cross-sector partnerships for public good. In: Proceedings of the 20th Annual International Conference on Digital Government Research, pp. 227–236, June 2019

Rukanova, B., Tan, Y.H., Huiden, R., Ravulakollu, A., Grainger, A., Heijmann, F.: A framework for voluntary business-government information sharing. Gov. Inf. Q. **37**(4), 101501 (2020)

George, J.J., Yan, J., Leidner, D.E.: Data philanthropy: corporate responsibility with strategic value? Inf. Syst. Manag. **37**(3), 186–197 (2020)

George, J.J., Yan, J., Leidner, D.E., Awasthi, P.: Does engaging in data philanthropy impact business value? Inf. Syst. Manag. 1–15 (2022)

Klievink, B., Van Der Voort, H., Veeneman, W.: Creating value through data collaboratives. Inf. Polity **23**(4), 379–397 (2018)

Micheli, M.: Public bodies' access to private sector data: the perspectives of twelve European local administrations. First Monday (2022)
Awasthi, P., George, J.: Harmonizing strategic advantage with social good through data philanthropy. In: Proceedings Annual Workshop of the AIS Special Interest Group for ICT in Global Development (2019)
Van Dijck, J., Poell, T., De Waal, M.: The Platform Society: Public Values in a Connective World. Oxford University Press, Oxford (2018)
Susha, I., Gil-Garcia, J.R.: A collaborative governance approach to partnerships addressing public problems with private data. In: Proceedings of the 52nd Hawaii International Conference on System Sciences, January 2019
Bannister, F., Connolly, R.: ICT, public values and transformative government: A framework and programme for research. Gov. Inf. Q. **31**(1), 119–128 (2014)
Porter, M.E., Kramer, M.R.: Creating shared value. In: Lenssen, G.G., Smith, N.C. (eds.) Managing sustainable business, pp. 327–350. Springer, Dordrecht (2019). https://doi.org/10.1007/978-94-024-1144-7_16
Austin, J.E., Seitanidi, M.M.: Collaborative value creation: a review of partnering between nonprofits and businesses: part I. Value creation spectrum and collaboration stages. Nonprofit Voluntary Sect. Q. **41**(5), 726–758 (2012)
Monge, F., Barns, S., Kattel, R., Bria, F.: A new data deal: the case of Barcelona. UCL Institute for Innovation and Public Purpose (2022)
Hummel, P., Braun, M., Tretter, M., Dabrock, P.: Data sovereignty: a review. Big Data Soc. **8**(1) (2021). https://doi.org/10.1177/2053951720982012
Mercille, J.: Inclusive smart cities: beyond voluntary corporate data sharing. Sustainability **13**(15), 8135 (2021)
Vigorito, A.: Government access to privately-held data: business-to-government data sharing: voluntary and mandatory models. Eur. J. Comp. Law Gov. **1**(aop), 1–22 (2022)
Sayogo, D.S., Pardo, T.A.: Understanding smart data disclosure policy success: the case of Green Button. In: Proceedings of the 14th Annual International Conference on Digital Government Research, pp. 72–81, June 2013
Klievink, B., Bharosa, N., Tan, Y.H.: The collaborative realization of public values and business goals: governance and infrastructure of public–private information platforms. Gov. Inf. Q. **33**(1), 67–79 (2016)
Susha, I., Grönlund, Å., Van Tulder, R.: Data driven social partnerships: exploring an emergent trend in search of research challenges and questions. Gov. Inf. Q. **36**(1), 112–128 (2019)
R Core Team: A language and environment for statistical computing. R Foundation for Statistical Computing, Vienna (2020). https://www.R-project.org/
Wickham, H., François, R., Henry, L., Müller, K.: dplyr: A Grammar of Data Manipulation. R package version 1.0.7 (2021). https://CRAN.R-project.org/package=dplyr
Fox, J., Weisberg, S.: An R Companion to Applied Regression, 3rd edn. Sage, Thousand Oaks (2019). https://socialsciences.mcmaster.ca/jfox/Books/Companion/
Hall, P.A., Soskice, D.: An introduction to varieties of capitalism. In: Varieties of Capitalism, pp. 1–68 (2001). https://doi.org/10.1093/0199247757.003.0001
Taylor, L.: The ethics of big data as a public good: which public? Whose good? Philos. Trans. Roy. Soc. A Math. Phys. Eng. Sci. **374**(2083), 20160126 (2016)
Vespe, M., Iacus, S.M., Santamaria, C., Sermi, F., Spyratos, S.: On the use of data from multiple mobile network operators in Europe to fight COVID-19. Data Policy **3** (2021)
Benjamins, R., Vos, J., Verhulst, S.: Mobile Big Data in the fight against COVID-19. Data Policy **4** (2022)
Ågren, K., Bjelkmar, P., Allison, E.: The use of anonymized and aggregated telecom mobility data by a public health agency during the COVID-19 pandemic: learnings from both the operator and agency perspective. Data Policy **3** (2021)

Johnson, B.R., Connolly, E., Carter, T.S.: Corporate social responsibility: the role of Fortune 100 companies in domestic and international natural disasters. Corp. Soc. Responsib. Environ. Manag. **18**(6), 352–369 (2011)

Robin, N., Klein, T., Jütting, J.: Public-private partnerships for statistics: lessons learned, future steps: a focus on the use of non-official data sources for national statistics and public policy. OECD Development Co-Operation Working Papers (2016). https://doi.org/10.1787/5jm3nqp1g8wf-en

Klein, T., Verhulst, S.: Access to new data sources for statistics: business models and incentives for the corporate sector. PARIS21, discussion paper no. 10, March 2017

Ozalp, H., Ozcan, P., Dinckol, D., Zachariadis, M., Gawer, A.: "Digital colonization" of highly regulated industries: an analysis of big tech platforms' entry into healthcare and education. Forthcoming in California Management Review (2022)

'Right to Be Forgotten': Analyzing the Impact of Forgetting Data Using *K*-NN Algorithm in Data Stream Learning

Caio Libera[1], Leandro Miranda[1](✉), Flávia Bernardini[1], Saulo Mastelini[2], and José Viterbo[1]

[1] Fluminense Federal University, Niterói, RJ, Brazil
{caiodellalibera,leandromiranda,fcbernardini,jviterbo}@id.uff.br
[2] University of São Paulo, São Carlos, SP, Brazil
mastelini@usp.br

Abstract. New international regulations concerning personal management data guarantee the 'Right to Be Forgotten'. One might request to have their data erased from third-party tools and services. This requirement is especially challenging when considering the behavior of machine learning estimators that will need to forget portions of their knowledge. In this paper, we investigate the impact of these learning and forgetting policies in data stream learning. In data stream mining, the sheer volume of instances typically makes it unfeasible to store the data or retraining the learning models from scratch. Hence, more efficient solutions are needed to deal with the dynamic nature of online machine learning. We modify an incremental k-NN classifier to enable it to erase its past data and we also investigate the impact of data forgetting in the obtained predictive performance. Our proposal is compared against the original k-NN algorithm using seven non-stationary stream datasets. Our results show that the forgetting-enabled algorithm can achieve similar prediction patterns compared to the vanilla one, although it yields lower predictive performance at the beginning of the learning process. Such a scenario is a typical cold-start behavior often observed in data stream mining applications, and not necessarily related to the employed forgetting mechanisms.

Keywords: Lazy learning · Stream learning · Right to be forgotten · K-NN · Data stream

1 Introduction

In the last decades, many works in literature have focused on dealing with incremental learning, for facing the catastrophic forgetting problem in machine learning [14,21]. These works evolved to the proposal of new algorithms for tackling recurrent issues in incremental learning, such as concept drift detection [11,16], novelty detection [1,18] among other aspects. More recently, frameworks bring together different data stream

Published by Springer Nature Switzerland AG 2022
M. Janssen et al. (Eds.): EGOV 2022, LNCS 13391, pp. 530–542, 2022.
https://doi.org/10.1007/978-3-031-15086-9_34

learning algorithms for some specific purposes, such as data stream clustering, classification, regression, and among other aspects. Examples of these kind of frameworks are *MOA* [3] and *WEKA* [12], implemented in Java and *Scikit-Multiflow* [20], implemented in Python.

On the other hand, in the last years, many laws around the world have been proposed to tackle data privacy issues, such as the General Data Protection Rules (GDPR) [6]. Among other specificities, these laws state that users have the right to be forgotten, asking that data must be deleted. This leaded the companies to establish mechanisms for forgetting data, which is simpler when the target information was not processed yet. However, many companies may have used these data to infer their models for recommending products or user profiles, predicting user behaviors, among other applications. Although these applications are not directly discussed in GDPR and related rules, multiple researchers are already discussing ethics in Artificial Intelligence (AI). The High-Level Expert Group on AI from the European Commission presented a document, called Ethics guidelines for trustworthy AI [5]. This document dictates that trustworthy AI should be lawful, respecting all applicable laws and regulations; ethical, respecting ethical principles and values; and robust, both from a technical perspective while taking into account its social environment. In our point of view, ethical principles and values include the discussion about not using data that should be forgotten in models constructed by learning algorithms.

In literature, we could observe that few authors discuss the impacts of the right to be forgotten in the artificial intelligence and machine learning domains, as discussed in Sect. 2. One important issue is analyzing the impact of forgetting data for future predictions. In this work, we consider some hypothetical scenarios, described in Sect. 3, in which we face the issue of having to remove data from the knowledge base to comply with the new regulations. Questions such as "how much prediction performance do the estimators lose in this forgetfulness scenario?" are yet to be answered. One issue related to this aspect is that there is not a widespread approach for evaluating the impact of forgetting data in machine learning.

Lazy learning approaches have the advantage of directly manipulating knowledge-base instead of creating models to be reused. *K*-NN algorithm memorizes a portion of the data, which leads to an easy adaptation for stream learning. Therefore, *K*-NN is available in many different machine learning frameworks, either for batch [9] or for data stream learning [3]. In this way, this algorithm easily allows forgetting past data to analyze the predicting behavior in future examples.

In this work, we present a methodology for conducting an experimental analysis of the *K*-NN behavior when forgetting data from the stream. As a contribution, we present a new algorithm called FGT-*K*-NN, which adapts *K*-NN for forgetting data from the data stream. In our experimental analysis, we used different types of datasets, which present different patterns of concept drift. These datasets were also used by Losing, Hammer and Wersing [16]. Our results show that FGT-*K*-NN can achieve similar predictive patterns over time compared to the original k-NN algorithm, although it shows lower performance in the beginning of the stream, as expected in data stream learning. It is worth noting that, as far as we know, this work is the first initiative of tackling the 'Right to Be Forgotten' principle directly by the stream learning algorithm.

This work is organized as follows: Sect. 2 presents a brief discussion regarding the 'Right to be Forgotten' and the problems this scenario may bring to Artificial Intelligence. Section 3 describes two fictitious scenarios of forgetting data in estimators constructed by machine learning algorithms. Section 4 presents the background in machine learning required for better understanding our proposal and results. Section 5 presents our methodology for conducting our experimental analysis. Section 6 presents the results of our experimental analysis. Finally, Sect. 7 describes our conclusions, limitations of this work, our next steps and future work.

2 Right to Be Forgotten and Artificial Intelligence

'Right to Be Forgotten' is essentially the concept that individuals have the right to request that their data (collected by others) must be deleted. European Union regulated, in 2016, "the protection of natural persons with regard to the processing of personal data and on the free movement of such data" through the General Data Protection Regulation (GDPR) [6]. Also, they state that "a data subject should have the right to have personal data concerning him or her rectified and a 'Right to Be Forgotten' ". According to Politou, Aleksis and Patsakis [22], there are many challenges related to forgetting personal data and revoking consent under GDPR, and they state that "privacy and big data are in many cases contradictory. Big data require massive amount of information to be collected with not a predefined and clear purpose at the time of collection. Users do not have any control on their personal information stored and analysed by the involved data controllers and the parties that participate in data dissemination may be numerous".

In this forgetting scenario, while data deletion may seem like a straightforward topic from the point of view of many regulators, this seemingly simple issue poses many practical problems in real machine learning environments. Thus, the estimators present in many systems need strategies to forget the data that must be excluded. The problem associated to the 'Right to Be Forgotten' in Artificial Intelligence (AI) may be due to our imprecise understanding of privacy in relation to AI [23]. Often, people see privacy as hiding their information from others. This is especially apparent when examining the 'Right to Be Forgotten' principle, under which individuals can request that information made public be deleted (and therefore made private). In the case of public information made private, the metaphor of the human mind forgetting some pieces of information applies well or, at least, no more humans in the future will be aware about the data turned private. However, this idea is not necessarily straightly translated into the era of AI and machine learning. Our current laws seem to treat human and machine memory in the same way, supporting a fictitious understanding of memory and forgetting that does not fit into reality.

However, the range of 'Right to be Forgotten' tools or techniques available in this context is still scarce nowadays. In the 'Right to be Forgotten' scenario, there are two possible approaches: (i) retrain the estimator using batch learning; or (ii) deleting data from the memory, in case of lazy learning. In the first approach, there is a need to store all records for the generation of new estimators. In the second approach, Villaronga, Kieseberg and Tiffany [23] use k-anonymity techniques in databases, for the protection and exclusion of information. However, the authors state that "it may be impossible to fulfill the legal aims of the Right to Be Forgotten in artificial intelligence environments". For the domain of stream learning, Mirzasoleiman, Karbasi and Krause [19] proposed a framework that offers instantaneous data summarization while preserving the right of an individual to be forgotten. They cast the problem as an instance of robust streaming submodular maximization, where the goal is to produce a concise real-time summary. They state that their framework outputs a robust solution against deletions from the summary at any given time, while preserving the same approximation guarantee. The authors tested their work on different scenarios. On the one hand, none of the found studies presents machine learning algorithms that incorporate such forgetting techniques, facilitating the use of machine learning algorithms in this context. On the other hand, the framework proposed by Mirzasoleiman, Karbasi and Krause [19] is an interesting approach, discussing the use of memories in the stream mining process. Their concepts inspired us to tackling memory process directly in stream learning algorithms, as well as studying other ways of adapting stream learning algorithms in the 'Right to Be Forgotten' context.

3 Forgetting Data in Machine Learning—Motivating Scenarios

In this section, we present two hypothetical scenarios where we make clear the challenges involved in forgetting data in estimators constructed by machine learning algorithms: (1) "An electricity supply company collects hourly energy consumption data to forecast the energy consumption of each customer in their home. The company uses this data to forecast energy consumption for the next hour, the next day and the next month. In this scenario, the company aggregates the forecast results to forecast the demand for energy consumption in a city. In the context of the new data privacy rules, the company's customers request the deletion of their historical consumption data."; and (2) "A social media company uses data from diverse users to predict consumption behavior. The usage of data was previously consented by users. However, many of them ask the company to forget their data". Both scenarios show that could be ethically necessary to chain the data deletion into the forecast estimators. We believe that scenarios like these hypothetical ones will be more and more common in future applications.

In our scenarios, we also consider that the estimators were constructed using supervised machine learning algorithms, which can be either (i) *eager algorithms* for constructing estimators through diverse approaches (such as symbolic learning, probabilistic learning, statistical learning and so on); or (ii) *lazy algorithms*, based on data memories. Also, they can be constructed either by batch or stream learning algorithms. In batch learning, the learning algorithm creates an estimator (a model or a set of memories) in only one step and, afterward, the estimator is used to predict the label for unlabeled instances that the estimator builder never saw [3,9]. In stream learning, an estimator is ready to do either one of the following at any time [4]: (i) Receive an unlabeled instance and make a prediction for it on the basis of its current estimator; or (ii) Receive the label for an instance seen in the past, and use it for adjusting the estimator. In the 'Right to be Forgotten' scenario, there are two possible approaches: (i) reconstructing the estimator if using batch learning; or (ii) deleting data from the memory [19,23].

Also, not only the data should be forgotten according to users requests, but also data may present data distribution changes over time. Such changes require the use of learning algorithms that tackle concept drift. Data stream learning is one of the approaches largely investigated in machine learning for constructing adaptive estimators when data stream is available and concept drift is present [3,10]. These data stream learning algorithms are applied mainly in scenarios where the data distribution happens in a non-stationary way. Consequently, in most cases, there is concept drift arising from the change in the data distribution over time [13]. Data stream learning has been applied and has shown good results in many different domains [15], such as monitoring and detection of solar energy consumption [7,24], intrusion detection in networks [2], anomaly detection [8], among others.

4 Stream Learning Characteristics for Classification Problems

Classification needs a set of properly labeled instances to learn an estimator, so that we can use this estimator to predict the labels of unseen instances. In this way, suppose we have a stream of continuously arriving instances. We need to assign a label from a set of nominal labels to each item, as a function of the other features of the item. A estimator can be trained as long as the correct label for (many of) the instances is available at a later time. Generally speaking, a stream mining estimator is ready to do either one of the following at any moment [4]: (i) Receive an unlabeled instance and make a prediction for it on the basis of its current estimator; or (ii) Receive the label for an instance seen in the past, and use it for adjusting the estimator, that is, for training. The most significant requirements for a stream learning algorithm are [3,4]: (i) Process an instance at a time, and inspect it (at most) once; (ii) Use a limited amount of time to process each instance; (iii) Use a limited amount of memory; (iv) Be ready to give a prediction at any time; and (v) Adapt to temporal changes. Typically, *a general data stream learning algorithm for constructing an estimator* follows these steps: (i) get an unlabeled instance $\mathbf{x}$; (ii) make a prediction $\hat{y} = \hat{f}(\mathbf{x})$, where $\hat{f}$ is the current estimator, under construction by the stream learner; (iii) get the true label y for $\mathbf{x}$; (iv) use the pair (x, y) to update (train) $\hat{f}$, and the pair $(\hat{y}, y)$ to update statistics about $\hat{f}$—the estimator performance. Although this estimator is too simple, it is useful for comparing data stream learning algorithms.

For evaluating the estimator in data stream learning, we used a technique called prequential [3]: Each individual instance is used to test the estimator before it is used for training, and from this, metrics such as accuracy can be incrementally updated. When the evaluation is intentionally performed in this order, the estimator is always being tested on instances that has not seen yet. This scheme ensures a smooth plot of accuracy over time, as each individual instance will become less and less significant to the overall average.

Concept Drift: Formally, concept drift is defined considering two time points t_0 and t_1, and is given by $\exists X : p_{t_0}(X, y) \neq p_{t_1}(X, y)$, where p_{t_0} denotes the joint distribution at time t_0 between the set of input features X and the target variable y [11]. Changes in data can be characterized as changes in the components of this relation. In other terms, the prior probabilities of classes $p(y)$ may change; the class conditional probabilities $p(X|y)$ may change; and, as a result, the posterior probabilities of classes $p(y|X)$ may change, affecting the prediction. In this way, Gama *et al.* [11] presents two different types of concept drift: (i) Real concept drift, which refers to changes in $p(y|X)$, and such changes can happen either with or without change in $p(X)$; and (ii) Virtual drift happens if the distribution of the incoming data changes (i.e., $p(X)$ changes) without affecting $p(y|X)$. In this way, only the real concept drift changes the class boundary and the previous decision estimator becomes obsolete. In practice, virtual drift changing prior probabilities or novelties may appear in combination with the real drift. In these cases, the class boundary is also affected.

Changes in data distribution over time may manifest in different forms, as illustrated in Fig. 1 on a toy one-dimensional data, constructed by Gama *et al.* [11]. In this data, changes happen in the data mean. A drift may happen suddenly/abruptly, by switching from one concept to another, or incrementally, consisting of many intermediate concepts in between. Finally, drifts may introduce new concepts that were not seen before (gradual), or previously seen concepts may reoccur (reoccurring concepts) after some time. Most of the adaptive learning techniques implicitly or explicitly assume and specialize in some subset of concept drifts. Many of them assume sudden non-reoccurring drifts. Typically, mixtures of many types of concept drift can be observed in real data.

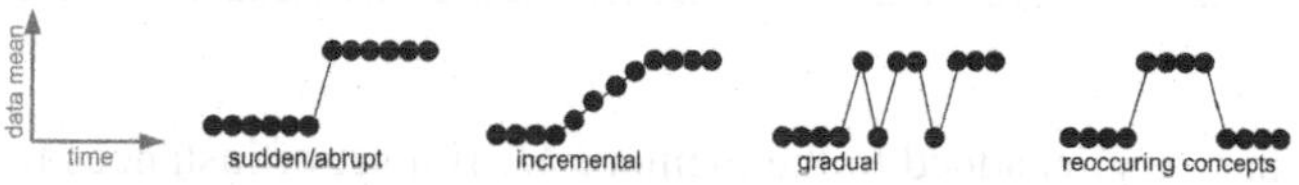

Fig. 1. Patterns of changes over time [11]

***K*-NN for Data Stream:** The estimator consists of keeping in the memory the last W instances of the stream. Given a new instance $\mathbf{x}_i$ to be classified, $\hat{y}$ is the most voted class label of the K closest instances in $S_W = \{(\mathbf{x}_1, y_1), ..., (\mathbf{x}_W, y_W)\}$. In other words, the K-Nearest Neighbor or K-NN algorithm outputs the majority class label of the K instances closest to the one to predict. Algorithm 1 shows the steps of K-NN for data stream.

5 Our Experimental Methodology

For conducting our experimental analysis, we firstly had to identify the main characteristics that must be considered by a learning algorithm in the 'Right to Be Forgotten' scenario. When considering the steps of a general data stream learning algorithm, we understand that step (iv) must be adapted to not only consider incorporating new labeled instances into the estimator, but also considering the possibility of forgetting past data from the stream. In this way, we extended K-NN (Algorithm 1) to create a new algorithm, called FGT-K-NN, whose steps are present in Algorithm 2. If a new instance $\mathbf{x}$ is presented in the stream to be classified then we call FGT-K-NN, with $Label = True$ and $Forget = False$. In this case, only Steps 1 and 2 are executed and $\hat{y}$ is returned to classify $\mathbf{x}$. If a new instance $(\mathbf{x}, y)$ is given to be added to the memory then we call FGT-K-NN, with $Label = False$ and $Forget = False$. Also in this case, only Steps 1 and 2

Algorithm 1. *K*-NN Algorithm.

Require:

M: K-NN memory—a queue of labeled instances given by the stream
Label: Boolean variable indicating if the instance arriving in the stream must be labeled (*True*) or loaded in M (*False*)
K: number of neighbors to be considered for classifying new instances
W: window size—defines the largest size of the memory for classifying new instances
$(\mathbf{x}, y)$: a new pair to be labeled ($y = \emptyset$) or used for being loaded in memory (y is the true label of $\mathbf{x}$)
L: set of labels in the data stream

if ($Label = True$) **then**
    $S_{near} = nearest\_neighbors(M, K)$
    return $\hat{y} = \arg\max_L (S_{near})$ ▷ Return the majority class of the nearest neighbors
else
    if ($|M| > W$) **then**
        dequeue(M) ▷ Delete the oldest instance from M
    end if
    enqueue($(\mathbf{x}, y)$) ▷ Put $(\mathbf{x}, y)$ in the beginning of M
end if

are executed, but $(\mathbf{x}, y)$ is added to the memory M. If a set of instances to be forgotten S_{Fgt} is given then we call FGT-K-NN, with $Forget = True$. In this case, only Steps 3 and 4 are executed, eliminating the instances of S_{Fgt} in the least N_{Fgt} elements of M.

For evaluating the behaviour of FGT-K-NN, we also extended the prequential technique. We simulated the forgetness selecting N_{Forget} instances from the N_{Recent} most recent instances loaded in memory M. For calculating accuracy over the stream, we firstly loaded the first 100 instances of the data stream, and calculated the mean accuracy of the next 100 instances for generating the graphs, shown in next section. We implemented both extensions using Scikit-Multiflow package[1]. Our implementations are available at GitHub[2]. We used the following parameters for our experiments: $W = 5{,}000$, $K = \{3, 5\}$; $N_{Recent} = \{1000, 5000\}$; $|S_{Fgt}| = \{100, 250, 500, 750\}$. We randomly selected from N_{Recent} instances a set S_{Fgt} containing $|S_{Fgt}|$ instances to be forgotten. We chose these fixed values because they are default values (K and W values) in most studies and allow different proportions of samples in relation to the number of samples present in the datasets.

We executed our experiments selecting seven datasets from the ones used by Losing, Hammer and Wersing [16]. Our selection was based on different patterns of concept drift. Table 1 shows the characteristics of the datasets used in our experiments. In this table, Name refers to the name of the dataset; N, the number of instances in the dataset; $|L|$, the number of labels in the dataset; M, the number of features in X; Drift, the concept drift properties of the dataset, which can be V (virtual), R (real), R+V (various, both real and virtual); AR (abrupt real), IR (incremental real) or ARV (abrupt reocurring

[1] Available at https://scikit-multiflow.github.io/.
[2] Available at https://github.com/dlcaio/research-project-data-stream-learning.

Algorithm 2. FGT-K-NN Algorithm.

Require:

M: K-NN memory—a queue of labeled instances given by the stream
Label: Boolean variable indicating if the instance arriving in the stream must be labeled ($True$) or loaded in M ($False$)
K: number of neighbors to be considered for classifying new instances
W: window size—defines the largest size of the memory for classifying new instances
$(\mathbf{x}, y)$: a new pair to be labeled ($y = \emptyset$) or used for being loaded in memory (y is the true label of $\mathbf{x}$
L: set of labels present in the stream
Forget: Boolean variable indicating if data must be forgotten ($True$);
N_{Recent}: number of the recent instances to be considered for forgetness in M
S_{Fgt}: set of instances to be forgotten

if ($\neg Forget$) **then** ▷ Call K-NN algorithm—Algorithm 1
    K-NN(M,$Label$,W,$(\mathbf{x}, y)$,L)
else ▷ Forget data in M
    Delete from the last N_{Recent} instances of M the instances pertaining to S_{Fgt}
end if

Table 1. Datasets used for our experimental analysis

Name	N	$\|L\|$	M	Drift	Type
Interchanging RBF	200,000	15	2	AR	Artif.
Mixed drift	600,000	15	2	R+V	Artif.
Poker hand	829,201	10	10	V	Real
Rotating hyperplane	200,000	2	10	IR	Artif.
Transient chessboard	200,000	8	2	ARV	Artif.
SEA concepts	50,000	2	3	AR	Artif.
Weather	18,159	2	8	V	Real

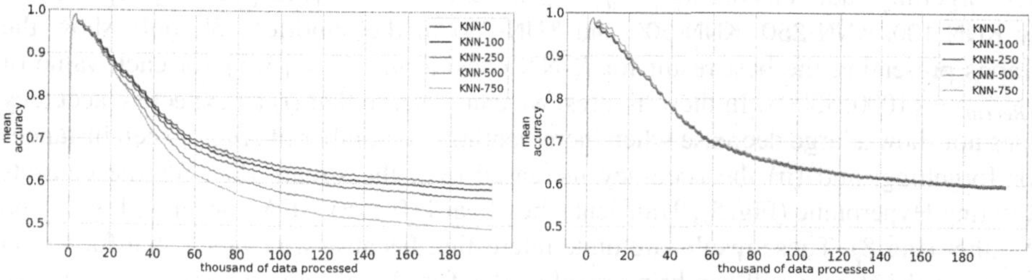

(a) $N_{Recent} = 1000, K = 5$ (b) $N_{Recent} = 5000, K = 5$

Fig. 2. Results using interchanging RBF dataset

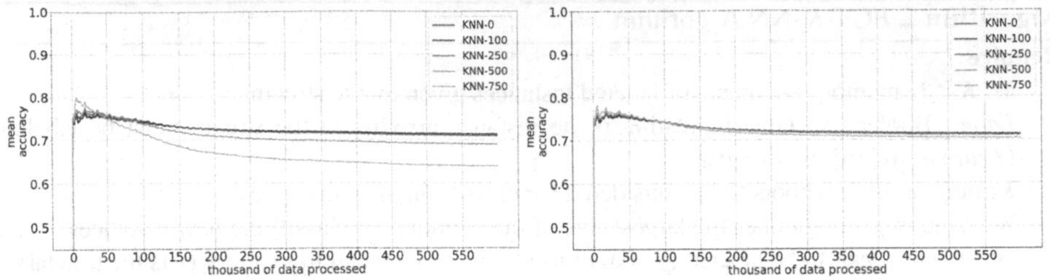

(a) $N_{Recent} = 1000, K = 3$ (b) $N_{Recent} = 5000, K = 3$

Fig. 3. Results using mixed drift dataset

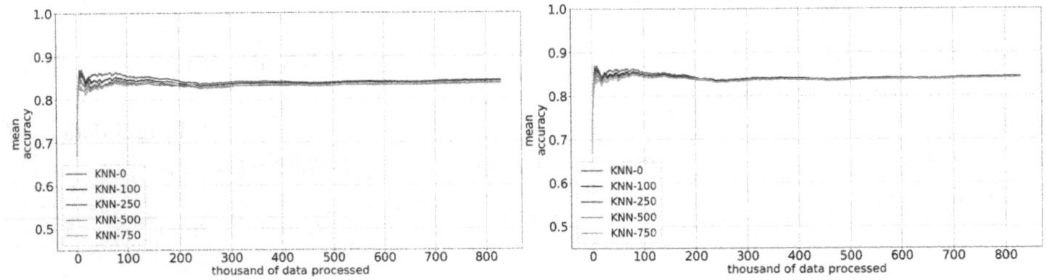

(a) $N_{Recent} = 1000, K = 3$ (b) $N_{Recent} = 5000, K = 3$

Fig. 4. Results using poker hand dataset

virtual); and Type, the type of the dataset, which can be Artif., meaning that the dataset was artificially generated, or Real, meaning that the dataset was collected from real world scenarios.

6 Experimental Results

Figures 2 to 8 shows the results obtained for each dataset using K-NN without forgetting data (shown as only KNN in the subtitles of each figure) and using FGT-K-NN forgetting data considering $|S_{Fgt}| = \{100, 250, 500, 750\}$, respectively represented by KNN-100, KNN-250, KNN-500 and KNN-750 in the subtitles. We only show the graphs presenting the best result for K-NN considering $K = \{3, 5\}$ for each value of $N_{Recent} = \{1000, 5000\}$. In these figures, we can observe that (i) as expected, accuracy does not show a large decrease when incrementing the number of N_{Recent} seen instances for forgetting; and (ii) the accuracy increased over the stream data for the datasets Rotating Hyperplane (Fig. 5), Transient Chessboard (Fig. 6), SEA concepts (Fig. 7) and Weather (Fig. 8). These results are quite interesting because we can see that forgetting data over the stream still can bring good results for classifying new instances. For the Poker Hand dataset (Fig. 4), we can observe that the accuracy remained stable over the entire stream data. For the Mixed Drift dataset (Fig. 3), we can observe that the accuracy decreased over the stream data. Finally, for the Interchanging RBF (Fig. 2), we can observe that the accuracy highly decreased over the stream data. This last result was

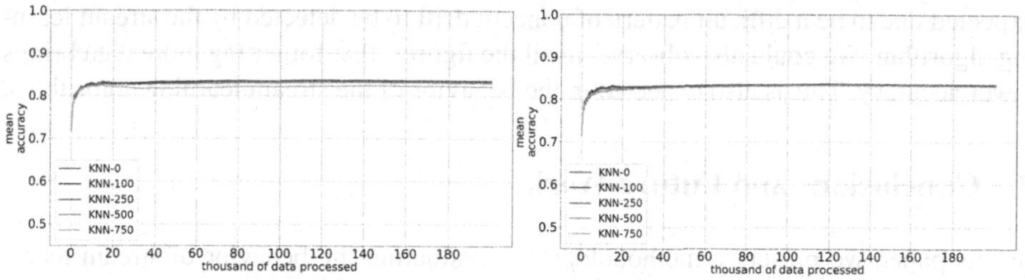

(a) $N_{Recent} = 1000, K = 5$ (b) $N_{Recent} = 5000, K = 5$

Fig. 5. Results using rotating hyperplane dataset

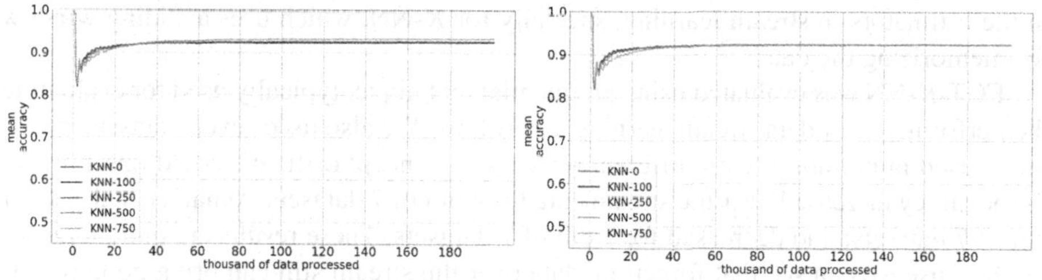

(a) $N_{Recent} = 1000, K = 5$ (b) $N_{Recent} = 5000, K = 5$

Fig. 6. Results using transient chessboard dataset

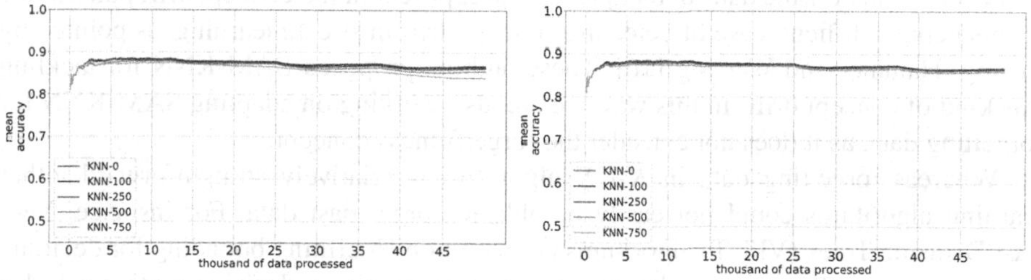

(a) $N_{Recent} = 1000, K = 5$ (b) $N_{Recent} = 5000, K = 5$

Fig. 7. Results using SEA concepts dataset

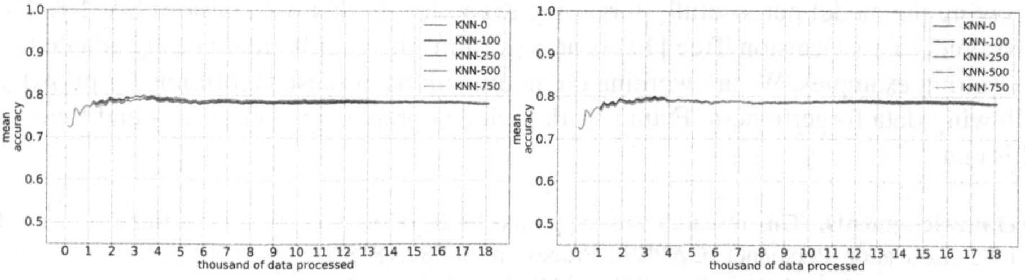

(a) $N_{Recent} = 1000, K = 5$ (b) $N_{Recent} = 5000, K = 5$

Fig. 8. Results using weather dataset

expected due to be a difficult pattern of concept drift to be detected by the stream learning algorithm. We could also observe, in all the figures, that forgetting more data brings lower accuracy. This is also expected in the behavior of the stream learning algorithms.

7 Conclusions and Future Work

In this paper, we present a methodology for evaluating the behavior of stream learning algorithms in the scenario of 'Right to be Forgotten'. We specifically used in our methodology the lazy learning algorithm K-NN. We extended this algorithm for forgetting recent data from the stream. We called our adaptation of FGT-K-NN. We explored forgetfulness in recent data due to the idea that more recent data is strongly represented in the estimators in stream learning, specially for K-NN, which uses a sliding window for memorizing the data.

FGT-K-NN was evaluated using prequential technique, typically used for evaluating the performance of data stream learning algorithms. We also used seven datasets, previously used in literature, with different patterns of concept drift. We could observe that the accuracy increased over the stream data for 4 out of 7 datasets; remained stable for 1 out of 7 datasets; and decreased for 2 out of 7 datasets. These results are quite interesting because we can see that forgetting data over the stream still can bring good results for classifying new instances. However, we could also observe that if we increase the amount of data to be forgotten then we achieve lower accuracy in the K-NN estimator. This is also expected in the behavior of the stream learning algorithms. We expected the worst results for the dataset that presents abrupt real in the concept drift pattern due to this being a difficult case of detecting concept drift in stream learning, as pointed by Losing, Hammer and Wersing [16]. These authors proposed SAM-KNN for tackling this kind of concept drift. In this way, we are also working on adapting SAM-KNN for forgetting data, as it does not consider the forgetfulness concept.

Whereas forgetting data in K-NN algorithm is relatively straightforward, other learning algorithms could not easily be able to forget past data. For instance, Very Fast Decision Trees (VFDT) algorithms are based on Hoeffding bounding for deciding how many examples must be observed before constructing a decision node. Such this one, stream learning algorithms focus on growing the model to incorporate new knowledge and adapt new data distributions. However, because of the historical catastrophic forgetting of the batch machine learning algorithms, they were not created to allow growing the model purposefully forgetting examples. In this way, besides SAM-KNN, Extremely Fast Decision Tree [17] is an algorithm that can be more easily adapted to forgetting examples. We are working on modifications of these algorithms for properly allowing data forgetfulness. Future work includes proposing frameworks and tools to this end.

Acknowledgments. This research was supported by the Coordination for the Improvement of Higher Education Personnel (CAPES), Process n. 88882.183880; and PIBIC/CNPQ/UFF. We also gratefully acknowledge Albert Bifet and Paristech University, who hosted Flávia Bernardini for a week and allowed us to have discussions to achieve these results.

References

1. Albertini, M.K., de Mello, R.F.: A self-organizing neural network to approach novelty detection. In: Machine Learning: Concepts, Methodologies, Tools and Applications. IGIGlobal (2012)
2. Alves, C., Bernardini, F., Meza, E.B.M., Sousa, L.: Evaluating the behaviour of stream learning algorithms for detecting invasion on wireless networks. Int. J. Secur. Netw. **15**(3), 133–140 (2020)
3. Bifet, A., Holmes, G., Kirkby, R., Pfahringer, B.: MOA: massive online analysis, vol. 11 (2010). http://portal.acm.org/citation.cfm?id=1859903
4. Domingos, P., Hulten, G.: Mining high-speed data streams. In: Proceedings of 6th ACM SIGKDD International Conference on Knowledge Discovery and Data Mining, pp. 71–80. ACM (2000)
5. European Commission: ethics guidelines for trustworthy AI (2019). https://ec.europa.eu/digital-single-market/en/news/ethics-guidelines-trustworthy-ai. Accessed 17 July 2020
6. European parliament: general data protection regulation (2016). https://eur-lex.europa.eu/legal-content/EN/TXT/PDF/?uri=CELEX:32016R0679. Accessed 18 May 2020
7. Faial, D., Bernardini, F., Meza, E.M., Miranda, L., Viterbo, J.: A methodology for taxi demand prediction using stream learning. In: 2020 International Conference on Systems, Signals and Image Processing (IWSSIP) (2020)
8. Faial, D., Bernardini, F., Miranda, L., Viterbo, J.: Anomaly detection in vehicle traffic data using batch and stream supervised learning. In: Moura Oliveira, P., Novais, P., Reis, L.P. (eds.) EPIA 2019. LNCS (LNAI), vol. 11804, pp. 675–684. Springer, Cham (2019). https://doi.org/10.1007/978-3-030-30241-2_56
9. Frank, E., Hall, M.A., Witten, I.H.: Data Mining: Practical Machine Learning Tools and Techniques, 4th edn. Morgan Kaufmann, Burlington (2016)
10. Gama, J.: Knowledge Discovery from Data Streams. CRC Press, Boca Raton (2010)
11. Gama, J., Žliobaitė, I., Bifet, A., Pechenizkiy, M., Bouchachia, A.: A survey on concept drift adaptation. ACM Comput. Surv. (CSUR) **46**(4), 1–37 (2014)
12. Hall, M., Frank, E., Holmes, G., Pfahringer, B., Reutemann, P., Witten, I.H.: The WEKA data mining software: an update. SIGKDD Explor. **11**(1), 10–18 (2009)
13. Holzinger, A., et al.: Machine learning and knowledge extraction in digital pathology needs an integrative approach. In: Holzinger, A., Goebel, R., Ferri, M., Palade, V. (eds.) Towards Integrative Machine Learning and Knowledge Extraction. LNCS (LNAI), vol. 10344, pp. 13–50. Springer, Cham (2017). https://doi.org/10.1007/978-3-319-69775-8_2
14. Jantke, P.: Types of incremental learning. In: Proceedings of the AAAI Symposium on Training Issues in Incremental Learning (1993)
15. Lemaire, V., Salperwyck, C., Bondu, A.: A survey on supervised classification on data streams. In: Zimányi, E., Kutsche, R.-D. (eds.) eBISS 2014. LNBIP, vol. 205, pp. 88–125. Springer, Cham (2015). https://doi.org/10.1007/978-3-319-17551-5_4
16. Losing, V., Hammer, B., Wersing, H.: KNN classifier with self adjusting memory for heterogeneous concept drift. In: Proceedings of the 2016 IEEE International Conference on Data Mining (ICDM), pp. 291–300 (2016)
17. Manapragada, C., Webb, G., Salehi, M.: Extremely fast decision tree. In: Proceedings of the 24th ACM SIGKDD International Conference on Knowledge Discovery and Data Mining - KDD 2018, pp. 1953–1962 (2018)
18. Mellado, D., Saavedra, C., Chabert, S., Torres, R., Salas, R.: Self-improving generative artificial neural network for pseudorehearsal incremental class learning. Algorithms **12**, 206 (2019)

19. Mirzasoleiman, B., Karbasi, A., Krause, A.: Deletion-robust submodular maximization: data summarization with the "right to be forgotten". In: Proceedings of 34th International Conference on Machine Learning, Proceedings Machine Learning Research, vol. 70, pp. 2449–2458 (2017)
20. Montiel, J., Read, J., Bifet, A., Abdessalem, T.: Scikit-multiflow: a multi-output streaming framework. J. Mach. Learn. Res. **19**(1), 2915–2914 (2018)
21. Polikar, R., Udpa, L., Udpa, S.S., Honavar, V.: LEARN++: an incremental learning algorithm for multilayer perceptron networks. In: Proceedings of 2000 IEEE International Conference on Acoustics, Speech, and Signal Processing (2000)
22. Politou, E., Alepis, E., Patsakis, C.: Forgetting personal data and revoking consent under the GDPR: challenges and proposed solutions. J. Cybersecur. **4**(1), tyy001 (2018)
23. Villaronga, E.F., Kieseberg, P.T.L.: Humans forget, machines remember: artificial intelligence and the right to be forgotten. Comput. Law Secur. Rev. **34**(2), 304–313 (2018)
24. Zamora-Martínez, F., Romeu, P., Botella-Rocamora, P., Pardo, J.: On-line learning of indoor temperature forecasting models towards energy efficiency. Energ. Build. **83**, 162–172 (2014)

Towards a Transdisciplinary Evaluation Framework for Mobile Cross-Border Government Services

Gregor Eibl[1] (✉), Lucy Temple[1], Rachelle Sellung[2], Stefan Dedovic[3], Art Alishani[3], and Carsten Schmidt[3]

[1] University for Continuing Education Krems, 3500 Krems, Austria
gregor.eibl@donau-uni.ac.at

[2] Fraunhofer Institute for Industrial Engineering, Nobelstraße 12, 70569 Stuttgart, Germany

[3] Johan Skytte Institute for Political Studies, University of Tartu, Lossi 36, 51003 Tartu, Estonia

Abstract. The evaluation and assessment of project results and their impact are still a recurring challenge in the digital government discipline. Many technologically driven projects or products have faced challenges, where the technology is advanced, but the market adoption and user acceptance are still lacking. To counter these challenges, this paper presents a transdisciplinary evaluation framework and how it could be applied. The foundation for the evaluation framework was a literature review on the most recent and relevant academic publications on transdisciplinary evaluations, which was narrowed down by using selected relevant search terms. This theoretical background was enhanced by a series of practical workshops to validate the findings. By using a transdisciplinary approach, this paper presents a transdisciplinary evaluation framework that enhances the evaluation process of project results in the digital government discipline with six pillars to reflect (1) the real word context, (2) interdisciplinary research, (3) going beyond science, (4) interaction (5) integration, and (6) relevance. Alongside these pillars, dimensions of measurement for the evaluation are also presented and elaborated on. While this evaluation framework could be adopted for many types of projects or products, this paper showcases how it is applied for an international digital government pilot research project throughout its development process. It presents the methodology and process used in establishing the evaluation framework, the evaluation framework itself, and a short discussion.

Keywords: Transdisciplinary research · Evaluation · Assessment · Research evaluation framework · Digital single market · Cross-border · Digital government · Sustainability

1 Introduction

The digital transformation landscape of European public administrations is evolving and capturing interest from various stakeholders. The share of projects that support a digital transition has grown, the scope of digital government research has expanded, new

Published by Springer Nature Switzerland AG 2022
M. Janssen et al. (Eds.): EGOV 2022, LNCS 13391, pp. 543–562, 2022.
https://doi.org/10.1007/978-3-031-15086-9_35

legislative and regulatory frameworks are being introduced, and public administrations continue exploring new opportunities that digitalization offers [1, 2]. While digital government is a relatively new research field, it derives knowledge from several established disciplines, and it includes elements of both practice and academia [3]. This is largely due to the nature of the problems that digital government research addresses. It often requires solutions that extend beyond a single research discipline [2] to support further improvements in how public administrations are governed [4]. For this reason, developing new knowledge and innovative solutions demands collaborative engagements between academic and non-academic actors who possess contextual knowledge and unique expertise to address the problems at hand. This requires projects encompassing diverse disciplines and a taking a transdisciplinary approach to creating spaces where science, policy, and industry can meet to address issues.

Transdisciplinarity is a complex concept adopted to address knowledge fragmentation by linking intellectual frameworks or disciplines initially separated from each other [2]. The outcome is often a new transdisciplinary field with its own conceptual structure [2]. Transdisciplinary projects focus on real-world and wicked problems, tackle issues in an interdisciplinary manner, extend beyond science, include various heterogeneous stakeholders, and integrate everyone's knowledge to enhance relevance for the active stakeholders but also society as the recipient. By nature, digital government projects are often transdisciplinary or have transdisciplinary elements [5]. They draw on knowledge and experiences from different research domains, including public administration, information systems, and computer sciences [2]. In the digital government domain, transdisciplinary projects are beneficial for complex undertakings, where the goal is to support different technological or governance changes [6]. However, implementing these types of projects is not an easy endeavour. They require different interactions between law and technology [7], bring together different kinds of expertise and often deploy artefacts that deliver real impact on public administrations. The design of activities and artefacts often occurs after complex negotiations and compromises between different views, interests, strategies, values, and regulations. For this reason, the implementation of transdisciplinary projects needs to be carefully monitored and evaluated against the expected impact and the attainment of the planned objectives.

In the digital government discipline, one of the challenging areas remains the evaluation and assessment of project results and the impact that initiatives deliver [8, 9].

The transdisciplinary nature of digital government projects could be noted as one of the causes, especially when establishing rules in assessing and evaluating the actual value that existing projects deliver. Evaluation becomes even more challenging if there is a discrepancy in how the value delivered by a project is understood in public sector-led initiatives against those led by the private sector [10]. Furthermore, according to Sellung and Rossnagel [11], when different disciplines are included in the evaluation stages, it becomes challenging to provide well-rounded evaluations. Especially in complex research projects.

Currently, in the research there are existing several evaluation frameworks that have been presented to measure the societal impact of transdisciplinary projects (e.g., [12–14]), yet there is still no unique way to include the different views of all stakeholders, i.e., research and practice, into the evaluation of a transdisciplinary project (see [14–16]). This research gap, is in line with the practical Horizon 2020 and Large-Scale Pilots (LSP), which involvement of various disciplines in a project causes critical issues for researchers and practitioners to assess and evaluate the successfulness of a project [10]. This mainly occurs due to unfamiliarity with the evaluation techniques [17] and most likely the lack of a transdisciplinary evaluation framework for digital government projects. Thus, a custom approach, based on project particularities, needs to be co-developed by the stakeholders, considering the particularities of the desired impact, i.e., in the case of our project, the three pilots. Furthermore, there is little guidance concerning how to design an appropriate evaluation strategy [18]. Based on this research gap our objective is following.

The objective of this paper is to provide researchers and practitioners involved in digital government transdisciplinary projects with an explanation of the process followed through for developing an evaluation framework in addition to providing evaluation framework a transdisciplinary aspect. This study also develops an evaluation framework that not only provides essential information on how to evaluate and design the pilots, but also important aspects concerning the cooperation of partners, their exchange, and knowledge integration throughout the project. Thus, the research question we aim to answer in this paper is *how to develop an evaluation framework that is suitable for transdisciplinary digital government projects*?

In this paper, we present the digital government field as a transdisciplinary domain and provide an evaluation framework for digital government transdisciplinary research projects, in addition to the description of the methods used in the development of this evaluation framework.

The rest of this article is structured as follows. Section 2 provides a practical background overview and shapes the context for this study. Section 3 breaks down the processes and methods that were used to collect the data and conduct this study. Section 4 presents the key findings from the structured literature review and introduces the transdisciplinary framework for evaluating digital government pilots. Section 5 demonstrates the implications of this study and suggests areas for future research. Section 6 summarizes the key findings from this study.

2 Practical Background

The Digital Single Market (DSM) is a key element of the European Single Market that is grounded on the four pillars of free movement for goods, services, capital, and people between the Member States. The approach was always focussed on services that fosters the development of the Single Market. The Single Market began in the mid- 20th century with collaboration in coal and steel. By the end of the century the European Commission (EC) and the Member States had come to recognize the importance of fostering technological and digital development. Consequently, this has led to the preparation of new online services. The implementation of these new services was accompanied by several political steps.

The first step was the implementation of Directive 1999/93/EC on a Community framework for electronic signatures. The EC continued this by supporting electronic and online services through the instruments of so-called action plans, the "eEurope 2002 Action Plan" and the "eEurope 2005 Action Plan" [19, 20]. Their main aim was to strengthen the digital infrastructure in Europe and to increase the digital skills of the potential users. A next step was the 'i2010 digital government Action Plan' of 2005. The way for the DSM was further paved by activities of the EC and the Council of the European Union, which issued further action plans and ministerial declarations. The 2009 'Malmö Declaration' and the 2010 'Digital Agenda' were essential to further pushing the digitization of the EU [21]. The eIDAS Regulation, established in 2014, was a key objective of the '2011–2015 digital government Action Plan', replacing the 'Electronic Signature Directive' by incorporating citizen identification, electronic seals and thus providing a European framework for accepting and using foreign digital identities for citizens and businesses in cross-border digital government services [22, 23]. The 'Tallinn Declaration' in 2017 and the 'eGoverment Action Plan 2016–2020' encouraged the ongoing implementation of the DSM [24]. These strategies and policy action plans required market transition by EU and EEA countries.

The transition of the common market of 28 Member States into a digital market is a very complex undertaking for which no blueprint existed. To showcase its technical feasibility on the one hand and to gather policy input on the other, the EC has started an initiative of so-called Large-Scale Pilot Projects (LSP) [25].

The EC has defined LSPs as targeted, goal-driven initiatives that propose approaches to specific real-life challenges (e.g., administrative, societal, or industrial). Pilots are autonomous entities that involve stakeholders from several sides. The focus is set on a European and national level. The supply and the demand side are covered, and contain all the technological and innovation elements, the tasks related to the use, application and deployment as well as the development, testing and integration activities [26]. To co-finance the LSPs the EC, with the consent of the Member States, has setup, beginning in 2007, several financial frameworks. The first one was the ICT Policy Support Programme (ICT PSP) as part of the Competitiveness and Innovation Framework Programme (CIP) that lasted until 2013. It was followed by the Horizon 2020 research and innovation funding programme from 2014–2020. As already mentioned, these projects involve multiple stakeholders with transdisciplinary approaches and aim to solve real-life challenges; they also require a coherent assessment of the project and project success.

For all LSPs and especially Horizon 2020 projects, evaluation of pilots is required as a requisite project deliverable, leading to the creation of multiple context-specific evaluation frameworks for each project and pilot. Until now, a coherent, generic, and extensible framework for the evaluation is still missing. These evaluation approach differences can also be seen in deliverables submitted by projects, such as DesignScapes, MAZi, ReFLow, and WeCount. Therefore, an ongoing LSP should be used as a nucleus for the development of a transdisciplinary evaluation framework. The mGov4EU project is on the one side a testbed for the technical approaches and the other side provides the frame and basis for this research. It is an undertaking that is driven by its members and originates from five European Member States. It will lift cross-border services supported by the Single Digital Gateway Regulation (SDGR) and by the eIDAS Regulation to new levels by enabling them for a mobile-device use we naturally expect nowadays

[27]. This will come with unprecedented user journeys by making extensive use of automatic attribute provision and SDGR's once-only principle, complemented by mobile identification so that the so-far cumbersome filling in of complex forms gets replaced by user-controlled and user-consented releasing of authoritative data. The project will, therefore, research, design, implement, and evaluate an open ecosystem for secure mobile government services to be used across Europe and beyond. This is accomplished by combining and enhancing the existing eIDAS layer and SDGR layer with modules for mobile devices that are generic enough that they can be reused in the emerging and thus still heterogeneous European mobile-government landscape. Thus, the project will provide a trustworthy federation of collaborative platforms. The outcomes of the project, software and architecture will facilitate the co-delivery, reuse, and trustworthy provision of accessible and easy-to-use public services. The project will implement the core once-only, digital-by-default, and mobile-first principles in a user-centric and user-friendly manner [28].

The results of mGov4EU project will be validated by multiple pilots implementing the enhanced infrastructure services for internet voting, smart mobility, and mobile signing. A key aspect of the pilots is the reuse of existing technical building blocks. It aims to integrate the solutions in day-to-day business and activities around the life-situations of the citizens where they use their mobile phones, to showcase that this is the key to a true cross-border, pan European public service provision [29].

The results (tangible and intangible) of the project will be content agnostic, reusable and extensible solutions [30]. They will provide several options for evaluating the outcomes.

3 Method and Process

This section describes the methodology and processes used in establishing the transdisciplinary evaluation approach. There are two main factors that were used as a basis for this multi-method qualitative research. The first is a literature review, which serves as a foundation and consisted of desk research on various elements of transdisciplinary evaluation frameworks. This presents the inductive coding methodology that was used in conducting the desk research that led to establishing the foundation of how, what, and why this type of evaluation is used and performed. The second factor was a series of workshops that were conducted and provided practical feedback to ensure a common understanding, requirements, and objectives for the evaluation. This allows the evaluation to be continuous throughout the development process, following an action based design science research, by seeking to develop scientific knowledge while solving the lack of a sufficient transdisciplinary evaluation approach [31].

3.1 Literature Review

To establish a foundation and to design our transdisciplinary evaluation framework, a thorough literature search was conducted, seeking the most recent and relevant academic publications on transdisciplinary evaluations. Due to transdisciplinarity being an interdisciplinary field of study, the search for the publications was conducted in two of the largest peer-reviewed literature databases: Scopus and Web of Science. The search string that was used to conduct the search has as a starting point transdisciplinarity as it is at the core of the framework and includes the following:

TITLE-ABS-KEY ((transdisciplin* AND (framework OR model) AND (evaluation OR benchmark* OR assessment))).

This way publications that focused on transdisciplinary frameworks or evaluations could be found. The search resulted in 806 results in Scopus and 631 in Web of Science. These were further filtered to those papers available in English, reducing the starting amount to 776 and 605 respectively, a total of 1381. After duplicates were removed, the search revealed 1006 papers. To be able to narrow down the number of publications by filtering those that were deemed unsuitable for the topic at hand, two researchers conducted a deep review of the title and abstract of the list of publications, removing publications for the following criteria: Duplicates that had not been detected before; Publications that were too specific: Focus on the field of medicine, Veterinary, ecology; Not a publication on transdisciplinary evaluation; Lack of indicators or relative sources of information for the goal of this desk research.

The sample was narrowed down to 185 publications, and finally, a conjoint examination with three researchers discussing those articles that were slightly unclear if they should be included in the analysis or not, brought the final sample down to 75. Out of these, 73 were available for download and were further reviewed and explored in their entirety.

To be able to move forward with the analysis, MAXQDA was selected as the software for coding the literature. An inductive approach was selected as the best option for this research, where a coding schema was defined after a sample of the literature was reviewed. First, three researchers reviewed and coded the same five papers that were deemed highly relevant when screening the databases. Next, a workshop with the academic researchers was set up to discuss the individually found codes and sub-codes for segments to understand transdisciplinarity at its core and how to evaluate it. A final set of codes and sub-codes were defined, alongside guiding principles on how to select a specific code for a segment. The rest of the papers were divided equally into the three partner organizations participating in the design of the evaluation framework. A total of 1375 segments were extracted in the texts and the categories in which they were coded are the following:

- Characteristics of transdisciplinarity
- Frameworks
- Dimensions
  - Purpose
  - Timing
  - Scope
  - Actors
  - Impact
  - Mix/Granularity

- Indicators
- Challenges of transdisciplinary evaluation

3.2 Workshops

Another goal of this methodology was to create an evaluation framework that included not only a sound theoretical background, but also a practical foundation. To accomplish this, workshops were conducted to tailor the evaluation framework to meet and set realistic expectations, requirements, and objectives for the pilot project. While this evaluation framework is being applied to a research pilot project, this evaluation framework could also be applied to other artefacts or types of digital government research projects.

There were two types of workshops: the initial alignment workshop and a series of pilot workshops. The initial alignment workshop took place with all the project partners involved in the evaluation of the project in an online environment. This included three scientific partners of various disciplines, and an industry partner belonging to the digital services and electronic voting field. These moderated discussions led to a common understanding of the roles of the partners, a first draft of expectations.

Following the alignment workshop, a series of three pilot tailored workshops were conducted. The knowledge and know-how gained from the literature review and the initial workshop established a foundation for the framework. Next, the scientific partners conducted and moderated the pilot workshop, as this was the focal point of this project. This workshop was divided into a series of phases. The first two phases were conducted in a hybrid setting, with most partners working face to face whilst some were present online. A total of 16 participants attended the workshop in situ, and 10 participated virtually. The workshops included all partners from the mGov4EU consortium, therefore there were partners with scientific focus, focused both on the eGovernment and identity disciplines, to economics, information science and social sciences, technical specialises with a focus on software development, legal specialists and govtech companies. The first of the series focused on pilot leaders answering the "5 Ws" [32] in order to provide the scientific partners with a current state of the pilot definitions. These questions refer to: i) what the pilots are about; ii) why the pilots are necessary iii) when and iv) where they are going to happen; and v) who is going to be involved and targeted respectively. In the subsequent second phase, the project partners guided by the pilot leaders were asked to elaborate on potential, pilot-specific indicators, which could either be provided by the indicators defined in the transdisciplinary evaluation framework or derived by the pilot development and design. The third and fourth phases of the workshop were continued online by all the relevant project partners. During the third phase, the participants separated the jointly developed indicators into two categories, i.e., related to the design process of the pilots, and the implementation itself. In case of a high number of indicators, participants were also requested to prioritize the indicators. In the final phase, the pilot specific groups were asked to reflect on how to measure each indicator, where information for the assessment and analysis could be found, and if the indicator could be a generic one, applied to all pilots, and not just one. Moreover, the groups were asked for approval and agreement on all the indicators established.

4 Transdisciplinary Evaluation Framework

Often a broader conceptual framework is needed as traditional bibliometrics for evaluation are insufficient for transdisciplinary projects [33, 34]. Defining a conceptual evaluation framework may involve not only searching through existing literature but consulting with experts, practitioners, and experienced stakeholders in a variety of fields [34]. By having a transdisciplinary evaluation framework, it aims to elevate interdisciplinary evaluation frameworks. The transdisciplinary evaluation framework aims at providing a comprehensive method to ensure that technical solutions developed in research (or other) projects meet needs required for market adoption and societal success. It does this by elevating interdisciplinary evaluation methods by including context on how to integrate a real-world viewpoint of the solution to create a solution that is 'beyond science'. In addition, it involves interdisciplinary perspective through relevant stakeholders and creating an environment that encourages interaction between those stakeholders throughout the entirety of the development process and integration to help ensure relevance.

As discussed previously, the research findings were extracted through a thorough literature analysis of scientific publications, and a series of workshops conducted to present the desk research results and have a common understanding of the requirements and objectives of a transdisciplinary evaluation. This section will present the six main pillars of the transdisciplinary evaluation framework, (1) real-world context, (2) interdisciplinarity, (3) beyond science, (4) interaction, (5) integration, and finally (6) relevance. An overview of each pillar will be presented, which will additionally showcase how the framework can be applied in a digital government project, and some possible indicators to consider. Indicators help aggregate information, allowing for the analysis of complex issues and adding value to thus help decision-makers make a suitable decision [35]. The second subsection will present some key measurement dimensions to be considered when applying the framework.

4.1 The Six Pillars of the Transdisciplinary Evaluation Framework

As a result of the literature analysis, there are six main pillars of transdisciplinary research to be highlighted, which in turn stand as the foundation for the transdisciplinary evaluation framework. Transdisciplinary research is embedded in a real-world problem context, is tackled in an interdisciplinary way, extending beyond science stakeholders, is done together in an interactive joint engagement by making sure that everyone's knowledge is integrated and transferred to enhance relevance for the active stakeholders, but also society as the recipient (See Fig. 1). All six pillars will be explored further below. Figure 1. Depicts how the six pillars interact with each other.

Real-World Context

The first pillar of the evaluation framework is the real-world context. At the beginning of transdisciplinary research, there is a problem of everyday life that needs to be solved [35]. For practitioners, it is of particular importance that the solution to an everyday life problem is addressed. These everyday life problems are examined to shape real processes. In addition, legal frameworks and possible actions have to be considered in their context [35]. In other words, transdisciplinary research focuses on solving real and

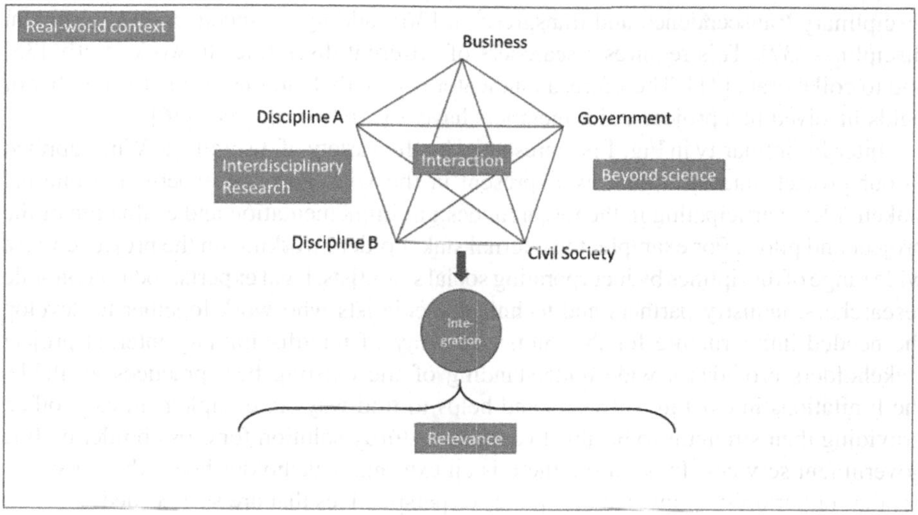

Fig. 1. Six pillars of transdisciplinary research

complex problems and questions aiming at creating knowledge that is solution-oriented to societally-relevant problems [36, 37]. Also, other authors [38] consider this problem – and the solution approach essential for transdisciplinary research. Its knowledge emerges from a particular context of an application by addressing societally-relevant problems as drivers for posing scientific research questions [39]. As shown in Fig. 1, the real-world context is represented by the grey rectangle, encompassing all the other pillars, as it is the starting point, the root of the transdisciplinary process. Some of the indicators associated to the real-world context, found in the literature, are that the research must manifest itself in actual practice and should meet policy interests [40].

On that note, when applying the evaluation framework to our project, the real-world context can be described as the backdrop and goal of the project pilots, implementing and validating enhanced infrastructure services for electronic voting, smart mobility and mobile signing. The project and the pilots have as a goal to leverage the SDGR and eIDAS together for mobile-device usage, pushing forward the practical use of inclusive mobile government services in Europe.

Interdisciplinarity

Interdisciplinarity is another key pillar of this evaluation framework. Transdisciplinary research includes interdisciplinary research, where transdisciplinary is the broader term for both concepts. The main purpose of transdisciplinary research is to search for solutions to a matter or a complex problem that cannot be solved with knowledge and techniques from a single discipline [36]. In other terms, it frees itself from its specialized or disciplinary boundaries, defining and solving its problems independently of disciplines. This is not to dismiss specialized and disciplinary knowledge, but to ensure that problems are not seen in a one-dimensional way, i.e., from a solely specialized or disciplinary perspective [39]. Interdisciplinary research includes considering the context of multiple disciplines and their intrinsic knowledge gathered in the same environment through disciplinary transcendence and transgression [36], adding perspectives from different disciplines [37]. This requires researchers of different disciplines to work jointly [35] and to collaborate [41]. Therefore, an indicator is exactly that, measuring the number of fields involved in a project and if members have a variety of degrees [36].

Interdisciplinarity in Fig. 1 is represented by the variety of disciplines. When applied to our project, interdisciplinarity is present in the wide array of experts and internal stakeholders participating in the research, design, implementation and evaluation of the project and pilots. For example, the internal stakeholders working on the project cover a wide range of disciplines by incorporating social scientists, legal experts, socio-economic researchers, industry partners and technical specialists who work together to develop the needed infrastructure for the pilots. An array of interdisciplinary internal project stakeholders provides a wide understanding of the existing best practices available, the limitations in existing software, and helps to find ways to complement each other, providing their strengths to be able to achieve a sturdy solution for cross-border mobile government services. In addition, there is an external stakeholder board that serves as another opportunity to involve disciplines or perspectives that are still needed.

Beyond Science

Another important aspect of the transdisciplinary evaluation is its bridging function between science and practice, transcending the boundaries between scientific disciplines and societal actors, understanding that a project must go beyond just science [38, 39]. The involvement of various non-academic stakeholders is an essential characteristic of transdisciplinary research projects [35], which can span everything from business or government to civil society, or from industry to societal entities, seeking application of the research results [36].

First, societal problems have to be related to scientific problems [42] so that researchers can work jointly with practical experts [35] on an equal basis [37] involving scientific and non-scientific sources or practices [43]. This alignment of partners' needs and desires makes the process relevant to all parties [44], contributes to both societal and scientific progress, accounts for the diversity of perspectives [39], and can create a culture of accountability [36]. Stakeholders need to feel heard, represented and somehow trust researchers to take into consideration their input [37, 45–47]. It is important for project leaders to facilitate the collaboration process[48], which is a complex undertaking and requires assessments of who should be involved in designing for almost all citizens, how many stakeholders are needed, who decides what should be a goal for a design initiative, and on what basis and legitimacy [49] As shown in Fig. 1, the beyond science pillar is represented by the parties interacting with the disciplines, such as businesses, governments and civil society. A relevant indicator would be to identify if there is interaction between academia, productive sector and society and if there is participation by extra-academic professionals [36].

The beyond science pillar is present in the project not only in the core consortium of the project, which includes academics in the fields of digital government, iVoting, transdisciplinary and technical skills, but also includes industry and businesses with expertise in iVoting systems and digital government services provision. Moreover, external stakeholders are consulted both from private enterprises and government. The key external stakeholders are represented in an External Stakeholder Board for the project, which holds workshops and opportunities for exchange throughout the project to incorporate their insights into the project as it develops.

Interaction

Interaction is the third main pillar of transdisciplinarity, as already mentioned, with very different actors from different disciplines and beyond the scientific field work together in a transdisciplinary project. In many definitions and descriptions of transdisciplinary research, this interaction is emphasized and referred to in different ways. The term co-production is considered a core concept of transdisciplinary research, representing the importance of interaction between the stakeholders [36]. Others emphasize the notion of research collaboration [37, 39], or the cooperation of different algorithms and approaches [43]. The goal is to connect skills and knowledge through teamwork and collaborative networks [36], cooperative learning and problem solving [43], active participation of all stakeholders [35], and engaged participants in processes of reflection, deliberation, and negotiation [41]. Interaction is depicted in Fig. 1 by the lines connecting the different stakeholders, the disciplines, and the private and public representatives. A suitable indicator refers to the amount and frequency of participatory events and networks created and/or expanded throughout the process [41].

Since the beginning of our project, interaction has been key to the development and progress of the project. Regular meetings are held between the consortium partners and joint work has been produced between the academics and industry members. Also, a series of workshops have been key to the understanding of different topics to further design the pilots. The interaction with the external stakeholders began almost simultaneously with the project start when interviews were conducted with government experts and public servants to establish the need's elicitation of the pilots and project context. Interaction is a key role in exchanging, gaining, and generating knowledge that will be further incorporated in the integration pillar throughout the development of the project.

Integration

Given the purpose of the above-described interaction, terms such as integration, synthesis, or transition are mentioned. Transdisciplinary research seeks to overcome the fragmented view of science and hyper-specialization through dialogue and integration of knowledge [36]. Integration is the fourth pillar of transdisciplinary evaluations. Integration is the cognitive operation of establishing a new, previously non-existent connection between the distinct epistemic, socio–organizational, and communicative entities that make up the given problem context [39]. Thus, it produces new knowledge by integrating these different scientific and extra-scientific findings [42], which others refer to as synthesis of the individual findings [37]. While the term integration implies the integration of disparate entities into a new entity, others emphasize the term transition, which refers to the successful solutions or applications to a distinct application domain [43]. In Fig. 1, integration is represented as the sum of the stakeholder's interaction, the outcomes, results and learning of this process. Indicators associated to this pillar are changes in attitude of participants, new insights and learning processes and new scientific knowledge gained [37, 50].

Within the project, integration is the continuous learning and improvement of processes, adapting of goals and development of solutions brought forward by the constant interaction between internal and external stakeholders. The workshop results, interview analysis and working meetings sum up the valuable outcomes of the interaction.

Relevance

Finally, the last pillar of transdisciplinary evaluations is the relevance. The promises of transdisciplinary research can be divided into benefits for project members (internal) and benefits for external stakeholders (external). Within the project boundaries, the most fruitful engagements will occur in environments and partnerships that provide mutually beneficial and relevant learning opportunities for both users and researchers [44]. Mutual learnings should be facilitated in successful transdisciplinary projects [37]. Other internal effects besides shared learning include mutual accountability, ownership, and leadership among project participants [41]. Outside the project boundaries, transdisciplinary research contributes to both societal and scientific progress [39, 42], which is guaranteed by the broad stakeholder engagement beyond science, mentioned above. In turn, other authors emphasize the practical benefits to society, e.g. by initiating public health programs, generating land-use plans, developing environmental policies, and excluding some of the standard academic outputs such as peer-reviewed publications or academic journals [41] or stress the need to secure the promised societal benefits [37].The final pillar of the transdisciplinary evaluation framework is depicted in Fig. 1., as the final overarching outcome, the final bracket. The relevance of transdisciplinary research can be linked to indicators such as existing changes in practice, new institutional frameworks created, and decisions made [37].

When inserting the framework in the project, relevance sums up all the aforementioned pillars that have shaped the design and development of the pilots. These pilots have the relevance of addressing the real-world context and promote the development of cross-border mobile services to the end users. Ideally, the relevance will facilitate market acceptance and sustainable success of the project beyond the project timeframe and results.

Overall, transdisciplinary research aims to provide a fundamental understanding [35] to generate knowledge that is solution-oriented, socially robust, and is transferable to both scientific and societal practice [39]. The above-mentioned pillars are six core aspects project evaluators must consider when delineating and designing their evaluation process, making sure all parts are addressed throughout the project. Embedding the framework within the project allows for a deeper understanding of how the framework can be used in future projects. To summarize, the real-world context is depicted as the main goal the pilots and project are trying to address within the EU digital government field. Interdisciplinarity is present in the variety of disciplines represented by the different consortium partners experts in the academic, legal and industry fields. Moreover, the beyond science pillar is present with the internal and external stakeholders involved in the project throughout the interaction in the form of interviews, meetings, and workshops. The integration pillar is the valuable results and input received through the interaction process of the project. Finally, the relevance pillar reflects the constant improvement and steps throughout the development process and how all the pillars have impacted and shaped the overall outcome and its relevance.

In the following subsection the dimensions of measurement of transdisciplinary evaluations will be discussed.

4.2 Dimensions of Measurement for Evaluation

The term "evaluation" can be described as "the systematic collection of information about the activities, characteristics, and outcomes of projects" that aims to assess the achievement of the objectives, the efficiency, effectiveness, impact, and sustainability of a plan [17]. The formative evaluation of the engagement process and its impacts, including demonstration of the success of both process and outcomes is essential [22]. In this context, activities can be seen as actions performed by the project, leading to output generated by the project. They steer outcomes, which are changes in knowledge, attitudes, skills, and relationships, manifested as changes in behaviour. These changes, which are changes resulting wholly or in part from a chain of events to which the project has contributed, finally create impact [23].

Below, we summarise the five major dimensions of measurement that were identified during the literature review process. These serve as a guiding tool for evaluators, each of these dimensions can dictate one or several indicators, process timings and process steps within the evaluation framework and the corresponding pillars.

The first dimension concerns the overall purpose of the evaluation; it has been proposed that a differentiation be made according to the following categories: accountability, strategy, broader purposes like learning and marketing, or multiple purposes [51]. In addition, it was suggested to make the evaluation on the basis of the following four principles: relevance, credibility, legitimacy, and effectiveness [45].

Another possible dimension is the timing, which can be separated into ex-ante, ongoing, ex-post, ex-ante + ex-post, or interactive [46]. In terms of general evaluation phases, often authors refer to classical ex-ante and ex-post evaluations [38]. A long-time frame for evaluation may be required to evaluate the outcomes of an initiative as the consequences, contributions and long-term effects may appear gradually [33, 52]. Evaluating a project immediately may be skewed by the impressions of the recent activities in the project [12], but measuring the long-term contributions can also be a complicated task. Defining when to evaluate, and how, either in a continuous loop through multiple iterations [53], or at a single instance, is a key dimension to be considered when designing an evaluation.

The third dimension to highlight is the scope; assessments could be categorized into a single assessment of an individual object of analysis or performing a networking assessment, studying the interaction between linked groups or institutions [36]. Assessments can also span products, entire projects, or programs [42]. One possible distinction is what happens internally within a project and what happens externally primarily in the organizations of the stakeholders, but also within society [54]. Transdisciplinary scientific collaboration can be evaluated on different scales ranging from proximal/micro to distal/macro levels of analysis [55].

Actors are a key dimension to be considered. During the evaluation, different actors can be identified. For example, the researchers conducting a study can also be the evaluators, or different persons can take over this role [12]. Another possibility to form an evaluation could be a coaching model, facilitating self-reflection about what members are supposed to be doing and how well they are doing it in comparison to a jury model [53]. One differentiation is how interdisciplinary teams integrate disparate bodies of knowledge in 4 types: common group learning, modelling, negotiation among experts, and integration by a leader [38].

The impact of a project or activity is a key dimension to be measured, and usually the most well-known and adopted evaluation dimension throughout evaluation frameworks. Societal impacts of research projects range from direct impacts (e.g., knowledge generation) to long-term community impacts (e.g., community well-being) [12]. Another possibility can be found when following the principles of citizen science. The evaluation of engagement can be considered in three dimensions: (i) scientific impact; (ii) participant learning and empowerment; and (iii) impact on society at large [48] (See Fig. 2).

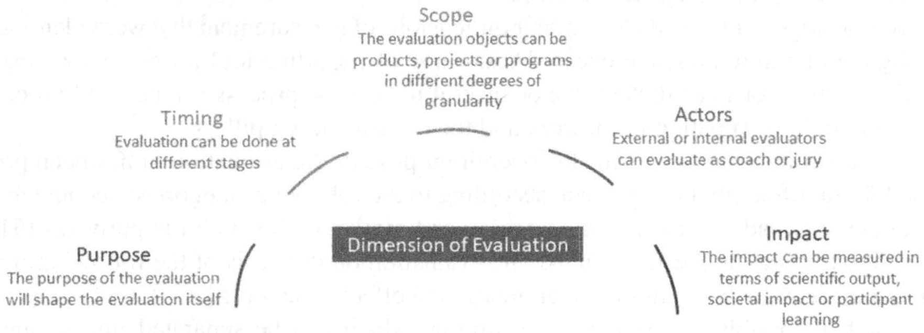

Fig. 2. Dimensions of evaluation

To summarize, we can see that purpose, timing, scope, involved actors, and impact are five measurable dimensions to focus on while creating an evaluation framework. Moreover, these are five recurring dimensions, but others might appear in a different project as each project is embedded in a particular context.

5 Discussion

This chapter discusses the main findings of our transdisciplinary evaluation research in comparison to other scientific work, surprising and unexpected results, the limitations of our findings and suggestions for further research.

Firstly, the evaluation framework presented above could be used in practice as a blueprint for adapting a context-specific framework to the needs of research projects. Most often evaluations of digital government research projects focus on evaluating functional requirements as stated in a deliverable usually produced at the beginning of a project. By utilizing the six pillars of the transdisciplinary evaluation framework, research evaluators will think beyond functional testing and include broader assessment criteria, which then increases the likelihood that the project results will be relevant in a real-world context.

Secondly, our findings make it clear that there exist a variety of different definitions of transdisciplinary research [52], many of which share the same characteristics. Thus, several authors come up with their own definition after reviewing existing ones [5, 19]. In contrast to setting up our own definition, we distilled the main characteristics reoccurring in existing definitions throughout the literature, without formulating our own new one.

Thirdly, our results show that evaluation frameworks propose different dimensions for measurement [36, 56]. Knowledge of these dimensions helps to make informed decisions about evaluation needs in the development of a broader evaluation framework.

Moreover, each process needs to adapt to a specific context, the needs of both scientists and non-academic parties, and reach the desired outcomes, taking into account the limited amount of money and time [57]. Selecting the appropriate methods for collaboration, knowledge integration, and evaluation is important to accommodate each particular project's context [58]. This need of adaption to specific contexts underlines the importance of good process models for adapting evaluation frameworks.

Generally accepted methods suggested by evaluation frameworks are mostly missing. In scientific sources, the aspect of understanding dominates over action-oriented perspectives, while implementing agencies emphasize the need for collaborative action over a knowledge-oriented perspective [59]. Action design research emphasises the importance of building and evaluating ensemble artefacts in their organisational environment, which makes it possible to identify organisational paradoxes that are contradictions between interdependent elements [60]. A transdisciplinary evaluation framework should be broader in terms of the elements to be measured and go beyond the mere measurement of scientific contributions.

A surprising outcome of the pilot workshops was the participants' strong focus on indicators to assess the technical feasibility of the artefacts. After the participants had been presented with possible indicators from the literature review, a broader range of indicators was identified.

Limitations of this study include the missing test of the framework in different digital government projects. Future empirical research can build upon the present article by testing the proposed framework in different digital government projects. Within the remaining project duration this limitation should be addressed by applying the framework with the planned pilots. Outside the project, the case study research that follows the evaluation model also has the potential to further refine the model and identify specific challenges in other settings. Research that uses reliable and valid measures of processes and outcomes would be particularly helpful in testing the model and identifying appropriate improvements or extensions. Another limitation mainly lies in the short timeframe of this study. A long timeframe may be required to evaluate the outcomes of an initiative [33, 52] and it is difficult to capture the long-term contributions of activities that extend through several months or years [61]. As the technical artefacts prepared for the pilot projects are only produced later in the project, the first round of evaluation can only cover the evaluation of the design phase of the pilot projects. One advantage of a shorter timeframe is that participants will still be in the process of forming their opinion about the study [12].

The third limitation is the strong focus on transdisciplinary evaluation frameworks mentioned in Sect. 3.1, while much could be learned from research on the evaluation of interdisciplinary projects. Since the literature search already yielded 806 papers, the search was not extended beyond transdisciplinary evaluation frameworks. Future research could additionally build on the framework and propose a general set of indicators that are in principle suitable for assessing transdisciplinary aspects. This general set of indicators could serve as an impetus for discussion on adapting the framework to the specific research projects.

6 Conclusion

Since digital government projects draw their knowledge from several established disciplines and include elements from both practice and academia, these projects have a strong transdisciplinary orientation, which translates into a challenging evaluation of project outcomes. Our guiding question was therefore how to develop an evaluation framework that is suitable for transdisciplinary digital government projects.

The developed framework builds on six pillars of transdisciplinary research, namely (1) real-world context, (2) interdisciplinary research, (3) interaction, (4) beyond academia, (5) integration, and (6) relevance, and proposes a few indicators from the literature grouped according to the six pillars as food for thought for adopting a context-specific evaluation framework. Furthermore, knowing possible dimensions will help in developing specific evaluation frameworks. It also shows an example of how this framework has been applied in a European Union research and innovation project under Horizon 2020.

Next, it is envisaged that the proposed model will be tested during the remainder of the project, which leaves open an important part of transdisciplinary research evaluation, namely capturing the long-term contributions of activities that go well beyond the project boundaries.

Future research could further elaborate this framework and develop the indicators from the literature into a more general set of indicators that, together with a process model for adoption, could form a blueprint for the context-specific development of transdisciplinary research evaluation frameworks. Incorporating a transdisciplinary approach that creates spaces where science, policy and industry can meet to address specific issues in digital governance projects, could go beyond this area and contribute to better market acceptance of newly developed technologies in general.

Acknowledgement. The mGov4EU project has received funding from the European Union's Horizon 2020 research and innovation programme under grant agreement No 959072.

References

1. Ndaguba, E.A., Ijeoma, E.O.C.: Exploring the epistemology of transdisciplinarity in public policy and administration in South Africa. TDSA **13**, 1–13 (2017). https://doi.org/10.4102/td.v13i1.406
2. Hans, H.J.: Discipline or interdisciplinary study domain? Challenges and promises in electronic government research. In: Chen, H., et al. (eds.) Digital Government, pp. 21–41. Springer US, Boston, MA (2008). https://doi.org/10.1007/978-0-387-71611-4_2
3. Heeks, R., Bailur, S.: Analyzing e-government research: perspectives, philosophies, theories, methods, and practice. Gov. Inf. Q. **24**, 243–265 (2007). https://doi.org/10.1016/j.giq.2006.06.005

4. Fedorowicz, J., Dias, M.A.: A decade of design in digital government research. Gov. Inf. Q. **27**, 1–8 (2010). https://doi.org/10.1016/j.giq.2009.09.002
5. Gil-García, J.R., Luna-Reyes, L.F.: Integrating conceptual approaches to e-government. In: Encyclopedia of E-commerce, E-government, and Mobile Commerce, pp. 636–643. IGI Global (2006)
6. OECD, International Telecommunication Union: M-Government: Mobile Technologies for Responsive Governments and Connected Societies. OECD (2011). https://doi.org/10.1787/9789264118706-en
7. Höchtl, B., Lampoltshammer, T.J.: Rechtliche Rahmenbedingungen und technische Umsetzung von E-Government in Österreich. In: Stember, J., Eixelsberger, W., Spichiger, A., Neuroni, A., Habbel, F.-R., Wundara, M. (eds.) Handbuch E-Government, pp. 135–161. Springer, Wiesbaden (2019). https://doi.org/10.1007/978-3-658-21402-9_10
8. Esteves, J., Joseph, R.C.: A comprehensive framework for the assessment of eGovernment projects. Gov. Inf. Q. **25**, 118–132 (2008). https://doi.org/10.1016/j.giq.2007.04.009
9. Qureshi, H.A., Salman, Y., Irfan, S., Jabeen, N.: A systematic review of e-government evaluation. Pak. Econ. Soc. Rev. 37 (2017)
10. Liu, J., Derzsi, Z., Raus, M., Kipp, A.: eGovernment project evaluation: an integrated framework. In: Wimmer, M.A., Scholl, H.J., Ferro, E. (eds.) EGOV 2008. LNCS, vol. 5184, pp. 85–97. Springer, Heidelberg (2008). https://doi.org/10.1007/978-3-540-85204-9_8
11. Sellung, R., Roßnagel, H.: Evaluating complex identity management systems – the futureid approach, 7 (2015)
12. Walter, A.I., Helgenberger, S., Wiek, A., Scholz, R.W.: Measuring societal effects of transdisciplinary research projects: design and application of an evaluation method. Eval. Program Plann. **30**, 325–338 (2007). https://doi.org/10.1016/j.evalprogplan.2007.08.002
13. Wolf, B., Lindenthal, T., Szerencsits, M., Holbrook, J.B., Heß, J.: Evaluating research beyond scientific impacthow to include criteria for productive interactions and impact on practice and society. GAIA-Ecol. Perspect. Sci. Soc. **22**, 104–114 (2013)
14. Klein, J.T.: Evaluation of interdisciplinary and transdisciplinary research. Am. J. Prev. Med. **35**, S116–S123 (2008). https://doi.org/10.1016/j.amepre.2008.05.010
15. Binder, C.R., Absenger-Helmli, I., Schilling, T.: The reality of transdisciplinarity: a framework-based self-reflection from science and practice leaders. Sustain. Sci. **10**(4), 545–562 (2015). https://doi.org/10.1007/s11625-015-0328-2
16. Zscheischler, J., Rogga, S., Weith, T.: Experiences with transdisciplinary research: sustainable land management third year status conference. Syst. Res. Behav. Sci. **31**, 751–756 (2014)
17. Grimsley, M., Meehan, A., Tan, A.: Evaluative design of e-government projects: a community development perspective. Transforming Gov.: People Process. Policy **1**, 174–193 (2007). https://doi.org/10.1108/17506160710751995
18. Venable, J., Pries-Heje, J., Baskerville, R.: A comprehensive framework for evaluation in design science research. In: Peffers, K., Rothenberger, M., Kuechler, B. (eds.) DESRIST 2012. LNCS, vol. 7286, pp. 423–438. Springer, Heidelberg (2012). https://doi.org/10.1007/978-3-642-29863-9_31
19. European Commission: Communication of 8 December 1999 on a Commission initiative for the special European Council of Lisbon, 23 and 24 March 2000 - eEurope - An information society for all (1999)
20. European Commission: Communication of 28 May 2002 from the Commission to the Council, the European Parliament, the Economic and Social Committee and the Committee of the Regions - The eEurope 2005 action plan: an information society for everyone (COM(2002) 263 final) (2002)
21. European Union: Malmö Declaration - Ministerial Declaration on eGovernment (2009)
22. Krimmer, R., Webster, W.: Trust, security and public services in the digital age. Forthcoming (2021)

23. European Commission: Regulation (EU) 910/2014 of the European Parliament and of the Council of 23 July 2014 on electronic identification and trust services for electronic transactions in the internal market and repealing Directive 1999/93/EC. 2014 (2014)
24. European Union: Tallinn Declaration on eGovernment. 2017. p. at the ministerial meeting during Estonian Presidency of the Council of the EU on 6 October 2017 (2017)
25. Schmidt, C., Krimmer, R.: How to implement the European digital single market: identifying the catalyst for digital transformation. J. Eur. Integr. **44**, 59–80 (2022). https://doi.org/10.1080/07036337.2021.2011267
26. European Commission: Large Scale Pilots (2016). https://cordis.europa.eu/programme/id/H2020_IoT-01-2016. Accessed 16 March 2021
27. European Union: Regulation (EU) 2018/1724 of the European Parliament and of the Council of 2 October 2018 establishing a single digital gateway to provide access to information, to procedures and to assistance and problem-solving services and amending Regulation (EU) No 1024/2012 (2018)
28. Krimmer, R., Kalvet, T., Toots, M., Cepilovs, A., Tambouris, E.: Exploring and demonstrating the once-only principle. In: 18th Annual International Conference on Digital Government, pp. 546–551 (2017). https://doi.org/10.1145/3085228.3085235
29. Schmidt, C., Krimmer, R., Lampoltshammer, T.J.: "When need becomes necessity" - the single digital gateway regulation and the once-only principle from a European point of view, p. 6 (2021)
30. Krimmer, R., Prentza, A., Mamrot, S., Schmidt, C., Cepilovs, A.: The future of the once-only principle in Europe. In: Krimmer, R., Prentza, A., Mamrot, S. (eds.) The Once-Only Principle. LNCS, vol. 12621, pp. 225–236. Springer, Cham (2021). https://doi.org/10.1007/978-3-030-79851-2_12
31. Collatto, D.C., Dresch, A., Lacerda, D.P., Bentz, I.G.: Is action design research indeed necessary? Analysis and synergies between action research and design science research. Syst. Pract. Action Res. **31**(3), 239–267 (2017). https://doi.org/10.1007/s11213-017-9424-9
32. Klock, A.C.T., Gasparini, I., Pimenta, M.S.: 5W2H Framework: a guide to design, develop and evaluate the user-centered gamification. In: Proceedings of the 15th Brazilian Symposium on Human Factors in Computing Systems, pp. 1–10 (2016)
33. Piggot-Irvine, E., Zornes, D.: Developing a framework for research evaluation in complex contexts such as action research. Sage Open **6**, 215824401666380 (2016). https://doi.org/10.1177/2158244016663800
34. Pregernig, M.: Transdisciplinarity viewed from afar: science-policy assessments as forums for the creation of transdisciplinary knowledge. Sci. Public Policy **33**, 445–455 (2006)
35. Heilmann, A., Reinhold, S.: Evaluation of a transdisciplinary research project for a sustainable development. In: Leal Filho, W., Skanavis, C., do Paço, A., Rogers, J., Kuznetsova, O., Castro, P. (eds.) Handbook of Theory and Practice of Sustainable Development in Higher Education. WSS, pp. 201–214. Springer, Cham (2017). https://doi.org/10.1007/978-3-319-47889-0_15
36. de Oliveira, T.M., Amaral, L., Pacheco, R.C.D.S.: Multi/inter/transdisciplinary assessment: A systemic framework proposal to evaluate graduate courses and research teams. Res. Eval. **28**, 23–36 (2019)
37. Zscheischler, J., Rogga, S., Lange, A.: The success of transdisciplinary research for sustainable land use: individual perceptions and assessments. Sustain. Sci. **13**(4), 1061–1074 (2018). https://doi.org/10.1007/s11625-018-0556-3
38. Hoffmann, S., Pohl, C., Hering, J.G.: Methods and procedures of transdisciplinary knowledge integration: empirical insights from four thematic synthesis processes. Ecol. Soc. **22**(1), 17 (2017). https://doi.org/10.5751/ES-08955-220127
39. Hoffmann, S., Pohl, C., Hering, J.G.: Exploring transdisciplinary integration within a large research program: empirical lessons from four thematic synthesis processes. Res. Policy **46**, 678–692 (2017). https://doi.org/10.1016/j.respol.2017.01.004

40. Czúcz, B., et al.: How to design a transdisciplinary regional ecosystem service assessment: a case study from Romania. Eastern Eur. OE. **3**, e26363 (2018). https://doi.org/10.3897/oneeco.3.e26363
41. Wiek, A., Talwar, S., O'Shea, M., Robinson, J.: Toward a methodological scheme for capturing societal effects of participatory sustainability research. Res. Eval. **23**, 117–132 (2014). https://doi.org/10.1093/reseval/rvt031
42. Jahn, T., Keil, F.: An actor-specific guideline for quality assurance in transdisciplinary research. Futures **65**, 195–208 (2015). https://doi.org/10.1016/j.futures.2014.10.015
43. Pyshkin, E.: Designing human-centric applications: transdisciplinary connections with examples. In: 2017 3rd IEEE International Conference on Cybernetics (CYBCONF), pp. 1–6. IEEE, Exeter, United Kingdom (2017). https://doi.org/10.1109/CYBConf.2017.7985774
44. Eanes, F.R., Silbernagel, J.M., Hart, D.A., Robinson, P., Axler, M.: Participatory mobile- and web-based tools for eliciting landscape knowledge and perspectives: introducing and evaluating the Wisconsin geotools project. J. Coast. Conserv. **22**(2), 399–416 (2018). https://doi.org/10.1007/s11852-017-0589-2
45. Belcher, B.M., Rasmussen, K.E., Kemshaw, M.R., Zornes, D.A.: Defining and assessing research quality in a transdisciplinary context. Res. Eval. **25**, 1–17 (2016). https://doi.org/10.1093/reseval/rvv025
46. Pinto, L.G., Ochôa, P.: Information science's contributions towards emerging open evaluation practices. Perform. Meas. Metrics **20**, 2–16 (2018)
47. Hohl, S.D., Knerr, S., Thompson, B.: A framework for coordination center responsibilities and performance in a multi-site, transdisciplinary public health research initiative. Res. Eval. **28**, 279–289 (2019). https://doi.org/10.1093/reseval/rvz012
48. Kliskey, A., et al.: Thinking big and thinking small: a conceptual framework for best practices in community and stakeholder engagement in food, energy, and water systems. Sustainability **13**, 2160 (2021)
49. Gidlund, K.L.: Designing for all and no one-practitioners understandings of citizen driven development of public e-services. In: Proceedings of the 12th Participatory Design Conference: Research Papers, vol. 1, pp. 11–19 (2012)
50. Holzer, J.M., Carmon, N., Orenstein, D.E.: A methodology for evaluating transdisciplinary research on coupled socio-ecological systems. Ecol. Ind. **85**, 808–819 (2018). https://doi.org/10.1016/j.ecolind.2017.10.074
51. Ormiston, J.: Blending practice worlds: Impact assessment as a transdisciplinary practice. Bus. Ethics: A Eur. Rev. **28**, 423–440 (2019). https://doi.org/10.1111/beer.12230
52. Schulte, R., Heilmann, A.: Presentation and discussion of an evaluation model for transdisciplinary research projects. EJSD **8**(3), 1 (2019). https://doi.org/10.14207/ejsd.2019.v8n3p1
53. Klein, J.T.: Afterword: the emergent literature on interdisciplinary and transdisciplinary research evaluation. Res. Eval. **15**, 75–80 (2006)
54. Belcher, B.M., Ramirez, L.F., Davel, R., Claus, R.: Retraction: a response to Hansson and Polk (2018) Assessing the impact of transdisciplinary research: the usefulness of relevance, credibility, and legitimacy for understanding the link between process and impact. Oxford University Press (2019)
55. Stokols, D., et al.: Evaluating transdisciplinary science. Nicotine Tob. Res. **5**, S21–S39 (2003)
56. Sakao, T.: Research series review for transdisciplinarity assessment—validation with sustainable consumption and production research. Sustainability **11**, 5250 (2019)
57. Woltersdorf, L., Lang, P., Döll, P.: How to set up a transdisciplinary research project in Central Asia: description and evaluation. Sustain. Sci. **14**(3), 697–711 (2018). https://doi.org/10.1007/s11625-018-0625-7

58. Verwoerd, L., Klaassen, P., van Veen, S.C., De Wildt-Liesveld, R., Regeer, B.J.: Combining the roles of evaluator and facilitator: assessing societal impacts of transdisciplinary research while building capacities to improve its quality. Environ. Sci. Policy **103**, 32–40 (2020). https://doi.org/10.1016/j.envsci.2019.10.011
59. Hitziger, M., et al.: EVOLvINC: evaluating knowledge integration capacity in multistakeholder governance. E&S **24**, 36 (2019). https://doi.org/10.5751/ES-10935-240236
60. Danneels, L., Viaene, S.: Identifying digital transformation paradoxes. Bus. Inf. Syst. Eng. 1–18 (2022).https://doi.org/10.1007/s12599-021-00735-7
61. Williams, S., Robinson, J.: Measuring sustainability: an evaluation framework for sustainability transition experiments. Environ. Sci. Policy **103**, 58–66 (2020). https://doi.org/10.1016/j.envsci.2019.10.012

Towards a Research Agenda for Personal Data Spaces: Synthesis of a Community Driven Process

Sander Van Damme[1](✉), Peter Mechant[1], Eveline Vlassenroot[1], Mathias Van Compernolle[1], Raf Buyle[2], and Dorien Bauwens[3]

[1] imec-mict-UGent, Miriam Makebaplein 1, Ghent, Belgium
sander.vandamme@ugent.be

[2] imec-IDLab-UGent, Technologiepark-Zwijnaarde 126, Ghent, Belgium

[3] Digitaal Vlaanderen, Koningin Maria Hendrikaplein 70, Ghent, Belgium

Abstract. Data are increasingly underpinning important actions and processes in both governmental and non-governmental environments. However, the consolidation of data in silo's limits its ability to be reused while also restricting the control that people have over how their data is used. To mitigate these issues, decentralised storage and personal data store technologies have been put forward as an alternative. Such technologies have gained momentum in Flanders (Flanders is the northern part of Belgium) and became a key policy aspect and a driver for innovation. To support the adoption of these technologies, the Flemish government initiated 'Solid Community', a platform for academia, governments, citizens and industry to collaborate on the development of Solid, a technology specification for decentralised data storage. Through ten plenary sessions, the potential challenges that relate to the adoption of Solid were discussed within Solid Community. The reports of these sessions were analysed through qualitative content analysis, leading to the identification of four domains in which these challenges can be situated: social, technical, legal and network (ecosystem) challenges. This paper discusses these challenges and contributes to the development of an interdisciplinary research agenda to help shape the framework conditions for the further diffusion of socially robust, ethically justified and legally supported personal data space initiatives in Flanders.

Keywords: Personal data space · Personal data store · Decentralised storage · Digital platform ecosystem · Solid

1 Introduction

While data underpin almost every action or process in our society it proves difficult to achieve a state of 'data liquidity' in which data can be reused where and when needed. Most data continue to stagnate in silos, controlled by data holders and inaccessible to its subjects or parties who could use it. In addition, people (e.g. social media users) have little meaningful options to control their personal data and information flows [1] and have barely any agency on how their data are 'packaged' and 'sold'.

M. Janssen et al. (Eds.): EGOV 2022, LNCS 13391, pp. 563–577, 2022.
https://doi.org/10.1007/978-3-031-15086-9_36

To mitigate these issues of autonomy and power asymmetries, decentralised storage of data has been put forward as an important response [2] and start-up or research companies are bringing to market applications supporting decentralised storage of personal information, e.g. Cozy Cloud, Meeco, OpenPDS and Solid. These applications, often called Personal Data Pods, are also being investigated by larger companies and (governmental) institutions. Examples are public broadcasters such as the BBC [3] or the VRT [4] which are experimenting with personal data store technologies that empower its viewers and listeners with their own data or the Flemish government (Flanders is the northern part of Belgium) which is founding a 'data utility company' to become one of the parties that will provide each of Flanders' millions of citizens with their own Personal Data Space or Personal Data Pod [5].

For Flanders, the focus on Personal Data Spaces (PDS) or Personal Data Pods as a key policy aspect and as a driver for innovation in Flanders was formalized in September 2021 during the annual policy declaration of the Flemish Government [6] and a real momentum has grown in Flanders to become a region that takes the storage and processing of digital personal data serious. In this light, PDS are considered as a valuable alternative for giving individuals granular control over the data that is captured about them and over how this data is shared and used, but also as a means for organisations to more easily develop data-based services and to stimulate a data economy.

Solid is a W3C specification [7] that supports such PDS that are under the control of an individual or organisation. This enables individuals to reuse their data among different applications while also providing them with a sense of control over how their data is used. The introduction of PDS puts individuals at the heart of the management of personal data and gives them an important role in the current data ecosystem. Due to the possibility of actively engaging with their data, people can obtain a consolidated view of their personal data. For example, using Solid-based applications [8], individuals can conveniently switch between data storage providers and application providers. They can give third parties, such as companies, permission to access certain data for a specific purpose and for a limited time (e.g. processing a loan application or delivering a personalized ad).

Implementing PDS in society should create an ecosystem where individuals control the sharing of their data between interoperable data sources and endpoints [9], with companies, institutions and governments accessing individuals' data with permission and for a specific purpose. In this article we focus on PDS enabled by Solid.

The goal of this paper is threefold. First, the architectural design of Solid is described. Secondly, the foundation and operations of the Flemish 'Solid Community' are discussed. The scope of the community, launched on April 20th, 2021, and consisting out of a variety of private and public stakeholders, includes both technical and non-technical facets, with a focus on architecture and user experience, use cases, business models, legal aspects and information security. The third goal of the paper is to describe, structure and reflect on the hurdles and challenges, with regards to making Solid enabled PDS a reality in Flanders, that emerged during the first year of the Flemish 'Solid Community'.

2 Solid Architecture

Solid is a W3C specification [7] that provides individuals with one or more online storage spaces, similar to commercial services such as Dropbox. These are referred to as Personal Online Data Stores (pod or pods) and may be offered by public or private parties and differ in their pricing, security features and accessibility [10]. Research has shown that local connected devices, such as smartphones, might also be used as a Solid pod [11]. As the Solid specification prescribes that data should be stored in a standardised and interoperable format (i.e. Linked Data) [12], users are able to switch between pod providers with relative ease, thus achieving a form of decentralization. In addition, individuals may grant organisations and applications granular access to read or write certain data to a Solid pod (e.g. a recruitment agency requesting access to diploma data). This access grant can be withdrawn at any time, to the extent legally possible, allowing individuals to retain a sense of control. As data is stored in a standardised format, applications are able to use data that was previously written by another application [13]. This means that individuals may be able to more easily switch between applications, as the switching costs are lowered. This also contributes to the decentral nature of Solid.

3 Flemish Solid Community

The Flemish 'Solid Community' was initiated by the Flemish government to promote cooperation between academia, governments, citizens and the industry (public and private companies) around the development of Solid based PDS [14]. The main objective was to stimulate the acceptance and usage of Solid by end users and service providers, to give individuals more control over their data and to increase data sharing within Flanders and Belgium. To achieve these goals in a responsible and durable way the project focuses on sharing knowledge, creating ecosystems, developing partnerships, executing projects and incentivizing the use of Solid [15].

The community originally operated through monthly plenary sessions where the various stakeholders were represented and given the opportunity to contribute ideas, ask questions and establish collaborations. These sessions initially explored the possibilities of Solid PDS within the domains of healthcare, mobility and culture, with an extensive reflection on how these applications can meet societal needs and challenges. These explorations included both conceptual considerations on what the main focal points should be but also demonstrations of prototypes, as contributed by members, to further the discussion. The topics discussed included user experience, identity and consent management, business models, interoperability and ecosystem architecture, legal and ethical issues, information security and ecosystem governance. This was complemented by various presentations of PDS pilot projects from both private parties and the Flemish government, of which the topics are listed below.

- Mobility PDS: mobility budget management, sharing mobility data to improve traffic management, personalised ride sharing applications, more appropriate mobility services for people with a disability, demand-driven mobility, simplified driving license check for car rentals

- Media & culture PDS: cross-service media curation, personalised media guide, exposure to new cultural content
- Health PDS: involving people in their own health (food, diabetes, exercise, BMI), informed decision making in the context of a pandemic
- Finance PDS: simplified social security application, simplified handling of fines
- Administration PDS: simplifying address changes, giving control over sharing of personal data when applying for a job, more personalised job recommendations

These projects were considered from both a technical and a non-technical viewpoint. In addition, there were reflections on key legal aspects such as the proposed European Data Governance Act [16]. The main challenges that were identified during this process are discussed in Sect. 4.

Based on these insights a governance model was developed to accommodate and optimise cooperation between stakeholders and to allow for the fruition of the community. This entailed operating through four working groups of which two focused on the technological and social dimensions of challenges related to PDS, one on translating these insights to concrete use cases and one on disseminating knowledge to external parties. The frequency of these sessions varied between bi-weekly and bi-monthly. The general principles of the Flemish Solid Community were bundled in a charter and entailed a focus on control over data, centrality of user requirements, stimulating partnerships between stakeholders, providing social added value, providing room for innovation and experimentation, knowledge sharing, transparency and stimulating intercommunity collaboration.

4 Methodology

In order to reflect on the prominent challenges that were put forward within the community, the notes of the past working group sessions were analysed. These sessions were facilitated and led by the Flemish government, Ghent University and the authors. Information about their contents and the attendees can be found in Table 1. Written notes were created by the authors during these sessions as recording was not possible due to privacy constraints. To accommodate for the potential loss of detail and context associated with this method of data collection, presentation slides of the speakers were included in the analysis if available. The analysis was based on the principles of Grounded Theory [17] and divided in three stadia. Firstly, the initial concepts were explored by selecting and coding fragments that relate to certain hurdles or challenges with Solid PDS. While describing these fragments, care was taken to stay close to the original wording of the attendees ('open coding'). However, it should be noted that due to the unavailability of a transcription, certain nuances might already have been lost. Secondly, the fragments were compared with the aim of reducing the number of codes and finding overarching categories ('axial' and 'selective' coding). Thirdly, this process was repeated to create an overall typology of the identified categories.

This coding effort structured the identified challenges in four domains: social, technical, legal and network (ecosystem) level challenges. As some concepts were discussed multiple times and from different perspectives, they may be located within multiple domains. This analytical approach was chosen for its ability to identify what issues attendees engage with and how this translates to a general picture.

While the large number of topics discussed within the Flemish Solid Community allowed for a broad analysis that covered a range of domains, this also limited the depth of the analysis. Later publications may focus on reports from a specific working group within the Flemish Solid Community, such as the working group for social dimensions, to allow for a more profound reflection on how these challenges are conceptualised. In addition, the near exclusive focus on Solid PDS in the analysed reports might limit the applicability of the results to other PDS technologies. Further research may consider related developments and technologies to broaden the perspective on Personal Data Spaces. It should also be noted that the analysis depicts the challenges related to PDS as perceived by members of the Flemish Solid Community. The validity of these issues might vary, as might their comprehensiveness. The latter relates to the organic way in which topics for discussion were selected, i.e. community members were able to choose or emphasise certain subjects, meaning that certain challenges might remain out of scope of this analysis.

5 Challenges Related to Solid PDS

As indicated, the identified challenges could be situated within four domains: social, technical, legal and network (ecosystem) challenges.

5.1 Social Challenges

Social challenges are defined as challenges related to limitations in human understanding or to broader societal dynamics of inequality. This might encompass concerns about how users of PDS can be provided with control over their data, what new business models in PDS ecosystems will mean for privacy and integrity and how one can communicate about data management and privacy self-management.

Meaningful Control. A first challenge relates to how individuals can be provided with control over their data. One proposed contributing factor to this is an intelligible way to provide consent for sharing information. However, it was noted that challenges lie not only with implementing this in a user-friendly way but also with developing interfaces that do this in a meaningful way. The latter refers to considering problems as privacy fatigue, time constraints and cognitive biases that degrade the extent to which an individual can provide consent in a meaningful way. This issue has been referred to as the 'consent dilemma' [18].

Consent intermediaries were considered as a viable way to counteract this. These refer to services that bring together and simplify consent management while still allowing for some degree of individual control [19]. However, it was argued that such forms of delegated consent and the role of consent intermediaries also require a communication framework to clearly explain their purpose to individuals. Other suggestions to improve intelligibility included embedding consent flows in the content itself or standardizing the flow over multiple applications to support recognizability.

Table 1. Overview of the analysed working group sessions

Title	Description	Participants		
		Government agencies	Public research institutions	Private companies
Use cases (2022/11/19)	Identifying Solid PDS use cases for health, mobility and culture & media. Representatives from government agencies and private companies presented their projects and ideas. In addition, meetings were organised for each domain to discover synergies and identify challenges	4	2	10
Challenges (2020/12/17)	Further exploration of synergies and challenges. Based on these discussions, a first join roadmap was drawn up, stating a number of shared risks and efforts	4	2	13
Objectives (2021/01/14)	Further elaboration on the initial roadmap, with the aid of an online interactive whiteboard for brainstorming purposes. Various challenges were discussed with regard to Solid and cooperation within Solid Community	4	2	14
Modes of cooperation (2021/01/28)	Meeting on the modes of cooperation, and further reflection on the goals and challenges	4	2	13
Conclusions (2021/02/25)	Drawing conclusions and planning further collaborations. Discussion of the vision statement. In addition, a presentation on the technical components of Solid was given, with room for discussion	3	2	12

(continued)

Table 1. (*continued*)

Title	Description	Participants		
		Government agencies	Public research institutions	Private companies
Data vaults (2021/04/29)	Technical presentations by three Solid software providers and experts on the state of the art of data vaults and their experiences. Afterwards there was room for questions and discussion	No data (8 people)	No data (11 people)	No data (32 people)
Usability (2021/05/27)	Presentation and workshop usability and user experience. Demos of various architectures for inspiration with room for discussion	No data	No data	No data
Consent and Data Governance Act (2021/06/24)	Presentations and discussion on consent flows and the Data Governance Act	3 (12 people)	4 (8 people)	16 (20 people)
Working groups (2021/10/07)	Networking event with the aim of developing an ecosystem governance model. The participants were divided in four groups to aid discussion	No data	No data	No data
Charter (2021/11/09)	Feedback on the proposed community charter and its governance model	No data	No data	No data

Related to this is the concept of providing a holistic overview of all consent decisions made by an individual. While this might contribute to providing more control and transparency, it is unclear how this information might be presented in an understandable way. The importance of a holistic overview of an individual's data was also discussed. Solid PDS allow data to be stored in various locations and among different organisations. Through so called 'data browser' or 'data dashboard' applications one can gain control over their data in a centralized fashion. However, uncertainty remains as to how this concept of decentralized data shown in a central way can be translated to individuals and to what extent. It was questioned to what extent individuals desire control over where data should be stored and retrieved.

These challenges are augmented when derived data is considered, e.g. algorithmically processed personal data, and its impact on the aforementioned measures of control. Not only should be examined how individuals can determine what algorithms are allowed to process their data, but also how informed decisions can be made based on these data. This might not only entail behavioural choices, such as estimating the risk of meeting a friend in a COVID-19 context, but also insight in how personal data is valued by various stakeholders and how these valuations differ when data is traded individually or in an aggregated manner.

Privacy, Integrity and Inclusion. A second concern focuses on what new business models in PDS ecosystems will mean for privacy and integrity. It was argued that increased control over larger amounts of data might induce exploitative dynamics where individuals are required to supply more data than today to make use of services. Additionally, this would carry the risk of exclusion for those that are not willing to share the required information. It also remains unclear how the willingness to share data from a personal data store differs by context and by data type. It was suggested that an overarching ethical framework be put in place to manage these issues and to explore further ethical barriers that may limit the adoption of Solid and have undesired societal effects.

Another aspect in consideration was how PDS could work for a diverse group of people, including those with limited access to technology or those in a vulnerable situation. Further research is needed to define what easy access and accessibility might mean for Solid PDS, and how people can be adequately protected against exclusion.

Intelligible Communication and Tangibility. A third challenge targets understandable communication about Solid PDS to the general public. This refers to ways in which Solid can be made tangible to people, for instance through education and storytelling. More broadly it entails questions about how to communicate about data management and privacy self-management. The latter refers to measures that allow people to take control of their own data [18]. A focal point is the decentral nature of Solid. Not only should be investigated how individuals experience this decentral aspect and how the decentral architecture of Solid should be communicated, it was also questioned how such communication can be uniform when various parties are involved in a decentral ecosystem.

Another set of questions that arose were related to the ways in which PDS can be effectively marketed. This encompasses ways to show the added value of PDS and promoting trust between individuals and service providers. These require the identification of relevant use cases and adoption requirements that contribute to user trust. It was argued that user involvement is an important component in the development of a communication strategy.

5.2 Network Challenges

Network or ecosystem challenges concern the changing roles in Solid PDS ecosystems and include the identification of business models for adopting Solid PDS for the storage and exchange of data, hurdles with regards to interoperability and standardization as well as challenges on how responsibilities should be shared and on how governing frameworks can avoid multiple interoperable competing technologies.

Business Models. A primary concern was the identification of business models that make it interesting for both commercial and non-commercial organisations to adopt Solid PDS for the storage and exchange of data (e.g. customer data). It should be investigated how current business models can be adapted to the context of a decentralized market and how these models compare against, and compete with, data silo models. In addition, it was questioned how a tipping point could be reached, i.e. overcoming a chicken-and-egg problem where individuals nor service providers are willing to adopt PDS due to a lack of presence of the other. To this end, it was argued that a framework be developed that both maps current funding methods for PDS projects and that aims to involve and support adopting organisations in the early innovation phase which carries a high risk of failure. This should include a mapping of the various potential stakeholders in a PDS ecosystem, such as pod or identity providers.

It was noted that there is a fair amount of uncertainty as to the competitive dynamics that would exist when such business practices are adopted. This includes how to cope with current dominant market players and what future value exchange will look like, but also more specific inquiries such as what a competitive market for consent intermediaries might look like. Another important aspect is what the separation of data and applications will mean for organisations. It was suggested that the improved access to data might improve the innovative potential of SME's or contribute to a separation of power in value chains. However, concerns were expressed about the possible establishment of new data silos to due to extensive data monetization that limits data access to smaller organisations.

Interoperability and Standardization. To ensure that the aforementioned data exchanges are able to take place there is a need for standards that enable interoperability. While various local and international standards exist that allow for data exchange, such as the Flemish OSLO initiative for open standards and Linked Data [20] it is unclear to what extent these can be reused for or applied to Solid PDS ecosystems. There was an extensive focus on pod interoperation and pod browser interoperability. The former referring to the standardization of data storage locations and the latter referring to how data browsing interfaces for individuals can be standardised. It was noted that interoperability with legacy systems and interfaces, as well as other standards, is important to accommodate the adoption of PDS.

In addition, there might be a need to adapt existing standard development frameworks as to ensure broad support among stakeholders in decentralized environment. It was suggested that further research is required to investigate what actors might or should become responsible for ensuring such interoperability, but also how cases of non-compliance should be handled, and that interoperability might be studied from a technical, legal, organisational and semantic perspective [21].

Governance Models. It was argued that to combat such challenges, a governance framework that focuses on creating trust among actors is essential. However, it is as yet unclear what factors might fully contribute to this aspect and how this might depend on the mode of cooperation or sector. Governing rules for the compliance to Solid standards and the development of new standards were suggested as in important element to further trust within an ecosystem. A governing framework for PDS might include other factors that optimise vertical and horizontal cooperation such as a mapping of how individuals can cooperate to market their data collectively in so called data collaboratives [22] and the role of PPPP-models (public-private-people partnership) in a cross-sector data sharing context. In addition, further research might focus on how responsibilities should be shared between various actors and how governing frameworks can avoid multiple interoperable competing technologies to share and control data.

5.3 Legal Challenges

Legal challenges point to regional, (inter)national and European legislation issues that might arise when implementing Solid-based applications to afford people to conveniently switch between data storage providers and application providers. These include concerns about data control and portability (e.g. the impact of the upcoming European Data Governance Act), about assuring legal compliance of PDS and about how consent can be delegated, for instance to a consent intermediary.

Data Control and Portability. An important concern was related to understanding what the European Data Governance Act [16] might mean for Solid, and especially for the position that Solid pod providers can take and the functions that they can perform. In addition, there were concerns about where the limits of data portability lie in this context and how the difference between a data holder and a data subject can be communicated clearly to individuals. In addition, there were questions regarding to what extent the right to manage one's data might translate to the duty to manage one's data, meaning that it should be investigated to what extent individuals will be forced to manage their data themselves and whether this is desirable. In relation to this, further research might explore how individuals can be supported in managing their data consciously.

Compliance. Another primary concern was assuring legal compliance of PDS and how this can be guaranteed when various providers are active. This includes assurances for individuals that pod providers are not to have access to the content of a pod, and the ability to verify that data was not used for undesired purposes.

Another important aspect is how fragmented data can be consolidated through Solid technology while remaining in compliance with both the European General Data Protection Regulation and local, regional, federal and international regulation. To this end, questions were raised about legitimate interest, its scope, and what this means for organisations and individuals. In addition, it was posited that research on these regulations should focus on the legal barriers that limit data sharing between governments and private organisations. Such data transactions might include derived data that are algorithmically generated, which pose further questions about their potential use within legal limits. Further concerns were raised about the role of data protection officers in a decentralised context and the alignment of European and local regulatory frameworks and how this impacts stakeholders that operate in a PDS ecosystem.

Lastly it was noted that frameworks should be mapped or developed that not only allow for the ethical, transparent and safe use of data in a lawful manner, but that also exceed the current legal requirements. To this end it was suggested that research efforts should focus on what conformity and ethical labels are required to represent and protect these requirements and on how these might differ across domains (e.g. health and mobility).

Consent. There also lies a challenge with informing individuals in an intelligible way that, while Solid's focus lies with providing individuals control through consent mechanisms, the right to process one's data might be granted by another legal basis [23]. Associated to this is how individuals can be made aware of what data they are legally required to provide access to and what data they can control more freely through consent mechanisms. Other points of uncertainty included how organisations should manage the withdrawal of consent by individuals when data has already been duplicated, and to what extent and in what contexts these consent withdrawals are a possibility. Uncertainty also remained about how consent can be delegated, for instance to a consent intermediary.

Software Licensing. A last legal challenge concerns the ways in which software contributions or components for Solid PDS can be licensed or shared. This while protecting the interests of both the organisations that make these components available and the broader ecosystem.

5.4 Technical Challenges

Technical challenges refer to the management of identities and achieving information security, scalability and maturity in both the development and deployment of Solid PDS.

Identity and Pod Management. A first series of concerns is related to identities and how these can be managed when multiple identity or pod providers are involved, and especially how individuals can maintain overview and control in this context. In addition, it is unclear what kind of additional flexible identities, such as a tourist or a short stay identity, might be required and how this differs per domain or use case. This question also relates to how these identities might be extended to internet connected devices such as sensors, wearables or cars and what their requirements are. When regarding identities, there were questions about how Solid's identity mechanisms can be used in tandem with decentralised identity technology.

In addition, it was suggested that research efforts should focus on how pod management or pod browser applications can be made interoperable (e.g. allowing to control national data with local or foreign pod management tools). In this context it was argued that standardizing efforts should also extend to consent granting delegation to other parties.

Information Security. In terms of information security, it was noted that it would be beneficial to map the current malicious applications or malicious ways of using data and reflecting on how these issues will be handled in the context of Solid PDS. Such research might also include what security standards a pod must adhere to, how this differs per use case and what generic solutions can be used for this purpose. Specific interest was shown in the potential risk that allowing individuals to store verifiable credentials carries.

In addition, it was argued that there should be a focus on techniques that allow for the drawing of conclusions from fragmented data sources without copying whole datasets (e.g. multi-party computation) and other techniques that allow for data minimalization. Attention might be required for handling or preventing data duplication. Furthermore, it was posited that the ways in which end-to-end and other emerging encryption technologies can be linked to the Solid realm should be investigated.

Scalability and Maturity. A last topic under discussion concerns the ways in which Solid can scale and mature. Firstly, this refers to an architecture that can scale to a vast number of pods or resources, for instance through caching or aggregator solutions. Secondly it considers providing tools for developers and organisations that allow for the implementation of Solid PDS and applications with limited available time. This includes identifying common components that are required by various parties and aligning the architecture with current reference models (e.g. International Data Spaces and European Common Data Spaces). Attention must be paid to how participating organisations might manage the complexity of this architecture, which might include various decisions about whether, where and how to host pods and applications. Lastly it was noted that more research is required that show how PDS technologies like Solid perform and why they might be preferred as a solution.

6 Discussion

The analysis shows that the challenges associated with the development of Solid PDS by the Flemish Solid Community are complex and multidisciplinary in nature. Through their conceptualisation within four domains this paper aims to contribute to the development of an interdisciplinary research agenda for the diffusion of personal data spaces technologies that are socially robust, ethically justified and both technically and legally supported. However, as there is only a limited reflection on their scientific relevance, further research may focus on how these challenges can be theoretically framed. Such a reflection might contribute to the development of domain specific research agendas that are based on the current needs as experienced by governments, academia and the industry. In addition, further research may focus on whether the current results are applicable in different contexts. This might entail the comparison of Solid PDS challenges with related PDS technologies and data sharing paradigms, such as open data. From a legal perspective, the influence of differing legal frameworks may be considered, while from a network-level perspective, the future relevance of these challenges may assessed by framing them within emerging data sharing models [24].

It should be noted that although citizens were able to participate within 'Solid Community', their actual involvement was very limited. As a major goal of PDS technologies entails improving individuals' agency on how their data is used, their involvement during the shaping of a scientific agenda is essential. Further research should augment the current results with the perspective of citizens.

7 Conclusion

Taking these identified challenges into account, the Flemish 'Solid Community' is well aware of the needs and problems Solid implementations are confronted with nowadays. Functioning as a reflexive and interactive platform, the Flemish 'Solid Community' next steps are to formulate answers to these social, network, legal and technical questions confronting practical citizen centred PDS initiatives in Flanders. The 'Solid Community' partners are therefore in an excellent position to pro-actively help to shape the framework conditions for the further diffusion of socially robust, ethically justified, and legally supported PDS initiatives in Flanders.

The 'Solid Community' takes an interdisciplinary approach as it bundles knowledge and expertise from different disciplines and domains. Interdisciplinarity is then at the core of this community and reflected in the composition of the community. Each partner has strong experience in certain aspects pertaining to Solid ecosystems and brings this expertise together. By approaching the topic in these diverse ways, a more fundamental grip on PDS as a concept is gained. Finally, the 'Solid Community' supports an Open Science-approach as it enables early and open sharing of research and as it involves all relevant knowledge actors including governments, companies, civil society and end users. It acknowledges that research and innovation processes are embedded within societal and political discourses, cultural practices and institutional structures.

Acknowledgements. This research was supported by SolidLab Vlaanderen (Flemish Government, EWI and RRF project VV023/10).

Vlaamse overheid | DEPARTMENT OF ECONOMY SCIENCE & INNOVATION | Gefinancierd door de Europese Unie NextGenerationEU

References

1. Willson, M., Leaver, T.: Zynga's FarmVille, social games, and the ethics of big data mining. Commun. Res. Pract. **1**(2), 147–158 (2015). https://doi.org/10.1080/22041451.2015.1048039
2. Van Kleek, M., OHara, K.: The future of social is personal: the potential of the personal data store. In: Miorandi, D., Maltese, V., Rovatsos, M., Nijholt, A., Stewart, J. (eds.) Social Collective Intelligence. CSS, pp. 125–158. Springer, Cham (2014). https://doi.org/10.1007/978-3-319-08681-1_7
3. BBC. Personal data stores: building and trialling trusted data services - BBC R&D, 29 September 2021. https://www.bbc.co.uk/rd/blog/2021-09-personal-data-store-research. Accessed 16 Mar 2022
4. 'Datavillage', STADIEM, 14 January 2022. https://www.stadiem.eu/datavillage/. Accessed 31 May 2022
5. Digitaal Vlaanderen. The Flemish Data Utility Company. www.vlaanderen.be. https://www.vlaanderen.be/digitaal-vlaanderen/het-vlaams-datanutsbedrijf/the-flemish-data-utility-company. Accessed 16 March 2022
6. Vlaamse Regering. Septemberverklaring van de Vlaamse Regering (2021). https://www.vlaanderen.be/publicaties/septemberverklaring-van-de-vlaamse-regering-2021. Accessed 16 Mar 2022
7. Capadisli, S., et al.: Solid protocol, 17 December 2021. https://solidproject.org/TR/protocol. Accessed 22 Feb 2022
8. Solid Project. Solid Project (2022). https://solidproject.org/. Accessed 16 Mar 2022
9. Lehtiniemi, T., Haapoja, J.: Data agency at stake: MyData activism and alternative frames of equal participation. New Media Soc. **22**(1), 87–104 (2020). https://doi.org/10.1177/1461444819861955

10. Sambra, A.V., et al.: Solid: a platform for decentralized social applications based on linked data. MIT CSAIL Qatar Comput. Res. Inst. Tech. Rep. (2016)
11. Jesús-Azabal, M., Moguel, E., Laso, S., Murillo, J.M., Galán-Jiménez, J., García-Alonso, J.: Pushed SOLID: deploying SOLID in smartphones. Mob. Inf. Syst. **2021**, e2756666 (2021). https://doi.org/10.1155/2021/2756666
12. Attard, J., Orlandi, F., Scerri, S., Auer, S.: A systematic review of open government data initiatives. Gov. Inf. Q. **32**(4), 399–418 (2015). https://doi.org/10.1016/j.giq.2015.07.006
13. Buyle, R., et al.: Streamlining governmental processes by putting citizens in control of their personal data. In: Chugunov, A., Khodachek, I., Misnikov, Y., Trutnev, D. (eds.) EGOSE 2019. CCIS, vol. 1135, pp. 346–359. Springer, Cham (2020). https://doi.org/10.1007/978-3-030-39296-3_26
14. Informatie Vlaanderen. 'Succesvolle start voor het Solid ecosysteem', Vlaanderen Intern, 04 May 2021. https://overheid.vlaanderen.be/informatie-vlaanderen/nieuws/succesvolle-start-voor-het-solid-ecosysteem. Accessed 03 Mar 2022
15. Solid Community Flanders. Solid Community Charter. 09 November 2021
16. European Commission. proposal for a regulation of the European parliament and of the council on European data governance (data governance act) (2020). https://eur-lex.europa.eu/legal-content/EN/TXT/?uri=CELEX%3A52020PC0767. Accessed 16 Mar 2022
17. Bryant, A., Charmaz, K.: The SAGE Handbook of Grounded Theory. SAGE Publications Ltd. (2007).https://doi.org/10.4135/9781848607941
18. Solove, D.J.: Introduction: privacy self-management and the consent dilemma. Harv. Law Rev. **126**(7), 1880–1903 (2013)
19. Lehtiniemi, T., Kortesniemi, Y.: Can the obstacles to privacy self-management be overcome? Exploring the consent intermediary approach. Big Data Soc. **4**(2), 2053951717721930 (2017).https://doi.org/10.1177/2053951717721935
20. 'OSLO' 2022. https://www.vlaanderen.be/digitaal-vlaanderen/onze-oplossingen/oslo. Accessed 16 Mar 2022
21. European Commission and Directorate-General for Informatics, New European interoperability framework : promoting seamless services and data flows for European public administrations. Publications Office (2017).https://doi.org/10.2799/78681
22. Susha, I., Janssen, M., Verhulst, S.: Data collaboratives as "bazaars"? a review of coordination problems and mechanisms to match demand for data with supply. Transforming Gov. People Process Policy **11**(1), 157–172 (2017). https://doi.org/10.1108/TG-01-2017-0007
23. The European Parliament and the Council of The European Union, Regulation (EU) 2016/679 of the European Parliament and of the Council of 27 April 2016 on the protection of natural persons with regard to the processing of personal data and on the free movement of such data, and repealing Directive 95/46/EC (General Data Protection Regulation) (Text with EEA relevance). https://eur-lex.europa.eu/eli/reg/2016/679/oj. Accessed 25 Mar 2022
24. Micheli, M., Ponti, M., Craglia, M., Suman, A.B.: Emerging models of data governance in the age of datafication. Big Data Soc. **7**(2), 2053951720948087 (2020). https://doi.org/10.1177/2053951720948087

Correction to: Automated Topic Categorisation of Citizens' Contributions: Reducing Manual Labelling Efforts Through Active Learning

Julia Romberg and Tobias Escher

Correction to:
Chapter "Automated Topic Categorisation of Citizens' Contributions: Reducing Manual Labelling Efforts Through Active Learning" in: M. Janssen et al. (Eds.):
***Electronic Government*, LNCS 13391,**
https://doi.org/10.1007/978-3-031-15086-9_24

Chapter 24 was previously published non-open access. It has now been changed to open access under a CC BY 4.0 license and the copyright holder updated to 'The Author(s)'. The book has also been updated with this change.

The updated original version of this chapters can be found at https://doi.org/10.1007/978-3-031-15086-9_24

M. Janssen et al. (Eds.): EGOV 2022, LNCS 13391, p. C1, 2022.
https://doi.org/10.1007/978-3-031-15086-9_37

Author Index

Printed in the United States
by Baker & Taylor Publisher Services